hatred, violence, and injustice never can and never will be able to create a mental, moral, or material millennium. The only way toward it is the royal road of all-giving creative love, not only preached but consistently practiced."

Thirty-five years later, after continuous scientific studies and establishing the Harvard Research Center in Creative Altruism, Sorokin finds his earlier beliefs immeasurably reinforced. "Now more than ever before I believe in the following truths, which are fully confirmed by our experimental studies.

"Hate begets hate, violence engenders violence, hypocrisy is answered by hypocrisy, war generates war, and love creates love.

"Unselfish love has enormous creative and therapeutic potentialities, far greater than most people think. Love is a life-giving force, necessary for physical, mental, and moral health.

"Altruistic persons live longer than egoistic individuals. . . .

"Finally, only the power of unbounded love practiced in regard to *all human beings* can defeat the forces of inter-human strife, and can prevent the pending extermination of man by man on this planet. Without love, no armament, no war, no diplomatic machinations, no coercive police force, no school education, no economic or political measures, not even hydrogen bombs, can prevent the pending catastrophe. Only love can accomplish this miracle, providing, however, we know well the nature of love and the efficient ways of its production, accumulation, and use.

"Unfortunately, we know about 'love energy' much less than about light, heat, electricity, and other forms of physical energy."

To learn more about the power and nature of this energy through intensive study has been Sorokin's purpose in life for over a third of a century. In this book are the findings to date.

# THE WAYS AND POWER OF LOVE

# BOOKS BY PITIRIM A. SOROKIN

*Crime and Punishment* (1914). In Russian.

*Leo Tolstoi as a Philosopher* (1915). In Russian.

*Elements of Sociology* (1919). In Russian.

*System of Sociology* (2 vols., 1920–21). In Russian.

*General Theory of Law* (1920). In Russian.

*Today's Russia* (1923). In Russian.

*Essays in Social Politics* (1923). In Russian.

*Leaves from a Russian Diary* (1924). Revised ed. (1950).

*Sociology of Revolution* (1925). German ed. (1928).

*Social Mobility* (1926). Japanese ed. (in part, 1928). Chinese ed. (1930). Spanish ed. (1954).

*Contemporary Sociological Theories* (1928). German ed. (1930). Japanese ed. (in part, 1930). Yugoslav ed. (1932). Chinese ed. (1933). French ed. (1935). Second Chinese ed. (1936). Czechoslovakian ed. (1936). Spanish ed. (1951). Polish ed. (in preparation). Ukrainian ed. (in preparation).

*Principles of Rural-Urban Sociology* (1929).

*A Source Book in Rural Sociology* (3 vols., 1930–31).

*Time-Budgets of Human Behavior* (1939).

*Social and Cultural Dynamics* (4 vols., 1937–41). Spanish ed. (in preparation). Hindustani ed. (in preparation).

*Crisis of our Age* (1941). Portuguese ed. (1945). Norwegian ed. (1948). Czechoslovakian ed. (1948). Spanish ed. (1948). German ed. (1950). Dutch ed. (1950). Finnish ed. (1952). Japanese ed. (1954).

*Man and Society in Calamity* (1942).

*Sociocultural Causality, Space, Time* (1943). Spanish ed. (in preparation).

*Russia and the United States* (1944). Portuguese ed. (1946). British ed. (1950). Japanese ed. (1953).

*Society, Culture, and Personality* (1947). German ed. (in preparation). Italian ed. (in preparation). Spanish ed. (in preparation).

*Reconstruction of Humanity* (1948). Japanese ed. (1951). German ed. (1952). Norwegian ed. (1953).

*Altruistic Love: A Study of American Good Neighbors and Christian Saints* (1950).

*Social Philosophies of an Age of Crisis* (1950). German ed. (1953). Spanish ed. (in preparation).

*Explorations in Altruistic Love and Bahavior: A Symposium* (1950). French ed. (in preparation).

*S.O.S.: The Meaning of Our Crisis* (1951). Czechoslovakian ed. (in preparation).

*Estructura Mental y Energias del Hombre* (1952).

*The Ways and Power of Love* (1954).

*Forms and Techniques of Altruistic and Spiritual Growth: A Symposium* (1954).

# THE WAYS AND POWER OF LOVE

Types, Factors, and Techniques of
Moral Transformation

by

PITIRIM A. SOROKIN

THE BEACON PRESS · BOSTON

Copyright 1954
by The Beacon Press

*Second Printing, October, 1957*

L.C. catalog card number: 53-10323
Printed in U.S.A.

# Preface

Blessed are the meek: for they shall inherit the earth.
Blessed are the merciful: for they shall obtain mercy.
Blessed are the peacemakers: for they shall be called the children of God.

In 1918 I was hunted from pillar to post by the Russian Communist Government. At last I was imprisoned and condemned to death. Daily, during six weeks, I expected to be shot, and witnessed the shooting of my friends and fellow prisoners. During the subsequent four years of my stay in Communist Russia I underwent other painful experiences and observed, to the heartbreaking point, endless horrors of human bestiality, death, and destruction. Exactly in these conditions I jotted down in my diary [1] the following " observations of a cold intellect and plaintive murmurs of a saddened heart ":

Whatever may happen in the future, I know that I have learned three things which will remain forever convictions of my heart as well as my mind. Life, even the hardest life, is the most beautiful, wonderful, and miraculous treasure in the world. Fulfillment of duty is another marvelous thing making life happy. This is my second conviction. And my third is that cruelty, hatred, violence, and injustice never can and never will be able to create a mental, moral, or material millennium. The only way toward it is the royal road of all-giving creative love, not only preached but consistently practiced.

Some thirty-five years have passed since these lines were written. The tragic events of these years, as well as my scientific studies, immeasurably reinforced these beliefs, and led me even to the establishment of the Harvard Research Center in Creative Altruism. Now more than ever before I believe in the following truths, which are fully confirmed by our experimental studies:

Hate begets hate, violence engenders violence, hypocrisy is answered by hypocrisy, war generates war, and love creates love.

Unselfish love has enormous creative and therapeutic potentialities, far greater than most people think. Love is a life-giving force, necessary for physical, mental, and moral health.

Altruistic persons live longer than egoistic individuals.

Children deprived of love tend to become vitally, morally, and socially defective.

---

[1] All references are to the Notes (pp. 491–536).

Love is the most powerful antidote against criminal, morbid, and suicidal tendencies; against hate, fear, and psychoneuroses.

It is an indispensable condition for deep and lasting happiness.

It is goodness and freedom at their loftiest.

It is the finest and most powerful educational force for the ennoblement of humanity.

Finally, only the power of unbounded love practiced in regard to *all human beings* can defeat the forces of interhuman strife, and can prevent the pending extermination of man by man on this planet. Without love, no armament, no war, no diplomatic machinations, no coercive police force, no school education, no economic or political measures, not even hydrogen bombs can prevent the pending catastrophe. Only love can accomplish this miracle, providing, however, we know well the nature of love and the efficient ways of its production, accumulation, and use.

Unfortunately, we know about " love energy " much less than about light, heat, electricity, and other forms of physical energy. " It is amazing how little the empirical sciences have to offer on the subject of love," correctly says A. H. Maslow. " Particularly strange is the silence of the psychologists. Sometimes this is merely sad or irritating, as in the case of the textbooks of psychology and sociology, practically none of which treat the subject. . . . More often the situation becomes completely ludicrous. [As a rule] the word ' love ' is not even indexed [in psychological and sociological works]." [2]

At the present juncture of human history an increase in our knowledge of the grace of love has become the paramount need of humanity, and an intensive research in this field should take precedence over almost all other studies and research.

This present work, together with its companion volume, *Forms and Techniques of Altruistic and Spiritual Growth: A Symposium*, is my humble contribution to this great objective. Considering the immensity of the task, the contribution is very modest in comparison with the total sum of the necessary studies. Since, however, the better brains are busy with other problems, including the invention of means of extermination of human beings; since governments are preoccupied with promotion of warfare; since educators are largely engrossed in cultivation of the intellect and tribal patriotism of their pupils, while many a religious leader is absorbed in the intertribal crusades against various enemies — under these conditions somebody, somehow, must devote himself to a study of the miracle of love, no matter how inadequate is his capacity to do the work well. *Feci quod potui, faciant meliora potentes.* This is my excuse for the innumerable infirmities of this contribution.

It opens with an outline of various aspects of love, its five empirical dimensions, its power, and the ways of its production, accumulation, and distribution.

Part Two gives a basic revision of the prevalent theories of personality structure. The revision is due not only to the fallacy of the current theories, but also to their disservice to the task of creative integration and altruistic transformation of human beings.

The third part deals with the how and why of the moral growth of the apostles of sublime love. What are the main types of altruists? How did they succeed in becoming the incarnations of unselfish love? What factors conditioned their creative growth? What techniques did they use for achievement of their transfiguration? The analysis of these problems throws some light upon the mystery of creative genius generally and of the genius of unselfish love particularly.

Part Four consists of a systematic survey of the main techniques of moral ennoblement and of the Yoga, the monastic, and the secular brotherhoods' systems of altruistic education. These parts somewhat unravel the little-known processes of moral transformation.

The final part offers a blueprint for transcendence of individual and group egotisms by the universal love of everyone to all human beings and to mankind as a whole. It maps the main steps toward unification of mankind into one real, harmonious family.

It is my privilege to express my warmest thanks to the Lilly Endowment and to Mr. Eli Lilly for their financial help in the execution of this study. Dedication of the book to Eli Lilly is a feeble token of my deep appreciation of their generosity to the Research Center and myself. Among the many persons who helped me in this study I am particularly indebted to Dr. S. G. Pushkarev, Dr. C. Andrade, Dr. Ashley Montagu, Mr. Francis D. Smith, Mr. Robert C. Hanson, and to the students of Harvard University and Radcliffe College. I am deeply indebted also to Dr. Lucio Mendieta y Núñez and the National University of Mexico for permission to reprint here the English text of my *Estructura Mental y Energias del Hombre*, published by the National University of Mexico, as well as for the degree of *Doctor Honoris Causa* granted to me by this oldest university on the American continent at its four hundredth anniversary; to the Julian Press for permission to reprint my paper " The Power of Creative Love," published in its symposium, *The Meaning of Love*, edited by Ashley Montagu; to the *Archiv für Rechts- und Sozialphilosophie* and *La Revista International de Sociologia* for permission to reprint my paper " Polarizacion en la Frustracion y en las Crisis "; and to the foreign publishers and translators of my volumes into many of the chief Euro-American and Asiatic languages of humanity. Finally, I want to thank all those who have contributed — often from modest incomes — financial help to the Harvard Research Center in Creative Altruism.

PITIRIM A. SOROKIN

*Harvard Research Center in Creative Altruism*

# Contents

PART FOUR

# TECHNIQUES OF ALTRUISTIC TRANSFORMATION OF PERSONS AND GROUPS

PART FIVE

# TRAGEDY AND TRANSCENDENCE OF TRIBAL ALTRUISM

# PART ONE

# LOVE: ITS ASPECTS, DIMENSIONS, PRODUCTION, TRANSFORMATION, AND POWER

*Chapter One*

# The Manifoldness of Love and Its Main Aspects

Love is like an iceberg: only a small part of it is visible, and even this visible part is little known.  Still less known is love's transempirical part, its religious and ontological forms.  For the reasons subsequently given, love appears to be a universe inexhaustible qualitatively and quantitatively. Of its many forms of being, the following can be differentiated: religious, ethical, ontological, physical, biological, psychological, and social.

## A. *The Religious Aspect of Love*

On the religious plane love is identified with God, the highest value in the Christian and other great religions.  " Love is God," and " God is love and he that dwelleth in love dwelleth in God and God in him," says the New Testament.[1]  So also say the *Bhagavadgita*, the *Dhammapada*, and the Scriptures of practically all the great religions: Taoism and Confucianism, Hinduism and Buddhism, Jainism and Judaism, Mohammedanism, and the rest.  Since God is believed to be the absolute value, love participates in God's absolute value.  Since God is an Infinite Manifoldness love is also qualitative and quantitative infinity.  As such it cannot be defined by any words or concepts; at best these can be only symbolic indicators of the infinite cosmos of love.  Paul Tillich well expresses this infinity of love when he says: " I have given no definition of love.  This is impossible, because there is no higher principle by which it could be defined.  It is life itself in its actual unity.  The forms and structures in which love embodies itself are the forms and structures in which life overcomes its self-destructive forces." [2]

On this religious plane three conceptions of love have run throughout oriental and occidental religious, philosophical, and ethical thought: love as Eros, love as Agape, and love as a synthesis of Eros and Agape.

Nygren's delineation of love as Eros and love as Agape serves as an introduction to the problem.  He avers that love as Agape is fundamentally different from love as Eros; that the Agape form of love is specifically Christian as meant by Jesus, St. Paul, and the early Christians.

| *Eros* | *Agape* |
|---|---|
| Eros is a desire of good for the self. | Agape is self-giving. |
| Eros is man's effort to ascend. | Agape comes down from above (from God). |
| Eros is man's way to God. | Agape is God's way to man. |
| Eros is man's achievement, the endeavor of man to achieve salvation. | Agape is a free gift, a salvation which is the work of Divine Love. |
| Eros is egocentric love, a form of self-assertion of the highest, noblest, and sublimest kind. | Agape is unselfish love, which "seeketh not its own," and freely spends itself. |
| Eros seeks to gain life divine, immortal. | Agape lives by God's life, and therefore dares to "lose it." |
| Eros is a will to have and to possess, resting on a sense of need. | Agape freely gives and spends, for it rests on God's own richness and fullness. |
| Eros is primarily human love, and God is the object of Eros. | Agape is primarily God's own love, for God is Agape. |
| Eros is given only to those who deserve it; hence it is not spontaneous, but "caused," by the value of the object. | Agape is poured out on "the evil and the good"; hence it is spontaneous, "uncaused," and bestows itself on those who are worthy and not worthy of it. |
| Eros recognizes value in its object, and therefore loves it. | Agape loves, and creates value in its object. |

Thus "Eros and Agape stand as direct opposites." Agape is like the sun; it shines upon the sinful and the virtuous, redeeming the sinners no less than blessing the virtuous. Its inexhaustible richness spontaneously pours itself out upon all, without any "rational discrimination." In this sense Agape is inscrutable, and incomprehensible by the human rational mind. Eros is love "earned" by the positive efforts of the loved party.[3] It discriminates against the sinful.

Though the historical accuracy of this typology of Eros and Agape may be questionable in regard to Christianity and the oriental, Platonic, Neoplatonic, and Aristotelian conceptions of love; and though several thinkers of the past and of the present give the terms Eros and Agape essentially different meanings, [4] the typology as such is graphic and logical. Some forms of love are indeed nearer to the type of Eros, while others are nearer to that of Agape. We can, however, ask: can Eros be separated from Agape or are not these two aspects of love inseparable? Is not Agape the redeeming love, pouring itself out in its inexhaustible richness, especially on those who need it for their redemption, salvation, revival, and reintegration? Is not Agape this aspect of love which is "love for the sake of love"? If love were granted only to those who deserve it — the virtuous, the "elect" — would not such a love become a mere commercial prize-giving to the "good boys" for their good behavior? These remarks show that the Agape form of love is inherent in the very nature of love, in its redeeming, resurrecting, and all-forgiving functions. Such an Agape far transcends justice, in the sense of the *suum cuique tribuere*, as well as of a remuneration for service done.

On the other hand, Agape in no way excludes Eros-Love. Eros-Love is nothing but falling in love with love and trying to be more perfect in love, with all the mental, moral, aesthetic, and physical ennoblement such a perfection implies. The ultimate point of such an Eros-Love is to reach the inexhaustibility of all-redeeming, all-loving, all-forgiving, and all-ennobling Agape. A person's Eros-Love, reaching this level, becomes God's Agape. This inseparability of Eros-Agape explains why factually most systems of love contain both these forms.

If the transfiguration is possible only by the way of Nygren's Agape, then evidently one need not do anything; all efforts to achieve the goodness of love are of no avail; it may shine equally upon the virtuous and the sinful. If the transfiguration is possible only by the way of Nygren's Eros, then there is no need to pray for the grace of God or any super-individual power. Any love-seeker would become a sort of Prometheus who achieves his goal exclusively by his own efforts, regardless or even in spite of Zeus or any other force.

In the oriental [5] as well as the occidental ethico-religious and philosophical conceptions, the prevailing view has been a combination of Eros and Agape as the way of salvation and achievement of love at its highest and best. Personal effort reinforced by the grace of God is considered the only real way to accomplish the purpose. " God helps those who strive, not those who rest and slumber," says St. Tychon.[6] Either of these forms alone is insufficient by itself: without the grace of God or some super-individual power, man's efforts are inadequate. On the other hand, the love and justice of God are gladly granted those who earnestly labor for love and salvation. The thought and the practice of salvation in all great religions are based upon this postulate. Otherwise, all the calls to be good, to perform good deeds, to fulfill moral and religious commandments would be senseless.

Only a few minor streams of thought and practice, in the Orient [7] and the Occident,[8] singled out exclusively either the Eros or the Agape way; and even these minor currents now and then had to grant to the other way a subsidiary role.

From this standpoint D'Arcy justifiably critizes the one-sidedness of Nygren's, Rousselot's, de Rougemont's, and other conceptions of Eros and Agape. He rightly says that " that two [forms of love] egocentric and theocentric have to live together," that " we must not think of the two loves as separate and independent within the one self, even though, in order to bring out their distinct characteristics, we have to treat them as if they were alone." [9] " On the one side, there will be a man with a passion which seeks for deliverance [of his real self from his pseudo-self] "; on the other, " God, who respects man's integrity while lifting him up into a new relation of love with himself."

To sum up: properly understood, self-centered love, as an effort of man to liberate in himself his real and divine self and to reach union with God, and God-centered love, as divine grace helping man in this endeavor, are given in practically all true systems of love, oriental and occidental, though some systems stress the Agape, and others the Eros. Later on we shall meet this problem in its empirical ramifications.

## B. The Ethical Aspect of Love

*Ethically love is identified with goodness itself.* Love is viewed as the essence of goodness inseparable from truth and beauty. All three are unified aspects of the Absolute Value or God. Real goodness is always true and beautiful; pure truth is always good and beautiful; and genuine beauty is invariably true and good.

## C. The Ontological Aspect of Love

Ontologically love is, side by side with truth and beauty, one of the highest forms of a *unifying, integrating, harmonizing, creative energy or power*. Empedocles correctly noted the unifying creativity of love as the ontological essence of this power. As such it is opposite to the functions of strife as " separating apart in enmity " what is united in and by love.[10] In accordance with this, subsequent thinkers viewed even the unifying physical forces of gravitation, of the unification of electrons and protons in the atom, of chemical affinity, of magnetism, and so on, as the manifestation of love energy acting in the *physical* world; the " instincts " of sociality or gregariousness, biological mutual aid and co-operation, as the manifestation of love energy in the *organic* world; conscious love, sympathy, friendship, solidarity, as its manifestation in the *psychosocial* world. Everywhere in the inorganic, organic and psychosocial worlds the integrating and uniting role of love functions incessantly. Untiringly, it counteracts the dividing and separating forces of chaos and strife. Without the operation of love energy the physical, the biological, and the sociocultural cosmos would have fallen apart; no harmony, unity, or order would have been possible; universal disorder and enmity would have reigned supreme. As a creative energy of goodness, love unites what is separated, elevates what is base, purifies what is impure, ennobles what is ignoble, creates harmony in the world of enmity, peace in war. Love raises man as a biological organism to the level of divinity, infinitely enriches the human self, and empowers humanity with a mastery over the inorganic, organic, and sociocultural forces, up to the potential rescue of an individual and mankind from even biological death. Dostoievsky well expressed this ontological power of love in his *Brothers Karamazoff*. " Seeing the sins of men, one sometimes wonders whether one should react to them by force or by humble love. Always decide to fight them by humble love. If it is carried through, the whole world can be conquered. Loving humbleness is the most effective force, the most terrific, the most powerful, unequalled by any other force in the world." [11] All great apostles of love unanimously testify to this. Without love, neither the possession of the tongues of angels, nor the gift of prophecy, nor a complete understanding of all mysteries and possession of all knowledge amount to anything, says St. Paul, and then magnificently describes the ethico-ontological nature of love:

> Love suffereth long, and is kind; love envieth not;
> love vaunteth not itself, is not puffed up,
> Doth not behave itself unseemly, seeketh not her own,
> is not easily provoked, thinketh no evil;
> Rejoiceth not in iniquity, but rejoiceth in the truth;
> Beareth all things, believeth all things,
> hopeth all things, endureth all things;
> Love never faileth:
> And now abideth faith, hope, love, these three;
> and the greatest of these is love. [12]

A person who becomes a real incarnation of love "will yield an influence greater than that of the sceptred monarch," testifies Gandhi.[13] "Love is basically not an emotional but an ontological power, it is the essence of life itself, namely, the dynamic reunion of that which is separated": such is the recent reiteration of this ontological power of love.[14]

Among others, N. F. Fedorov (a little-known Russian thinker who notably influenced Dostoievsky and Leo Tolstoi), and under his influence V. Solovyev, have especially well developed and analyzed this ontological "energy" of love. They have shown that only through love, in cooperation with truth and beauty, can man rise from the level of a mortal biological organism to that of a conqueror of death and master of inorganic, organic, and sociocultural forces; that only in this way can man realize his truly divine nature and become "God-Man" (Bogotschelovek); that only thus can man fulfill his mission and redeem his historical existence; that only through such a real immortality are all the other values of humanity preserved, instead of becoming meaningless and perishing in vain.[15]

In this ontological conception, according to Solovyev, love is the power that counteracts the dark evil that permeates the world of raw nature.

Evil is a universal fact because each natural life begins with struggle and hatred, continues in suffering and slavery and ends in death and rottenness. . . . The first law of nature is the struggle for existence. All the life of nature in the raw takes place in an incessant enmity of creatures and forces. . . . Every creature in this natural world beginning with the smallest particle of dust and ending with man tells by its whole natural existence one and the same thing: "I am, and the rest of the world exists only for me as a mere means," and, colliding with others, it says: "If I exist, you cannot exist, there is no room for you with me." Each creature in brute nature says so, each attempts to fight all the others, wants to destroy them, and is destroyed in turn by the others. In so far as it is based upon egoism, life in brute nature is *evil* life, and its law is the law of *sin*. By the same law sin inevitably causes its own retaliation, one evil calling forth another. For if one creature inimically acts against the others, these others act as inimically against it. Such an enmity is *suffering* — another form of the world evil. Since everything in nature sins one against another, everything suffers from one another.

Owing to this egoism, which separates one creature from all the others, each creature is a stranger living in an inimical environment which presses and attacks it from all sides. . . . All its natural life consists in a struggle with this inimical environment, in self-defense against the rest of the world. But it cannot defend itself against the pressure of all these inimical forces: a given creature is one while its enemies are many. They naturally overcome it. This conflict between each and all the rest inevitably leads to the *destruction* of each creature: the overwhelming inimical forces finally destroy its life, and the struggle ends universally by *death and rotting*. Death makes only explicit the secret brute of nature's life; it shows that *life in nature is a hidden death*. Such is the fiery wheel of natural existence. Such is the universal evil, one in its nature and triple in its forms. Such is the tree of life in disintegrated nature: its root is *sin*, its growth is *sickness*, its fruit is *death*. [16]

Love is the universal creative force that counteracts this evil. Love replaces the struggle for existence by harmonious unity and mutual aid. It tends to make the whole universe one harmonious cosmos in which each particle is not fighting all the others but harmoniously working with the rest of the world. By the power of love each creature is not opposed to all the others, is not attacked by all the others, and therefore is not destroyed by the others. For this reason its life need not be ended by death and destruction. Love tends thus to destroy the death itself and to replace it by eternal immortality.[17]

So far in the natural world we have only a partial realization of this creative work of love energy. Only through it does the world continue to exist in spite of the all-pervading destructive forces of evil. Love keeps the world going and living. Love prevents the universal death and destruction of the whole universe. If and when love is realized more and more fully, sin, suffering, and death are bound to decrease — and with the full realization of love, to disappear. Such is the ontological role of love as the highest creative power.[18]

The foregoing gives one of the many variations of the ontological conception of love as the universal creative energy.

## D. *The Physical Aspect of Love*

According to Solovyev and others, the physical counterpart of love in the inorganic world is shown in all physical forces that unite, integrate, and maintain the whole inorganic cosmos in endless unities, beginning with the smallest unity of the atom and ending with the whole physical universe as one unified, orderly cosmos.[19]

### E. *The Biological Aspect of Love*

The biological counterpart of love energy manifests itself in the very nature and basic processes of life. This energy, still little known, and often called the "vital energy" that mysteriously unites various inorganic energies into a startling unity of a living — unicellular or multicellular — organism, is the first biological manifestation of the Empedoclean energy of love. The generation of practically all unicellular organisms from a parent cell, by fission of the parent cell either into four new individuals (zoöspores) or into thirty-two or sixty-four microzoöids with a subsequent conjugation of gametes into a new organism, is another manifestation of "biological love energy": "the two are for a time bound together in an interactive association"; "the life of either one or the other is at some time dependent upon the potential or actual being of the other." Without such an interaction — without the parent cell's supplying the vital tissues to the new organism, and without metabolic and physiological exchanges between parent and daughter cells — the appearance of a new organism is impossible; the very continuity of life itself becomes impossible.[20] Co-operation of two organisms in sexual reproduction of multicellular organisms, accompanied by the passion of biological attraction between them, is a visible form of this "biological love" necessary for the maintenance of all such species and, through that, of life itself. The parental care of the offspring, during its period of helplessness — the care that in some species, like *Homo sapiens*, must last several years — is a still more explicit manifestation of biological love energy. Without it such species would die out. This co-operation is rightly considered a "fundamental characteristic of life phenomena," as universal and basic as the trait of the "struggle for existence." [21]

The "co-operative forces are biologically the more important and vital [than the antagonizing forces]. The balance between the co-operative, altruistic tendencies and those which are disoperative and egoistic is relatively close [in biological organisms]. In the long run, however, the group-centered, more altruistic drives are slightly stronger" — such is a summary of this situation.[22]

To sum up: without the operation of a biological counterpart of love energy, life itself is not possible, nor its continuity, nor the preservation and survival of species, nor life evolution, nor the emergence and evolution of *Homo sapiens*.

### F. *The Psychological Aspect of Love*

Psychologically the experience of love is a complex consisting of emotional, affective, volitional, and intellectual elements. It has many qualitative forms, covered by such terms as: empathy, sympathy, kindness, devotion, admiration, benevolence, reverence, respect, adoration, friendship — to single out a few. Each of these " shades " of love as psychological experience has its own " color." [23]   These experiences are opposite those of hatred, enmity, dislike, envy, jealousy, antipathy, and other forms of hate. *In any genuine psychological experience of love, the ego or I of the loving individual tends to merge with and to identify itself with the loved Thee.* The greater the love, the greater the identification. The joy or sorrow of the loved person becomes joy and sorrow to the loving person. Genuine sharing of all the values of life follows. Sacrifice for the loved person becomes a sacrifice for the person himself.

In other words, *love as psychological experience is " altruistic " by its very nature;* whereas the opposite *experience of hatred is inherently selfish.* In a genuine love the loved person is experienced always as the *end* value; in the egoistic experience the other person is always only the *means* value. Aristotle and V. Solovyev have pointed out very clearly this characteristic of love *versus* the egoistic experience of hatred and pseudo-love. In a real love or friendship a friend is " one who does what is good (or what he believes to be good) for another for that other's sake, and one wishes his friend to . . . live for that friend's own sake," and not because the friend gives him pleasure or is useful to him. Pseudo-friendship, motivated by pleasure or utility, takes the other person as a means and not as the end value.[24]

Solovyev stressed this point especially well in his analysis of love and egoism. " True love is that which not only affirms in subjective feeling the unconditional significance of human individuality in another and in oneself, but also justifies this unconditional significance in actuality." [25] Egoism in its pure form, on the contrary, " affirms an unconditional oppositeness, an unbridgeable chasm between one's own ego and the others. The egoist says: I am everything . . . while the others are just nothing for me and become something only as a mere means for me; my life and well-being is an absolute goal, while the life and well-being of others are admitted only insofar as they are instruments for a realization of my goal. . . . I am the center, while the whole world is only a circumference." [26]

" Love is the justification and deliverance of individuality through the sacrifice of egoism. It rescues us from the inevitability of death, and fills our existence with an absolute content. . . . Sacrificing egoism and surrendering ourselves to love, we find in it not merely living, but also life-giving power, and we do not forefeit our individuality (personality) with our egoism, but on the contrary make it eternal."

Such a love cosmos is now only at its beginning in the empirical world of man, at about the same stage as is reason in the animal world. Love conquering death " exists in its beginning but not as yet in actual fact." Eventually it will grow and conquer death on this planet, in this world.[27]

More concretely, *love is the experience that annuls our individual loneliness;* fills the emptiness of our isolation with the richest value; breaks and transcends the narrow walls of our little egos; makes us coparticipants in the highest life of humanity and in the whole cosmos; expands our true individuality to the immeasurable boundaries of the universe.

Eliminating our loneliness and binding us by the noblest of bonds to others, love is literally a *life-giving force,* because, as the studies of suicide show, an empty loneliness is the main cause of suicide, and because altruists live longer than egoists do.[28] Making us full-fledged coparticipants in the lives of others, love infinitely enriches our lives by the greatest and noblest values of all humanity. In this sense it fills us with *knowledge,* because coparticipation and coexperience in the richest experience of all the generations of humanity — rather than only in one's pitifully poor individual experience — is the most efficient method of learning and the most fruitful way to truth and knowledge. In this sense the love experience leads to a true cognition and *love becomes truth* (see further on that).

*Love beautifies our life* because the love experience is beautiful by its very nature and beautifies the whole universe. To love anything or anybody means literally to immortalize the mortal, to ennoble the ignoble, to uplift the low, to beautify the ugly. Anything that one looks at through loving eyes becomes " lovely," that is, beautiful.

By its very nature *love is goodness itself;* therefore *it makes our life noble and good.*

Finally, *love experience means freedom at its loftiest.* To love anything is to act freely, without compulsion or coercion. And vice versa: to be free means to do what one loves to do. In this sense, *love and true freedom are synonyms; love is the loftiest form of freedom.* Compulsion and coercion are the negation of love. Where there is love there is no coercion; where there is coercion there is no love. And the greater the love the greater the freedom. A person who loves all humanity is free in this human universe; a person who loves the whole universe is free in the whole world. A person who hates the world is the greatest of slaves — subjectively and objectively. Anything or anybody is his enemy, anything or anybody hinders him, opposes him, presses upon him, limits his freedom incessantly, at every turn, in every action, in every thought, emotion, or volition. The whole world, from inanimate objects up to his fellow men, becomes his prison filled with innumerable executioners.[29] St. Paul's quoted statements are perfectly accurate in this respect. Freedom is love and love is freedom.

The love experience is marked further by a " feeling " of *fearlessness and power.* Love does not fear anything or anybody. It cuts off the very roots of fear. Where there is fear there is no love; where there is love there is no fear.

"Those that love God through fear are the lowest of human beings. They worship God from fear of punishment. . . . So long as there is any fear in the heart, how can there be love also? Love conquers naturally all fear. A loving mother does not hesitate to throw herself against any danger menacing her child; a loving person does not hesitate to lay down his life — is not afraid even of death — saving the loved ones. Fear comes from a selfish idea of cutting one's self off from the universe. The smaller and the more selfish I make myself, the more is my fear." [30] *The best and most scientific remedy for fear is love.* Without love there is no remedy for this disease.

*The fearlessness and freedom of love implies power.* A person who is not afraid of anything is subjectively (in his own experience) and objectively a powerful person. He cannot be intimidated; he cannot be bribed; he cannot be beaten into subjection. All his energies are coiled up into the single power of love "that beareth all things, endureth all things." Nothing in this coiled-up energy is wasted in inner conflicts and external friction; the whole of it is directed to one great purpose. And often the more it functions, the greater are the returns of the energies it generates in others; the more it expends itself, the greater are the returns that replenish its expenditure. In this sense it is a form of energy that is almost inexhaustible (like the energy of intra-atomic friction), an energy that sometimes actually grows through its expenditure. The more love expends itself the stronger it becomes. Herein lies the fact, noted above, of the majestic, gigantic power of love and gentleness, of the power of the great incarnations of love like Buddha and Jesus, St. Francis and Gandhi. Even from a strictly "positivistic" standpoint, the influence exerted by these apostles of love upon the whole of human history far exceeds the influence of the mighty conquerors, rulers, empire builders, and seeming controllers of millions of soldiers and subjects. (See, on the power of love further, Chapter Four.) Hence a scientific prescription. *The most effective and most accessible way to acquire the maximum of constructive power is to love truly and wisely.* The kingdoms built by the apostles of love prove to be more enduring than those built by hate and coercion. [31]

Finally, *the love experience is equivalent to the highest peace of mind and happiness.* Beginning with the somewhat puny "*peace of mind*" of Freudians and of our best sellers on "how to stop worrying," and the lollipop happiness of our dime-store hedonists and chamber-of-commerce utilitarians; passing through the short-lived "peace of mind" and "happiness" of contemporary sensual lovers; and ending with the unshakable peace of mind and unutterable bliss of an all-embracing, all-forgiving love: the love experience is the only experience that brings both of these graces of God — peace of mind and happiness — to their fruition. When love is slight and impure, peace and happiness are slight and fragile. When it is unbounded and pure, it is " the peace of God which passeth all understanding"; [32] happiness becomes the ineffable *summum bonum*.

" Love for love's sake is the highest happiness." [33] Without love there is neither peace of mind nor any sort of happiness. Hence, *the best and most accessible path to real peace of mind and supreme happiness is to love (wisely guided by truth).*

Such are some of the important characteristics of love as psychological experience.

In comparison with these, other psychological traits of the love experience are somewhat insignificant and puny. Farther on, however, in the discussion of the dimensional system of love, some of these secondary traits of love will be mentioned.

## G. *The Social Aspect of Love*

Finally, *on the social plane love is a meaningful interaction — or relationship — between two or more persons where the aspirations and aims of one person are shared and helped in their realization by other persons.* A loving person not only does not hinder the realization of the wise aims of the loved person but positively helps it. So far as he helps, he does not cause pain or sorrow to the loved person, but increases his happiness. It is the joy of giving and the joy of receiving; it is fulfilling oneself in others and by others. The terms " solidarity," " mutual aid," " co-operation," " unity of good neighbors," " familistic relationship," and the like denote various forms of love as social relationship. Its highest forms are magnificently defined in the Sermon on the Mount.

Love your enemies, bless them that curse you, do good to them that hate you, and pray for them which despitefully use you and persecute you.
Agree with thine adversary quickly.
First be reconciled to thy brother, and then come and offer thy gift [to the altar].
Ye have heard that it hath been said, An eye for an eye, and a tooth for a tooth: But I say unto you, That ye resist not evil: but whosoever shall smite thee on thy right cheek, turn to him the other also.
And if any man will sue thee at the law, and take away thy coat, let him have thy cloak also.
And whosoever shall compel thee to go a mile, go with him twain.
Give to him that asketh thee, and from him that would borrow of thee turn not thou away.

These norms outline the social relationships of love at their highest and best.

The religious, ethical, ontological, physical, biological, psychological, and social phases of love do not exhaust it; on the contrary, they show the infinite richness of this participant in the Absolute.

We shall concentrate in this study mainly on the psychological and sociocultural planes of love — love as a " visible " empirical psychosocial phenomenon. Concentrating on these planes, however, we shall always keep in mind the manifoldness of love as a whole, because without its religious, ethical, and ontological aspects we cannot truly understand a " visible " part of this cosmos, its psychosocial empirical aspects.

*Chapter Two*

# The Five-Dimensional Universe
## of Psychosocial Love

I

### FIVE DIMENSIONS

Even as an empirical psychosocial phenomenon, love remains a many-dimensional cosmos. It has at least five " dimensions ": (1) the intensity of love: (2) its extensity: (3) its duration; (4) its purity; (5) the adequacy of its objective manifestation in overt actions and material vehicles in relation to its subjective purpose.

### A. *The Intensity of Love*

In intensity love ranges between zero and the highest possible point, arbitrarily denoted as infinity. The zero point is neither love nor hate. Below the zero point is hate (which has a similar intensity dimension). We all know this range of love intensity. When we observe a person who preaches love but does not practice it, we know that the intensity of his love is near the zero point; when the highfalutin preaching of love is used to mask selfish and hateful actions of hypocrites, their actions fall below the zero point and become hateful actions of various intensities. Such actions as giving a few cents to the hungry (from large possessions of the giver), or offering a seat to another person on a streetcar, are actions of love, though of low intensity. Actions by which a person freely gives to others his greatest values — health, life, " soul," hedonistic or utilitarian happiness — are love actions of the highest possible intensity. Between zero and the highest points of love intensity there are many intermediary degrees.

As a whole, the range of love intensity is not scalar: in most cases we cannot say exactly how many times greater a given intensity is than another, or whether it is equal, or higher, or lower. Yet we can often see clearly *which intensity is really high and which low, and sometimes even measure it in quantitative units.* Thus, other conditions being equal, the act of merely offering the seat in a streetcar will be appraised by practically all normal beings as an action of much lower love intensity than the action of saving a life at the risk or sacrifice of one's own. Again, other conditions being equal, when the same person gives to others at one time 2 per cent of his wealth and at another 90 per cent of it, his second love action will be many times more intense than the first. When at one time he gives others one hour of his time and at another a week or a month, his second action will be many times higher in its love intensity than his first. To sum up: by and large *love intensity is not scalar*. This, however, does not hinder us from seeing the greatly different intensities of various love actions; nor even — here and there — from roughly measuring in numerical units these intensities. The same may be said of the scalar and nonscalar character of the four other dimensions of love.

### B. *The Extensity of Love*

*The extensity of love ranges from the zero point of love of oneself only, up to the love of all mankind, all living creatures, and the whole universe.* Between these minimal and maximal degrees lies a vast scale of extensities: love of one's own family, or a few friends, or love of all the groups one belongs to — one's clan, tribe, nationality, nation, religious, occupational, political, and other groups and associations. The maximal point of intensity is the love of the whole universe (and of God). Like St. Francis, one can love " a dear brother — earth," the moon, the wind, a river, a tree, and generally all animate and inanimate phenomena, and thus " reverently and lovingly walk the earth." And one can " hate the whole world " and view it as his enemy. The zero point of love extensity is a love of oneself only. As mentioned, the " *ordinate* " *of extensity is nonscalar, but this does not prevent its helping to distinguish contrastingly vast and narrow extensities of love and once in a while even to measure them in scalar units.*

### C. *The Duration of Love*

Again, *the duration of love may range from the shortest possible moment to years or throughout the whole life of an individual or of a group.* Not only love actions of low intensity, but many of the highest intensity may last but a short time, like the actions of a soldier on a battlefield who risks or sacrifices his life to save his comrade; having saved him, and having himself survived, a soldier may stop such activities and become a selfish, ordinary creature. On the other hand, love actions of low as well as high intensity may endure for a long period, perhaps throughout the life of an individual or group. A mother caring for her sick child through his and her life, a good neighbor for years giving financial or other help to this or that person, great apostles of love discharging their love mission for decades, even throughout life, are examples of enduring love.

### D. *The Purity of Love*

*The purity of love ranges from the love motivated by love alone — without the taint of a " soiling motive " of utility, pleasure, advantage, or profit, down to the " soiled love " where love is but a means to a utilitarian or hedonistic or other end, where love is only the thinnest trickle in a muddy current of selfish aspirations and purposes.* The statements of saints of the Occident and the Orient that each loved God and would love Him even if He were to condemn them to an eternal hell for such a love are perhaps the most striking expressions of the purest love. " I love Thee, Lord," says a hymn ascribed to St. Francis Xavier, " yet not because I hope for Heaven thereby; nor yet since they who love Thee not, must burn eternally. Not with the hope of gaining aught; not seeking a reward; but as Thyself has loved me, O ever loving Lord." And the Oriental: " I do not want wealth, nor many people, nor learning; no, not even do I want to go to Heaven. Let me be born again and again; but, Lord, grant me this, that I may have love for Thee, and that for Love's sake." [1]

Pure " love knows no bargain . . . no reward. Love is always for love's sake. . . . Ask not anything in return for your love; let your position be always that of the giver; give your love unto God, but do not ask anything in return even from Him." " Love knows no fear . . . no rival " — such are other traits of a pure love. [2] The quoted statements of Jesus, St. Paul, and Aristotle tell the same thing.

### E. *The Adequacy of Love*

*The adequacy* of the subjective goal of love to its objective manifestation ranges from a complete discrepancy between the subjective goal of love actions and its objective consequences, up to their identity. *Inadequacy may have two different forms:* (a) love experience may be subjectively genuine in the loving person, but the objective consequences of his love actions may be very different from, even opposite to, the love goal; (b) a person may have no love experience or intentions subjectively, yet the objective consequences of his actions, though motivated by something else than love, may be most beneficial for others, similar to the effects of genuine love. The first sort of love experience and activity is altruistic subjectively but not objectively. The second sort of experience and action is not altruistic subjectively but is altruistic objectively.

Let us briefly consider each of these two forms of *inadequate love.* We all know mothers who love their children intensely and want to make them " lovable " — that is, honest, industrious, and good. With this purpose they frequently pamper them, satisfy all their fancies, and fail to discipline them when they need it. Through such love actions they often spoil their children, and make them capricious, irresponsible, weak, lazy, dishonest. These objective consequences of love differ radically from the mother's goal of love. Another extreme case of such discrepancy is that in which a loving person, anxious to help a loved one, by mistake gives him poison instead of medicine. Such discrepant love actions are the forms of *inadequate, unwise, misled, ignorant,* or *blind love*. In all such cases love is not guided by truth and knowledge in the choice of the overt actions and instrumentalities of love. The necessary wisdom lacking, blind love miscarries in its objective manifestations and destroys itself; instead of benefiting the beloved person, it often harms him. Here we have an inadequate love which corresponds to de Rougemont's Eros as a dark passion moving to self-destruction.[3]

Beginning with a spectacular discrepancy between its aims and its objective consequences, this form of subjective love actions-reactions ranges upward in a series of ever-decreasing discrepancies, until we have adequate love: where the subjective aims of love and its objective consequences become identical. *Such an adequate love acts in complete union with the truth and knowledge that guide its objective manifestations in all its actions and interrelationships.*

In a purely " *objective love* action " a person may have no love motives in his activities, yet their objective consequences may be identical with those of genuine love actions of the highest intensity and purity. Many great creators of art values — Bach or Mozart, Beethoven or Shakespeare, Raphael or Michelangelo — were motivated in their creative activities not so much by love of goodness as by love of beauty, or by a creative urge, or by even prosaic motives (money, fame, popularity, etc.). Likewise many a scientist or inventor in his discoveries and inventions has been moved by his love of science or technology, or by a creative urge or some prosaic motive, and not by the motive of love as goodness. Even many saints aspired directly not for altruistic love but for union with God: they became " love-filled " only as a necessary condition of their main purpose. In spite of the absence of altruistic love motives in the activities of these creators, their achievements have nevertheless exerted the most potent love effects upon millions and millions. The works of Bach and Beethoven, Shakespeare and Michelangelo, Plato and Newton have exerted beneficial, ennobling, uplifting, spiritualizing, enjoyable, and gladdening effects upon uncounted generations. Objectively (though not always subjectively) they became by their achievements great benefactors; not only intellectual or aesthetic, but also moral educators of humanity.

The inadequacy of such " objective but not subjective " love actions ranges upward from those extreme cases where no motive of love is present, through those cases where it enters as one of the motives, to those highest instances where the love motive becomes dominant and finds its adequate expression in overt activities and achievements. As we shall see later, these *objectively altruistic actions are possible mainly through the*

*indivisible unity of goodness, truth, and beauty, and the possibility of
their mutual transformation into one another.* If in their ontological
nature they are inseparable — though distinct in their individuality — anyone who truly creates in one of these fields indirectly creates in the other
two: genuine goodness is always true and beautiful; genuine beauty is
always good and true; and genuine truth is always good and beautiful.
The great and small creators in the fields of truth and beauty may not
be directly motivated by goodness (love); yet when they are creative in
these fields they cannot help becoming creative also in the field of love,
because of the unity and mutual transformability of these "forms of
energies."

This unity of the greatest values and of the altruistic effects of the pursuit of truth, beauty, and God is stressed by the Hindu distinction of the
three ways to "the liberation": Karma Yoga, or the way of good deeds
or love of neighbors; Jnana Yoga, or the way of truth and enlightenment;
and Bhakti Yoga, or the way of complete devotion to God and love of
God.[4]

These, then, are the two main forms of the inadequacy of love.

## F. *The Theoretical and Practical Significance of the Five-Dimensional System of Love*

Because it is manageable and not too complex, this five-dimensional
system of love serves us in many theoretical and practical ways.

First, it allows us to "grade" roughly the total, five-dimensional magnitude of love. Such grading is not a strict measurement, because, as was
pointed out, each dimension is not strictly scalar. Yet when we are confronted with an unquestionably contrasting "small love" and "great
love," we can use a rough numerical indicator as a shorthand symbol of
obviously different magnitudes of love.[5] If we arbitrarily designate various values to each of the five ordinates by figures from 0 to 100, we may
use them as indicators for notably different magnitudes of the total, five-
dimensional love.

The greatest altruists, like Jesus, Buddha, St. Francis, would occupy
the highest possible place, denoted by 100 in all five dimensions. Persons
who are neither loving nor hating would occupy a position near zero.
Others would find a place somewhere between these points, some higher,
and some lower than the others. In this way a rough numerical denota-
tion may be used to indicate obviously contrasting magnitudes of love.

Second, the five-dimensional system allows us to compare and concisely denote various forms of love. For instance, if we take only the
dimensions of *intensity* and *extensity* of love, we can at once distinguish
several types.

1. There are many persons whose love is very intense toward a small in-
group (their family, their friends, their clique or sect or faction), but

whose love for anybody beyond this little universe is nonexistent. The extensity of their love is thus very low.

2. There are many persons who profess to love the whole of humanity. The extensity of their love is thus enormous. But their love of humanity rarely goes beyond speech-reactional declarations, and shows little in their deeds. This is *love of low intensity combined with vast extensity*.

3. There are persons who most intensely love their little in-group, then love *but in a decreasing degree of intensity* various larger groups: their neighbors, their village or town, their occupational or political or religious or national or state groups, then all humanity. This is a type of love decreasing in intensity as it increases in extensity.

4. We all know love actions of the *highest intensity* but of *very short duration*. A soldier impulsively risking his life to save his comrade on a battlefield is such a case. Many are heroes of love for a short moment; only a few are such for a long time!

5. There are persons *who love for a long time but with a low intensity*. Persons who for years contribute their reasonable donation to a community fund are examples of this type. Most " American Good Neighbors " in my collection of some 1,000 cases belong to this type.[6]

6. There are persons who love intensely, and for an indefinitely long time, either a small or an extensive human universe.

7. We have love activities in which *high purity* is combined with high or low intensity, small or vast extensity, short or long duration, low or high adequacy; and similar combinations of *low purity* with other dimensional values. Which of these combinations is more frequent in an ordinary human universe remains unknown and can be learned only by systematic studies as have yet hardly been begun.

All this shows that our dimensional system permits us to classify the types of love activities and of loving persons, and to learn which types and combinations are more frequent in a given human universe.

The third service of our system is that it permits us to set forth and study the meaningful-causal relationships among the dimension variables. Are they clearly connected with one another? If so, how? positively? negatively? Which dimension variable with which? How closely?

At present our knowledge of these relationships is rather meager. We need far more study before our knowledge of the problem can begin to be useful. With this reservation, a few tentative uniformities in this field may be pointed out.

## II

### UNIFORMITIES IN THE CAUSAL-MEANINGFUL RELATIONSHIPS OF LOVE'S DIMENSIONAL VARIABLES

#### A. *Self-Evident Uniformity*

*The greater the five-dimensional magnitude of love, the less frequent it is in the empirical sociocultural world.* The great altruists like Jesus, Buddha, St. Francis, Nil Sorsky, and Gandhi are as rare as the greatest genius in the field of truth or beauty.

#### B. *Less Self-Evident Uniformities*

1. *Uniformities between Intensity and Extensity.* Other conditions being equal, *the intensity of love tends to decrease with an increase of its extensity or the size of the universe of love.* Insofar as the empirical love of a person or a group is an energy of *limited magnitude,* the larger the love universe the thinner its spread. If a given reservoir of love supplies only three persons, its intensity is many times greater than if it supplies three thousand or three million persons. Herein lies the explanation of why frequently professed love of all humanity is so feeble in its intensity and rarely goes beyond a mere verbal declaration. If we assume that love is not energy or that its magnitude is unlimited, then the formulated uniformity becomes questionable.

As a variation of this uniformity, we have a *decreasing intensity of love (of the individual or group) with the passing from a small group dearest to them to ever larger and larger groups that are socioculturally more distant from them.* The logical reason for this is the same as that just pointed out for the main uniformity.

Factual observations and even a few experimental studies seem to corroborate these uniformities. Whether we take our own behavior or observe the behavior of other persons and groups, we see uniformly that our most intense love (in overt actions) applies only to a very limited number of persons (members of the family, a few friends, and generally a small in-group). Next comes a socially more remote circle, which we still love tangibly but less intensely. The larger and more distant the group becomes, the feebler becomes our love in its intensity, until it becomes intangible, merely speech-reactional.

This uniformity is well corroborated by a few experimental studies, beginning with my own. Here are the essentials of one or two of these studies and their summary results.

In one experimental study with children between the ages of 3 and 5 and high school children, the intensity of love or sociality was measured by the amount of work the subject did — carrying marbles and pails of sand from one corner of a garden to another, and other measurable forms of work: (a) for himself or herself; (b) for the dearest " pal " in the group; (c) for a member of the group he disliked or was indifferent toward. The results showed a decrease in the amount of work done by each child as we pass from the work " for himself or herself " to that for a " pal " and then for an indifferent or disliked member.

In 1928 the same problem was experimentally investigated with students of the University of Minnesota.[7] In this case the " thermometer of relative sociality (or love) " was measured by the amount of money the students were ready to give to three given causes. To be sure, this thermometer is wholly inadequate for measuring the comparative sociality of various individuals; a rich man may give more than a poor man and yet be less social. But the amount of money given by the same individual, at the same time, for the benefit of different groups seems to be a pretty good indicator of the individual's sociality toward these different groups.

Starting with this premise the author and, at his request, H. R. Hosea and O. D. Duncan, instructors in sociology at the University of Minnesota, one day addressed six classes of sociology at the University with the request that every student contribute as much as he could for the following three purposes: first, for diagrams and a computing machine for the class itself; second, for " three brilliant students in the sociology department who were financially ruined by the Mississippi inundations and who would be forced to leave the University unless we should help them "; third, in the name of the " International Students' Relief " for the students of Chinese and Russian universities who were dying of starvation. The students were told that the diagrams and computing machine would be exceedingly helpful to them in preparing for their examinations. We took care to describe most realistically the pitiful situation of the brilliant students whose families were ruined by the recent Mississippi inundation. And the terrible situation of the Chinese and Russian students was depicted realistically. In brief, each of us played an actor's role in order to make the students believe that we were sincere and were really collecting money for these groups. After this each student was given a slip of paper and instructed to write how much he could give — and give immediately — for each of these purposes. The slips were collected and the results studied.

The first group, then, was the class itself; the second, students of the same department and the same university, but not of the same class — thus more remote socially than the first; and the third group was still more remote socially, for though composed of students, they were students in Chinese and Russian universities. Thus the social distance increased from the first group to the third. On the other hand, the importance of the cause increased from the first group to the third. Whereas the Russian and Chinese students needed help to keep them from dying of starvation (danger of life), the second group risked only their university education; and the third cause was a mere convenience in preparing for examinations. The results are shown by the table which follows.

## CONTRIBUTIONS AND CONTRIBUTORS FOR THREE CAUSES

| Class | I — For Class Diagrams, etc. | II — For Impoverished Students of the University of Minnesota | III — For Chinese and Russian Students |
|---|---|---|---|
| Money contributed — A | $ 7.30 | $ 6.00 | $ 3.55 |
| B | 6.25 | 3.90 | 2.65 |
| C | 5.30 | 6.60 | 5.00 |
| D | 6.75 | 5.75 | 2.25 |
| E | 11.10 | 6.05 | 5.75 |
| F | 11.55 | 4.70 | 3.25 |
| Totals | $48.25 | $33.00 | $22.45 |
| Number of persons contributing — A | 43 | 33 | 23 |
| B | 27 | 16 | 11 |
| C | 40 | 36 | 29 |
| D | 23 | 22 | 10 |
| E | 20 | 15 | 14 |
| F | 32 | 16 | 12 |
| Totals | 185 | 138 | 99 |
| Comparative indices for money contributed (Cause I = 100) | 100.0 | 68.4 | 46.5 |
| Comparative indices for number of persons contributing (Cause I = 100) | 100.0 | 74.6 | 53.5 |

The table shows, first, that in spite of the least importance of Cause I, the same students contributed a greater amount of money to it than to Causes II and III, " self-altruism " or egoism being stronger here than altruism for others. Secondly, in spite of the fact that Cause III required the greatest amount of help, the contribution for it was the least. Thirdly, the picture is similar for the number of students who contributed to one or all of these causes. Out of a total of 202 students who responded to the appeal (those who gave nothing are excluded from the table), the greatest number, 185, contributed to the least important cause, and the least number, 99, to the most important cause. Of course there were individuals who contributed more to the second or the third cause than to the first; there also were individuals who contributed only to the third or the second, and gave nothing to the first; and Class C gave more ($6.60) to the second cause than to the first ($5.30).

This means that the equal love toward all human beings is still practiced only by very few, though it is professed by many.

All these students professed in their speech-reactions that "in helping other human beings we should not discriminate against race, nationality, religion, or any other characteristics, and should help them according to the urgency of their need." But in their overt behavior of helping other human beings, only 27.4 per cent of these students showed consistent overt actions and speech-reactions.

When American Good Neighbors were asked to choose those twelve persons in the world who were dearest to them, they chose spouse, children, parents, and siblings as the first six dearest; and personal friends and relatives as the next six. Even this group of Neighbors, who are somewhat above the average in their altruism, has a decreasing intensity of love with an increase of psychosocial distance.[8]

Similar results were obtained with Harvard and Radcliffe students.[9]

Similar results have also been recorded in other experimental studies of the problem.[10]

2. *Uniformities between Intensity and Duration of Love.* The relationship between these variables is little known. The subsequent uniformities are purely tentative.

(a) Assuming that the total magnitude of love energy in an individual is finite, *the intensity of love tends to decrease with an increase of duration, when the love expenditure of a given person is not correspondingly replenished by an inflow from other persons or other sources, empirical or transcendental.* And not only does the intensity decrease, but the more intensely love's reservoir is spent, the shorter becomes the period during which it is exhausted. Like any other limited amount of energy, love energy can be spent either very intensely in a short period or it can be spread more thinly over a longer time. Millions of love heroes manifest love energy at high intensity for a short time. Thousands of soldiers risk their lives, sometimes voluntarily sacrifice them, to save their comrades. Thousands of persons perform daily actions of love of high intensity. Even in heterosexual love there are millions who love "madly" for a comparatively short time. But these times are "short" indeed; having quickly exhausted their love energy, these persons soon become ordinary or even selfish in their love activity. *There are millions of heroes of love for a moment, but few for indefinitely long periods. And their number tends roughly to decrease as the duration increases.* This happens especially if and when their love intensity is not reciprocated, or is not replenished by some sort of public approval, by a compensating inflow of love from their fellow men, or through love actions from other sources, empirical or transcendental. In this respect love energy seems to behave like other forms of energy (heat, electricity, etc.).

(b) *When an intense expenditure of love is reciprocated by love of others or, more generally, is replenished by an inflow of love from ex-*

*ternal sources* [11] — whether this source be retroactive love, love generated by love actions themselves, public approval, popularity, fame, or other substitutes for love, or whether it be a love coming from mystical, little-known supraempirical sources — *the intensity of love does not necessarily decrease as its duration increases.* Since the expenditure of love is either fully or partly compensated by its inflow from these sources, the intensest love can function for an indefinitely long time, as long, in fact, as the inflowing equivalent continues. *If this equivalent is greater than the expended love, its intensity can even grow in the course of time.*

Here again, the daily observations of ordinary persons and especially of great altruists demonstrate to us the reality of the indefinitely long and intense love. We frequently observe that the intensity of love between two or more persons grows, rather than decreases, in the course of time. Many love relationships begin as a feeble sympathy and eventually grow in intensity and purity. This happens also in heterosexual relations. The behavior of the great apostles of love displays the most intense love pulsating for an indefinitely long time.

The discussed uniformity is explained in the above proposition, then, by an inflow of love or of its substitutes (transformable into love as other forms of energy are transformable into one another) from " outside the individual." The concrete forms of this inflowing love (or " feed-back ") are many: love reciprocation, kindness answered by kindness, sacrifice by sacrifice, public approval, glorification of the love hero, tangible appreciation of love by others through pecuniary and other means, and so on. From our own experience, and from observations of the love conduct of others, we know that such reactions to one's love serve to kindle it, and replenish it.[12] On the other hand, we also know that ordinarily an unrequited love, especially when it is responded to with animosity, tends to become discouraged, dried up, and disillusioned; sometimes this makes us bitter and even inimical toward those who thus " do not appreciate our kindness." Even the greatest apostles of love had their " dark nights " and moments of despair because of unrequited love.

To sum up: the secret of an undiminishing love intensity over long periods of time seems to lie in this inflow of love from outside the loving individual that replenishes his great expenditures of intense love energy. Without such an inflow, the intensity of love with an increase of duration tends to fall under the first uniformity discussed.

Sometimes there seems to be no inflow of love from other human beings, nor from any visible empirical source; instead, the response is open animosity. And yet the great martyrs of love, such as Jesus, or Al Hallaj, or Damien the Leper, or Gandhi [13] — to mention only a few spectacular cases — did not decrease the intensity of their love despite persecution, hatred, and even martyrdom. How then shall we explain such " miracles "?

In the first place, practically all such martyrs of love had an inflow of the intensest and purest love from a small group of their family, their followers, their friends and companions. We know of hardly any such martyr of love who stood indeed alone in the whole inimical world; almost without exception they had at least a small group of those who loved them intensely. Furthermore they doubtless had a much larger "reservoir of love" than ordinary people have; and this great reservoir must have permitted them to expend their love lavishly for a long time. These two reasons may suffice to explain many of the cases discussed.

But this still leaves unexplained those martyrs of love who have no observable "inflow of love" from outside. The most probable hypothesis for them (and in a much slighter degree for a much larger group of smaller altruists and good neighbors) is that an inflow of love comes from an intangible, little-studied, possibly supraempirical source called "God," "the Godhead," "the Soul of the Universe," the "Heavenly Father," "Truth," and so on. Our growing knowledge of intra-atomic and cosmic ray energies has shown that the physico-chemical systems of energies are able to maintain themselves and replenish their systems for an indefinitely long time. If this is true of these "coarsest" energies, then the highest energy of love is likely to have this "self-replenishing" property to a still higher degree. We know next to nothing about the properties of love energy. Theoretically love may have its own "fission forces" that make its reservoir inexhaustible. When a person knows how to release these forces of love he can spend love energy lavishly without exhausting his reservoir.

This hypothesis is corroborated by the purely empirical statements of the martyrs of love who were surrounded by an inimical world. In such an emergency they called for the help of an "intangible force" — God or His equivalent. Jesus, foreseeing and foretelling his crucifixion, says in his agony at Gethsemane: "My soul is exceeding sorrowful unto death. . . . And he went forward a little, and fell on the ground, and prayed that, if it were possible, the hour might pass from him. And he said, Abba, Father, all things are possible unto thee; take away this cup from me: nevertheless not what I will, but what thou wilt" (Mark 14:34–36). And on the cross, again appealing to his Father, he forgives and prays for his executioners: "Father, forgive them; for they know not what they do." Finally, in his last agony he prays, "My God, my God, why hast thou forsaken me?" (Luke 23:34, Mark 15:34).

Similarly the great Mohammedan mystic, thinker, and apostle of love, Al Hallaj, imprisoned and waiting for the cruelest execution (crucifixion, preceded by the cutting off of his arms and legs, and followed by burning the remains) forgives his enemies and also appeals to God for strength. "Here we are. . . . It is in Thy grace that we look for a refuge and in the pre-eternal splendour of Thy glory we look for clarity. . . . Thus it is Thou, my God, who assigned to this witness [Al Hallaj] Thy divine essence, Thy certain selfness. It is Thou who wanted my début. . . . It is Thou who made me to proclaim Thy essence through my created essence. . . . It has come to pass that now I am going to be exposed to death, executed, hanged on a gallows, burnt, my ashes thrown to the wind and currents. . . . Ah! . . . the smallest particle of my ashes promises to my body a glorious transfiguration [resurrection], a reality that is more certain than that of the greatest mountains." [14]

Practically all the martyrs of love in similar situations miraculously reinforce their love through prayers to God, the Invisible Power, the Self, or other transcendental sources. In prosaic language, they begin to draw their love energy from a transcendental source, by whatever name they call it (the Agape form of love). We find examples of such " drawing " in the biographies or autobiographies of the past, as well as of contemporary apostles of love. M. Gandhi and A. Schweitzer repeatedly indicate this in their autobiographies, when they were in difficult siutations surrounded by an inimical world. "After all, the real protector was neither I nor my brother, but the Almighty." " Without an unreserved surrender to his Grace complete mastery over thought (and all fears) is impossible." Praying " to the God of Truth that He may grant the boon of Ahimsa [nonviolence] in mind, word and deed " was Gandhi's method of " drawing his loving strength in all crucial situations of his life." [15]

" My life is completely and unmistakably determined by the mysterious experience of God revealing Himself within me as ethical Will and desiring to take hold of my life. . . . One day, in my despair, I threw myself into a chair in the consulting-room and groaned out: ' What a blockhead I was to come out here to doctor savages like these! ' Whereupon Joseph quietly remarked: ' Yes, Doctor, here on earth you are a great blockhead, but not in heaven.' " " Many a time I tried to settle what meaning lay hidden for me in the saying of Jesus, ' Whosoever would save his life shall lose it, and whosoever shall lose his life for My sake and the Gospel's shall save it.' Now the answer was found. In addition to the outward, I now had inward happiness." [16]

When Serafim of Sarov (1759–1833) was attacked in his eremitic retreat by two criminals, he did not resist their attack, though he was physically powerful and had at that moment an axe in his hands (he was clearing the forest). Remembering Christ's " resist not evil " and " they that take the sword shall perish with the sword," he dropped the axe and allowed the criminals to beat him almost to death. Instead of resisting or cursing the attackers, he prayed for them; and later when they were caught he categorically opposed their persecution. In this, as in other emergencies, he drew his loving strength from God, because " God loves those who love him." [17]

These three suggested sources — love of the martyrs' in-group, the vast reservoir of their love, and the self-perpetuating energy of love drawn from an intangible, supraempirical (but most natural) source — rather satisfactorily account for the inexhaustible expenditure of love through indefinitely long periods. These seeming exceptions are not exceptions at all to our second uniformity in the relationship of the intensity and duration of love.

3. *The Relationship between the Intensity and the Purity of Love.* The basically nonscalar nature of these particular dimensions makes it especially difficult to define their quantitative relationship. *Nevertheless, all in all their interrelationship seems to be positive. Love becoming increasingly purer also increases in its intensity; and vice versa.* Only the purest love is capable of the greatest sacrifice, of being most intense, because from the standpoint of an impure love of utilitarian and hedonistic calculations such a sacrifice is disutilitarian and antihedonistic. As such it is hardly possible. "Soiled love" is always fragile, weak, and short-lived. Hence it is of low intensity. And vice versa: the intensest love has to be the purest. It means a complete merging of the whole human ego (or egos) with those of the loved one: a complete identification of the intensely loving persons. Such an identification goes beyond any utilitarian-hedonistic motivations, which are inseparable from ego and egoism. Such a love is a "disinterested" love, free from "soiling ingredients."

These almost self-evident conclusions seem to be corroborated by all the data of observation and self-observation, however scarce they are. First, the love of the greatest apostles is simultaneously intense and pure. The greatest sacrifice they made testifies to its intensity. The absence of all selfish — utilitarian and hedonistic — motives from their love activities testifies to their purity. The love of Jesus, St. Paul, St. Francis of Assisi, Buddha, Dr. Theodore Haas, Serafim of Sarov, Damien the Leper, Gandhi, and of thousands of other apostles of love, had both these characteristics. On the other hand, millions of cases of love of low intensity invariably are a variety of "soiled love" in which selfish, utilitarian, and hedonistic motivations are conspicuous. Most such love relationships are not "familistic" but "contractual." By their very nature these are selfish and almost always are planned to get as much as possible for as little as possible.[18]

The above statement is equally applicable to heterosexual love based on "romance" and "pleasure." Such love activities may appear very intense: the persons may be "madly in love," for the only reason of expected sexual pleasure. Such "loves" have little if any relationship to the love studied here. No wonder therefore that the passion and intensity of this sort of heterosexual love wither quickly away; "mad" love cools, craziness passes, and the persons soon become mutual strangers, sometimes even enemies. If married, they soon divorce or desert each other. When, however, we have heterosexual love in which the lovers really merge into one " we," gladly sharing their joys and sorrows, each viewing the other as the end value, each identifying his self with the self of the other, then the sex factor becomes secondary and love becomes intense as well as pure. Readiness to sacrifice anything for the other is a thermometer for measuring this intensity and purity.[19]

4. *The Relationship between the Intensity and the Adequacy of Love.* Considering for a moment only the " subjective inadequacy " of love, its existence means that the *relationship between these variables is somewhat indeterminate and loose.* The love may be very intense and yet be utterly blind or inadequate in its objective manifestations — in overt actions and external instrumentalities. *Such instances are due mainly to a lack of knowledge or wisdom in the loving person, to a separation of love from truth and beauty.* Innumerable daily facts testify to the reality of this discrepancy. We all know persons who love intensely and make sacrifices for members of their family, for friends, or for others, which however make them objectively worse instead of better, and push them farther from the goals the blind love seeks to accomplish. In intergroup relationships a group with the most helpful intentions often hurts the other group instead of helping it. The destruction and death brought to Korea by the United Nations furnish a recent example. Facts of this kind are too numerous and too well known to need further corroboration. This being the case, these facts demonstrate the above indeterminacy in the relationship of intensity and adequacy.

On the other hand, *when the manifestations of intense love in its overt actions and instrumentalities are accompanied by wisdom and knowledge, then love intensity is positively connected with its adequacy.* This factor of sufficient wisdom or knowledge is essential if a loose or negative relationship of intensity and adequacy is to be turned into a positive one. It can turn a blind love into a wise one. Such wisdom or knowledge is not only the strictly " scientific " experience obtained through training, schooling, literacy, and that sort of education. In accordance with my theory of personality and the sources of knowledge (sensory, rational, and superconscious-intuitional) such wisdom may be obtained through each of these channels, including intuition.[20] A "loving heart" often knows or feels instinctively (that is, intuitionally) when and what is wrong and what is right for the loved one. An illiterate mother frequently intuits the right and wrong manifestations of love. Insofar as love is ultimately connected with truth, such intuitional wisdom operates fairly frequently. *When all these forms of cognition are considered, intensity, purity, and adequacy of love are somewhat more frequently associated positively than negatively or not at all.* Other conditions being equal, persons with intense love are likely to express it more adequately than persons with a low intensity of love. Only when there is a conspicuous deficiency of wisdom or knowledge does the relationship between our variables tend to disappear or turn negative.

In the relationship between love and the *objective consequences of creativity in the fields of truth and beauty* — creativity motivated otherwise than by love for goodness — we are confronted with the *phenomenon of transformation of the energy of truth or beauty into that of love or goodness, and vice versa*. As mentioned before, since real truth, real beauty, and real goodness or love are three inseparable aspects of the Supreme and Ultimate Reality, the possibility of the transformation of one of these "energies" into the other two follows logically from the hypothesis. Just as the energy of heat can be transformed into that of electricity or motion, so also can one of these supreme energies be transformed into the other two. Empirical facts and a careful analysis clearly show such transformation. *Real beauty*, whether in the form of great music, great literature, drama, painting, sculpture, or architecture, simultaneously *purifies and ennobles us morally*. This transformation of beauty into goodness and love was observed, studied, and confirmed long ago. Mimesis and catharsis effected by a tragedy or other real art creation were indicated by Confucius, Pythagoras, Plato, Aristotle, and a legion of other known and unknown thinkers and observers of ancient Egypt, Babylonia, India, China, Greece, as well as by recent thinkers and educators.[21] The morally ennobling educational effects of a genuine art creation are an axiom of contemporary educators as well as those of the past.

Likewise, a legion of thinkers in the past, in recent times (like F. Nietzsche), and today have pointed out convincingly that *real beauty or art contains in itself cognitive elements which in their own way impart to us something of truth and knowledge*.[22] Beethoven expressed this well. "Every art, all genuine feeling, is a moral progress. . . . He who truly understands my music must go free of all the misery which others bear about with them." "When I am alone, I am never alone. I prefer the spiritual realm and Him who stands above all spiritual and celestial monarchs. The Almighty, the Eternal, the Unending!" Finally, "Music is the sole incorporeal entrance into the higher world of *knowledge*, which comprehends mankind. It gives prophetic vision and . . . heavenly wisdom."[23]

That real *truth is beautiful and good* and transforms itself into beautiful and ethically good energies is nowadays an almost axiomatic proposition, questioned by hardly anyone. The aesthetic elegancy of a genuine mathematical, scientific, philosophical, or religious thought is obvious, as is its enormous role in aesthetic creativity itself; also obvious are its immeasurable benefits in enriching and ennobling the beauty-realm of every one of us.  The innumerable empirical facts of the most beneficial (altruistic) consequences of an important scientific discovery, constructive technological invention, enlightening philosophical thought, or genuine religious truth are well known and need not be demonstrated here.

On the other hand, *real goodness is always beautiful, in the noblest sense of the term.*  If real beauty produces catharsis in us, then real love or goodness impresses us as the purest and noblest beauty.  It is not incidental that the terms *love* and *beauty* are often used interchangeably as " lovely " and " beautiful."  Likewise, real love or goodness contains in itself cognitive elements that enrich us with either intuitive, or rational, or even empirical cognition or truth.  The ethical *summum bonum* has correctly been considered by Plato, Aristotle, and others as containing in itself also a true cognition.  An analysis of the *value judgments as cognitive propositions* by past and contemporary thinkers is general evidence of the transformability of goodness into truth.  Kant's " practical reason " is ethical as well as cognitive " reason."  E. Husserl's demonstration that the proposition " a soldier must be courageous " means " only a courageous soldier is a good soldier " is an example of the transformation of a value judgment (put in the imperative mood) into a cognitive proposition (put into the indicative mood).  C. I. Lewis's recent work has adequately demonstrated the truth that value judgments are at the same time cognitive judgments.[24]

All this shows the transformability of truth-goodness-beauty into one another.  This transformability explains why real creations in fine arts or discoveries in the cognitive field of truth have resulted in morally ennobling, beneficial effects for millions, though the creators of beauty and seekers of truth may not have been directly motivated in their activities by ethical or love impulses.

*Transformability being certain, it does not preclude a difference in the efficiency of transformation.*  Even the transformation of the physical energies of heat, electricity, and motion into one another never reaches 100 per cent of the efficiency of transformation: a part of the energy is always wasted in radiation and other ways, as the second law of thermodynamics or Carnot's principle (law of entropy) teaches us.  Something similar occurs in the transformation of the truth-love-beauty into one another.  Here also the efficiency of the transformation hardly ever reaches 100 per cent.  A part of the energy of beauty transformed into that of love is always partly " wasted," and always gives an efficiency of transformation below 100 per cent.

We do not know what factors govern this variation of the percentage of the efficient transformation; the problem has hardly even been investigated.  Offhand, one can tentatively point out one or two conditions that seem important.  One of these factors is the qualitative-quantitative magnitude of each energy in a given individual or group: *the intenser, purer, more extensive, durable, and adequate the given energy of truth or beauty is, the greater tends to be the percentage of its efficient transformation into goodness (love) energy; and vice versa.* The beauty of the great compositions of Bach, Mozart, and Beethoven seems to be much greater — intenser, purer, etc. — than, for instance, the beauty of third-class compositions or of the latest crooning or jazz " hit." The relevant facts seem to corroborate this expectation. It is uncertain that any such " hit " has ever ennobled, purified, or ethically uplifted anyone, and it is certain that it has stimulated sex, biological, and selfish aspirations in thousands; it is equally certain that Bach's, Mozart's, and Beethoven's compositions have given the purest bliss to millions, have ethically ennobled and uplifted them to the highest spheres of reality, to the *universalia ante rem* of Godhead of goodness.

The same can be said of any great art creation compared with the questionable " hits ": of Homer, Dante, Shakespeare, Dostoievski, confronted with various best sellers of our time; of the Parthenon or a great medieval cathedral compared with an ostentatiously glittering night-club building. The great art creations endure and continue to be transformed into goodness for generations, centuries, millennia. The splashy best sellers go into oblivion within a short time — a few months or a few years at the most.

Similarly, the great philosophical, religious, and scientific " truths " of Plato's system, of the religious systems of Taoism, Confucianism, Hinduism, Buddhism, Jainism, Christianity, Mohammedanism; of the fundamental principles and generalizations of the natural sciences, and of the true part of the social sciences; these have benefited, ethically ennobled, and uplifted millions of human beings for millennia. The efficiency of their transformability into goodness energy has been incomparably greater than that of " little " scientific, or philosophical, or religious truths, and especially of many big pseudo-truths in these fields and in the field of the social and humanistic disciplines. Many of these large generalizations, like the Marxian or Freudian, are at best true in only a small part; for the greater part they are sham truths. It is small wonder, therefore, that side by side with some goodness they have generated an incomparably greater amount of hate, enmity, struggle, war, bestiality, and other evils.[25]

The collective experience of humanity clearly perceives this in the statement that " sham truth or half-truth is more dangerous (socially and ethically) than complete ignorance." Herein also lies one of the reasons why a mere increase in literacy, in school training, in purely " technical " training in little special " tricks," the imbibing of many little truths in our schools and colleges, not for their own sake but to get a comfortable and well-paid position, even scientific discoveries and inventions of a destructive kind — why all these have exerted little if any moralizing influence on the " imbibers." This explains why an increase in schools, in literacy, and even in discoveries and inventions — in part constructive, in part destructive — has not decreased the selfishness of individuals and groups; why bloody wars, both international and civil, have not declined; and why criminality has not abated.[26]   In brief, it explains why the percentage of efficient transformation into love energy of these little truths, half-truths, ignorance parading as truth, and destructive semi-truths has been so low, and often resulted in the evil of strife instead of the unity of love.

Great truth, whole truth, and pure truth invariably give a high rate of efficient transformation into goodness; ignorance, half-truth, little truths, and destructive semi-truths always give a low or even negative efficiency of transformation.

Besides this main factor there are possibly many secondary factors that determine the variation of this efficiency.   But we know as yet little about them, and hence must leave the problem unsolved.

5. *The Relationship between the Extensity and the Adequacy of Love.* A very tentative uniformity appears to be that *with an increase in the extensity of love its inadequacy (subjective and objective) tends also to increase.*   There are several reasons for this tentative generalization.   First, small groups are loved more genuinely, more intensely, and less hypocritically than large ones.   Therefore the subjective motives of love are here more often genuine than when large groups are involved.   Secondly, the adequacy or inadequacy of the objective consequences of love actions become apparent sooner and more clearly with a small group than with a large one.   Whether one's love action hurts or helps the loved ones in a family, among friends, and in a face-to-face group shows itself clearly and quickly, whereas with vast groups the objective consequences of one's love actions rarely become apparent and clear, and still less rarely in a short time; usually these consequences remain unclear and unknown.   And this applies not only to the love actions of ordinary individuals, but also to the consequences of various laws enacted by supposedly competent legislators for the benefit of a nation, or a vast universal church, or a political party, or an international alliance.   Many laws of the best intent produce quite unexpected consequences; and practically all laws fall short of their expected results.   Some even achieve results opposite those intended.   This applies equally to states, nations, political parties, world religious bodies, international movements, international military alliances, the League of Nations, and the United Nations.   The history of governments is full of examples of measures which, though enacted to establish peace, resulted in war, and vice versa; of measures enacted to increase prosperity that resulted in depression, of the attempts at raising the birth rate that resulted in its decline, or reinforcements of order that produced disorders, and so on.

Such discrepancies are still more frequent in the activities of political parties, and of the policies of large religious bodies actively involved in social and political affairs. The Catholic Church did not expect the Inquisition to weaken and demoralize the Church. The League of Nations certainly did not expect its measures to result in its death; nor does the United Nations realize that its policies may result in its possible liquidation.

History is full of facts that illustrate this tragic discrepancy. If this happens persistently to legislators, rulers, and experts, it happens still more frequently to ordinary people.

Such are the reasons for the tentative uniformity between these variables.

6. *The Relationship between the Duration and the Purity of Love.* Other conditions being equal, *the purer the love the more lasting it tends to be.* This follows from the very nature of pure love. Being love for the sake of love, it endures all ordeals, sufferings, disadvantages, and disutilities. It is not afraid of anything or anyone. Hence it can bear " all things," and by bearing them it lasts an indefinitely long time, often up to the death of the loving person and beyond. Impure love, motivated by utilitarian considerations, hedonistic expectations, and other selfish advantages, functions in a " soiled form " only as long as these utilities, pleasures, and advantages are forthcoming. As soon as they cease or are replaced by their opposites, such love dries up and dies.

Empirical observation well corroborates this generalization. Heterosexual love motivated exclusively by sex pleasure lasts, as a rule, only as long as the libidinal pleasure continues. When it fades, or when erotic pleasure from copulation with another person becomes more attractive, such sexual love dies. Marriages based on it crumble; " romances " fade.

Any love or alliance of persons or groups that is based on the hatred of a common foe is also short-lived. Once the common enemy has disappeared that " love," "alliance," or " mutual aid " of the previously allied parties quickly dies out. Hitler, as a common enemy, cemented Communist and anti-Communist groups into an alliance, but as soon as Hitler and the Third Reich were defeated the alliance cracked and fell apart; previous comrades-in-arms became enemies. Similarly, Soviet Russia now cements the Western countries into one bloc; but if and when this " common enemy " disappears, the countries of the Western bloc may be fighting among themselves. Again, any love among partners based on a profitable business cools fast whenever the partnership ceases to be profitable for one or for all the parties concerned. For the same reason many highfalutin " brotherhood " communes, communities, associations, and sects turn out to be short-lived as soon as the profits, pleasures, and advantages of their " love " and " brotherhood " fade. But the pure love of a married couple, of members of a family, of true friends, of members of a genuine religious sect, of a leader and his followers, of a teacher and his pupils, or of any totality of individuals, endures and is virtually immortal. The loved one departed from this life is neither forgotten nor loved less than in life. Suffering, pain, sorrow, disadvantage, are often incapable of breaking such a love.

7. *The Relationship between the Duration and the Adequacy of Love.* For obvious reasons, *adequate love is likely to last longer than inadequate love.* From every standpoint adequate love is more satisfactory for all persons involved. The unlovely and harmful consequences of an objectively inadequate love weaken and sometimes kill not only the love of the loved person, harmed by inadequate results, but even that of the loving person himself, made resentful by the " ingratitude " of the other party or shocked by the harmful results of his own love activities. As a rule, such " blind love " is quickly resented (repudiated, rejected, protested) by the other person, who suffers from its inadequate consequences; and this resentment cools or ends the love of the blindly loving person. The " ingratitude " of children toward their mother whose blind love has spoiled them; the " ingratitude " of many subjects or dependents toward their patrons, superiors, and other " blind benefactors "; the " ingratitude " of employees toward their employers for the latters' blind benevolence: these are all too well-known, perennial phenomena. They demonstrate the tentative validity of our generalization when the inadequacy consists in a discrepancy between the objective consequences of love and those that were expected.

8. *The Relationship between the Purity and the Adequacy of Love.* There appears to exist, on the whole, *a tangible, positive relationship between the purity and the adequacy of love.* Pure love contains an element of true wisdom or cognition as to the best means and ways of its manifestation. It implies a notable lack of emotional blindness, and a notable knowledge of the adequacy or inadequacy of its manifestation. *This association, however, does not need to be close.* In reality we rarely find a strictly pure love; it almost always has some " soiling elements." Hence it is somewhat subject to emotional blindness in its manifestations. Then, too, the cognitive elements of even a pure love experience are always limited: pure love experience does not and cannot give all the necessary knowledge of the physical, biological, and psychological results of its manifestation. If such knowledge is not acquired by way of a cognitive experience, the objective manifestations of pure love may miscarry in its actual consequences.

These seem to be the main tentative uniformities in the relationship of the major dimensions of love.

## Chapter Three

# Tentative Considerations on Production, Accumulation, and Distribution of Love Energy

**A.** *The Production of Love Energy*

If love can be viewed as one of the highest energies known, then theoretically, at least, we can talk about the production or generation, the accumulation (or loss), the channeling, transmission, and distribution of this particular energy.[1] If at the present stage of our knowledge this talk has to remain largely theoretical and speculative, even now it has some practical possibilities. In order to see this, let us take first the problem of generation or production of love energy.[2]

This expression is not a mere figure of speech, but a formula that describes actual social process going on perennially in all groups and societies that maintain the necessary minimum of solidarity co-operation, good will, and peaceful relations among their members: in the family, community, state, nation, labor union, political party, or religious group. Love, solidarity, and peaceful relationships in any group do not fall by themselves from heaven; like food and other material necessities, they have to be produced. And this production must go on as incessantly as that of material commodities — heat and light, mechanical, electrical and other energies. If for a moment the production of love energy is totally stopped in any group, and there is not stored or accumulated love energy, that group at once begins to suffer from inner tensions, conflicts, antagonisms, and "civil wars," fueled by hate, discord, and similar negative energies unchecked by the positive energy of love.

The main difference between the production of love and of other more tangible energies is that in technologically advanced societies an enormous amount of time, means, and collective effort are devoted to the organized production of physical energies. For this reason, such physical production is highly efficient. It goes on incessantly in technological machinofacturing processes, based on the knowledge of physical, chemical, and biological phenomena. In contrast to this, the contemporary technology of love generation is in practically all societies given little thought, time, or effort; it still remains in the most rudimentary form, corresponding to the primitive manual technology of material production in preliterate tribes.

In practically all the societies of our time the generation of love energy still remains in its unorganized " natural " stage. It goes on only inasmuch as it goes " naturally," without any special effort to produce it, without special " factories," and adequate know-how of production — even without a clearly expressed desire to discover, to increase, and to learn this know-how. We " collect " and use love energy only insofar as it is " naturally " produced in our societies. So little effort is made to produce it deliberately (as we produce our material necessities) that most of us are hardly aware even that there is a process of love generation that goes on *urbi* and *orbi*, where an elementary social harmony and peace exist. To many, even these statements about love production may appear strange, either as a mere analogical figure of speech, or as something debasing the value of love itself; perhaps as fantastic as would have seemed, to the most primitive groups of collectors of nature's gifts, the idea of a systematic production of material necessities, with highly complex tools and gadgets, in special factories, with highly cultivated knowledge, and with experts trained for years in the know-how.

The time has come for humanity not only to begin to understand the nature, forms, and how and why of love, but also to endeavor to design more efficient techniques of its production. We already understand that *the " love commodity " is the most necessary commodity for any society; that without its minimum no other commodities can be obtained in abundance; and that at the present time it is a commodity on which depends the very life and death of humanity.*

Here, then, is the briefest summary of the essentials of where, how, and by what means the production of love energy goes on at present.

1. Love, in all its forms, is produced by the interaction of human beings. Any action of love, rendered by A to B, or mutually, or any love reaction of A to B's aggressive, offensive, hateful action would be a generation of love energy in human interaction.

The more intense, extensive, durable, pure, and adequate the love that pulsates in such actions is, and the more numerous the actions are, the greater the love production in these interactive processes.

2. Love is produced in these interactions for the most part haphazardly, side by side with hate and its varieties. There are hardly any safeguards or precautionary measures to prevent in these interactions the production of hate instead of love.

3. The purest and most intense forms of love have been spontaneously produced mainly in the interactions of members of the *same family, of the closest friends, of small, face-to-face in-groups* — scholastic, religious, political, occupational, ethnic, cultural, or other. With the expansion of such groups into larger and still larger units, the production of the intensest and purest forms of love progressively declines (per capita), and the production of hate and antagonisms tends to increase.

4. In the interactions of members of the same solidary in-group, the production of love goes on more successfully than in the interactions of members of different, unrelated out-groups.

5. In all these interactions the production of love goes on mainly "spontaneously" and "naturally," without special aims, devices, tools, or techniques to organize production on a more efficient level, in order to produce a greater quantity and a better quality of love energy for the group and for humanity.

6. Only a few persons and agencies have purposefully endeavored to improve in their own interactions this process of love production, or have devoted themselves to this task to a considerable degree.

7. Such "inventors and engineers of love production" have been *exceptional individuals* who themselves have been filled with love, who generously granted it to anyone, and who deliberately endeavored to improve the production of love in groups and in humanity at large, or who contributed to it indirectly. The following are examples of these:

(a) *All great apostles of love and moral educators of humanity:* Christ, Buddha, St. Francis of Assisi, Gandhi, and the many smaller "producers of love" — kind and good neighbors, and all who habitually perform unselfish acts of love.

(b) *Many great religious educators:* one of the central values of their religion has been the ethical or moral code of love, whether in the form of "love your enemy" and other moral precepts of Taoism; or the "reverence, benevolence, and reciprocity" of Confucianism; or the "compassion and love" of Hindusim, Buddhism, and Jainism; or the Ten Commandments of Judaism; or the commandments of "Mercy, Compassion, and Love" of Mohammedanism; or the sublimest norms of the Sermon on the Mount in Christianity. All great religions, through their founders and leaders, have tried — and now and then have succeeded to a notable degree — in increasing the production of love among their members in their interrelationship with God or the Highest Value, with one another, and with all human beings and all living creatures.

(c) *All great and small creators in the field of constructive truth* (science, philosophy, scientific technology) *and of real beauty* (all the fine arts). As I have indicated, these values are transformable to a degree into the values of goodness and love; in so far, all those who enriched humanity with truth and beauty have also contributed to a more efficient production of love.

8. Besides these kinds of individuals, a *few social groups or institutions* have contributed a great deal to the production of love and to its improvement. Such groups or institutions are similar to *small workshops and farms* in the production of the material necessities in agricultural and manufacturing (not machinofacturing) societies. Among such agencies the *family* has been the most important. Spontaneously — rather than deliberately — the family, compared with other groups, has been the most efficient agency in human altruization and socialization. In this sense it has been the most important " workshop in love production." Like a workshop producing mainly for a local market, the family production of love has also been limited mainly to the members of the family. Only indirectly and occasionally has the family produced love that extended beyond it for the human " world market." Of course this is only an outline of the general or typical role of the family in this business. It does not exclude the great variation in individual families, some producing an enormous quantity of the " best love," while other families — luckily a minority — produce either little love of low grade or even manufacture hate and its varieties.

Other love-producing groups are *groups of close friends, religious groups* that earnestly inculcate altruistic relationships among their members and partly toward outsiders, *small local communities, schools and educational institutions, occupational unions, castes and orders,* and other manibonded groups. To a degree each group that has some solidarity among its members generates a certain amount of love. Most groups, however, tend to generate a relatively weak, impure, short-lived, unextensive, and inadequate current of love. And besides, such love tends to circulate mainly or exclusively among the members of the group, often followed by the generation of hate and animosity toward some common enemy or by their common exploitation of outsiders for the benefit of the group. As a result some groups produce more hate than love and solidarity in the human universe. All this shows the astounding lack of organized effort for an abundant production of love energy in the human world. At present this neglect threatens the very future of humanity. Hence the imperative need for a decisive improvement in the production of love.

B. *A Preliminary Plan for the Improvement of the Production of Love Energy*

1. *The Increase of Creative Heroes of Love.* The first step toward a greater output of a better quality of love is an increase in the exceptional

apostles of love and the creative geniuses of goodness among us. The total influence of the heroes of love, of science, of beauty, of religion, far transcends their direct, face-to-face influence. Just as the aesthetic and other effects of the works of Homer, of Dante, of Shakespeare have been inestimably great upon generations of humanity; just as the effects of the compositions of Bach and Mozart and Beethoven have been great beyond all calculation; just as the total influence of the achievements of Plato, of Kant, of Galileo, of Newton has been enormous on all philosophy and science, and through these has affected millions of human beings: likewise the total effects of the life and activity of the great altruists like Buddha, Jesus, St. Francis, Gandhi have been almost infinite, both for the production of love and for the enrichment of humanity. Each of them is like a great power station, endlessly generating an enormous amount of the best love energy. For centuries and millennia this energy incessantly issues from these " fountainheads of love," spreads over millions, permeates social institutions and cultures, and maintains the necessary minimum of solidarity in groups. Even the deaths of these heroes of love do not stop the process of love generation started during their lives: after their deaths Buddha and Jesus have possibly radiated more love than they did during their lifetimes. This shows that love energy is as imperishable as any other form of energy.

These observations show that an increase in the number of heroes of love means an increase of love output far beyond a mere numerical increase of altruistic persons. Any society that wants to be animated by an abundant energy of love must have, must produce, and must cultivate such heroes of love. Without such great power stations it can hardly have an abundance of love energy.[3]

Herein lies the enormous significance of such heroes of love. Their outward appearance changes from period to period, from society to society. Now they appear as religious leaders; now as pious nobles; now as hermits; now as monks; now as social reformers; now just as good neighbors, secular persons of this or that occupation, or as housewives and husbands. Their external garb changes, but their real function remains the same: they act as power stations generating the energy of love for humanity.

This most vital function of these heroes is still poorly understood by many radically minded talkers. They fail to see, beyond and beneath the " garb of a crazy hermit " like St. Anthony, or an " insane priest " like Ramakrishna, the real function that these " athletes and fools of God " have performed among their contemporaries and in human history: namely, the function of great power stations producing love for generations of human beings.

How these heroes of love emerge and become such heroes will be discussed elsewhere.[4] Here we may note that *truly heroic techniques and specific genius are needed to produce the heroes of love.* Ordinary techniques adequate for molding ordinary good neighbors are insufficient for molding the heroes of love. What these heroic techniques must be will be discussed further. Here we note again that many scholars fail to understand this point. For them such techniques of altruization as eremitic isolation for years with various ascetic practices; as the "superman" technique of Yoga; the "spiritual exercises" of Loyola; the serving of lepers by St. Francis or Father Damien; the techniques of many monastic orders, and so on, appear as something strange, superstitious, or stupid. We shall see that these scholars are mistaken: these and many other techniques are but varieties of the "heroic techniques" necessary for the self-education of the heroes of love, or of God's athletes (*athletae Dei*), as the word *ascesis*, the training of the athlete, means in application to the ascetic altruists.

Such is the first provision to be carried out if a given society or humanity at large wants to increase its production of love.

2. *The Increase of Creative Heroes of Truth and Beauty.* Each great creator in the fields of science, philosophy, religion, technology, or the fine arts is also a gigantic power station generating the energies of truth and beauty. So far as these energies are transformable into the energy of love (and vice versa), an increase in the number of these heroes of truth and beauty leads indirectly to an increase in the production of love (and vice versa). Therefore all measures that facilitate an increase of constructive creativity in the fields of truth and beauty also serve the purpose of increasing creativity in the field of goodness. Just as ordinary techniques are not adequate for producing a hero of love, so also such techniques are insufficient for producing a hero of truth or beauty. Corresponding heroic techniques are also necessary for producing a genius in science, religion, philosophy, or fine arts. Mere "rational training" is insufficient. The opening and release of the "egoless" energy of the suprarational genius is an indispensable condition here, just as it is in the field of the "athletes of love." This is the second step toward our goal.

3. *The Increase of Love Production by the Rank and File.* However important, an increase in the production of love by the heroes of goodness, truth, and beauty is not enough. It must be paralleled by at least a modest increase in love generation by ordinary persons and groups. Nothing greatly heroic can or need be expected from the rank and file, either in increased output or the quality of love generated, or in the techniques of the generation. The overwhelming majority of human beings cannot become either Yogis, or Bodhisattvas, or Altruistic Saints, or great heroes of love. Likewise, the heroic techniques of love generation are inapplicable and inaccessible to the rank and file.[5] Moreover, no such hero-

ism is needed here. *If the bulk of ordinary mortals would simply abstain from murdering other human beings; if they would cut in half their daily actions of hate and would double their daily good deeds, such a modest improvement in their moral conduct would enormously increase the output of love and decrease the output of hate, and thereby the general ethical and social level of humanity would be raised to a much higher level.* This modest elevation of the ethical behavior of mortals would be quite sufficient to prevent new catastrophes of war, and would improve enormously the social harmony of humanity. It would increase the love output and decrease the hate production incomparably more than has ever been done or can be done by the activities of the League of Nations, the United Nations, legislative enactment, or any other activities of political, legal, and religious agencies. Without such improvement in the ethical conscience and behavior of the rank and file these agencies hardly ever even try to enact laws and rules demanding a higher ethical behavior and relationship. As a rule most such laws have been enacted and such agencies created precisely by the pressure of the ethically ennobled rank and file. If in a few cases the initiative came from the agencies themselves, their laws and activities had small success unless they were supported by the bulk of the people. This holds true not only for democracies, but also for monarchical, autocratic, and dictatorial groups. No heroic techniques are needed for this modest increase in love production by the rank and file; it can be achieved through means and techniques that are quite accessible to all human beings. All that is required is better organization and expert use of these ordinary means. (See on this further Parts Four and Five of this work.)

4. *An increase in the Production of Love by Groups and Institutions.* In the preceding section the human population is treated as a sum of individuals. Factually all these individuals belong to various organized groups or institutions, from the family to the state and the various national and international organizations. Practically all the behavior and all the social relationships of each individual follow the patterns prescribed or recommended by the groups of which he is a voluntary or involuntary member. For the overwhelming majority of persons an improvement in their altruistic standard is possible only when that standard is improved by each and all the groups to which they belong. With the possible exception of a few individuals, altruists can hardly be expected in egotistic groups. And contrarily, there are few egotistic individuals in a universe of altruistic groups.

This means that an increase in love production by the rank and file is possible only when an increase occurs also in the groups or institutions to which they belong. As a rule, the altruization of an individual is possible only through the altruization of his groups or institutions; and vice versa, the altruization of institutions or groups is possible only through that of their members.

If within each group the love relationship among its members grows, the production of love by the group and by its members increases.[6] Up to the present time an increased generation of love within a group has often been followed by an increase of discrimination and antagonism toward outside groups and persons. In other words, an increase of the in-group intensity of love has not been followed by a proportionate expansion of its extensity. If anything, a greater devotion to one's in-group has often led to an increased discrimination against, exploitation of, and animosity toward, the outside groups and persons. This has tended to cancel the increase of love generation within the group. As a result, humanity as a whole has profited little from this double process of an *increase of love generation within a group followed by an increase of hate output toward the outside world.*

This mutually canceling process is senseless; and it must be replaced by *the increase of love within each group without an increase of antagonism toward the outside world.* It is indeed possible to increase the love of the members of a family or group toward one another without increasing antagonistic discrimination against the rest of the human universe. When such a change is made, an increase in the love generation of each group will lead to an increase of the total love output of all humanity. Under these conditions the fresh air of love will not be polluted by the poisonous exhaust of hatred. (See further Part Five.)

Such is the main operation that the groups or institutions must undertake in order to make possible an increase in love production by the rank and file, by groups or institutions as such, and by humanity as a whole. As soon as we succeed in canceling a group's counteracting generation of antagonistic discrimination toward outsiders we " automatically " increase the total output of love in the human universe.

But can such an operation be achieved? Does it not require some heroic effort by each and every ordinary mortal and by their groups? Strange as it may appear, the task is well within the reach of all persons and groups. This problem will be dealt with in Part Five of this work.

5. *The Increase of Love-Production by Cultural Systems and the Total Culture.*[7] Finally, most of the cultural systems and cultural congeries must also increase their generation of love and decrease their radiation of hate and antagonism. All cultural systems (and congeries) of science, philosophy, religion, ethics, law, fine arts, humanistic and social disciplines, as well as applied technology in all fields of human activity, must be permeated by the value of love and freed from the negative value of hate to a much greater degree than they have been up to the present time.

Contemporary science serves not only the God of love, but also the

Satan of hate and destruction. Contemporary philosophy and pseudo-religion exert upon human beings not only morally ennobling and loving effects, but to a hardly less degree the opposite effects of hate and strife. This is still more true of most of the contemporary fine arts: literature, music, painting, sculpture, and drama. It also applies to contemporary law and pseudo-ethics, social theories, and humanistic ideologies, not to mention the contemporary " technology " of physical, biological, and social sciences. They all play a double role in their influence on individuals and groups. In one role they generate love, make human beings ethically nobler and more creative, and integrate them into one human family of mutually respecting and loving members. In the other role they radiate hate and discord, demoralize and debase ethically, disintegrate intellectually; and they destroy and kill.[8]

If we need to increase the love output of humanity, then all the main cultural systems and even the congeries must evidently be so reconstructed as to radiate only the positive love rays and cease generating the negative hate rays. This double radiation has been one of the main reasons why the positive effects have been largely canceled by the negative ones, and why, as a net result, all the enormous progress of scientific discovery, technological invention, philosophy, the fine arts and other cultural systems has not resulted in a decrease of hate and interhuman warfare.[9] Humanity of the twentieth century cannot boast of being better morally than the humanity of the Stone Age. If we *can reconstruct these cultural systems so as to eliminate their hate generation*, we shall incalculably increase the love production of all humanity. If, in addition, we can increase the love production of most of the cultural systems, we shall doubly increase the output of love. This is the operation to be performed in the field of culture.

Can it be done? Is it within human possibility? Are the necessary means and ways accessible to ordinary mortals? The answer is that the operation is quite within the reach of human possibility; its means and techniques are also accessible for the purpose. When co-ordinated with the changes outlined above, the reconstruction of the main cultural systems can be brought about without any superhuman hardships or capacities. (See on this further Part Five.)

6. *Summary*. Through these five steps the production of love in humanity can be increased and the generation of hate can be decreased enormously. The total net result will be an amount of love energy quite sufficient to prevent bloody strife or enmity on a large scale, and to build a harmonious human order, far nobler and happier than any hitherto known. If and when humanity or its leaders earnestly decide to carry it out, they will discover that the plan is quite realizable, and free of utopianism.

## C. *The Accumulation and Distribution of Love Energy*

*Accumulation.* Like other forms of energy, love energy can also be accumulated or stored (a) *in individuals,* (b) *in social institutions,* and (c) *in culture.* The storing of love energy in *individuals* means making their love actions and reactions *spontaneously habitual,* interiorized and rooted to such an extent that they become second nature. Love energy, as man's second nature, flows spontaneously, neither hindered by any internal friction, nor demanding any special effort for its manifestation; it is ready to pour itself out abundantly when and where it is needed. If the habituation is begun during earliest childhood and continuously practiced thereafter, it would indeed amount to a great accumulation of love energy in individuals, and through them in humanity as a whole. The total reservoir of love energy thus stored would be sufficient for the needs of humanity.

*The storing of love energy in social institutions (or organized groups) and in culture* will be achieved through the permeation of cultural systems and institutions — their structures and functions, their agencies and vehicles — with the grace of love energy. Constructed and reorganized in conformity with the principles of love, animated mainly by an effective love at its best, these cultural systems and social institutions would become a multitude of gigantic power systems, incessantly generating love, storing it, and radiating it upon all human beings. In the gentlest but most effective way love, radiated by culture and by social institutions, would form a permanent atmosphere that would pervade all human beings from the cradle to the grave. Under these conditions they would breathe it incessantly, be inspired, motivated, and molded by love into its own image. The productive capacity of social and cultural " power systems of love " is practically unlimited; potentially unlimited also is the magnitude of its accumulated energy. Its total amount, stored in individuals, institutions, and culture, can be sufficient for all the practical purposes of humanity: (a) for the prevention and elimination of crime, revolutions, wars, and other forms of conflict where there is underlying hate, envy, and unhappiness; (b) for the maintenance and growth of man's creative activity; (c) for decreasing and eventually eliminating the worst forms of suffering, unhappiness, loneliness, illness and unnecessary death; (d) for making the whole world a friendly, warm, and inspiring cosmos for everyone and for all.

If humanity and its wise leaders earnestly set out to accomplish this task, much love energy can be produced and accumulated even now, with the human world in its present stage.

*Distribution.* Like other forms of energy, accumulated love can also be distributed according to the particular needs of various persons and groups. When an urgent need arises, demanding a release of an unusually intense or large amount of love energy — as when a catastrophe or dreadful conflict impends, or to extinguish a conflagration of hate — its accumulation would make possible such a release.

Through various general and special agents, friends, neighbors, everyone and all, and through special channels for its circulation, love energy can be directed to those groups or persons who at any given moment need it most. An individual struck by a great tragedy can best be consoled by the intensive love focused on him by his closest friends, neighbors, and large groups. A person or groups afflicted by the disease of hate, mental depression, or suicidal tendencies, can often be cured by a concentrated love that understands, forgives, and cures. In these and thousands of similar cases, love energy can be poured on the persons, the groups, and the danger spots in such abundance and intensity that the threatening conflagration is extinguished, hate epidemics are cured, catastrophe is averted. Life again becomes worth living for the afflicted persons and groups, and the world once more appears as a sunny and warm marvel.

It should be noted that this whole matter of accumulation and distribution of love is *realizable* and not utopian.

## D. *General Summary*

These outlined aspects of love, its properties, its empirical dimensions, the relationships between its dimensional variables, and, finally, the problems of the efficient production, accumulation, and distribution of love energy — all these open a vast, little known, and desperately important field of exploration. At the present time mankind perhaps needs to explore this field more than any other. A greatly increased knowledge of love is essential if there is to be a greater production, accumulation, and circulation of love energy in the human world. Both a better knowledge and a greater production of love are desperately needed for the very survival of mankind and for the continuation of its creative mission.

Subsequent chapters of this work give a development and validation of the statements of this introductory part. Their validity depends greatly upon the problem of whether love is a real power. Chapter Four deals with this question.

*Chapter Four*

# Power of Creative Love

## I

### PREVALENT VIEWS

In the atmosphere of our Sensate [1] culture we are prone to believe in the power of the struggle for existence, selfish interests, egoistic competition, hate, the fighting instinct, sex drives, the instinct of death and destruction, all-powerful economic factors, rude coercion and other negativistic forces. Yet we are highly skeptical in regard to the power of creative love, disinterested service, unprofitable sacrifice, mutual aid, the call of pure duty and other positive forces. The prevalent theories of evolution and progress, of the dynamic forces of history, of the dominant factors of human behavior, of the " how " and " why " of social processes unanimously stress such negativistic factors as the above. They view them as the main determinants of historical events and of the individual life courses. Marxism and the economic interpretation of history; Freudianism and its libidinal-destructive explanation of human behavior; instinctivist, behaviorist, and physiosomatic theories of personality and culture; Darwinistic and biological theories of the struggle for existence as the main factor of biological, mental, and moral evolution; even the prevalent motto of the chambers of commerce that " rivalry and competition made America great " [2] — these and similar theories dominate contemporary sociology, economics, psychology, psychiatry, biology, anthropology, philosophy of history, political science, and other social and humanistic disciplines. These ideologies have an enormous appeal to the prevalent Sensate mind, are eagerly believed by Sensate man, and are considered by him as " the last word in modern science."

In contrast to that, Sensate minds emphatically disbelieve the power of love, sacrifice, friendship, co-operation, the call of duty, unselfish search for truth, goodness, and beauty. These appear to us as something epiphenomenal and illusory. We call them " rationalizations," " self-deceptions," " derivations," " beautifying ideologies," " opiates of the people's mind," " smoke screens," " idealistic bosh," " unscientific delusions," etc. We are biased against all theories that try to prove the power of love and other positive forces in determining human behavior and personality; in influencing the course of biological, social, mental, and moral evolution; in affecting the direction of historical events; in shaping social institutions and culture.

This penchant to believe in the power of negative forces and to disbelieve the influence of positive energies has nothing to do with the scientific validity of either type of theory. It is mainly the result of the congeniality of the "debunking theories" and the noncongeniality of the positive "idealistic" theories with our negativistic and decaying Sensate culture. The negativistic theories are "the flesh from the flesh, and the bone from the bone" of the negativistic Sensate world. As such they are at home in that culture and appear to be valid to the Sensate mind. They easily infect Sensate individuals, including Sensate scientists and scholars. Their "facts" appear to be convincing; their logic persuasive; their "evidence" undeniable: hence the success of these theories in the Sensate sociocultural world.

Because of their noncongeniality, the positive "idealistic" theories are doomed to be the stepchildren in this Sensate culture of ours. They are destined to be unpopular, and unsuccessful in the Sensate milieu; they appear to be unconvincing, unscientific, prejudiced and superstitious to Sensate society and to Sensate man.

When both kinds of theories are carefully tested, their comparative validity becomes quite different from that determined by the extra-scientific, existential factor of their congeniality and noncongeniality with the dominant Sensate culture.

The purpose of the subsequent pages is to sum up a vast body of evidence in favor of the enormous power of creative love, friendship, and nonviolent, nonaggressive conduct in human affairs and social life. The corroborative cases are grouped into classes and several typical facts are given in each class. The paucity of typical cases is motivated by consideration of space: otherwise the facts of each class could be multiplied ad libitum.

## II

### Love Stops Aggression and Enmity

"A friend of mine, an elderly Quaker lady, entered her Paris hotel room to find a burglar rifling her bureau drawers where she had considerable jewelry and money. He had a gun which he brandished. She talked to him quietly, told him to go right ahead and help himself to anything she had, as obviously he needed it more than she did if he had to be stealing it. She even told him some places to look where there were valuables he had overlooked. Suddenly the man let out a low cry . . . and ran from the room taking nothing. The next day she received a letter from him in which he said, 'I'm not afraid of hate. But you showed love and kindness. It disarmed me.'" (The fact communicated by C. Foster in a letter, November 7, 1951.)

"During the Revolutionary War William Rotch, a Friend, living on Nantucket island, invited an enemy officer bent on plunder of the island to dinner. Thinking Rotch to be a loyalist the officer asked him how and where to begin the plunder. Rotch replied: 'I don't know any better place for thee to begin than here at my house, for I am better able to bear the loss than anyone else.' After meeting other persons in the village who had the same attitude as Rotch, the officer went back to his ship and left the island in its original condition." [3]

"Lotte Hoffman and her 16-year-old daughter were home in the suburbs of Berlin in 1945 when Russian soldiers burst into their room. She prayed silently, then walked over to her piano and began singing German folk songs. Instead of shouting and threatening, the soldiers began to listen to the music. From then on, as long as half-drunk troops were about, one or two Russian soldiers, armed, would sit up all night in Mrs. Hoffman's room to make sure that she and her daughter would be safe." [4]

In a detailed, twelve-page analysis of her own experience, a young American lady from California describes how on the eve of her departure from Colombo, in March, 1948, she was " cornered " in her hotel room by her neighbor in the adjacent room. The "neighbor" was determined to have sexual relations with her, willingly if she consented, to rape her if she opposed. In India the lady had learned the method of "rational dealing with an opponent, omission of violence, necessity for understanding, 'love,' if the word is admissable in my situation." She applied this method. It required enormous courage and a steady nerve. With some difficulty it worked: she was able to convince the aggressor to go away without molesting her. "The struggle in my mind was too much for me. I was immensely fatigued," concludes the lady (in a personal communication to the author).

The Brazilian government tried to destroy the Chavantes Indians (a tribe of 6,000 Indians living in the northeast corner of Mato Grosso) in the eighteenth century. During the nineteenth century the government ignored them; missionaries failed also and several were killed. In 1907 Gen. Candido Rondon founded the "Brazilian Indian Protection Service." Its policy was: "Pacification through Love." During his first attempt at contact Gen. Rondon was badly injured, but ordered his men not to resist. In this behavioral way he established his policy: "Die if necessary, but never kill." He brought about enactment of the law according to which no white Service man may kill an Indian even in self-defense; no Service man can carry arms in Indian territory. The "Protection Service" brought gifts to the Indians (by airplane and by leaving presents in temporarily abandoned villages).

Though a number of Service men were killed in the period of 1907–1946, no reprisals were made. The results of this policy have been more successful than those of the previous policies of extermination and aggression: several tribes of the Chavantes were pacified; others, formerly destructive, have become helpful to the government; still others can now be contacted without fatal consequences. Chavantes are now accepting gifts; the hostile actions of the white people are reduced. An expedition of twelve unarmed men in 1946 was successful: an amicable meeting with 400 Indians took place. All in all the policy of "Pacification through Love" succeeded better than the aggressive policy. [5]

It is well known that in early America, the Quakers, the Mennonites, the Moravians, and the Schwenkfelders, of Pennsylvania — all partisans of non-violent resistance to evil, and all practicing the policy of unarmed friendship — lived in peace with the Indians. Though a few, without offering resistance, were killed by the Indians, all in all they suffered less from the Indians and lived in much greater peace with them than all the groups that fought, exterminated, and aggressively treated the Indians. The unarmed, peaceful policies of the Quakers and other pacifistic groups were more successful in preventing and hindering the aggressive retaliation of the Indians than the militant, aggressive policies of other groups.[6]

When the Hun destroyer, Attila, in 452, was marching towards Rome, Pope Leo I went forth unarmed to meet the ruthless invader. Somehow he managed to gain an interview with him and made an appeal so powerful (and perhaps offered a considerable ransom, as some cynics conjecture) that Attila turned back, spared the city, and never returned. Whether or not Attila was well paid, the important fact is that an *unarmed* great spiritual leader could stop a terrible sacking of Rome.

In May, 1922, in Russia, during the great famine, a band of plundering Kurds stopped a group of Quaker relief workers and started to take their food supplies. After finding out the help-rendering mission of the Quakers, the Kurds rode away without harming anyone or taking any of the supplies.[7]

At Pec, Serbia, during the famine, a young relief worker assigned to drive oxcarts over robber-ridden mountain roads, refused a military escort. When robbers did stop him after many unmolested trips, he asked them to help him to transport the food to the starving people. Instead of attacking him, they helped him.[8]

In Berlin in 1921 during the *Putsch*, an Englishwoman, a Quaker leader, not only succeeded in making Communist and government soliders guard the Quaker supplies but, having introduced the enemy soldiers to one another in the storeroom, engaged them in pleasant conversation with one another and made them mutually friendly as they sat watching the supplies together.[9]

New York City, 1925: the treasurer of a Jewish hospital fund was stopped with $15,000 in his pocket by two robbers. When told that the money was for a hospital, the robbers threw in a ten-dollar bill of their own.

In 1924 a doctor in a slum district of New York was stopped by robbers. When the doctor told them he was attending a sick woman in the area, they waited until his work was done and then escorted him to a safer part of the city.[10]

During and after World War I nearly one thousand Quaker relief workers went unarmed into hostile countries. None met a violent death, nor were any of the relief goods plundered by robbers or the needy people.[11]

Hundreds of similar facts, including the pacification of civil war factions in Chinese villages and other places, are recorded in the annals of Quaker relief missions in European countries, in Syria, in China, Nicaragua, Haiti, etc., during and after World War I and up to the present time. Altruistic relief work of thousands of agents, acting often in areas of bloody civil and international conflicts, has been able to overcome numerous aggressions, has calmed many enmities, and led to very few, if any, violent deaths or serious harm among the workers.[12]

On December 31, 1937, in Shaktu Valley, Waziristan, British-led troops pulled out alive a few laborers of the Kakari clan who had been buried in a landslide. The clan hitherto fighting the British troops stopped its hostile actions and sniping: the action of saving a few laborers more successfully stopped the attacks of the Kakari than all the military operations against them.[13]

During the extensive railroad building in the United States in the first half of the nineteenth century, construction engineer W. P. Thompson fired a trouble-making worker. This man threatened to kill Thompson. Thompson refused to arm or to retaliate. When Thompson surprised the worker who was waiting in ambush for him, and even gave the worker a very good reference as to his ability and character, the worker became a changed man: he gave up his guns, stopped getting into arguments, and successfully advanced in his work for another railway.[14]

In the Civil War the Shaker community of Pleasant Hill, Ky., was unharmed during the border violence of the time of John Morgan, a guerilla leader: he had grown up to respect and admire the quiet, kindly Shakers.

A similar thing happened to Jacob Gooff, Joseph Haughton, and other Quaker families during the rebellion in Ireland, about 1798. Their reputation for kindness saved them and their property during the terrible persecutions and destruction around them.[15]

An American missionary in China, Merlin Bishop, politely but firmly refused to hand over to Japanese officers the keys of an abandoned American university entrusted to his care. The time finally came when an officer demanded the keys or the missionary would be shot. Bishop said he wished the Japanese no harm, but that he could not turn over the keys. Three men were selected and lined up with their rifles aimed at the missionary. He smiled and waited. " The officer seemed uncertain, the men uneasy. Then, one at a time they relaxed. Rifles lowered, sheepish grins replaced their looks of grim determination." But one of the soldiers apparently was disgusted at this outcome. He charged the missionary with a fixed bayonet on the end of his rifle. At the last instant the missionary dodged, grabbed the shorter soldier and the butt of the rifle, pulling him toward him. " Our glances locked and held for seconds that seemed ages long. Then I smiled down at him, and it was like a spring thaw melting the ice on a frozen river. The hatred vanished and, after a sheepish moment, he smiled back! " Then Bishop gave them tea before they left on their return journey.[16]

A Japanese Christian, Osamu Ishiga, refused conscription in Japan, was investigated and found to be neither a Communist nor a coward. "What baffled [the authorities] was his sheer goodness, his vital personality. Finally, they let him out of prison. There didn't seem to be any *other* way they could dispose of him! " (From a letter published in Peace Notes [F.O.R.], April 14, 1949.) [17]

On May 8, 1945, Russians were entering the city of Dresden, Germany, looting and sometimes raping. An American woman, a long-time resident of

Dresden, calmly greeted the Russian soldier who barged into her room, and shook hands with him. After examining the room he spied her watch. But instead of violently taking it, he cupped his hands and asked for it. She nodded yes as he emptied his pockets and rolled up his sleeves to show that he had picked up no loot. Then he left with a fleet kiss on her forehead and with a radiant smile.[18]

Incidents in the life of Bayard Rustin (present College Secretary, Fellowship of Reconciliation):

Once in a restaurant Rustin was ignored after asking for a hamburger. Finally, catching the attention of the woman proprietor, he succeeded in getting her to agree to his proposition: " He would sit before a cold hamburger, refusing to touch it for ten minutes. If any one came in and objected to the presence of a Negro in her restaurant, he would instantly leave without fuss." Before the time was up her resistance broke down and she brought him a hot dog and coffee. She then explained that her patrons did not want Negroes around because they were dirty. Instead of challenging this remark, Rustin said that it was true sometimes because many Negroes couldn't afford baths in their houses. He gave other statements about the condition of the Negroes in the town, which the woman later took the trouble to verify. She then became interested in getting justice done to the Negroes in the community and became a real friend to them.

On another occasion, while riding in an elevator in a Spokane hotel, Rustin was ordered by a white man to lace up his shoes. He did not object, but laced up the white man's shoes, then refused the offered tip, saying that he he had done it not for money, but because he had assumed the man needed help. The white man was apologetic and invited Rustin to his room to talk about racial problems.[19]

Three Dutch sisters were in danger because they were sheltering a Jew — the Gestapo men were quartered across the street from them. Nevertheless, when a Gestapo man called on them they invited him in since they decided that Jesus would have done so. The man then made it a practice to take part in their evening prayers and songs. At first the German had hated the Jews. As time went on the arguments and behavior of the sisters began to tell. On his last visit the German grew white when the younger sister said that the " Jews are to the Lord as the apple of the eye." He whipped out his revolver, but instead of using it he handed it over, saying he was a sinner. After their evening prayer and hymn he left. They never saw him again.[20]

When the Kingsley Hall neighborhood house was threatened by attack from persons drawn from nearby saloons by a disgruntled lady (who blamed the Hall for her trouble with her daughter), the leader, Miss Muriel Lester, let them come in, heard the tirade of " Mrs. Smith," then asked all to join in prayer about it. The drunks took off their hats during the prayer. Miss Lester offered her arm to the surprised lady immediately after the prayer, and marched out of the house, followed by all the rest. No damage was done, and " Mrs. Smith " sobered up on the way home, declaring her eternal friendship to Miss Lester from which she has never wavered.[21]

During the Nazi regime, Wilhelm Mensching, pastor in Petzen, Germany, was openly against the Nazis. He refused to say " Heil Hitler " or to put the Nazi flag in his church. When he was told that a certain Nazi was going to

have him thrown out of the church, he went straight to the man and told him
that his allegiance was to Christ, that since the Nazi now had the relevant information, he could get the pastor kicked out. But the Nazi refused to take
action. Though Mensching openly prayed for the enemies, kept in touch
with English friends, voted against the Nazis, etc., he was never arrested. The
mayor and all the people loved him and told the Nazis that he would not
betray anyone but be friends to all.[22]

In a mopping-up operation during World War I, Michael once came face
to face with a German fighter. Michael immediately walked toward the enemy, his rifle on his shoulder, smiling and exclaiming "Kamerad!" The
puzzled German advanced toward him with his bayonet, but stopped just a
few feet away as Michael continued to smile and tried to speak German,
Michael said "Liebe mannen, alles mannen." The incredulous German asked,
"Alles mannen? Deutsch?" "Ya, alles mannen," answered Michael. Gradually the German came to understand his position and broke out with "Freund!
Freund!" They chatted a while, then each went his own way.[23]

Toyohiko Kagawa had just finished speaking at a church service in Japan.
Ten hooligans arose and attacked him with large bamboo sticks. He stood
with no change of expression on his face as the blows fell and the blood
streamed. When they stopped, Kagawa led the congregation in the closing
prayer. He then invited the hooligans into his study to talk to them. Before
long they were apologizing.
Kagawa "has so much security inside that he can afford to go without any
outside." Alone in his tiny room on the Shinkawa slums, he was awakened
one night by a drunk or half-drunk gangster, with sword uplifted. Kagawa
got to his knees and bowed his head in prayer as he awaited the blow. Instead the man said, "Kagawa, do you love me?" Kagawa answered, "Yes,
I do." Soon the man said, "Here's a present," and he left Kagawa his sword.
Hearing one day of the march of 10,000 destruction-bent strikers toward
dockyards which were guarded by armed police and soldiers, Kagawa abruptly
closed his sermon, and averted the impending slaughter by checking and di-
recting the first row of marchers down a side street. Alone he faced the
strikers and as the first row approached him, he looked into the eyes of each
man, praying "Let there be peace." They swerved down a side street and
the dockyards were left untouched. No shots were fired; the union was
saved.[24]

In the satyagraha campaign in Vykom, South India, Travancore Province,
Brahmins refused to let Untouchables walk along a highway near their quarters. An Untouchable and a young Christian started it off by walking down
the road. Both were beaten. They did it again and were arrested. Others
took their places until authorities stopped the arrests and put a line of police
across the road. Then the satyagrahis started to stand opposite the policemen
in an attitude of prayer. They went on six-hour shifts and persisted in their
nonviolence despite threats, insults, etc. *A year and four months later* the
Brahmins gave in and opened up not only this road but other roads in the
province to use by Untouchables.[25]

During World War II a young American was being marched at bayonet
point toward Japanese lines. He began to speak Bible passages and sing
hymns as he went along, to build up his courage. As he found strength in his

voice and soul, his singing became contagiously relaxed. Soon his Japanese captor was walking beside him and singing along with him. When the hymn ended they stopped and swapped experiences. They prayed together. Then instead of killing his prisoner, the Japanese decided not to kill any more. The two made their way together toward the American camp.[26]

Kees Boecke, Dutch Quaker, teacher, missionary, and war resistor, had allowed a Jew to sleep in his office during the Nazi occupation. It turned out that this man was active in the underground, had been caught, and now the Gestapo were waiting for Boecke in his office. He admitted allowing the Jew to sleep there, saying that he followed a different faith from theirs. He said he believed in the brotherhood of men and taught this in his school. Despite the finding of an article he had written for postwar publication which condemned dictatorship and the Nazi occupation, no harm came to him.[27]

A German orphanage outside of Berlin was wanted for quarters by the Russians. But the director of the school, Isa Gruner, had planned how to maintain the school, should this happen. When the Russians came they were greeted by the youngsters who had learned Russian songs. Soon the soldiers were singing with them. When the officer said the buildings would have to be cleared out, Isa said that the school teachers would take care of the Russians — cook, wash, iron, etc. She had a sign put up saying that the school was under the protection of the Russian soldiers. This plan worked for nine months. Then another group of Russian soldiers came who wanted all the buildings for their use. This officer refused to listen when Isa said the school was under the protection of the Russian army. Then she began to cry. The other teachers cried, and the children. The officer couldn't stand this and told them to go back to their cottages. Then he and his soldiers left.[28]

Mr. Arima was administrator of the Kosuge prison of Tokyo. Before a man was released Arima would often find a job for him. He treated and fed the men well, gave them interesting things to do, both in skills and in recreation. When a released man broke faith and was returned to prison, he was treated to new clothes and a good meal, and once more became a co-operative member of the group. The results of this kind of administration were tested in the great earthquake of 1923. Walls of the prison were broken. Arima went around letting the prisoners out of the crumbling cells. Although there was nothing to hold them anymore, the prisoners rallied around their warden and remained true to his trust in them. The detachment of soldiers that arrived to guard them were refused by Arima. To prove his faith, the roll was called and practically every one of the 1300 was there to answer the test.[29]

Leonard, a 4-year-old member of a nursery school group, had been very irritable and out of sorts for a time. Aggressive behavior is unusual in this particular group, and the children did not respond in kind to his attacks against them. They discussed and lamented his " trouble " and agreed that he needed to be treated " extra nice." One afternoon when it was time to go home, he refused to put on his snow suit. When the teacher ignored his angry demands for help, he began to flail the children near him with the pants of his suit. The teacher removed him to the corridor. There he cried, stamped, and hit at everyone who came by him. The teacher accidentally stepped on his scarf as she passed him. At this he dissolved in tears, and

Eileen, who had just been struck hard on the shin by the buckle on one of his pants straps, rushed to his rescue. Firmly, but soothingly, she said, "Sit down, Leonard, I'm going to help you." And as she did so, three other children came to help, too. Together they pushed and poked the placated child into his wraps, while he repeatedly sighed, "These are my friends." [30]

More than 23 centuries ago, Moh-Tze walked for ten days and ten nights, according to the story, to reach the office of a state engineer who had invented a new weapon and was making plans to invade a neighboring state. Moh-Tze convinced the inventor to give up the plan to start a war. [31]

Telemachus, a monk in Asia Minor, made his way to Rome, a thousand miles away, to see what he could do to stop the slaughter of human life in the huge Roman gladiatorial shows. In the middle of a fight he ran from his seat in the amphitheater and called upon the combatants to cease their attempts to kill each other. The furious spectators rushed in and beat him to death with sticks and stones. But the sacrifice had its effect on Honorius the Emperor. He issued a rescript forbidding all gladiatorial combats. The evil spectacle was never held again. [32]

Thomas Lurting, a former war hero of the British navy, had become a Quaker and was on his civilian ship when it was captured by Turkish pirates. His captain and some others were taken to the Turkish ship, leaving Lurting and the crew behind with only ten Turks to guard them. By a skillful maneuver Lurting managed to get the Turks locked into the hold. Then he sailed into port planning to release the Turks there. Upon regaining his command, the captain decided to deceive Lurting and sell the captured Turks as slaves. Lurting heard of this plan, however, and with three helpers, loaded the Turks into a small boat and rowed them to shore where they were set free. There they parted "in great love." After that Quakers alone were allowed by the people of that region to come among them without hostility. [33]

Mrs. Grace Olive Wiley feels perfectly safe handling deadly rattlers and cobras. She attributes her years of success in handling these snakes to an application of the Golden Rule. She tries to "communicate confidence" to them until a relationship of mutual trust is built up.

When wolves were needed for the Hollywood movie "The Call of the Wild," Larry Trimble undertook to train twenty of them. They were let loose in a twenty-acre stockade. Larry would leave pieces of meat out in the open, then curl up in his sleeping bag in the same area, defenseless but confident. Before long the wolves were eating out of his hand and sleeping within a few yards of him. [34]

Helen Keller insisted — despite warnings — upon becoming more familiar with a lion, which she had heard of, but could not see or hear. She walked into the lion's cage without fear and inquiringly knelt before the surprised lion, which strangely offered no resistance to her touch. As she explored the lion's muscles, mane, paws, tail, etc., it roared (but Helen didn't hear); nevertheless, it made no effort to stop her, as if it sensed the friendliness of its visitor. [35]

Sundar Singh had become a wandering Christian sadhu living a dedicated life of voluntary poverty in India. A leopard was on the loose near a village where Sundar happened to be. The villagers were frantically searching it out, but Sundar sat defenseless and alone in a clearing near his host's house. As the night wore on his host became anxious for him, and looked out the window just in time to see the leopard crawling toward Sundar. Too late to call out, he stared in wonder as Sundar reached out and serenely stroked the leopard's head. When he came into the house and answered his host's questions, Sundar said, " Why should the leopard harm me? I am not his enemy."

When a listener once struck Sundar Singh a savage blow, Sundar merely washed off the wound with water from a ditch and came back singing to his audience. By the end of the hour the man who had struck him wanted to go along with Sundar.

In the bandit-ridden mountains Sundar was once attacked, but upon seeing the tranquillity on his face, the bandits changed their minds and invited him to their cave for a chat. Before he left the leader had become a Christian.[36]

The Maori in New Zealand had no weapons to fight the white imperialists taking possession of their land. One wise leader, upon hearing that the English were marching to attack his village, summoned his people together and told them to prepare for a feast, to meet and welcome the soldiers with songs, dances, and games. The soldiers were baffled by their reception and followed the procession into the village where they were met by the chief with friendliness and hospitality. They could do nothing but accept the spirit of their hosts. They finally withdrew, leaving the tribe in possession of the land, and never made another expedition against them.[37]

Baiko San had been asked to become priest for her village in China after the previous priest — her husband — had died. One night she was awakened in her little shrine by a robber demanding the money from the last night's meeting. She calmly said she would not give it to him. When he threatened her with a sword, she said she was old and ready to die, but that she was concerned about him and his future should he kill her. Then she said that he could have her own personal money given her by the villagers, told him where it was, and went back to sleep. The next morning she found that none of the money had been touched.[38]

When Richard Baxter was working in an English mine, he decided to turn over a new leaf — not to get drunk and not to get into fights any more. On his job one day he found a fellow worker bullying one of the small boys in charge of a coal-carrying wagon. After Richard had helped the boy get back the wagon, the worker growled that he felt like smacking Richard in the face. Richard told him to go ahead and the man hit him several times without receiving any resistance. When Richard saw this worker the next time he went down into the mine, the worker broke out into tears and asked for forgiveness. Richard said he had forgiven him. They shook hands and became friends.[39]

During the Civil War William Hockett was drafted into a North Carolina regiment. He refused to participate in the military system and was finally ordered to be shot. As the rifles were raised, he raised his arms and said, " Father, forgive them, for they know not what they do." Not a trigger was pulled; the guns were lowered without orders. Members of the company were heard to say they could not kill such a man.[40]

In the year 1917, bands of ruffians roved southern Russia marauding, raping, killing. A Mennonite community, though long-time pacifists, were frightened into arming to protect their women and children and " to fight fire with fire." The attack came; many were killed, the women raped and brutally treated. After the invaders left a council was held and it was decided to go back to the old way. The next time the raiders came the men went out to meet them without guns. Instead, they knelt and prayed for their loved ones and also for their enemies. " The impact of this spirit got through. It reached the conscience of their attackers. The marauders apparently sensed that they were up against a superior, even if invisible power. They left and did not return." [41]

When Dr. Theodore Pennell went into the Northwest Frontier in India, a price was put on his head by the local Mowlahs (Mohammedan clergy). As soon as Pennell found out the name of one of these persons, he paid the man a visit. The surprised Mowlah could not carry out his own orders — after all, you can't stick a knife into a guest; you must be hospitable. So Pennell became the Mowlahs' friend and lived unarmed among them for years. The commander of the British army on the frontier said Pennell's being there was worth two battalions for the peace which followed his presence.[42]

An old Hindu and his servants stopped to rest in a spot infested by robbers. Despite his servants' warnings the old man sat down alone to watch the setting sun. A robber, believing the old man to be wealthy, crept up on him with a dagger in his hand. The old man's eyes turned on the robber with quietness and love. The surprised robber dropped the dagger and fell at the man's feet, confessing his sin. Instead of admonishing the robber, the old man rose and threw his arms around him indicating that the robber was now his disciple. The robber became a new man and lived a life of service.[43]

A converted New Hebrides chieftain, an ex-cannibal, sent a message to a fellow chieftain that he and four attendants would pay a visit the next Sunday to tell of their new ideas. He received the answer that if anyone came trying to preach to them at any time, all would be killed. The chieftain sent another message saying that he had learned to return good for evil, and would appear unarmed with his attendants the next Sunday. Again the blunt reply was that if they came they would be killed. When the chieftain and his little band appeared walking toward his village, the nonco-operative chief begged them to leave, but nothing would stop the others. Soon spears began to fall around them; before long they were dodging and expertly catching the close ones. Out of wonder the villagers stopped throwing their spears and listened to the Christian chief. Eventually the other chieftain with his people became pupils of this new way of living.[44]

In the 1905 Russian Revolution in southern Russia, a small Mennonite community was threatened by rebels who were destroying everything in their path. One family met the situation by preparing a good rich supper the day of the expected raid. The husband asked his wife to set the table for guests, and sent the children to bed. When the band appeared and asked the father to surrender, he invited them in to the prepared dinner, saying that anything of his was theirs, but that they must want refreshment first. They hesitated, then sat down to eat. After the supper the father showed them beds he had prepared in the next room. After their sleep the leader appeared again, this time smiling, and said: " We have to go. We came to kill you, but we can't." [45]

In an experimental study of the Harvard Research Center in Creative Altruism, we set a task to change the inimical relationship between members of each of five pairs of Harvard and Radcliffe students into an amicable one. Five pairs of mutually hating students were dealt with. The method of good deeds was selected for the desired transformation. One of the students of each pair was persuaded to start to do some kind deed to the disliked partner. Within a period of some four months the inimical relationships in four pairs were replaced by amicable ones. Performance of small deeds of kindness (inviting to a dance, giving a ticket for theater, helping in study work, teaching the other party to crochet, etc.) began to change retroactively the performer and then the other party in replacing their dislike by better understanding and then friendship.[46]

In another experimental study of changing the attitude of dislike toward certain nurses by certain patients of the Boston Psychopathic Hospital, the technique of good deeds and unfailing kindness of the disliked nurses towards the disliking patients succeeded in replacing the previous antagonisms by friendly relationships.[47]

*Conclusion.* The foregoing set of facts has been selected intentionally to be diverse. In spite of their diversity all these facts show the power of love subduing enmity, aggression, or hate. Facts of this sort can be multiplied without end. In the experience of everyone of us similar facts have probably happened many times. Sometimes they become unforgettable; at other times they are forgotten. Whether remembered or forgotten, they occur. When they are registered at least as carefully as the facts of enmity overcoming friendship, the facts of love overpowering animosity appear to be much more frequent than we habitually think. Facts of this sort give a firm basis for the contention that unselfish love, true kindness, and friendship have real power, and that this power is much greater than Sensate individuals believe. The subsequent series of empirical data tremendously reinforce this conclusion.

### III

### LOVE BEGETS LOVE, HATE BEGETS HATE

Next evidence of the power of love is supplied by innumerable facts showing that unselfish love is at least as " contagious " as hate and that love influences human behavior as tangibly as hate does. If and when an individual or group approaches other persons or groups in a friendly manner, the respondents' answer to such an approach is also kindly in the overwhelming majority of cases. And the frequency of the friendly response to the friendly approach is at least as high as that of an inimical response to an aggressive approach.

Of numerous observations of this uniformity, only a few typical cases can be mentioned here. Dr. R. W. Hyde and H. Eichorn studied the approaches and responses of a group of patients of the Boston Psychopathic Hospital, and received the following results: to friendly approaches the respondents reacted friendly in 73 per cent of actions-reactions; in 16 per cent they responded in an aggressive manner; and in 11 per cent, in a neutral way. To aggressive approaches the respondents answered aggressively in 69 per cent, friendly in 25 per cent, and indifferently in 6 per cent. The authors remark that the 6 per cent of aggressive response to the friendly approaches is possibly due to the "superficiality of friendly approach hiding an undercurrent of hostility or of disinterestedness." Likewise, a friendly response to the seemingly aggressive approach "may have been accepted by the recipients as compliments regarding their sexual potency." Whatever is the cause of the aggressive response to friendly approach and of the friendly response to the aggressive approach, the main rule that love begets love and begets it as frequently as hate generates hate is clear from the data. The per cent of the friendly response to the friendly approach is even slightly higher than that of the unfriendly response to the unfriendly approach.[48]

In Sorokin's study of the relationship between each of 548 Harvard and Radcliffe students and his or her "best friend," the friendship was initiated in 23.7 per cent of cases by an action of kindness, help, sympathy and care of one or of both parties; in the remaining 76.3 per cent of the cases it was due to the desirable traits, and mutual supplementation of the values and experiences of the parties involved. There was not a single case of a friendship initiated by aggression of one or of both parties. The inimical relationship between each of these students and his or her "worst enemy" started in 48.1 per cent of the cases by an action of aggression or unfriendliness of one or of both parties involved. In the remaining 51.9 per cent of the cases the enmity was due to the undesirable personal traits, to the incompatibility of the values, ideals, and aspirations of the parties involved. Here again friendliness tends to beget friendliness and aggression generates enmity.[49]

In another, more detailed investigation of how friendship started and developed with the "best friend" of each of 73 Harvard and Radcliffe students, and how the enmity with the "worst enemy" of each of these students grew, the results were fairly similar to the above: 24.2 per cent of the friendships were started by actions of kindness, generosity, help, sympathy of one or of both parties; 42.7 per cent of the enmities were started by aggressive and inimical actions of one or of both parties. The remaining percentage of friendship was due to hidden and somewhat milder actions of sympathy and mutual supplementation of the parties involved, while the rest of the percentage of enmity was due to a lack of sympathy, indifference, and a milder form of animosity of the parties in question.[50]

Here again the emergence and development of either friendship or animosity follows the formula: love begets love, enmity produces enmity.

In a number of other clinical, observational, and experimental studies similar results were obtained.

A group of 10-year-old children under autocratic and aggressive conditions displayed thirty times more frequent hostility and eight times more frequent aggression among its members than the same group under nonaggressive and democratic conditions.[51]

M. E. Bonney's study has shown that the technique of praising, complimenting, helping, and initiating friendly discussion is the best answer to " how to make friends." [52]

In M. D. Fite's experiment, the technique of helping aggressive children to find a good solution to their immediate problems proved to be more successful in curing their aggressiveness than the techniques of reproofs, repression, and punishment.[53]

In a large number of other investigations the rule of love begetting love has well been confirmed.[54] The rule means that any genuine (and adequate) [55] love or friendship effectively (though not always) changes the human mind and overt behavior in a friendly direction towards the friendly acting person(s). In this inner and overt transformation the power of love seems to be as effective as is the power of hate or animosity.

## IV

### Love as an Important Factor of Vitality and Longevity

Other conditions being equal, of two persons with identical biological organisms, the kind and friendly person tends to live longer and to have better health than the unkind and especially the hate-possessed individual. Love in its various forms proves to be one of the most important factors of longevity and good health; being loved by others and loving others seems to be as important a single factor of vitality as any other.

The first important evidence for this is supplied by the life durations of the Christian Saints. An overwhelming majority of these Saints were eminent altruists. Sorokin's study of 3090 Christian and Catholic Saints and 415 Russian Orthodox Saints from the beginning of Christianity up to the present time has shown that they had notably longer life duration than their unsaintly and less altruistic contemporaries. Though the duration of life of 37 per cent of these Saints was cut off by a premature death through martyrdom; though most of them lived an ascetic life denying the satisfaction of many bodily needs; though many of them lived in nonhygienic conditions; and though the average life duration of the populations in the centuries before the nineteenth was notably lower than that of the United States population in 1920 — in spite of all these adverse conditions the life duration of the Saints as a group was somewhat higher than that of the American population in 1920. This can be seen from the following rough comparison.

Frequency of distribution of ages in percentages among: [56]

| Age groups (years) | Those who died in the United States in 1920 at the age of 20 years and above | The Saints' group (years) | Percentage |
|---|---|---|---|
| | % | | |
| 20–39 | 22.7 | 16–40 | 15.8 |
| 40–59 | 28.6 | 41–60 | 27.5 |
| 60–79 | 38.1 | 61–80 | 39.0 |
| 80 and above | 10.6 | 81 and above | 17.7 |
| Total | 100.0 | | 100.0 |

If anything, these statistics are loaded against the Saints: the first age group of the Saints is taken at a younger age (16 to 40) than the first group of the general American population (20 to 39). In spite of this the per cent of the Saints who died at the ages 61 and above is tangibly higher than that of the ages 60 and over in the general population of the United States of the twentieth century.

On the other side, the life-giving and life-sustaining power of love is strikingly demonstrated by the fact of *suicide*. We know now that the main cause of suicide is psychosocial isolation of the individual, his state of being lonely in the human universe, not loving or caring for anybody and not being loved by anybody. Each time when the love ties of a person are breaking down, especially breaking abruptly, when his attachments to other persons weaken, when he becomes an unattached and disattached human atom in the universe, his chances of suicide are increasing. Each time when one's love and attachment to one's fellow men multiply and grow stronger, the chances for suicide are decreasing.[57] This means that love is indeed the intensest vital force, the central core of life itself. Further on this conclusion will be reinforced by other basic evidence.

## V

### CURATIVE POWER OF LOVE

This conclusion that love has curative power is corroborated by a vast body of evidence which demonstrates the tangible curative power of love in regard to certain physical and mental disorders. Modern psychosomatic medicine correctly views the strong emotional disturbances, especially of an aggressive, inimical, hateful, and antagonistic kind, as one of the basic factors of cardiovascular, respiratory, gastrointestinal, eliminative, skin, endocrine, genito-urinary disturbances, and others such as epilepsy and headache. " The great anatomist, John Hunter, is reputed to have said concerning his angina pectoris, ' My life is at the mercy of any rascal who can make me angry.' " [58]  Among other things, a strong hateful, angry, inimical emotion robs one of peace of mind and through that (and other ways) undermines one's health and vitality.  On the other hand, emotions of love, sympathy, and friendship tend to build one's peace of mind, one's equanimity towards fellow men and the world at large; for this and other reasons they exert revitalizing and curative effects upon the organism and its disturbances.

For babies motherly love is a vital necessity.  Deprived of warm love they sicken and die as quickly as they sicken and die because of infection or hunger or improper diet.  One of the latest studies along this line is that of René A. Spitz.  He reported and filmed the death of thirty-four foundlings in a foundling home.  They had all the necessities and care in the foundling home except motherly love.  Its lack was sufficient to cause their deaths.  The whole process of the withering of their vitality was filmed by Dr. Spitz, and can be seen and followed by the film's on-looker.  After three months of separation from their parents the babies lost appetite, could not sleep, and became shrunken, whimpering, and trembling.  After an additional two months they began to look like idiots.  Twenty-seven foundlings died in their first year of life, seven in the second.  Twenty-one lived longer, but " were so altered that thereafter they could be classified only as ' idiots.' " [59]

The therapeutic power of love is especially important in preventing and healing mental and moral disturbances.  As we shall see in the subsequent sections of this book, the grace of love — in both forms of *loving* and *being loved* — is the most important condition for newly born babies to grow into morally and mentally sound human beings.  Deprivation of love in childhood ordinarily leads such unfortunate persons to moral and mental disturbances in their youth and adult periods.

In our age of psychoneuroses, and of extensive juvenile delinquency, the Mennonite and Hutterite communities in the United States yield either the lowest quota of delinquents, criminals, and mentally sick persons or none.  The main reason for this is that these communities try to practice in the interrelationship of their members the precepts of the Sermon on the Mount as closely as possible; they not only preach love but realize it in their daily behavior.  No member of the communities is deprived of love and all are united into one real brotherhood.[60]

The power of love, sympathy, empathy, and understanding appears to be the main curative agent in diverse therapies of mental disorders.  How curative the various psychiatric techniques actually are is exceedingly difficult to establish.  The difficulties are due to a lack of objective criteria of improvement, diagnosis, record-keeping, etc.  Various attempts to measure the curative effects of diverse psychiatric therapies give discrepant results from a very low percentage of patients, with temporary and slight improvement, up to some 40 to 60 per cent of cases is psycho-neurotic, sexual, and character disorders; and much lower percentages in epilepsy, migraines, stammering, chronic alcoholism, and psychoses.[61]

Regardless of the uncertainty and contrariety of the curative results of various psychiatric methods, on one vital point the psychiatrists seem to be in essential agreement, namely, *that the main curative agent in all the diverse psychiatric techniques is the " acceptance " of the patient by the therapist, the rapport of empathy, sympathy, kindness, and love established between the therapist and the patient.* In other words, the essence of curative therapy consists in the patient's exposure to the " radiation " of understanding, kindness, and love of the therapist, instead of the atmosphere of rejection, enmity, reproof, and punishment the patient is usually living in.

Concluding his study of the percentages and the degrees of improvement of patients subjected to various psychiatric therapies, K. E. Appel concludes that " the therapeutic statistics of psychiatry appear to justify . . . that any therapy [in the sense of friendly rapport between the therapist and the patient] *is* in itself more fundamental than the type employed. There is something basically effective in the process of therapy in general which is independent of the methods employed." [62]

The same conclusion is reached by F. E. Fiedler [63] in his studies of the effectiveness of various psychiatric methods and especially of the " ideal therapeutic relationship." These studies show that in spite of wide differences in the theories and specific techniques of various psychiatric methods, the curative results of expert psychiatrists are fairly similar and the eminent psychiatrists of different schools all agree in what is the best or the " ideal therapeutic relationship." It is marked by the following characteristics: complete empathy between the therapist and the patient; good rapport; an atmosphere of mutual trust and confidence. The therapist sticks closely to the patient's problems; the patient feels free to say what he likes. The therapist accepts all feelings which the patient expresses as completely normal and understandable (according to the old precept: " to understand all is to forgive all "). The patient assumes an active role in his own improvement. There is, in other words, a full understanding and sympathy between the parties.

In contrast to this ideal therapeutic relationship, the worst and least effective therapy is marked by a punitive therapist, making the patient feel rejected and having little respect for the patient; by an impersonal, cold, often inimical relationship of the parties; by treatment of the patient as a child or irresponsible, dangerous, stupid, and inferior person.[64]

In another study of the problem Fiedler concludes:

This investigation supports the theory that relationship [of understanding, communication and sympathy between the therapist and the patient] *is* therapy, that the goodness of therapy is a function of the goodness of the therapeutic relationship [in the sense of the "ideal therapeutic relationship"] . . . that the patients who cannot establish interpersonal relationship with others do not seem to improve as a result of psychotherapy.

A patient must have "support, security, and understanding," as well as "acceptance and warmth" from the therapist if any cure can occur, sums up S. G. Estes' study of this problem.[65]

The "positive transference," that is, the affectionate and warm feeling of the patient towards the therapist — in contradistinction to the "negative transference with its feeling of hostility" — is generally regarded as the necessary condition for improvement of the patient. "When the transference is positive, the analytic work proceeds smoothly. Sometimes a negative transference dominates. Then the work goes on slowly, with difficulty, without signs of benefit to the patient."[66]

One of the patients sums up the situation as follows: "As a result of my own experience as a client, I am convinced that the counselor's complete acceptance, his expresssion of the attitude of wanting to help the client, and his warmth of spirit expressed by his wholehearted giving of himself to the client in complete cooperation with everything the client does or says are basic in this ['the client-centered'] type of therapy."[67]

C. R. Rogers describes the process of curing as follows:

The client moves from the experiencing of himself as an unworthy, unacceptable, and unlovable person to the realization that he is accepted, respected, and loved, in this limited relationship with the therapist. "Loved" has here perhaps its deepest and most general meaning — that of being deeply understood and deeply accepted.[68]

Similar is the conclusion of competent therapists of practically all the schools of psychiatry.[69]

Since the real curative agent in mental disease is love in its various forms, this explains why many eminent apostles of love have been able to cure the mental disorders of legions of persons, though these altruists did not have any special psychiatric training. Their sublime love and supraconscious wisdom have been an excellent substitute for the "little or no love" and the professional training of ordinary psychiatrists. It is true that for a successful cure of especially serious mental disorders, a mere blind, inadequate love and too-dried-up "intellectualized" love is not enough. Elsewhere it has been pointed out that truly creative and curative love must be not only pure and intensive, but also "adequate" or wise, choosing the adequate means for the realization of its supreme objective. Otherwise, it may miscarry and harm rather than benefit and cure.[70] Though love seems to be the main curative agent in therapy, it must be adequate and wise love, guided by the supraconscious genius or scientific training of the therapist. The need for an important role of adequate scientific training is not canceled by the thesis that love is the main agent.

To do its work effectively, love needs to be competently guided, channeled, and used. For the geniuses, their supraconscious supplies this guidance. For the ordinary therapists, their scientific training performs this function.[71] Stressing the importance of either supraconscious or scientific guidance of love, then, the curative power of love remains indispensable for practically all successful therapeutic treatments of mental disorders.

## VI

### Love as the Mainspring of Life and of Life Evolution

The discussed curative and life-giving functions of love follow from the very nature of love as the concentrated form of life and from the nature of life as a form of a love energy. This conception of life has been outlined above, in Chapter One, and has been well demonstrated by Ashley Montagu [72] and by others.[73]

The co-operative forces are biologically the more important and vital [than the antagonizing forces].[74]

To sum up: without the operation of a biological counterpart of love energy, life itself is not possible, nor its continuity, nor the preservation and survival of species, nor life evolution, nor the emergence and evolution of *Homo sapiens*.[75]

In the last few decades [76] an enormous body of evidence has been produced showing that the principle of cooperation has possibly been even more important in the evolutionary process than that of egoistic struggle for existence. From the simplest protozoa up to man, mutual aid in various forms is found to function among all species, especially among those that have to nurture their offspring. For man mutual aid has been the condition of survival of the species. Owing to its helplessness, a newly born child has to be taken care of for a number of years. The very biological interdependence of the two sexes of *Homo sapiens* dictates their living together, their cooperation and mutual aid. Before human culture and weapons were developed, men could defend themselves against stronger species and many destructive forces only by living together, in groups with co-ordinated collective activities.[77]

## VII

### Integrative and Creative Power of Love in the Life of an Individual

Love not only cures and revitalizes the individual's mind and organism; it proves itself to be the decisive factor of vital, mental, moral, and social well-being and growth of an individual. The unwanted, unloved, rejected babies, deprived of the grace of love at an early age, tend to die or to grow into distorted " human plants." They are like seedlings planted in an unfertile soil and deprived of the necessary ingredients for normal growth and activity. If in these conditions such seedlings do not die they grow stunted, misshapen, weak, and ugly. Babies and children not blessed by the grace of love of their family, playmates, and neighbors, grow into unhappy, defective, and often delinquent human beings. To love and be loved turns out to be the most important " vitamin," indispensable for the sound growth of an individual and a happy course of human life.

This is well corroborated by two opposite sets of evidence. On the one hand, children unloved, unwanted, and rejected by their parents, siblings, and others, yield a much higher quota of juvenile delinquents, adult criminals, and physically and mentally defective persons than do children who are adequately loved by the members of their family, playmates, and others. Unloved and unloving children give a higher rate of warped, hostile, and unbalanced sort of persons than do children blessed by the grace of love. The evidence supporting this generalization is substantial and adequate.[78]  On the other hand, almost all of those Christian Saints who quietly, without any tragedy and sudden conversion, grew into apostles of love came from harmonious families where they were wanted and loved.[79]

The positive and negative sets of facts confirm the indispensable grace of love in forming a sound, integrated, and creative personality. This constructive function of love is one of its many forms of power.

## VIII

### Love as Creative Power in Social Movements

With the exception of love as the mainspring of life and of biological evolution, we have dealt so far mainly with the influence of love upon individuals and interindividual relationships. Fortunately, the power of love is not limited by this influence. It goes far beyond individual relationships and cases; it effects the whole social and cultural life of humanity. It operates as the driving force of mankind's creative progress towards ever-fuller truth, ever-nobler goodness, ever-purer beauty, ever-richer freedom, and ever-finer forms of social life and institutions. Throughout human history each positive step in this direction has been inspired and " powered " by love, while any regressive step away from these values has been moved by hate.

Let us begin with a few cases of love's influence upon vast social movements. We can start with concrete questions: Can the nonviolent power of love stop war and give peace? Can the peaceful power of love achieve important social reforms and constructive changes? Can it compete with the social reconstructions inspired by hate and carried on by means of violent and bloody struggle of clashing parties?

A number of clear-cut historical events give an answer to these questions. As a first case of the power of love in regard to war and peace, Asoka's experiment can be mentioned. After his accession to the throne in 273 B.C. Asoka, like his predecessors, spent the first twelve years of his reign in wars of consolidation of his Indian empire. The conquest of the province of Kalinga in 261 B.C. was his last war. From Asoka's own inscriptions we learn that the horrors and miseries of wars aroused in him a deep remorse, a sense of profoundest shame, and an understanding of the utter futility of war as a means of pacification and of social improvement. As a result, in 261–260 B.C. he was converted into Buddhism, as a lay disciple, and in 259 he entered a Buddhist order as a monk. This date marks the complete transformation of Asoka and of his policies. The successful emperor-warrior changed into a zealous apostle of peace, compassion, love, and good works. He began now to preach, to practice, and to carry on " the policies of goodness, mercy, liberality, truthfulness, purity, and gentleness," — especially towards the conquered peoples — and the policies of liberation from " depravity, violence, cruelty, anger, conceit, and envy." Specific duties required from his followers and officials were: nonslaughter of animate beings, noninjury to " existing creatures "; hearkening to father and mother; reverence to teachers; liberality and seemly behavior towards friends, acquaintances, fellow men, and ascetics; compassionate and seemly conduct towards slaves and servants; and " small expense and small accumulation."

His *works of charity* consisted in planting the roads with shade trees and orchards, building rest houses and watering sheds, and digging wells; in construction of hospitals and dispensaries (for men and animals), in distribution of medical drugs, in planting medicinal herbs and fruit trees; in outright grants of money and organized relief to the poor, the aged, the helpless, prisoners, the infirm, and needy people generally.

His *political administration* was marked by the complete cessation of wars and establishment of undisturbed peace — internal and external — and by the organization of a special class of high officials (Dharma-Mahamatras) whose duties were concerned solely with the temporal and spiritual welfare of the people. All political officers were to follow Asoka's example in their personal behavior. They were exhorted to carry on the policy of good will, sympathy, and love to their own people, as well as to the peoples of the bordering territories. The officials thus were missionaries and moral leaders. One of their main functions was to be " peacemakers " between all sects, races, parties, and peoples, building their mutual good will and decreasing their enmities. Asoka revised the existing law and judicial administration, making these more just, human, and uniform. He made himself available for the business of the people at any and all times, and so on.

Asoka's *cultural activities* resulted in spreading mental and moral education among the people; in reconstructing the fine arts, particularly the art of the stage. The amphitheaters were used, among other things, for dramatization of the enjoyments which would follow from a life of virtue, from improvement of economic conditions of the people, and so forth.

To sum up: here we have a striking example of a peaceful, *love-motivated* social, mental, moral, and aesthetic reconstruction of an empire.[80] Was Asoka's experiment successful? It certainly was. He secured internal and external peace in his empire, not only up to his death in 232 B.C., but for an additional thirty to forty years after his death — that is, for a period of some sixty to seventy years. A systematic study of all the wars in the history of Greece, Rome, Austria, Germany, Holland, Spain, Italy, France, England, Russia, Poland, and Lithuania from 600 B.C. up to the present time shows that out of each one hundred years of their history from twenty-eight to sixty-seven years had an occurrence of war. In other words, in average these countries had a war in one-fourth to one-half the years of their history.

This does not mean that the years of war and peace in the history of any country have been evenly distributed; some periods had uninterrupted war during two, five, ten, or thirty, and so on, years; other periods have had several years of undisturbed peace. But periods of peace as long as one-quarter of a century have been exceedingly rare in the history of all countries, and a period up to 100 years or more of peace is almost unique, given in the history of Holland; in some of these countries long periods of peace did not occur at all. Almost every generation (25 to 30 years) in the past, with very few exceptions, have been a witness of, or an actor in, war phenomena.[81]

In the light of these data, the period of uninterrupted peace for some sixty to seventy years achieved by the love-inspired, nonviolent, peaceful policy of Asoka is an exceptionally rare achievement in the history of all countries at all times. It is the policy radically opposite to the Roman policy of *si vis pacem para bellum* ("if you want peace, prepare for war") or its contemporary version of "peace through armed power."

From the remotest past up to the present time this predatory policy of "peace through armed power," intimidation, coercion, and destruction has been followed by an overwhelming majority of governments of all countries. In spite of its past and present glorification, in spite of the endless repetition of this "enmity-fueled" policy, it has neither given lasting peace to humanity nor yielded even relatively long peaceful periods. After numberless applications of this predatory and hate-loaded policy for millennia, mankind of the twentieth century finds itself in the bloodiest, most militant, most inhuman, and most destructive century of the twenty-five centuries studied.[82]

A detailed study of war and peace periods in the history of the twelve countries named above shows that an overwhelming majority of the relatively long peaceful periods, of some fifteen years and over, occurred in the times when the ruling groups and the people of the respective countries neither were ambitious for military glory, nor believed much in the sheer power of arms, nor were anxious to conquer their neighbors, nor hated other countries. On the contrary — like the governments and the people of The Netherlands during the nineteenth and the beginning of the twentieth century when that country had a century of peace, or like the governments and the peoples of Switzerland and Belgium during their long neutrality period — the ruling groups during the long periods of peace were more humanitarian and peace-aspiring than the carnivorous, war-intoxicated and conquest-inspired ruling groups of the long war periods. In other words, comparatively long periods of peace are closely correlated with peace-aspiring and humanitarian governments, while the long periods of war are associated with the militant, and hate-inspired, expansionist, and domineering governments trusting mainly the power of arms, coercion, and destruction of enemies. If we take one by one all the long periods of peace and all the periods of long and frequent wars in the history of the twelve countries mentioned, and if we carefully study the prevalent types of governments and of ruling groups in peace and war periods, we find the above generalization well corroborated. Peace-aspiring and humanitarian governments are prevalent in the long peaceful periods; and carnivorous, warlike, timocratic governments are prevalent in the particularly belligerent periods.[83]

From these statements it is clear that the extraordinary success of Asoka's peace and love policy is not accidental, but is a conspicuous case of a fairly general uniformity. *In the internal and external policies of nations and empires, love also begets love and hate produces hate.* It is highly regrettable that our statesmen, diplomats, and contemporary ruling groups still transgress this rule, believing still in peace through the power of limitless arming, unbounded hating, and pitiless crushing of the actual or potential enemy. No wonder they have utterly failed in establishing peace and strikingly succeeded only in starting and expanding the bloodiest and the most destructive wars in the whole human history. In fact, their policies well demonstrate the truth that hate produces hate, physical force and war beget counterforce and counterwar, and that rarely, if ever, do these factors lead to peace and social well-being.

Asoka's policy was highly successful also internally. Without any violence and bloodshed it fruitfully carried on one of the greatest reconstructions — vital, social, economic, political, legal, mental, moral, spiritual, and aesthetic — in the entire history of humanity. For its time and for all times, Asoka's reconstruction was deeper, greater, and more constructive than any reconstruction done through bloody revolutions and violence. Again, the success of Asoka's internal policy was not accidental. It was but a conspicuous case of a fairly general uniformity that the *love-inspired reconstructions, aspiring for the real well-being of the people and carried out in a peaceful manner, are more successful and yield more lasting positive results than the social reconstructions inspired by hate and carried out mainly by violence and bloodshed.* Though in our age of violence and bloodshed this truth is entirely ignored, it remains still a valid truth. In addition to the peaceful reforms and bloody revolutions of the past, the events of our age also convincingly prove its validity. They prove it positively and negatively. The unlimited violence and the hate-inspired war policies of World War I, of World War II, of the Korean War, and of the Chinese, the Russian, the Fascist, and the Hitler revolutions strikingly demonstrate the utter futility of hate-driven wars and revolutions in improving the total well-being of humanity. First of all, empires quickly built by unlimited war and violence — like the empires of Alexander the Great, Caesar, Genghis Khan, Tamerlane, Suleiman the Magnificent, Napoleon; up to the quickly expanded empires of Japan, 1941–1945, of Hitler, or Mussolini — all such empires crumbled within a few years or decades after their establishment. Within one decade the empires of Japan, of Hitler, and of Mussolini enormously expanded and then shrunk to limits smaller than they were before the expansion.

The World Wars aimed to improve the welfare of mankind, and to make the world safe for democracy and freedom. Instead, they destroyed about one-sixth of the most inhabited regions of this planet, killed and wounded more than one hundred million human beings, brought misery, disease, and poverty to the greater part of humanity, blew to pieces all the great values, spread insanity and demoralization, unleashed in man " the worst of the beasts," and created an unprecedented chaos and anarchy. Instead of freedom and democracy, they gave unlimited tyranny, autocracy, totalitarianism, and universal coercion. The Korean war has utterly ruined the country of some thirty millions, and already has killed several millions of innocent Koreans. The net balance of these wars is quite negative: they greatly decreased the vital, mental, moral, social, and economic well-being of humanity. For all persons who have their eyes open and their minds sound, this conclusion is quite certain.

The same can be said of the recent Chinese, Russian, Fascist, Nazi, and other smaller revolutions. The Chinese revolution was started in 1911 and is still going strong. The net result of some forty years of this revolution is millions of victims, an untold ocean of suffering and bestiality, and a notably lower level of the total well-being of the Chinese nation in comparison with the prerevolutionary level. Almost all the loudly advertised " achievements " of the revolution remain mainly " paper achievements," " empty shells," without real value content. The negative balance of the Fascist and the Nazi revolutions is evident: their boasted " conquests " have already vanished and so did all their temporary triumphs. Millions of killed and wounded human derelicts, destruction, and misery is all that remains from their " achievements."

Similar is the net balance of the Russian revolution. In spite of at least twenty million direct and indirect victims of the revolution and notwithstanding all the boastful five-year plans, and all the Soviet propagandized "successes" of the revolution, the Russian nation now has a more tyrannical regime than the Czarist regime at its worst; the economic well-being is still lower than it was before 1914; the creative work of the nation is less exuberant in most fields of culture than it was before the revolution; and the moral and mental well-being of the Russian people is hardly higher now than it was before the revolution. Of course, pitilessly exploiting the great nation, the Soviet regime could not help but achieve a few positive results; these results look modest, however, in comparison with those that were peacefully achieved before the revolution, and those which would have been achieved if the revolution had not occurred.[84]

The evidence of these wars and revolutions is confirmed also by the wars and revolutions of the past. Beginning with the oldest recorded Egyptian revolution (*ca.* 3000 B.C.) and ending with the recent revolutions, they all testify to the utter futility of hate-driven mass violence for realization of the well-being of the populations and mankind.

All this negative evidence of war and revolution is confirmed, on the other hand, by the fruitfulness of peaceful and love-inspired, orderly social reconstructions.

Striking historical examples of such reconstructions are supplied, first, by peaceful transformations of peoples, culture, and social institutions by *the founders, apostles, and early followers of religions and ethics of love, compassion, and mutual service.* After all, Jesus, Buddha, Mahavira, Lao-tzu, Confucius, and Francis of Assisi had neither arms, nor physical force, nor wealth, nor any of the worldly means for exerting influence upon millions and for determining the historical destinies of nations and cultures. Nor to obtain their power did they appeal to hate, envy, greed, and other selfish lusts of human beings. Even their physical organism was not that of the heavyweight champion. And yet, together with a handful of their followers, they reshaped the mind and behavior of untold millions, transformed cultures and social institutions, and decisively conditioned the course of history. None of the greatest conquerors and revolutionary leaders can even remotely compete with these apostles of love in the magnitude and durability of the change brought about by their activities. What is still more important, the great apostles of love succeeded in working out the gigantic and imperishable change in the "upgrade" direction of creative love instead of the much easier "downgrade" direction of hate and bloody struggle.

If for a moment we subtract Christianity from the historical life, social institutions, and culture of the West; Confucianism, Taoism and Buddhism from the life and culture of China; Hinduism, Buddhism, and Jainism from the sociocultural universe of India; after such subtractions only a chaotic mass of debris would be left from the culture, social institutions, and historical life of these countries. Without their ethico-religious systems the whole history of these countries becomes incomprehensible.

Likewise, without the gigantic stream of sublime love poured by the apostles of love into it, the life of humanity would have been sorely lacking the very minimum of moral foundation necessary for its existence and survival. *Bellum omnium contra omnes* and suicidal mutual extermination would have been the lot of humanity were this sublime love absent.

And how, by what force, have these moral leaders been able to exert this gigantic influence? *Only through the grace of sublime love they were blessed with and through the wisdom of love they discovered and opened to their fellow men.* As mentioned, they did not command any armed force or machinery of state organization; nor did they possess wealth and power of money; neither were they the great intellectual scientists, nor gigantic artists. Their only weapon was the mysterious power of love. For this reason their influence stands as an indisputable demonstration of the virtually unlimited power of love. By this power they ennobled, maintained, and re-created the biological, social, and cultural life of mankind. By this power they counteracted and limited the destructive influence of the forces of strife — and are doing so up to the present moment.

This power of love is not responsible for the bloody movements and deeds perpetrated often in the name of Jesus or Buddha, or other geniuses of creative love. Religious wars and persecutions, religious political machineries and their great inquisitors have nothing to do with the teachings and activities of the great apostles of love. If anything, these machineries, bureaucratic inquisitors, wars, persecutions, intolerance, and hypocrisy are the negation and perversion of the power of love of the founders of the great religions of love. These machineries are mainly the prison structures built by the forces of enmity to stem the stream of harmonizing love, and to envelop it by the muddy waters of selfish lusts. The militant activities of these machineries are mainly the manifestations of the forces of ego-centered domination and not of the forces of love. No wonder therefore that, like other forces of enmity, these " religious " activities have wrought mainly death and destruction in the historical life of humanity.

The recent reorganization of India can serve as a modern example of the reconstructions inspired and " fueled " by the power of love. It has been started and carried on under the leadership of Gandhi and his co-workers. Their policy has been motivated by creative love at its purest and best. Hate and enmity have been explicitly ruled out from their movement — so also any violent means and methods. Throughout its whole history the Gandhi-led movement was peaceful and orderly, and its constructive results have been truly astounding. It achieved the complete political independence of an India of some 400 millions of people. This result alone exceeds the political achievements of practically any violent revolution known in human history. Gandhi's movement succeeded in the liberation and equalization of some 60 million outcasts in India — another result hardly rivaled by the "liberation" of any violent revolution. The peaceful crusade of Gandhi and his co-workers in this movement has already achieved a most significant amelioration of vital, economic, mental, moral, and cultural conditions of the vast population of India. Besides the inestimably fruitful reconstruction of India, it has produced gigantic reverberations in the entire human universe. The whole world has been constructively affected by Gandhi's policy and by its results. The reconstruction of India has convincingly shown the boundless effectiveness of the policy of love, sympathy, and good will carried on by nonviolent means, without hate and inhuman destruction. If all its positive results are summed up, they unquestionably exceed the constructive results of any violent revolution or war. India's modern reconstruction is an eloquent demonstration of the gigantic power of love in the truly creative rebuilding of a vast nation and of the possibilities for the whole of mankind.

This power of love continues to work in India, not only in the policies of Gandhi's successors in the present Indian government, but in hundreds of other movements, private and public. The activities of one of the disciples of Gandhi, "the holy man," Acharya Vinoba Bhave, give an example of these other movements. Practicing the principles of love he preaches, this gentle ascetic — by merely appealing to the goodness of human nature — has already achieved astounding results in his "one-man crusade." His speeches on nonviolence as the only fruitful solution to economic and social problems have won thousands of oppressed peasants away from Communism, and have convinced many a landlord to give up freely part of his land to the needy cultivators. "Single-handed, he attacked India's grave land problem, which is the source of rural unrest, and swiftly brought about the redistribution of 35,000 acres of land by landlords to their tenants, without coercion or the payment of an *anna*." Going from village to village this gentle ascetic has been getting about 300 acres a day freely granted by the landlords to the needy. "The Central Ministry of Food and Agriculture has been sufficiently impressed with his methods to offer 10,000,000 acres of Government-owned cultivable wasteland for him to distribute, personally, among the landless." His goal is 50,000,000 acres — one-sixth of the total cultivable land of India — to be given freely by landlords for the distribution among the landless and the needy.[85]

The fruitfulness of social reforms inspired by love rather than by hate is demonstrated by practically all such reconstructions in the history of various countries. The "Great Reforms" of 1861–65 in Russia that liberated serfs and basically reorganized political, social, economic, and cultural institutions is another highly successful peaceful reconstruction. The westernization of Japan and the basic reorganization of its institutions, carried on in orderly fashion during the second half of the nineteenth century and the beginning of the twentieth, is another successful reconstruction. Its positive success becomes especially clear when it is contrasted with Japan's violent experiments to reconstruct herself and Asia as the "co-prosperity area." Started with the Pearl Harbor attack, this "reconstruction," carried on by means of unlimited bloodshed, resulted in the catastrophic self-destruction of Japan and in a deadly devastation of China and other Asiatic countries. This has shown indeed that "it does not pay" to be violent and destructive.

The reason for this contrast is at hand. After all, violent and hate-inspired revolutions and wars are but a form of "social sickness" similar to the sickness of an organism. As long as all its parts co-operate harmoniously and maintain inner and external equilibrium, the organism lives a healthy life and is free from sickness. When the harmonious co-operation of the parts of the organism with one another and of the organism with its milieu is broken, it becomes sick. Sickness means the breakdown of the internal and external co-operation of the organism's life forces. Sickness does not cure, but needs to be cured by life forces if the organism is to be recovered. A successful cure of sickness cannot be achieved by application of bloody, hateful, and violent means. Instead, a scientifically competent, orderly, and sympathy-inspired therapy is needed. When an operation is prescribed, it is to be an operation by a competent surgeon and aimed at the recovery of the sick, but not a violent and hate-inspired butchery. In application to an organism this is well known and understood by all.

In regard to social sickness this understanding is still lacking. As long as the members of a given society or of a universe of societies co-operate with one another, as neighbors, the societies live a peaceful and harmonious life. When the co-operation, with underlying mutual sympathy and tolerance, dries up, then social tensions, enmities, and antagonisms emerge. Society or the universe of societies becomes "sick." Social sickness generates social suffering, fever, and social movements. Intentionally or not, the movements aim to get rid of the sickness. As in biological illness, mere violence and blind bloodshed cannot effect the cure. Scientific competence and sincere love for the patient are no less necessary here than in medical sickness. If even "a social operation" is in order, it must be a competent surgical operation, but not blind social butchery. It must be aimed at curing the patient, and not at killing him. It has to be peaceful and orderly therapy, and not a violent and destructive bloodshed. These conditions explain why social reconstructions, animated by sincere sympathy, competently planned and systematically carried on, turn out to be more successful in curing social sickness and in improving the well-being of society than hate-inspired wars and revolutions. In social as well as medical operations, hate-laden butchery harms rather than cures, kills rather than revives, destroys rather than builds. If something good comes of such wars and revolutions, it is due to a current, however small, of unselfish love and disinterested desire to help the suffering multitudes. In addition, most of the positive results of such violent movements are obtained through spoliation of some other groups, at the cost of their suffering, their well-being, and often their very life. Most of the " achievements " of wars and revolutions are the mere plundering of the defeated party by the victorious group. " Transference " of goods from one ruling gang to another does not enrich the whole society; neither does it increase the total sum of the goods, nor eliminate mutual hates, antagonisms, and injustices, nor cure the social sickness. It merely changes the ruling actors and the forms of tyranny, exploitation, misery, injustice, hate, and tensions without notably decreasing the total fund of social evils.

While the victorious ruling faction profits by war or violent revolution, the bulk of the populations of both struggling parties must bear the cost. And the bloodier the struggle, the greater the cost — in life, property, and happiness — for the large masses. In protracted and bloody struggles, the vital, economic, mental, and moral losses of the vast strata of both parties ordinarily far exceed their gains. While the small ruling groups of Genghis Khan or Napoleon, of Marius or Sulla, of Caesar or Anthony, of Cromwell or Robespierre, of Lenin or Hitler for a short time enormously profited by their victories, the vast multitudes of their peoples were about ruined by the struggle. Sometimes the ruin was irreparable and eventually led to the decline of the " bled " nations and their cultural creativity. Bloody civil strifes and the Peloponnesian war ushered in the decay of Greece; the costly wars and civil struggles of Marius and Sulla, of the First and Second Triumvirate started the decline of the Roman Empire. The bloodshed of the French Revolution and of the Napoleonic wars prepared the subsequent eclipse of France. The same can be said of the wars of Suleiman the Magnificent in regard to the Turkish Empire, or of the decay of the Old Kingdom, of the Middle and the New Empire in Egypt. Finally, the bloodiest revolutions and the World Wars of our time have brought the whole of mankind, especially the belligerent and turbulent West (including Russia), to the brink of an Apocalyptic catastrophe. Hate-inspired butcheries do not improve social well-being; neither do they cure social illness. Only wisely guided forces of love and free co-operation can perform these functions. Where they are lacking, no constructive results for humanity can be expected.

## IX

### Love as the Supreme and Vital Form of Human Relationship

Human relations of interacting individuals to one another can be *compulsory*, like the relationship of master and slave, of executioner and executed, of prisoners and guard, of victim and victor. The ties binding individuals into a group can also be *contractual*, with each party trying freely to get from the other parties as much advantage as possible for as little as possible, as in the relationship between buyer and seller, free employee and employer, " free " prostitute and customer. Again, the social bonds can consist of a *love relationship* sought and aspired to for its own sake. In a love relationship, the egos of the parties are freely merged into one " we "; the joys and sorrows of one party are the joys and sorrows of the other(s); the ego of one person is fully identified with that of the other(s); and if separated, the parties feel unhappy and spontaneously try to be together. Their mutual love is the end value for them. Each party gladly does and gives anything for the well-being of the other party. There is no bargain, nor calculation of profits, pleasures, and utilities. The relationship between loving mother and her child, between truly loving husband and wife, between true friends, and between all those who practice the love precepts of the Sermon on the Mount are examples of the love relationship.

It goes without saying that the finest, the noblest, and the happiest human society is the society of individuals bound together by a love relationship. This is the freest society, because the very meaning of " I love to be here," or " I love to do this," or " I love to be a member " is the highest expression of the free desire, action, and preference of a person. It is the happiest society because loving and being loved is the highest form of happiness in human relations. It is the most peaceful and harmonious society; it is also the most creative, most beautiful, and noblest.

The love relationship is not only the best, but its minimum is absolutely necessary for a long and enjoyable existence of human society and social life generally. A society bound together only by coercive bonds is but the worst " prison " society permeated by mutual hate, deprived of any freedom, joyless and drab. Prisoners always try to escape from it. It is a social hell hardly worth living in. If mankind were destined to live in such a universal prison, neither mankind nor its social life could survive.

Contractual society is much better than the prison society, but when completely deprived of the love relationship it also cannot successfully survive for a long time. Fully egoistic individuals contractually taking advantage of one another soon will find themselves engaged in a merciless struggle for existence, a mutual cold and hot war, the Hobbesian *bellum omnium contra omnes.* In unlimited free competition, the stronger individuals are soon "freely" exploiting and subjugating the weaker ones; the society is divided into the rich and the poor, the aristocracy and the plebs, the victors and the victims, the masters and the serfs, the "superiors" and the "inferiors" mutually hating each other and inevitably degenerating into a compulsory type of society. Only the strands of love relationship interwoven into the bulk of contractual relationships warm the otherwise cold society, moderate its unlimited struggle for existence, and prevent it from turning into a compulsory prison with frequent riots and "civil wars" of the prison population. In addition, if the relationships of the members of the competitive-contractual society were fully deprived of love, if the members did not love anyone and were not loved by anyone, the incessant free-for-all struggle for existence would have soon become tiresome, joyless, and senseless. Bargaining for the sake of bargaining, cutthroat rivalry for the sake of rivalry is not an end value that can be continued for its own sake forever. It has some sense and value only when the bargainers love somebody and want to help them, or to use the accumulated means for higher ends. These higher aims always contain love to something or somebody and the well-being of other human beings.

If at the present time the Western "capitalist-contractual society" is crumbling in the conflagration of multitudinal hates, strifes, and wars, one of the reasons is exactly the lack of the necessary minimum of the love relationship. Through this lack, its unlimited rivalry has degenerated into an unlimited "war of everybody with everyone," and its free contractual relationships have turned in an ever-increasing part into compulsory ones.

Only a notable infusion of the love relationship into this society can save it from its further degeneration into either compulsory totalitarian society or chaotic human flotsam.

To sum up: the love relationship is not only the supreme form of social relations, but it is an absolute necessity for the harmonious existence and survival of any social group. Without it no good social life is possible. Plato and Aristotle were quite right in their statement that the true friendship or love is the most vital stuff of all true social relationships. Often overlooked, this function of love shows its unique power in social life and in man's historical process.[86]

## X

### Love Power in Knowledge, Beauty, Goodness, Freedom, and Happiness

Finally, love furnishes considerable driving force to the total power of each of the highest values of human life: to the power of truth and knowledge, of beauty, and freedom, of goodness, and happiness. Each of these end values has its own power that tangibly effects, enriches, and ennobles the life of individuals, of groups, and the course of human history. Entering as a component into each of these values, love adds to their power. Thus *love of truth* makes the search for truth more forceful, enjoyable, and indefatigable than a pursuit of truth either coercively imposed or contractually stipulated. Most of the valid truths of humanity have been discovered through the love of truth rather than through coercion or obligation. The love of truth not only stimulates scientific discoveries, inventions, philosophical and religious verities, but *love directly contributes to our knowledge and learning.* Through empathy and communion with, and co-participation in the experience of all who are loved, love enormously enriches our poor individual experience. When love embraces the whole of humanity, each man becomes a co-participant in the richest experience of all generations. This empathic, sympathetic, loving way of learning is possibly one of the surest and most efficient methods of cognition and most fruitful way to truth and knowledge. Love, then, transforms itself into truth and knowledge. In these two ways the power of love greatly reinforces the power of truth and knowledge.

Similarly *love greatly increases the power of beauty.* Love of beauty is a pre-condition of all the innumerable actions of aspiration, enjoyment, and creative achievement of the beautiful in human life, in the fine arts, and in human history. In a sense *love is beauty's indispensable component.* Anything that one loves and looks at through loving eyes becomes " lovely," that is, beautiful. Anything unloved appears " unlovely," often ugly. Since the love experience is beautiful in its very nature, everything that love touches becomes beautiful. Love generates the search for beauty and supplies an immense driving power to the energy of beauty itself. Through the factor of beauty, love notably affects our life and the course of history. Love power has been working in and is embodied in all the fine art phenomena, beginning with the enjoyment of a sunset and the beauty of the beloved, and ending with Homer's epic poems, Shakespeare's tragedies, Beethoven's and Bach's music, Michelangelo's sculpture, and all great paintings and architecture.

Likewise, *love for freedom* has been instrumental in all movements for the realization of freedom in human history. Even more: love experience is freedom at its loftiest and best. To love anything is to act freely, without compulsion or artificial stimulation. To be free means to do what one loves to do. In this sense, *love* and *true freedom* are synonyms. Compulsion is the negation of love. Where there is love there is no coercion; where there is coercion there is no love. And the greater the love the greater the freedom. Without love, all the Bills of Rights and all the constitutional guarantees of freedom are but empty shells.

There is no need to argue that *love is the heart and soul of ethical good-*

*ness itself and of all great religions.* Their central command has always been love of God and of neighbor. Their main verity is " God is Love and Love is God." Without love there is no morality and no religion. If the stream of love in religion or ethics dries up, both become empty and dead.

Finally, *love experience is the supreme form of happiness.* Love contributes to it in many ways; first of all, as the most powerful antidote against fear and insecurity. Love " beareth all things, endureth all things . . . never faileth." Love does not fear anything or anybody. Love transcends our ego; it identifies our self with the Infinite reality-value. Disarming fear, love contributes to our happiness by blessing us with the highest peace of mind. When love is slight and impure, its peace of mind is impure and vulnerable. When love is unbounded and pure, it is " the peace of God that passeth all understanding."

The experience of a truly great love is the highest form of happiness itself. It is the *summum bonum.* Each experience of loving and being loved, however simple and impure, is already a happy experience, " a moment of sunshine " in our grayish life process. An experience of a great love is the highest bliss of human life. And vice versa. Any life deprived of love is a mere miserable existence. Such a life becomes often unbearable and leads its victims to suicide.

Thus the power of love generates, inspires, reinforces, and operates in all the individual and collective actions of the realization of truth and knowledge, of goodness and justice, of beauty and freedom, of the *summum bonum* and happiness, throughout the whole creative history of humanity. When all the manifestations of love power are rightly understood, one can but agree with Gandhi's and Dostoievsky's restatements of the old truth on the power of love. Dostoievsky wisely counsels: " Love all God's creation, the whole and every grain of sand in it. Love every leaf, every ray of God's light. Love the animals, love the plants. Love everything. If you love everything, you will perceive the divine mystery in things. Once you perceive it, you will begin to comprehend it better every day, and you will come at last to love the whole world with an all-embracing love."

PART TWO

# STRUCTURE OF CREATIVE PERSONALITY

## Chapter Five

# Mental Structure and Energies
# of Man

## I

### Main Blunders of the Prevalent Theories

The ultimate task of these studies is to find out the efficient ways of making persons more creative and altruistic. In order that this purpose may be fruitfully advanced, one has to have an adequate theory of the mental structure of human personality and of the energies generated in and operating through the human organism.

The prevalent theories in this field are grossly defective. The first of the blunders consists of merging into the category of the " unconscious " or " subconscious " (E. von Hartmann, P. Janet, S. Freud, and others) two radically different energies of man: the *biologically unconscious* that lies below the level of the conscious state of mind and the *supraconscious* (" genius," " creative *élan*," " divine inspiration," etc.) that lies above the level of any conscious and rational thought or energy. The " depth psychology " of the prevalent theories of personality is in fact quite shallow. It either flattens the mental structure almost exclusively to the level of the unconscious or subconscious, with a sort of epiphenomenal and vague " ego " and " superego," or just depicts it as a " two-story building " — the unconscious (subconscious) and the conscious (rational). In harmony with the negativistic character of the disintegrating Sensate culture, the prevalent theories of personality also move mainly in the region of the " social sewers." They see mainly the lowest form of man's energies (the unconscious and subconscious) and are blind to man's highest supraconscious genius. They emphasize man's animal, sadistic, and masochistic tendencies and pass by man's sublime, creative, and altruistic properties. They interpret the highest creative *élan* as a mere biological reflex or drive; the sublimest sacrifice as masochistic tendency; the noblest inspiration as this or that subnormal complex; the genius as an abnormal neurotic; and the saint as a doubtful " deviant."

From a strictly scientific standpoint, all such theories are but pseudo-scientific ideologies — flesh from the flesh of the disintegrating Sensate order, its children, created in its image and indebted for their success to their negativistic parental culture.

This blunder must be emphatically corrected. An adequate theory of personality must emphasize the highest aspect of its mental structure no less than its lower region, and must emphasize the supraconscious energy operating in human beings no less than the unconscious energy.

The second defect of the prevalent theories of personality is an unpermissible oversimplification of the " conscious " and " unconscious " energies of man.

The third shortcoming is their vagueness in spelling out the relationships between the structure and energies of the individual and those of the groups and culture the individual lives in. These and other shortcomings of the prevalent theories are largely responsible for a lack of real success in applied educational, psychiatric, and other techniques, in their treatment of psychoses and neuroses, and in their efforts to make human beings more creative and less selfish.

The subsequent outline of the fourfold structure and energies of personality tries to correct these blunders and to give — in black and white — a roughly adequate conception of these phenomena.

## II

### The Fourfold Mental Structure and Energies of Man

Four different forms of energies — four mental levels and activities — can be distinguished in our total personality and behavior: 1) the biologically unconscious (subconscious); 2) the biologically conscious; 3) the socioculturally conscious; and 4) the supraconscious. Figuratively speaking, man appears to be a sort of four-story building, instead of the two- or one-story structure depicted by the prevalent theories.

### 1. The Unconscious in Man

Man is an animal, and all the reflexological, instinctive, and unconscious excitations and inhibitions, drives and activities of the human organism necessary for animal life, growth, and survival make up the lowest aspect of human personality — its biological needs, drives, energies, and activities. Breathing, eating, drinking, micturation, defecation, sleeping, freedom of action without physical or other restraints, sexual conjugation, rest after fatigue, activity after inactivity, avoidance of pain and of danger to life and health; seeking and co-operating with other human beings and often caring for helpless offspring; attacking and fighting other human beings in the struggle for existence; crying, laughing, yelling, or growling: such are the main purely biological drives, needs, energies, and activities inherent in the human organism. These biological forces determine also the specific differences (anatomical, physiological, and behavioral) of different sexes, races, and age groups. Beginning with the simple pupillary or knee reflexes, passing through the complex processes of breathing, heart-beating, blood circulation, or food digestion — all automatically controlled by our autonomic nervous system — and ending with the most diverse and intricate actions and reactions, excitations and inhibitions, satisfying the above inherent needs of our organism and resulting in its growth and change from childhood to old age: these unconscious activities occupy an important part in the total biomental structure of human personality and behavior. Through this part, the human being is connected with the vital forces of the outside universe of life and through this universe with the forces of the inorganic cosmos, as the matrix of life generally and of human life particularly. This biological part of a human individual manifests, and is conditioned by, the biophysical properties of the total cosmos.[1] Being unconscious, this part of the personality's mind does not have a conscious experience of " ego " or " I." Strictly automatic reflexes occur without any ego accompanying them. The activities of breathing, heart-beating, or digestion normally proceed without any consciousness of the ego. Only when these activities become inhibited or disordered do they enter the field of consciousness and attract the attention of the conscious ego. Otherwise, they go on in the organism unconsciously and " egolessly."

The unconscious part of our mental apparatus and the reflexological, instinctive activities of the human personality are something much more complex than Freud's unconscious " id "[2] and complexes. In some of his works Freud identified the id with general energy of life; in other places he identified it with libidinal energy or sex instinct. In still other works, Freud filled the id with two instincts or energies: the sex and destructive death instincts. Whichever of these three variants of the Freudian " unconscious " is taken, each is eminently inadequate from logical as well as factual standpoints.

If we identify the total unconscious in man with the id, and this id with life energy generally, our id or unconscious becomes just another term designating the undifferentiated total life energy of man's organism. In that case, id means no more than the terms *life* or *vital force* without any further differentiation and specification. A mere replacement of these terms by *id* does not add anything to them, nor does it advance our knowledge at all. The artificial id is, if anything, darker and vaguer than *life* or *vital energy*. It just replaces the undifferentiated " darkness by blackness."

When id in the sense of undifferentiated life energy is, at the same time, identified with sex or libidinal energy, as Freud now and then does, he commits the still worse error of writing two mutually discordant equations: Equation No. 1: "Id is identical to life energy," and Equation No. 2: "Id is identical to sex energy, muscular, cutaneous, genital, anal, oral." If sex energy, with sex organs and activities, means a specific form of life energy — different, for instance, from nutritional energy with its organs and activities or from breathing energy, organs, and activities — then Equation No. 2 obviously contradicts Equation No. 1. In that case Freud commits the error which the old logicians called *pars pro toto* — identification of the whole with its part, of a specific *differentia* with its *genus*. If the libido (sex) means just undifferentiated life energy, then by calling it *sex energy* Freud only confuses us; not a scintilla of knowledge is added through such a misleading identification of sex with life. In that case the second equation is nothing but an obscured tautology of the first equation.

If, as Freud claimed in some of his other works, the realm of the unconscious id means not one but two energies — of sex and death instincts — then he gives to us three mutually contradictory formulas, beautifully repudiating one another. 1: "The unconscious id is identical with life force"; 2: "The unconscious id is identical with libidinal (sex) energy"; 3: "The unconscious id is identical with libidinal and death-destruction instincts (energies, activities)." The whole Freudian conception of the unconscious thus becomes a logical hash.

It is no better from the standpoint of factual accuracy. As soon as we begin to differentiate and specify the undifferentiated unconscious life energy of the human organism, it at once divides itself into several specific forms, organs, needs, and activities, indicated above: breathing, eating, drinking, etc. Each of these biological activities is specific and is quite different from the others and from sex activity; each has its own organs in human beings (these again different from sex organs). Breathing and its organs are different from sex organs and copulation; both are different from eating and its organs; all three are different from sleeping, and so on. Each function can inhibit and be inhibited by the others when two or more of these become antagonistic. Sex activity can inhibit hunger and vice versa; fleeing from danger can inhibit the sexual and hunger drives and their corresponding activities. Each tries to monopolize for a moment almost the whole human organism and turn it into a mere instrumentality for its satisfaction — e.g. of hunger or thirst, or sex, or defecation, and so forth.

In brief, as soon as we begin to differentiate the specific forms of the unconscious vital energy and activities of the human organism, we find not one nor even two specific forms of it, irreducible to one another, but a much greater number — a dozen or more, depending upon the classification. There is not the slightest possibility of reducing all the main differentiated forms to a mere " libidinal plus death " forms. Insofar as Freud and the Freudians try to do so, they fall into several gross — logical and factual — errors; insofar their conception of the unconscious mind, energies, organs, and activities of man is notably distorted.

The distortion becomes excessive in additional embellishments ascribed by Freud to the unconscious, such as: the id's destructive tendency directed either against others or the id's own organism and ego. In this self-aggression of the id, the Freudian proposition turns again into tautological nonsense, i.e., " the id as life energy is sadistically directed against the id as life energy," or " the id contains in itself sadistic death instinct directed against the id," or " life energy in itself contains death energy."

The notion of *life* thus becomes identified with that of *death;* the notion of *libido* with *life, destruction, death,* and with all sorts of *erotogenic sensations* (*genital, anal, oral, muscular,* etc.), often hardly distinguishable from *sensation generally*. Even the notion of *aggression* — which for Freud means an act of infliction of pain upon others or of depriving others of pleasure, an act due to one's frustration and carried on for the sake of protection of one's own libido, life, health, ego — loses any clear meaning through its extention into " self-aggression " or " aggression directed against the self." In this latter case, aggression turns into " an act of infliction of pain upon oneself or of depriving oneself of pleasure for the sake of avoidance of pain or for obtaining an enjoyment of pleasure, an act which is generated by one's frustration and tries to cure this frustration by imposition of a new frustration." In brief, it turns again into tautological nonsense and meaningless vacuity. Like the correlative notions of father and son, each of which has a meaning only in conjunction with the other notion, aggression has a meaning only as an act directed against others. As soon as we make it also " self-aggression," its meaning is canceled just as the meaning of " father " is canceled when it is taken without " son " or when " father " is identified with " son." Freudian manipulation of these terms turns them into the foggiest mass of empty tautologies and self-contradictory notions.

Still more erroneous are the Freudian theories about the child's incestuous sexuality which tries to satisfy itself on and through the parents, a girl tending to seduce her father and a boy his mother (the Oedipus complex). Also in error are the theories about the boy's fear of castration for his incestuous libido; about the female envy of the male penis; about libido directed towards sexual objects and libido gratified on the self (the narcissistic ego-libido). Through this boundless extension of the meaning of libido, it again is deprived of any clear meaning and turned into a term which can mean anything or nothing. Even more phantasmagoric are Freud's analyses and classifications of human characters on the basis of the oral, anal, phallic, urethral, and genital eroticisms.

These and other characteristics of the Freudian unconscious make out of it a grotesque phantasma, fallacious logically, wrong factually, ugly aesthetically, and demoralizing ethically.

The considerable success of Freudianism is due mainly to its congeniality with the dominant, disintegrating Sensate culture of the West in which
Freudianism was born and diffused.  Freudianism is possibly the most
typical child of this disintegrating culture.  Both are moving mainly in
the region of the " social sewers "; both are negativistic; both drag into the
social muck everything ennobling and beautiful, beginning with God and
ending with childhood, motherhood, parenthood, love, and sacrifice.

Finally, contrary to Freud, the unconscious energies of man do not constitute a single hydraulic system with a constant libido energy circulating
through various channels.  The total quantity and qualitative forms of
these biological energies vary according to the biosocial conditions.  To
a certain extent they can be transformed into one another; but there are
definite limits to these transformations.

One last remark on the unconscious: due to the development in man of
the conscious and the supraconscious, the whole realm of the unconscious
in man is somewhat disorganized and does not function as well as, for instance, the whole reflex-instinct mechanism in most of the other species.
Our total reflex-instinct unconscious apparatus is tangibly upset and needs
some supervision and control on the part of the conscious and the supraconscious.  About this something more will be said further on.  For the
present this concise characterization of the unconscious in man is sufficient, and we can pass on to the next level of the human mind and personality, the bioconscious.

## 2. The Bioconscious in Man

Next to the unconscious energies and activities come the bioconscious
energies and activities associated with a set of biological egos and roles in
personality.  When a person is aware of his biological tension, and the
tension enters the field of consciousness, the biological energy becomes
bioconscious and leads to bioconscious activities on the part of the corresponding biological ego.  Thus, when one grows aware of a pain and consciously strives to alleviate it, or when one says, " I am hungry," or
" thirsty," or " tired," and consciously seeks to allay his hunger, thirst, or
fatigue, the purely unconscious energies and activities assume a bioconscious form and involve a set of corresponding biological egos.  When an
individual becomes aware of his race, sex, or age characteristics, thinking
or saying: " I am a Negro," or " I am acting like a woman," or " I am just
like a baby," or " I am too old for that," or " I am young yet," the unconscious race, sex, and age forces become the bioconscious race, sex, and age
egos of the individual.  These energies, roles, and egos constitute a second
stratum of personality adjacent to the stratum of the unconscious.  Like
the latter, the total quantitative energies of this stratum vary; still more
variable is the qualitative set of biological egos and roles.  It is constantly
changing, one biological ego appearing and, after its satisfaction, being

replaced by another. When one is hungry, his " nutritional ego " emerges and occupies a large area of the field of consciousness and conscious activities. When his hunger is satisfied, it recedes into the field of the unconscious, giving place to another biological ego — for instance, the sex ego.

Side by side with these short-time numerous replacements of one biological ego by another in the course of each day, there is an irreversible, long-time succession of the age egos of the individual: the egos of baby, adolescent, mature man, old man. The irreversible succession of these bioconscious age egos occurs in the life cycle of every individual who lives a full span of human life. It is basically determined by biological forces and is accompanied by a legion of important anatomical, physiological, and psychosocial changes in the individual, his behavior, his relationships with others, and his position in his social groups.

Like the unconscious drives, these bioconscious forces and egos are inherently neither antisocial nor social in character. If their propensities are sanctioned by the sociocultural egos — for instance, if hunger or the sex urge is satisfied in forms approved by the norms of law or religion or mores — they operate in harmony with the corresponding sociocultural egos. If such propensities are disapproved by the sociocultural egos — for instance, if the satisfaction of hunger is achieved through theft, or that of the sex ego through rape — the biological egos conflict with the sociocultural egos. Biological egos and their energies may be harmonious with one another; for instance, when cold and hunger together impel one to seek food or warmth or both. They may also conflict with or act independently of one another; for instance, when hunger impels a person to actions inconsistent with those dictated by the sex drive, either weakening or inhibiting the sexual impulse, or else as in the case of prostitution, forcing one to perform sexual actions in the absence of the sex impulse.

## 3. *The Socioconscious in Man*

Above this bioconscious stratum lie the conscious sociocultural energies, activities, egos, and roles. They are derived from and generated by the conscious, meaningful interaction of mindful persons in their collective living, experience, and learning. Through this collective experience, they are accumulated and transmitted from person to person, group to group, generation to generation. In the process of this interaction, they are patterned into specific scientific, philosophical, religious, ethical, artistic, political, and technological forms of sociocultural thought, norms, values, activities, and institutions.

*A person possesses as many sociocultural egos, roles, and activities as there are sociocultural groups with which, voluntarily or not, he is connected.* Most of us have our *family ego* and activities, our *state-citizenship ego* and activities, our *nationality ego* and activities, our *religious ego* and role (if we belong to an organized religion), our *occupational ego* and activities, and the *lesser egos* of the societies, clubs, and associations to which we belong or with which we are interacting. Each of these egos, roles, and activities is different from the others. In the midst of our family, our ego and role is that of a father, mother, brother, sister, son, or daughter; the ego is imbued with the appropriate ideas, values, volitions, emotions and feelings; our role assumes certain definite forms, and even our costume (such as a bathrobe and slippers) is of a typical kind. When we leave home and reach the scene of our occupation, the family ego gives place in the field of our consciousness and behavior to that of the occupational ego and actions of a doctor, professor, pastor, engineer, businessman, farmer, clerk, or the like. Our occupational ego considers and discusses quite different things, in a different way, and with different emotions as compared with the family ego. In our occupational role, compared with the family role, we perform very different activities, in a different setting, with different co-actors (bosses, co-workers, and subordinates), in a different garb. If our occupational ego were to think, talk, and behave as our family ego does, we should be looked upon as " queer " and should probably soon lose our position. Our occupational ego frequently does things of which our family ego disapproves, and vice versa. These two egos are, in fact, as unlike in their mentality and activities as two different persons.

When we go to church, our religious ego replaces the family and occupational egos. This religious ego is again quite different from both others in its mentality and activities. It is concerned with God, sin, and salvation; in its religious role it prays, sings hymns, kneels, and performs other acts of religious character, quite different from the actions of the family ego or the occupational ego. A similar transformation of our egos takes place when we attend a political rally. Our political ego may think, say, and do many things of which our family ego or religious ego is ashamed.

Each of these egos is a reflection of the meanings, values, and norms of the particular group which it represents. The activities and the role of each of our sociocultural egos are defined by their respective social group. Some of the groups where the membership is involuntary — like the army for a drafted soldier, the totalitarian state for its citizen, the prison for an inmate — compulsorily impress their own image upon their members and coercively regiment the members' bodies, souls, and activities in many fields up to the smallest detail: what a member has to eat or drink, what he has to wear, where he has to live, whom he has to meet, obey, or boss, when and how much he has to sleep, what he has to believe, think, and say, what he has to read, and in general where and when he has to do what. Such coercive groups compulsorily install their representative egos into an individual, with all the values, beliefs, and actions pertaining to the respective ego.

Other groups, where membership is voluntary, do the same but in a less painful way. They also inculcate into an individual their representative ego, with this ego's values, ideas, beliefs, rights, duties, and behavior. One can remain a member of any social group only as long as he complies with its demands and fulfills the membership duties. One remains a citizen of the United States or a member of the Roman Catholic Church only as long as he performs the duties and maintains the values and standards (in thought and actions) prescribed by the United States laws and government or by the Catholic Church, respectively. Otherwise, he is penalized or else forfeits his group status for the violation of his duties.

The same is true of any organized group. Each seeks to impress upon a person its own image, in the form of a particular ego; each attempts to mold the individual after its own pattern; each demands a portion of his time and energy, a pound of flesh and a part of his soul or conscious mind; each prescribes in detail his activities, functions, rights, and duties. The group incessantly subjects its members to various demands and the members incessantly respond to these through the respective egos, roles, and activities.

The state requires from us now payment of our taxes, now services as a soldier or a member of a jury, and would not accept instead of these state duties, say, our prayers in church or our taking care of our children. Our occupational group demands from us six or eight hours of a specified work and would not accept instead, say, our political activities. Our family demands from us a wide set of activities, of a husband or wife or parent, and would not be satisfied instead with the activities of our recreational group, and so on.

This explains the proposition that *each of us has as many conscious sociocultural egos and roles as there are organized groups with which we are in contact. The totality of these egos occupy almost the whole field of our conscious mentality; and the totality of these sociocultural roles and activities fill an overwhelmingly major part of our time, activities, roles, and life.*

During each twenty-four hours, almost all our activities consist in discharging the functions and duties of the groups to which we belong. Even the purely biological activities like sleeping, micturating, eating, or sex relations are not entirely exempt from control of the groups we are affiliated with. Our occupational group now and then puts us on a night shift, forcing us to sleep in the daytime instead of at night, as is more natural. The regiment of a soldier on a battlefield sometimes deprives him of sleep for twenty-four or more hours (in spite of the biological tendency to fall asleep); sickness of a member of our family sometimes demands our vigilance for many hours far beyond the biological disposition to stay awake. Various social groups notably determine what sort of food one has to eat and what sort is tabooed (though chemically the tabooed food is often perfectly good), when one has to eat and when one has to fast, including such details as how many meals a day, at what hours, and so on. From early infancy the family and other groups begin to train the child to control his defecation and micturation. Social groups also tangibly control many aspects of sex activities, such as who may have sexual relations, with whom, when, under what circumstances, how often, etc. In brief, even most of the bioconscious activities of an individual are controlled by the totality of social groups of which he is a voluntary or involuntary member. To sum up: *the diversity and multiplicity of the groups to, which we belong account for the plurality and diversity of our sociocultural egos and roles. The totality of one's sociocultural egos and roles is a microcosm reflecting the sociocultural macrocosm in which one is born and reared and in which one acts and interacts.*

The ideology, behavioral patterns, and cultural values of the groups of our interaction also account for the major part of the cultural content of the individual mind and of the cultural values of the individual. The individual does not invent his religion, his morals, his laws, his aesthetics, his language, the patterns of his everyday behavior with his equals, superiors, and inferiors, his manner of eating, or most of his ideas and actions. All this one receives ready-made — thanks to education, instruction, and language — from his family and the groups of which he is a member. For instance, when the religious culture of the group is a set of animistic or totemic beliefs and practices, the individual's religious orientation will also be animistic and totemic. If his religious group is Christian or Buddhist, his religious ego ordinarily also becomes respectively Christian or Buddhist. The same can be said of all the other aspects of the individual personality. Since the scientific, religious, ethical, and other ideas, beliefs, and values are not biologically inherited, the individual acquires these mainly from the groups with which he interacts. As long as the individual belongs to a group, he must adopt its culture to some extent or his position will become untenable.

The *major part* of the individual's culture, let us repeat, is determined by the culture of his groups. This means that a lesser portion of the individual's culture consists of cultural meanings and values not acquired from organized groups, but from other sources — through reading, seeing, and coming in contact with them. These may include (a) personalities like Plato or Beethoven long deceased, yet still active agents of a great culture; or (b) cultural elements with which the individual becomes familiar as a tourist in a foreign country, or as a visitor at archeological excavations of ancient civilizations, or as a reader of books. There are hundreds of other ways in which elements of alien cultural systems may enter into our own.

Finally, the individual's culture depends upon his *selectivity and creativity*. These are determined partly by one's unconscious tendencies, by the total constellation of one's groups and their cultures, and partly by the "supraconscious" part of our mental structure — to be discussed further. No individual can absorb all the cultural elements of his milieu. In one way or another he must select some and reject the rest. This explains why the personalities of members of the same groups are never identical. In secondary points, at least, they differ from one another.

No one is entirely passive. Every person selects, combines, and sometimes even creates, and to that extent he is an active agent in the social process. True geniuses display great creativity. Out of the existing cultural values they combine something conspicuously different. Though most of us display very modest creativity, nonetheless through creativity and selection we function also as active agents. A person is not a *tabula rasa* on which society writes its cultural teachings.

In spite of this selectivity and creativity, however, the totality of our social groups and their cultures — let us repeat — define most of our conscious egos and their cultures. These sociocultural egos occupy the major part of our conscious mentality and behavior.

From these basic propositions a series of further conclusions follow. First, *if the groups to which a given individual belongs are in a solidary relationship with one another, if they all urge the individual to think, feel, and act in the same way, if they push him towards the same goal and prescribe to him the same duties, values, and rights, then the different egos of the individual which reflect these groups will also be in harmony with one another.* In that case all the sociocultural egos of the individual will be integrated and unified into a single, large, harmonious, conscious ego free from inner conflicts. If one's bioconscious egos do not conflict with one another and with one's sociocultural egos, and if the sociocultural egos are mutually harmonious, the individual will experience a unity of his personality. He will be like a ball pushed by several forces in the same direction (the case of addition of forces in mechanics). He will be blessed with peace of mind and consistency in his conduct. What his rights and duties are, what he shall or shall not do, will be clear to him. No conflict of duties, no inner struggle, no doubt and indecision will worry him. If the family, the state, the church, the occupational group, the political party and the other groups of the individual issue to him similar commands — for instance, to go and fight the enemy — then all the egos of the person will be unanimously urging him to do this duty and he will gladly do it, even sacrificing his life if needed. Happy are the persons who are in this situation. Only such persons present a personality fully integrated and unified on the conscious level.

*If the groups to which an individual belong are in conflict; if they urge him to contradictory actions, duties, values and convictions* — if, for instance, the state demands what is disapproved by the church or the family — *then the individual's respective egos will be mutually antagonistic.* The individual will be a house divided against himself, split by inner conflicts. There can be no peace of mind, no unclouded conscience, no real happiness, no consistency in such an individual. He will be like a ball pushed in opposite directions by several forces (the case of subtraction of forces in mechanics). His conduct will be irresolute and contradictory; so will be his thoughts and utterances. Like Hamlet he will worry and consume his energy in futile indecision. If the pressure of one group is stronger, then he will follow its orders, but with diminished enthusiasm and power, for the opposition of his other egos will decrease his power of action.

During World War II, and again at the present time, the state has demanded from certain workers relentless effort in war industries. Their unions, now and then, have ordered the workers to strike. This objective conflict of the state and the union generates conflicts within the workers. Their national egos disapprove what their occupational egos demand, and vice versa. The result has been hesitant, contradictory conduct.

A similar conflict between the national and the religious egos has been generated in thousands of sincere Christians by the war. Jesus' Sermon on the Mount commands them not to kill but to love their enemies; the belligerent state orders them to be patriotic and to kill their enemies. In some (for instance, in conscientious objectors), the religious and ethical egos prevail; but their religious enthusiasm is greatly diminished by the conflict with their patriotic state duty. In others — in the majority of " Christians " — the national or state ego prevails, but its impetus is widely tempered by the doubt and reproach of their religious ego. All sincere Christians who are at the same time good citizens have experienced divided loyalties. Their peace of mind has been profoundly disturbed and their total personality deeply hurt.

We must not think that such split personalities are rare in a population differentiated and stratified into many groups. If not in a sharp then in a mild form, such inner conflicts are a frequent occurrence with most individuals in differentiated societies. In our society there are few individuals who do not now and then undergo a conflict of duties and a clash of loyalties. Sometimes it is only a superficial conflict between two unimportant values. But there are much more painful conflicts — between our duties to our family, state, church, occupational group, political party, nationality, our friends, and neighbors — which frequently beset us with all their attendant worries and indecisions. When our religious and ethical egos predominate, we are all for the brotherhood and equality of man, and against racial or religious discriminations. When we are acting as a Southern Democrat, however, or as a member of a particular ethnic group, we think, speak and act in the opposite way. Our ethical ego proclaims the equal sovereignty of all nations and their right to determine their political regime and policies. But when our national ego gets in the saddle, we dictate our commands to weaker nations, interfere in their inner policies, and demand their compliance with our orders on pain of economic, political, or military sanctions. And so this tragic comedy of human inconsistency and self-contradiction goes on. It is not conscious hypocrisy, but the unavoidable result of belonging to many different and antagonistic groups. *This explains also why not only the plain citizen, but even the most prominent thinkers and leaders display so many contradictions in their speeches, writings, and actions.*

To conclude: in regard to the above three levels of human mental structure — the unconscious, the bioconscious, and the socioconscious — the ideally integrated person may be defined as one whose unconscious drives, and bioconscious and sociocultural egos are in a state of mutual harmony. Such a person experiences himself as one, unified ego. The poorly integrated person, on the other hand, is one whose unconscious drives, and bioconscious and sociocultural egos are constantly at war with one another. As we shall see, such a person is likely to become a suicide, an inmate of a mental asylum, a sophisticated and cynical human animal, or a demoralized brute, a self-contradictory Hamlet, or a human being exceedingly unhappy and " gone to pieces."

To finish the portrait of the sociocultural conscious mentality and behavior of a person, it must be mentioned that a small part of each conscious ego with its respective activities, and of the whole field of sociocultural consciousness, is in a state of *secondary, subconscious automatism.* This small part comprises the totality of the actions and respective states of mind which are learned, which at the beginning of the learning require conscious attention, but which after many repetitions become habitual and are performed automatically, without entering into consciousness. When we learn how to play the piano or write or drive an automobile, the initial stages of our learning require our full attention. After many repetitions, the respective actions come to be automatic and are performed " subconsciously." They sink into this subconscious state and function smoothly until some obstacle appears. Then, at once and without any difficulty, they become a conscious part of our sociocultural egos and mentality. Generally, all these secondarily automatic actions easily shift from subconscious into conscious, and vice versa. Their subconsciousness and automatism is something quite different from the unconsciousness of the truly reflexological and instinctive actions.

The *conscious, sociocultural part of our mentality and behavior is directly connected with the sociocultural human world.* The totality of our sociocultural egos and activities reflects this world, is molded by it, and is molding it. They are mutually interdependent. Any important change in our social groups and their culture affects the total constellation of our egos and activities; and any important change in the constellation of egos and roles of the members influences the constellation of social groups and

their culture.  While the unconscious and the bioconscious parts of the
individual are strongly influenced by the biophysical, cosmic, and vital
forces, the sociocultural part of our personality is especially dependent
upon the sociocultural world in which we are born and live.

If my conception of the unconscious and the bioconscious in man has
little in common with Freud's unconscious (and "pre-conscious"), the
outlined structure of the sociocultural egos of the individual is entirely
different from Freud's "ego" and "superego."  In contrast to the unconscious and pre-conscious which, rightly or wrongly, Freud tried to
elaborate in detail, in regard to his concepts of "ego" and "superego"
he never went beyond the vaguest, shifting, and self-contradictory delin-
eations.  At the beginning, the ego was defined as a conscious surface
agency situated above the unconscious and pre-conscious, and trying to
regulate the eruptions of the unconscious and pre-conscious against itself.  Later on the ego was made partly unconscious and growing from
the unconscious.  At one time, the ego was ascribed its own instincts
and drives, different from the libido of the unconscious; at others, the
ego was conceived as having libido of its own, and so on.  Still darker
have been Freud's manipulations with the superego.  Now it was viewed
as "an unconscious conscience" that "unconsciously" censored and scru-
tinized instinctive urges of the unconscious and of the ego; another time it
meant the conscious superpersonal parental and societal mores regimenting
the ego and repressing the urges of the unconscious.  Still again it meant
something else.  It would be a fruitless loss of time and energy to follow
in detail all the odd peregrinations of Freudian thought about his ego and
superego.[3]

It suffices to say that the very terms "unconscious ego," "unconscious
consciousness and conscience" are self-contradictory logically, like
"white blackness" or "wooden iron."  Factually, Freud's notions do not
answer the questions, What are the real natures of ego and superego?
Whence and how do they arise?  Where do they get the power for the
control, especially repression and suppression, of the libidinal and destructive urges of the unconscious?  Some answers which Freud attempts to
give, especially in such works as his *Totem and Taboo,* are grotesquely
fantastic from the logical, and especially from the factual and historical
standpoints.  The whole Freudian theory about the emergence and development of the superego is based upon nothing but the phantasmagoric
imagination of the author.

### 4. The Supraconscious in Man

Finally, there is a still higher level in the mental structure of man, a still
higher form of energies and activities, realized in varying degrees by different persons — namely, the supraconscious level of energies and activities.  These constitute the fourth and highest stratum of man's personal-

ity, energies, and activities. They are frequently designated as "the divine in man," "the manifestation of Godhead," "the sublimest energy of truth, goodness, and beauty," "the highest creative genius," and so on. The supraconscious manifests itself in the greatest creative victories of man in the fields of truth, beauty, and goodness. These are the main forms of the supraconscious, transformable, as we have seen, into one another.

## Chapter Six

# The Supraconscious in Man's Mental Structure, Creativity, and Cognition

### I

### Its Characteristics

While the existence of the first three levels of personality structure (described in Chapter Five) is hardly questioned, the existence of the supraconscious mentality, energy, and activities is either denied or seriously questioned by many scholars of both the social sciences and humanities. Its admission goes against the dominant materialistic and mechanistic metaphysics, still prevalent in contemporary psychology and social disciplines. For this reason, and also because of the exceptional importance of the supraconscious for creative altruization, it is advisable to stop at this problem somewhat longer than at the elucidation of the unconscious, the biological and the sociocultural consciousness in man. The purpose of this chapter is to lay down the very minimum of evidence for the reality of the supraconscious and to describe some of its properties.

The supraconscious is known very little. What is known can be summed up as follows:

A. The supraconscious seems to be the fountainhead of the greatest achievements and discoveries in all fields of human creative activity: science, religion, philosophy, technology, ethics, law, the fine arts, economics, and politics. Without its genius and operation, through merely conscious and unconscious activities, only mediocre achievements are possible; never the greatest. A professor of English or of musical composition may know excellently all the rational rules and techniques entering into the composition of a literary or musical masterpiece; and yet, if he is devoid of the supraconscious genius, he never can become even a remote relative of the Shakespeares and Chaucers, the Bachs and Beethovens. The same is true of a professor of scientific method: if he is not graced by the supraconscious, he has no chance to become Galileo or Newton, Plato or Kant. In this sense, the supraconscious is the highest creative energy known.

B. The supraconscious creates and discovers through *supraconscious intuition*. It is different from all sensory intuitions — perception, observation — and from logical, mathematical, and syllogistic reasoning. 1. In contrast to senses and reason, intuitional inspiration or cognition comes as a momentary flash, different from a patient sensory observation or mathematical, logical analysis. 2. The time moment and the circumstances of this flash can hardly be foreseen, predicted, or voluntarily produced. 3. The flash often occurs in the least expected moment and conditions. This is true of nations and other organized groups as well as of individuals. The stream of their creativity — measured either by the number of creative geniuses or by that of scientific discoveries, great philosophical, religious, and ethical systems, by fine art's creations, or technological inventions — this stream in each and all fields of creativity swells and dries, rises and falls, shifts from one group to another, in an unpredictable and fairly erratic manner.[1] 4. The intuitional flash intuits adequately the central or most essential nature of the intuited phenomenon, noumenon, or relationship or of the new creative value. 5. During the process of supraconscious intuition the person (creator or cognizer) and the intuited object tend to become united into one whole in which there is no separation between the subject (person) and the object: they become one identity. 6. For this reason, the supraconscious intuition delivers to us the unmediated, adequate knowledge or experience of the intuited phenomenon or noumenon instead of the mediated, inadequate, and always uncertain cognition or idea derived through sense organs and logical reasoning. 7. This means that the supraconscious intuition deals with the essence and not with the appearance of its object. 8. As such the supraconscious intuition lies at the basis of the whole sensory and logical knowledge or value experience. The ultimate bases of our cognition and the ultimate standards of our moral, aesthetic, and other values are intuitional. For the same reason, in the functioning of the supraconscious intuition, a person's ego entirely disappears; the individual becomes one with his object and loses any awareness of ego or I. *The supraconscious is egoless:* it transcends ego entirely and unconditionally. The field of any ego or its constellations is strictly limited to the *bioconscious and sociocultural conscious levels of personality*. Ego disappears below this level and above it; there is no experience of ego or I in the unconscious or subconscious fields of an individual, nor in the supraconscious. Dominated by the supraconscious an individual becomes its egoless instrument, lifted far above the limitations of an ego. 9. The supraconscious with its creative intuition and other characteristics was noted long ago and called by different terms. The " self " (vs. " ego "), " atman," " purusha " of the Upanishads, the

Bhagavadgita, and of the Yoga system of Patanjali are the Hindu names given to the supraconscious and its cognitive and creative intuition. The "self," the "enlightenment," and the state of "satori" are its forms in Buddhism and Zen Buddhism.[2] "Eternal reason," "sublime stupidity," "intuition" vs. sensory and intellectual knowledge are the names for it in Taoism.[3] The "divine madness" of Plato and "nous" are the Greek names. "Divine wisdom" (vs. "foolishness of the world"), "grace of God," "divine or mystic revelation," "pneuma," the *docta ignorantia* of Nicolas of Cusa, up to the "inner light" of the Quakers are other terms for it used by many thinkers and groups. "Genius," "inspiration," "creative *élan*," the "sovereign intelligence which sees in a twinkle of an eye the truth of all things in contrast to vain knowledge" (J. J. Rousseau), "celestial inspiration," "supramental wisdom that goeth beyond all knowledge" (Ibn-Khaldun), the "oversoul" (Emerson), and "intuition," "creativity," and the "unconscious" (E. von Hartmann) are still other names. With different terminology almost all eminent oriental and occidental thinkers assert reality and characteristics of the supraconscious in man.[4]

Having outlined the essentials of the supraconscious, let us glance at the concrete evidence of its existence and operation. We can begin with mathematics.

## II

### The Role of the Supraconscious in Mathematical and Natural Sciences

The so-called "calculating boys" or "arithmetical prodigies" give an example of an instantaneous operation of the supraconscious, quite different from conscious mathematical calculation. These persons, often of a low intelligence and incapable *consciously* of an elementary mathematical reasoning or understanding, have been able to make instantaneously a complex mathematical calculation, like determining the logarithm of any number of seven or eight places, or finding intuitively "what factors would divide any large number, not a prime; thus given the number 17,861, they can say instantly that it is $337 \times 53$. . . . He [Mr. Bidder] could not explain how he did this; it seemed a natural instinct to him."[5]

Another prodigy, Benjamin Hall Blyth, at the age of six years was able to calculate instantly how many seconds he had lived, including two days for the leap years (1820 and 1824) omitted by his father in his calculations with pen and paper (172,000 seconds). When Arago in the presence of the French Academy asked Vito Mangiamele (10 years old and otherwise uneducated) what is the cubic root of 3,796,416, in a space of about half a minute the child responded 156. Asked "What satisfies the condition that its cube plus five times its square is equal to 42 times itself increased by 40? " in less than a minute Vito responded that 5 satisfies the condition. Asked to extract the 10th root of 282,475,249, Vito found in a short time that the root is 7.[6] And so on.

The subsequent list taken from F. W. H. Myers' work concisely sums up the age when the calculating gift was observed, duration of the gift (which lasted only for a limited time with most of the prodigies), and finally their conscious general intelligence.

### TABLE OF PRINCIPAL ARITHMETICAL PRODIGIES

| Name (alphabetically) | Age when gift was observed | Duration of gift | Intelligence |
|---|---|---|---|
| Ampère | 4 | ? | eminent |
| Bidder | 10 | through life | good |
| Buxton | ? | ? | low |
| Colburn | 6 | few years | average |
| Dase (or Dahse) | boyhood | through life | very low |
| Fuller | boyhood | ? | low |
| Gauss | 3 | ? | eminent |
| Mangiamele | 10 | few years | average |
| Mondeux | 10 | few years | low |
| Prolongeau | 6 | few years | low |
| Safford | 6 | few years | good |
| "Mr. Van R.," of Utica | 6 | few years | average |
| Whately | 3 | few years | good |

Among these thirteen names we have two men (Ampère and Gauss) of eminent ability, and three rated good. The rest are of low or average intelligence. Some of these, like Dase, were devoid of mathematical grasp and could not understand an elementary mathematical proposition or Euclidean theorem. It is also to be noted that the gift lasted only a few years with most of them, mainly in their youth. Later on it disappeared.[7] Whatever is the nature of this gift, one thing is certain: it is something quite different from ordinary arithmetical calculation and cognition. Since it shows itself neither in an unconscious nor subconscious state of the prodigies (they were wide awake and conscious of what they were doing), and since their operations radically differ from ordinary conscious mathematical calculation (with pen and paper, slow and gradual, requiring a conscious knowledge of arithmetic or algebra or geometry), these operations are of the supraconscious kind, inexplicable and impossible otherwise.[8]

As to the main *mathematical discoveries*, the role of the supraconscious intuition has been enormous and indispensable. Henri Poincaré's own experience is typical here. "During fifteen days I tried to demonstrate that no functions analogous to what later on I called *les fonctions fuchsiennes* could exist. All these days I sat down at my working table, and attempted a great number of combinations and arrived at no result. One evening I took black coffee and could not fall asleep; ideas appeared in crowds; I felt as though they were pushing one another until two of them hooked each other and made a stable combination. In the morning I established the existence of the class of the *fonctions fuchsiennes*. All that I had to do was to repeat the results, which took only a few hours from me." Another time the solution of a mathematical problem over which he had fruitlessly worked came to him instantaneously and unexpectedly when he was stepping into a bus, " with the same traits of brevity, suddenness and immediate certitude." [9] Poincaré also shows that a great many mathematical discoveries have been achieved in a similar intuitive way,[10] and other mathematicians corroborate this conclusion.

Poincaré, G. Birkhoff, Arago, and the whole Intuitional School in mathematics all assert further that " intuition and faith " serve as " the foundations for the rational superstructure erected by means of deductive and inductive reasoning," that they are " heuristically valuable," " of supreme importance," and are " beyond reason." [11] Other eminent mathematicians like J. Hadamard, Kronecker, A. Fraenkel, P. Boutroux, F. Gonseth, H. Weil, and eminent physicists like N. Bohr, W. Heisenberg, L. de Broglie, F. Klein, and so on, reiterate these ideas, stating that the notion of number is an inherent or intuitive property of our mind, which lies at the foundation of any mathematical or logical proof and without which no thought is possible. Furthermore, these scientists explicitly point out the intuitional foundations of their theories.[12]

Jacques Hadamard, himself a well-known mathematician, recently made a special study of the psychology of mathematical inventions. Among other sources, he used the answers of the eminent living mathematicians to his questionnaire. The main results well corroborate all the above characteristics of the supraconscious (which Hadamard calls the " unconscious," following the prevalent mixing of these different orders).

All these mathematicians state that their discoveries were " sudden and spontaneous," " without any time for thought, however brief." They report experiences resembling Gauss's. Gauss for many years fruitlessly struggled with a mathematical theorem. Finally, he reports:

I succeeded, not on account of my painful efforts, but by the grace of God. Like a sudden flash of lightning the riddle happened to be solved. I, myself, cannot say what was the conducting thread which connected what I previously knew with what made my success possible.

In the opinion of many mathematicians the supraconscious does not originate in the mathematicians but comes from the cosmos and connects the inventor with the supraconscious cosmic mind. Aristotle, Leibnitz, Schelling, and Fichte called it " participation in divinity." F. Myers, W. James, O. Spengler, W. Schubart, and others expressed a similar idea.

Further on, many of the inventor mathematicians, among them Albert Einstein, think not in words, notions, or concepts, but in various symbols, signs, syllables, visual forms, and so on.

Almost all discoveries are started intuitionally. " There is hardly any completely logical discovery. Some interaction of intuition [from the supraconscious region] is necessary at least to initiate the logical work." And finally, among the motives of discoveries, " the sense of scientific beauty " is stressed by many mathematicians.[13]

What is said of the role of the supraconscious intuition in mathematics still more certainly can be said of other natural sciences. Supraconscious intuition has been the starter of most of the important discoveries in these sciences; intuitional verities lie at the very foundation of all the valid scientific propositions; and the intuitional flashes have occurred there unexpectedly, often in surprising conditions.

Sir Isaac Newton's discoveries of the mathematical method of fluxion, of the law of gravitation, and of the composition of light are classical examples of great discoveries that were started intuitionally. His biographers rightly describe these discoveries as " nothing short of miraculous " on the part of a youth who did not distinguish himself in college, who retired after graduation into a lonely village, worked there unaided, and made the discoveries in two years. An apple falls with a thud . . . and starts a chain of creative thought ending in the discovery of the law of gravitation.[14]

Similarly, Galileo sees a swinging lamp in a church and, through a " short circuit of intuition," discovers the law of oscillation of the pendulum. From two chance occurrences during a voyage, Robert Meyer " with a sudden leap of thought . . . derived the law of the mechanical equivalence of heat." [15] The same is true of discoveries of Haller, Black, Gauss, Ampère, Liebig, Humphreys, Faraday, E. H. Moore, M. Planck, Davy, Berthelot, B. Russell, and others. In biology, the role of intuition was well stressed by C. Bernard.[16] Eighty-three per cent of 232 natural scientists queried by the American Chemical Society admitted an unpredictable flash of insight; this insight, they said, illuminated the essentials of a solution to some problem with obvious adequacy and finality.[17]

It is not surprising, therefore, that a large number of great scientists — like Pascal, Kepler, Newton, Galileo to some extent, and others — were not only intuitionists, but mystics in the narrow sense of this term.

As to the intuitional bases of the valid logical and sensory propositions of these sciences, these bases have been explicitly recognized by the leading empirical and positivist methodologists of these sciences, among them Auguste Comte and John S. Mill. " The truths known by intuition are the original premises from which all others are inferred " is the formula of J. S. Mill. The foundation of all conclusions from experience

and of our belief in the uniformity of nature necessary for the validity of
any inductive knowledge is " instinctive law of belief " (Reid and others),
" custom and habit " (Hume), " belief and intuition " (J. S. Mill), " intuitive insight " (A. Comte).[18] Similar are the statements of hundreds
of contemporary scientists and scholars.[19]

Philosophy also recognizes intuition. Beginning with the Upanishads
in India and Taoism in China, passing through all the mystic philosophies
of the East and the West; through Plato, Aristotle, the Neoplatonists
(Plotinus, Porphyry, Proclus), the Neo-Pythagorians and Gnostics; St.
Augustine and the Church Fathers; Pseudo-Dionysius, J. S. Erigena,
Nicolas of Cusa; most of the great scholastics of the late Middle Ages
(including St. Thomas Aquinas, especially in the last period of his life);
up to the more modern philosophers — even such apparent rationalists
as Descartes and Spinoza; such skeptical-critical philosophers as Hume
and Kant, not to mention Schopenhauer, Fichte, Schelling, Nietzsche,
and such objective idealists as Hegel — V. Solovyev, L. Tolstoi, H. Bergson, N. Lossky, W. James (in his later period), A. N. Whitehead, E. Husserl and other " phenomenologists "; N. Berdyaev, followers of Soren
Kierkegaard, J. Maritain, and the Neo-Thomists; M. Scheler, K. Jaspers,
M. Heidegger, and some of other Existentialists: these and many other
philosophers — practically an overwhelming majority — recognize some
sort of intuitional axioms, " forms of mind," or intuitional truths as the
basis of all the mathematical, logical, and sensory-observational verities in
all fields of human cognition and creativity.[20]

## III

### THE SUPRACONSCIOUS IN TECHNOLOGICAL INVENTIONS

The supraconscious intuition plays perhaps a still more important
role in initiation of technological inventions than in scientific discoveries.
A detailed study of how inventors happen to conceive their inventions
shows unmistakably the role of intuition; in most of these cases the first
idea of the invention came like a flash, unexpected, often in peculiar conditions, with all the other traits of the intuitional insight.

" In my own experience, many decisions were made on the basis of
intuition," says I. I. Sikorsky,[21] inventor of clippers, helicopters, and so
on. J. Rossman collected, by questionnaire, many details of how technological inventions have been made by a large number of American
inventors. The answers of the inventors corroborate Sikorsky's experience. One of the inventors says that when a need for a certain invention
comes, " I cease to labor over it, and consign it to the ' subjective department ' of my mind." There it spontaneously ripens until it " comes out."
Another states: " Ideas come when I least expect them, often when I am
half asleep, or day-dreaming." Others say that the first idea comes " in a

flash," "quite unexpectedly," "suddenly," when the inventor is engaged in a different kind of work, in "the period of relaxation," "in a bathtub," "at the moment of waking," and so on.[22]

"The veritable man of genius is he who acts by impulse. . . . And genius is a grace." Thus J. de Maistre succinctly sums up the situation in his excellent criticism of Bacon's *Novum Organum*.[23] Practically all historians of technological inventions assert the startling and indispensable role of the supraconscious intuition.[24]

## IV

### THE SUPRACONSCIOUS IN THE FINE ARTS, PHILOSOPHY, AND THE SOCIAL SCIENCES

Still more decisive is the role of the supraconscious intuition in the discoveries and creativity in language, the fine arts, philosophies, humanities, and social sciences. All great creators in these fields have been persons graced by a generous magnitude of the supraconscious and this supraconscious — in co-operation with the consciously learned skills and techniques — has been responsible for their achievements.

Language is an indispensable condition for human thought and creativity in many fields. Its invention and creation is one of the greatest marvels of humanity. Since it is a condition of rational thought, it could not be invented consciously and rationally. Creation of all natural languages was largely supraconscious. (None of them, except the artificial languages like Esperanto, was created "rationally"; Esperanto and other rationally created languages have not had any success.) [25]

The main philosophies, the main ethical systems, the main codes of law, and the basic humanistic and social science theories were formulated in the sublimest form long ago, when neither laboratories, nor statistics, nor the rational techniques, nor the enormous body of observed facts existed. Any rationally conscious generalization can be achieved only when these sources and data are available. Since the greatest philosophies, theories, and generalizations were made long ago, when these sources and data did not exist, these great philosophies and theories evidently were formulated and created intuitively, through the operation of the supraconscious.

Only through the supraconscious could Plato have created his great philosophical system to which, A. N. Whitehead believes, the subsequent history of philosophy has been but a footnote. The same may be said of the place of the supraconscious in other great philosophical systems of the past, as well as in the great social science theories, in ethical and (to some extent) juridical codes. The sublimest ethical systems of the great religions were formulated long ago. All the ethical-intellectual theories have not created anything equal to the norms of the Sermon on the Mount, or to the similar norms of Taoism, Confucianism, the Upani-shads, the Bhagavadgita, of Yoga, Buddhism, Jainism, Judaism, and Mo-hammedanism. All the subsequent ethical theories and codes are but mere footnotes to these great ethical systems. The purely utilitarian, "rational" and "empirical" ethical theories have often been either a questionable "discovery," or a sort of instruction book for Chevrolet drivers. But even with these derivative theories, the supraconscious in-tuition often has been a participant in their birth and formulation.

F. Nietzsche well describes this role of intuition or "inspiration." In the state of creative inspiration:

one becomes nothing but a medium for supermighty influences. That which happens can only be termed revelation; that is to say, that suddenly, with unutterable certainty and delicacy, something becomes visible and audi-ble and shakes and rends one to the depth of one's being. One hears, one does not seek; one takes, one does not ask who it is that gives; like lightning a thought flashes out, of necessity, complete in form. . . . It is a rapture . . . a state of being entirely outside oneself. . . . Everything happens in the highest degree involuntarily, as in a storm of feeling, freedom, of power, of divinity.[26]

Many great poets similarly described the basic transmutation they experienced when "inspired" or possessed by the supraconscious. " Until Apollo calls a poet to his sacred sacrifice he is vulgarly silent; his soul is asleep; and among the insignificant children of the world he is per-haps the most trifling. But as soon as the Divine word touches his sensitive ear, the poet's soul rouses as an awakened eagle. He is bored amidst amusements of the world; he is a stranger to the gossips of the mob; he does not bend his proud head to the feet of the popular idol." In this way Pushkin, the greatest poet of Russia, describes this transmu-tation; and similarly it is described by others, Horace, Schiller, Goethe, Wordsworth, Browning, Shelley, Spenser, and Gogol among them.

"What, you ask, is my method in writing and elaborating my large and lumbering things? " writes Mozart. "I can, in fact, say nothing more about it than this: I do not know myself and can never find out. When I am in a particularly good condition . . . then the thoughts come to me in a rush, and best of all. Whence and how, I do not know and can-not learn." Further on he describes how "the crumbs" spontaneously combine with one another until they assume a finished form in his head. "All the finding and making goes on in me as in a vivid dream." Finally, he starts to write and since it is ready in his mind " it goes pretty quickly on to paper." [27]

Quite similar are the descriptions of the process of creativity by others in the fine arts. Beethoven states:

You will ask me where I get my ideas. I am not able to answer that ques-tion positively. They come directly, indirectly; I can grasp them with my hands. Out amidst the freedom of nature, in the woods, on walks . . . called forth by . . . moods. I carry my thoughts about with me long before I write them down. . . . Then begins the mental working out of this stuff. . . . [Finally] it is put on paper. . . .

What we conquer for ourselves through art is from God, divine inspiration. . . . Every genuine creation of art is independent, mightier than the artist himself, and through its manifestation, returns to the Divine. With man it has only this in common: that it bears testimony to the mediation of the Divine in him.

Beethoven clearly stresses the insufficiency of the rational mind for creativity. "Kings and Princes may be able to create professors and privy counselors . . . but they cannot create great men. . . ." "I sit and [rationally] think, and get it all settled, but it won't come on paper." "The new and original is born of itself without one's thinking of it." [28]

Similarly Richard Wagner in a letter of July 20, 1856, says that ideas of his musical compositions came to him "like a flash of light in the greatest clarity and definiteness, but not altogether in complete detail."

Brahms states about his early years: "I was always composing. . . . My finest songs would come to me early in the morning, while I was cleaning my boots." [29]

In still greater detail Tchaikovsky describes this process.

Usually the seed of a future musical creation germinates instantaneously and most unexpectedly. If the soil is eager, if there is a disposition to work, that seed takes root with an amazing power and speed, appears above ground as a little stalk which puts forth leaves and branches, and, finally, flowers. This simile is as near as I can come to a description of a creative process. If the seed appears at a favorable moment, the main difficulty is passed. The rest grows of itself. [A new idea gives to Tchaikovsky a boundless joy. . . .] One forgets everything; one is a madman. . . . Sometimes inspiration takes flight, one has to seek it again — often in vain. Frequently one must rely here upon a quite cold, deliberate technical process of work. Perhaps such moments are responsible, in the works of the Great Masters, for those places where the organic coherence fails, and where one can trace artificial coherence, seams and patches. But this is unavoidable. If that spiritual condition of the artist called inspiration . . . should continue uninterrupted, the artist could not survive a single day. . . . The strings would snap and the instrument would fly to pieces. One thing, however, is indispensable: the main idea of the piece, together with a general outline of the separate parts, must not be found through searching, but must simply appear as a result of that supernatural, incomprehensible and never-analyzed power called inspiration.

In another place he says that in his musical creativity the idea comes usually in a fully orchestrated form. "I never compose in the abstract. . . . So I find the musical thought simultaneously with the orchestration."

Only the music moved by inspiration can touch and take possession of the hearer. There is no doubt that even the greatest musical genius has sometimes worked unwarmed by inspiration. *It is a guest that does not come on first invitation.* In the meantime one must work. . . . If one waits for inclination (to compose) instead of advancing to meet it, one easily drifts into laziness and apathy. One must hold fast and have faith, and inspiration will come.

Further on he insists upon the necessity for any great artist of acquiring all the technical skill: without it his genius may be wasted and may give only a half-baked product. Nevertheless, without a genius or inspiration, no technical skill can produce anything great and valuable.[30]

M. Proust reiterates: "Every artist seems thus the citizen of unknown fatherland, forgotten by himself. Each of them remains forever unconsciously [rather *supraconsciously*, P.A.S.] tuned in a certain unison with it; he is delicious with joy when he sings in accordance with his fatherland." [31]

Paul Chabaneix, T. Ribot, and E. von Hartmann each collected (by questionnaire and interview) a number of answers of eminent poets, writers, artists, and scholars about the process of their creativity. All answers were similar in the emphasis on the supraconscious (which they, however, like many others call the "subconscious" or "unconscious").[32]

Here are a few of many examples given in these works:

Corneille composed the scene between Horatius and Curiatus just as the bird builds its nest. (Voltaire's testimony)

In writing these dramas I seemed to be a spectator at the play; I gazed at what was passing on the scene in an eager passionate expectation of what was to follow. (Sully-Prudhomme)

With Chopin, creation was spontaneous, miraculous; he wrought without foreseeing. It would come complete, sudden, sublime. (Testimony of George Sand)

In the course of my life I have had some happy thoughts, and I often noted that they would come to me involuntarily, and when I was not thinking of the subject. (Du Bois-Reymond)

You feel a little electric shock striking you in the head, seizing your heart at the same time — that is the moment of genius. (Buffon)

On ne travaille pas, on écoute, c'est comme un inconnu qui vous parle à l'oreille. (De Musset)

Ce n'est pas moi qui pense; ce sont mes idées qui pensent pour moi. (Lamartine)

My conceptions rise into the field of consciousness like a flash of lightning or like the flight of a bird. (Remy de Gourmont)

Saint-Saëns had only to listen, as Socrates to his daemon. T. Ribot, summing up a number of similar cases, says: "It is the unconscious [the *supraconscious*, P.A.S.] which produces what is vulgarly called inspiration. This condition is a positive fact, accompanied with physical and psychical characteristics peculiar to itself. Above all, it is impersonal and involuntary, it acts like an instinct, when and how it chooses; it may be wooed, but cannot be compelled. Neither reflection or will can supply its place in original creation. . . ."

The testimony of Schiller (in his "Happiness"), Goethe (see his *Autobiography* and how he created *Egmont, Iphigenia, Werther*), R. Wagner, Wordsworth, Browning, Shelley, Spenser, Tolstoi, Carlyle, Descartes, Walter Scott, Schopenhauer, Michelet, Voltaire, Gogol, Condorcet, Coleridge, Tartini, Rosny, Schumann, Diogenes Laërtius, Balzac, and of many others depicts the creative process "as something that passes in ourselves, without us and sometimes against us. Artistic inspiration is not devoid of any of the aspects of religious inspiration because it has the same psychological characteristics." In the words of Schelling:

Just as the man of destiny does not execute what he wills or intends, but what he is obliged to execute through an incomprehensible fate under whose influence he stands, so the artist . . . seems to stand under the influence of a power which . . . compels him to declare or represent things which he himself does not completely see through, and whose import is infinite.[33]

## V

### The Supraconscious in Religion and Ethics

Finally, the role of the supraconscious is overwhelmingly decisive in religious and moral creativity. The greatest religious creators — the founders of great religions, the great prophets and apostles — all explicitly state that either they themselves are an incarnation of the supraconscious (God, Brahma, "Father," "Mother," and their equivalents) or that they are revealing the suprarational, supraconscious, suprasensory Truth or Gospel. Lao-tzu, Zoroaster, Buddha, Moses and the Hebrew prophets, Mahavira, Christ, Mohammed, all the great moral teachers, up to the more recent charismatic religious leaders, explicitly profess this role. Even when ordinary persons become religiously and morally inspired, they consider themselves emptied of their egos and turned into the instrumentality of the supraconscious or God. This is implied by the term "complete surrender to God" or his equivalent or by the idea of "complete transcendence of our little egos." "When we are emptied of our self, God takes possession of us." [34] Religious and moral creators have said:

"I and the Father are one." (Jesus: John 10:30)
"Thou [God] art the doer thereof." (Jayminiya Upanishads)
"I live, yet no longer I, but Christ liveth in me." (St. Paul: Gal. 2:20)
"The works of a man who is led by the Holy Ghost are the works

of the Holy Ghost rather than his own." (St. Thomas Aquinas, *Summa Theol.* II, i, 96, 6 and 1)

" If any man is to come to God, he must be empty of all works and let God work alone." (John Tauler, *Following of Christ*, 16, 17)

" Not me, but God working through me." (St. Theresa)

" It is Thou who wanted my debut and who took my essence in order to serve Thee as a symbol among men." (Al Hallaj)

" To be like wax before the fire ready to receive every impression of the divine will." (Thomas Schillitoe and other Quakers) For Quakers, the enemy is ego or self-centeredness. It is at war with the divine " inner light." In spiritual growth, man completely surrenders to God and becomes His instrument.[35] The same idea is stressed by mystics in their statement that the ego must die before one can reach the union with God.

We see here the same transmutation of man into an instrument of the supraconscious which we saw in all fields of creativity. In religious and ethical fields this " becoming obsessed by the supraconscious " is especially conspicuous.

Since the great religions have been as great as any creations of man, since their basic verities seem to be immortal and eternal, and since the great religions were created long ago (when rationally scientific and sensory knowledge was meager), this testifies that they could be created only through the supraconscious and not through the empirical and logical mind. The conclusion is reinforced by the invariable failure of all attempts to create " rational and scientific " religion, " reasonable, sensible, verifiable empirically." Such " religions " never have gotten any where and at the best remained a third-class vulgarized philosophy and pseudo-science, spread among a mere handful of " rational intellectuals " devoid of the grace of the supraconscious.

Finally, as in the field of truth, the ultimate bases upon which the whole sensory and rational structure of the beautiful and the good are built are again supraconscious intuitions.

The very division of all the phenomena into " beautiful and ugly," " right and wrong," is intuitive. Their concrete forms (erected by reason and senses) are diverse and varying; but the very difference of the beautiful and ugly, of the right and wrong, of the good and bad, is eternal, universal, and constant. As such it can be only supraconsciously given.

Many other basic traits of the good and beautiful are likewise intuitional. With good reason, B. Croce says that " art is perfectly defined when simply defined as intuition." [36] " Aesthetic associations are intuitive in type. . . . Aesthetic judgment acts intuitively and rapidly," says an eminent mathematician on the basis of his study of aesthetic proportions and mathematical relationships in art phenomena.[37] Even more, as is the case with ethical values, the relativity of concrete aesthetic phenomena is greatly exaggerated by many sociologists, anthropologists, and historians. It is true that the concrete forms of the beautiful are conditioned by subconscious and conscious custom, mores, habit, and rational-sensory considerations of pain and pleasure. But all this diversity concerns the concrete "superstructure" of the beautiful, erected upon its eternal intuitional bases by senses and reason. Even in regard to this superstructure, there is more similarity than discord in the aesthetic evaluations of various groups and persons. Admiration of Gothic architecture does not hinder an admiration of the Parthenon or of the great architectural achievements of the Hindu, the Chinese, the Arabic, and other cultures. Their diversity is not an evidence of the relativity and oppositeness of aesthetic phenomena, as it has been interpreted by sociocultural "relativists"; it is evidence that manifestations of the beautiful are manifold. Admiration of different sorts of roses, of azaleas, of a blue sky or a stormy ocean, of Beethoven and Bach is not an evidence of the contrariety of aesthetic perception, evaluation, and phenomena, but of the rich diversity of the beautiful. Its diversity and manifold richness is not its relativity and contrariety. Our "relativists" confused two different orders: the manifoldness of the beautiful (in which there is no antagonism, no contradiction, no conflict between the diverse but equally beautiful forms), and nihilistic, mutually exclusive contrariness. Bach is different from Beethoven, Homer from Shakespeare or Mahabharata, a rose from an azalea, but this difference is mutually supplementary and it is free from either-or mutual contrariness; all are beautiful in their own way. Diversity is not relativity, let us repeat; the fullness and richness of manifestations of the beautiful are not evidences of its relativity, conventionality, or nonexistence. The diversity of the sounds (words) used for designation of the object called in English "the sun," in French "le soleil," in Russian "solntze," — the object now shining, now clouded, now hot, now seemingly cold — does not make the sun relative or conventional or nonexistent or not universally and for an indefinitely long time given and existing in its solid reality. Even in their concrete manifestations, the aesthetic phenomena are much less relative and contradictory than our nihilistic relativists try to convince us.

Still more true is this in regard to ethical values and manifestations. Their ultimate bases are intuitional. All the main moral commandments of practically all religious ethical codes are essentially similar to that of the Ten Commandments, and especially of the Sermon on the Mount. On supraconscious intuition is based also what is called "natural law" (as *aeternum quiddam, quod universum mundum regeret imperandi prohibendique sapientia*), the Golden Rule, or the categoric imperative. Kant, denying that the "pure reason" of our conscious, rational mind can know the true reality, as it is in itself and for itself, affirmed that we can and do know it through the supraconscious moral intuition or "practical reason." Even more, the ethical norms of almost all preliterate groups assert altruistic love and its derivatives as *good and right* in regard to the members of the in-group, and hate or harming as bad and wrong. The basic norms of the good and right and of the bad and wrong are truly universal and eternal. The main difference is not in the norms and commandments, but in the extensity of the universe to which they have been applied.

Not only the basic ethical norms but even most of the main concrete law norms of various groups, persons, and periods, beginning with preliterate ones and ending with contemporary, are essentially similar in what they prohibit and punish when done to a member of the in-group and in what they recommend and demand. They all prohibit murder of an in-group member, infliction of various physical and other harms upon him, violation of his basic values, health, etc. Here again, our superficial cultural relativists enormously exaggerate the contrariety, nihilistic relativity, and changeableness of ethical values and evaluations.[38] In many of their empirical details, built by sensory-rational experience, law norms have to be different and now and then even contradictory; but in their foundations and basic traits, as well as in many details, they have been universal, eternal, unchangeable. It may even be said that in the changeable details, they have shown mainly manifold diversity rather than contradictory relativity.

To sum up: the supraconscious " furthers the conscious process of thought by its inspiration in small as in great matters." [39]

" New directions of thought arise from the flashes of intuition." [40]

Human spirit as " something that knows " is not quite so narrow a description as " the observer." Consciousness has other functions besides those of a rather inefficient measuring machine; and knowledge may attain to other truths besides those which correlate sensory impressions. . . . Deeper than any " forms of thought " is a faith. . . . In the age of reason, faith yet remains supreme; for reason is one of the articles of faith.[41]

## VI

### The Supraconscious in Extrasensory Perception, Psychokinetics, Etc.

A specific aspect of the supraconscious appears in extrasensory perception, psychokinetics, and related phenomena.[42] At the present time the reality of these extrasensory and suprarational processes is well demonstrated. Their nature apparently differs basically from sensory and purely rational processes. They open to us one of the many aspects of the little-known supraconscious.

## VII

### Uneven Distribution of the Supraconscious

*The supraconscious or the creative genius seems to be of different magnitude and of different kinds with different individuals and groups.*

*It is distributed unevenly among different persons and groups; and this distribution greatly varies in time.* Some individuals — the greatest geniuses — have it in its maximal magnitude and of the highest quality; others, common mortals, have only its minimum and this of an inferior quality. Some, like Plato or Aristotle, had the philosophical form of genius; Buddha, Lao-tzu, Confucius, and Jesus manifested its religious form; Phidias, Homer, Beethoven, Michelangelo, its artistic form; Galileo, Newton, Darwin, its scientific form; Archimedes, Stephenson, Fulton, Edison, its technological creativity; Hammurabi, Moses, Manu, or the jurisconsults of the *Corpus Juris Civilis*, its juridical form; and so on.

The supraconscious of smaller magnitude and of possible inferior quality seems to be present in every normal individual. If it is not stifled by the individual's unconscious, bioconscious, and conscious forces, as happens in some cultures and periods, every individual has his moments of domination by the supraconscious. When the individual's egos and drives are forgotten in the purest religious ecstasy, in the sublimest altruistic sacrifice, in the ineffable experience of beauty (of nature, the fine arts, the loved one); in the complete immersion into cognized phenomenon, however elementary; in the flare-up of creativity in any field, however simple: all these and similar moments occurring in the life of practically every normal individual are moments of pulsation of the supraconscious. The "moments" which T. S. Eliot describes are further illustrations of these occurrences of the supraconscious in daily life. Eliot's "moments in the rose-garden," "the moment in the draughty church at smokefall," "lost in a shaft of sunlight," in the "whisper of running streams and winter lightning," or the moments when "music [is] heard so deeply that it is not heard at all, but you are the music while the music lasts," or the moments "I can only say, there we have been: but I cannot say where . . . beyond any meaning we can assign to happiness" — these and similar supraconscious moments occur in the life of almost all individuals. They are the highest peaks of creativity reached by an individual in his whole life.

The supraconscious makes every human being an inestimably great value, the end value — one that should not be used as a mere means for anything and anybody except the supraconscious itself. For when a person becomes an instrumentality of the supraconscious, he is rising above all means and all other ends; he increasingly becomes the ultimate end value. Further on, we shall see that this pulsation of the supraconscious can notably be increased in the life activity of all of us, if a proper care and effort is taken for that purpose.

## VIII

### MANIFOLDNESS OF THE SUPRACONSCIOUS

The above aspects of the supraconscious show its manifold character. It seems to have many forms and manifests itself in all the infinite richness of supreme creativity. Theoretically it can be defined as the Manifold Infinity, the *coincidentia oppositorum* transcending the contradictions of rational thought and inexhaustible in its creativity.  It possibly connects man with the cosmic supraconscious, as man's unconscious connects him with the biophysical universe and his conscious with the sociocultural cosmos.

*Chapter Seven*

# Forms and Ways of Personality Integration and Creativity

## I

Between Integrated Genius and Degenerated Human Animal

The preceding outline of the fourfold structure of man's mentality and energies permits us to define the types of the integrated, unintegrated, and disintegrated personality structures. These structures objectively range themselves from the ideally integrated genius to the utterly disintegrated human animal, with numerous variations in between these poles.

At the top we have a *perfectly integrated creative genius*. From the standpoint of our theory, this type is characterized by the following traits:

1. Its supraconscious is fully developed to the greatest creative magnitude. The ideally integrated creative genius is objectively realized in the highest creativity in the fields of truth or goodness or beauty or in all these fields. Without strenuous effort or rough means the supraconscious easily controls the individual's conscious egos and especially the unconscious energies and activities. The control is so perfect that the conscious and the unconscious forces spontaneously follow the suggestions of the supraconscious. As a result, all four levels and energies of the human personality are in full, mutual harmony.

2. All the sociocultural egos with their cultural content are harmonious with one another; this results in *one conscious unified ego* with its integrated cultural system free from inner conflicts. Being gracefully controlled by the supraconscious, the unified ego, in its turn, delicately controls its bioconscious egos and unconscious energies.

3. All the bioconscious egos and energies are harmonious and free from mutual friction. Directly subjected to the control of the conscious sociocultural egos, indirectly they are controlled by the supraconscious.

4. The unconscious drives and needs, guided by the conscious knowledge and the supraconscious wisdom, are mutually harmonious, each being satisfied without painful inhibition of the others. The drives disapproved by the higher energies are painlessly limited or eliminated.

The control of man's unconscious energies by the conscious and the supraconscious is necessitated by the fact that in the process of evolution of the human species, the unconscious (instinctive and reflexological) mechanisms of Homo sapiens have been notably unsettled or disorganized. In the history of man these mechanisms have not always functioned as unfailingly as they do in many other species that live in comparatively static conditions and have not developed their conscious energies to a great extent.[1]

The dynamic character of the milieu in which the human species developed and the emergence in man's mentality of conscious and supraconscious thought have probably been the main reasons why man's instinctive mechanisms have become markedly unsettled in the process of evolution. In the increasingly complex and feverishly changing environment of modern man, these unconscious mechanisms are still more inadequate than before. The automatic, reflexological, and instinctive responses are perfect reactions only to very specific and static stimuli. In ever-changing and different conditions, they become progressively disserviceable. They begin to maladjust rather than adjust the organism to its environment; to misfire rather than to hit the bull's eye. Under these conditions the unconscious activities turn out to be malfunctioning even within the narrow region of the instinctive stereotypes.

An example of this is given by the pleasure-pain signals of the unconscious mechanisms. The main biological function of pleasure feeling seems to have been to signal the forces and processes that are useful to the life and health of the organism. Pain has been a signal of the processes and agencies harmful to the body. The existing deteriorated mechanisms of the unconscious often mislead with these signals: many processes signaled as pleasurable are objectively deadly and harmful to the organism, while some pains are healthy and useful. If in the evolutionary process man had had to rely solely upon the disorganized unconscious activities and their mechanisms, Homo sapiens would hardly have had much chance to survive and no chance to elevate himself above the creativity of other vertebrate species. Without the supraconscious and conscious creativity, such a man would have become but a " degenerated monkey."

These are the reasons why the unconscious part of contemporary man needs guidance and control by the conscious and the supraconscious in order to function harmoniously within itself and within the whole personality structure. Left alone, the unconscious tends to turn the whole organism into a chaos of conflicting destructive forces.

Such are the four characteristics of an integrated genius at its noblest and best. Such a perfectly integrated individual has hardly ever existed. Even the greatest geniuses have had tensions between their egos, energies, and activities. The perfect integration here outlined, however, serves as the *highest standard of personality integration and creativity*. The closer the individual's mental structure to it, the higher his creative integration; the further his mental make-up from this standard, the lower his creative unity.

The deterioration of personality integration from this standard can proceed along three lines.

a. When in the total mental structure of personality the proportional power of each higher energy, beginning with the supraconscious, decreases in favor of those of a lower, especially the unconscious, energy: the proportional decrease means a withering of the highest creativeness in man, and a progressive replacement of the creative genius by an uncreative human animal. Indirectly it means also a deterioration of the integration.

b. When the "vertical" control of man's lower energies by the higher ones decreases: such a change means a loosening of the connections between various levels of the mental structure, anarchy of the uncontrolled unconscious drives, and an increase of friction between the three main energies and respective activities.

c. When solidarity between different egos and forces of each and all strata decreases and friction between these increases.

A change of mental structure along each of these lines means a decline in the creative integration of personality. A simultaneous change along all three lines signifies a threefold deterioration of personality's unity and creativity. The extreme limit of this deterioration is either an insane human animal or Plato's and Aristotle's man as "the worst of the beasts."

Between the poles of the perfectly integrated superman and the utterly disintegrated human animal there are many intermediary types of personality structure. The overwhelming majority of human beings belong in these intermediary types.

## II

### TRIPLE SET OF OPERATIONS FOR DEVELOPMENT OF MAN'S ALTRUISTIC CREATIVITY AND INTEGRATION

If an individual wants to improve his creative integration generally, and his altruistic integration specifically, he must perform several operations in the mental and behavioral structure of his personality; and he must parallel this by corresponding operations in the totality of his cultural values and in that of the social groups of his affiliation. The basic reason for this triple — personal, cultural, and social — set of operations is that the personal, cultural, and social aspects of sociocultural phenomena are inseparable from one another.

If we want to change in a certain direction our personality structure, for instance, we have to change in the same direction our cultural values and our group affiliations.  If we want to change radically our group affiliations, we must respectively change our cultural values and the structure of our personality.  Otherwise, the desired change would be miscarried and result in failure.  This triple change is initiated sometimes in the structure of personality and then followed by a corresponding change in the cultural values and group affiliations of the individual.  Sometimes it is started in his cultural values or in his group affiliations.  In whichever of these three fields it is started first, however, it must be followed by a respective change in the two other fields, if it is going to be successful.  If the change is not threefold, it remains superficial or miscarries, assuming forms quite different from the expected one.[2]

We already know that each of the bioconscious and the sociocultural egos of an individual is a reflection and manifestation of a corresponding biological drive or of a group of which he is a member.  We know that the overt behavior of each of the bioconscious and sociocultural egos is respectively an execution of the pressure of biological drives and of the legal commandments and ethical recommendations of the respective group. We are well aware also that an individual ordinarily belongs not to one but to several groups: his family, clan, or tribe, his sex and age groups, ethnic and racial group, his neighborhood or territorial group, his occupational, religious, state, political, and other groups.[3]  If the values and demands of the various groups to which an individual belongs are contradictory, as we have seen, the values and sociocultural egos of the individual will be contradictory.  So also his ideas, interests, wishes, and actions.  An individual placed amidst such contradictory groups and values cannot help being divided against himself, incapable of durable kindness and warm love.

If he wants to free himself from all these conflicts, then, the necessary means is a reorganization of his biological and sociocultural egos, of his set of values, and of his group affiliations.  All his egos and their activities must be harmoniously centered around his highest " self " identified with the supreme value of love or its equivalents: Love as God, as Truth, as Supreme Beauty, as the Cosmic Self, as Tao, Atman, the Oversoul, etc. The egos and their activities that contradict this " self " must be dropped or erased from the totality of the individual's egos and activities.

All his values likewise must be organized into one harmonious value system sublimated to the supreme value of love or its equivalents.  He must be affiliated only with those groups that are predominantly altruistic and whose altruism extends far beyond the group itself, eventually over the whole of mankind.  When these operations are done successfully, the individual finds himself identified with one supreme self, one unified system of values, and with one unified set of altruistic groups.

When a person begins to perform this triple reorganization of his egos, values, and group affiliations, he makes the first decisive step towards unity of his personality and conduct. His ultimate results are peace of mind and freedom from inner conflicts; a clear understanding of his duty; quiet happiness and self-confidence, kindness and love towards all human beings.

Expressed in this brief form, the triple reintegration of egos, values, and group affiliations sounds simple and easy. In its actual realization, however, it is a long, difficult, and complex process, as almost all creative processes are. It requires constant effort, undivided attention, determination, courage, and skillful ability to solve the hundreds of secondary problems involved. Here are some of the operations to be performed in each of the three fields — personal, cultural, and social — in order that the triple reintegration may be successfully achieved.

| Personality structure | Culture structure of values | Social structure of groups and institutions |
|---|---|---|
| 1. Development of the supraconscious to its possible maximum. In the case of altruists, development of creative love (and connected values of truth and beauty) to the greatest possible intensity, extensity, purity, duration, and adequacy. | Reassessment of all the values of a given culture and development of the supreme value of creative love (and truth, and beauty) as the central value of the culture and of the value system of its individual members. Respective devaluation of all pseudo and negative values in the structure of the culture and of its members. | Increasing termination of affiliation with all selfish groups and increasing affiliation with all altruistic and creative groups in the fields of love, truth, beauty, and other positive values. Organization of concerted efforts aimed at replacement and reconstruction of all aggressive and egotistic groups into more altruistic and creative ones. The replacement and reconstruction is to be done by nonviolent means in the spirit of love and creative ennoblement. |
| 2. Development of the conscious mind up to its possible maximum; dedication of the conscious energy to the service of love, truth, beauty, and other positive values, and denial of its service to hate, enmity, and all pseudo and negative values. | Rational rearrangement of all secondary cultural values into one unified system subordinated to the supreme values of love (and truth, and beauty) in the total value system of a given culture and of its members. Invention, learning, and mastery of the ways and techniques for creation of new positive values, and for acquisition, possession, and cultivation of the rearranged values in the culture and in the value | Rational rearrangement of all group affiliations of individuals, and of the total institutional and group structure of a given population, in accordance with the supreme values of love and other positive values. Invention, learning, and mastery of the most fruitful organization of the total group structure of the population as well as of the functions, duties, and role of each member in each of the positive groups he is |

| Personality structure | Culture structure of values | Social structure of groups and institutions |
|---|---|---|
| | system of its members. Increasing permeation of the total culture by the spirit of love and truth and beauty. | affiliated with. Increasing permeation of all groups and institutions by the creative spirit of love, truth, and beauty. |
| 3. Tightening of the vertical control of man's lower energies by his higher energies: of the unconscious by the conscious; of the conscious by the supraconscious. Development of the control's efficiency to the highest limit and ennoblement of its means by making them milder, nobler, freer from coercion and more spontaneous in following the directions of the higher energies by the lower ones. Increasing harmonious co-operation of man's supraconscious, conscious, and unconscious energies. | Tightening of the vertical control of the lower cultural values by the higher ones in the culture as well as in the value sets of its members. Ennoblement of the means of this control by a progressive elimination of the rude, coercive means in favor of the free and spontaneous means of such control. Increasing co-operation and integration of the supraconscious, conscious, and unconscious values into one cultural supersystem dominated by its supreme values. | Tightening of the control of carnivorous groups and of uncreative institutions by the altruistic groups and creative organizations. Ennoblement of the means of control through an increasing replacement of violent force and predatory fraud by nonviolent means, creative inspiration, and by mimesis of the positive examples of creative groups by the selfish and less creative collectivities. Similar tightening of the control of group affiliations of the members of the groups. |
| 4. Subsequent elimination of friction between all egos, drives, and activities in each and in all levels of mental structure. Unification of all conscious egos and unconscious drives into one harmonious unity sublimated to the egoless, suprapersonal and supraconscious " self." | Elimination of friction between all values of a given culture and between the values of each individual. Unification of all cultural values into one many-sided unity centered around the supreme value of love, truth, and beauty, or the ultimate value of God of which these values are the main manifestations. Similar unification of the values of each individual member of the culture and of the interindividual values of all members of the human race. | Elimination of friction between all groups and institutions of a given population. Unification of all organizations into one multilinear unity dedicated to the service of the supreme values and bound together into one solidary human family by the bonds of mutual love and collective creativity. Similar elimination of friction between various group affiliations of each individual and unification of all his affiliations into multilinear membership in the whole of humanity. |

A fully successful performance of these triple operations is a tremendous undertaking for any individual and for mankind as a whole. Its complete realization can be achieved only in the remote future, if it can be achieved at all. For a long time it will stand as an ideal, the port of destination towards which the ship of humanity must set its course. This does not hinder, however, the incessant movement of the ship towards this final port.  Each mile traveled along this course brings the ship nearer and nearer to the ideal.

The outlined plan of the betterment of man and the human universe is based on a maximal realization of the supraconscious and conscious potentials of man.  Only through the fullest possible release of the highest energies of a person can his unconscious forces be successfully ordered and used as means for the purposes of vital, mental, moral, and social ennoblement of man and his sociocultural cosmos.  (See further on this Chaps. 23 and 24.)  In this respect the plan contrastingly differs from the prevalent psychoanalytical and other therapies which are aimed mainly at an " adjustment " of the unconscious drives and at their release from the so-called repressions and inhibitions of the conscious and supraconscious forces.  In spite of all talk about the " sublimation " of the unconscious drives to the control of the ego and the superego, these therapies tend to adjust the supraconscious and conscious forces to the demands of the unconscious drives, rather than to adapt these to the requirements of the higher energies of man.  In the first part of this chapter the reasons have been given why man's disorganized mechanisms of instincts and reflexes have become disserviceable long ago and are miscarrying especially in modern times.  A mere tampering with these unconscious drives can hardly adjust even functional disorders of the unconscious and conscious minds; still less can it change a human animal into a rational Homo sapiens, and this *Homo* into a genius.  If anything, it is liable to extinguish the creative flame in the morass of the unconscious " id " or chaotic " libido."

In the following chapters we shall test whether the mental structures of great and small altruists correspond to the structure defined by our standard of creativity and integration, and whether the process of their altruization has consisted in the successful performance of the above triple operations in their personality structure, in their cultural values, and in their group affiliations.  An affirmative answer to these inquiries would validate our " therapy " as well as our theory of mental structure.

These preliminary points proved, further on we shall study what are the best available techniques for the successful performance of each of the operations.  For an elucidation of these problems we shall investigate, first of all, the ways and techniques used by the great altruists.  Since these altruists succeeded in becoming geniuses of goodness, they obviously discovered, somehow, some of these conditions, ways, and techniques.  The knowledge derived from their experience may be supplemented then by other sources.  The total knowledge available from all sources can supply the best practical prescription for unfolding and developing altruistic creativity and integration to the maximal limit possible for every individual and group.

PART THREE

# THE WAYS OF ALTRUISTIC GROWTH

*Chapter Eight*

# Supreme Love and the Supraconscious

Ego-centered amity — of low intensity, narrow extensity, and short duration, impure and inadequate — can be easily developed in persons and groups without participation of the supraconscious, through purely bio-conscious and socioconscious motivations. This may be accomplished through the ego-centered techniques of conditioned reflexes, mechanical drilling, rude punishment and reward, or even through the technique of hate cultivation. Motivated mainly by hate of the enemy or coercion of their commanders or by some utilitarian and hedonistic reasons, thousands of soldiers on the battlefield risk their lives for their countrymen or near-by comrades. All forms of low-grade amity actions can be performed and usually are performed without any help of the supraconscious. Even the participation of conscious utilitarian and hedonistic motives is not always necessary for such behavior: well-drilled soldiers fight the enemy automatically, through the disciplined conditioning of their reflexes and actions. There are millions of superficial friendships motivated merely by threat of punishment, by conscious considerations of convenience, utility, pleasure, or profit, without any participation of the supraconscious agent. In brief, low-grade amicable actions are effected through ego-centered conscious and unconscious forces.

Quite different seems to be the situation with the supreme forms of creative love — intense, extensive, durable, pure, and adequate. Like supreme creativity in the field of truth or beauty, *supreme love can hardly be achieved without a direct participation of the supraconscious* and without the ego-transcending techniques of its awakening. Its grace seems to be as necessary here as it is for the highest creativity in science and technological inventions, in philosophy and religion, in the fine arts and other creative fields. The evidence for this hypothesis is logical as well as empirical.

# I

## LOGICAL EVIDENCE

Supreme love transcends our conscious egos and their rational — hedonistic, utilitarian, and eudaemonistic — interests. If it remains ego-centered it is not supreme altruistic love but its low-grade modicum. Supreme love often urges a sacrifice of the important interests of our egos. Once in a while it dictates even a free sacrifice of the life of the individual. Evidently from the standpoint of the ego-centered person there can be no logical reasons for such a sacrifice.

This explains why the logic of all the consistent, ego-centered ethics — hedonistic and utilitarian — has always been the logic of calculated selfish interests and not the logic of altruistic love. No logical ego-centered ethics can urge the individual to transcend his ego(s). Still less can it urge the individual to sacrifice his interests. The major premises of such a logic forbid any plea for sacrifice. If it does present such a plea, it becomes self-contradictory: "For the benefit of your egos and your ego-centered personality you have to transcend your egos and your ego-centered *I;* for the benefit of your egos you have to sacrifice their vital interests; for the benefit of your personal life you have to sacrifice your life." The second parts of these propositions deny what their first parts affirm.

In brief, viewed by the logic of the rational ego(s), the logic of the Sermon on the Mount is a non-sense and a complete illogicity. And vice versa: from the standpoint of the ethics of the Sermon on the Mount, all rational, ego-centered ethics are but "the moral arithmetics" of the selfish interests of the individual viewing the whole world as a mere means for satisfaction of his advantages. Such an ego-centered ethics has only a very distant relationship to supreme love and to genuine friendship. No individual — even Jeremy Bentham or John Stuart Mill — who rationally and consistently follows such an ethics can ever soar to the heights of supreme love and become either a Jesus or Buddha, a St. Francis of Assisi or a Gandhi or any apostle of this sort of love. If some of the hedonists and utilitarianists reached these heights, they did it by breaking their ego-centered rational ethics and by becoming "possessed" by the grace of the supraconscious. The forces of the unconscious (in man) and of the conscious egos cannot generate supreme love as they cannot produce the supreme achievements in other fields of creativity.

# II

## EMPIRICAL EVIDENCE

As to the empirical evidence, there is a considerable body of relevant facts favorable to our hypothesis.

## A. *Testimony of Altruists*

The first category of this factual evidence is *the unanimous testimony of the eminent apostles of love*, from Buddha and Jesus up to Gandhi and Schweitzer, and *of practically all the ethics of supreme love*. In different terms the supreme altruists of the most different nations and periods unanimously state that in doing their acts of sublime love they act as a mere instrument of the supraconscious, called by different names: God, Heaven, Heavenly Father, Tao, the Great Reason, the Oversoul, Brahma, Jen, Chit, the Supra-Essence, the Divine Nothing, the Divine Madness, the Logos, the Sophia, the Supreme Wisdom, the Inner Light. Without almost any dissenting voice they state that in their acts of love a complete humility and transcendence of the egos and the ego-centered conscious mind (not to mention the subconscious propensities) is necessary in order to soar to the supreme forms of love. The same is unanimously told by practically all the ethical systems of love.

Here are a few typical statements of the altruists and then of the ethics of love.

"Betwixt me and Thee there lingers an 'it is I' that torments me. Ah, of Thy grace, take away this 'I' from between us! I am He whom I love, and He whom I love is I, We are two spirits in one body. If thou seest me, seest Him, and if thou seest Him, thou seest both." This is the exact formula of Al Hallaj, a great Muslim altruist and mystic.[1]

"The stage of being lost in God," "intermixture" (*haloul*), "identification" (*ittihad*), "intimate union with God," (*wasl*) are expressions used for this self-identification with the supraconscious. "But all these expressions are inadequate," because "the intuitions of the truths by means of ecstasy or inspiration" are indescribable by words, says Al Ghazzali (1059–1111 A.D.), the great Muslim philosopher, mystic, and altruist. After his conversion into altruistic mysticism, he considered the identification with God in mystic ecstasy as the necessary condition for cognition of truth as well as for becoming morally good.[2]

"The contempt of the world and of self" or an unconditional humility was the first necessary condition for anything good in her actions, says St. Theresa. And "anything of this good kind is [God's] and not mine because I am neither learned nor of good life, and I have no person of learning or any other to teach me." "We must neither imagine nor think that we can of ourselves bring about" these good things. God is doing them through us. For that purpose He "suspends our understanding" (conscious mind) and "puts before it that which astonishes and occupies us: so that, without making any reflections, we shall comprehend in a moment more than we could comprehend in many years with all the efforts in the world. . . . He teaches everything in a moment, so that I am lost in wonder." Stressing her own stupidity and dullness of mind, and her inability to learn from the learned persons through her rational, conscious mind, St. Theresa repeats again and again that anything good in either her writing or her actions is due entirely to God. " God gave me to understand with all distinctness in a moment " and we cannot and should not " raise our spirit [conscious mind] ourselves, if our Lord does not raise it for us; and if He does, there can be no mistaking it." [3]

In entirely different terms, a contrastingly different altruist, Albert Schweitzer, states a similar point. He tells how by sudden intuition he decided to become doctor-missionary among the savages, and how the suprarational functioned in his altruistic activities, in spite of his strong rationalism. He goes further, and contends that " neither world-and-life affirmation nor ethics can be founded on what scientific knowledge of the world can tell us about the world. . . . Ethics have nothing to expect from any theory of knowledge." Neither the sublime actions of love nor the ethics of reverence for life can be based, derived, and motivated by purely rational, conscious, scientific thought. For that a deeper, intuitive, and mystic will-to-live with its direct insight is necessary. " Reverence for life means to be in the grasp of the infinite, inexplicable, forward-urging Will in which all Being is grounded. It rises above all knowledge of things." " World-and-life affirmation and ethics are nonrational." They are based upon suprarational mysticism. On it are based also the supreme acts of love and reverence for life in an individual — in Schweitzer himself.[4]

" Thus God laid the foundations of my life in South Africa and sowed the seed of the fight for national self-respect," states Gandhi. Again and again he stresses that practically all his altruistic activity was motivated by the supraconscious, which he calls by the names of Truth, God, Love, and so on.[5]

Telling how in England he was saved from sexual sin by a sudden suprarational impulse, Gandhi states that " only vaguely I understood that God had saved me on that occasion. On all occasions of trials He has saved me. In all my trials — of a spiritual nature, as a lawyer, in conducting institutions and in politics — I can say that God saved me. When every hope is gone, I find that help arrives somehow, from I know not where. Supplication, worship, prayer are no superstitions . . . they are acts more real than the acts of eating, drinking or walking. It is no exaggeration to say that they alone are real. . . ." [6] He sums up his life experience thus: " What I have been striving and pining to achieve these thirty years is self-realization, to see God face to face, to attain Moksha. . . . I live and move and have my being in pursuit of this goal. . . . The instruments for the quest of Truth are as simple as they are difficult. They may appear quite impossible to an arrogant person, and quite possible to an innocent child." An unconditional humility, a transcendence of all sorts of egoism, and ahimsa (nonviolence) are the suprarational ways for obtaining the Truth. Mere rational knowledge of even religion and ethics is quite insufficient and inefficient for seeing the Truth (God) and for following the path of supreme love.[7]  The grace of the supraconscious activated through prayer, supplication, concentration, self-surrender, and humility is indispensable for such achievements.

In fiercely intellectualistic and at the same time most mystic terms, the supraconscious is stressed by a still more modern " sister to all sufferers," Simone Weil (1909–1943).  Bitterly rejecting the Catholic, the Jewish, and other institutionalized religions, this anarchistic, pacifistic, revolutionary, and unorthodox altruist characterized the supraconscious as " something that is not affliction, not joy, something that is the central essence, necessary and pure, something not of the senses, common to joy and sorrow: the love of God." [8]  Her own fierce charity actions were generated by this suprarational " something " that transcended any and all ego-centered rational motives, including even peace of mind or of soul.  " As for the spiritual direction of my soul, I think God himself has taken it in hand and will keep it."  In her unorthodox prayer she prays: " Father, since Thou art the good, and I am the mediocre, take from me this body and this soul and make them Thy things.  Let nothing of me remain even to eternity."  She adds: " Such words are only effective if they are dictated by the Holy Spirit.  One cannot voluntarily demand such things. One reaches this point despite oneself.  Despite oneself but consenting to it.  Consent is entire and unreserved."

In more religiously orthodox terms the supraconscious, as God's grace, is stressed in the experience of another modern altruistic soul, Dorothy Day, the founder of the *Catholic Worker* and " subversive " Catholic friend to all sufferers.  Humility, renunciation and transcendence of ego, and the divine grace are constantly mentioned by her as the necessary conditions for genuine and sincere actions of charity or love.  " Not much time for prayer these busy days.  And not much time to think of self either; or comfort, physical, spiritual or mental.  So that is good, too. ' Self ' is the great enemy.  ' Deny yourself, take up your cross and follow Me.' . . .  Most of us have not the courage to set out on this path wholeheartedly, so God arranges it for us." [9]

Similarly St. Serafim of Sarov ascribed to God everything good he did, including healing, consoling, pacifying, and instructing morally thousands of people who flocked to him when, after forty-seven years of eremitic, ascetic, and spiritual preparation, he returned to the world and dedicated himself to the service of his fellow men and women.  " Not me but the Holy Ghost did it through the prayer of the humblest and poorest Serafim," was his usual statement.[10]

" When the Lord gave me some brothers [first companions] no one showed me what I ought to do, but the Most High Himself revealed to me that I ought to live according to the model of the Holy Gospel," writes St. Francis of Assisi in his *Testament*.

" God in his goodness has not called us merely for our own salvation, but also for that of many men. . . . Be not fearful on the ground that we appear little and ignorant. . . . Have faith in God, that his Spirit will speak in you and by you. . . . My brother, commit yourself to God with all your cares, and he will care for you." Such were the first directions which St. Francis of Assisi gave to his first companions and disciples.[11]

John Woolman called himself " a trumpet, through which the Lord speaks " when Woolman was speaking truth, and viewed himself but a mere instrumentality of Jesus. When he was on his own, he says, his talks were foolish and his actions were selfish. " Resignation," dying to self-love and complete surrender to " a principle which is pure, placed in the human mind, which had different names, but proceeds from God," this " inward stillness " is the source of sublime love.[12]

Practically all great Christian educators of humanity — St. Basil the Great, Pachomius the Great, St. Benedict, St. Cyprian, St. Bernard, St. John Climacus, St. Dorotheus, John Cassian, St. Isaac the Syrian, St. Francis de Sales, St. Ignatius Loyola, and others — reiterate similar experiences.

" There are three kinds or degrees of Truth; we rise to the first by humble effort, to the second by loving sympathy, to the third by enraptured vision. . . . The work of the Persons of the Holy Trinity is leading men through the three degrees of Truth. . . . The first degree appears to be due to the action of the Son, the second to that of the Holy Spirit, and the third to that of the Father. I recognize humility as the way. I long for truth as the reward . . . ," says St. Bernard in his detailed analysis of the problem.[13] Different in terms but essentially similar is the testimony of the other Christian Fathers mentioned.[14]

Similar also is the experience of the non-Christian, oriental altruists and moral leaders. The testimony of Sri Ramakrishna and of Swami Vivekananda can serve as examples. " It is on account of the ego that one is not able to see God. . . . Unless one renounces the ego, one does not receive God's grace." " Through the Divine Mother's grace the people attain liberation. She is called the Savior, and the Remover of the Bondage that binds one to the world and entangles in ' woman ' and ' gold.' " [15]

And here are similar testimonies of the moral leaders of certain sects which are marked by a comparatively high level of unselfish service among their members and in regard to the human world at large.

" Within ourselves we become conscious of the [Divine] Spirit [the ' Inner Light ' or the ' Christ within '], and as we submit ourselves to its leadings, we also are enabled to live in conformity to the will of our Heavenly Father. Love, the outworking of the Divine Spirit, is the most potent influence that can be applied in the affairs of men, and this application of love to the whole of life the Society of Friends conceives to be the core of the Christian gospel." [16] Such is the central principle of the Quakers, distinguished for their high altruistic service.

"The main bases of religious and moral views of our community [of Dukhobors] are as follows: To Love God with all our heart and soul and to love our neighbor as oneself. . . . Loving neighbor we realize our love of God. Cultivating love we acquire through that God in our heart. . . . A mere intellectualism, literacy, and education are entirely insufficient for becoming altruistic. If anything, they help subjugation and exploitation of man by man. . . . They hinder finding the real truth and enlightenment, and make human beings selfish rather than unselfish." Such is the testimony of the eminently altruistic, distinguished leader of the Dukhobors, Peter V. Verigin.[17]

Further, there is the testimonial experience of the Mennonites, the Hutterites, and other sects marked by their high moral standard and unselfish service.[18]

If from these contemporary sects we move to the German prophets and moral leaders of the seventeenth and eighteenth centuries (D. Peterson, E. L. Gruber, J. F. Rock, E. S. Gleim) who founded the Christian Communities in Europe and eventually in the United States, we find testimony again essentially similar in this point. "Abandon ego, with all its desires, knowledge, and power," they say. The first condition of real altruization and spiritualization is complete humility, complete "emptying and purgation" of our (conscious, ego-centered) mind, "the spiritual death of the sinful man" (conscious and unconscious minds), followed by an unconditional surrender to the supraconscious. "Before the Spirit of God can flow into the soul the soul must be empty and pure; the Spirit of God must first work on the soul to purify it, and the soul must suffer being purified, which is a sort of death for it. . . . The old man must die in a baptism of suffering." Selfishness, self-love, ego-centered ideas, presumptions, and impurities all must be "cut away with God's sharp blades."[19]

Finally, some 30 per cent of the American Good Neighbors (who are somewhat above the rank and file in their service to fellow men) confess that in doing their good-neighborly deeds they are inspired, moved, and helped by God, "the Divine call," by the "irresistible voice of duty," by "spontaneous urge," and by other agencies of the supraconscious, called by different terms.[20]

This kind of testimony by altruistic persons about the supraconscious as the fountainhead of their own love activities can be multiplied by hundreds of other cases. So far as it sums up real experience of the real altruistic behavior of real persons, the testimony becomes objective, relevant, factual evidence. Unanimous similarity of this objective evidence strongly corroborates our hypothesis. Such, then, is one series of factual proofs.

## B. *Testimony of Ethical Systems of Love*

Another series of factual corroboration of the hypothesis is given by practically *all ethical systems of love*, beginning with the oldest and ending with the newest ones. Let us concisely sum up the situation.

The Taoist ethics of " recompensing injury with kindness," of loving not only friends but also enemies, is rooted neither in the unconscious nor in the rational mind, but in the supraconscious " Great Reason " or Tao. A quiet immersion into this supraconscious, in the form of calm meditation and inaction, is the Tao way to become wise and good, to obtain stillness of mind and freedom from desires. " When no desire any longer arises, there is the true stillness and rest. . . . In constant stillness there is the constant purity." " I consider doing nothing to obtain enjoyment to be the great enjoyment. Heaven does nothing, and thence comes its serenity. Earth does nothing, and thence comes its rest. All things in all their variety grow from this inaction." " Doing nothing is better than to be busy doing nothing." [21] One of the main conditions either for the altruistic transformation of man or for harmonious and solidary society is precisely this process of " emptying one's mind " of all rational and conscious knowledge and filling it with Tao, the supraconscious and suprarational " Great Reason " as the fountainhead of supreme creative love.

" The holy man when he governs empties the people's hearts [or minds] but fills their souls. Always he keeps the people unsophisticated and without desire. . . . He who disciplines his soul and embraces unity cannot be deranged. . . . Through inducing tenderness he can become like a little child. By purifying and profound intuition he can be free from faults. In loving the people and administering the country he can practice non-assertion. . . . Like a mother-bird, he can be unsophisticated. He acts but claims not. He excels but rules not. This is called profound virtue. . . . He who with Reason [the supraconscious] assists the master of mankind will not with arms conquer the empire. Reason always practices non-assertion, and there is nothing that remains undone. If princes and kings could keep Reason, the ten thousand things would of themselves be reformed. The simplicity of the unexpressed [the supraconscious] will purify the heart of lust. Where there is no lust there will be rest, and all the world will thus be blessed. Superior virtue is un-virtue. [It transcends any conscious virtue and any rational awareness of virtue.] Inferior virtue never loses sight of virtue [always is conscious and egoistically proud of it]. Therefore it has no virtue. Superior virtue is non-assertion and without pretension. Inferior virtue asserts and makes pretensions."

" The ancients who were well versed in Reason [the supraconscious] did not try thereby to enlighten the people [to fill them with rational knowledge and rational ethical rules]. They intended thereby to make them simple-hearted. If people are difficult to govern [and are demoralized], it is because they are too smart [too sophisticated rationally]. . . . To govern the country with smartness is the country's curse. . . . Profound virtue verily is deep. Verily, it is far reaching. But then it will procure great recognition." [22]

Supraconscious also is *Jen* — perfect virtue and perfect love for others — in Confucianism and in the ethics of universal love of Mo-tzu (*ca.* 475–393 B.C.) and his followers.[23]

Except the Materialists (Cārvāka-Bārhaspatya), all the main religious philosophies of India — Jainism, atheistic Sankhya, Yoga, Vedanta, the orthodox Mimāmksakas, the Nyāya-Vaišesika, and Buddhism — have similar precepts for union with the Absolute, for full realization of the supraconscious egoless Self or Atman, for clear manifestation of the purusha, for reaching nirvana and stopping the endless cycle of births and deaths, or, finally, for reaching the highest wisdom and sublime love. "This am I. I, the human individual, of limited consciousness, steeped in delusion, spellbound by Maya, actually and fundamentally am This, or He, namely the Atman, the Self, the Highest Being, of unlimited consciousness and existence. I am not to be identified with the perishable individual, who accepts as utterly real and fatal the processes and happenings of the psyche and the body. 'I am He who is free and divine,'" so it is said in the *Song of the Inner Gander* (Vishnu), listened to by Markandeya.[24]

Complete control of the unconscious drives and the conscious emotions, an elimination of egos, a thorough calming and stilling of the conscious mind, and a release of the supraconscious, even its help, are the necessary operations for achievement of "friendliness towards all living beings that are happy; compassion towards those in pain; joy towards those whose character is meritorious; indifference towards those whose character is de-meritorious." A first step towards such an objective is Yoga; "Yoga is concentration" and a complete "restriction of all the fluctuations of the mind-stuff," or a complete quieting of the inherently restless ego-conscious mind (*chitta*) incessantly disturbed by emotional *rajas* and *tamas*.[25]

Insofar as the techniques of all the above-mentioned religions and philosophies of India for achievement of their supreme goal are essentially similar to the technique of Yoga, to this extent the insufficiency of the unconscious drives and the ego-centered conscious forces in man for sublime altruization of person is stressed by all of them. Similarly they all emphasize the necessity of the functioning and grace of the supraconscious (the Self, Atman, Isvara, Brahman, "the purifying elements" of early Buddhism) for that purpose.[26] With some variations in their philosophies these precepts are enunciated by the Upanishads, the Bhagavadgita, by the Patanjali Yoga, the Dhammapada, and by all the main texts of these religions of India. They outline the way for reaching the state of samadhi or liberation in Sankhya, Yoga, Vedanta, Jainism, the orthodox Mimāmksakas, and the Nyāya-Vaišesika. They sum up "the Path towards Quiescence" (nirvana) — the "Small Vehicle" of early Buddhism or the "Grand Vehicle" of later Buddhism; and the way of opening "the third eye" and reaching the state of satori in Zen Buddhism.

" When one has conquered one's self (lower) [the ego-centered conscious mind] and has attained to the calm of self-mastery, his Supreme Self abides ever concentrate, he is at peace in cold and heat, in pleasure and pain, in honor and dishonor. . . ." He " is master of his senses." " When one does not get attached to the objects of sense or to works, and has renounced all purposes, then he is said to have attained to Yoga. . . ." Through " abandoning without exception all desires born of (selfish) will, restraining all the senses . . . quieting his mind by fixing it on the Self . . . supreme happiness comes to the Yogin, whose mind is peaceful, whose passions are at rest, who is stainless and has become one with God." [27]

With some variation, these conditions of reaching the high levels of altruistic love are reiterated by all the main currents of Indian religious, ethical, and philosophical thought.

Very similar are the precepts of Plato and Aristotle, and of other Greco-Roman ethics of absolute principles, ethics of love, and of the sublimest eudaemonistic ethics.[28]   Plato's views in this matter, especially in his *Phaedo*, are almost identical with the above precepts of Taoism, Hinduism, and Buddhism.  The supraconscious " divine madness " is for him the only source of any supreme creativity, whether cognitive, moral, aesthetic, or other.  In cognition our sense perception gives only the least certain empirical notions (which he contemptuously calls " mere opinions " or " dancing shadows "); mathematical and syllogistic logic gives more valid knowledge; but only the supraconscious " divine madness " grants to the few perfect wisdom.  In the field of virtue and goodness, the body with its unconscious and conscious strivings is an obstacle rather than a help toward anything good, be it courage, temperance, justice, friendship, or love.  The more our supraconscious " soul " is free from the body — from its desires, from its ego, from its passions, from its pleasure-pain objectives and its sense perceptions — the purer and more virtuous it actually becomes.  In this light the death of the condemned Socrates is viewed by Plato as the real liberation of the supraconscious self or soul from all the imperfections of the unconscious and conscious forces of the body.

" Thought is best when the [suprarational and supraconscious] soul is gathered into herself and none of these things trouble her — neither sounds nor sights [nor any other sense perception], nor pain nor pleasure — when she has as little as possible to do with the body, and has no bodily sense or feeling but is aspiring after being herself."  The true and virtuous " philosopher dishonours the body; his soul runs away from the body and desires to be alone and by herself."

" And he attains to the knowledge of [absolute truth, and beauty, and justice, and goodness] in their highest purity who goes to each of them with the mind alone, not allowing the intrusion of sight or any other sense," . . . getting " rid of eyes, ears, and of the whole body which he conceives of only as a disturbing element " and " the source of endless trouble," " hindering the soul from " reaching these values.

A person who is " not the lover of wisdom but a lover of the body is at the same time usually a lover of money or power or both." Motivated mainly by fear, pain, and pleasure, such a utilitarian and hedonistic person has " a shadow of virtue only," devoid even of " any freedom or health or truth " or courage or justice or any other real virtue.

In such a person even his " soul is dragged by the body into the region of the changeable and is confused; she is like a drunkard under their [the sense organs] influence. . . ." " But when returning into herself she reflects; then she passes into the realm of purity, and eternity, and immortality, and unchangeableness, which are her kindred. . . . The soul resembles the divine. . . ." " And this is the reason, why the true philosophers abstain from all fleshly lusts, and endure and refuse to give themselves up to them " and not because of fear of poverty or dishonor or pain or any other motives of the body's unconscious and conscious forces.[29]

In a somewhat stronger empirical vein and with variations in secondary points, similar principles were enunciated by Pythagoras, Heraclitus, Empedocles, and others before Socrates and Plato; and after Plato by Aristotle, Theophrastus, Zeno, Cleanthes, Chrysippus, Diogenes, Poseidonius, Philo, Seneca, Marcus Aurelius, Epictetus, Apuleius, Plotinus, Porphyry, Proclus — by practically all the leading thinkers of the Platonic, Aristotelian, Neoplatonic, Stoic, Pythagorean, Gnostic, and Mystic schools in Greco-Roman philosophy and ethics.[30]

Indeed, the Christian ethics of love stressed these precepts particularly clearly. This ethics made the supraconscious Agape or God's grace the only fountainhead of any sublime love, hope, and faith, and of salvation itself. Without the supraconscious grace, all the unconscious, subconscious, and rational forces of a person cannot lift him or his mind and behavior into the spheres of pure love and sublime altruistic creativity. Even Jesus himself ascribed his sublime deeds of love to the Father (as the supraconscious).

" I am in the Father, and the Father in me. . . . The words that I speak unto you I speak not of myself: but the Father that dwelleth in me, he doeth the works . . . for my Father is greater than I. . . ." Addressing his apostles and all followers he indicates Himself, the Father, and the Holy Ghost as the fountainhead and the real force of all their good deeds.

" I am the way, the truth, and the life. . . . He that believeth in me, the works that I do shall he do also; and greater works than these shall he do. . . . And whatever ye shall ask in my name, that I will do. . . . The Holy Ghost . . . shall teach all things, and bring all things to your remembrance." "I am the vine, ye are the branches. He that abideth in me, and I in him, the same bringeth forth much fruit: for without me ye can do nothing. . . . If a man abide not in me, he is cast forth as a branch, and is withered." [31]  St. Paul reiterates all this, saying: "We have the mind of Christ," [32] and "I live, yet no longer I, but Christ liveth in me." [33]  St. Augustine and practically all the Church Fathers see in the body's unconscious, subconscious, and conscious forces the source of sin, selfishness, and moral degradation rather than the power of love to God and fellow men. Without the supraconscious grace, these forces of sin cannot even be controlled and mastered.

"And all my hope is nowhere but in Thy great mercy. Give what Thou enjoinest, and enjoin what Thou wilt. . . . Thou enjoinest us continency . . . for no man can be continent, unless God give it. . . . Verily Thou enjoinest me continency from the lust of the flesh, the lust of the eyes, and the ambition of the world. . . ." While without the help of the supraconscious (God) all these temptations would be irresistible, with God's help they all are mastered. "I can do all things through Christ that strengtheneth me." [34]

These ideas and precepts are the common fund of all Christian ethical thinkers, from St. Paul to St. Francis de Sales, not to mention still later leaders in Christian ethics of love. [35]

Clothed in different terms — now and then perfectly secular terms, free from any religious affiliation and denomination — these ideas and precepts are common to practically all the partisans of the ethics of love, regardless to what religion they belong or whether they belong to any institutional religion at all. This is true about virtually all altruistic mystics of all institutional and noninstitutional religions. Buddha, Chaitanya, Tukaram, Ramakrishna, Vivekananda, Gandhi, Sri Ramana Maharshi, and Sri Aurobindo in Hinduism and Buddhism; Al Hallaj, Al Ghazzali, Dhu'l-Nūn, Abū Sáïd, Ibnu'l-Arabī, Rūmī in Mohammedanism; and Hillel in Judaism are examples of such mystics. About all of them one can say, with E. Underhill, that "the business and method of mysticism is Love" (to God, men, and the whole world). And they all reach their objective — union with the Absolute or the supraconscious — through the "mystic way." This mystic way consists of these steps: 1. the awakening of the supraconscious self; 2. its preliminary purgation from the negative unconscious and conscious temptations, values, and influences; 3. illumination of the self; 4. the "mystic dark night" or "mystic death," followed by a complete surrender of the self to the absolute supraconscious (God); 5. union with the Absolute; 6. final purification and liberation from the control of all the finite things, including one's conscious and unconscious forces. At the end of this difficult process, a true "mystic enjoyeth all creatures in God and God in all creatures." "The Cosmos belongs to you and you to it." [36] The mystic becomes an instrument of the supraconscious with a complete mastery of the unconscious and conscious forces of his human person.

This is true also, as we have said, of all the partisans of the Christian and the Western ethics of Love, secular as well as religious, positivistic as well as mystic. In different terms the precepts discussed are stated by Church Fathers like Justin the Martyr, Clement of Alexandria, Origen, Athanasius the Great, Basil the Great, St. Ambrose, Gregory of Nyssa, St. Augustine, Gregory the Great; by Dionysius, Maximus Confessor, J. S. Erigena, Alcuin, Photius, Bernard of Clairvaux, Hugo of St. Victor, Peter Abelard, Joachim de Floris, Albertus Magnus, St. Thomas Aquinas; by Dante, Meister Eckhart, J. Tauler, H. Suso, Ruysbroeck, Nicolas of Cusa, Thomas à Kempis, St. Theresa, G. Bruno, St. John of the Cross; by J. A. Comenius, F. Froebel, J. H. Pestalozzi, A. A. S. Shaftesbury, J. J. Rousseau, I. G. Herder, A. Schopenhauer, I. H. Fichte, R. W. Emerson, J. Ruskin, A. Comte, L. Tolstoi, F. Dostoievsky, V. Solovyev, R. Wagner, C. Renouvier, M. Maeterlinck, M. B. Eddy, and many others.[37]

If someone should ask about my rules of life, I would show the Decalogue, for I am sure that no one can say better what is pleasing to God than God himself.

The School of God's Wisdom is divided into three classes: The School of Nature, or the Physical School, for the learning of this we are provided with our five senses. The second school is the Metaphysical School, here we are taught by our mind. The third school is the Hyperphysical, here God alone is the teacher.

This last school is called by Comenius also by the term "the Eternal Light." It shines on and influences man's will, affections, and conscience and leads to the "serenity and happiness of heart which come from the sense of knowing the Truth and partaking in holiness." [38]

Such is the formula of the great educator, J. A. Comenius. In different terms it is reiterated by another notable educator, F. Froebel.

In all things there lives and reigns an eternal law. . . . This all-controlling law is based on an all-pervading, energetic, living, self-conscious, and hence eternal Unity. This Unity is God. . . . It is the destiny and life-work of all things to unfold their essence — to reveal God in their external and transient being. It is the special destiny and life-work of man . . . of the divine effluence in him, and, therefore, of God. . . . Education consists . . . in leading man, as a thinking intelligent being, growing into self-consciousness, to a pure and unsullied, conscious and free representation of the inner law of Divine Unity, and in teaching him ways and means thereto. . . . Education should lead . . . to peace with nature, and to Unity with God.

All the pedagogical means are but instruments for a realization of this purpose — which is helped by the supraconscious (God).[39]

As a further variant of these precepts, the statements of Auguste Comte and Tolstoi can be mentioned. "Love is our principle, Order is our basis, Progress is our end," is the motto of the Father of Positivism, and of the High Priest of the Religion of Humanity. Moral ennoblement of mankind in the sense of an increase of altruistic love appeared in Comte as the main way out of the chaos, towards a nobler and better social order. This goal could not be reached through the merely unconscious and conscious (intellectual) forces in man.

"The supremacy of reason is an utter illusion. Individual happiness and public welfare are far more dependent upon the heart than upon the intellect."

"If the intellect aspires to become supreme, its ambitious aims, which are never realized, result simply in the most deplorable disorder . . ." and selfishness. The unconscious forces alone, not guided either by intellect or by affections or by something like the supraconscious, would lead to chaos, to a "barren, even dangerous contention." Only when affections and social instincts are guided by intellect and all three are united under the control of the supra-intellectual universal love and of the ethical religion of Humanity, only then the necessary moral, mental, and physical progress of mankind can take place.

"Intellectual life is always liable to these mischievous and anti-social illusions of pride; and it can only be preserved from them by the constant control of religion, guiding it ever back to its high purpose." [40]

In his insistence on the unconditional and incessant following of the rules of the Sermon on the Mount in our behavior, including love of the enemy and nonviolent resistance to evil, as the only way towards building a harmonious, happy, and creative human universe, Leo Tolstoi strongly emphasizes the need of the grace of the supraconscious ("the Divine Will" etc.). In his opinion the merely subconscious and rationally conscious forces of an individual are quite inadequate to produce such truly Christian conduct and society.

The life we lead . . . is getting madder and madder, unhappier and unhappier, because men, instead of keeping to a spiritual, moral principle [of love] that would unite them in a society of peace and concord, are guided by their *bestial instincts* which they seek to satisfy by trading on their *intellectual faculties.* . . .

Christ founded no church, established no State, made no laws, imposed no government, or exterior authority; he simply set himself to write the law of God in the hearts of men in order that they might govern themselves. The doctrine of Christ is based on the metaphysical principle of love, the supreme law, that should guide us in our daily life and which admits of no exception.

When you can say with entire truth and with a whole heart: "Lord God, lead me wherever Thou desirest," then, only, do you deliver yourself from servitude and become really free.

Do what you have to do in life according to divine will, and in that way you will improve the lives of everybody.

State violence [wars, revolutions, etc.] will disappear, not with the aid of external means, but thanks only to the calls of conscience of men who have awakened to the truth.

Accomplish your task in life by obeying the divine will, and you will be certain to help towards the betterment of social life in the most efficient way.

We possess a single infallible guide and this is the Universal Spirit that lives in men as a whole. . . . It is the spirit that commands . . . to reach out towards God, and by so doing become united to each other.[41]

To sum up: this similarity, even unanimity, of the precepts of all ethical systems of love, and of a large number of eminent ethical teachers is significant. It is real evidence in favor of our proposition. It cannot be explained away as a mere chance concordance of a number of chance opinions of a number of chance ideologists. It is in fact the similarity derived from a vast body of experience of altruistic love observed and practiced by a large number of apostles, teachers, propagators, investigators, and observers. For this reason it is an important factual evidence.

## C. *Testimony of the Nature of the Techniques of Awakening and Realization of Supreme Love*

A third series of evidence for the supraconscious as the necessary fountainhead of supreme love is given by the character of the techniques used by eminent altruists for the awakening and development of their love conduct and activities. In subsequent parts of this work these techniques are analyzed in detail. For the present it is enough to say that the *main body of these techniques neither is aimed at nor does it lead to a development of man's conscious or unconscious mind*. If such a development occurs, it is a mere by-product of these techniques and not their objective. *Their objective is the awakening and development of the supraconscious for the difficult realization of the actions of supreme love*. Prayers to the supraconscious (called by different names) in various forms; eremitic isolation from all human beings and from the whole civilization with all its sources for the development of rational knowledge — books, libraries, lectures, instruction, etc.; sustained meditation and concentration which neither aims at nor deals with the problems of the development of man's intellect and its " scientific knowledge "; silence for long periods; semi-ascetic and ascetic training in the control of man's unconscious and conscious propensities; ecstatic trances; most peculiar deeds of altruism like St. Francis' sudden act of embracing a leper and kissing his horrible wounds: these and hundreds of other techniques are neither designed nor effective for the intellectual development of man or for the most pleasurable, spontaneous play of his unconscious and bioconscious propensities. If, however, in the experience of practically all the eminent altruists these and similar techniques are practiced, regarded necessary, and found effective for their purpose, this means that the presence and functioning of the supraconscious may indeed be necessary for the development of supremely altruistic deeds.

This conclusion is corroborated also by the experience of millions of ordinary persons who at some time must make the supreme sacrifice or do a deed of supreme love. In such situations these ordinary persons also invoke the help of the supraconscious and use some of the techniques of the eminent altruists. We shall see that on the whole these techniques, when used expertly and in the proper conditions, are effective indeed for their purpose.

### D. *No Close Relationship between Intelligence and Altruism or Criminality*

The fourth series of empirical evidence shows the nonexistence of a close positive connection between intelligence (or conscious mind) and altruistic love and criminality. The existing body of evidence shows that:

1. Criminals (that is, on the whole, the most antialtruistic persons) are all in all no less intelligent than the noncriminals, or at least have as good conscious minds. If the rational mind or intelligence were an important factor of altruism, the criminals should have been less intelligent in comparison with the noncriminals. Factual evidence, however, points in a different direction.

On the basis of a study of 163,000 cases of the relationship between intelligence and criminality, no significant uniform relationship between these variables was found. The coefficients of correlation between these variables fluctuated in various investigations from minus .52 to plus .76, most of the studies giving the coefficients near to zero. Insignificant also are the coefficients of colligation between delinquency and illiteracy (between minus .09 and plus .24); between delinquency and amount of schooling (between minus .12 and plus .19); between criminality and school progress (between .46 and .52: it is to be remembered that the coefficient of colligation is still less reliable than that of correlation); between intelligence and morality (between minus .35 and plus .84, remaining low — about .1 to .3 — in the most careful studies).[42]

2. Other conditions being equal, groups and persons brighter in their intelligence (with higher I.Q. and grades) are no more altruistic in their conduct than groups and persons who are duller intellectually.

3. With the progress of intellectual growth, measured by the increase of schooling, literacy, number of schools beginning with kindergarten and ending with university, by the enormous increase of scientific discoveries and technological inventions, from the earlier periods to the present time and specifically from the twelfth century on to the twentieth century — with such intellectual progress the most antisocial, and antialtruistic phenomena: international and civil wars, crime, violence, exploitation, etc., have not decreased at all. If anything, with some

fluctuation, they have increased from the twelfth to the twentieth century. This is shown by the following data.[43]

| Centuries | Index of magnitude of wars (measured by war casualty per million of Europe's population) | Index of magnitude of important internal disturbances in Europe | No. of universities and higher institutions of learning in the Western World | No. of scientific discoveries and technological inventions |
|---|---|---|---|---|
| XII | 2 to 2.9 | 763 | 5 | 12 |
| XIII | 3 to 5.0 | 882 | 18 | 53 |
| XIV | 6 to 9.0 | 827 | 30 | 65 |
| XV | 8 to 11.0 | 748 | 57 | 127 |
| XVI | 14 to 16 | 509 | 98 | 429 |
| XVII | 45 | 605 | 129 | 691 |
| XVIII | 40 | 415 | 180 | 1574 |
| XIX | 17 | 766 | 603 | 8527 |
| XX (1900–1925) | 52 | 295 | 753 | 862 (only for 1900–1908) |

With a steady growth of scientific discoveries and inventions, institutions of higher learning and literacy — from the twelfth to the twentieth century — wars and bloody revolutions do not decrease, but with strong fluctuations they rather increase, reaching an unprecedented explosion in the twentieth century. (The indexes for the present century are only for its first quarter; if they are computed up to 1953, they would greatly exceed the indexes for any of the preceding centuries.) Likewise — with the progress of schooling, science, and technology — crime, insanity, and various forms of interindividual and intergroup conflicts have not decreased at all. At the present time they are as high and probably higher than in most of the preceding centuries. All this means that purely intellectual progress does not lead to moral progress.

If the conscious mind were an important or sufficient factor of altruistic love, we should expect a) that criminals, as the least altruistic persons, should be the least intelligent or anyhow less intelligent than the noncriminals; b) that intellectually brighter persons and groups would be more altruistic than duller ones; c) that with an enormous progress of intellectual development of humanity from the earlier periods to the present time, the most antisocial actions, especially wars, bloody revolutions, grave criminality, and grave violence in various forms, would be decreasing. Factually the situation is very different from these expectations. Therefore, *either the conscious intellect is impotent, or is not sufficiently strong, or is not the factor positively connected with altruistic phenomena generally and with their sublime forms especially.*

With still greater reason the same can be said of the unconscious forces in man. Though the human biological organism contains not only the forces of the struggle for existence, but also those of mutual aid; not only egoistic but also altruistic propensities (often called " social or gregarious instincts "),[44] these unconscious altruistic drives are hardly much stronger than the unconscious forces of enmity. As mentioned, the instinctive mechanism of the altruistic propensities has been notably disorganized in the process of evolution and its equilibrium is easily upset by adverse environmental factors as well. For these reasons the species Homo sapiens is one of the very few species whose members regularly fight, kill, harm, and hate one another: *man's main enemy is man.*

Even when not upset, the " social instinct " of man hardly can reach the level of sublime love in its intensity, universal extensity, purity, lasting continuity, and adequacy. As biological instinct it was molded to be narrow in its extensity, with mutual aid limited to the circle of the small family or tribe, rather than the whole of mankind. As an instinct, biological sociality hardly ever was universal in its extensity, as supreme love must be. Similarly, biological sociality cannot be pure; and especially can it not be adequate in the dynamic conditions of man's environment and change. Its reflexological rigidity makes it inadequate in the ever-changing conditions of man's life. If biological sociality can be sporadically intense (as shown in the heterosexual love relationship) this intensity is neither extensive, nor durable and pure. It is sporadic, hedonistic, sometimes even very harmful. Even in favorable conditions, purely biological sociality in man is incapable of ascending to the heights of sublime love.

For all these reasons *the unconscious forces in man cannot serve as the fountainhead of the most intense, universal, pure, durable, and adequate love.* When properly controlled by the conscious and the supraconscious forces, these unconscious drives can greatly reinforce and fuel the energy of love, but alone they can deliver only haphazard and erratic altruistic deeds of a low degree, interspersed by similarly erratic deeds of hate and enmity. Since neither the conscious nor the unconscious forces alone can be the fountainhead of the supreme altruistic actions discharged by the altruistic geniuses, the only source of such deeds and geniuses therefore can be the supraconscious in man. Only persons blessed by such an energy apparently can be eminent creators in the field of love as well as in the field of truth and beauty. The logical reasons and the four series of factual evidence given make our hypothesis fairly probable. In the light of this total evidence it seems to be true that indeed *no supreme love behavior can occur without the supraconscious energy in action.*

All the debunking attempts to degrade the supraconscious to the level of autohypnosis do not stand the slightest test: there have been millions of individuals, especially among the patients of psychopathic hospitals, who have experienced various forms of autohypnosis and similar pathological states of mind. And yet, none of them has achieved any significant creative results in any creative field, including moral creativity. This fact alone is sufficient for invalidation of all theories of this kind. No real theory can identify moron with genius and the supraconscious with autohypnosis or other pathological states of mind.

Let us now inquire how the supraconscious has been awakened and developed, how it has operated in the apostles of supreme love, and what techniques have helped them in activating it in their own personalities.

*Chapter Nine*

# Three Types of Altruists and Three Courses of Altruistic Growth

I

## OUR DARK IGNORANCE OF THE PROBLEM

Altruistic growth or transfiguration of the eminent apostles of love ordinarily begins with the operation of self-identification with the supra-conscious.  As soon as one begins to study this process, one is confronted with many dark and baffling problems.  The mystery of altruistic genius is a case of the mystery of creative genius generally.  We little know why some individuals become Beethovens and Bachs, Phidiases and Michel-angelos, Platos and Newtons, Christs and Buddhas, while others go through life without creating anything great, and still others become subnormal mental cases.  Likewise, we are largely ignorant of the reason why at a given period one cultural group or nation becomes greatly creative, while at another period the same nation or group shows itself strikingly sterile.  Why out of many ethnic groups do only a few be-come creative, while many others pass through their historical life span without notable creative accomplishments?  Why does one group dis-tinguish itself by creativity in science, another in music, and a third in religion?  Why does the leadership in this or that creativity shift in the course of time from one group to another, and why is this other now group A, now group C, now group M, but not group B, or N, or X? [1]

And we know even less about why and how some individuals become altruistic geniuses, while others distinguish themselves only by the rudest selfishness.

What is known about these problems is fairly thin, fragmentary, and uncertain.  We can mention, for instance, *five factors of supreme crea-tivity* whose constellation is necessary for an individual or a group to be-come eminently creative: 1. a favorable biological heredity or, in other terms, " creative grace," " spiritual grace," " genius," etc.; 2. an urgent sense of need for a great new creation, invention, or discovery in a given individual or/and group; 3. the exposure of an individual or group to the cross-currents of different ideas, beliefs, patterns, and values relevant to the new creation, invention, or discovery; 4. cultural freedom; 5. good luck, especially in the form of an event that serves as a spark for the subsequent creative process.[2]

Granting that each of these factors is necessary for a notable creative process, this still helps little in the matter. The factors of fortunate heredity (or creative grace) and of good luck remain as unpredictable and mysterious as the mystery of creativity itself. On the basis of existing knowledge, we cannot predict (with the exception of organically defective newborn babies) which of a given group of babies has "fortunate" or "unfortunate" heredity, "creative grace" or "creative sterility," "good luck" or "bad luck." Likewise, existing knowledge cannot satisfactorily explain why most of the Australian tribes did not create a great civilization, while the Egyptians and Babylonians, Greeks and Romans, and a few other groups did. Why did each of these "historical nations" display an exuberance of creativity at one period, and creative sterility at another? [3]

In the field of supreme creativity, the supraconscious seemingly blowest where it willest. This is also true of supreme, creative love. We know little how it is awakened and developed, and we cannot predict when or whom the supraconscious grace will visit and empower to soar to the summits of creative love.

All that we can do in deciphering the mystery of its awakening is to observe the conditions in which it occurs and the technical ways of the eminent altruists. Such an observation supplies us at least with some knowledge about where, when, in what conditions, how frequently, and through what techniques supraconscious love has been generated and developed, until it overflowingly filled the life, mind, and activities of its apostles. Since these conditions and techniques have proved efficacious with these great men, they may prove to be helpful also with others potentially capable of sublime altruism.

Let us then observe some of these conditions and techniques, as far as they are supplied by the life histories and operations of altruistic geniuses. The inventory will certainly be incomplete, but even an incomplete inventory is better than no inventory at all, as the situation is at the present time.

## II

### The Meaning of Self-Identification with the Supraconscious

As mentioned before, one of the first operations of eminent altruists in their strivings towards and their practice of sublime love is purely ideological self-identification with the supraconscious. Widely varying in forms and details, the *essential part of this procedure consists in a progressively growing awareness by the maturing altruists that their true self is neither their body, nor their unconscious, subconscious, or preconscious energy, nor their bioconscious or socioconscious egos with all their trappings, but rather the supraconscious, whatever name and properties they give to it. The supraconscious is the embodiment of the altruist's very highest ideal. It is his highest value.* In this sense it is his Absolute. As to the name, the supraconscious is called by widely different names by various altruists.

1. The most common name for it is that of God or the equivalent, in personified and transpersonal forms: God, Tao, Chit, Jen, Nirvana, Jehova, Ahura-Mazda, Indra, Vishnu, Brahma, Siva, Buddha, God the Father, God the Son, Holy Ghost, Jesus, Allah, Osiris, and so on.

2. Another common name is a term derivative from the name of God and the equivalent: the Divine, the Absolute, the Divine Madness, the Oversoul, the Soul of the World, the Spirit, Heaven, Logos, Sophia, Soul, Atman, and others.

3. Often the supraconscious is called by various abstract metaphysical or mystic terms: the Supra-Essence, the Ever-Living Fire, the Ever-Progenitive Nature, the Infinite Manifold, the Ground, the *coincidentia oppositorum*, the Inexpressible, the Nameless, the Divine Nothing, and so on.

4. Frequently it is called by diverse psychological and ethical terms: genius, inspiration, categoric imperative, moral duty, call of conscience, inner voice, highest social responsibility, social instinct or sentiment, gregarious or paternal instinct, noblest and highest ego, superego, and so on. On the part of the atheistic altruists (see further about them), their highest ideal and value is often called by various "prosaic" names: the greatest happiness, the greatest good, the main pleasure, the most important social value, the deepest emotional drive, the greatest social need, libido, life energy, and the like. These terms denote in such cases something far transcending their literal meaning. In these denotations and connotations the term *matter* often means about the same as the term *God*, for a believer; the term *life energy* becomes co-identical with that of the *supraconscious;* and so on.

Each of these classes of names is usually symbolized by various visible or audible or sense-perceived signs, as for instance, the symbol of the "eye in a triangle" in Christian churches, the shriyantra in Hindu religious art, the cosmic lotus in Buddhism, and hundreds of other religious and secular symbols denoting the supraconscious in its various names and representations.[4]

Self-identification with the supraconscious does not mean a mere intellectual self-assertion or rational conclusion that my true "soul," my "ego," my "self," my "I" or "me" is identical with the supraconscious in whatever concrete form I as a given individual conceive it. Such a purely intellectual conclusion is only one of the first steps in altruistic growth. To be effective the self-identification must be not only ideological but also behavioral, practiced in overt actions, and manifest in the set of egos, the values, and group affiliations of the individual. Self-identification in this tangible form means a very difficult operation, sometimes demanding years of strenuous effort. Before it can reach this full development, however, self-identification has to be started and somehow cultivated at its earliest stage when it is as yet weak and powerless. Therefore, our study of the techniques of self-identification will begin with a deeper analysis of this early phase. How is it started? In what conditions? Through what forces? What actions are done to start and to keep it going? These and a host of other questions are to be cleared in order that we may know the nature, the techniques — the *why* and *how* — of self-identification.

## III

### THREE TYPES OF ALTRUISTS AND SELF-IDENTIFICATIONS

At the outset of our analysis three different types of eminent altruists must be pointed out. One can be called "the early-fortunate," another "the late-matured" or "the late-catastrophic," the third "the intermediary" type. Some eminent altruists show themselves altruistic from the earliest years of their life. Whether through the good fortune of being born and reared in a good family or through other conditions favorable for altruistic development (this will be discussed further), such altruists show themselves identified with the supraconscious at their earliest age. Their set of egos, system of values, and group affiliations corresponds to this self-identification and needs no basic change; but only its unfolding and development. Such individuals are loving and friendly from childhood. In the course of time they grow graciously in their love behavior, without any catastrophic conversion or sharp change in their egos, values, or group membership. And so they continue on up to their death. They can be called the "*fortunate altruists*."

Their development is similar to the growth of beautiful plants: from their seeds they silently grow, quietly flower and bear fruit, without convulsions and serious crises. No difficulty seems to be formidable for these geniuses of goodness. The initial creative force carries them through all obstacles "on the wings of love," as it carried Mozart or Schubert through seemingly insurmountable impediments to their musical creativity.

Notably different is the life course of the "*late altruists*." Here there is a sharp turning point that divides their life into two parts: pre-altruistic

and altruistic. In the life of some late altruists the sharp turn is marked
by a catastrophic precipitant. Before their "conversion" they do not
display any sublime love; some exhibit even a conspicuous egoism.
Their system of egos, values, and group affiliations is notably different
before and after the turning point. The period of change in their life
consists of a painful and difficult process of basic reintegration of their
unconscious drives, conscious egos, values, group affiliations, and their
overt behavior. Sometimes this reintegrative phase is comparatively
short; sometimes it is long.

Finally, the "*intermediary type*" of altruists and of self-identification is
in between the early and the late types. As such, it is marked by the characteristics that in milder form belong to both extreme types. Being
intermediary, this type has gradations: some of its representatives are
nearer to the early type; some others are more like the late type. After
these preliminary sketches of each type, let us look closer at their real
representatives and at the first steps in self-identification of these representatives with the supraconscious.

## IV

### VIRTUOSI TECHNIQUES OF THE FORTUNATE ALTRUISTS

We begin with the techniques and methods of self-identification of the
early-fortunate altruists. A. Schweitzer (1875–     ), Damien the Leper
(1840–1889), John Woolman (1720–1772), Dr. T. Haas (1780–1853),
Serafim of Sarov (1759–1833), Francis de Sales (1567–1622), St. Tychon
(1724–1783), B. Franklin (1706–1790), Henri Lasserre (1878–1945), and
many others — including the majority of the living American Good
Neighbors and the Christian Catholic and Russian Orthodox Saints in
my study — are the examples of the fortunate altruists.[5] Reading their
autobiographies and biographies, letters and other sources, one does not
come upon any catastrophe or event after which their mind and conduct
suddenly become notably different.

One meets some events which seemingly accelerated the process of
altruization, but this process was already under way before the event.
Thus, John Woolman mentions killing a robin, after which he "was
seized with horror, at having killed an innocent creature." He also tells
of his "undutiful reply" to his mother, and finally of the sickness which
filled him first with confusion and distress and then "in the multitude of
God's mercies I found inward relief."[6] But before he was even seven
years old, he already was "acquainted with the operations of Divine
love."[7] The mentioned incidents in Woolman's life seemingly only reinforced and facilitated the course of altruization already in full flow
instead of creating it or radically changing the direction of his life.

The whole process of altruistic growth, as in the case of Woolman and other altruistic Quakers,[8] has certain typical stages. These are: 1. " divine revelation in childhood "; 2. uneasiness over youthful frivolity; 3. search with slight conflicts; 4. convincement; 5. conversion; 6. period of discouragement; 7. entrance upon ministry; 8. simplification of dress and manner of living; 9. curtailment of successful business and liberation from all " superfluities of life "; 10. advocacy of social reforms and active service to all the needy.[9] This whole process does not have any great breaks or sharp turning points. All ten stages are factually one continuous, steady, and fairly even development of altruization or self-identification with the supraconscious.

The same process can be said to have developed at the time of the death of Dr. Haas's father in 1814;[10] or in the stirring of A. Schweitzer's early altruistic sensibilities and at similar periods in the life histories of this type of altruist. These individuals seem to have been born and reared in an environment that developed their altruistic or spiritual propensities early. While their early " package " of harmonious egos, centered around one supreme value and group, dictated to them altruistic conduct, their altruistic conduct in its turn reinforced their self-identification with the supraconscious. This incessant interplay explains *their harmonious spiritual and moral growth in the course of their life, and their ability to make a vital decision and sacrifice, almost at a moment's notice.*

Damien the Leper gives an example of such spontaneous action. When the bishop called for a volunteer to go to and remain for life amidst the Molokai lepers (with the certainty of the volunteer's becoming a leper himself), this was a call for a truly momentous sacrifice. " As the Bishop said this, his voice faltered. Even he could not demand such a sacrifice of anybody." " No sooner were his words ended, when four priests, one of whom was Damien, sprang to their feet and pleaded to be allowed to live and work among the lepers." Without any hesitation, Damien pleaded for the privilege of this " slow death sentence " to be granted to him. Within a few moments " the affair was settled," with the bishop pronouncing the death sentence " in a low and trembling voice ": " This employment is of such a nature that I would not have imposed it on anyone, but I gladly accept your offer." [11]

Not many ordinary men can make such a decision at a moment's notice. When it is done, it becomes a " pregnant event " whose consequences decisively chart the subsequent life of such an altruist.

Take Albert Schweitzer. Quietly he makes the momentous decision that when he reaches thirty years of age, he will leave his most successful scholarly, artistic, and other creative activities, with their popularity and fortune, and will bury himself for the rest of his life in African jungles in order to serve preliterate natives as their physical, mental, and moral doctor. Very few men, if any, would be willing to do this even after a long period of consideration — and especially to do it "light-heartedly," without feeling the enormity of the sacrifice. Schweitzer did it seemingly "easily," naturally, without any "sense of tragedy of ruined life." From his boyhood he had felt that he was somehow not entitled to have comforts and luxuries which others could not have. " It struck me as incomprehensible that I should be allowed to lead such a happy life, while I saw so many people around me wrestling with care and suffering." This idea never left him during all the happy years of his studentship and distinguished scholarly and artistic activities.

" Then one brilliant summer morning [in 1896] there came to me, as I awoke, the thought that I must not accept this happiness as a matter of course, but must give something in return for it. Proceeding to think the matter out at once with calm deliberation, while the birds were singing outside, I settled with myself before I got up, that I would consider my-self justified in living till I was thirty for science and art, in order to de-vote myself from that time forward to the direct service of humanity. Many a time already had I tried to settle what meaning lay hidden for me in the saying of Jesus: 'Whosoever would save his life shall lose it, and whosoever shall lose his life for My sake and the Gospel shall save it.' Now the answer was found. In addition to the outward, I now had inward happiness."

Quietly following this decision, in 1905 he entered medical school and then became " a jungle doctor," to the astonishment of the public and many of his friends who tried to persuade him not to ruin his bril-liant life career.[12]

A similar picture is given by the life histories of Serafim of Sarov and of Dr. T. Haas. Born in the pious family of a building contractor, Serafim early showed his religiosity. " The building of the Church to the Mother of God in Kursk by his mother was one of the child's early memories; he played about the growing structure." At the age of ten, during his sickness, he had a vision of the Mother of God who promised his rapid recovery. From that age on, he voraciously read the Bible and other religious books. At the age of seventeen he took a vow of chastity and went as a pilgrim to the famous Kiev Pechersky monastery. Two years later, blessed by his mother and friends, he entered the Sarov monastery and stayed there for fifty-five years. The first few years he lived together with the other brethren; then he spent several years in eremitic isolation as an ascetic, silent person, living on herbs, and spending his time in prayer and meditation, " accumulating the grace of the Holy Ghost." During these years his self-identification with God was ac-complished. After many years of this training he returned to the world and marvelously served it in love. Beginning with members of the Czarist family and ending with criminals, the sick, the insane, the un-happy, the psychoneurotics, thousands and thousands flocked to him in order to receive wise counsel, recovery from mental, moral, and physical illness, consolation in sorrow, enlightenment in confusion, or help in tragedy. At the age of 74, in a kneeling position of prayer, he quietly fell asleep forever.[13]

Dr. Haas started life with an integrated constellation of egos and "self," identified with Christian love. He became an eminent physician and served humanity, especially the poor, in the way of love. Then he concentrated his altruistic activity upon the physical, moral, and mental improvement of criminals and the general amelioration of the conditions of prisons and punishment. He spent his life in this task, giving to it all his time, energy, money — everything he had. No conflict of values and egos, no inner split, no "precipitants," and no "conversion" mark the life of either Serafim or Haas.[14]

The same is true of John Woolman. Early integrated in his egos, values, and groups, early self-identified with the God of Love, he quietly grows in his altruism and seemingly easily eliminates all the conflicting values, egos, and groups that life confonts him with: he refuses to write a will for a neighbor who wants to will his slaves; he liquidates and gives up his prosperous business in order not to be engulfed in "superfluities"; he works for the abolition of slavery; he frees himself from membership in groups and values contradictory to his supreme value. And so he quietly grows in his "inward life, wherein the heart doth love and reverence God; learns to exercise true justice and goodness, not only toward all men but also toward the brute creatures." [15]

Similar is the course of St. Francis de Sales' self-identification with the God of Love and Joy. His childhood was a happy one, a fact due especially to his loving and pious mother. Though the child of a Catholic family living amidst a Protestant population, he early displayed his values and egos well harmonized with each other through their subordination to the supreme value — God — and through his affiliation with mutually harmonious Catholic groups. In his early childhood, at school in Paris, he clearly showed his specific "cheerful religiosity." From an early age, his God was the loving God of Joy and not the God of vengeance, mortification, and cruel punishment. In regard to man, his religiosity demanded mainly love of God and a cultivation of the whole man — his body and his mind — in the highest values of the true, the good, and the beautiful. *Libido sciendi, vivendi, sentiendi* was his motto from the earliest age up to his last moment. In his teens, when he was living in Paris as a student of the Clermont college, he had for about six months an inner struggle between the strong temptations of worldly values and his ethico-religious aspirations. This struggle for a time undermined even his health; but finally the inner conflict was terminated by his vow of chastity and his decision to devote himself to the "service to souls." His self-identification with the God of Joy and Love was accomplished, and his character as a *humaniste, gentilhomme, un homme du monde, un être sensible et bon* (as a humanist, a well-cultured man of the world, a good and sensible man) came out clearly and remained for the rest of his devout and altruistic life. No sharp turn and no catastrophic tragedy mark the whole course of his life. It appears, again, as a steady unfolding of the same trend, from his earliest years up to his death.[16]

Though in his childhood St. Tychon lived in extreme poverty (his father, a mere "reader" in a poor church, died soon after Tychon's birth) the boy was graced by the love of his mother, brothers, and sisters, and by the kindness of their neighbors, especially of the mail-coachman, who wanted to adopt him. Except perhaps for the brief period of decision as to whether or not he was to be given for the adoption, no catastrophes are recorded in his childhood. He worked from an early age as a hired hand and farm laborer to earn his bread, and from the beginning he showed his pious inclination. When a theological school was opened in the neighborhood, as a son of a cleric, he entered it; still struggling with poverty, he quietly grew in his studies, religiosity, and kindness. His subsequent life was but a gradual unfolding of this trend through his official progression from abbot of a monastery to rector of a theological seminary and then to bishop. He finally became a semi-eremitic recluse in the poorest cell of the Zadonsk monastery, helping many needy people with both material and spiritual blessings. Once in a while there were moments of melancholy but they were short, few, and caused mainly by doubts as to whether he had not missed his true vocation of rendering the greatest possible service to God and human beings. Otherwise, the main trend of his self-identification with the God of Love is free from any sharp turn or a "before and after the conversion." [17]

Benjamin Franklin represents a secular type of a good person, altruistic above the level of his contemporaries. Viewed as such he belongs to the fortunate type of altruist. His life course is also free from a sharp or disruptive turn. It represents a steady development of an inquisitive and inventive mind, of a rational and moral utilitarian at his best, of a good and helpful fellow citizen.

He himself stresses this by calling his life "felicitous" and "happy."

That felicity has induced me sometimes to say, that were it offered to my choice, I should have no objection to a repetition of the same life from its beginning, only asking the advantages authors have in a second edition to correct some faults of the first. . . . But though this were denied, I should still accept the offer.

He had, of course, some conflicts with his elder brothers and with a few other persons, but all these "sinister accidents" were peripheral and short-lived. In no way did they make his life unhappy, uneven, or catastrophic.

And now I speak of thanking God, I desire with all humility to acknowledge that I owe the mentioned happiness of my past life to His kind providence, which led me to the means I used and gave them success.[18]

Coming from a family circle prominent for its notable contribution to
many good causes — among them participation in the foundation of the
Red Cross and amelioration of the conditions of labor — Henri Lasserre
belongs also to the fortunate altruists. From an early age up to his death
in 1945 he worked creatively for the great cause of integral co-operation,
giving to it his fortune, energy, and time. His ultimate goal was the
Christian society based upon the principles of the Sermon on the Mount
not only preached but practiced. "*Live* your Christian brotherhood. . . . The *deeds* of Christianity unite men in true fellowship, the
*words* of Christianity [hypocritically paraded, but not practiced] have
in them the seeds of discord and division." He agrees that "the individuals must give themselves to the highest Cause which is God, or
unity or love," leaving each individual to realize this along the principles of the Sermon on the Mount.[19]

My own study of the living American Good Neighbors shows that
among them an overwhelming majority belong to this fortunate type of
altruist, while only 3 per cent belong to the late-converted, catastrophic
type, and some 10 to 12 per cent to the intermediary type. A study
of all Christian Catholic and Russian Orthodox Saints shows that 43.0 per
cent of the Catholic Christian and 69.9 per cent of the Russian Orthodox
Saints were the fortunate type of altruist, the rest of the percentage being
either the late-converted or intermediary or "martyr" types.[20]

The above material gives a fairly clear idea of the fortunate type of altruists and of their self-identification with the highest value of love. First,
from their earliest childhood they display a harmonious constellation of
drives, egos, and values; second, this constellation appears to be subordinated to the highest value with which they self-identify themselves; third,
their main affiliations with social groups happen to be free from sharp
mutual conflicts. In the course of their lives they naturally make some
changes in their group affiliations, but these changes are neither notably
painful, nor greatly contrasting in the groups changed. They are changes
in congenial group affiliations rather than in opposite ones; the differences
between the membership groups dropped and those newly taken are
rather small. Often the new groups represent a logical substitute at the
altruist's later age for a similar group of his earlier age. In the life histories of the typical representatives of the fortunate altruists we rarely
meet with tragic or dramatic scenes in the change of their group affiliations. As we shall see, however, such dramas and tragedies are fairly ordinary in the course of life of the late-catastrophic altruists.

What perhaps is most important about the fortunate altruists is the fact
that notwithstanding temporary "black hours," especially at the begin-

ning of their conscious service, the more they seemingly sacrifice, the happier they become. They seem to say what Athanasius, Archbishop of Alexandria, said of St. Anthony: "Let no one who hath renounced the world think that he hath given up some great thing . . . the whole earth set over against heaven's infinite is scant and poor." [21]

## V

### THE TECHNIQUES OF SELF-IDENTIFICATION OF THE LATE-CONVERTED AND CATASTROPHIC ALTRUISTS

Other eminent altruists are less "fortunate." They begin their lives with their egos, values, and groups either poorly integrated or wrongly integrated around egoistic and Sensate values. *They eventually pass through sharp crises of disintegration and reintegration,* shocked or not by "a precipitant." They have to redefine their identification with the supreme value, to rearrange their egos and group affiliations, and only after a short or long, sharp or mild, but always painful stage of depression, disillusionment, hesitation, inner struggle, and "dark hours" do they succeed in performing the above triple operation. Such seems to have been the spiritual and altruistic career of many eminent and ordinary altruists. Here are several examples of this type.

*Gautama Buddha* (563?–483?) found himself at an early age torn between opposing egos, values, and groups. On the one hand, there were the Sensate (hedonistic) egos, values, and groups — the wife, the family, and the court of his father with its multitude of Sensate distractions, worldly values, and groups. On the other hand, at an early age in his culture there appeared the imperishable values of Brahman, Atman, or Self, free from the sorrows of death, disease, and old age, and there emerged a need for group affiliations that demanded a realization of these eternal values and self-identification with the immortal Self.

This inner conflict of egos, values, and group affiliations lasted for several years, until it seemingly became unbearable and resulted in Buddha's leaving his court, his wife and child. This was an abrupt breaking of most of his group ties, and the dropping of most of his values. He became a wanderer in search of a new self-identification. In this way the process of reintegration of his egos, values, and group affiliations began.

"I have left my home to seek some way of rescue [from the sorrows of old age, disease, and death, and the impermanency of all Sensate values]. I search for the happiness of something that decays not, that never perishes, that never knows beginning, that looks with equal mind on enemy and friend, that needs not wealth nor beauty, the happiness of one who finds repose alone in solitude, all thoughts about the world destroyed." "Separation and association." [22] Having thus broken all his ties with his previous groups, values, and egos, Buddha, an itinerant wanderer, spent many years in his efforts to reintegrate his new egos, values, and group memberships. He tried to identify himself with the values and groups of ascetic hermits and self-torturers. Finding their way of salvation hopeless, he then tried to find the way out in the worldly-wise groups who preach the advisability of sowing wild oats in youth, then settling down, marrying, becoming rich, and at old age turning ritualistically religious. This way was also hopeless. And so were several other ways experimentally tried by Buddha. None of these groups and values could satisfy him. Finally, he found the "Enlightenment and Illumination," that completed his self-identification with the suprarational and suprasensory nirvana, with a corresponding rearrangement of all his egos, values, and group affiliations. This led him to the liberation through "giving up" all group affiliations except a small group of his disciples and all living creatures, all egos, and all Sensate values.

The restless busy nature of the world this I declare is at the root of pain. Stop then the end by choking up the source [that is, the belief in the reality of sensations, perceptions, objects, substances, even God, soul, personality, names, things, and ego]. Desire not either life or its opposite. All is empty. Neither "self" nor place for self, but all the world like a phantasy, this is the way to Nirvana.[23]

"I have no master; no honorable tribe; no point of excellence; self-taught in this profoundest doctrine, I have arrived at superhuman wisdom. . . . Wealth, riches, self all given up; unnamed, I still am named 'Righteous master.'"[24] So Buddha sums up the total triple operation of reintegration of his egos, values, and group affiliations (which resulted in severing ties with all groups except the small group of the recluse-disciples);[25] reidentification of himself and of the disciples with the supreme value of nirvana.

As in many similar cases, many trial and error efforts were made and many extreme techniques were tried, before the operation was satisfactorily completed.

*St. Francis of Assisi* (1182–1226). Still sharper and clearer is the triple operation in the transfiguration of Giovanni Bernardone into St. Francis of Assisi. After spending his youth in merry banqueting and festivals, dissipation and vainglory, his transfiguration began at the age of twenty-two years, and took about two years to be completed. As "precipitants" of his conversion several painful events served. Among these was his short participation in war and the life of a military prisoner for about one year, after which he "returned home and took up again his life of good cheer as of old."[26] As a result of too many "fetes, games, festivals, and dissipation" after his return home from imprisonment, he fell gravely ill. "For long weeks he looked death so closely in the face that the physical crisis brought about a moral one." During the long convalescence "the miserable emptiness of his life suddenly appeared before him." " He was seized with a disgust of himself, his former ambitions seemed to him ridiculous or despicable." [27]

In this way a conflict of his egos, values, and group affiliations was started. In this conflict the influence of his loving mother gave an example of love that lives under all conditions. A companion in his walks, one of the spiritual " Brothers of Love," and a poor priest, planted in their conversations with Francis the idea of serving God, humanity, and the whole world by love, humility, and poverty. However, a series of new blows were necessary in order that the process of reintegration could be about completed in its preliminary stage. In spite of his inner conflict he returned again to his previous life of dissipation; but " the joy in his heart was dead. . . . At every day his restiveness grew." [28] He attempted to get glory for his old egos through a military action (" I shall come back a great knight "). He strangely failed in this and was ridiculed, especially by the nobles whom he tried to imitate.

From then on a quest for solitude appeared and increased, and more and more he frequented a deserted cave alone. Once more, however, he returned to the banquets and festivities, but now they gave him no joy. At the beginning vague and nonintentional, his self-identification with the God of Love, humility, and poverty grew spontaneously until, after one of the night banquets, being moody and asked by one of his merry companions what he was dreaming about, perhaps about marriage, he answered to his own and his companion's amazement: " You are right. I intend to be married, but to a lady purer and more lovely than you have ever seen. Her name is Lady Poverty." " This answer came over his lips without his consent. It had usurped power over his will, for he had not thought of saying what he said." [29]

" This reply marks a decisive stage in his inner life. By it he cut the last links which bound him to trivial pleasures." [30] It also terminated his affiliations with most of the " merry-making " groups of the preceding period of his life.

This decision notably changed his behavior. Among other things he began often to give merchandise of his father to the poor and to sell it for money to rebuild a dilapidated church. His father strongly objected to this, and a violent conflict between Giovanni and his father followed.

The scene in the court where he was brought by his father dramatically sums up the situation. At the advice of the presiding bishop that he give up all his property, St. Francis " retired to a room in the bishop's palace, and immediately reappeared absolutely naked, holding in his hand the packet into which he had rolled his clothes." He laid down this only property of his and said: " Until this time I have called Pietro Bernardone my father, but now I desire to serve God. This is why I return to him this money and clothing and all that I have had from him, for from henceforth I desire to say nothing else than ' Our Father, who art in heaven.' " [31] This completed cutting all his affiliations with previous groups, even his own family. Reintegration of all his previous egos and values was effected and self-identification with the God of Love and Lady Poverty. Giovanni Bernardone was now transfigured into St. Francis.

His self-identification with poverty and the God of Love was cemented by a few subsequent actions of St. Francis. These impulsive actions were, in fact, ingenious inventions of effective techniques for self-altruization.

One day while riding a horse he met a leper. His first reaction was to give his horse the spur, to avoid the horrible encounter with the leprosy-eaten individual. Instead of following this natural impulse, the next moment — under some influence — he stepped down off his horse, embraced the leper and kissed the repulsive open sores of the leper's hand. After that, every day he entered the Lazarists' house of the lepers and helped them as their brother and servant.[32] This incident must have been decisive, because St. Francis himself in his *Testament* or *Will* specially mentions it. " When I lived in sin, it was very painful for me to see lepers, but God himself led me into their midst, and I remained there for a while. When I left them, that which had seemed to me bitter had become sweet and easy." [33] This action was followed by St. Francis' giving up everything, putting on the rags of a beggar, eating (deliberately) the poorest food, living in a grotto or anywhere he could " lay down his head," and depriving himself of all comfort. At the same time he strained what he called his " donkey-body " or " brother-body " to the utmost limit in rebuilding the St. Damien Church entirely by himself; courageously withstood the insults, mockery, and persecution of his former fellow townsmen; and he did all this with songs and cheerfulness. These actions indeed cemented the transformation of Giovanni Bernardone into St. Francis, into the ever-singing Knight of Lady Poverty, the joyful " troubadour of God," the ever-cheerful " jester of Lord," (*jongleur de Dieu*), " Brother " to the Sun, the Moon, Hunger, Fatigue, to all human beings, to all animals, and the whole world.

The self-identification was firmly established and began decisively to determine his whole life — all his actions, feelings, emotions, volitions, and ideas.

*Brother Joseph (Ira Dutton) (1843–1931).* Up to about his thirty-ninth year of life, Wisconsin-born Ira Dutton did not exhibit any extraordinary altruism. His unhappy marriage, in 1866, to a woman who proved to be unfaithful and who in 1867 ran away with another man, deeply disturbed his life and ushered into it the " secret years " of Ira Dutton. (For fourteen years, up to 1881, he took no action for divorcing his wife. Only in 1881 did he divorce her, charging her with adultery.) He himself describes these years as a period of " a truly dual life that I lived. At night there would be one sort of associations, and then by day a care for sobriety and respectable company." [34]   His greatest vice of these " secret years " seemingly was his heavy drinking, with " its attendant folly."

Perhaps I never injured anyone but myself; but I was subject to various follies that attend the use of strong drink, a habit acquired in this reckless period.

Then, on July 4, 1876, he took " a voluntary, private vow: my declaration of independence. . . . A declaration against John Barleycorn. Since that, I have kept my vow, being free of intoxicants and of all the attendant folly; " " never felt any desire to use intoxicants after I stopped." Beginning with this date, " the idea of doing penance " to " Almighty God " for " the wicked capers I cut " entered his mind, and he started his self-identification with the supraconscious (God) and Love. As to the factors that started this new epoch in his life, he says that he " cannot recall any particular incident that caused me to change my life; think it was a shame for acting so among capable, sober, well-balanced men, and feeling that having even a little authority I should have a clear head, and feeling so mean after my sober Civil War record. Anyway, I determined to kick John Barleycorn out of my house, and so it was." [35]

Perhaps Dutton's appointment in 1875 as a War Department investigating agent; then the influence of a few close friends, especially Mrs. Benedict J. Seemes, with whom Dutton quite frankly discussed his troubles, and received the heartfelt advice and first suggestions about starting a new life; then strong health, participation in the Civil War, and a rather orderly life before his " secret years ": perhaps these were additional factors of Dutton's liberation from alcoholism and its attendant follies.

This vow and freedom from alcoholic folly were his first decisive steps in the self-identification with the religious and moral supraconscious: God and the duty " to get along with everyone, to ask no special favor, not to make anyone the slightest difficulty that I could reasonably avoid, and to do what I could to help my neighbor in every way." [36]

After that, still discharging his governmental and business duties, he began to visit churches of various denominations, to compare their beliefs, to talk of his " wild years " and " sinful capers," and to do the work " of penance for the rest of my years." In 1882 " I decided that the penitential system of the Catholic Church was best suited for my condition. [His family and he in his early life were Protestant.] After a daily study of the catechism for a month . . . I was received into the Church on my fortieth birthday, April 27, 1883."

Simultaneously with this conversion he also changed his name from Ira to Joseph. " I always had a special respect for the name of Saint Joseph. . . . At the close of 1883 I was disposed to be a new person, Joseph Dutton, a servant of our Lord; so reverently laying aside the ' Ira B.,' I was Joseph, stepping out to a new life." [37]

In the same year, 1883, he terminated his government service and started the life of a penitent. As such he entered first (but never took the monastic vow) the Trappist monastery at Gethsemane, Kentucky. The Trappist order attracted him by the ascetic severity of its monastic life. After some twenty months of staying there, however, he realized that the Trappist *life of contemplation* did not meet his desire for a severe, penitent *life of action*. As a result, he left the monastery and after several explorations, *incidentally* heard about the work of Father Damien in the Molokai colony of lepers.

" It was in the New Orleans convent, in the reading room, that I saw for the first time the mention of Father Damien — a brief item in an old-time Catholic paper about the Molokai and the Father. I had never heard of him. Why this *suddenly impressed me with the certainty* that I had found my real vocation, I have never tried to elucidate; but have acted as if there were need only to go ahead, leaving the whys and wherefores to any who like such problems." [38] (Note again how unforeseen and unplanned the event was, and how instantaneously the decision was made with a feeling of complete certainty that this was the vocation looked for.)

Brother Joseph (as he was called now, though he never took any monastic vow) quickly rounded up his affairs, and went to the isolated island of Molokai where the lepers' colony was situated. He stayed there and served the lepers for the remaining forty-four years of his life, taking no pay for his services, and contributing more than $10,000 of his own money to the colony. Without any publicity, without much of religious talk, unassumingly and quietly, he did the extremely difficult work of a good Samaritan for these long years, and earned indeed the halo of the " real brother to all."

After his vow against alcohol in 1876, and especially after his conversion into Catholicism, his self-identification with the God of Love was accomplished. Started by the precipitant of his unhappy marriage, the triple operation of self-identification in his case is crystally clear: the reintegration of his egos and values was followed hand in hand by a radical rearrangement of his group affiliations. The whole process took at least seven years, from 1876 to 1883, in his case.

*St. Ignatius Loyola* (1491 or 1495–1556). St. Ignatius tells in his *Autobiography* that up to the age of twenty-six years he was given to the vanities of the world and particularly to the military glory and courtly ambitions. On May 20, 1521, while defending the fortress of Pampelune against the French, he was severely wounded: the bone of one leg was broken by a cannon ball and the other leg was seriously mutilated. He underwent two painful operations. For some time his life was in the balance, and the subsequent convalescing period lasted several months.[39]

During this convalescence his self-identification with the supraconscious

— Christ, Our Lady, chastity, poverty, humility, the ideals of St. Francis and St. Dominic — was started and practically completed, all in a period of about one year.

His long painful illness induced Ignatius's brooding over the why and wherefore of life and death. The first self-identification in this vague brooding occurred around June 28th. His illness turned out to be so serious that around this time his life was in balance and doctors had practically no hope for his survival. June 28th was the vigil of the feast of St. Peter and St. Paul, and Ignatius always had a particular reverence for St. Peter. On that day the crisis came and was followed by subsequent recovery. Ignatius ascribed the recovery to the intercession of St. Peter. In this way the first step in the self-identification with the supraconscious was taken, or rather occurred: unplanned and unforeseen.[40] The next step also occurred *incidentally*, rather than being intentionally arranged.

As the convalescence was slow, in order to pass the time Ignatius asked for books of adventures of knights errant and of chivalrous romances — the only entertaining novels that existed at that time (like *Amadis of Gaul*, etc.). There happened to be none in the house. Instead, he was given a substantial volume, the *Life of Christ* by Ludolf of Saxony, and another book on the lives of saints (*Legenda Sanctorum Aurea*). He "frequently read" these books with an increasing pleasure, and often interrupted his reading by meditation on what he read. These books, especially the *Life of Christ*, quite definitely helped him to make another step in his self-identification.[41]

Though his dreams and thoughts on his sick bed often wandered to regions of romance, most lovely ladies, knightly exploits, and fame; though for several weeks he fluctuated between these worldly ambitions and pilgrimage to Jerusalem, barefoot and living on herbs; with the help of Jesus (as he says) the final victory was won by the ideals of the *Life of Christ*. Ignatius decided to "imitate Him in the three-fold way He trod — the way of poverty, humility, and hardship" (as it is said in the book) and to lead the life of St. Francis of Assisi or St. Dominic.[42]

The third step in this self-identification was made under the influence of a visitation by Our Lady with her Child in her arms. This happened during one of the sleepless nights in his convalescence. This vision greatly consoled him and "left him with such a disgust for all his previous life, and especially for all the lusts of the flesh . . . that beginning with that moment up to this present month of August, 1555, when this autobiography is being written" he never had known any temptation of the flesh.[43]

This step practically cemented his self-identification. It was followed by a radical rearrangement of his group affiliations. His membership in the courtly, military, and worldly groups was canceled, and memberships in new groups corresponding to his new self-identification were entered in. His immediate steps — the refusal to re-enter his promising military career, his penitential pilgrimage to the far-famed monastery of Montserrat, his complete confession immediately after his arrival in the monastery, his vow to the Virgin of perpetual chastity, his change of worldly clothes for the pilgrim's garb of sackcloth with the vow of perpetual poverty, his self-dedication to the life of St. Francis — all these steps were mere consequences of the already achieved self-identification. All these actions were performed within a period of one year from the moment of his being wounded. They completed his self-identification and made it the major factor determining his whole subsequent life, his thoughts and deeds.

*St. Augustine* (354–430). Much more protracted and slow was the conversion and self-identification of St. Augustine. Though from his childhood he was exposed to the Christian way of life and belief through the example and instruction of his Christian mother, Monica; though he earnestly strived for a satisfactory solution of the basic questions of life; though he tried to identify himself with the pagans, and the Manichaeans; only at the age of twenty-nine years did he finally choose Christianity as the highest value. But even this self-identification with the Christian God and system of values was only rather tentative and purely ideological; it was not behavioral, in spite of the powerful influence of his mother, of St. Ambrose, Simplicianus, and other agencies of Christianity. And even though he became a catechumen in the Christian church at the age of twenty-nine years, his effective self-identification with the Christian God and values did not become definite — i.e., not only ideological but also behavioral — until he was thirty-two.

The main reasons for this protraction were the temptations of flesh, wealth, honor, fame, vanity, and especially of sexual lust. He had neither rearranged his egos and values, nor changed his group-affiliations.

Though theoretically, in abstract, St. Augustine made an ideological self-identification with Christianity even earlier than his twenty-ninth year, the temptations of the world and the persisting set of egos, values, and membership in the worldly groups kept him from an actual, behavioral transfiguration.

When Thou didst on all sides shew me, that what Thou saidst was true, I, convicted by the truth, had nothing at all to answer, but only those dull and drowsy words, " Anon, anon," " presently," " leave me but a little." But " presently," had no present, and my " little while " went on for a long time; in vain I delighted in Thy law according to the inner man, when another law in my members, rebelled against the law of my mind, and led me captive under the law of sin which was in my members.[44]

I, wretched, most wretched, in the very commencement of my early youth had begged chastity of Thee, and said, " Give me chastity and continency, only not yet." For I feared lest Thou shouldest hear me soon, and soon cure me of the disease of concupiscence, which I wished to have satisfied, rather than extinguished.[45]

Even at the age of thirty-two, when "my desires no longer inflamed me, as of old, with hopes of honor and profit . . . still I was enthralled with the love of woman." [46] "The very toys of toys, and vanities of vanities, my ancient mistresses, still held me." [47]

The slow but steadily increasing drift of St. Augustine into Christianity was notably reinforced when he was thirty-two by several factors: by the public conversion into Christianity of Victorinus, a most powerful rhetorician of that time and influential councilor of statesmen and politicians; by the rapidly growing power of the Christian church; by the continued influence of his mother and that of Simplicianus; and by other forces pushing him towards final self-identification with God and the values of Christiantiy. The necessary final spark was the famous call: *Tolle lege*. One day he heard a voice of a boy or girl, seemingly from the neighboring house, chanting and repeating: *Take up and read; take up and read*. "Interpreting it to be no other than a command from God, to open the book, and read the first chapter I should find. . . . I seized [the volume of the Apostles], opened, and in silence read that section, on which my eyes first fell: 'Not in rioting and drunkenness, not in chambering and wantonness, not in strife and envying: but put ye on the Lord Jesus Christ, and make not provision for the flesh,' in concupiscence. No further would I read; nor needed I: for instantly at the end of this sentence, by a light as it were of serenity infused into my heart, all the darkness of doubt vanished away." [48]

Immediately St. Augustine communicated this to Alypius and his mother, Monica. After this his self-identification with God was established; and it led to a radical change of St. Augustine's mind, behavior, group affiliations, and total way of life. Unobtrusively and quietly, he vowed to devote his life to God, without delay abandoned the profession of rhetoric, retired to the country to prepare himself for the grace of baptism, was baptized with his son Adeodatus, and Alypius, and entered upon the religious life and moral activities of St. Augustine, the great Church Father.[49]

*Simone Weil* (1909–1943). Born in Paris in 1909, daughter of a Jewish doctor, Simone Weil was educated in the Lycée Duruy, and then received her *Agrégation* in Philosophy at the École Normale in 1931. "It was when she was appointed professor in the Lycée at Puy that she first became aware of the hardships suffered by the working classes." Like the unemployed, she tried to break up stones on the road by pickaxe and then became a factory worker. In this experimental way she found out that unemployment, the conditions of factory workers and even their employment all were highly harmful to their bodies and souls. These things made the workers serfs in a moral and mental sense. In this way, she " deliberately identified herself with the anonymous masses, their unhappiness entered into her soul and body. . . . As she said herself, this contact with misery destroyed her youth." [50]

From that time " she was always on the side of the vanquished and the oppressed." This unselfish self-identification with the underdog of any sort led her to participation in the Spanish Civil War; to political activities of the extreme left. Without belonging to any party, she defended the weak and the oppressed, making no distinction of race or opinion. Then she worked in the Free French Broadcasting services. All the time she tried to live under the conditions of self-imposed deprivation in order not to be privileged in comparison with the poorest classes.

The behavioral self-identification with the oppressed and the vanquished was followed eventually by her ideological and heartfelt identification with Christ, Christ's passion and his death, with the Son of God, Crucified. This and only this aspect of Christianity she accepted and lived by. Other aspects, especially the institutionalized forms of Christianity or of any other religion, including the Jewish, she, being a Jewess, harshly denounced as " tainted and horrible." For her " faith is to believe that God is love and nothing else. . . . Faith is to believe that reality is love and nothing else." Everything else, including theological dogmas and " the unconditional and global adherence to all that the Church teaches, has taught and will teach, which St. Thomas calls faith, is not faith, but social idolatry." " The spirit of truth is almost lacking entirely in religious life. . . ." Arguments in favor of official Christianity, she said, " sound like the slogans for ' Pink Pills for Pale People.' . . . To look for shelter or consolation in religion is error." " Religion as a source of consolation and of peace of mind becomes a sort of an advertised patent medicine." As such " it is an obstacle to true faith. In this sense atheism is a purification." [51]

Misery and deprivations ended Simone Weil's life at an early age. In her short life, however, she early achieved her self-identification with love and the God of Love and practiced it. This was paralleled by a corresponding reintegration of her egos, values, and group affiliations. She serves here as an example of a modern altruist, believing only in the God of Love and Sacrifice and harshly rejecting the dogmatic, ritualistic, and hierarchical paraphernalia of all religions and moralities.

*Sri Ramakrishna* (1836–1886). From an early age Ramakrishna seems to have had a constellation of somewhat integrated egos, values, and group affiliations, but it apparently had many " loose ends," was amorphous, and even self-contradictory. Side by side with his religious values of a Brahmin son, now and then he deviated into entertainment of men and women; into the semi-religious activities of an actor. He entered the Dakshineswar temple as a priest, violating the rules of Brahmins and in spite of their protest. He was often in the reprehensible company of persons with doubtful reputation and behavior; and so on. These conditions and obstacles made his transfiguration difficult and painful: for months and years he behaved like a real lunatic; had many dark hours; burned himself and his health up to the extent that he was brought to the brink of serious physical illness and mental disequilibrium. He was ready to commit suicide.

Only after some twelve years of strenuous, strange (for us), and certainly torturous efforts, the process of a complete reintegration of his egos, values, and groups, a cutting of all ties with contradictory groups, an identification with God in His various forms (personal, Kali or Divine Mother, and impersonal), was concluded. "Oh, what days of suffering I passed through! " he used to say later on to his disciples. "You cannot imagine my agony at separation from [the Divine] Mother. That was only natural. I knew that the Mother, full of infinite bliss, compared with which all earthly possessions were as nothing, was there, quite close to me. How could I be satisfied with anything else? I had to seek her. I became mad for her." "I was then suffering from excruciating pain because I had not been blessed with a vision of the Mother. . . . I was overpowered by a great restlessness, and a fear that it might not be my lot to realize Her in this life. . . . Life did not seem worth living." [52]

His old egos, values, and groups were all destroyed without any possibility of restoration; his new values, egoless "self," and new group affiliations were not as yet finished products. Finally, reintegration and self-identification were completed. He began to have samadhi and the vision of the Mother. An "ineffable bliss" descended upon him. From that time he became a counselor, real healer, pacifier, moral educator, psychiatrist, even a sort of a "miracle-maker," for the thousands who began to come to him with their anxieties, doubts, fears, mental and physical troubles, quests for God, for goodness, for illumination, and the like.

Possibly none of Ramakrishna's many " crises " was very serious; but in their numerous totality they made his transfiguration long in time and torturously difficult in degree.[53]

*St. Paul* (?-67 A.D.). St. Paul's observable reidentification can serve as an example of a transfiguration achieved in the shortest time, though latently it might have been ripening for a much longer period. St. Paul's conversion, externally, was fulfilled within a few days: a blinding stroke, and a fall to the earth in a fit of disease while en route to Damascus; then a few days of suffering, recovery and baptism. Such was the externally observable period of transfiguration during which all three operations were completed: reintegration of previous egos and values; severance of previous memberships in non-Christian groups and affiliations with Christian groups; self-identification with Jesus Christ, whose followers he had pitilessly persecuted before. This external course of conversion was probably preceded by a much longer inner restlessness, precipitated by his participation in and supervision of the stoning of St. Stephen and reinforced by his cruel persecution of many Christians, including Christian Jews. All this led him to a conflict of egos, values, and groups, and undermined his identification with the supreme value of the Jewish religion. The final outcome was almost instantaneous conversion.[54]

The type of the late-catastrophic altruists is probably less frequent than the early-fortunate type. In a sample of the living American Good Neighbors only some 3 per cent had the late course of self-identification and altruization. Among the Christian Catholic Saints 11 per cent, and among the Russian Orthodox Saints some 17 per cent belong to this type of altruists.[55] Three per cent is probably too low for the total altruistic populations at large; 11 and 17 per cent look nearer to reality. Whatever is the typical per cent of this type of altruists, it is very probable that the late altruists are a minority among altruists of all types. It seems it is much easier to mold babies into altruists from their earliest childhood, as with the fortunate altruists, than to reshape a grown-up selfish person into altruistic form, as with the late altruists. Only a small fraction of grown-up egotists can be transfigured into creative altruists. This way is not only less effective, but also much more painful, wasteful, and difficult.

The above examples of late altruists clearly show the common characteristics of this type of self-identification. We see that the "conversion" comes somewhat late in the life of this kind of converts. Their life course has indeed a sharp turning point of "before and after the conversion." The process of self-identification itself is marked by stress, strain, and sometimes by catastrophic and other "precipitants." In most of the cases this process lasts for some time — from a few days to several years. So far, no single case of a truly momentary conversion (or self-identification) is observed: the shortest cases, like St. Paul's, took several days and in their latent period of ripening they probably went on for a much longer time.[56] In all these transfigurations, at their pre-identification phase, we observe a notable disorganization and mutual conflict of the egos, values, and group affiliations of the respective person, with "cracked" or incomplete self-identification with a higher value. Such a state of intense inner war and chaos produces restlessness, distress, depression, and "aridity" in the respective person. Sometimes this inner state becomes unbearable; it relentlessly urges the suffering individual to find a way out of this distress. Numerous detailed tech-

niques (discussed further) are used for a successful performance of the
" rebirth."

Let us turn now to the intermediary course of self-identification and
the third type of altruists.

## VI

### THE INTERMEDIARY COURSE OF SELF-IDENTIFICATION AND TYPE OF ALTRUISTS

The intermediary type has many gradations between the early-fortunate
and the late-converted types. Its least pronounced variations are barely
different from these types. Only its central forms are tangibly intermediary and clearly differ from the early-fortunate and the late-converted types. Subsequent actual cases illustrate the main gradations of
the intermediary type.

*St. Theodosius* (?–1074). If we disregarded the sharp and prolonged
conflict of St. Theodosius with his mother and the group of kinsmen
who opposed his early self-identification with Christ of Love, Poverty,
and Humility; his love of an " uncouth garb "; his manual work with the
family's serfs; his early aspiration to become a pilgrim and then a monk;
his actual service to the poor and the needy — if we disregard this sharp
conflict of his group affiliations, then St. Theodosius in his religious and
altruistic growth belongs to the type of the fortunate altruists. Born in a
pious and harmonious well-to-do family, " Theodosius grew up under the
tutelage of his parents. God's grace was with him, and he had the light
of the Holy Ghost from his first years. . . . As he matured in body and
spirit, he was drawn by the love of God to go to church daily, devoting
all his attention to the sacred books. He wore coarse and patched garments, and when his parents tried to make him put on fresh clothing
and play with other children, he would not obey, for he wanted to be
identified with the poor."

After his father's death, when Theodosius was thirteen years old, he
" applied himself even more zealously to his undertaking ": went into the
fields with his serfs and did the humblest work, and still more earnestly
than before imitated Christ in His poverty, humility, and love. All this
displeased his mother: she began to lock him indoors and even to beat
him. " But he would not obey her."

Then *an unforeseen circumstance* intervened: pilgrims going to the
Holy Land came to the town where Theodosius lived. He, " rising in the
night, left home secretly, taking nothing with him except the poor
clothes." After a long pursuit his mother caught up with him. In her
fury " she seized him by the hair, flung him to the ground, and trampled
on him." Bound like a criminal, Theodosius was taken home and locked
there.

The conflict continued for a fairly long time, until Theodosius secretly left home again and came to the blessed Anthony, the hermit. Anthony permitted Theodosius to live with him in a cave outside of Kiev. There Theodosius was given the tonsure and invested with the monastic robe. After a four-year search, his mother again found him and tried to take him back; she failed. (Eventually, under the influence of Theodosius, she entered a convent and became a nun.) The subsequent life of Theodosius was a creative growth in love, humility, and service to especially poor classes. In some respects he resembled St. Francis of Assisi; in other traits, St. Dominic. Thus, if he had not had the sharp conflict with his mother and the family group, he would have belonged to a clear type of the early-fortunate altruist. This conflict forced him to reintegrate slightly his egos and values, and to rearrange sharply his group affiliations, especially with his family group. According to Nestor, his earliest biographer, the conflict with his family was reinforced by Theodosius' hearing " the words of the holy Gospel; ' He that loveth father or mother more than Me, is not worthy of Me.' " [57]

A somewhat similar conflict with family and caste occurred in the cases of Gandhi and St. Theresa. Buddha abandoned his wife and child. Generally among all Christian Catholic Saints, 18.9 per cent were relentlessly opposed by their parental family in their religious aspirations; 10.1 per cent were temporarily opposed, but later on approved; 5.7 per cent were reacted to indifferently by their parental family; 65.3 per cent were encouraged.[58] These data show that a conflict of an altruist with his family is not a rare phenomenon. At least a mild conflict with some group has been the unavoidable experience of practically all altruists, including the fortunate type.

*St. Basil the Great* (329–379). If St. Basil had not been converted into Christianity by his sister at the age of twenty-seven years, he would also belong to the early-fortunate type of great religious and altruistic leaders. So far as the details of his early life are known, from his childhood he had a " good " constellation of egos, values, and group affiliations. Coming from a noble and rich family, he seems to have spent a happy childhood on the parental estate, and then was given the most brilliant education at the most advanced schools of Constantinople and Athens.

After returning to his native region, at the age of twenty-seven he adopted Christianity and immediately plunged himself into the most creative ascetic, altruistic, and organizational activities. He, with his sister, turned their estates into two monasteries; built a great hospital in Caesarea, organized large-scale hospices for the poor and infirm (called Basileias), sold the remaining part of the estate and gave the money to the poor. He practiced indeed what he preached: " The love of God and the love of neighbor, is to be the chief motive of the Christian life, whether in the cloister or in the world." And " the bread you hoard belongs to the hungry; the cloak in your wardrobe belongs to the naked; the shoes you let rot belong to the barefoot; the money in your vaults belongs to the destitute." [59]

To sum up: except for his comparatively late conversion into Christianity and his late but extraordinarily creative dedication to religious and altruistic activities, St. Basil would have fallen into the class of the fortunate altruists. A post-conversion rearrangement of his egos, values, and especially group affiliations was considerable, but neither too difficult nor too painful. This rearrangement displayed the relentless driving force of the fortunate altruist, easily overcoming obstacles, spontaneously making enormous sacrifices, creating new forms of communities, and most effectively educating — morally, mentally, and socially — a large portion of the humanity of his time and of subsequent generations.

*M. Gandhi* (1869–1948). All in all the course of self-identification of Gandhi was fairly close to the fortunate type. There were, however, two tangible differences: a) Gandhi's self-identification occurred only at the age of some sixteen to eighteen years; before this age Gandhi's altruism was hardly greater than that of the rank and file of Hindu teenagers; b) to achieve the self-identification Gandhi had to rearrange some of his egos, values, and group affiliations. Because he had a favorable constellation of these from his childhood, this rearrangement was neither too difficult nor too radical; yet, it had to be done. Small conflicts among his egos, values, groups occurred now and then: between those of his family and the " reforming friend," those of his sociocultural egos and carnal sex ego (his visiting a brothel); between " gentleman's groups-values-egos," and his other egos (in London during his first year); between his caste and other groups to which he belonged. But all these conflicts were easily solved through not too painful rearrangement of his values, egos, and group memberships.

When his self-identification was accomplished Gandhi could " easily " make momentous decisions of the utmost sacrifice, without hesitation or regrets: the decision to undergo many serious discomforts; to abstain from carnal lust; to give up his property; to deprive himself of many enjoyable associations; to take upon himself the most strenuous and heartbreaking tasks; to separate from his loving and loved family; to risk his life; to go to prison; to be vilified by many; to be expelled from his caste; to give up sexual life; not to mention his numerous hunger strikes and life-endangering fastings. When one reads his autobiography and other documents, one is surprised at how seemingly easily all these vows were made and sacrifices performed. Let us glance more closely to the concrete details of his self-identification with the supraconscious.

The first two steps in this process happened when he was about twelve years old. They were *neither planned nor deliberately arranged. They just occurred.* They consisted of the accidental reading of a book, *Shravana Pitribhakti Nataka*, a play about Shravana's devotion to his parents, and seeing it enacted by itinerant showmen. A little later Gandhi saw another play about a truthful hero, Harishchandra. Gandhi says about the book: " I read it with intense interest. The book . . . and the picture left an indelible impression on my mind. 'Here is an example for you to copy.'" About the Harishchandra play he tells us that " it haunted me and I must have acted Harishchandra to myself times without number. 'Why should not all be truthful like Harishchandra?' was the question I asked myself day and night. *To follow truth and to go through all the ordeals Harishchandra went through was the one ideal it inspired in me.*" [60] In this way the process of self-identification with Truth and Love as the supreme value was started.

Other important events consisted of the advice of Gandhi's old nurse to repeat the verses of *Ramanama* to cure his fear of ghosts and spirits; and then in reading the great epic *Ramayana* to his father. Both of these events were again unplanned and unpremeditated.

In contrast to their enormous influence, the planned religious and moral instruction of Gandhi through the school and religious authorities, through attendance of the temple services, through the preaching and other works of Christian missionaries " never appealed to me." They utterly failed to impress young Gandhi. He even developed a dislike for them, especially for Christianity that " abused religion " of Gandhi's ancestors, and " compelled one to eat beef, drink liquor and change one's clothes." [61]

While the organized instructions and education by the established religious and educational authorities utterly failed, Gandhi " kept on picking up things here and there from [his] surroundings." The incidental advice given by the old nurse — devoted to and loved by Gandhi — and the reading aloud of the great epic of the *Ramayana* " took deep root in me . . ." leading to " the conviction that morality is the basis of things and truth is the substance of all morality. Truth became my sole objective. It began to grow in magnitude every day."

About the same time " a Gujarati didactic stanza likewise gripped my mind and heart. Its precept — return good for evil — became my guiding principle." [62] (As an important detail, Gandhi tells that the same great books, for instance the *Bhagavadgita* or the *Ramayana*, did not impress him when they were read poorly or by persons whom Gandhi did not love or respect.)

These *positive events were combined with several temptations and moral failures.* Under the influence of a friend, Gandhi became for a time a meat-eater — a considerable sin for a Vaishnavite and something that would have greatly aggrieved his parents if they had known of this. Then, he became a smoker, and to buy the cigarettes he stole from his brother a piece of gold. Further on, under the influence of the same bad friend, he went to a brothel, though in shame he fled and did not commit the sexual act. Finally, he was lustful with his wife even when his father was dying.

Due to the positive self-identification already started, Gandhi felt *deeply guilty* for these failures. Finally, he wrote a clean confession to his father, " asked adequate punishment," and pledged himself never to repeat the sins in the future.

His father (sick in bed) read the confession, then with tears streaming down his face, tore the paper. " I also cried. . . . These pearl-drops of love cleansed my heart, and washed my sin away. Only he who experienced such a love can know what it is. . . . This was, for me, an object-lesson in *Ahimsa* [nonviolence, nonhurting]. When such *Ahimsa* becomes all-embracing, it transforms everything it touches. There is no limit to its power." [63]

Such are the beginning and the first steps in Gandhi's self-identification with the supraconscious Truth (God, Love, the Highest Value).

Seven points are significant in this course. First, most of the instrumental events that awakened and developed the self-identification of Gandhi were positive moral values, patterns, heroes, and actions. The devotion and sacrifice for the parents of Shravana, the truthfulness and love of Harishchandra surmounting all the ordeals; the Gujarati stanza about " returning gladly good for evil done " by the heroes of unselfish courage, sacrifice, and creative love; then the love of his nurse, and the lesson in pure Ahimsa given by his father — all these stimuli were positive. In all these there was nothing pathological, debased, or morally dirty.

If several moral misdeeds happened with Gandhi at that time, they occurred either simultaneously or *mainly after the exposure to the above values and establishment of a positive moral foundation.* Having fallen on such a foundation, the vices could not set forth deep roots and, under the pitiless criticism of a sense of guilt and heartfelt remorse, they quickly withered. Their net effect was mainly an acceleration of the self-identification discussed: serving as first temptations and tests, they helped Gandhi to " pass his first ethical, social, and spiritual examination." These events have to be stressed because nowadays many mental and moral therapies consist largely in exposing the patient to primarily the negative, pathological, criminal, and insane patterns; in keeping him mainly in the atmosphere of the " social sewers "; in eliminating any sense of guilt in the patient or pupil; in making him believe that he or she is mainly an id or libido or masochistic and sadistic destroyer or a perverted animal organism. Gandhi's experience is quite opposite to this negativistic therapy and negativistic education and interpretation of man given by many contemporary mental and moral " healers."

The second point is that all the starting events were unplanned and unpremeditated. Third, they happened to be somewhat incidental in their nature: reading and seeing a play, the advice of an old, illiterate nurse,[64] reading a great epic to his sick father, and so on. This suggests that one can hardly know what sort of events can awaken the self-identification in different individuals. Fourth, the official religious and moral agencies with their supposedly perfect techniques utterly failed in any awakening of the self-identification, in development of altruistic élan or even of religious belief in the dogmas, deities, and ritual.

Fifth, though not shown at the earliest age, the supraconscious potential seemingly was present in Gandhi: in his teens he shows already a strong moral sensitivity and actually begins the practice of the moral virtues he believed in. From the first event, Gandhi became active in his moral aspirations and in various forms (repeating the noble verses, re-acting many times " psychodramatically " the role of his hero, etc.) he started to strive actively towards a fuller self-identification with the supraconscious, not only in phantasy and thought but also in overt actions.

Sixth, unexpected pure love, instead of punishment, granted to Gandhi by his father after Gandhi's frank confession, played a decisive role in Gandhi's moral maturation.

Seventh, freely repented and mastered moral misdeeds did not stop the developing process of the self-identification. All in all, three techniques appear to be basic: 1. Early exposure to and behavioral imitation of positive moral examples. 2. Grace of love unexpectedly granted (by his father). 3. Behavioral practice of good deeds. In Gandhi's subsequent growth into an apostle of love, his active efforts to serve the God of Truth and Love are to be mentioned. Many events that gave opportunity for such service were accidental — just happened, without plan and arrangement. They were not permitted to go by, however, without the eager and active, sometimes painful and difficult, sometimes dangerous efforts by Gandhi to use them for his service to Truth and creative Love. Like all geniuses in any field of creativity, a genius in the field of love uses any random event for the incessant development of his creativity; he turns the adverse, bad events, into instruments of creative victory. Active, creative Eros thus always co-operates with Agape. The various techniques used by Gandhi in his life work will be analyzed further. For the present, the above sums up his first steps on the road of self-identification with the God of Truth and Love.

*St. Theresa* (1515–1582). A remarkably good father and mother, both very religious and notably altruistic; reading and listening to the good books read at home and at her uncle's home; a devout brother and sisters; playing the roles of hermits, nuns, and giving alms — such were the early forces that moved St. Theresa to self-identification with God and to the desire to become a martyr. The early motives of this, however, were rather impure: fear of death, fear of eternal damnation, and various utilitarian and hedonistic calculations.

I had a great desire to die a martyr's death, not out of love of Him [God] of which I was conscious, but that I might most quickly attain to the fruition of those great joys of which I read that they were reserved in heaven [and] were forever, and ever, and ever.

I was more influenced by servile fear than by love to enter religion.[65]

After the death of her mother (when Theresa was twelve years old) "I went in my affliction to an image of our Lady of Charity, and with many tears implored her to be my mother. I did this in my simplicity, and I believe that it was of service to me." [66]

These early aspirations were counterbalanced for a time by the girl's passionate reading of books of chivalry, by increasing care about dress, appearance, perfume, "all vanities within my reach," and especially (at the age of fourteen) by a close friendship with her kinswoman (cousin) who was "light and frivolous" and from whom she "learned every evil." "I am amazed at the evil one bad companion can do." (Compare the similar influence of such a companion on Gandhi.) "The conversation of this person so changed me that no trace was left of my soul's natural disposition to virtue." [67]

After three months of this "life of vanity," Theresa was sent to a convent for education and correction. The first eight days in the convent she felt very uncomfortable, but after that she began to like the nuns and the surroundings; the rules of the convent put an end — first mechanical then psychological — to her "vanity life," "vanity contacts," and eventually vanity desires. One of the nuns there "began to root out the habits which bad companionship had formed." After one year and a half in the convent, she notably progressed in her self-identification with God, though she was still reluctant to become a nun. Such was the change in her group affiliations, values, and egos. Then came a serious illness and repeated fainting fits with fever. During these days of illness, Theresa experienced deeply the precariousness of the vanity of the world and the short-lived nature of its values. These experiences were followed by the most charitable kindness to her shown by her married sister and her husband, by the desire of her brother to become a monk, and by other positive influences. As a result, her self-identification with the supraconscious became so strong that contrary to the will of her father, she and her brother simultaneously entered two cloisters and became respectively a nun and a monk. Her enormous struggle to overcome obstacles can be seen from the following few lines of the saint's writings.

The pain I felt when I left my father's house was so great, that I do not believe the pain of dying will be greater . . . for, as I had no love of God to destroy my love of father and of kindred, this latter love came upon me with a violence so great that, if our Lord had not been my keeper, my own resolution to go on would have failed me. But, He gave me courage to fight against myself. . . . When I took the habit . . . at that moment I was filled with a joy so great, that it has never failed me to this day; and God converted the aridity of my soul into the greatest tenderness.[68]

Though subsequently St. Theresa (as any eminent creator) had many temptations and tribulations throughout her life, after taking the nun's habit, her self-identification with the supraconscious became firmly established. It began decisively to control her life, mind, and actions. Other techniques and factors of St. Theresa are examined further on.

The essential points in the first steps in her self-identification are: a) good family and good examples her parents and kin gave in her childhood; b) good books she was exposed to; c) kindness she had from relatives and neighbors; d) early utilitarian and hedonistic ("cheaply purchased kingdom of God," as she accurately says) motives in her religious and moral strivings later replaced by purer motivation; e) death of her mother; f) her serious sickness, fainting fits and fever; g) similar religious desires of one of her brothers and martyr-death (as she believed) of another brother in America; h) strong "sinful" counter forces — books of chivalry and love stories, temptations of the body, of the vanity of the world, of passion of love; frivolous cousin infecting her with "evil" aspirations; i) mechanical termination of the dangerous drift by being sent into a convent school and thus rearranging her group affiliation; j) influence of the cloistered environment, regime, education, and especially of some of the nuns; k) an illness and her brother's decision to become a monk. These stimuli helped her overcome her "sinful tendency" and helped to establish a firm self-identification with "our Lord." The whole process of self-identification consisted in a series of reintegrations of the early egos, values, and group memberships. The change was continuous, not abrupt, radical, or particularly difficult.

These cases give an idea about the various gradations of the intermediary type of creative altruists and of the course of self-identification with the supraconscious.

## VI

### . .  CONCLUSION

Such then is the nature of the triple operation of self-identification with the supraconscious performed by all creative altruists as the first decisive step towards their goal. And such are the main three courses of self-identification and the three main types of creative geniuses of love:

1) the early-fortunate, evenly, gradually, and quietly growing in creative altruism; 2) the late-catastrophic and converted, whose life is divided
into the "before and after the conversion," and whose self-identification
process is punctuated by sharp crises, stresses, suffering, and "precipitants"; 3) the intermediary or the residual course marked by minor
stresses.

Before making an analysis of the factors responsible for each of the
three types and courses of altruistic growth, we shall analyze further the
essentials of altruistic self-identification in order to avoid possible mis-
understanding of this all-important process.

## Chapter Ten

# Ideological and Behavioral Altruistic Self-Identification

## I

WHAT KIND OF SELF-IDENTIFICATION HELPS ONE TO BECOME ALTRUISTIC?

Not all self-identifications help in the altruistic transformation of individuals. Only when self-identification means not a mere *ideological acceptance* of a certain value as supreme, but *also a deep permeation by this value of the body of one's ideas, emotions, feelings, volitions and, eventually, actions;* only when, in addition, the supreme value is *positive* and contains in itself *sublime love*, does such self-identification become a decisive factor in molding one's personality and overt conduct into the living incarnation of love. It is not incidental that explicitly or implicitly all eminent altruists identify themselves with the highest and sublimest values: God, Tao, Jen, Logos, the Inner Light, etc., and always Love at its purest and best. Though called by different names, the central core of these values, especially their common denominator — an unbounded love at its best — is really similar. Paraphrasing the Vedantist motto that the "Truth is one, but men call it by different names," we can say that " The supreme value of self-identification of all great altruists is one, but they call it by different names." To sum up: only this sort of self-identification is instrumental in altruistic transfiguration of human beings.

The validity of this proposition is witnessed by an overwhelming majority (from 90 to 99 per cent) of all eminent altruists, of all Christian Saints, and of all Good Neighbors studied. Their ideological self-identification is perfectly positive and contains the value of love as the main value.[1]

## II

### ALTRUISTIC SELF-IDENTIFICATION IS NOT CONFINED TO ONE CONCEPTION OF SUPREME LOVE

The eminent altruists appeared in different societies, and in different cultures. They are not confined to either one religion, or one ethical, political, or philosophical system. They lived and created in Taoist and Confucianist China, in Hindu, Buddhist, and Jainist societies, among the purest currents of Christianity, Mohammedanism, Judaism, as well as among the Stoics, the Cynics, and other " pagan " groups and nations.

What is still more important, eminent altruists have identified themselves with differently named and conceived supreme values: personalistic and suprapersonal Gods; theistic, deistic, and pantheistic Gods; with the diversely conceived " theological " Gods of Judaism and Christianity, of Mohammedanism and Hinduism, and of other religions; with the " Godless " Tao, Jen, Nirvana, and so on; with Love, Truth or Beauty, with Moral Supreme Value, even with prosaic-sounding terms of " social welfare," " well-being of man and mankind," " moral duty," and so on. *Since we find great creative altruists self-identified with widely diverse ideological conceptions of the positive supreme value, this means that none of religious dogmas and beliefs, philosophical systems, or ethical teachings has a monopoly on the production of eminent altruists. Many of the diverse ideologies seemingly have served the purpose and helped in the ideological and behavioral self-identification of the altruists.* Whether the diverse positive ideologies serve the purpose with equal success, remains unknown: we do not have even the roughest statistics on the frequency of creative altruists in the groups with different religious, philosophical, political, and ethical ideologies. We know still less about the frequency of the eminent altruists identified with various conceptions of the supreme value. For these reasons we cannot contend, for instance, that the self-identification with the Christian God yields a greater ratio of altruists than that with the Hindu or Buddhist, Taoist or other supreme values. The same is true of other conceptions of the *summum bonum*.

## III

### What Kind of Self-Identification Impedes Altruistic Transformation?

The situation is very different with the values of self-identification which do not contain the value of love, and which are " pathological," ugly, insignificant, negative, not only in name but in their nature, in the properties ascribed to them by their followers. *A self-identification with such negative and " ugly " values devoid of the value of love cannot and does not make the individuals creatively altruistic.* One hardly meets any eminent altruist who has such a self-identification. If a person sincerely identifies himself (ideologically and behaviorally) with " anal, oral, and genital libido," or with " id," made up of the instincts of sex and death, or with " man eat man ego," or with a bundle of masochistic and sadistic propensities, or with the " devil," " satan," and other " loveless " negative values, such self-identification can produce only a selfish, aggressive, abnormal, sadistic and masochistic person, now and then turning into " the worst of beasts." One hardly meets a real altruist who performs actions of love in the name and for the sake of the devil, anal libido, sadistic instinct, or hate. By rudest force, punishment, reward, and similar means, egotists of this sort can be kept within the limits of law, and can be inhibited from an unrestrained manifestation of their selfish propensities. But now and then even the rudest means of control are insufficient to prevent them from turning into vultures, rampant egotists, and well-disguised hypocrites.

Herein lies an enormous potential danger of ideologies and therapies which try to identify man mainly or only with stomach, or sex, or id, or body, or animal organism and similar values. If and when individuals become convinced (ideologically and behaviorally) of this sort of " self-evident scientific truth "; when ideologists, psychologists, psychiatrists and counselors base their practice on this kind of theory about man's nature and inculcate this kind of self-identification into their disciples and patients, rarely, if ever, are altruistic and creative results produced. If anything, such counselors rather harm their patients, pupils, or followers and the society in which they live. Viewed in this light, these people have been one of the potent poisons that demoralized and " bestialized " the Western world in the twentieth century, when their number enormously increased and their activities became influential. This sort of self-identification builds and can build only a " hell on earth," where *homo hominis lupus est.*

The validity of the proposition is supported by the ever-present groups of " unrepentant " criminals, undisguised human vultures, given in any large society at all periods of human history. When carefully studied their main aspirations are found to consist in ideological and behavioral efforts to use the whole world as a mere means for their " ego " and its lusty propensities. In contrast to the hypocrites (mentioned further) they do not pretend to disguise their selfish views and aspirations by any " noble and charitable ideology." Whether in the form of a highly sophisticated ethics of egoism and an ideology of " the struggle for existence as the supreme law," or in the form of the most primitive belief in " man eat man " and " eat, drink, and be merry for tomorrow we die," these persons and groups are fairly consistent in their negativistic ideology and behavior, preached and practiced. They identify themselves with the negative egoistic value and behave respectively, without any hypocritical pretenses.

" George Cvek, who had sneered about the fifteen housewives he had murdered, raped, or robbed . . . when he came into court for sentencing, sneered and spat at Judge James M. Barrett. He told Judge Barrett not to say, ' and may God have mercy on your soul! '. . . A cynical

smile played about his lips while attendants adjusted head and leg elec-
trodes " (in the death house).² Cvek gives an example of the unrepentant
consistent criminal.   J. D. Tuggle, 23 years old, who died in the Mc-
Alester penitentiary electric chair for the murder of his aunt and uncle,
gives another example of a person consistent in his negativistic ideology
and behavior.   He " calmly puffed on a cigar " while walking into the
execution chamber and cynically told the warden to take care of himself.   Many *condottieri* and intellectuals of the Italian Renaissance give
a high-brow example of persons consistent in their negativistic value-
ideology and overt conduct.   Werner von Urslingen with his motto
" The enemy of God, of pity, and of mercy," practiced the cruelest deeds.
An intellectual openly addressing God as " Thou, thoroughly wicked
God . . . truly I would tear thee to pieces," he behaved accordingly.
" Among those at the top (the Visconti, the Sforzas, the Borgias, and
such *condottieri* as Braccio di Montone, Tiberto Brandolino, Malatesta)
' the disinterested love of evil, the thirst for blood for its own sake, the
devilish delight in destruction' reigned supreme.   The same was true of
the intellectuals and of a part of the lower classes." ³

This type of person makes up a considerable part of any human society at any period.   In some periods it increases, in others decreases, but
in some proportion it always exists.   In our age, its proportion is especially considerable in the contemporary materialistic, Communist populations as well as among the nominally Christian Western peoples.   Further
on it will be pointed out in what sort of society and culture each of these
types increase or decrease.

## IV

### What Kind of Self-Identification Is Insufficient and Ineffective?

*When self-identification with positive or negative values remains purely
ideological, without changing respectively the overt behavior of a person; or when it is purely intellectual, and does not permeate one's " heart,"
emotions, and volitions, such a purely ideological self-identification remains largely ineffective; ordinarily it even fosters egotism.*

In the individuals who do not practice what they preach and do not
preach what they practice, whose ideological (and vocal) utterances are
fairly independent from the rest of their overt actions — such a purely
ideological self-identification with God, Jesus, Love, or other supreme
value is not always followed by godly and altruistic behavior.   Due to the
autonomy of their speech-reactions from the rest of their overt behavior,
such individuals can preach the noblest ideology, can identify themselves
with the highest positive values, and at the same time act overtly in the
ignoblest manner quite contradictory to their ideological self-identification.   This self-identification, indeed, is often *intentionally used* by them

as a beautifying screen for their hypocritical selfishness. In other cases their noble ideology helps them to believe *sincerely* that their overt conduct is also as noble as their ideology, though objectively it is gravely selfish and rapacious. There is a vast legion of human beings who are very susceptible to this sort of self-gratifying and self-justifying illusion. Calling themselves devout Christians, followers of the Sermon on the Mount, they easily convince themselves that they are really such, though their actions strikingly repudiate their ideological claims.

This inconsistency between ideological self-identification and overt behavior once in a while manifests itself also in the form of persons who ideologically identify themselves with atheism, materialism, irreligiosity, animal nature of man, egotism, and other negative values, and who in their overt actions show themselves conspicuously altruistic and truly Christian. When, however, the seemingly negativistic self-identification of these behavorial altruists is carefully analyzed, it is found to contain the values of sympathy, love, and supreme moral law hidden in the mass of negativistic verbiage.

The validity of this proposition is witnessed by the perennial existence of three types of persons in particular: 1. hypocrites and liars who intentionally use noble preachings to hide their ignoble practices; 2. persons who sincerely fail to see the enormous contrast between their noble preachings and ignoble deeds, who sincerely believe that as soon as they profess a noble ideological self-identification ("I am a Christian," "Jesus is my Lord," "I believe in God's commandments," "I love my neighbor," etc.), they become noble in their nature and behavior; 3. individuals whose ideologies and speech-reactions are fairly autonomous from the rest of their overt actions, who have an unbridgeable chasm between their "ideological preachings" and overt behavior. While the existence of a considerable group of hypocrites and liars in any large society is well ascertained, many of us do not realize that the category of the "sincere" beautifiers of their ugly egos and behavior by a noble ideology is also large.[4]

During the last several hundred years such individuals have composed a very large part of the population in the Christian West. "During the past few centuries the most belligerent, the most aggressive, the most rapacious, the most power-drunk section of humanity has been precisely the Christian Western world. During these centuries Western Christendom has invaded all the other continents; its armies, followed by its priests and merchants, have subjugated, enslaved, robbed, pillaged, and exterminated most of the non-Christian peoples, beginning with the preliterate tribes and ending with the non-Christian nations. . . . Somewhat similar has been the conduct of Christians toward one another during these centuries."[5] Endless religious wars of Christian denominations and nations with one another, and a multitude of bloody revolutions and civil wars of one Christian faction with others glaringly testify to the enormous chasm between the Sermon on the Mount which the Christians preached and their fratricidal, most selfish, and un-Christian conduct. A large bulk of these Christians have sincerely failed to see this contradiction and earnestly believed they have been good Christians, carrying Christian " love " to all the pagans and fellow Christians as well. At the present time this tragic chasm is as great as at any time before.[6]

A very high per cent of this type of person occurs especially among the ruling groups of all countries and periods. Publicly, kings, presidents, prime ministers, influential politicians, captains of finance and industry, and other power-holding individuals profess the noblest preachings and frequently invoke God and other highest values. In their overt behavior, however, the ruling groups give a much higher ratio of criminality than their subjects or plain citizens. Lord Acton's motto that " power corrupts and absolute power corrupts absolutely " is essentially correct.[7]

To this type of " sincere " beautifiers of their behavior by noble self-identification belong also a considerable part of the sudden so-called religious converts. After almost any revivalist meeting of a popular preacher, there usually is a crowd of " momentary converts." When, however, one studies whether this " momentary conversion " changes altruistically their overt conduct, for a large part of such converts the answer is *no*. For another part, the change is short-lived and rapidly evaporating. For instance, in a collective study of seventy-three Boston converts (1948–1950),[8] one reported no change at all; thirty-seven reported only slight ideological change; thirty-three reported some behavorial change, but mainly in the form of attendance at church, Bible reading, preaching " Repent: the kingdom of heaven is at hand! " and other ideological changes. Of these thirty-three only a small fraction mention an altruistic behavioral change. Other studies of religious conversion bring a body of similar evidence. Even when a tangible behavioral change like the Welsh miners' giving up alcohol occurs (after a revivalist mass-conversion), it proves to be short-lived, and within a few days or weeks it evaporates (the converted miners resumed their alcoholic habit). Of one hundred converts studied by Starbuck, 93 per cent of the women and 77 per cent of the men had backsliding of some sort.[9]

Among other things this shows that *the behavorial altruistic transfiguration is much more difficult than the purely ideological one.* A purely ideological conversion of thousands and a purely ideological revival of religion are comparatively easy. But such a religious or moral revival does not mean much. It does not necessarily improve the overt behavior and social relationships of the respective population. At the best it changes only their speech-reactions, without changing their mind, heart, or deeds in a truly religious or altruistic direction. Often it makes the converts even worse, turning a hitherto frankly " irreligious " or " sinful " person into a liar and hypocrite, into a sham-altruistic and sham-religious pharisee. For these reasons most of the mass-conversions and religious revivals, especially those widely advertised and financially exploited by various individuals, firms, and publishers, should not be overestimated in their positive effects. As often as not, the effects are very modest; sometimes, they are even negative.

Though the number of persons who sincerely beautify their ignoble actions by noble ideological self-identification is much greater than the number of *persons who hide their noble, altruistic activities behind a seemingly ignoble ideological self-identification*, this latter variety of persons exists and is found among both eminent and ordinary altruists.

As mentioned, the altruists who hide under shabby ideological clothing a beautiful body of good deeds, ordinarily have the supreme values of love and moral duty hidden in the mass of their negativistic ideology. Insofar their ideological self-identification is positive rather than negative, while their " heart " is entirely altruistic.

Buddha and the early Buddhists serve as a great example of the type of behavioral altruists with seemingly " atheistic " ideology. Gautama Buddha and the early Buddhists denied the reality of God, of soul, of ego, of personality, of matter, of any substance, and of any substantial agents. The whole world was viewed as an incessant stream of momentary " point-flashes " of energy. Insofar, the Buddhist ideology was utterly atheistic. But the chaos of these momentary point-flashes in this ideology was ordered by the causal and moral law (karma). The supreme imperative of this moral law was an unbounded empathy, compassion, and love to all living creatures and nonharming any living being by thought, word, or deed. This ideology was consistently realized in the overt behavior of the early Buddhists, and has been largely practiced by Buddhists up to the present time. Most of them do not kill even poisonous snakes and other dangerous creatures. Here the apparently negativistic atheistic ideology contained the value of sublime love with which the early Buddhists identified themselves.[10]

About 2 per cent of the American Good Neighbors declared themselves ideologically " atheistic," " materialistic," " egoistic," and generally irreligious. Nine per cent of the Good Neighbors did not attend any church service, and were not affiliated with any of the institutionalized religions. In a group studied, 13 per cent of the Harvard students and 6 per cent of the Radcliffe students felt themselves to be " doubtful " as to whether they needed any religion, except an ethical code of conduct.[11] The irreligious American Good Neighbors are more altruistic than the rank and file of the " religious " American population. The Harvard and Radcliffe students who declared themselves " doubtful " are in no way less ethical and moral than the students who declared themselves religious. The real situation here is similar to that of the early Buddhists. "Explicitly or implicitly, the irreligious Good Neighbors all take the moral values of the Golden Rule, of the Sermon on the Mount, and so on, as the supreme values, regardless of their denial of God and other kinds of authority. . . . When carefully analyzed, their "atheistic" phraseology reveals a person with a supreme set of moral values and deep ethical convictions of right and wrong — a person who practices what these convictions preach." [12] Similarly, "the religiously doubtful" Harvard and Radcliffe students identify themselves with the ethics of love as the supreme value.

In practically all cases of behavioral altruists who hide their good deeds under a seemingly negativistic ideology, one always finds a supreme value of love in the apparently negative self-identification. Some of these behavioral altruists do it intentionally, following Jesus' advice: "Take heed that ye do not your alms before men, to be seen of them: otherwise ye have no reward of your Father." "When thou doest alms, let not thy left hand know what thy right hand doeth: that thine alms may be in secret. . . . Pray to thy Father . . . in secret." [13] Either explicitly or implicitly practically all real altruists identify themselves only with the positive values, and among these always with the value of supreme love taken as the highest value. Insofar the behavioral "atheistic" altruists do not make an exception to the first proposition of this chapter.

## V

### TECHNIQUES OF DEVELOPMENT OF IDEOLOGICAL SELF-IDENTIFICATION INTO BEHAVIORAL ONE

Our next step in the analysis of self-identification with the supraconscious is to find out the ways and techniques by which it grows from the merely ideological to the behavioral sphere, from an ineffective intellectual idea into a dynamic force decisively determining the mind, the heart, and the conduct of the individual. A careful analysis of the factors and techniques by which eminent altruists have solved this problem throws light on this dark process. Accordingly, we turn now to a study of the factors and ways of deepening ideological self-identification into behavioral altruism.

Since the course of altruization of the early-fortunate and of the late (converted and catastrophic) altruists is very different in the first parts of their life cycles, our analysis of this problem must be carried on somewhat separately for these different classes of altruists. Regarding the first part of the life course of the early altruists, the problem consists in how and why they received their "lucky package" of egos, values, and group affiliations in their earliest childhood; and then how they developed and maintained it throughout their life.  For the late (converted and cata-strophic) altruists the problem is to unravel how and why they had a turn-ing point in their life course, and what forces started and carried on their altruistic conversion.

In accordance with this, we turn now to the problem of the " lucky package " of the fortunate altruists.

*Chapter Eleven*

# Factors in the Early Integration of the Fortunate Altruists

I

UNPROVABLE, DOUBTFUL, AND INSUFFICIENTLY KNOWN FACTORS

The fortunate altruists are marked by having from childhood a " lucky package " of well integrated egos, values and group affiliations, all subordinated to the supreme supraconscious value. The main mystery is how did they happen to acquire such a " lucky package " in their early childhood? What agencies or factors are responsible for such an inestimable fortune?

In our elucidation of this problem, let us first eliminate the factors which are either unprovable or improbable or very doubtful.

A. *Unprovable Theories*

Most popular of the unprovable theories are those of the divine grace (Agape), of the " spiritual heredity," of blissful karmic influence or of the effects of a certain constellation of planets, of a mysterious influence coming from interplanetary regions, or of dianetics' engrams and the " reactive mind bank," and the like.

Most pious biographers of the saintly altruists, as well as many of the altruists themselves, believe in a *divine grace* or Agape as the cause of their *early altruistic* disposition and of subsequent altruistic growth. Even if we accept this belief, it does not help us much: since the ways of the divine Agape are inscrutable, nobody can either predict to whom and when such a grace will be granted or comprehend why it is granted to some children and is not granted to other children who are seemingly as good as the " lucky " ones. Thus, empirically the theory of the divine grace does not elucidate the mystery at all. It simply replaces one unknown $x$ by a no less unknown $y$.

The same argument is applicable to the theory of a " *spiritual inheritance*." It claims that at the moment of birth or conception each child receives its " spiritual personality " or its " individual soul." The early altruists are those who become the bearers of an "altruistic spiritual personality or soul"; the early egoists or juvenile delinquents are those who receive an egoistic or criminal soul. There are several — more primitive and more sophisticated — versions of this theory. Like the theory of the divine grace, the hypothesis of the "spiritual inheritance" does not dissipate the darkness: it does not supply any basis for a prediction either of what sort of "spiritual personality" will be granted to each newly born baby, or why one baby receives a most aggressive spiritual soul while another gets a more altruistic one. The hypothesis remains unprovable and empty as an explanatory principle of empirical phenomena.

A special variation of this is the hypothesis of the *karmic consequences of one's good deeds in one's previous incarnations*. The partisans of this theory believe in transmigration of souls and the law of karma. According to this law, all our actions have inevitable consequences that visit upon us either in our present life or in one of our future incarnations. If in one's previous existence one behaved virtuously, the causal consequences of such a life may manifest themselves in the form of a "lucky package" of egos-values-group affiliations manifested in one's new incarnation, from its childhood. Previous criminal conduct may result in a retributive catastrophe and punishment in one's subsequent incarnations. Such is the essence of this karmic hypothesis.[1]

However intriguing the hypothesis is, empirically it is no more provable and no more helpful than the previous two beliefs. Its only use is purely residual and dogmatic: if we cannot account for the properties or events in the life of a given individual by "natural reasons," we can say (as Edgar Cayce said) that his fortune or misfortune is due to the karmic law of reward or retribution for good or bad deeds done by him in one of his previous incarnations. In such an explanation everything remains unproved, including the fact of the existence and immortality of singular-individual souls, the fact of their transmigration and incarnation, and the fact of the karmic "savings bank" of good or bad habits. Likewise, the hypothesis cannot predict or determine in which of the endless incarnations a retribution or reward for which deeds of which preceding incarnations is going to fall upon their author; and so on. All these beliefs remain entirely unproved and unknown. Instead of one unknown $x$ (what are the factors of the early "lucky package" of the fortunate altruists?), the hypothesis introduces a dozen still less-known enigmas. For these reasons it is meaningless.[2]

No better is the situation with the theories of *astrological and interplanetary influences*, or of even unduly inflated *influences of cosmic, astrophysical, and geographic factors*. In spite of the hoary antiquity of astrological interpretations of man's properties and of humanity's life course; in spite of a very wide diffusion of astrological beliefs in many countries in the past and at the present; in spite of thousands of repetitions and variations of the basic patterns of these theories; nevertheless, at the present time they stay as much unproven as they were in the time of ancient Chaldean or Egyptian astrologers. As a matter of fact, all astrological theories of the last fifteen centuries hardly improved much the classic version given in C. Ptolemy's *Tetrabyblos*. They all are still in the state of conjectures without even a minimum of the necessary evidence. Especially unproven remain their "horoscopic" diagnoses of the characteristics and life course of each individual born under a given constellation of planets. All this remains still mere belief — in many cases demonstrably wrong belief.[3] No better evidenced are the theories of mysterious interplanetary influences that determine the properties and life course of individuals, as well as the creative rise and decline of nations. The more recent variations, given by O. Spengler, W. Schubart, and others, are stated as dogmatically as before, without any shred of evidence. In the authors' own words, these forces are inscrutable, unforeseen, and unpredictable.[4] As such, these theories are *guesses* which remain unknown and unproved.

In the same situation are the theories that look for an explanation of the "lucky or unlucky package" of this or that child in the impressions which a newly conceived embryo receives in its prenatal existence, especially immediately after its conception. According to the tenets of dianetics, *each slightest impression experienced by the human fetus is recorded forever as an "engram" or a permanent trace on its protoplasm and is stored forever in its "bank of the reactive mind"* (different from the "analytical mind" with its ordinary memory). Anything that happens to the organism of the pregnant mother during her pregnancy is recorded in the "engrams" of the newly conceived baby, and decisively determines whether after birth it is going to be a "cleared" or "uncleared" person, altruistic or egoistic, good or bad. The whole secret of what we are is locked in the "engrams" received by our organism during its prenatal development and stored, without any evaporation, in the bank of our "reactive mind."[5] In a less crazy form this belief is shared by Freud and many Freudians.

This theory of the permanent, prenatal "engrams" is a sort of "devilish" version of the theories of the divine grace, spiritual inheritance, or astrological influences. It is an ugly, "social sewer" counterpart of the beautiful theories of the "heavenly" influences. With this difference, the theory of the engrams or forever-stored prenatal influences is as unprovable and unproved as the above "heavenly" theories. Of course, from the standpoint of the law of preservation of matter and energy, or of the law of karma, nothing is lost in the universe, including each infinitesimal influence upon an embryo. Theoretically, from the standpoint of these laws, your or my sneezing in some infinitesimal way influences the course of the cold war or the movement of Jupiter — or of even the remotest galaxy of stars. For practical purposes, however, all such infinitesimal influences are equivalent to zero-influences. As such they can be dismissed and clearly distinguished from the tangible and provable influences. Viewed in this light, most of the infinitesimal influences upon the human fetus are equivalent to zero-factors and as such can be disregarded.

As to the engrams, their storage in the bank of the reactive mind, their decisive role, and so on, the whole of this theory is mere conjecture and nothing more. The very existence of the engrams is entirely unproved; their unerasable, permanent character is unproved; the existence of the " reactive mind " is unproved; its ability to store unerringly forever each engram is wildest phantasy; the decisive role of the engrams is unproved; and so on. Nothing in this theory is proved or even can be proved. Furthermore, it is entirely empty as a predictive and diagnostic tool. Its authors do not know what sort of engrams are stored in each embryo in its prenatal existence and in each child in its postnatal period. They do not deduce, from an examination of the observable, or perceived, or calculable kind of the engrams in an embryo or child, the child's or grown-up's characteristics. Instead, they go backward from the empirically given characteristics of a person or child to their conjectural " engrams." These remain perfectly parasitic and useless as diagnostic or explanatory principles. In addition, the whole theory is but a bundle of logical contradictions: the perfectly unconscious " reactive mind " is at the same time perfectly conscious and unerringly registers everything; the memoryless reactive and somatic minds turn out to be perfectly memorizing everything; and so on. The whole theory with its technique of recall, etc., is a peculiar mixture of some shreds of science, and notions of oriental philosophy, mixed up with the wildest speculation and conspicuous charlatanish claims.[6]

To sum up: the theory of dianetics can be dismissed as unprovable and in its greater part demonstrably wrong. In a milder form this criticism is applicable also to the Freudian theory of the decisive importance of prenatal influences upon the fetus and of the trauma of birth upon the newly born child. Side by side with a sound part, this theory contains some unproved and unprovable notions and also something which is proved to be wrong. After all, Hubbard's dianetics is but an extreme variation of essentially Freudian theory.

The theories surveyed above represent the most popular theories of the unproved and unprovable kind.[7]

## B. Doubtful Factors

Among the doubtful explanations of the " lucky package " of the fortunate altruists, three kinds of theories can be mentioned. The first interpretation is *geographic*, the second is *somatic*, and the third is *grotesque*, exemplified by the swaddling theory of the properties of nations and " the swaddling philosophy of history."

*Geographic* theories try to account for psychosocial traits of persons or populations, including the traits of aggressiveness or altruism, through climate, flora, fauna, and other geographic conditions. If the claims of the geographic theories in regard to many sociocultural phenomena are often exaggerated and sometimes are even baseless,[8] in the problem of the "lucky package" these theories hardly supply any evidence at all. Nobody has proved as yet that one group of specified geographic conditions favors an early development of altruism, while another group facilitates an early development of egotism. Nobody has shown as yet that the countries with a certain climate produce a high frequency of fortunate altruists, while those with a different climate give a low frequency of these. So far as I know, there exists no study of the frequency of distribution of altruists by geographical regions, except perhaps my own study of the distribution by the countries of birth and death of the Christian Catholic saintly altruists. (Of these, 21.8 per cent were born in the British Isles; 27.0 per cent in Western Europe; 26.5 per cent in Italy; 9.3 per cent in Central and Northern Europe; 10.1 per cent in Asia; 5.1 per cent in Africa; and 0.2 per cent in the North and South Americas.) This distribution and its dynamic changes in the course of some twenty centuries of the history of Christianity cannot be explained at all geographically, while it is easily explainable through a combination of sociocultural factors.[9]

For the reasons given, then, we can dismiss geographic theories in our specific inquiry. They cannot account for the essentials of our problem.

In the last few years there has been a sort of revival of various *somatic* interpretations of personality traits, characteristics of groups, and sociocultural processes.[10] In their essentials the recent somatic theories represent a variation of numerous somatic and racial theories of the preceding centuries.[11] Just as these contended that a series of mental, moral, and social traits of personality are causally connected now with blondness or brunetteness, now with the color of skin, now with cephalic index, now with stature or weight, now with structure of hair, now with various bodily disproportions and abnormalities, now with some combinations of these and other somatic traits; in a similar manner the recent theories claim that certain somatic types are connected with a series of psychological traits of personality. Thus W. H. Sheldon's endomorphic somatotype — fattish, round, broad in hips and narrow in shoulders — tends to be sociable, tolerant, amiable, and complacently pleasing (viscerotonic temperamental type and manic psychiatric type). Sheldon's mesomorphic somatotype — broad in shoulders, narrow in hips, muscular "he-man type" — is connected with aggressiveness, callousness, ruthlessness, lust for power and domination (somatotonic temperamental type and paranoid psychiatric type). His ectomorphic somatotype — slender, flat-chested, small-boned — tends to be secretive, a lover of privacy and solitude, and sociophobic (cerebrotonic temperamental type and heboid psychiatric type). Following the old theories of C. Lombroso, Garofalo and others, recent somatic theories contend also that not only is an individual's becoming a criminal largely determined by somatic factors, but that specific somatic character-istics are responsible for one criminal's being a murderer, for another's be-ing a rapist, for the third's being a forger, and so on. In a similar manner the theories claim that there are specific somatic types of professors, mili-tary men, business executives, politicians, government bureaucrats, and so on. The Glasgow study of Ferguson and Cunnison discovers that short boys leave their jobs more often, and are more likely to be juvenile delin-quents and rabid film fans, than their taller brothers.

The weakest point of the recent somatic theories is the same as that of the old somatic hypotheses: they give very little evidence for their claim that somatic types are closely connected with specific psychosocial traits. The psychological characteristics ascribed to the endomorphic, meso-morphic, and ectomorphic types are asserted without a minimum of the necessary proofs. The same is true of the connections of certain somatic traits with either criminality or with its specific forms (murderer, rapist, etc.). Among other things, the alleged somatic characteristics of criminals or delinquents given by one of the somatologists do not fully agree with those given by another (for instance, Hooton's with Sheldon's). Even more, Sheldon's study of delinquent youths shows that their somatic indices are fairly similar to those of military men, business executives, and psychiatrists; that 68 youths committed before the age of nineteen to cor-rectional institutions do not differ in their somatic traits from 132 youths not committed to such institutions. When his data are analyzed more carefully, they do not show any significant difference between the somatic types of the juvenile delinquents and of the normal youths.[12] Schluessler and Cressey summarized [13] some 113 studies of the personality traits of criminals compared with those of noncriminal control groups through ob-jective tests. Their conclusion is that these 113 studies (that cover almost all existing " objective " studies) do not show any consistent difference of personality traits of criminals compared with those of noncriminals. To sum up: the recent somatic theories are as doubtful in their validity as their earlier predecessors. If they fail to show the existence of causal con-nection between somatic and psychological traits generally, and especially between the somatic types and criminality, they still less succeed in con-necting altruism with somatic factors.

This does not exclude either a tangible influence of serious somatic de-fects, especially of organic defects of the nervous system or glands, upon mental and other properties of constitutionally defective persons. But the discussed somatic theories go far beyond this narrow and specific influence in their broadest claims of the almost all-determining role of somatotypes and characteristics. Likewise, the fallacies of the theories considered do not hinder hypothetical admission of a *subtle important function* which somatic constitution plays in influencing behavioral and psychological personality traits. The difficulty with the existing somatic theories lies in their failure to find out the somatic factors which are truly instrumental in a tangible conditioning of some specific psychological and behavioral traits. The traits, measurements, and types of the theories discussed are too coarse, too mechanical, too external, and too much of a surface nature to be the subtle, microscopical, inner, all-permeating somatic agents tangibly influencing man's conduct and mind. The genes and chromosomes of the geneticists can serve as an example of these subtle, inner, microscopical somatic factors. As the agencies of biological heredity in their interaction with the environment, they seem to be truly important somatic instrumentalities in determining several psychological and behavioral personality traits. Further on, in discussion of the role of biological heredity, something more will be said on this. For the present the above conclusions sum up the situation with the recent somatic theories.

*Still more untenable are the theories which ascribe all-decisive influence upon the main psychosocial traits of whole nations to a very narrow, external, superficial, and largely incidental factor.* These theories are replicas of the most primitive and most untenable somatic theories which ascribe all-decisive influence to a single somatic trait, like the color of eyes, curvature of nose, texture of hair, or stature, or cephalic index, and so on. The theory of the *swaddling of infants,* held by G. Gorer, J. Rickman, and in part M. Mead,[14] as one of the main factors of national character and culture, serves as an example of the grotesque theories. According to this particular theory, a legion of cultural and national characteristics of the Russian people stand in tangible connection with the Russian variety of infants' swaddling. Abundance of rage and fear; widely spread feelings of omnipotence and helplessness; switching from kindness to cruelty and vice versa; overdeveloped feelings of guilt and gratification; orgiastic feasts; pentecostal emphasis in religion; emphasis of " dark eyes "; depressive moods; Dostoevsky's novels; ritualistic religion; little concern for economy, cleanliness, and physical suffering; an autocratic regime punctured by riots and revolts; idealization of the leader and fear of authority; ambivalence in love and " avalanche fantasies "; desire of either absolute equality or complete subordination — these and a host of other characteristics are viewed as forthcoming from the factor of infant swaddling.

The theory represents a fantastic inflation of the Freudian belief in the importance of the ways and manner of early treatment of babies and of their early training in relieving their physiological needs. If the much more moderate Freudian theory is doubtful in a number of points, Gorer-Rickman-Mead's theory is entirely untenable. It is partly wrong in mapping the areas of the diffusion of certain ways of swaddling. It is perfectly dogmatic in ascribing to the factor of swaddling numerous psychosocial effects upon the personality of the swaddled infants and grown-ups.  It is wrong in viewing these effects as permanent.  It is wrong in asserting a series of traits as belonging to the whole nation.  It errs in viewing these national traits as specifically Russian or American.  It is doubly wrong in regarding the factor of swaddling as tangibly responsible for the alleged main characteristics of nations, of their history, culture, and institutions.  In these sweeping claims, the theory hardly gives any evidence for its corroboration.  What it presents as an evidence is a sham-evidence: a beggarly knowledge of the shreds of relevant factual material drowned in a mass of misinformation and plain ignorance, aggravated by a nonlogical interpretation due to the distorted Freudian biases of the authors.  The theory can be dismissed as a curious example of a grotesque fallacy parading in the uniform of science.

Without mentioning them, we can dismiss other theories of this kind, which like bad weeds continue to grow in the field of contemporary social, anthropological, and psychological sciences.  What has been said of the swaddling theory is applicable to all such " weed " theories.

## C. *Insufficiently Known Factors*

The factor of *biological heredity* belongs to this class.  It potentially determines a number of physical, psychological, and behavioral properties of an individual.  Among other things, without the hypothesis of a " fortunate " heredity, an early development of an altruistic genius — as well as a creative genius generally — can hardly be accounted for.  Likewise, the factor of a " bad " heredity seems to account for congenital — physical and mental — defects.  Broad temperamental dispositions, favorable for a development of either kindness and amiability or irritability and aggressiveness, also seem to be inherited to some extent.  Insofar the factor of biological heredity appears to be one of the potential factors of the " happy package " of our fortunate altruists.

On the other hand, an insufficient knowledge of this factor limits its heuristic value in the clarification of our problem.  The geneticists do not know exactly what kind of genes and chromosomes facilitate the development of a genius, and what kind produce a mediocrity; what sort contain a potential altruist, and what kind hatch an aggressor.  By a most careful examination of chromosomes and genes, the biologists cannot predict the potential type of personality they contain and can develop.  So far, their induction, diagnoses, and prognoses have followed the other way around: from the given traits of personality they deduce the kind of the chromosomes inherited.  With the exception of the fairly tenuous rule that talented parents tend to produce a higher rate of capable children than do mentally dull parents and that organically defective parents are likely to give defective progeny more frequently than do organically sound parents; in regard to the complex mental and moral traits, geneticists cannot predict with any accuracy which of the parental mental and moral characteristics will be inherited by their children, which will be not inherited, and what new characteristics will appear in the progeny. In these respects the factor of biological heredity has about as little predictive value as the factors of the divine grace, spiritual heredity, or karmic consequences. For this reason, the scientific role of the heredity factor in our problem is mainly *residual:* if and when we cannot account for some of the properties of a given person through tangible, manageable, and observable factors, these unaccountable traits can be referred to the residual factor of biological heredity. Such a reference should not, however, disguise the fact that by putting this factor in the place of the unknown $x$ we largely replace this unknown $x$ by a not much better known $y$. Therefore, the less we leave for accounting through this residual factor, the better: a substitution of one unknown for another does not increase our knowledge of the phenomena studied.

## II

### KNOWN, VERIFIED, AND VERIFIABLE FACTORS

#### A. *The Family*

Of all the known factors, the family seems to be the most important agency in determining the properties of individuals and groups, including the " lucky package " of the fortunate altruists. This was fully understood even by Confucius and was clearly formulated in his doctrine of filial piety.

Filial piety is the root of all virtue, and the stem out of which grows all moral teaching. Our bodies . . . are received from our parents, and we must not presume to injure them: this is the beginning of filial piety. When we have established our character by the practice of the filial course, so as to make our name famous in future ages, and thereby glorify our parents: this is the end of filial piety. It commences with the service of parents; it proceeds to the service of the ruler; it is completed by the establishment of the character. . . . He who loves his parents will not dare to incur the risk of being hated by any man. . . . For teaching the people to be affectionate and loving, there is nothing better than filial piety. . . . The services of love and reverence to parents when alive, and those of grief and sorrow to them when dead — these completely discharge the fundamental duty of living men. . . . By the practice of filial piety, the people are brought to live in peace and harmony [without any] ill will between superiors and inferiors.[15]

Subsequently a legion of social thinkers have indicated the decisive role of the family in molding the biological, mental, moral, and social properties of its offspring, the reasons for and the way of such a decisive influence, and what sort of family exerts a positive influence and what sort a negative influence.

The main reasons for all this is the uniquely multibonded character of the family, and the extremely vital biosocial and cultural functions it performs. As a socially sanctioned union of husband(s) and wife(wives), parents and children and relatives, the family members are bound together, ordinarily for life, by a large number of strongest psychosocial ties and by a satisfaction of the most vital needs: a) sexual; b) procreation of posterity; c) securing the race continuity; d) taking care of infants and children for the many years of their helplessness and inability to survive by themselves; e) procuring the means of subsistence for the members of the family; f) socialization, acculturation, and education of especially the younger generation — through linguistic, religious, moral, occupational, behavioral and other trainings — to fit it for adult life (in this respect the family has been the most important school for moral and altruistic molding of its young members); g) protection of the life, integrity, and values of the members from all enemies and dangers; h) mitigation of psychosocial isolation; i) promotion of happiness and creative development.

The overwhelming influence of these bonds and functions of the family is reinforced by the fact that the family is the first social group ordinarily entered by a newborn baby. It remains under the family's monopolistic influence during the formative years of its life, when the organism is plastic and when each influence leaves a lasting impression. Beginning with birth, and during the first few years of their life, the family continuously controls and " sculptures " its members by precept and example, persuasion and suggestion, constraint and punishment, and especially by abundant love in good families. It molds decisively most of the mental, moral, and social characteristics of personality. Even now, when the family is notably weakened in most of the urbanized and industrialized countries, it still remains the most important agency in the sociocultural and psychological molding of children. Even in such countries children follow a) the occupation of their parents in a higher proportion than any other occupation; b) the religion of the parents some 70 to 90 per cent of the time; c) the moral ideas, standards, mores, and manners of the parents more than those of any other group.[16]

The family not only decisively influences its members, but collectively influences practically the whole of mankind, because at least 95 per cent of human individuals are born in some sort of family, and pass through its decisive influence during the early part of their life. For all these reasons there is much truth in the statement that " what the family is, such will society be."

To be sure, in such a form the statement is one-sided; for just as the family tangibly conditions the other groups, these in their turn influence the family. However, the statement is substantially accurate in that the family formation essentially determines all the important groups and institutions of a given population. This fact has been well demonstrated in the past, especially by Confucius, and by P. LePlay and his followers in recent times. They have shown that in a population with a *dominant patriarchal type of family* the other groups and institutions and the entire sociocultural life assume the patriarchal character. Its concomitants comprise the absorption of the individual into the family " we "; domination of the familistic and paternalistic relationship in the state and other groups; stability and conservatism of the personality and conduct of the people; controlling power of tradition in contrast to that of modern fashion; meager scientific and technological inventions; and a slow tempo of sociocultural change. The reason is to be sought in the character of the training which the younger generation receives in the patriarchal family. In populations with a *dominant particularist type of family*, according to LePlay, the institutions and groups, the modes of thinking and acting, are permeated by a spirit of individualism. The prevailing characteristics are the development of self-reliance, initiative, energy, and creativeness; the spirit of innovation versus tradition; a multiplicity of scientific, technological, and other inventions and discoveries; a rapid tempo of progress; the control of the state and the state government by public opinion, and so on. Again, the explanation is that the particularist family molds the younger generations according to this pattern.

Finally, populations dominated by an *unstable type of family* neither educate the new generation to have respect for authority nor train them to be independent. Such a type of family develops individuals relying neither upon a stable patriarchal family nor upon themselves, but primarily upon the state. They are trained by the family for bureaucratic positions in the military and civil hierarchy of the state. Hence such societies are marked by a centralized bureaucracy which regulates and controls most of the social relationships; by an underdeveloped public opinion; by the absence of the traditionalism and the rational modernism of the patriarchal and particularist types of society, respectively; and by a general instability signalized by inconsistent and often irrational changes, sometimes of an explosive character.[17]

Such are the basic types of family and the corresponding national types, according to LePlay and his school. Apart from the one-sidedness of their thesis, it is approximately valid.

Molding most of the mental, social, and cultural traits of personality, the family strongly determines also the *moral* properties of the individual, including the presence or absence of the " lucky package " of the fortunate altruists. This influence of the family can be summed up in the following two propositions.

Proposition One. *As a general rule the families with prevalent discordant relationships among their members, especially between husband and wife, where a newly born baby is unwelcomed, where it is deprived of the grace of love and from its early days breathes the poisonous air of discord and enmity in the relationship of the members of the family to itself and to one another; where there is neither a set of high values preached and practiced, nor wise and loving discipline combined with creative freedom; such families tend to produce morally erratic persons, little capable of self-control, selfishly irresponsible, careless of the interests and well-being of others, and frequently criminal or delinquent.*

Proposition Two. *The families with a set of high values preached and practiced by their members, where harmony prevails in their relationship to one another and to the world at large, where intense and especially wise or adequate love permeates the whole life of the family, where a baby in its prenatal and postnatal life is welcomed and blessed with the grace of abundant and wise love; such families tend to produce well-disciplined persons with kind and happy dispositions, the potential possessors of the " lucky package " of the fortunate altruists.*

As to the first proposition, it is well ascertained by an enormous number of the existing studies of the factors of criminality and delinquency. All significant studies show 1. that discordant families and broken homes produce a much higher rate of delinquents and criminals than harmonious and strong families do; 2. that children unwelcomed and rejected by their parents and other members of the family, or children deprived of the grace of love in their early age, yield a much higher rate of demoralized, delinquent, and criminal individuals than children blessed by the grace of love; 3. that the broken and discordant families " manufacture " human beings hostile towards other human beings and the world at large in a much higher proportion than the harmonious families living in the " climate of love "; 4. all this means that the demoralized, poorly integrated, discordant families produce a low per cent of the potential fortunate altruists and an extremely high per cent of egotistic, erratic, neurotic, demoralized, and delinquent individuals; 5. in all these " productions " the family influence is possibly much greater than that of any other agency.

Out of an enormous body of evidence, only a few illustrative data taken from recent studies can be mentioned here. The bulk of the evidence is to be looked for in the studies referred to and in the vast literature given in these works.

In the Gluecks' study, " no cohesiveness " (or solidarity) in the delinquent families gives 24.7 per cent, while in the nondelinquent control families it is only 0.8 per cent; the families with " marked cohesiveness " make only 16.0 per cent in the delinquent families, while they make 61.8 per cent in the nondelinquent families.[18] Similarly, the families of the delinquents compared with those of the nondelinquent control group are found to be poorer in recreation, in supervision by the parents, in conduct of the parents at home, in conjugal relationships of parents, in self-respect of the family, and in many other cultural, mental, moral, and economic conditions. The difference is all the more significant because the control group is similar to the delinquent group in all the important respects: age, sex, economic level, neighborhood, ethnic, I. Q., and other conditions.[19]

In E. Shilder's study from 40 to 70 per cent of the delinquents came from broken homes, while only 25 per cent of the nondelinquents came from such homes.[20]

In C. Burt's investigation the ratio of broken homes among the delinquents and nondelinquents was 131.3 for delinquents to 35.2 for nondelinquents; 79 per cent of the delinquents had a poor family discipline, compared with 11.5 per cent of the nondelinquents.[21]

In a recent study by W. Warren of some 548 children in Maudsley Hospital in London, 90 cases of delinquents and 70 cases of nondelinquent children with neurotic disorders were selected for a special investigation. The results showed that the delinquent children came from families notably more deteriorated than the families of the neurotic children. The delinquent group had a much higher incidence of epilepsy and psychopathy among their parents and siblings than the neurotic group had. The delinquent group had a much higher percentage of bad neighborhoods and companions than the neurotic group. A much higher percentage of the delinquents showed lack of parental care, under-solicitude, hostility to both parents, and so on, than the children with neurotic disorders. In a number of other ways the home and the family of the delinquent children turned out to be more discordant and demoralized than those of the neurotic children.[22]

Of the matched 300 delinquents and 300 nondelinquents in a California study, 50.7 per cent of the delinquents had broken homes and 49.3 per cent were living with parents, while only 26.7 per cent of the nondelinquents had broken homes, and 73.3 per cent were living with parents. Compared with the nondelinquent children, a much higher per cent of the delinquents were poorly adjusted, did not like their home or living at home, hated their parents, had faulty discipline, and showed other defects in their family and home.[23]

H. Witmer's study showed that in clinical cases of children with an extreme lack of parental affection for the child, there was no improvement in 64 per cent of the cases in contrast to 97 per cent of the cases of complete improvement for the children blessed by a normal affectional relationship with their parents and members of the family.[24]

P. Wiers's study gave the following coefficients of correlation: .77 between divorce (in the family) and delinquency of the children; .77 between parental neglect of children and delinquency; .76 between employment of mother (with her absence from the children during the employment hours) and delinquency.[25]

A large number of other studies give similar results.[26] The total body of existing evidence hardly leaves any doubt that a discordant, disorderly, demoralized, broken and divorced family rejecting its children and depriving them of parental loving care is perhaps the main producer of selfish, disorderly, demoralized, delinquent and criminal human beings.

Many other agencies participate in this "unholy production," but the comparative role of each of these seems to be notably more modest than that of the bad family.

These conclusions are well sustained by the body of evidence that shows a close relationship *between a good family and the good human material produced by it for the human universe*. The total body of evidence here is not so vast as in the case of broken homes and delinquency; nevertheless, the existing studies uniformly show the causal connection between a good family and the good human material molded by it.

Of 484 Harvard and Radcliffe students who describe their childhood as happy, 72.8 per cent ascribe it to the family: parents' love and care, loving and loved siblings, and harmonious and good family organization. The same study disclosed that of the students who had a happy childhood, 67 per cent view the world and human nature affiliatively and kindly, while only 50 per cent of the students who had an unhappy childhood due largely to broken homes have an affiliative attitude towards their fellow men.[27]

A recent study of some 500 American Good Neighbors — persons who are somewhat above the average in their unselfish activities — shows that 70.6 per cent of them had a very happy and 18 per cent a fairly happy childhood, due mainly "to understanding and loving parents" (42 per cent of the reasons), to "love and respect in home" (32 per cent), "being kept busy with useful and interesting activities in the family" (14 per cent). Only 6 and 17 per cent (in two groups) mention an incompatibility of their parents, and zero per cent in one group, and 7 per cent in another report some troubles of delinquency.

The same study disclosed further that an overwhelming majority of the Good Neighbors with a happy childhood have grown in their "good neighborliness" along the path of the fortunate altruists, while most of the Good Neighbors with an unhappy childhood and parental home followed the path of the late altruists with the turning point of the "before and after the conversion." It is needless to add that practically all Good Neighbors with a happy childhood have a most friendly attitude towards social reality and the world at large.

Like their parental families the families of Good Neighbors themselves "are well integrated and function harmoniously." Only one family (out of some 500 families) reports delinquency trouble among its offspring.[28]

A study of all Christian Catholic and Russian Orthodox Saints show that some 70 per cent of them belong to the fortunate type of altruists. These came from harmonious families and were encouraged by their families in their activities which eventually led to their sainthood.

My studies show further that the *family still remains the most efficient agency in inculcating in the individual intensest affections and love towards its members*. No other agency or factor can compete with the fam-

ily in this " production of the intensest love and attachment of one individual to another." *The members of one's family are still one's dearest persons
in the whole world.* Asked to designate the ten dearest persons in the
whole world in a decreasing order of affection, a group of Harvard and
Radcliffe students gave the following results: 1. mother (51%); 2. father
(43%); 3. sibling (45%); 4. sibling (32%); 5–10. relatives and outside
family friends.[29]

Similarly for American Good Neighbors among "twelve dearest persons in the world," the first six places are occupied by kinsfolk. Only beginning with the seventh, do nonkinsfolk dearest become prevalent (mainly
because six persons about exhaust the members of one's immediate family).
Of the most dearly loved persons in this group the first place is occupied
by spouse (40.3%), parent (20.9%), and child (11.4%); the second place
is occupied by child (39.7%), parent (17.5%), and spouse (6.3%), and so
on.[30] Of 358 sympathetic responses observed in children under five years
of age, 285 were toward members of their family; 73 toward other people.[31]

Thus, in spite of a notable disintegration of kinship and the family in
the United States and other industrialized countries, the family still is a
far more efficient " manufacturer " of the intensest, most durable, purest,
and possibly most adequate love of one individual to several others, than
any other social group or factor. Herein lies the deep significance of
these data.

Several other studies disclose the general fact that a good family exerts
a no less powerful good influence upon its young generation than a bad
family generates a bad influence upon its members, and that the positive
influence of the family is still about the most powerful among the positive
influences of all other agencies.

For instance, the moral opinions of children show much greater resemblance to the moral values of their parents than to those of other persons.
In the study of Hartshorne, May, and Shuttleworth the correlation

| between children's moral ideas and those of their parents = | .545 |
|---|---|
| children's friends | .353 |
| club leaders | .137 |
| school teachers | .060 |
| Sunday school teachers | .002 |

Thus, the main source of children's knowledge of right and wrong is still
their home and the family.[32]

W. Lunden's study of socio-legal norms disclosed that students from
good families rank highest in Law Norm Scores, while students from
broken homes rank lowest. G. Allport's investigation of the factors of
religiosity among Harvard-Radcliffe students shows that parents are
mentioned in 67 per cent of the cases, while all other factors are mentioned
in notably lower percentages.[33]

The study of Havighurst and Taba [34] likewise disclosed the following correlation between good family relationships and the character of the children at different ages.

| Traits | Correlation for age groups | | |
|---|---|---|---|
| | 10 years | 13 years | 16 years |
| honesty | .65 | .40 | .24 |
| moral courage | .51 | .22 | .25 |
| friendliness | .71 | .35 | .24 |
| loyalty | .69 | .36 | .24 |
| responsibility | .79 | .43 | .34 |

The more harmonious the family, the better the child's moral reputation and behavior. With the passage of years, the parental family's influence tends naturally to weaken.

A considerable number of other studies well corroborate our Proposition Two.

Further corroboration of both propositions is given by pediatric, psychological, and psychiatric studies of the physical and mental well-being of children and their aggressive or affiliative tendencies. Almost unanimously these investigations show that, first, *love, and especially mother's love and real or artificial mothering, is a necessary condition for an infant's well-being and normal growth;* second, that *" rejected " infants and children, deprived of the bliss of love, develop anxiety, mental trouble, aggressiveness, and warped personality more frequently than the children blessed by wise and warm love;* and third, that *well-loved infants more frequently mature into persons with kind and friendly dispositions than " love-starved " children.*

Studies of marasmus or wasting away of infants, especially in well-to-do homes and hospitals where they have everything to satisfy their needs, show that one of its main factors is a lack of mother's love or warm love generally. Hence, the treatment of this disease is through giving them either genuine or artificial mothering.[35]

Lack of a warm mother's love — drinking from the mother's breast, mother's caresses, etc. — is one of the important factors in " unsocial behavior, hostile aggression, lack of patterns for giving and receiving affection, inability to understand and accept limitations, much insecurity in adapting to environment " which so frequently occur with the children and persons who spent their infancy in institutions with their " cold simulacrum of love." [36]

A series of careful researches shows further that such unloved children develop aggressiveness, hostility, and other mental and moral troubles much more frequently than loved children cultivated by loving families. Sometimes, when infants and children are suddenly separated from their families, as happened in England during the World War II bombings, the results of such a sudden separation by evacuation in the middle of the night from the bombed buildings turned out to be more injurious than the effects of the terrifying bombing itself. Of the evacuated children 61 per cent showed signs of strain for a period of three weeks to two months, but the majority recovered after this time from the shock of the air raid. The strain of separation from parents was generally greater, however, and the effects were more disastrous, especially upon the mental health of the children.[37]

At the present time almost all currents of psychiatry, psychology, and pediatrics fairly unanimously affirm the close relationship between a discordant family and the aggressive and hostile type of personality hatched by it.[38]

These lines of evidence are in an essential agreement with other lines given here.

On the basis of the total body of existing evidence we must conclude that *the most important factor of the " lucky package " of fortunate altruists is a good family as defined in our Proposition Two.* Though in most of the industrialized, urbanized, and Sensate countries the prevalent type of family is somewhat weakened and demoralized; though the quantity and quality of love in such families seem to be tangibly deteriorated; nevertheless, there still is a sizable portion of good families. Together with morally " fair " families, the good families allow the family to remain still the most powerful agency of creative altruization of its members and, through that, of the whole human population. Among the existing socializing and moralizing agencies there is none that can compete with the family in this respect. Even the school, and the church, the occupational group and neighborhood community, the state and other agencies are less influential in this respect than the family. In it lies the main secret of the " lucky package " of fortunate altruists.

## B. *The Other Agencies*

These conclusions do not mean that the family completely and monopolistically determines the properties of its members and, through them, of the human population. The above evidence shows only a preponderant influence of the respectively bad or good family. The data demonstrate that the discordant family yields a much higher quota of delinquents than the harmonious family, and the harmonious family a much higher quota of altruistic persons than the disharmonious family. The results do not prove that all discordant families actually deliver only delinquent posterity, and that all harmonious families produce only saints or good neighbors. Instead, the data show that some of the demoralized families do not produce delinquents and that now and then they even yield good persons. The same paradox is true of the harmonious families. A minor portion of these do not produce altruists or now and then they even yield a delinquent progeny. This means that in all such cases the influence of the family is overcome by that of a nonfamily agency.

The preceding chapter described, for instance, the case of St. Theodosius who had to struggle with his mother for several years in order to be able to devote himself to his altruistic and saintly activities. Gandhi had to overcome the resistance of his parental family and caste in order to carry on altruistic activities far more extensive than his parents and caste approved. A considerable number of other altruists collided with their parental family in their strivings for altruistic and saintly activities. Twenty-nine per cent of the parental families of the Christian Catholic Saints opposed their religious aspirations and the saints had to surmount their opposition in the realization of their saintly vocation.[39] Though in most of these cases the initial saintly and altruistic propensity was planted by the harmonious parental family, the extensity, purity, and adequacy of this family love happened to be insufficient or below the level and extent of love aspired to by the altruists and saints. Hence the conflict with the family, whose resistance was eventually overcome by the influence of nonfamily agencies working at variance with the family. This means that a special constellation of these other agencies can take the upper hand in overriding the good or bad influence of the family.

What are these agencies? This is answered by Proposition Three. *They are all the groups, persons, and forces with whom a child or youth directly interacts and to whose influence he is directly exposed. Other conditions being equal, the intenser and longer the interaction and exposure, the greater the influence of the group, or person, or nonhuman agency.*

The proposition assumes that the concrete important agencies satisfying these conditions are perceptually not always the same for different children and youths, in different human populations, cultures, societies, and periods. In other words, the concrete forms of these agencies are shifting. For one child such an agency may be a *gang of neighborhood children or playmates;* for another, a *nursery school, kindergarten, or elementary school* with its teachers, playmates and children; for the third, *the church,* its priest, service, and preachings; for the fourth, an *old illiterate nurse-poet* impressively telling fairy tales and heroic legends; for another, *a book* that incidentally is read or listened to; for still another, a *show* of itinerant players, *a movie, a pageant, a parade, a baseball or football or some other game, a radio or television program.* Sometimes the important agency can be a magnificent sunset, or a terrible thunderstorm, or a singing bird or the scene of killing an animal or ruining a bird nest or any other event in the inorganic or organic worlds. As a matter of fact, some of these agencies were actually met in the analysis of self-identification of the altruists described in the preceding chapter. The concrete character of such agencies is far more varied than the above enumeration suggests.

This diversity does not mean, however, that all these agencies actually play an equally important part. Some of them seem to function more frequently and exert a stronger effect than the others. All in all, *human groups, persons, and man-made culture, instrumentalities and environment play a more important role than the nonhuman forces.* Second, of human groups and individuals, the most important are: *the playmates, the school* with all its teachers, pupils, and cultural instrumentalities, if a child regularly participates in such activities; the *sport and recreational agencies* with their movies, television, radio, and other instrumentalities; *the church and the state,* insofar as its laws condition the organization and activities of all other social groups; a *specific* person, playmate, friend, sweetheart, counselor, doctor, spiritual leader, worshiped hero, etc., if a child interacts with such a person; and at a later age, the *occupational and economic groups* are especially important.[40]

All in all these human agencies generate their effects more frequently, more continuously, and more intensely than most other human and nonhuman agencies. If these influential agencies function well and their influence is vitally, morally, and mentally sound, they contribute an important share to the " lucky package " of the fortunate altruists. If their effects are poisonous, they supply their quota of delinquents, neurotics, and egotists. Sometimes, under specific conditions, their effects are as strong as, or even stronger than, the influence of the family. The comparative power of these nonfamily agencies varies in accordance with different situations.

The following actual data give an idea of the varying comparative role of nonfamily agencies in their conditioning of saintliness, altruism, happiness, unhappiness, length of time exposure, and so on.

In about 43 per cent of the Christian Saints the *family and kinship* agencies determined their first steps on the road to sainthood. In the remaining 57 per cent, 27.9 per cent of the Saints were determined in their first steps by *specific persons,* and 29.2 per cent by *religious, monastic and educational institutions.*[41]

American Good Neighbors ascribe their good-neighborliness in 29 per cent of the cases to the parental family; in 28 per cent to cultural factors and social institutions (other than the family, religion, and school); in 21 per cent to religion; in 8 per cent to schools; in 11 per cent to personal life experience in the sense of the retroactive effects of thoughts, emotions, and actions. Only in 1 per cent is it ascribed to books.[42]

Four hundred and eighty-four Harvard and Radcliffe students ascribe their childhood happiness in 72.8 per cent of all factors mentioned to their parental family; in 26.8 per cent to their playmates and friends; in 13.6 per cent to their school. On the other hand, 171 students who felt unhappy in childhood ascribe their unhappiness in 26.2 per cent of all factors mentioned to the unharmonious parental family; in 29.1 per cent to a lack of playmates or to uncongenial playmates; in 16.3 per cent to school;

in 44.4 per cent to poor health, physical handicaps, and other maladjustments.[43]

Judged by similarity of moral opinions of children with those of other persons and groups, the influence of children's friends (r = .353) comes next to that of the family (r = .545), in the study of Hartshorne, May, and Shuttleworth previously cited.

If we take grown-up persons, the urban (Boston) white-collared unemployed, the time of their exposure to and interaction with specified groups is appraised by the following indices: alone, 36.14; with friends, 35.67; with family members, 24.09; with business associates, 8.85; with relatives, 3.15; with casual acquaintances, 1.26; with neighbors, 0.78; with strangers, 0.20.[44] Since these are grownups, living away from the parental families, and unemployed, and mostly unmarried, their exposure to the family is less than to friends; next after the friends and the family come the business associates.

These figures illustrate the main nonfamily agencies and their varying character for the different persons studied. If these agencies generate integrating and creatively altruistic effects, they contribute to the "lucky package" of the fortunate altruists. If their influence is negative, they contribute to demoralization and delinquency.

Finally, the influence of a specific *person* playing a decisive role in the life of a given child or youth is to be added to the above factors. Whatever are the reasons for the exceptionally strong influence of such a person — be it a teacher, psychiatrist, spiritual guide, doctor, chum, benefactor, enemy, lover, etc. — and whether the effects are healthy or poisonous, for some children and youths (though not for all) this sort of *personal* actor sometimes is one of the strongest.

Such, then, seem to be the tangible and testable agencies of the "lucky package" studied. The most important role of these agencies consists exactly in *supplying the child with the initial " lucky package," and in starting him thus along the path of the creatively altruistic life career.*

## C. The Factor of the Retroactive Influence of the First Good Deeds

Once started by these agencies in performance of altruistic and creative actions, the child puts himself under the influence of the retroactive effects of his first good deeds. These leave strong positive traces upon the child's physical, mental, and moral personality and begin to shape his behavior altruistically. The retroactive influence of his good deeds reinforces his creatively altruistic propensity for further altruistic actions. In this way the child enters a happy circle of mutual reinforcement of his altruistic propensity by his good deeds and of his good deeds by the retroactive reinforcement of his altrustic tendencies. The more and the longer he acts altruistically, the stronger becomes his altruistic disposition; the stronger the disposition becomes, the more vigorous becomes his altruistic overt behavior.  Once started along the right path, the child thus begins to build his own personality and his own life through his actions and their retroactive consequences.  Among other things he easily completes *self-identification* with the supraconscious value.

With each additional performance of an unselfish deed, his altruistic behavior and mentality become increasingly *habitual,* deeper and deeper grounded in the child's whole personality, until the *habit turns into a second nature.*  As explained in Chapter Three, an increase in habituation of creatively altruistic actions means an *accumulation of the energy of creative love in a given individual.*  The more this supreme energy accumulates, the more transfigured the individual becomes from an instrumentality of the coarse, selfish forces into an agent of sublime love.  In these happy conditions the altruistic children quietly grow in their altruism and overcome " road blocks " on their royal highway to the kingdom of creative love.

D. *The Residual Factor of " Fortunate Heredity " or " Divine Grace " or " Spiritual Heredity "*

With the exception of the geniuses of love, the outlined tangible and testable factors fairly well account for the how and why of the " lucky package " of fortunate altruists.  What these factors do not sufficiently explain is the phenomenon of the geniuses of inexhaustible love: how and why do they happen to be endowed with an extraordinary amount of sublimest love far in excess of the love endowment of most ordinary persons?  The geniuses of creative love are in the same enigmatic position in which are the creative geniuses in science, religion, philosophy, art, technology, and other fields of human creativity.  The greatest creators in all these fields also seem to be inexplicable through the totality of observable and testable environmental factors.  For an adequate explanation of genius, the residual factor of " fortunate heredity " or " divine grace " or " spiritual heredity " is to be invoked.  I pointed out before that unfortunately such an untestable residual factor does not help much empirically; we cannot either predict its operations or satisfactorily explain the how and why of the distribution of this " mystical energy."  If it does not help much empirically, however, it helps logically: it fills the hole of the unaccountable force, and urges heuristically to bring to the light of our knowledge its nature and mode of operation.  With an increased concentration of research at this residual factor, its mysterious nature can be somewhat elucidated.  It may eventually be clarified empirically and used for practical purposes.

## III

### Summary and Practical Prescription

The preceding analysis strongly suggests that *it is much easier to grow in the family garden a large crop of creative altruists from newborn babies than it is to transform a grown-up egoist into an altruist or to graft an " altruistic scion " onto a coarse, selfish stem.* The methods of transformation and grafting are much more wasteful and require much greater energy, time, economic, mental, and moral efforts than the method of " growing " altruists in the good family gardens supplemented by those of the mentioned nonfamily groups.

If all parents take necessary pains with their " family gardens " and cultivate each newborn baby with all the care of a wise and adequate love, in the short span of one or two generations they can multiply many times the beautiful altruistic flowers at the cost of the weeds of stupid selfishness and poisonous criminality. So far, the *method of " family gardens " is the easiest and most fruitful way of transformation of the human universe from an ugly wilderness into a magnificent garden of Eden.*

*Chapter Twelve*

# Inner Conflicts and Precipitating
# Factors of the Late Altruists

## I

### Preconversion Disintegration of Their Egos-Values-Group Affiliations

Having elucidated the how and why of the "lucky package" of fortunate altruists and of their quiet creative growth, we now turn to the how and why of the conversion in the life cycle of late altruists. Why and how do they undergo a conversion from a selfish way of life into an unselfish one? What are the forces that work it out and what are the stages of their self-identification and transfiguration? These are the problems to be elucidated now.

*Three sets of factors seem to be instrumental in preparing, precipitating and accomplishing the transformation:* 1) *an increasingly painful discord of the egos, values, group affiliations of the prospective convert, in his preconversion period;* 2) *the precipitating factors;* 3) *the factors leading to completion of self-identification and altruistic transfiguration.* The preconversion state of a late altruist is marked by increasingly painful conflicts of his values-egos-groups with one another. These conflicts rob the individual of his peace of mind, elementary comfort, and happiness. The person's unity increasingly deteriorates. He turns into a self-contradictory, confused, and frustrated "sick soul." Now deeply depressed, now irritated, he experiences life as increasingly painful and meaningless. Escape from such an inner anarchy becomes an overpowering urge and commanding necessity.

Unfortunately, these efforts do not always lead to an altruistic or religious conversion, or to a creative transformation generally (scientific, artistic, philosophical, etc.). *Only a minority of the "sick souls" find their way out along the path of creative reintegration of their egos-values-group affiliations.* A majority of such souls are less lucky. They try to scape along the roads which are more accessible and easier than the way of creative overcoming of the obstacles.   These accessible roads bring the unfortunate pilgrims either to a) suicide, or b) officially certified mental disorder, or c) " unofficial " mental confusion, " split soul," and psychoneurosis, or d) moral and mental regression to the level of a brutal, aggressive, and selfishly sensual human animal, or e) semi-animal submissive passivity and dumb patience, or f) a cynical sensualism of the " enjoy yourself, it is later than you think " type.

These are the typical ways taken by the majority of individuals out of torturous conflicts of their egos-values-group affiliations.

Now let us see, first, whether the prospective altruists do experience at their preconversion stage the described conflicts of their egos-values-group affiliations; and second, whether the outlined typical " ways out " of the painful inner warfare are really taken by the respective minority and majority.

The total body of evidence available clearly confirms the hypothesis of the disintegrated " inner package " of the prospective converts.   *Logical evidence* tells us that if they were not in this painful state of inner conflict, they would not have needed at all to look for a way out of it.

*Empirically*, an overwhelming majority of the moral and spiritual converts display such a preconversion state.

Beginning with Gautama Buddha, passing on to St. Augustine, St. Francis, Ignatius Loyola, and ending with Brother Joseph, all the late and almost all the intermediary altruists, described in Chapter Nine, experienced these painful inner conflicts.   A careful study of hundreds of other religious and altruistic converts displays a similar inner warfare of their egos-values-groups at their preconversion phase (Leo Tolstoi, Bunyan, George Fox, Pascal, Cardinal Newman, Manzoni, F. J. Kinsman, Paul Bourget, G. Papini, Madame de la Vallière, and other religious and moral converts).[1]

Leo Tolstoi's description of his own state of mind before his altruistic reintegration excellently depicts the situation.   His inner disintegration appeared when he was about the age of fifty.

I felt that something had broken within me on which my life had always rested, that I had nothing left to hold on to, and that morally my life had stopped.   An invincible force impelled me to get rid of my existence, in one way or another. . . .   I did not know what I wanted.   I was afraid of life. . . . All this took place at a time when so far as all my outer circumstances went, I ought to have been completely happy.   I had a good wife who loved me and whom I loved; good children and a large property. . . .   I was respected more than I had ever been; I was loaded with praise; and without exaggeration I could believe my name already famous.   Moreover, I was neither insane nor ill.   And yet, I could give no reasonable meaning to any action of my life. . . . My state of mind was as if some wicked and stupid jest was being played upon me by someone. . . .[2]

James gives several other autobiographical descriptions of the preconversion state of the " sick soul." For example:

> I was both a burthen and terror to myself, says Bunyan; nor did I ever so know, as now, what it was to be weary of my life, and yet afraid to die. . . I found myself as on a miry bog that shook if I did but stir. . . .[3]

Henry Alline, a noted evangelist of the eighteenth century, states: " Everything I saw seemed to be a burden to me." [4]

In a varied form this confused, conflicting, depressed and " aimless ' state of mind is experienced by practically all the late religious and moral converts. Like the late converts-mystics, they pass through the stage of " a dark night of the soul," often " the most terrible of all the experiences of the mystic way " with its sense of an utter loneliness, aimless drift, and absence of any divine or other inspiring force.[5]

In our recent study of seventy-three religious and moral converts in Boston, thirty-eight conversions were found to be quite superficial: they did not tangibly change the moral behavior of the converts. The remaining conversions appeared to be moderately genuine in the sense of a tangible ideological and speech-reactional change. These tangible convert report dissatisfaction, depressive mood, mental confusion and various inner conflicts: intellectual, religious, moral, sexual, and other, up to the state of an utter loneliness and insecurity. A notable physicist writes about his preconversion state of intellectual conflict between the strictly deterministic (Newtonian) viewpoint and the creatively indeterministic view suggested by reading Toynbee's work and by the quantum theory. " Quantum theory breaks with Newtonian science in that you look at the inanimate world statistically, and this allows for variety, within a statistical framework. . . . This coupled with Toynbee made me realize that man is a free agent. . . ." Eventually, the latter standpoint prevailed and led to the resolution of the conflict in acceptance of a belief that " conforming through free will and choice means to conform to the Divine will. If a man conforms to the Divine will, he is content. Contentment is a magnificent gift of God, and is worthy to be called God-Love."

Another convert was greatly troubled by the " sin " of masturbation for a period of seven years, which " sin " led to several other inner conflicts of his egos, values, and group affiliations. Another convert was led into the state of a rebellion against God by a paralysis that afflicted her brother. " Since my brother became paralyzed, I hadn't been able to view God as good." A conflict between her previous religious beliefs and the new disbelief followed, reinforced by other moral conflicts.

Another " intellectual " convert reports that " at the age of seven prayed to God, and made a bargain with Him. He didn't keep his part of the bargain. . . . I made a clay image of God. After two weeks broke it to pieces. I was victorious. Later on, I considered this as a sign

hat the Protestant God had rejected me." In this rebellious way he
started his long quest for religious and ethical values and satisfactory group
affiliations. "At 13 I attended a Baptist Revival Meeting. I left it in utter
disgust. I felt everything but Jesus. I was converted at that point decisively from Protestantism to Atheism." This, however, did not satisfy
him or clear his confusion. At the age of seventeen he became a Unitarian
Humanist and tried to help people in various ways. One time he even
thought about going into a Humanist ministry, but gave it up. On the
one hand he "felt himself too smart to be among unintellectual people
as those in Sunday School" and "I had no respect for any preacher: they
all seemed to be something between villains and fools." On the other, he
became a Sunday School teacher, and was "still something of anti-Chris-
tian in my teaching and preaching." This self-contradictory vacillation
continued, with an increasing dissatisfaction, up to 1947, when finally he
was converted to Catholicism, by the tolerance, kindness, and love of the
monsignor at the Roman Catholic Cathedral in Raleigh.

Another convert's preconversion depression and conflicts were created
by the death of her mother, sister, and father — all within a few years they
"walloped" her and left her in utter loneliness and confusion. The conflict was reinforced by a self-contradiction of her father during his illness.

My father was a man who preached that sudden death was sudden glory.
Yet, when he was ill, he was afraid to die. I wondered about this. We could
not even put the lights out at night, he was so afraid. I remember one day I
said, "Something is wrong with this religion; it gives no fortitude." All during my father's illness, he kept the Bible closed. He did only what the doctor
said and took medicine. . . . This waiting for him to die had a great effect
upon me. *I got to the place I could not sleep or eat. I felt myself just going,
going . . .* [depressed and confused].

Another convert, a 30-year-old divorcee, reports about her conflicts
arising from her divorce. The problem of living alone after living with
someone for five years created feelings of loneliness and depression. She
also felt that men had a tendency to think that she was easily approachable
sexually, and she was constantly bothered by sexual advances. Formerly
an ardent churchgoer she felt also that others looked down upon her because she was a divorcee. Her own sex impulses added to these conflicts.
On their basis a number of other moral and religious confusions arose.
In their totality they induced a state of depressive lonesomeness, mental
and moral conflicts.

The above examples are only a few out of many variations of the inner
conflicts and confusions at the preconversion stage of religious and moral
converts. Other cases of this sort were given in Chapter Nine; and still
others will be met subsequently in Chapter Fourteen.

In somewhat different form a state of discomfort, severe frustration, depressive moods, and psychoneurotic symptoms are experienced by most

creative thinkers in other fields of creativity at the preliminary phases of
their creative efforts, when they are groping for the solution to their
problems.  These preliminary stages in scientific, philosophical, artistic
or technological creativity correspond to the preconversion phase of altruistic and religious creativity.  Most scientific, artistic, technological, or
philosophical creators pass indeed through this state of conflict of their
egos-values-group affiliations.  E. D. Hutchinson correctly indicates that
the first two stages of the process of creative discovery in science and of
creative achievement in the fine arts are the stages of " preparation and
frustration."  The first " preparation stage " of trial and error in thinking
of the problem and of " hit and miss " experimentation induces " the beginning of severe frustration."  Subsequently, until the solution of the
problem is found — and often this takes a long time — the frustration develops and is marked by the creator's restlessness, irritability, inferiority
feelings, recession, depressive moods, renunciations and involuntary re-
calls of the problem, and mild psychoneurotic symptoms.[6]

Hutchinson gives a considerable number of cases showing this " pre-
creative phase."  Thus Bertrand Russell says: " In all the creative work
that I have done, what has come first is a *problem, a puzzle involving discomfort.*"[7]  Other creators similarly testify to having at the preliminary
phase " headache and daze," " fatigue and depression," " sense of immi-
nent failure," " gloomy mood," " irritability," and so on (Sir W. M
Flinders Petrie, Dr. Banesh Hoffman, Dr. John Yellot, M. A. Rosanoff
Dr. H. Alling, and others).

Anyone who even in a small degree has participated in a truly creative
work knows by his own experience this preinvention, prediscovery, or
precreation depressive, irritable, and uncomfortable state of mind.  Altruistic creativity is but a variety of creativity generally.  The similarity
of the preconversion stage in this field with the precreation phase in other
fields of creativity is but an additional evidence of the accuracy of the
proposition discussed.  The tension of the preliminary phase in all creative
fields is the driving force that does not allow the creator to stop at this
painful stage.  Creative pregnancy with its pains and tensions precede
and leads to the either creative or abortive birth of altruistic, or religious
or scientific or artistic achievement.  So much about the preconversion
state of the late altruists and the force that drives the " sick souls " to find
some way out.

## II

### THE NONCREATIVE " SOLUTIONS " OF THE INNER CONFLICTS
### OF EGOS-VALUES-GROUP AFFILIATIONS

The creative solution of the disintegrated state of one's egos, values
and group affiliations is accessible only to a limited minority.  Only Bee

thoven or Smetana, stricken with deafness, could overcome it by soaring to new heights of musical creativity; common musicians can hardly do that. Only stuttering Demosthenes could conquer his defect by becoming one of the greatest orators of all times. Only Schubert and Mozart, well aware of their approaching death, answered its challenge by the creation of their greatest immortal masterpieces. Only Milton after becoming blind in 1652 could write his greatest works: *Paradise Lost, Paradise Regained, Samson Agonistes,* and his best sonnets. Only altruistic and religious geniuses can turn the disintegration of their egos, values, and group affiliations into a supreme moral or religious transfiguration.

The rank and file of the disintegrated " souls " solve their inner conflicts, painful confusions, and depressive moods through the more accessible but less creative methods, enumerated above.[8]

Some of them become the victims of *suicide.* The conflicts of egos-values-group affiliations lead to this tragic " solution " by two ways or for two reasons. The inner conflicts are followed by depressive moods, by anxiety and melancholia, or, in other terms, by retarded and anxious depressions. In these depressions " the danger of suicide is very great, many acutely depressed persons being unremitting in their plans and attempts at self-destruction." [9] In spite of the vigilance in hospitals, a number of these " sick souls " end their life by suicide. The inner conflicts enormously increase the psychosocial isolation or lonesomeness of their victims. The victim's social bonds start to break and are cut off. A social vacuum begins to surround him. He becomes increasingly shut in his own sick shell. This sort of psychosocial isolation appears to be the main cause of " an egoistic suicide " as an intentional preference of death to life.[10] For these two reasons a small portion of the disintegrated persons " solve " conflicts of their egos-values-group affiliations in this tragic way.

*A much larger portion of the disintegrated souls " solve " their problem by becoming " official " mental cases,* called by the terms of maniac, melancholiac, depressive, sometimes schizophrenic, paranoiac, and the like. Whatever the name, the sick soul becomes one of numerous patients of psychopathic hospitals.

*A still larger portion turn into " split souls," the utterly confused individuals whose right hand denies what their left hand affirms.* These inconsistent and self-contradictory persons remain at large, outside of mental hospitals, though they are as " abnormal " and dangerous as the officially diagnosed mental cases. In the periods of great social upheavals, when the inner conflicts enormously multiply and appear in millions of human beings, this " solution " of the conflicts becomes particularly " popular." Millions of our fellow men belong to this type of split souls, confused minds, and self-contradictory Hamlets.[11]

*Perhaps a still larger portion of the disintegrated souls turn into the human " broken reeds."* Having failed after several attempts to resolve their conflicts creatively, they lose the very capacity to fight them, and acquiesce in an equilibrium of dumb patience and submissive passivity. They become the apathetic "masses" subjugated and manipulated by dictators, tyrants, and by all sorts of autocratic bosses. Their inner pseudo-equilibrium is established on the lowest — the unconscious and the bioconscious — levels of human personality. They do not resolve the conflicts by soaring above them and overcoming them through creative forces. Instead, they "regress" to the primitive level of a human animal; they lose the superconscious and finest conscious levels of their personality (as the main seats of most of the inner conflicts). With their loss they "get rid" of most of the inner conflicts. Figuratively speaking, they get their semi-animal "peace of mind" through a sort of mental and moral "lobotomy." In our age millions and millions of human beings are resolving their inner conflicts in this regressive manner.

*Millions of other human beings try to end their inner conflicts by a similar regression to the level of an aggressive brute.* They are an active counterpart of the spiritually "broken" human animals. Instead of submissiveness, these brutes attack, destroy, and subjugate by rudest force and fraud everybody who stands in their way.[12] Having lost their moral, religious, civic, and other inhibitions, they are not hindered by any inner scruples in their aggressive activities. Beginning with the habitual murderer and ending with all "crusaders" clamoring for war and extermination of all their opponents, these "carnivorous" human beings get rid of their inner conflicts by reverting to the level of the cunning human brutes. They use their intellect mainly for aggressive purposes. In times of great social upheavals millions of people resolve their inner conflicts in this way. Side by side with the millions of human "broken reeds," in our times there are millions of "crusading" aggressors. They have been killing their victims and one another in untold numbers in World War I and II, in the gigantic civil wars of the Chinese, Russian, and other revolutions, in endless riots, "suppressions," and "police actions," and in the less bloody but still brutal strifes of various "crusaders" with one another.

*A "resolution" of the inner conflicts intermediary between those of "dumb passivity" and "brutal aggressiveness" consists in a regression to the level of a cynical, sensual human animal.* This way out of the inner conflicts exists in primitive and sophisticated forms. Both forms are identical in their central motto: "eat, drink, and be merry, for tomorrow we die." The cynical sensualists disvalue all the moral, religious, or other high values, principles, and commandments. They "empty" themselves of these "foolish and embarrassing superstitions." They free themselves from all the "naive" inhibitions that hinder sensual pleasure or impose sensual pain. They do not believe in any justice or God or karma or retribution, except the physical punishment imposed by physical agents. Being primitive hedonists and utilitarianists, they strive by any means available to get as much of the sensual pleasures, and to avoid as much of the sensual sufferings, as possible. *Carpe diem*, " Enjoy yourself as long and as much as you can," and " Don't give a hoot for anything or anyone else " are the rules of their life. These cynical sensualists are found among the human brutes as well as among the submissive human animals. They make an intermediary variation of these two types.

Such are the noncreative " resolutions " of the inner disorganization of egos, values, and group affiliations practiced by a vast majority of individuals infected with inner conflicts. Further on we shall see that in the periods of mass suffering and frustration, both creative and uncreative ways of resolution of inner conflicts appear and grow. Their growth results in a uniformity called the law of polarization. " In a generalized form the *law of polarization states that a crisis, calamity, suffering, frustration, or inner conflict tends to make explicit and open the implicit and hidden contradictions, whether in one's mind and conduct, or in a social group and institution, or in a given culture.*" [13]

Further on we shall return to the law of polarization. For the present the above gives an adequate description of the preconversion crisis of egos-values-group affiliations of the late altruists, and of its driving force toward resolution, whether creative or noncreative.

## III

### The Precipitating Factors of Altruistic Transformation

In the process of the " bumpy " life career of the late (and to some extent of the intermediary) altruists, there is a critical period. It divides their life into two parts — *before* and *after* the conversion. It involves also the operation of what can be called the precipitating factors of the transformation. *Any event or events that make overt the hitherto covert inner conflicts, that bring them out and render them behaviorally observable, can be called the precipitating factors.*

These appear when the inner conflicts reach a high tension, and are ready to burst into the open or to pass from the inner " state of mind " into the observable actions. Though the precipitants are part and parcel of the numerous factors that start and maintain the inner conflicts in their covert form; nevertheless, they appear as a definite event or a series of tangible events that stand out as a landmark of a sharp turn in the individual's life. They start and greatly accelerate the overt behavioral change.

*Diverse Precipitants.* In their concrete forms the precipitating events are diverse. Let us glance at their main forms. The meetings by Gautama Buddha in his luxurious and carefree milieu with a *senile man, then a sick man, then a dead man* seem to have started him on the path of his Enlightenment and liberation from the sorrows of old age, disease, and the endless round of deaths and births.  These meetings, plus *ennui with a hedonistic life, and the difficulties in his marriage*, served as the precipitants to bring into the open his inner conflicts.  These precipitants made him secretly leave his luxurious home and become a wandering pilgrim in quest of the path of true liberation.[14]

More reliable is the information about Sri Chaitanya (the great apostle of Vaishnavism, 1485–1533 A.D.).  His fairly sudden change from a proud, aristocratic pundit, conscious of his intellectual superiority, delighting in the defeat of his opponents, full of life, fun, and play, into the humblest of the humble, serving the old, the infirm, and the lower castes, was started by the *death of his first wife from a snake bite, and then by meeting, during his pilgrimage, a venerable Vaishnava guru, Mityananda,* who initiated him into the mysteries of the bhakti cult at Gaya.  The crisis was so sharp that at its beginning he tried to commit suicide.  " His whole spiritual [and behavioral] outlook was changed " within a short period of a few years.[15]

The conversion of Pelagia from a prostitute into a saint was started by a *sermon* by Bishop Nonnus which she happened to hear.  The conversion of St. Mary, the Harlot, from a prostitute into an eremitic saint was decisively influenced by the blessed Abraham, her hermit-uncle, who came to her city.  By his *action of unbounded love and readiness to take upon himself her sins*, he eventually succeeded in returning her to the hermitage in the desert.

A prostitute hired to seduce a hermit was converted into a saintly and good woman by the hermit's *action of burning* one by one his five fingers while she tried to seduce him.[16]

St. Tychon of Zadonsk (1724–1783) tells that two events played an important part in his change of position from a lay teacher in a theological seminary to that of an altruistic monk, and finally to a bishop.  One event was *an escape from a fatal fall* from a highly elevated position in a church building when the rail suddenly fell down and he was thrown back as though by some unseen force; and the other, *a mystic vision of an open sky* " with a glow such as mortal tongue is unable to describe." [17]

*An escape from death or a deadly danger* and a *beatific vision* played the role of precipitant in a great many lives of notable altruists.

An eminent mystic, John of Ruysbroeck, sums up the situation as follows: " The grace of God touches a man from without and from within.  From without through sickness; or through the loss of external goods, of kinsmen, and of friends; or through public disgrace.  Or he may be stirred by a sermon, or by the examples of the saints or of good men, their words, or their deeds; so that he learns to recognize himself as he is." " Sometimes a man is touched also from within through remembering the sorrows and the sufferings of our life." From this " prevenient grace arises a natural repentance of sins and a natural goodwill." Then come efficacious grace (Agape), supernatural light, " the free conversion of the will, in a single moment of time," " the union of love of God and Soul." " Of these two things — the grace of God and the free conversion of the will enlightened by grace — charity, that is, divine love, is born." [18]

*Unexpected Kindness as Precipitant.* One of the fairly general events starting conversion is *an act of unexpected kindness or unmerited love towards the future convert*, especially when he had reason to expect hate, anger, retaliation, and the like on the part of the other party. The typical pattern of this kind of precipitation of altruistic and spiritual conversion is magnificently described by Victor Hugo in his *Les Misérables*. An ex-convict, Jean Valjean, bitter against the whole world, robbed the good bishop who gave him hospitality. Caught with the goods on him, Jean Valjean was brought back to the bishop to certify that the goods were stolen from him. The bishop's statement to the police, that he had given these goods to Jean Valjean, first dumbfounded the ex-convict, and then shook him to the bottom of his heart. This shock decisively turned the man on the path of subsequent transfiguration.

In various forms this kind of action serves frequently as a most powerful precipitating factor. Thus, among the saintly hermits we are told of several cases quite similar to that of Jean Valjean. The wisdom of the Desert Fathers generalized it in the form of a rule: " It is not possible that by dint of harshness and austerity a man shall lightly be recalled from his [bad] intent: but by gentleness shalt thou call him back to thee." [19] Jesus' " Love your enemy " and requite by love for hatred; similar precepts of Taoism, Hinduism, Buddhism, and of most of the great religious and ethical systems, as well as the moral teachings of L. Tolstoi, F. Dostoievsky, and M. K. Gandhi, are in fact among the most efficient, verified, and valid educational and therapeutic prescriptions. Of course, as any medicine, these precepts do not work unexceptionally — cases of failure of the rule are certainly known; but for the purposes of altruization it works much more frequently than the opposite rule of revenge, hateful retaliation, punishment, compulsion, anger, and animosity.

One of the poor patients of Dr. T. Haas (treated by him free of any charge) stole his watch and then was caught. Dr. Haas informed the police that he gave the watch to the thief; then he invited him in, talked to him cordially, and gave him money. The patient was radically cured from his antisocial tendencies. [20]

" One day St. Tychon of Zadonsk heard of a squire who mistreated his serfs." He intervened and betook himself to the lord. In the dispute the nobleman forgot himself so much as to strike the bishop on the cheek. St. Tychon left the nobleman's house, but on the way changed his mind, returned to the nobleman, fell at his feet, and begged his forgiveness for " having led him into such a temptation."

" This unexpected act of the pastor, who knew no anger, so deeply impressed the nobleman that he himself fell upon his knees at the Bishop's feet, imploring forgiveness. From that day on his behavior towards his serfs was completely altered." [21]

Before meeting Sri Ramakrishna, Swami Vivekananda was a sophisticated student, " sceptic, with no faith in the Hindu Gods," and full of mockery at the Hindu scriptures. He regarded Ramakrishna as a maniac, a self-hypnotized fraud, possibly having some mesmeric power. Just for the sake of curiosity he and his friends decided to visit Ramakrishna. The first and the second visits were the decisive precipitating events in Vivekananda's subsequent life. Ramakrishna's unusual kindness and peculiar love, together with his answer to Vivekananda's sarcastic question: " Have you seen God, Sir " (" Yes, I see Him just as I see you here "), combined with the " mystic touch " by Ramakrishna's right foot — these actions of Ramakrishna changed the whole direction of Vivekananda's life in a comparatively short period of time. [22]

Many facts of this sort have been given in Chapter Four. To mention them again, from 3 to 7 per cent of the living American Good Neighbors were precipitated in their altruism by *an unusual and unexpected kindness granted to them.* So were also many of the Christian Saints. [23] Among Harvard and Radcliffe students 2.3 per cent were positively influenced by unexpected kindness. [24] Two and nine-tenths per cent of seventy-three Boston converts were precipitated by kindness of a believer to them. In 37 per cent of the cases studied, gratitude is mentioned as a factor of awakening religious sentiment of Harvard and Radcliffe students. [25] Kindness aroused kind reaction among the patients of the Boston Psychopathic Hospital, [26] among Harvard and Radcliffe students, [27] children, [28] and other groups. [29]

In an experimental transformation of five pairs of inimical relationships of Harvard-Radcliffe students into amicable ones, the factor of *kind and good deeds,* rendered by one party to the other in each of five pairs, was the most successful precipitant and technique. [30] In R. M. Brickner's clinical treatment of a paranoiac, the technique of a constant, prolonged, and persevering friendliness succeeded in dissipating the patient's suspicions and aggressiveness. In a study of M. E. Bonney, the techniques of praising, complimenting, highly valuing, initiating friendly discussions, helping, and stimulating to a higher level of behavior proved most successful in " how to make friends." [31] In M. D. Fite's experimentation, the technique of *helping* aggressive children to find a good solution in their immediate problems proved to be much more successful in curing their aggressiveness than the techniques of reproofs, repression, and punishment. [32]

In contemporary psychotherapy, as we have seen, the technique of kindness to the patient is a basic precept for every competent psychiatrist. In many successful treatments the kindness and love are possibly the most important factors in the cure of the patients.[33]  Still more the technique of love is used in any successful moral and social education of normal children.

Use of the precipitant of kindness in spectacular and unspectacular form is a daily occurrence.  Generally speaking, a very large proportion of persons are " precipitated " in an altruistic direction by actions of unmerited, unexpected, or gratuitous kindness.  Beginning with the daily altruization of members of all good families, where the technique of love and kindness is used as the main method of the members towards one another, and ending with hundreds of truly socializing interrelations between persons and groups, *the therapy of overwhelming kindness has been one of the main forces maintaining the necessary minimum of justice, peace, harmony, and altruism in all societies and at all times.*

## IV

### CATASTROPHES, SUFFERING, AND FRUSTRATIONS AS PRECIPITANTS

Side by side with the precipitant of kindness, these are very frequent precipitants of altruistic transformation.  In comparison with the precipitant of kindness, catastrophic and frustrating precipitants have much more diverse, often opposite (positive and negative) influence upon different persons and groups.

In view of the widely accepted erroneous theories about the character of the moral influence of suffering, frustration, or catastrophe, we shall stop at this problem somewhat more than we do in regard to other precipitants.

*Two Prevalent Theories.*  Prevalent views on this matter are expressed by two diametrically opposite theories.  Since almost immemorial times, one view contends that sufferings and calamities purify, spiritualize, and altruistically ennoble the individuals and groups involved.  Aeschylus' " it is through suffering that [moral] learning comes "; the motto of the New Testament, and of other religions, that " whom the Lord loveth, He chasteneth; and scourgeth every son whom He receiveth " — these are ancient formulas of this belief.

Not only John of Ruysbroeck but also John Woolman expresses this belief, saying that a smallpox epidemic and other calamities " are the messengers from the Almighty to be an assistant in the course of virtue and to incite us to consider whether we employ our time only in such things as are consistent with perfect wisdom and goodness." [34]

Numerous recent examples are represented by the statements of Father Yelchaninov and A. J. Toynbee.  " Our Lord has infinite pity for us, and yet He sends us suffering; it is only when we are stricken by calamity that we are able to yield a certain sacred fire." [35]  Toynbee repeats this, saying that " after all, one of the deepest spiritual laws that we know is the law that ' it is through suffering that learning comes ' "; that suffering is the way "for getting into closer communion with God, and becoming less unlike Him"; that "in this world we do learn by suffering." [36]

The opposite view — also very old — has been more fashionable in recent times. S. Freud, and in his wake a legion of psychologists, psychiatrists, sociologists, and moralists, maintain that suffering, calamity, and tragedy are a variety of frustration; and frustration invariably produces aggression against the direct and indirect agencies of frustration. Since aggression is possibly the sharpest form of an active egoism attacking and inflicting pain upon others, this means that suffering-frustration tends to generate aggression, enmity, and strife in all their forms, from the bloodiest to the mildest, from the most overt up to the hidden tendencies of animosity. Freud, viewing the search for pleasure and avoidance of pain as the primordial force of human nature, saw frustration in each instance that pleasure-seeking or pain-avoiding was thwarted. Aggression is thus "the primordial reaction" to any frustration or suffering.[37]

*Frustration and Aggression* by J. Dollard, N. E. Miller, L. W. Dobb, O. H. Mowrer, and R. R. Sears can serve as a conspicuous example of Freudian views among contemporary psychologists and social scientists. Trying to show themselves to be "quite scientific," the authors open their study with the categorical "basic postulate" that "aggression is always a consequence of frustration," and that "aggression inevitably follows frustration." [38] Following this postulate, the authors deduce a series of dogmatic "generalizations," that are based (with a very few exceptions) on practically nothing but "illustrative and imaginary cases." By uncritically accepting Freud, they extend the meaning of "aggression" to "self-aggression" (self-criticism, self-control, suicide, self-altruization, "catharsis," etc.), thus depriving the term of any definite meaning and covering by it a series of quite different — and often opposite — phenomena.[39]

Such are the two prevalent theories concerning the egoistic or altruistic, aggressive or spiritualizing effects of calamities, miseries, suffering, and frustration upon individuals and groups.

The mutual contradiction of these hypotheses is already evidence of their invalid one-sidedness. What serves as factual and logical evidence to support and corroborate one theory is evidence of the one-sidedness and fallacy of the other theory. In addition, a long series of experimental, semi-experimental, observational, statistical, and historical facts openly contradict the one-sided claim of either of the theories considered.

## V

### Main Types of Responses to Frustration, Suffering, Calamity

Contrary to the theory that suffering always ennobles, the body of evidence shows that in many cases suffering, frustration, and calamity produce not altruization — the spiritual and moral ennoblement of persons and groups — but either dumb passivity and stultification, or an increase of egoism, selfish aggression against persons and groups, and spiritual and moral degradation.    On the other hand, the relevant factual evidence also shows that frustration does not always lead to aggressive reaction.    Aggression is only one of several main reactions.    In many cases, contrary to the theory of frustration-aggression, frustration in the form of calamity, misery, grief, sorrow, tragedy, or the thwarting of pleasure-seeking and pain-avoiding actions, produces not an aggression against others, but several types of reaction different from aggression: a) submissive passivity and dumb patience; b) redoubling of the creative efforts by frustrated persons, especially creative geniuses, to transcend the frustrating obstacles; c) searching self-criticism, self-control, decrease of selfishness, increase of altruism, religious spiritualization, and moral ennoblement; d) mental disorders and confusion; e) cynical sensualism; f) suicide.    Leaving the last three types without discussion here, let us comment briefly on the other effects of the catastrophic precipitants.

1.  It is a daily occurrence that frustrations develop in many persons and groups an unaggressive submission and dumb patience towards all the forces that block their desires and objectives.[40]   Without any aggressive protest they submit to the misfortunes in the same way that many of us submit to bad weather, snow, rain, drought, and storms.   We may suffer from this inclemency, but we do not shake our fists at the heavens, nor curse and attack anything or anybody.   We just patiently endure and suffer.   This attitude develops especially well when our first efforts to overcome the frustration fail.

The development of this sort of reaction to frustrations is particularly evident when a given group is conquered either by an external enemy or, in internal revolutions, by the victorious faction.   At the beginning of such a conquest, part of the conquered population tries to fight the conquerors and reacts aggressively; while another part passively submits and tries to do its best under the circumstances.   If the attempts of the aggressive part repeatedly fail, it also becomes " tamed," and gradually turns into a dumb and submissive broken reed that cannot be straightened and aggressive.   Like trees that, having been slightly bent, tend to straighten but lose this " aggressiveness to straighten " if they are broken or kept bound by a rope for a sufficiently long time, so individuals and groups lose their inclination to fight the conqueror after being " broken " or kept " bound " for a sufficiently long time.   Some individuals and groups do not show such aggressiveness at all.

It is exactly on this passive submissiveness that many conquerors and dictators build their domination over the subjugated populations.   If, at the beginning, the dominant group must use the rudest means of coercion, punishment, and terror, after a certain period of bloody tyranny their domination becomes " natural ": the population submits to the conquerors without any severe coercive measures. Slaves and serfs, outcasts and lower castes, the conquered peoples that have accepted their lot for many generations without even questioning the right of their masters — these serve as solid, perennial, and universal evidence of the existence of this passive submissivity as one of the typical reactions to frustrations. History, and the daily observation of the relationships between various bosses and their subordinates (who are frequently frustrated by their bosses), supply unlimited examples of these sorts of phenomena. Some of the disabled and infirm also react in this way.[41]

2. In other cases frustration is reacted to by increased creative efforts on the part of artists, scientists, inventors, thinkers, and moral and religious creators. Lord Byron's lameness reinforced his efforts to be a great poet. Mirabeau's ugliness made him " boil with ambition, ravenous for fame." [42] Such a catastrophic frustration as deafness did not make Beethoven or Smetana more aggressive, but increased and improved their creative work. The same is true of the blindness of Milton. The incessant frustration of poverty, the death of his mother, the lack of appreciation on the part of his early patron, the Archbishop of Salzburg, up to later frustrations in his efforts to obtain the position at the Hapsburg court, failed to make Mozart aggressive, but rather stimulated his creative endeavor to overcome these difficulties by redoubling his creative activities. Frustrations of poverty, nonrecognition, and other painful obstacles did not stop the creative achievements of Schubert, and of many other musical, literary, and artistic men of genius, nor did they make them more aggressive. The catastrophe of being condemned to death and then to many years of hard labor in the worst of prisons did not crush Dostoievsky; neither did it make him aggressive. On the contrary, it seems to have awakened his creative bent. Many eminent scientists and technological inventors — beginning with Archimedes and ending with the Edisons, the Sikorskys, the Curies, and a legion of others — experienced very serious obstructions and frustrations before they succeeded in their purpose. And yet, these frustrations did not make them aggressive, but only stimulated, redoubled, and tripled their energies.

Moreover, *some amount of frustration is rather necessary to stimulate the efforts and creativity of all persons*, ordinary individuals as well as geniuses. When things are too easy and no frustration blocks their activities, their energies may remain latent or only a small fraction of their potential talent may become active.[43]

3. Finally, in many cases, frustration and catastrophe, or suffering, is reacted to by an increase of altruism and decrease of egoism, by a religious

and moral transfiguration, by the elimination or weakening of aggression instead of its emergence or reinforcement. So many relevant, easily observable, and testable facts of this sort exist, that only a few typical ones need be mentioned here.

In the first place, the transformation of a number of persons from self-centered egoists into altruistic beings, from irreligious or little religious into religious and from sinful into saintly individuals, was precipitated precisely through intense frustration, suffering, or calamity.

The frustrations of a *long illness, of being a prisoner of war, of humiliation at the hands of nobles, and of sharp conflict with his father* were the precipitants of St. Francis' transformation from a dissipated golden youth into an incarnation of the deepest, purest, unbounded love.[44] Similarly, the conversion of St. Ignatius Loyola, "up to twenty-six years of his age given to the vanities of the world," was started during the *long sickness, and painful surgical operations* described before. Dunstan was going to marry but, becoming *severely sick*, sent for the bishop (instead) and received monastic consecration.[45]

The first step in the transformation of Augustine from a lusty sophisticated intellectual into a saint was started by the *death* of his dear friend.[46] The Irish *plague* of 685 A.D. and the *death of a dear companion* precipitated the religious and altruistic transfiguration of Egbert.[47] St. Theresa's transformation was precipitated by her *sickness* and *fits*, and especially by her most serious illness soon after her entrance into the monastery.[48] St. Paul's conversion, as we have seen, was precipitated by his *sudden fit, blindness, fall from a horse and injury* that occurred on his way to Damascus where he was to "purge" the Christians.[49] "And he fell to the earth, and heard a voice saying unto him: Saul, Saul, why persecutest thou me? . . . And trembling and astonished . . . Saul arose from the earth. . . . And he was three days without sight, and neither did eat nor drink." [50]

*Sickness*, followed by two years of solitude, marks the beginning of the conversion of Al Ghazzali, the greatest Islamic theologian and saint (b. 1058).[51]

The *loss of his wife* marks the beginning of Tukaram's (1608–1649) altruization.[52] *The death of his beloved Fiametta, plus sickness* in 1374 and other misfortunes changed Boccaccio from a libertine and freethinker into a religious and ethical man. *The shock* which Raymond Lull (b. 1235) experienced when the woman he wanted to seduce reproachfully and dramatically exhibited to him her cancerous breasts marks the radical change in his life.[53]

*The death of her child* played a similar role in the conversion of Jacopone da Todi. *The death of his mother* was "the first and bitterest grief" in the life of Ruysbroeck, and it accelerated his piety and led him to the priesthood.[54]

*The death of his wife* from a snake bite precipitated the spiritual and moral transfiguration of Chaitanya.[55]

*Escape from a deadly danger* played the role of precipitant for St. Tychon.[56]

*The shock of his first imprisonment* by the English precipitated Sri Aurobindo's conversion from an atheist and radical political fighter into a saintly Yogin.[57]

*A grave illness of three years' duration,* culminating in a vision of the Mother of Jesus, accelerated and accentuated the saintly progress of Serafim of Sarov.[58]

A similar precipitant, namely *sickness,* marks the beginning of Mohammed's religious career and the conversion of St. Hildegard of Bingen. *Illness and the cooling off towards her of Louis XIV* caused the conversion of Madame de la Vallière, as did *disease* in the case of H. Cohen and F. Coppée, and the loss of his wife in the case of F. Leseur. Cardinal Newman's conversion to Catholicism was started by *the condemnation of his tracts and the moral abandonment* by his Protestant colleagues and friends.[59] *A death sentence,* commuted to long imprisonment under the harshest conditions in "the House of the Dead" changed F. Dostoevsky into an intensely religious and ethical man. *Deafness, followed by grave sickness* (abdominal inflammation) in 1825, and other misfortunes, mark Beethoven's increasing religiosity.[60] *Imprisonment* precipitated the religious conversion of G. Papini. *Sickness and various misfortunes* were responsible for spurts of religiosity and moral ennoblement in the lives of F. I. Kinsman, Paul Bourget, Alfred de Musset, Pascal, Heinrich Heine, van Gogh, and St. John of the Cross. *A bad wound* received by Brother Lawrence in the Thirty Years' War, together with the horrors of the war, "kindled in him such a love of God that he could not tell whether it had increased in the more than forty years that he lived since." [61] *An unlucky marriage and five years of "desolation"* led to the almost instantaneous conversion of Catherine of Genoa.[62]

*Grave sickness and the danger of death* turned many Renaissance libertines, like Perpaolo Boscoli, Codrus Urseus and others, into religious persons.[63] Eleven per cent of 3090 Christian Saints, about 2 per cent of some 700 American Good Neighbors, and about 15 per cent of the Harvard and Radcliffe students studied were made more religious or/and more altruistic by some sort of catastrophe. For 46.9 per cent of the students who experienced a notable change in their life, the catastrophic precipitants were as follows: *illness,* 8.6 per cent; *bereavement,* 6.2 per cent; *dear person's misfortune or illness,* 3.9 per cent; *accident,* 2.3 per cent; *disappointment in love,* 2.3 per cent; *family breakdown,* 1.6 per cent; *military service,* 1.6 per cent; *war,* 2.3 per cent. Of 73 Boston converts, 8 conversions were precipitated by the death of a dear person or by fear of their own death; 9 by unhappy marriage; 1 by unfortunate sex experience; 6

by sickness; 3 by other misfortunes. Of some 500 students studied by G. Allport and others, 8 per cent credited their religious awakening to sex turmoil, 17 per cent to sorrow and bereavement, and 42 per cent to fear and insecurity.[64] Moreover, a misfortune, such as being condemned to death, causes some of the recently condemned to repent, turn to God, and become more moral, while others become yet more hardened in their criminality and go to death without any repentance, cursing God and everything of moral value.[65]

A *positive ethico-religious polarization* (paralleled by a negative one) *almost invariably occurs on a mass scale in a city or region, nation or other group subjected to an important calamity, whether it be war, pestilence, famine, revolution, earthquake, flood, and so on.* It is clearly exemplified by a polarization in the population of Halifax, Nova Scotia, which occurred when an explosion of two ammunition ships, on December 6, 1917, destroyed a large part of the city, killing hundreds and wounding thousands. Deeds of sublimest altruism, contrasted with actions of human "ghouls and vultures," exploded at once on a large scale.[66]

During World War II a similar polarization took place in several "thickly populated areas" which were exposed to ammunition explosion, mass bombing, atomic bombing, eruption of Vesuvius and other volcanoes, or some other catastrophe. The population directly involved in a catastrophe has invariably exhibited a spectacular increase of altruism and spiritual ennoblement, side by side with a striking eruption of demoralization, human bestiality, and criminal egoism.

A systematic study of practically all important wars, bloody revolutions, famines, pestilences, earthquakes, floods, volcano eruptions, and other forms of catastrophe clearly shows that invariably this double-faced uniformity of polarization occurs.[67]

Moreover, a systematic verification of this uniformity shows that in the history of ancient Egypt, Babylonia, the Greco-Roman world, China, India, and Europe *almost all the important steps in their ethico-religious progress occurred precisely in periods of short or long catastrophes, or immediately after these had reached their peak.* (These steps were *paralleled by demoralization and bestialization of another part of the population.*)[68]

*To sum up:* there is hardly any doubt that an intense frustration, great suffering, or notable calamity has functioned as a precipitant for altruization of persons and groups. This effect of frustration is no less general and uniform than the effect of aggressiveness, selfishness, and animalization.

The net result of this analysis is to demonstrate that both theories discussed are one-sided and fallacious. *They assume that there is only one way of reacting to frustrating circumstances* (either by positive transfiguration or aggression) *whereas in fact there are several* (at least six) *outlined patterns of response: a*) *egoistic aggression* (*brutalization and demoralization*); *b*) *dull apathy and patient submissiveness; c*) *redoubling of creative and other — nonaggressive — efforts; d*) *spiritual and altruistic transfiguration; e*) *mental disorders and confusion; f*) *suicide.*

All six types of reactions to frustration-suffering-calamity have occurred on a mass scale during the calamitous period 1940–1954.[69] *Millions of persons and many social groups on almost all continents of this planet have exhibited an extraordinary explosion of arch-bestial and bloodiest aggression against other human beings and groups.* The twentieth century before World War II was already the bloodiest of the preceding twenty-five centuries of Greco-Roman and Western history, so far as wars are concerned; it was also the bloodiest and most turbulent century with respect to revolutions, civil wars, and important internal disturbances; and, finally, it was at least as criminal as any other century before.[70] The period 1940–1953 continued this exceptionally bloody, merciless, and gigantic aggressiveness of the preceding period. World War II, with its victims numbering into the millions, the Apocalyptic destruction of almost one-sixth of the inhabited territory of this planet, numerous civil wars, endless guerilla wars, exceptionally high criminality, anarchy, and demoralization — these phenomena testify to the elemental planetary explosion of aggressiveness as a response to the extraordinarily frustrating, painful, and catastrophic conditions of the period. Mercy, compassion, and sympathy seem to have vanished. Man the killer continues to run rampant in his sadistic and masochistic orgy. The decade stoutly confirms that for many millions aggression naturally follows frustration, or develops hand in hand with it.

No less eloquently does the period demonstrate the *passive submissiveness of yet more numerous millions to frustration, suffering, and calamity.* After several unsuccessful attempts to defend or regain their freedom from the dictatorial, tyrannical, or intolerable regimes of Lenin-Stalin, Hitler, Mussolini, Tito, Franco, the " democratic regimes " of Quirino, Syngman Rhee, Mao Tse-tung, and other Communist, Fascist, and " democratic "-totalitarian and colonial governments — millions of revolters against such regimes, after repeated merciless suppressions, have turned into broken reeds, unable to straighten and oppose the oppressors and tyrants. They simply became dumb human animals, patiently bearing anything their rulers imposed upon them. Moreover, after one or two decades of such passive submissiveness, they have become genuine supporters and glorifiers of their tyrannical bosses. If not the whole population, then at least substantial parts of it, in Soviet Russia or China, Indonesia or North Korea, in the Third Reich or Italy, in Spain or in several Latin American countries, in Morocco, Malaya, Tunisia, South

Africa, and other colonies, have changed from being bitter opponents of the regime to loyal and enthusiastic followers of their previous oppressors. The total number of such people has to be computed by tens, perhaps even by hundreds, of millions on this planet. The period strikingly corroborates the conclusion that apathetic submissiveness (which sometimes turns into loyal adherence) is an unquestionable reaction to frustration, as common and frequent as the reaction of aggression.

*The transcendence of frustration by creative effort is generally a much less frequent response than aggressive or submissive reactions.* Creativity is a very rare flower in comparison with the weeds of aggression and submissiveness. It becomes especially rare in periods like ours, when a hitherto existing dominant (Sensate) form of sociocultural order disintegrates and a new form is only at its inception.[71] Nevertheless, a few of these rare flowers have blossomed as a reaction of creative geniuses to the period's frustrations. A number of scientists made important discoveries in the mathematical, physico-chemical, and biological sciences. Atomic discoveries were only a part of these. A number of inventors and engineers created and constructed atomic plants, new types of airplanes, and many other things. Several biologists discovered new medical preparations. Unfortunately, a large part of the discoveries and inventions in the physical and biological fields turned out to be destructive and deadly, rather than constructive and vitalizing. In this respect they were one of the important manifestations of the aggressiveness of the period. However, a part of these discoveries and inventions were peacefully constructive. They served the needs of life and not of death; and they facilitated the forces of harmony, co-operation, and good will, instead of those of hate, death, and destruction. Therefore, this part of the discoveries and inventions was a manifestation of a creative response to a frustrating calamity.

The same is true of the decade's creativity in the field of religion, philosophy, ethics, law, social sciences, humanities, and the fine arts. Though the total creativity in these fields was relatively insignificant; though a large part of revived beliefs, philosophies, theories, ideologies, and art creations was negative rather than positive, hate-laden rather than love-laden, demoralizing rather than integrating, debilitating rather than revitalizing — nevertheless, a small portion of these creations were mentally, morally, and aesthetically ennobling and inspired the love of God, the world, and one's fellow men. To this extent, their authors transcended the endless frustrations of the period by creative effort; and this effort is likely to grow in the future.

The period also witnessed a notable upsurge of altruistic love, compassion, empathy, unselfish sacrifice, ascetic stoicism, revived spirituality, and revitalized religiosity. Almost each act of aggression has been followed by actions of sympathy and help to its victims. Thousands of unrecorded deeds of heroic sacrifice have been performed daily by the relatives, friends, neighbors, and strangers of the victims of all sorts of aggression. Often whole communities and nations rendered most unselfish help to the suffering parts of humanity. Though our press, radio, and television record such altruistic actions less frequently than the aggressive deeds, nevertheless the former have been almost as frequent as the latter. An altruistic and spiritual response to the period's endless frustrations also emerged and grew, side by side with the other three responses.

Finally, the period has been marked also by an increase of official and especially unofficial mental disorders and of depressive suicide.

This means that all the other variations of the one-sided theories of " frustration-aggression " or " frustration-altruistic spiritualization " are also one-sided: as, for instance, the theory that claims the invariable increase (or decrease) of criminality in periods of crisis and catastrophes, or the theory that asserts there is an invariable increase of religiosity (or atheism), spiritualization (or demoralization), creative renaissance (or creative decay) in periods of calamities. Each of these one-sided theories sees only one effect of frustration-suffering-calamity instead of the above six effects, and especially the polarized effects of increased aggression and altruistic love, demoralization and moral ennoblement, spiritualized religiosity and sensual atheism, dumb submissiveness and dynamic creativity.

Having indicated this, we can now examine more closely the forms of individual, social, and cultural polarization which take place during the catastrophic periods generally.

# VI

## THE LAW OF POLARIZATION IN FRUSTRATIONS, CRISES, AND CALAMITIES

This basic law of psychosocial uniformity is still unknown to the public at large, as well as to social scientists and psychologists. Defined, analyzed, and demonstrated elsewhere,[72] it can here be formulated in a still more generalized form than in its earlier delineation. In this generalized form the law of polarization states that *a crisis, calamity, or frustration tends to make explicit and open the implicit and hidden contradictions, whether in one's mind and conduct, or in a social group and institution, or in a given culture.*

### A. *Polarization in an Individual*

If there is a covert split in the mind or in the conduct of a person, under the conditions of calamity or crisis this becomes overt. The polarization assumes one of the following three forms: a) If the contradictory tendencies are about equal in strength, then the mind and conduct of a person remain split into two irreconcilable parts that war with each other, the one denying what the other affirms, the one destroying what the other constructs. The individual becomes a split personality. b) If there are several multilateral contradictory tendencies, the individual's mind and behavior disintegrate, becoming devoid of unity and consistency. Both turn out to be jerky, confused, incoherent, and abnormal. c) If the contradictory tendencies in the individual are unequal in strength, then the stronger tendency overcomes the weaker ones. As a result the individual now becomes more consistent and intense in his dominant (stronger) tendency or trait. If for instance, in the contradictory tendencies of sinfulness and saintliness, the sinful bent happens to be stronger, such a person during a crisis or calamity becomes more intense and consistent in his sinfulness than before the crisis. If the saintly bent in him is potentially stronger, then under conditions of some tragedy he becomes much more saintly than before. Tragedies and frustrations tend to split the soul and behavior of the same person into two contrasting parts: the black soul of an aggressive beast, and the white soul of a self-sacrificing, unselfish, and loving person. In normal conditions this split does not exist or is only latent. Misfortune tends to make it explicit with a deep chasm between the two parts. The Nazis or the Communists or soldiers during wartime show this split of the soul clearly. One of their main egos kills, tortures, destroys, rapes, and plunders "enemies" without any remorse and uneasy conscience; their other main ego sacrifices their own life, well-being, property, and other values for their Nazi party and the Third Reich; for their Communist party and the Soviet Fatherland; for their "My country, right or wrong." And this sacrifice is altruistic in its nature.[73]

The same is true of any contradictory tendencies in the thought, words, deeds, or relationships of an individual. Polarization in a person expresses itself either in the appearance of an open and unbridgeable split in the mind and actions (when the contradictory bents are about equal in strength), or in a psychoneurotic disintegration of his personality (when there are several or multilateral contradictions), or in an intensification of the strongest contradictory tendency, elimination of its opponents, and a corresponding polarized, fanatical integration of the person.

## B. *Polarization in a Group or Institution*

Under the conditions of calamity, a covert and potential contradiction among the members of a group becomes overt and actual; it grows in its intensity and splits the group into openly opposed factions. Its extreme poles tend to grow at the cost of its central, balanced majority. For instance, under normal conditions the majority of a social group is neither particularly saintly, nor particularly sinful. It tries to render unto God what is God's and unto Caesar what is Caesar's. Under conditions of calamity this majority begins to melt from both ends: a part of its previously balanced members become more sinful, while another part become more saintly than before the crisis. Some become brutalized, others intensely socialized. Some disintegrate morally, mentally, and biologically; others are steeled into an unbreakable unity. In adversity some lose their sense of honor; others are ethically ennobled and spiritually reinforced. In certain respects adversity or frustration is destructive in all fields of culture; in other respects it proves to be a stimulating and constructive force, making for a cultural renaissance. In calamity, two trends appear in a group: one is a trend toward irreligiosity and demoralization; the other is a trend toward extreme spiritual and moral exaltation. The group thus becomes polarized, and an open conflict flares up between its opposed factions.

Under normal conditions the political majority of a group is made up of the totality of balanced, moderate parties. The extremely reactionary or revolutionary parties are almost always a minority. When a severe catastrophe befalls the group, it drastically splits: its extreme parties tend to grow at the expense of its moderate parties. Political conflict becomes intense and violent. The group polarizes politically.

A similar polarization in a group may occur around other contradictory values and interests, if and when these are important for a given group at a given moment. Religious, economic, artistic, political, philosophic, ethical, juridical, and other contradictory values and interests cause the polarization of many social groups. In a great calamity the group polarization tends to become "multilateral" or "total," involving many sets of contradictory values and interests, and splitting the group into two or more irreconcilable factions warring ruthlessly with one another.

## C. Polarization in a Culture

Under the conditions of catastrophe, a hitherto hidden contradiction between meaningful cultural values or phenomena becomes explicit. Becoming open, the contradiction leads to an open fight for survival or domination among the contradictory values. In this struggle sometimes the weaker value — defeated by the stronger — disintegrates, whereas the stronger value grows in integration and power; at other times competitors mutually destroy each other, giving a victory to a *tertius gaudens* — to a third value that either transcends both fighting values or synthesizes their positive merits, or just happens to be favored by lucky circumstances. In both cases the defeated cultural values disintegrate, become increasingly incoherent, and lose their prestige and influence.

The polarization in cultural values is paralleled concretely by an enormous intensification of the struggle between the partisans (individuals and groups) of each competing value. The competing values appear to their partisans as the end values, as the absolutes that do not permit any reconciliation, any compromise. As a result the struggle itself often turns into a bloody strife in which each party tries to destroy its opponent to the *majorem gloriam* of its cultural value. The struggle for domination and existence of various religious values, with their religious wars and bloody suppression of heretics; the struggle of various political values of monarchies or republics, with their civil wars and revolutions; the fight between capitalism and communism, regimented and free enterprise, democracy and despotism, with corresponding " cold " and " hot " wars, are examples of this sort of cultural polarization.

Such, in brief, is the central point of the law of polarization and its personal, social, and cultural forms.[74]

## VII

### OTHER PRECIPITANTS

The above patterns do not exhaust all the varieties of the precipitants. A *book, sermon, lecture, play, movie, etc.*, may play this role. Two per cent of our Boston converts, 4 per cent of the American Good Neighbors, and 10.9 per cent of the students studied had these sorts of precipitants.

An *extraordinary person* — father, mother, sibling, spiritual guide, pal, preacher, teacher, lover, altruist, friend, doctor, etc., — often serves the role of a precipitant. Twenty and six-tenths per cent of our students, 6 per cent of the Good Neighbors, 10 per cent of our Boston converts, and 41.1 per cent of the Christian Saints studied were affected by the influence of specific persons.

An *injustice, discrimination, or unexpected unkindness* was the precipitant for 3 per cent of American Good Neighbors, and 4.3 per cent of Harvard-Radcliffe students studied. *War* was a precipitant for 5 per cent of the Good Neighbors and 2.3 per cent of the students.[75] Terrible or happy events experienced or observed; the sight of a starry sky; the fury of a storm; migration and travel; and hundreds of other diverse phenomena served as precipitants for various persons and groups. Practically anything and anybody can serve this role under certain conditions. The influence of the precipitants is due not so much to their physical, chemical, biological, or sociocultural traits as much as to their role of a match at the proper time touching the inflammable material. Their real role consists in *making open and explicit the disharmony and conflicts of the egos, values, and group affiliations of respective persons and groups.* This " inner warfare " — with the concomitant dissatisfaction, restlessness, lack of peace of mind — must become intense, must be vaguely or clearly experienced by a person, in order that the precipitant can bring it into the open. Without this tension, no event can play the role of the precipitant. When the tension is " ripe," any event can play this role. The enumerated kinds of precipitants seem to play this role especially frequently and successfully.

*Prescription.* From this analysis the following practical prescription follows: *For persons and groups that are in a state of the inner warfare a precipitant can be prescribed. But its nature must well fit the specific conditions of the persons and groups. A well-selected precipitant may open the hidden " inner war."* In this way *it may precipitate the process of altruization.*

*Precipitants in the Conversion of the Intermediary Type of Altruists.* Between the course of the fortunate altruists, where no precipitants are necessary, and the contrasting course of the " converted " apostles of love, stand the cases of the intermediary altruists where there is no specific event changing the life course abruptly. Instead, a series of events is observable that in their *cumulative totality* after some period of time lead to a tangible change. Among these events there may be one or two tangibly accelerating the transformation, but they are just links in a chain of several events.

# VIII

## CONCLUSION

The above accounts for the preconversion state of the late altruists. The deep inner war of their egos-values-group affiliations becomes a stern driving force coercing them to find a resolution of their painful inner conflicts. If they succeed in choosing a creative method of resolution (in contrast to the noncreative ways out: suicide, mental disorder, brutalization, cynical sensualism, dumb submissiveness), they are precipitated in their endeavors by a number of different events, forces, and agents. Most common of these precipitants are: unexpected, expected, and gratuitously granted love, kindness, or help; different catastrophes — illness, accident, death of a dearest person, happy or unhappy love, expectation of one's own death and disaster, fear and insecurity, other tragedies, misfortunes of one's friends or close relatives, war, and so on; unexpected and undeserved unkindness and discrimination; extraordinary influence upon the future convert of a specific person — a close relative, spiritual guide, teacher, doctor, lover, chum, etc.; book, lecture, sermon, play, movie, and similar stimuli; an example of heroic and sublime love observed by the potential altruist; a magnificent event of nature; and so on.

In discussing the precipitants and the creative and uncreative methods of resolution of the inner conflicts, the utter one-sidedness of two prevalent theories in the field has been demonstrated and the law of polarization has been discussed. If we put into one *class of the creative resolution* of the inner conflicts altruistic and all other creative overcomings of the inner warfare, and into *the class of the uncreative resolution:* suicide, mental disorders, brutalization, increase of selfishness, dumb submissiveness and cynical sensualism, then *the law of creative and uncreative polariza-*

*tion is the only valid, general uniformity occurring in persons and groups
visited by catastrophe, frustration, or suffering.*

## IX

### IMPORTANCE OF THE FIRST STEPS AFTER PRECIPITATION

The preceding analysis shows that the precipitants push some persons
to the creative and some others to the uncreative solution of their inner
warfare. Among the totality of the forces that determine the kind of
solution for each individual, *the role of the first ideological and behavioral
responses to the precipitants is to be specifically mentioned.*

The first few deeds they do after the precipitation, and the first ideological self-identification they happen to construct in the state of their
inner warfare, often have a decisive influence on the course they follow
in the resolution of their conflicts. In the state of their utmost disequilibrium, the slightest force can throw them on either the creative and
altruistic path of resolution, or upon the noncreative ways of apathy,
cynical sensualism, brutalization, mental insanity, or suicide. If the first
self-identification is made with creative love or some other great value,
and if the intentional or unintentioned first deeds are altruistic or creative,
the consequences of such ideas and deeds help to break the unstable equilibrium in favor of a creative life course. If both factors are negative,
they tend to send the respective person along one of the noncreative high-
ways mentioned. St. Francis' post-precipitant self-identification with the
Lady Poverty and the God of Love, his first steps of rebuilding the
dilapidated church and kissing the leper quite tangibly conditioned his
subsequent altruistic course. After the deepest despairs caused by his
deafness, Beethoven's determination to overcome it by intensified creative efforts and his actual realization of these efforts (we know this from
his " Testament "), led him to new heights of creative achievements. On
the other hand, the first responses to the precipitants in the form of alcoholism, sensuality, ideological cynicism, brutality, lasting depressive
moods, and the like, have dragged down the uncreative life course many
a potential creator and millions of ordinary human beings. For these
reasons *all persons who are in the state of this unstable equilibrium need a
careful, helping hand in guiding them towards the creative first deeds and
self-identification in the period of their inner warfare, and during and
after their exposure to the precipitants.* The role of these first deeds and
self-identification is always important and now and then it is decisive for
the subsequent life course of respective persons.

Chapter Thirteen

# Types of Altruistic Rearrangement of Group Affiliations and Environment

## I

### SELF-ISOLATIONIST, EREMITIC SOLUTION

All the late, the intermediary, and in a lesser degree, the fortunate altruists undergo the operation of rearrangement of their group membership as a part of the trilateral operation. This change of group affiliations consists not only in dropping membership in the predominantly selfish groups and in continuing it in the mutually harmonious altruistic groups, but also in the establishment of a new group or in the selection of one of the altruistic groups as their main organization. In the latter case, the growing altruists fully identify themselves with such a main group; invest most of their energy into it; and make it their alter ego. This main group's ego becomes the dominant ego or egoless self among the egos of each of the altruists. *The Society of Buddha's Disciples, the Group of the Apostles of Jesus, St. Francis' Order, Loyola's Society of Jesus, the Monastic Order of St. Pachomius, of St. Basil the Great and of St. Benedict,* the *Molokai Colony of Lepers* for Damien or Brother Joseph, even *Alcoholics Anonymous* or " *We Are Not Alone,*" are examples of such central groups for the respective altruists and persons. An establishment of a new altruistic group or the selection of one of the old altruistic groups as the central group for a given convert is one of the necessary steps in the long and difficult process of reintegration of one's group affiliations, egos, and values.

Without an altruistic organization of group membership, no great progress in altruistic growth is possible.

A successful performance of this operation is closely connected with the *organization or reorganization of human environment in which the growing altruist has to live and act.* Let us now glance at how the eminent altruists have solved these problems. Their solutions can be reduced to four main types: 1) eremitic isolation; 2) altruistic wayfaring; 3) establishment of a special group and environment; 4) remaining in the world, but selecting only positive groups and environments from it.

The first important type of solution to the problems of group member-ship and environment favorable for altruistic growth has been a volun-tary *self-isolation or eremitic retreat from all human groups and the hu-man world into solitude* — of a desert, forest, island, mountain, cave, or other uninhabited part of this planet. Any voluntary self-isolation from direct interaction with human beings and " civilization " in whatever place, even in one's city room, is a variety of this type of solution.

As a general rule, *involuntary* physical and psychosocial isolation of ordinary individuals from other human beings and from human culture, or an imposed confinement within a solitary prison cell, secluded house, or other place, is harmful rather then beneficial. A vast body of evidence shows that such an isolation and confinement leads ordinary individuals to vital, mental, and moral deterioration. It facilitates suicide and mental regression.

The situation is quite different, however, when we have a *voluntary* retreat into solitude by the seekers of self-identification with the creative supraconscious. Religious, moral, artistic, scientific, and other potential creators retreat into solitude voluntarily. They carry with themselves the highest values of their culture; they strive to cultivate these values up to the highest limit, and they want to identify themselves with these values as much as possible. Under these conditions, physical and mental soli-tude seems to exert a positive rather than negative influence upon strong creative souls. Such a seclusion seems to be beneficial physically, men-tally, and morally for such people; for the rank and file, however, its ef-fects may be negative.

The reasons for its positive influence are fairly clear and were dis-covered long ago by all the creative hermits, anchorites, and self-isola-tionists. By retreating from the sociocultural world into mental and physical solitude, the hermits and the self-isolationists abruptly break off all their social ties with their groups. By cutting off their social bonds, they free themselves from all group conflicts and other social forces that generate their inner tensions and hinder their altruistic self-identification. Previous group affiliations terminated, most of the egos, generated and supported by the groups, lose their ground and begin to crumble. So also do most of the values of each ego. When these egos and their values fade away, their mutual conflicts fade away also·in the inner experience of the hermits. In this way voluntary solitude brings about a clearance of the inner life from the debris of one's discordant egos and conflicting values. In this manner it prepares the inner forces for building a new universe of harmonious values and egos subordinated to the supreme egoless self.

The voluntary solitude helps also to calm down most of the turbulent unconscious drives and bioconscious temptations. Since these are aroused mainly by human beings, by their activities, and by their " civilizational intoxicants," the absence of these stimuli in physical solitude helps to keep the drives and temptations dormant and at a low voltage. In such a state they do not too violently disturb one's peace of mind, and can be more easily controlled than at a state of high intensity.

Besides the services of cleansing the inner life and of quieting the passions, voluntary solitude helps also in building the new universe of harmonious egos and values, united into one self. Voluntary solitude sets the seeker face to face with himself. In his seclusion he is exposed to himself in all his " stark nakedness." He begins to see not only his noble virtues, but also his ignoble ugliness. All his false pretenses rapidly fall down. Most of his " social roles," with their " civilizational " make-ups, superficial masks and glittering costumes, begin to " peel off " the hermit. Most of his hollow values become now obviously worthless. Solitude does not have any demand for these empty toys. Being a pitiless tester and the sternest " lie detector," solitude incessantly tests all the egos, values, and affiliations of the voluntary recluse. By this testing it helps the hermit to keep the gold and to throw away the trash; it assists in reintegration of his self and his system of values.

By its undisturbed peace, solitude facilitates deep meditation and by lack of human rush it helps an unhurried creative effort. By its stark sternness it discourages man's preoccupation with trivia, and by its magnificent grandeur it induces the mood of viewing everything *sub specie aeternitatis*. By freeing one from pseudo-values, lilliputian egos, and " encumbering superfluities," solitude invigorates the seeker in his quest for the supreme value and immortal self.

These functions of solitude explain why the eremitic solution has been widely practiced throughout human history, from the remotest past up to the present; and why flight into solitude has repeatedly increased in the periods of great crises of complex civilizations. In such times, inhabitants of Megalopolis try to find salvation from their inner warfare in an eremitic retreat from the turbulent social world.

Religious and altruistic hermits have been well aware of these services of voluntary solitude. Firmly believing that the ordinary social environment is inimical to their objective, they sought solitude in order to achieve the aspired union with the supraconscious and love for their neighbors. Some of the great anchorites like St. Anthony, St. Paul of Thebes, and a host of Christian hermits of the fourth, the fifth, and the sixth centuries spent most of their life in Egyptian deserts or in other wildernesses. During the last two millennia many Hindu, Buddhist, Taoist, Jainist, and

Mohammedan altruistic hermits (there are still living ones, like Bhagavan Sri Ramana Maharshi) lived the greater part of their life in physical and mental isolation.[1] St. Anthony spent some 85 years out of 105 years of his life in his hermitage on the Egyptian desert. Only four times was his long solitude interrupted by short visits to the human world that called for his help in an emergency. In the almost absolute isolation of the Egyptian desert, hardly seeing any human being, St. Paul of Thebes spent some 90 years out of 113 years of his life. St. Serafim of Sarov (1759–1833) lived in solitude, with short interruptions, from 1794 to 1815.

Training themselves for their religious and altruistic mission, many self-isolationists for several years carried on a solitary life in uninhabited or little-inhabited places. Having " arrived " at their goal and become firmly established in their self-identification, they returned later on to the human world to discharge their religious and altruistic services.

Still others like Buddha, Moses, David, Chaitanya, Jesus,[2] St. Paul, Mohammed, St. Basil the Great, St. Benedict, St. Gregory the Great, St. Francis of Assisi, Al Hallaj, Abū Sáïd, Al Ghazzali, St. Ignatius, John Woolman, and other altruists, preparing for their mission in the human world, lived in an eremitic isolation for shorter periods. Discharging their duties in the social environment, now and then they used to go back into such a retreat for renewal of their spiritual and altruistic powers.

Many religious and moral guides explicitly prescribe periodic retreats of this sort as a " tonic " for mental and moral invigoration. St. Ignatius' formula is an example of these prescriptions. He recommends periodic retreats, by " separating oneself from his friends and acquaintances, and from human affairs. A Retreat has three advantages: 1. Of banishing things which do not tend of the service of God. 2. It prevents intellect from being drawn in different directions. 3. The soul, finding itself solitary and separate, the more easily seeks and finds its Creator." [3]

To achieve union with God, " the first condition demanded . . . is seclusion, not from our neighbor, but from the distraction of the world. . . . Spiritual retirement is essential, but this will be found impossible apart from physical retirement, since the sights and sounds of the world are bound to distract one from prayer. . . ." " A retired habitation is a help to the soul in avoiding distraction," says St. Basil the Great.[4]

Such short-time retreats from the hustle and bustle of the human world into a secluded spot of nature or other quiet place have been practiced by a legion of altruists, artists, thinkers, and creators of various kinds. These seclusions have helped them in preparation and development of their creative activity: religious, ethical, scientific, artistic, philosophical, technological, etc.

Lifelong seclusion is undertaken mainly by contemplative minds, by passive Ideationalists, or meditative introverts for whom action is but a low-grade contemplation. Shorter solitudes have been practiced by active Ideationalists, Idealists, and Sensate altruists. For these, overt behavioral realization of their ideals is more important than a mere contemplation of the supreme value in its pristine purity.[5]

The wide use of eremitic methods for millennia and in most different cultures testifies to its fruitful efficacy for solution of the problems of group affiliations, of inner conflicts, and of the environment favorable for spiritual and altruistic growth. Otherwise, it would hardly be used to such an extent in different societies for such a long period of human history. A long or short withdrawal from the world into solitude seems to have been an essential prerequisite for religious and altruistic leadership. The retreat has notably helped in rooting the leaders' self-identification with the supraconscious.

A long or short solitude seems also to have been a prerequisite for other forms of creative achievements: in science and philosophy, fine arts and technology, even politics and economics. A. J. Toynbee correctly states that " a withdrawal and return " is one of the general characteristics of either individual or collective genius.[6]

The disengagement [from social milieu] and withdrawal make it possible for [a creative] personality to realize individual potentialities which would have remained in abeyance if the individual . . . had not been released for a moment from his social toils and trammels.[7]

Before returning to the world to fulfill their mission, practically all founders of great religions — Lao-tzu, Confucius, Buddha, Moses, Christ, Mahavira, Parçva, Zoroaster, Mohammed, to mention but a few names — and most religious and moral leaders underwent a long-time or short-time self-isolation or withdrawal. So also — for short periods and from time to time — did many a genius in all fields of creativity.

Let us glance more closely at the most conspicuous examples of the eremitic retreat from the world as it was practiced by the great hermits of Christian and other religions.

We note, first, that these hermits were well aware of the inimical nature of the ordinary human environment to the task of religious and altruistic transfiguration they sought.

Fish, if they tarry on dry land, die: even so monks that tarry outside their cell or abide with men of the world fall away from their vow of quiet [says the hermit Anthony].

Arsenius, flee from men, and thou shall be saved [the voice of the Lord said to this hermit while, as a notable man of the world, he was praying for] the way of deliverance.

He who abides in the midst of men, because of the turbulence, he sees not his sins; but when he hath been quiet, above all in solitude, then does he recognize his own default.[8]

St. Tychon of Zadonsk (1724–1783) put the matter very clearly:

If we flee men, it must not be because of men, but because of sin. We must hate sin, not men: men we must love, and we must pray for them. It is our need which moves us to pray for ourselves, but love persuades us to pray for our neighbors.

The desert and the monastic cell accumulate riches, but the temptations of the world disperse them. In the cell man gathers up his whole past life in his thoughts, and contemplating it, turns to Christ with sighs and asks for His mercy. Nothing causes a man to sin so often as his tongue. In seeking solitude, he flees the occasion of sin. Our eyes and ears are like windows through which temptations penetrate to our heart and strike at it. In solitude this is avoided and temptations refused. . . . Solitude collects spiritual treasures, a journey or visits disperse them. . . . It is rare that a man [after a visit] returning to his cell is the same as when he left it.[9]

Similar have been the views of the Hindu, the Buddhist, the Taoist, the Jainist, the Sufist, and the Judaist eremitic altruists. In Hinduism, Buddhism, and Jainism the eremitic abandonment of the world is recommended as the last phase of the fulfilled human life. It comes after the preceding three phases of student, householder, and ascetic.[10]

I have left my home to seek some way of rescue [from old age, disease, and death], says Buddha. . . . I search for happiness of something that decays not; that never perishes . . . that looks with equal mind on enemy and friend, that needs not wealth nor beauty, the happiness of one who finds repose alone in solitude, in some unfrequented dell.[11]

The same is still more true of Jainists. "The duties of an ascetic consist in subduing his senses, withdrawal from worldly things and from communication with people."[12] Similar ideas and practices have existed also in Taoism, with its motto "the mind of man loves stillness, but his desires draw it away";[13] among the Sufist hermits and Mohammedan mystics,[14] and many others.

For thousands of years, in the most different cultures, groups, and religions it has been repeatedly asserted that "the way to steady and purify the mind is to retire into solitude,"[15] and that "without solitude, neither the carnal lusts can be tamed, nor the evil thoughts can be eliminated."[16]

An important question arises now. In spite of the universal use of this method, has it indeed made the self-isolationists and hermits truly altruistic? Has not such an isolation from the rest of the world precluded altruistic service to humanity? Is not the method in its very nature egoistic, the hermits selfishly seeking their own salvation only, caring nothing for the rest of humanity?

These questions and doubts have been raised not only by secular critics of religious anchorites, but also by the great founders of cenobitic monastic orders like St. Pachomius the Great, St. Basil the Great, St. Theodore of Studium, St. Benedict, and others. A number of secular critics like E. Gibbon, Voltaire, Lecky, and others, and even theologians like A. von

Harnack, most venomously denounced the hermits as "hideous, distorted, emaciated maniacs; without knowledge, patriotism, natural affections, spending their life in a long, useless, and atrocious self-torture; quailing before the ghastly phantoms of their delirious brains" and exerting "the most stultifying effects on the world." Statements like these are comprehensible coming from the pens of the secular, irreligious, and progressive "Sensate" ideologists.

Much more important than this, however, is the criticism of the extreme forms of eremitic solitude by the great founders of the cenobitic orders. They themselves repeatedly withdrew into solitude for comparatively short periods (of several days, weeks, or a few years), and now and then approved true hermits. They do not deny the virtues of the eremitic way of life, but find it less perfect and less effectively leading the rank and file to religious and altruistic transfiguration than the cenobitic monastic system.

The best example of their criticism is given by St. Basil the Great. His statements are especially significant because of his own eremitic experience, because of his unexcelled interpretation of Christianity as the religion of the sublimest Love, and because of his being one of the greatest founders and organizers of the cenobitic order of communal life. "Being a persistent propagandist of the cenobitic ideal of communal life, St. Basil did not deny in practice the eremitic order, and himself organized several solitary retreats; but the pure and most perfect type of monkhood he saw in the cenobitic ideal of social organization." [17] His monastic community is a union "of like-minded persons who have chosen the object of religion," who "are of one heart and one soul and have all things in common," and "are harmonious with one another in the love of Christ as members in a body." [18] "The Love of God, involving also the love of our neighbor, is to be the chief motive of the Christian life, whether in the cloister or in the world." [19]

[For St. Basil] it is necessary, with a view to pleasing God, to live with like-minded persons. . . . Solitude is difficult and dangerous. . . . I recognize that the life of a number lived in common is more useful in many ways. To begin with, none of us is self-sufficient even as regards bodily needs, but we need one another's help in getting necessaries. . . . But apart from this the fashion of the love of Christ does not allow us to look each at his own good. For "love seeketh not its own." [I Cor. 13:5.] Now the solitary life has one aim, the service of the needs of the individual. But this is plainly in conflict with the law of love. . . .

Secondly, in such separation the man will not even recognize his defects readily, not having anyone to reprove him and to set him right with kindness and compassion. . . . Such a guide it is difficult to find in solitude. . . . And many commandments are easily performed by a number living together, but not by a solitary man. . . . We are one body having Christ as head, and we are severally members one of another. But if we are not joined together harmoniously in the close links of one body in the Holy Spirit, but each of us

chooses solitude, not serving the common welfare . . . how, when we are
thus separated and divided off, can we preserve the mutual relation and serv-
ce of the limbs one to another? . . .

In the next place, no single man is sufficient to receive all spiritual gifts. . . .
When a number live together a man enjoys his own gift, multiplying it by
imparting it to others, and reaps the fruits of other men's gifts as if they were
of his own. . . .

Further, to the sinner it is easier to depart from sin when he fears the condemnation passed by a number in agreement. . . .

But the solitary life has another danger . . . that of self-pleasing; for having
no one to test his work, a man will think he has reached perfection in the
commandment. [In solitude] man neither recognizes his defects nor knows
his progress in good works. . . . For wherewith shall a man show humility,
f he has no one in comparison with whom to show himself humble? Wherewith shall he show compassion, when he is cut off from the communion of the
many? If a man says he finds the teaching of the divine Scriptures sufficient
o correct his character, he makes himself like a man who learns the theory of
building, but never practices the art.[20]

Such is a sober criticism of one who visited the solitary desert Fathers,
who himself underwent eremitic experience, and who certainly knew it
firsthand. His reasons sound quite modern and scientific.

Fairly similar is St. Benedict's evaluation of the comparative merits and
demerits of the eremitic and the cenobitic orders. In his opinion of four
kinds of monkhood " the first [and the best] are the cenobites. . . . They
are the strongest race of monks. . . ." The second best are " the anchor-
tes or hermits." Still lower are " the Sarabaites who have been tried by no
rule nor by experience the master as gold by the furnace. . . . These in
twos and threes, or even singly without a shepherd . . . make a law to
themselves of their own pleasures and desires. . . ." These are " the
detestable kind of monks." Still worse are the Gyrovaques, " who spend
all their lives long wandering about divers provinces, staying in different
cells for three or four days at a time, ever roaming. They are worse in
all things than the Sarabaites." [21]

Not different is the viewpoint of other leaders of the cenobitic orders,
like St. Pachomius the Great, founder of the cenobitic monasteries, St.
Theodore of Studium, St. Dorotheus, and others.[22]

What shall be the conclusion from this criticism and from the total
body of the evidence available on this problem?

As to the attitude of the great leaders of the cenobitic orders, their
criticism concerns only the *comparative merits and demerits of the eremitic and the cenobitic orders so far as the rank and file of monkhood and
of secular individuals* are concerned. In the opinion of these leaders, for
this ordinary rank and file the cenobitic system is more efficient, more
applicable, and more fruitful than the eremitic order. Otherwise, especially for the heroic solitaries, the eremitic order is as good as any. St.
Basil himself practiced it, set it forth several times, and approved it for the

strong "athletes of God." Through his angel St. Pachomius explicitly says:

I gave this [not too difficult] rule so as to make sure that even the little ones [the rank and file] keep the rule and are not afflicted. But *the perfect have no need of legislation, for by themselves in their cells they have surrendered the whole of their life to the contemplation of God.* But I have legislated for as many as have not a discerning mind, in order that they, like house-servants fulfilling the duties of their station, may live a life of freedom.[23]

In other words, for the religious and moral heroes the eremitic with-drawal for even a long time is perfectly good. Short-time solitude is good for even "the little ones." As to the malicious jibes of the Sensate critics, they hardly give sufficient evidence to support their biased ac-cusations. The total body of evidence seems to indicate that the strong seekers of the supraconscious did become in the voluntary solitude more spiritual, more ethereal, and more altruistic. Solitude seems to have helped their transfiguration, reinforced their self-identification with the supra-conscious, and assisted in an accumulation of the "coiled up" altruistic energy in such hermits.

Whether the hermits aimed directly at becoming altruists or at the realization of the rule "Thou shalt love thy God," and, as prerequisite to it, "thou shalt love thy neighbor as thyself," [24] these "athletes of God" (*athletae Dei*, as they called themselves, *ascesis* meaning the training of the athlete) have indeed succeeded in their self-altruization, have become altruistic in their relationship with one another, have transfigured them-selves into the greatest moral leaders of humanity, and, finally, by the objective consequences of their ascesis, have exerted gigantic altruistic in-fluence upon humanity.

The greatest temporary hermits — among them Lao-tzu, Confucius, Buddha, Chaitanya, Moses, Jesus, Mohammed, Mahavira, Parçva, Zoroas-ter — have become the most influential and sublime moral leaders, and the greatest educators of humanity. Even lesser short-time hermits of the past, like St. Paul, St. Francis of Assisi, St. Ignatius, and of recent time, Serafim of Sarov, Gandhi, Sri Ramakrishna, Vivekananda, Sri Ramana Maharshi, Albert Schweitzer, Sri Aurobindo, and a legion of others are the most effective instrumentalities of altruization of the human world (while their Sensate denunciators have hardly exerted any such influence and in their own life have shown little, if any, unselfishness).

As to the hermit's self-altruization, Rufinus' impressions from his visits in 394 A.D. with the Egyptian hermits — supposedly the most "ferocious" and "maniacal" among the hermits seems to sum up the situation well.

I have seen among them fathers that lived the life of heaven in the world. . . . I have seen some of them so purged of all thought or suspicion of malice that they no more remembered that evil was still wrought upon the earth. . . . They dwell dispersed throughout the desert and separate in their cells, but bound together by love. . . . Quiet are they and gentle. . . . They have indeed a great rivalry among them . . . it is who shall be more merciful than his brother, kinder, humbler, more patient.[25]

When one reads the brief portraits of the hermit fathers like Benus, Theon, and of many others; when one studies their lives, actions, and sayings — "If a man have humility and poverty and judgeth not another," he is good, or " no one in this world ought to be despised," even a thief or murderer or sinner; when one follows their actions of not only mutual help, but sacrifice of their life, even of their soul, by taking upon themselves the sins of others; there hardly remains any doubt that the real hermits (but not the many fakes who later on began to imitate them) have fully succeeded in their self-altruization.

The very fact that ordinary people used to flock to their hermitage seeking help in their troubles; the fact that around their hermitage soon grew vast monasteries of thousands of followers (Pachomius' Tabenna monastery had seven thousand members; five thousand monks on Mount Nitria; Serapion ruled over ten thousand, and so on); the fact that the number of persons cured by such hermits (after they had finished their training and returned to the people) from their troubles, physical and especially mental, has to be counted by hundreds and thousands, one hermit sometimes curing more patients than does a legion of psychoanalysts taken together: all these facts give a clear verdict in the matter.

Add to this the hermits' services of pacifying vast political and religious bodies when such groups were rent by dissensions and when, being unable to calm themselves, they repeatedly called St. Anthony or other great hermits to pacify their discordance — which service of love the hermits did successfully. Moreover, examine the enormous influence which these hermits have exerted upon the altruistic activities of the religious bodies acting in the world; upon the formation of their dogmas and beliefs; their institutions of charity and their moral renaissance when they have become corrupted. By instilling the spirit of love, humility, and sacrifice into the public religious bodies, the hermits are largely responsible for the heroic level of their ethics. By vigorously denouncing corruption, and by fearlessly opposing it, the hermits have been instrumental in most of the positive reformations of the bodies — religious, political, and social. The enormous influence of Christian hermits upon the growth and formation of Christian religion, and upon its reformations and cleansings, is an example of the similar influence of occidental and oriental hermits upon their religious and other institutions.

Finally, by their very existence the heroic athletes of God incalculably influenced humanity in the same decisive way in which any great hero in any field influences the ordinary folk by striking their imagination, and by becoming a fascinating myth of heroic — religious and moral — achievement. Their shining example grows into an irresistible and enchanting image calling forth mimesis and catharsis of the masses. Heroic images of Plato in philosophy, of Newton in science, of Phidias and Michelangelo in architecture and sculpture; of Alexander the Great in military art; of Homer and Shakespeare in literature; of Bach, Mozart, and Beethoven in music; of a great athlete in sport: each of these images has become an unforgettable myth for imitation by their followers. In a similar way the athletes of God have been one of the important forces in the moralization of humanity. They have discharged this role by their very existence and by becoming heroic symbols of creative love and spirituality.

About the eminent anchorites one can say what H. Bergson says about the mystics generally. Viewing them as superhuman creators he regards each mystic — and all great hermits have been mystics — as a "new species" composed of one unique individual. Each of them marks "in an élan of love" an attainment of a new height in the evolution of Life and of the human species; "and each has manifested in a new form a love which seems to be the very essence of creative effort. . . . The great mystic feels the truth flow into him from its source like a dynamic force. He cannot stop himself from spreading it just as the Sun cannot stop itself from pouring out its light. His desire is with God's help to complete the creation of the Human Species" and to turn mankind "which is essentially created thing, into a creative effort." [26]

When these and similar facts are considered, the proposed question is answered positively. Years-long solitude has notably helped the athletes of Goodness in their religious and altruistic growth. For many of those who strive to eliminate their inner conflicts, to reintegrate their egos and values, and to deepen their self-identification with the supraconscious, shorter temporary solitudes also seem to have been re-creative. More than that. Either repeated short-time retreats or a lasting solitary withdrawal have been favorable for development of any creative activity. A temporary withdrawal within one's self from the rush and hustle of the external world is a condition necessary for any creative achievement: in religion and ethics, science and philosophy, the fine arts and technological invention, economics and politics. For any such achievement a deep and intense concentration is required. Such a concentration is exceedingly difficult amidst the noise and rush, passions and conflicts, worries and trivia of ordinary life. A person who spends his daily hours in "being busy doing nothing," in rushing from crowd to crowd, from excitement to thrill, from one routine activity to another, such a person simply does not have time to do any creative thinking and concentration. His time and energy are spent in futile excitations, bores, and routine motility.

Still more true is this about a moral achievement. For altruistic growth also one has to be now and then in solitude, in order to examine his conscience, to talk face to face with his soul and God, in order to see his hypocrisy, false pretensions, self-admiration, and other failings. "So great is the hurry in the spirit of this world, that in aiming to do business quickly and to gain wealth the creation at this day doth loudly groan," rightly observes John Woolman, repeating Lao-tzu's " quiet doing nothing is better than to be busy doing nothing." [27]

In the light of these considerations for the strong souls, the eremitic, and self-isolationist solutions of the problems of group-affiliations, of the inner conflicts, of the reintegration of egos, these solutions appear to be sound and fruitful. If factually available, the solutions can be prescribed for many who earnestly seek an altruistic or creative transfiguration generally, and for many who suffer from inner warfare and official psychoneuroses. Such a prescription is likely to be much more effective than the prescriptions and environment of the psychoanalyst's couch; or of fashionable resorts, crowded rest homes, and sanatoriums; or the therapy of aimless traveling from hotel to hotel, from city to city, or from show to show, not infrequently prescribed by educators, psychiatrists, and psychoanalysts.

It is true that the prescription of a long solitude is good mainly for the strong souls, capable of standing this powerful medicine. *For the weaker souls " solitude therapy " is dangerous*, especially when it is prolonged, involuntary, and experienced away from all human beings. Instead of reintegration, it may demoralize; in place of developing their creative potential, it can destroy it. For these reasons only a short-time and " light solitude " can be prescribed for the rank and file. For the ordinary souls different therapies seem to be more suitable than the therapy of eremitic solitude.

## II

### The Solution of the Unattached Pilgrims of Goodness

One can get out of the constellation of the mutually antagonistic groups, and of the respective conflicts of egos and values, by severing membership in all groups; by becoming a wayfaring " stranger," living in the world but not settled in any place, acting among groups, but not becoming a part of them. Like a comet passing unattached through a solar system, " a wayfaring stranger travels through this world of woe," doing good deeds wherever he is and to whomsoever he meets. In order to be able to do that, a pilgrim of goodness, after detaching himself from his conflicting groups and purging himself of his antagonistic egos, must be able to reintegrate his inner world and closely identify himself with the supraconscious love and value. Otherwise, he runs the risk of becoming just an ordinary hobo, gypsy, demoralized wanderer, or a criminal on the move.

This solution is intermediary between the hermit's abandonment of the world and the creation in the world of a special environment favorable for altruistic growth. Buddha wandering from place to place with his disciples; itinerant Jesus with his apostles; wayfaring St. Francis with his companions; Al Ghazzali turning into a pilgrim in the period of 488 to 499 A.D.; [28] itinerant prophets, wandering dervishes, preachers, helping pilgrims, having no place of their own and no property except their staff and clothes: such good-doing wanderers are examples of this solution to the problem. In contradistinction to the lifelong hermits, these altruists do not flee the world physically (except for short-time retreats now and then). They live their life in the sociocultural universe, but do not attach themselves to any specific group or tribe. They are loyal only to the supreme value, to the supraconscious that transcends all other values and groups. As the children of the supraconscious they are above all tribal limitations; they are citizens of the whole cosmos, being good and kind to everyone and to all. *The Song of the Sannyâsin* (wandering monk) by Swami Vivekananda depicts the type.

> Have thou no home? What home can hold thee, friend?
> The sky is thy roof; the grass thy bed; and food,
> What chance may bring, well cooked or ill, judge not.
> Go thou, the free, from place to place, and help
> Them out of darkness, Maya's veil. Without
> The fear of pain or search for pleasure, go
> Beyond them both, Sannyâsin bold. Say —
> "Om tat sat Om."

*The Song of Angya* by a Zen Buddhist master gives another portrait of the holy wanderer.

Determined to leave his parents, what does he want to accomplish?
He is now a Buddhist, a homeless monk now, and no more a man of the
   world; his mind is ever intent on the mastery of the Dharma.
His conduct is to be as transparent as ice or a crystal,
He is not to seek fame or wealth,
He is to rid himself of defilements of all sorts. . . .[29]

In contradistinction to the ordinary vagabonds and hoboes, the altruists wander because of their renunciation of all " tribal " ties and values, and of their desire to complete their self-identification with the supreme value, and to serve in love their God and neighbors. Their refusal to be entangled in the Sensate affairs of the world and their cult of Lady Poverty are mere consequences of their self-dedication to the highest purpose.

In some way, and for some periods, this method of altruistic growth has been practiced by a number of altruists. Many a religious and secular missionary, many a good-doer like John Woolman, many an itinerant doctor, teacher, and reformer has been a *peregrinus* of this kind. In the history of almost any country there have been hundreds of cases where persons have given all their possessions to the poor and have turned into unattached pilgrims. "Through the hands of such as these God speaks, and from behind their eyes He smiles upon the earth." [30]

Viewed scientifically, this method of solution of group affiliation, of inner conflicts, and of altruistic growth is accessible only to a minority of strong souls, and to those who have already completed self-identification. Having accomplished their altruistic transformation, they can return to the world and, as unattached pilgrims, fruitfully serve it. Such individuals run no danger of becoming mere hoboes doing no particular good either to themselves or to others.

*For the rank and file, however, the method is highly dangerous.* Without a preliminary training in creative altruism, ordinary individuals turned into vagabonds can easily become uprooted human flotsam. Freed from the control of their groups, rootless and rudderless, they certainly run a high risk of moral and mental disintegration. These human rolling stones yield an abnormally high rate of delinquents, semi-delinquents, and morally irresponsible individuals.[31] These remarks do not concern recreational trips and travels for rest, relaxation, health improvement, entertainment, and enjoyment. Tourist trips do not imply either severing of social ties or permanent change of residence. Neither do they aim to transform the tourists into altruistic pilgrims. For these reasons tourist travels are neither good nor bad from the standpoint of altruistic ethics.

Although highly dangerous for the moral rank and file, the method of altruistic pilgrimage is highly fruitful for those strong souls and established altruists who have a wanderlust and roving disposition. By satisfying their bioconscious urge, the altruistic pilgrimage uses the vital energy of the urge for highly creative purposes. Freed from their bonds to tribal groups and values, unencumbered by narrow partiality, undismayed by worry or trouble, self-identified with their highest value, they become free instruments of universal compassion and love. Their self-dedication to the sublime Agape insulates them against moral corrosion and mental regression; against anxiety, fear, and neuroses; even against many physical hardships. It enables them to radiate inexhaustible good will and untiringly to perform their good deeds as their main mission.

To sum up: for these strong souls with wanderlust dispositions, altruistic pilgrimage is an effective method for creative growth. For the untrained and unprepared rank and file it is dangerous. In mild form, under wise guidance of an altruistic counselor, and as a temporary measure, it can be prescribed to ordinary individuals suffering from an inflation of their egos and from the fear of losing their egos' possessions, prestige, comfort, and the like. Otherwise, its application is to be limited to the strong seekers of goodness and already established altruists.

## III

### SOLUTION THROUGH ESTABLISHMENT OF OR AFFILIATION WITH INSTITUTIONALIZED GROUPS FOR ALTRUISTIC EDUCATION AND LIVING

The preceding methods of eremitic withdrawal and altruistic wandering have been applicable to and fruitfully used by only a comparatively small minority of the strong souls.  Since a minimum of altruism or solidarity among its members is necessary for any society to live and to survive; since this minimum does not come automatically by itself; and since the rank and file of the members have to be trained somehow in this minimum of solidarity, it is evident that other methods different from the above two have been used for that purpose.  One of these other methods has been a creation of special groups or institutions designed for the purposes of altruistic training of the rank and file, as well as of the geniuses of altruistic creativity.  All educational agencies of a given society — beginning with the family, nursery school, kindergarten, elementary and Sunday schools, and ending with college, religious, occupational, or industrial group, even police, court, and other agencies — are trying to perform this task in a good or bad way.[32]

These institutions are designed, however, not so much for altruistic molding of their pupils, as for their intellectual training or for the punishment of the delinquents.  Except perhaps in the family and the special schools for religious and moral education, in most contemporary groups the altruistic molding of pupils' personality plays a modest and sometimes even a negligible role.  This task of altruistic training is largely neglected by the schools of our age.

Even when serious attention is paid to the problem, the schools cannot perform quite successfully the tasks of rearrangement of one's social affiliations, of liberation from inner conflicts, of reintegration of one's egos and values, and of complete self-identification with supraconscious love.  First of all, schools try to instill in their pupils egoism and the value of competition as much as the egoless self and value of love; they glorify the cult of success and victory over all competitors more than that of humble service.  When the schools teach altruism it almost always is a tribal altruism, of low intensity, narrow extensity, inferior — utilitarian and hedonistic — purity, inadequate, and of short duration.  It is a bargaining love, trying to get from others as much as possible for as little as possible.

Then, too, schools are institutions with which one is actively connected only for a limited time.  The pupils are not expected to live their whole life in the schools and to make the schools their permanent home, their working place, and their permanent creative center.  If one breaks off his membership in all groups, for such free persons school cannot become the central or supreme group that replaces all the broken affiliations.  For this reason schools cannot efficiently eliminate one's conflicting egos and values, and give the integration centered around the egoless self.

For similar reasons schools are not the best agencies for training geniuses of altruistic creativity.  Only special institutional groups intentionally established for the purposes of altruistic training and living can meet this requirement.

The most rigorous, most developed, and probably most efficient eximple of these institutionalized groups has been the best monasteries, cloisters, convents, and brotherhood communities (like the Mennonite, the Hutterite, and other brotherly groups), with all their charitable establishments and activities. Hinduism, Buddhism, Taoism, Jainism, Christianity, Judaism, Mohammedanism, and practically all great religions and many sects have created such monasteries or "special environments" for training and living in service to God and humanity. In this general sense religious monasteries and secular communal brotherhoods or sisterhoods are universal and perennial schools of spiritual and moral training.

The monastery in its heroic age was something much more important than the best school. For its members, the monastery or brotherhood group was the central community — their home, their permanent workshop, their center of creative activity, their church, their family, their labor union, their recreational agency — in brief, their everything. It took into its monopolistic possession their body, soul, and whole life. This is clearly demonstrated by the fact that before their admittance into full membership in a convent or brotherhood, before taking their monastic vow, they had to publicly renounce their allegiance to practically all groups, including the family, and they had to break all previous social ties. Such renunciation was an important part of their initiation ritual. They thus became completely identified with the monastery or brotherhood and with its values. It replaced all their previous groups; its egoless "self" took the place of all their previous egos. Instead of a chaos of conflicting egos and values, now one egoless self and the supreme value of God or the *summum bonum* presided in the inner experience of a monk or brother. Deep peace of mind, often an ineffable bliss, descended into his inner world. His life progressively tended to be an unselfish service to the supreme value, fellow men, and to the whole animated cosmos.

In all these functions the genuine monastery or brotherhood (but not their degenerated simulacra) represents an unexcelled agency for the total transfiguration of human beings. Their creation was one of the greatest inventions in the field of social engineering.

These services of monasteries and communal brotherhoods are the reasons behind their universal spread and perennial existence. While differing in many details, in discharge of these great services monastic and brotherhood institutions of various countries are essentially similar. Thus the organization and life of the Buddhist monastery, or of the Zen Buddhist "Seat of Perfect Wisdom," specifically built for the purpose and of the Zen "Meditation Hall" consists of: " 1. life of humility; 2. life of labor; 3. life of service; 4. life of prayer and gratitude; and 5. life of meditation. After his initiation to the Brotherhood, the monk is to be trained along these lines. . . ." "The Brotherhood is a community of men pursuing one common object, and the spirit of mutual help and service is everywhere evident in its life." It is democratic organization. Its members are trained in " the active and concrete realization of love." " Each monk . . . endeavors to give others the least trouble for his own sake while . . . he will do his utmost to do the most good he can for the general welfare of the community." " A life of disinterested service is closely related to that of humility and gratitude." [33] As practically in all monasteries, the Zen monks have all things in common and no private property.

Similarly, St. Basil's monasteries are the brotherhoods of " like-minded persons . . . of one heart and one soul and having all things in common," " harmonious with one another in the love of Christ." Their objective is to " love God and neighbors." " Monastery provides quiet and complete freedom from the disturbances of the outside world." [34]

According to St. Benedict's *Rules*, a monastery is " a school of the Lord's service (*Dominica schola servitii*) . . . for the amendment of vices or the preservation of charity," for the realization of the supreme commandments: " to love the Lord God (*ex toto corde, tota anima, tota virtute*) and to love one's neighbor as oneself."

Similar are the functions and objectives of the monasteries of St. Pachomius, of the Franciscan order, of the order of St. Theodore of Studium, and of practically any genuine monastery or brotherhood community. Training and living in love with one another and with the whole world is their common objective (besides training in love to God). " Peace and harmony and competition in humbleness " must dominate in relationships of the members of Pachomius' monastery. (*Sitque inter eos pax et concordia . . . et invicem de humilitate certantes*.) [35]

The friars of St. Francis, unlike the earlier orders, " were instituted to do a special work, not merely to save their own souls. Theirs it was to minister to the outcast, to seek the down-trodden and the afflicted." [36] " The friars were essentially an order of social laborers. They should save themselves by losing themselves in saving others." [37] Respectively, St. Francis' *Rules of the Friars Minor* indicate " humility and patience, pure simplicity, and true peace of mind, and always . . . the divine love " as the objectives of their training. [38]

The whole life in the monastery or brotherhood has been organized in such a way as to make the realization of these objectives possible.

Beginning with their geographical place, their buildings, and their total material culture, and ending with the most detailed regulations of the life, mind, and behavior of their members — everything has been ingeniously arranged with a view to making their members religious and moral leaders. Whether it be a Buddhist, or Taoist, Hindu or Christian, Jainist or Mohammendan " monastery " or sectarian brotherhood, thousands of their material, cultural, organizational, and behavioral characteristics all have been created for this purpose. The monastery resembles a self-centered state or city. Surrounded by walls, with its workshops, its farms, its gardens, its mill, and so forth, it is a religious house resembling the family, with the abbot held in place of the father, and all the members as brothers or sisters. "In St. Benedict's conception a monastery existed for the service of God and the spiritual welfare of its inmates. It was to be spiritually and actually a family living for God." [39] Each twenty-four hours of the life of the inmates were arranged in detail; their work, meals, sleep, prayer, confessions. "There was very little time during the day which was not occupied by liturgical or community duties." [40] When carefully studied, many of these characteristics and regulations appear ingenious indeed and effectively serve the purpose. Many of these are real inventions in the field of religious and moral training.

These characteristics will be studied further (see Chapters Twenty and Twenty-One). Here it suffices to point out that the monasteries tried to be an abode of the concentrated cultivation of love, spirituality, and wisdom.

At their heroic age they well succeeded in this task, possibly better than any other educational institution. After all, in spite of the fact that their total population always has been an insignificant fraction of the total worldly population, their share in the total number of true saints, religious and moral leaders, outstanding altruists, and ethically noble persons has been extraordinarily large, many times exceeding their share in the total population. So far as *outstanding* altruists, religious, and moral leaders are concerned, they have come from monastic and eremitic environments in far greater proportion than from any other environment. In the total number of Christian Saints enumerated and described in many volumes of the *Acta Sanctorum* or in Migne's *Patres Latine* and *Patres Graeci*, a majority came out of monastic, eremitic, and pilgrim environment. Among all Christian and Christian Catholic Saints, abbots and abbesses make 8.1 per cent; hermits (as hermits) 2.7 per cent; monks (as monks) 0.2 per cent; all in all 11 per cent. Considering, however, that most of the Church hierarchy — pope, cardinal, bishop, priest, missionary, many martyrs and confessors — were also monks promoted to these positions, the total per cent of saints with monastic background is well above 50 per cent of all the saints. Purely secular persons (kings, princes, matrons, actors, patrons, etc.) make only 11.4 per cent of all the saints. Of the remaining 88.6 per cent of the religious or clerical saints, at least 50 per cent came from monasteries. Among all the Russian Orthodox Saints, monastic saints make 61.3 per cent.[41]

This evidence is sufficient to demonstrate the practical effectiveness of these institutions. This does not mean that all who lived in monasteries and brotherhoods — for instance, all monks and nuns — have become saintly and altruistic; however, the tangible number of religious and moral failures of these institutions is not an evidence against their efficacy and ingenuity. The reason is the same as that for which the large number of failures and mediocrities among the students of the best university is not an evidence of its inefficacy and inadequacy in the intellectual training of its students. Most of the eminent scientists and scholars, thinkers and inventors, creative artists and worldly leaders have come from such universities; and the greater the university, the greater its share of intellectual leaders trained within its environment.

Consider further the remarkable success of the Christian monastic educators in the moral transformation of the bulk of the population at the beginning of the Middle Ages, when they had to deal with the decadently Sensate population of the urbanized Greco-Roman world, and with the barbarians morally disintegrating under the impact of the decadent urban culture. The very fact that the religious-monastic educators succeeded in taming their animal proclivities and in ennobling the age morally is eloquent evidence of the extraordinary success of their mission and of the high moral stamina of the missionaries themselves.

Similar has been the situation with the saints and moral leaders of the oriental and other great religions: quite a large per cent of these have come also from monasteries and brotherhoods, and these spiritual and altruistic leaders have also played a very important role in promoting and maintaining the moral standards of the vast oriental populations.

It is true that monasteries and brotherhoods, as any institution, have had their ups and downs concerning the successful discharge of their tasks. In their heroic age they did it much more successfully than in their decadently "opulent" age when they became rich, large, ritualistic, hierarchical, and worldly. But such degenerations happen with any institution, including universities. And they usually occur when the rigor and the morally vibrant atmosphere of such institutions in their heroic age are replaced by an external simulacrum of the intensest spirituality, altruistic *élan*, and the manner of life of the creative age. The whole character of the organization, material culture, mentality and conduct, rules and regulations of any institution at its degenerated stage are entirely different from those of its heroic age.

In modern times the heroic monastic institutions have been decreasing in number and in quality.[42] Secular educational institutions have been taking their place. Whatever are the merits of these secular institutions — private and public schools — in purely intellectual training, they cannot boast of being better schools of altruism than the monasteries of the past. If anything, as we have seen, they are much poorer schools for altruistic character education than the old monasteries and communal brotherhoods. The total body of evidence shows that with an enormous increase of the secular schools, beginning with nursery schools and ending with universities, from the twelfth century on up to the present time, neither international and civil wars, nor crimes decreased, nor has the altruistic and moral level of the Western population improved. If anything, wars and crimes increased and reached in the twentieth century — the most schooled, the most literate, the most scientific, and the most educated century — their unprecedented height. A vast body of evidence shows further that in the modern times there has not been any close relationship between intellectual brightness, excellent school grades, I.Q., the amount of school education, on the one hand, and criminality, or altruism, or high ethical conduct on the other.[43]

One of the main reasons for this moral impotency of the secular schools is a lack in these schools of most of the educational techniques of the old monasteries and communal brotherhoods. A great deal more about that will be said further. For the present, the above suffices to show the essentials of the monastic way of the solution to the problems discussed, and the high degree of success of this method.

## IV

### THE MAIN SOLUTION: ALTRUISTIC LIVING IN THE ORDINARY WORLD

Finally, an overwhelming majority of good neighbors and a number of outstanding altruists have been born and raised in an ordinary sociocultural environment. They have not withdrawn into a hermitage, nor have they become wandering pilgrims, nor have they entered a monastery or brotherhood. Without leaving the busy world of social life, hundreds of thousands of individuals have become good neighbors, and many have grown into eminent lovers of man and of all living creatures.

How is such a miracle possible? For the same reasons by which fortunate altruists are possible, and by which selfish persons are converted into late altruists. Besides the normal organism and the insufficiently known factor of fortunate heredity or grace, the main known factors of the fortunate altruists, as we have seen, are: 1. a harmonious and loving parental family; 2. mutually harmonious social groups amidst which the fortunate altruist is born, reared, and interacts; 3. the retroactive influence of the first good deeds and of subsequent altruistic actions (see Chapters Eleven and Twelve).

The point to be stressed now is that the *total* sociocultural world of each individual is so unbelievably rich, that one can place oneself or be luckily placed in it amidst conditions identical with those of the fortunate altruists. The total sociocultural world contains in itself not only forces of egoism, but also agencies of love; not only stimuli of stupidity, but also of creativity. Though the proportion of these two classes of forces is not constant in various sociocultural environments — some being saturated more by creatively altruistic stimuli, others by uncreatively selfish agencies — in any and even in the worst possible sociocultural milieu, there always function some agencies of creative altruization. If a person wants to live mainly amidst such forces, he can pick them up from his total ordinary environment, and thus surround himself with forces working for his al-truization.

For instance, if he is born and reared in a good family permeated by the spirit of love; if he is exposed mainly to the truly socializing forces — good playmates, friendly school atmosphere, good friends and neighbors; if he sees mainly good pictures, reads good books, listens to good music, interacts with good fellows; if, from early childhood, he is taught to be unselfish, generous, and kind; if he is inculcated with strong moral convictions and begins to act and react according to these norms; if further he experiences profound catharsis through some tragic or happy event: through these and similar agencies of an ordinary sociocultural environment he is powerfully molded into a reasonably unselfish, now and then eminently altruistic, person.

By careful selection of his group affiliations from the total sociocultural world, he can pick up only the " good groups " and leave alone the " bad groups." When membership in a group, like the state or the army, is obligatory and does not depend upon the choice of the individual, he can inwardly depreciate its value and in a nonviolent way can refuse to discharge the vicious duties imposed by such a coercive group. Though he is forced to be affiliated with it, he is not a part of it, and in his inner world he is free from its doubtful values and the poisonous ego which the group tries to install into him.

In this way, in the total imperfect world one can place oneself amidst a well-integrated and mutually harmonious group membership and altruistic value system. We already know that in one's inner world such a group situation tends to result in a universe of harmonious egos and values all sublimated to the supreme self and the value of love. Without withdrawing from the busy and selfish world, one can actually live in a pre-eminently altruistic universe built up out of selected positive elements and forces of the total world.

Throughout his life the individual can considerably control his group affiliations by dropping membership in new conflicting group(s), if by the circumstances he happens to be involved in them; and by adding membership in new group(s) that are creative, altruistic, and consonant with his other groups. Through this continuous adjustment of one's changing group affiliations, one can maintain the unity of his incessantly changing egos and values.

The same procedures have been used by the late altruistic converts immediately before, during, and after their conversion. Their first step consists in dropping membership in all selfish, uncreative, and anti-suprasensory groups with which they are affiliated; their second step is contracting membership in the most important altruistic groups and unification of these around the supreme group value into one harmonious cosmos.

Such is the answer to the question of how the altruistic integration of group membership, and of the inner world of egos and values, is possible for persons living and acting in the ordinary total world. This has been precisely the way of altruistic growth of a legion of good neighbors and of many recent altruists like M. K. Gandhi, Albert Schweitzer, Brother Joseph (successor to Damien the Leper), Dorothy Day, and others. This has been the path followed by millions of ordinary good persons, known and unknown, whose moral integrity and unselfishness keep the world going. The American Good Neighbors studied give an example of these millions.[44]

As mentioned, even in the seemingly worst moral environment a constellation of altruistic forces can always be found, if one earnestly seeks them. Even in the hideouts of murderers, prostitutes, thieves, and hypocrites, such regenerating agents and stimuli are not entirely lacking. This explains the striking fact that a number of prostitutes, murderers, thieves, and the like now and then turn into very good persons, and once in a while into eminent altruists and saints like Mary Magdalene, St. Pelagia the Harlot, St. Mary the Harlot, to mention but a few. Jean Valjean of Hugo's *Les Misérables* is a literary example of such a person.[45]

Hence, the more altruistic is the total sociocultural environment, the greater are the chances for a larger crop of unselfish persons in its total population. The more hellish is this total environment, the lesser are the chances for such a crop. This partly explains why in the periods of great demoralization and desocialization of groups, persons, and culture, the crop of truly altruistic persons, even of good neighbors, is meager, and vice versa.[46]

## V

### SUMMARY

Such are the four main types of solution to the problem of altruistic reintegration of group affiliations, of egos, and values, and of the environment favorable for altruistic formation of individuals and groups. The first two solutions are accessible only to the minority of strong souls. The third, the monastic and brotherhood way, is accessible to a comparatively larger portion of humanity, but this portion is still small. At its heroic phase each of these three methods has been effective, and has produced a vast number of ordinary and outstanding altruists. Finally, the bulk of humanity has solved the task through a selective arrangement of group affiliations, egos, and values picked up from the ordinary sociocultural environment. Taken as a whole, this method has been used by vast multitudes of human beings, and has produced a large crop of ordinary good neighbors, as well as a number of extraordinary altruists. When we consider the altruization of an overwhelmingly large part of humanity, the last method appears to be the most important as the only accessible method for the vast masses. Its functioning thus acquires a primary importance for any society and for humanity as a whole. Any improvement in the method, and in the ordinary sociocultural world, produces perhaps unspectacular but general altruization of the masses on a vast scale. Altruistic effects of these improvements spread upon the whole human universe in contrast to the spectacular but few heroes of altruism generated by other three methods.

*Chapter Fourteen*

# Trials and Pains of Reintegration
# of Behavior

## I

### NO AUTOMATIC INSTANTANEOUS REINTEGRATION

In the study of altruistic arrangement and rearrangement of group membership in the preceding chapters it has been stated that one's harmonious group affiliations result in a concordantly harmonious integration of one's egos, values, drives, and activities.

The statement being true, *it does not mean that a harmonious group membership automatically and instantaneously produces an altruistic harmonization of egos, values, biological drives, and overt activities.* It means only that if an individual starts earnestly to work over his group affiliations, he will also be working over his egos, values, drives, and overt actions; and vice versa. A change along each of the three lines indicated requires strenuous effort on the part of the individual.

Let us look more closely at what happens with one's egos, values, and actions when one drops membership in a previous group and acquires it in a new organization. When an individual drops membership in an important group, say, his occupational group, this cuts off the very roots of his occupational ego, values, and activities. He ceases to perform during six or eight hours daily his occupational activity; about one-third of his time thus becomes unfilled; his occupational office and environment, his bosses, co-workers, and subordinates likewise fall out of his life; his occupational values and standpoint become unimportant; his occupational wages or income ordinarily stop; his occupational rights and duties, interests and ambitions lose their ground. Finally, his occupational ego withers. In brief, with dropping or losing a given occupational position, the occupational ego, values, and activities lose their fountainhead, and are bound to dry up and sooner or later to die.

In the total field of one's egos, values, and activities, the membership termination eventually produces an empty, blank spot or " debris " where before were the occupational ego, values, and activities. With a proper modification the same can be said of severing an affiliation with any important group.

When one becomes — willingly or not — a member of a new group — for example, when he is drafted into the army or marries and sets up his own family — the new membership leads to the "installing" in the field of one's egos-values-activities of a new member: the army or the family ego, values, and activities. Such an installation seriously changes the inner world and the external behavior of the respective person. If diagramed, the change would show itself in the form of the appearance of a new ego, with its activities and values, where before was a blank, empty space. If one simultaneously takes membership in many important groups or if one of the new groups becomes dominant, a drastic revolution occurs in the total field of his personality, in his inner world as well as his external behavior.

Stressing the basic importance of the structure and change of one's group membership, *I do not contend that the corresponding changes in the total field of one's personality occur synchronously, immediately, and automatically with those in group affiliations.* As a rule, and especially when the changes in group membership are radical, the respective substantial rearrangement of one's egos, values, drives, and activities takes time and strenuous labor. Generally, it is a difficult operation.

The reason for the difficulty in the altruistic reintegration of one's egos, values, and activities is that our inner experiences, especially repeated ones, and our overt actions, especially habitual activities, do not disappear at once, at a moment's notice. Most of the experiences of each of our main egos are particularly persistent, and tend to live for some time after their fountainhead — the respective group affiliation — dries up. The same is true of the experiences and activities satisfying the biological needs of our organism. They cannot be erased or suppressed. They cannot be easily canceled at a moment's notice. They vigorously resist any attempt aiming at their extinction or restraint.

Similarly, many new experiences and new actions (required by new group affiliations) cannot be at once and easily interiorized by one's organism, and installed in the field of one's egos, values, drives, and activities. The new egos, activities, and values are actively resisted by all the old egos and activities antagonistic to them. The newcomers have to fight a strenuous battle before they can install themselves in the total field of one's egos, values, drives, and activities. Many difficult efforts and many repetitions are necessary to make them " second nature " to the person.

This explains why the altruistic or religious transformation of the late and intermediary altruists has not been accomplished by a mere rearrangement of group affiliations and why, having performed this rearrangement, they had to labor strenuously and for a long time before they succeeded in reintegrating their egos, values, drives, and activities. The operation is so difficult that many could not do it and irrevocably failed. Most of the altruists who completed it have also had one or several set-backs before they become " firmly established."

## II

### REINTEGRATION IN EREMITIC SOLITUDE

A number of actual cases and the relevant facts confirm and well illus-trate the difficulty of the operation discussed. One of the Church Fathers, St. Jerome (345–420 A.D.), gives us a striking account of his own experiences in this sort of operation.

At the age of about 28 years he decided to become a hermit, broke off practically all his social affiliations, left Rome and his native Aquileia, and went into the Syrian desert; and started there his five-year long soli-tary hermitage. The reader must keep in mind that before going into the desert, St. Jerome had the best possible education of his time; he was one of the foremost intellectuals of the period, and had many affiliations with the pagan and Christian high-brows, with the upper and the middle class groups, societies, and organizations in Rome, Dalmatia, Italy, France, and surrounding regions. Before starting his solitary hermitage in the desert of Chalcis he established and for three years headed his first society of ascetics at his native Aquileia. This means that he had a long preliminary training for ascetic life before entering the desert hermitage. In spite of this — and notwithstanding the radical termination of all his previous so-cial affiliations — his previous egos, values, drives, and activities persisted and vigorously resisted their extermination. The operation of the rein-tegration of these was very difficult and painful. St. Jerome tells of his experiences in this operation:

Oh, how often, when I was living in the desert, in that lonely waste, scorched by the burning sun, which affords to hermits a savage dwelling-place, how often did *I fancy myself surrounded by the pleasures of Rome!* I used to sit alone; for I was filled with bitterness. My unkempt limbs were covered in a shapeless sackcloth; my skin through long neglect had become as rough and black as an Ethiopian's. . . . Tears and groans were everyday my por-tion; and if sleep ever overcame my resistance and fell upon my eyes, I bruised my restless bones against the naked earth. Of food and drink I will not speak. Hermits have nothing but cold water even when they are sick, and for them it is sinful luxury to partake of cooked dishes. But though in my fear of hell I had condemned myself to this prison-house, where my only companions were scorpions and wild beasts, *I often found myself surrounded by bands of danc-ing girls.* My face pale with fasting; but though my limbs were cold as ice, my mind was burning with desire, and the *fires of lust kept bubbling up* before me when my flesh was as good as dead. . . .

And so when all other help failed me, I used to fling myself at Jesus' feet; I watered them with my tears; I wiped them with my hair; and if my flesh still rebelled, I subdued it by weeks of fasting. I do not blush to confess my misery. . . . I remember I joined night to day with my wailings, and ceased not from beating my breast till tranquility returned to me at the Lord's behest. . . . Filled with stiff anger against myself, I would make my way alone into the desert; and when I came upon some hollow valley or . . . precipitous cliff, there I would set up my oratory, and make that spot a place of torture for my unhappy flesh. . . . There sometimes also after many a tear . . . I felt myself in the presence of the angelic hosts and in joy and gladness would sing: " Because of the savor of thy good ointments we will run after thee." Such are the temptations of men whose bodies are emaciated with fasting.[1]

Besides the persistence of sex and other biological drives, the previous sociocultural egos, values, interests, and activities tended to persist also.

Many years ago for the sake of the kingdom of heaven I cut myself off from home, parents, sister, relations, and, what was harder, from the dainty food to which I had been used. But even when I was on my way to Jerusalem to fight the good fight there, I could not bring myself to forgo the *library* which with great care and labor I got together at Rome. And so, miserable man that I was, I would fast, only to read Cicero afterwards. I would spend long nights in vigil; I would shed bitter tears called from my innermost heart by the remembrance of my past sins; and then I would take up Plautus again. Whenever I returned to my right senses and began to read the prophets, their language seemed harsh and barbarous. With my blind eyes I could not see the light: but I attributed the fault not to my eyes, but to the sun. While the old serpent was thus mocking me, about the middle of Lent a fever attacked my weakened body and spread through my innermost veins. The ravages it wrought on my unhappy frame were so persistent that at last my bones scarcely held together. . . . My whole body grew gradually cold, and life's vital warmth only lingered faintly in my poor throbbing breast. Suddenly I was caught up in the spirit and dragged before the Judge's judgement seat: and here the light was so dazzling, and the brightness shining from those who stood around so radiant, that I flung myself upon the ground and did not dare to look up. I was asked to state my condition, and replied that I was a Christian. But He who presided said: " Thou liest; thou art a Ciceronian, not a Christian. . . . For where thy treasure is, there will thy heart be also." Straightway I became dumb, and amid the strokes of the whip — for He had ordered me to be scourged — I was even more bitterly tortured by the fire of conscience. . . . At last the bystanders . . . prayed Him to pardon my youth and give me opportunity to repent my error, on the understanding that the extreme of torture should be inflicted on me if I ever read again the works of Gentile authors. . . . Taking oath I called upon His name: " O Lord, if ever again I possess worldly books or read them, I have denied Thee! " After swearing this oath I was dismissed, and returned to the upper world. There to the surprise of all I opened my eyes again, and they were so drenched with tears, that my distress convinced even the incredulous. . . . And I acknowledge that henceforth I read the books of God with a greater zeal than I had ever given before to the books of men. . . . [For] what concord hath Christ with Belial? What has Horace to do with the Psalter, Virgil with the Gospels and Cicero with Paul? [2]

Here the *library* and the *Ciceronianus es, non Christianus* stand for all artistic, literary, philosophical, political, cultural and " the society " groups (and values) with which St. Jerome was associated in Rome, Dalmatia, and elsewhere before he undertook the pilgrimage to Jerusalem and eremitic solitude. St. Jerome's description of his own experience gives a good idea of the enormous difficulty of the religious-altruistic reintegration of his egos, values, drives, and activities, in spite of the earlier termination of his membership in almost all his previous groups and a good rearrangement of his new affiliations. All his five years of hermitage were taken for his inner transfiguration and even then the task was not wholly accomplished: the learned Church Father retained the traces of quarrelsomeness to the end of his life.

The typicalness of St. Jerome's experience is confirmed by other saintly and secular altruists who had to undergo the operations of a sharp rearrangement of their group affiliations and of a radical reintegration of their egos, values, drives, and activities. Like St. Anthony, with his well-known sex temptations, most of them were tortured by unruly biological drives, and could not easily and quickly get rid of their previous egos, values, and pleasurable activities. These stubbornly lingered and sometimes flared up in a powerful revolt, defying all the efforts of an eremitic or monastic or secular altruist.

## III

### REINTEGRATION IN SEMI-SOLITUDE OF TEMPLE AND PILGRIMAGE

In recent times Sri Ramakrishna gives the oriental example of experience similar to St. Jerome's. After severing all his previous social ties, and entering the Dakshineswar temple, although this was contrary to the Brahmanic rule, he spent several years in incessant, strenuous, and painful efforts to arrive at the union with the Divine Mother (God) before he achieved his purpose.

So great was his yearning for God that twelve strenuous years passed in a state of divine intoxication, during half of which period he did not close his eyes in sleep. . . . Unconscious of hunger, thirst, or any of the cravings of the body, or of the things happening around him, Sri Ramakrishna, during that period of Sadhana [spiritual discipline] was almost like a madman.[3]

During these years he experimentally tried the most varied techniques for achievement of his goal. One of these was spiritual meditation during afternoons and nights in the jungle, under an amalaka tree, naked and without the Brahmin's sacred thread. When his young nephew and helper asked him: " Why have you taken off your cloth and the sacred thread? " Ramakrishna answered:

Why, don't you know that is the way one should think of God, *free of all ties?* Since our very birth we have the eightfold fetters of hatred, shame, pedigree, culture, fear, fame, caste and egoism. This sacred thread means that I am a Brahmin and therefore superior to all. When calling upon the Mother [God] one has to set such ideas aside. So I have removed the holy thread.[4]

" Thus the realization of God — the vision of the Divine Mother — became the one passion of Sri Ramakrishna." In spite of all his efforts, however, union with the Divine was not achieved for a long time. Ramakrishna used to cry:

" O Mother! Where are Thou? Reveal Thyself to me. Am I a wretch that Thou dost not come to me? Pleasure, wealth, friends, enjoyments — I do not want any of these. I only desire to see Thee, Mother." Tears flowed continuously from his eyes. The day would pass, and when the peal of evening bells in the temple announced the close of day, he would become sadder still and cry, " Another day is spent in vain, Mother, for I have not seen Thee! Another day of this short life has passed, and I have not realized the Truth! " He would often rub his face against the ground in his agony. His plaintive moans would attract crowds of people, who whispered to one another, " Poor young man! Has he really lost his mother? "

Referring to this tremendous thirst for God Sri Ramakrishna would often say to his disciples later on, " Oh, what days of suffering I passed through! You cannot imagine my agony at separation from Mother! " [5]

At one moment he behaved like a demented person, at the next he would cry like a child. . . . He took less food and slept very little.

He says again: " I was then suffering from excruciating pain because I had not been blessed with a vision of the Mother. . . . I felt as if my heart were being squeezed like a wet towel. I was overpowered by a great restlessness, and a fear. . . . I could not bear the separation any longer: life did not seem worth living. Suddenly my eyes fell on the sword that was kept in the Mother's [Kali] temple. Determined to put an end to my life, I jumped up like a mad man and seized it, when suddenly the blessed Mother revealed Herself to me, and I fell unconscious on the floor. What happened after that externally, I do not know, but within me there was a steady flow of undiluted bliss altogether new, and I felt the presence of the Divine Mother." [6]

After this first vision of the Divine, " the darkest night " of his self-identification was essentially over. Though subsequently there were some dark periods, they progressively decreased and the God-intoxicated state of *samadhi* became more frequent. Ramakrishna arrived at his goal. His reintegration of egos, values, and activities around the supreme value of God was fully achieved. With it, a profound peace of mind, interrupted frequently by the ecstatic state of blissful samadhi (union with God), became the normal state of Ramakrishna.

" It is ego that is the cause of all trouble. The wretched ' I ' is almost indestructible." [7]  " When the ego dies, all troubles cease to exist," he sums up. [8]

The great Muslim philosopher, one-time skeptic, and then Sufist mystic Al Ghazzali (1058–1111) gives our next case. As professor, philosopher, ethical, political, and religious leader, he reached the summit of fame, prosperity, and influence in the Muslim Arabic world and beyond it. In his search for truth he, like St. Augustine, however, became deeply skeptical about the validity not only of his own teachings but also of the theories of the scholastic theologians who professed to follow reason and speculation and of the empiricists and philosophers who called themselves masters of logic, observation, and demonstration. Eventually he identified himself with " the Sufis, who call themselves the elect of God and possessors of intuition and knowledge of the truth by means of ecstasy." [9] From the purely intellectual self-identification to the completed mental, moral, and behavioral transfiguration, however, there was an enormous distance to be covered.

I acquired a thorough knowledge of their researches, and I learned all that was possible to learn of their methods by study and oral teaching. It became clear to me that the last stage could not be reached by mere instruction, but only by transport, ecstasy, and the transformation of the moral being. . . . To define health and satiety [or drunkenness], to penetrate their causes and conditions, is quite another thing from being well and satisfied [or being drunk]. . . . In the same way there is a considerable difference between knowing renouncement, comprehending its conditions and causes, and practicing renouncement and detachment from the things of this world. I saw that Sufism consists in experiences rather than in definitions, and that what I was lacking belonged to the domain, not of instruction, but of ecstasy and initiation. . . . *I saw that one can only hope for salvation by devotion and the conquest of one's passions, a procedure which presupposes renouncement and detachment from this world of falsehood in order to turn towards eternity and meditation on God. Finally, I saw that the only condition of success was to sacrifice honours and riches and to sever the ties and attachments of worldly life.*[10]

With truly scientific precision, Al Ghazzali describes the emergence of the inner conflicts in himself, identifies himself intellectually with the Sufist system of religious, philosophical, and moral values and clearly sees that without renunciation of all his social ties and reintegration of his egos, values, and behavior he cannot reach the objective. A mere intellectual self-identification with the Sufist supraconscious did not solve his problems. Subsequently he tells us about his hesitations, struggles, and difficulties before he succeeded in severing all his ties, and his ten years of struggle to achieve the sought-for reintegration of his inner world.

Coming seriously to consider my state, I found myself bound down on all sides by these trammels. Examining my actions, the most fair-seeming of which were my lecturing and professorial occupations, I found to my surprise that I was engrossed in several studies of little value, and profitless as regards my salvation. . . . I perceived that I was on the edge of abyss. In these reflections I spent a long time. Still a prey to uncertainty, one day I decided to leave Bagdad and to give up everything; the next day I gave up my resolution. I advanced one step and immediately relapsed. . . . In the morning I was sincerely resolved only to occupy myself with the future life; in the evening a crowd of carnal thoughts assailed and dispersed my resolutions. . . . Thus I remained, torn asunder by the opposite forces of earthly passions and religious aspirations, for about six months [A.D. 1096].

Then a precipitant of sickness occurred:

At the close of six months my will yielded and I gave myself up to destiny. God caused an impediment to chain my tongue and prevented me from lecturing. Vainly I desired to go on with my teaching, but my mouth became dumb. The silence to which I was condemned cast me into a violent despair; my stomach became weak; I could neither swallow a morsel of bread nor drink a drop of water. [Doctors gave up hope of saving his life.]
Finally, conscious of my weakness and the prostration of my soul, I took refuge in God as a man at the end of himself and without resources.

When the religious and political authorities and his friends learned about his decision to retire from the world, they did not take it seriously "because they considered my position as the highest attainable in the religious community," says Al Ghazzali.

"At last I left Bagdad, giving up all my fortune." During the next ten years he spent two years in Syria in "retirement, meditation, and devout exercises." He "used to live a solitary life in the Mosque of Damascus," then as a pilgrim he visited Jerusalem, Mecca, Medina, Hejaz. "Ten years passed in this manner. During my successive periods of meditation there were revealed to me things impossible to recount." He was able "to purge his heart of all that does not belong to God" by the mystic "cathartic method of the Sufis" and became "lost in God." The operation of the spiritual and altruistic reintegration of his group affiliations, egos, values, activities, including the mastery over his biological impulses, was about completed. His prayer to God to "cleanse from all defilement, that nothing remain in him except Himself" was seemingly heard. As a transfigured person now he could return to the world to carry on his religious and moral mission.[11]

Carefully studying the process of altruistic transfiguration of the late, the intermediary and some of the fortunate altruists, one finds that they all had to fight somewhat similar struggles before they were "over the hump." Altruistic reintegration has ordinarily been painful and has taken some time before it was complete.

## IV

### Reintegration in Monastery and Brotherhood

The great educators of mankind — the eminent religious and altruistic leaders — well knew of this difficulty of reintegration. They learned of it by their own experience. This explains why in establishing their monasteries, brotherhoods, and other institutions for moral and religious training, or when counseling aspiring novitiates, they made a number of special provisions for dealing with the difficulty. Their rules aim at weeding out all the weak aspirants for membership in these institutions, and admitting only those who can pass a long series of severe tests designed to reveal whether a candidate can successfully reintegrate his egos, values, drives, and activities. Those who pass these life-like tests are admitted and promoted; those who fail are barred from admission to the membership and demoted.

One of these provisions is a *most careful selection of the candidates for membership in the monastery or brotherhood.* Another rule is a *fairly long (from one to several years) period of probation of the selected candidates before they are permitted to take the monastic or brotherhood vow and admitted to full membership.* The third rule *is the requirement of a complete renunciation of all social ties by the initiated monk or brother, and a complete self-identification of the initiate with the monastery or brotherhood.* Fourth, there is the *special kind of training during the period of probation and the requirement of complete obedience from the novice.* Fifth, *a spiritual father (" spiritualis pater "), guru, sheik, or spiritual, moral, and mental counselor is given to each novice, to guide him in all his thoughts, words, and deeds.*

These rules and conditions are almost universal in monasteries, communal brotherhoods, and in other agencies for moral education in the East and West. Thus, in ancient India a candidate for moral and social leadership had to undergo during his studentship such a long and severe testing that only a few men could meet the requirements without a failure. The course of study of the Vedas continued from twelve to forty years. During this period the student " shall obey his teacher, except crimes "; he must not contradict him; must care for him, feed him, take food only after the teacher has finished his eating. Furthermore, " he shall not look at the sun; he shall avoid honey, meat, perfumes, garlands, sleep in the daytime, ointments, collyrium, a carriage, shoes, a parasol, [sexual] love, anger, covetousness, perplexity, garrulity, playing musical instruments, bathing for pleasure, cleaning the teeth, elation, dancing, singing, calumny and terror; he shall avoid the gaze and touch of women; gambling; low service; taking things not offered; injuring animate beings; making bitter speeches; he shall speak the truth "; and so on.

Contrariwise: " If these rules are transgressed, study drives out the knowledge of the Veda, acquired already, from the offender and from his children; besides, he will go to hell and his life will be shortened " (not to mention that he loses all chances to become a man of high order).[12]

In practically all Hindu monasteries, communal brotherhoods or ashrams of the past and of the present, all five rules given above are found to be functioning and enforced.

For Zen Buddhist monks, " A Zen monk is no Zen monk unless he goes through at least a few years of severe discipline at this institute [Zen monastery]." [13] Selection and testing of a novice by a local Zen master begins even before the candidate comes to the Zen monastery. " Determined to leave his parents . . . he is a homeless monk now, and no more a man of the world. . . . He is to rid himself of defilements of all sorts." Such is the aim of the candidate even at this initial stage of the selection and testing.[14] His tests are continued during his traveling on foot to the monastery; at its gates where he is kept for a day or so before he is admitted into the yard or campus of the monastery. Then, if he is admitted, he must pass a long series of living tests of his moral, social, and mental stamina before he becomes a full-fledged member of the Zen brotherhood. Renunciation of all his social ties and possessions, identification with the Zen brotherhood, and obedience to his moral and mental advisors are also a part of the long selection and severe testing during the several years of the " probationary period." [15] Many fail to complete the severe process of the reintegration of the novice's egos, values, drives, and activities. Those who pass it become full-fledged members of the brotherhood.

Similar is the situation in the Taoist or Mohammedan (Sufist) brotherhoods or monasteries. Also, the constitutions of practically all Christian monastic orders have similar " safety valves." Thus the *Rules of Pachomius* prescribe that all those whose earlier life rendered them unsuitable are not to be admitted even for probation. Of other candidates, every aspirant must be tested before admittance inside the walls of a monastic community. Therefore, a newcomer is placed for a few days outside the monastery, and the seriousness of his intention to enter the monastery is tested. Can he renounce the world, including his parents? Can he obey the rules, etc.? If he passes the tests, then he is taught the prayers and the rules of the establishment, and only after that he is admitted to a " low-grade " membership. After admittance he must unconditionally obey the rules and the authorities.[16]

St. Basil's *Rules* state that " we must examine their [the aspirants'] characters, whether they are unstable and prone to sudden decisions," and " to submit them to an appropriate course of training." " And when each man, after full examination by those who are competent to make skillful investigation, has been accepted as vessel serviceable unto the Master and ready for every good work, then let him be numbered with those who have dedicated themselves to the Lord. . . . It is necessary that the newcomer be received with knowledge of all the brethren in order that they may rejoice and pray together." " True and perfect obedience of subordinates towards the leader is shown in this; namely, in not only refraining from wrong things according to the counsel of the Superior, but not doing even praiseworthy things without his approval." [17] Since " no man can serve two masters," complete renunciation of all previous social ties and groups and the values of the world, including the family bonds, is the necessary condition for monastic membership.

" Renunciation is a loosening of the chains which bind us to the present material and transitory life, a freeing from human obligations, making us more ready to start on the God-ward way." [18]

Very similar are the *Rules of St. Benedict.*

> To him that newly comes to conversion, let not an easy entrance be granted, but, as the Apostle says, " Try the spirits if they be of God." If, therefore, he that comes persevere in knocking, and after four or five days seem patiently to endure the wrongs done to him [or the harshness shown him] and the difficulty made about his entrance, and to persist in his petition, let entrance be granted him, and let him be in the guesthouse for a few days. Afterwards, let him be in the cell of the novices. . . . Let there be assigned to him a senior, who is skilled in winning souls, who may watch him with the utmost care and consider anxiously whether he truly seeks God, and is zealous for the work of God, for obedience, and for humiliations. Let there be set before him all the hard and rugged ways by which we walk towards God.

After two months of this probationary period, the novice is acquainted with the *Rules,* warned about the austerities of his vocation, and is returned to the cell of the novices where he " again is tried in all patience " for another six months. The *Rules* are read to him again, and " if he stands firm " he is returned again to probationary cell for another four months. Then the *Rules* are again read to him, " And if, having deliberated with himself, he promises to keep all things, and to observe everything that is commanded him, then let him be received into the community." [19] Renunciation of all previous social ties, of his property, of his parents or family, of all the values of the world, up to " renunciation of his own will," and the vow of " the holy obedience," are further obligatory requirements.[20]

Similar are the requirements of the *Constitution* of St. Theodore of Studium,[21] and of the *Constitutiones* of the Society of Jesus. Especially detailed, severe, and long are the tests of the preliminary and probationary periods of the Society of Jesus. Any candidate for even the novitiate is carefully selected. Persons guilty of heresy or homicide, of membership in another order, mental deficiency, of doubtful habits and inclinations are not admitted. Then follows two years of novitiate training, the purpose of which is " a complete destruction of pride and spirit of the world." The novice is subjected to six kinds of trials: one month to a study and practice of Loyola's *Spiritual Exercises;* one month to the service of the sick in hospitals; a month to a pious pilgrimage, without other resources than the alms begged and received along the way. Then each novice shall be employed in the humble duties of the house; he shall teach Christian doctrine to the children and the ignorant; shall practice in preaching, and, if he is a priest, in hearing confessions. If all the recommendations from all the persons he serves during these months are satisfactory, he is admitted to a house of the Order where he must unfailingly perform all the duties required. " The novices must keep watch and ward over eyes, ear, and tongues; they shall speak in words apt for edification, wear modest looks, walk with unhurried gait, and never a gesture showing pride or impatience; they . . . should look upon themselves as the inferior . . . and shall give themselves over to a perfect obedience, looking upon the Superior, whoever he may be, as in the place of Christ. . . . Novices shall love poverty like a mother; they shall strive after righteousness," and so on.

A retreat of eight days must precede the novice's taking the vows of poverty, chastity, obedience, and of a special unconditional obedience to the Pontiff. Before pronouncing the vows, the novice must beg from door to door for three days. He must renounce all of his personal possessions, and sever all contacts and communication with his friends and family. Each coming and going letter is examined by the superior, who decides whether it is to be sent or given to the novice. Each novice is given a regular confessor or spiritual counselor, " to whom he should make known all the good and all the ill he has done," and " an exact and detailed account of conscience."

The requirements and training continue after the novice is taken into the Order, if he is to progress from the lower rank of " the indifferents," through the ranks of " the scholastics," then " the spiritual and temporal coadjutors " and, finally, to " the professed " who are all priests. In brief, the selection and tests are severe and are likely to bar from the Order most of the weak and " soft " individuals.[22]

According to the " First Rule of the Friars Minor " of St. Francis of Assisi, if a preliminary investigation of the candidate does not rule him out, " let the ministers receive him [the candidate] kindly and encourage him, and diligently explain to him the tenor of our life. This being done, if he is willing and able, let him sell all his goods and endeavor to distribute them to the poor. . . . Then let the minister grant him the habit of probation for a year. The year of probating being finished, let him be received to obedience." Then like other brothers he " ought to live in obedience, without property and in chastity," and as Jesus says, " let him deny himself and take up his cross." [23]

St. Basil and St. Jerome excellently sum up the significance of these rules and of the monastic community generally. They correctly indicate that life and membership in the monastic community is an all-powerful factor that enormously reinforces the limited efforts of an individual, and incalculably helps him in realization of his difficult purpose. In their writings they clearly point out that the monastic community " is not to be a mere physical neighborhood . . . but rather an idea bearing fruit in every department of life and spirit." [24] By merely becoming a member, an individual increases his power by the far greater power of the community, and since the community is dedicated to and participates in the infinite power of God, the individual member becomes thus a participant in a power far transcending his own limited potential. His endeavors are thus backed by the power of the community and the grace of God. In this way he is incalculably helped in achievement of his objective. St. Basil and other founders of monastic orders lay down clearly and in great detail all the reasons which nowadays we hear from the founders of "Alcoholics Anonymous," "We Are Not Alone," "Group Therapy" and other therapeutic organizations.

Some of St. Basil's statements have been quoted in the preceding chapter. Here are a few lines of St. Jerome's summary of the situation:

No art is learned without a master. Even dumb animals and herds of wild beasts follow leaders of their own. . . . The purpose of these examples is simply . . . to show you that you had better not be left to your own discretion, but should rather live in a monastery under the control of one father and with many companions. From one of them you may learn humility, from another patience, this one will teach you silence, that one meekness. You will not do what you yourself wish; you will eat what you are ordered; you will take what you are given; you will wear the dress allotted to you; you will perform a set amount of work: you will be subordinate to some one you do not like; you will come to bed worn out with weariness and fall asleep as you walk about. Before you have had your fill of rest, you will be forced to get out of bed and take your turn in psalm singing. . . . You will serve the brethren; you will wash the feet of guests; if you suffer wrong you will say nothing; the superior of the monastery you will fear as a master and love as a father. Whatever precepts he gives you, you will believe to be wholesome for you. You will not pass judgment upon your elders' decision, for it is your duty to be obedient and carry out orders. . . . You will be so busy with all these tasks that you will have no time for vain imaginings. . . .

St. Jerome indicates that in the world there are many who " had renounced the world — in garb and in verbal professions, but not in reality . . . . [They] changed nothing of their former mode of life " and have even more luxuries, servants, and live more sinfully than before their verbal renunciation of the world. In contrast to this hypocrisy and deceit, the monastic discipline changes one's mind, heart, and behavior. What appears to be at first a compulsory drilling imposed upon the novice eventually turns into a freely self-imposed, welcomed, and pleasurable method of self-transformation.

Habits will gradually grow on you, and finally you will do of your own accord what was at first a matter of compulsion; you will take pleasure in your labors; and forgetting what is behind you will reach out to that which is before; you will not think at all of the evil that others do, but only of the good which it is your duty to perform.[25]

The above shows clearly the difficult operation of integration or reintegration of one's egos, values, and activities, before, simultaneously, or even after a successful rearrangement of one's group membership. With whatever step the trilateral operation starts, the successful reintegration of the inner cosmos and the external activities of the individual is an effortful, sometimes painful, prolonged, and almost always difficult process.

Only the fortunate altruists do it comparatively easily. For most of the late and the intermediary altruists it is a most strenuous operation.

## V

### REINTEGRATION IN THE CONDITIONS OF A NORMAL WORLDLY LIFE

This is equally true of the late and the intermediary altruists living and growing in the ordinary social world. Whether the reintegration of their egos, values, drives, and activities is done after, simultaneously, or before a reorganization of their group membership, again it is almost always an arduous and time-consuming operation. In this respect it is similar to the painful and difficult process of a " reorganization of self " [26] of the subnormal clients of psychiatrists. In order to be " adjusted " or " cured," the patient's disorganized and self-contradictory inner world has to be reorganized, too. When the reintegration of egos, values, drives, and activities is slight, it involves only " a slight discomfort." When it is substantial, " the client may go through the most racking torment of pain, and a complete and chaotic confusion." [27]

Here are a few examples of reintegration by the " worldly altruists."

Before his conversion Brother Joseph (I. Dutton) was bookstore clerk, soldier, distillery superintendent, railroad agent, U. S. Government investigator of claims; a Protestant, unhappily married. As we have already seen, the beginning of his conversion after his " sinful years " was marked by his resignation as railroad freight agent, by his divorce in 1881, and then in 1883 by his retirement from the government service. In 1883 he became a member of the Catholic church. In the same year he changed his name, " reverently laying aside the ' Ira B.' " for " Joseph, a servant of our Lord." Thus, in 1883 he entirely reorganized his social affiliations, and, to a considerable degree, reintegrated his egos, values, drives, and activities. Among other things, he stopped his drinking, and among his new egos, the ego of a " penitent " or " brother to everybody " began to be dominant. Nevertheless, it took from two to three years after 1883 before his reintegration was completed and before he found his altruistic life mission. During these years he wandered from place to place, and entered for some twenty months the Trappist monastery at Gethsemane, Kentucky. Not entirely satisfied with even the severe discipline of the Trappist monastery, he left it. Finally, having incidentally heard in the Redemptorist house in New Orleans about the work of Damien the Leper at Molokai, he was

attracted by it wonderfully. I became convinced that it would suit my wants for labor, for a penitential life, and for seclusion as well as a complete separation from the scenes of all past experiences.

Having settled all his affairs, in the garb he was to wear for the rest of his life — a suit of cheap blue denim — he started from Memphis to San Francisco. Though I had ample means along, I came on an immigrant ticket, and from San Francisco on a sailing vessel — the cheapest way — carrying out the idea of making it a sort of pilgrimage.

He served the leper colony at Molokai as its leader or director for forty-four years. But before he found his vocation, and even after a basic re-arrangement of his group affiliations (in 1883), he still had to struggle with the reintegration of his inner world for several years.[28]

Gandhi gives another example of a secular altruist living and growing in the very thick of the busy world. In the preceding chapter we saw how his altruistic transformation was started and developed. Since he never stopped in his altruistic growth and continuously set forth ever-higher and stricter moral demands for himself, an ever-better rearrangement of his group affiliations and an ever-finer reintegration of his egos, values, drives, and activities continued, with ups and downs, throughout his life.

With the start of his altruization he began to " disaffiliate " himself from, or was dropped by, doubtful friends, acquaintances, groups, caste; he continued this disaffiliation up to the end of his life. Simultaneously he affiliated himself with many persons, groups, associations, clubs, and so-cieties that helped his altruistic objectives. Parallel with this process, he arduously worked over a better and purer reintegration of his egos, values, drives, and activities. He took one moral vow after another, and strenu-ously kept them unbroken, no matter how difficult fidelity to them might prove. The following lines tell something about the effortful struggle involved.

Brahmacharya means control of the senses in thought, word and deed. Every day I have been realizing more and more the necessity for restraints of the kind I detailed above [control of sexual lust, of the palate, of pride, and so on]. There is no limit to the possibilities of renunciation, even as there is none to those of *brahmacharya*. Such *brahmacharya is impossible of attainment by limited effort.* For many it must remain only as an ideal. . . . So long as thought is not under complete control of the will, *brahmacharya* in its fulness is absent. . . . Curbing of thought . . . is even more difficult to curb than the wind.

Among many vows, in 1906 he took the vow of sexual chastity in the relationship with his wife. He decided it (but did not take the vow) in 1901, but twice failed. " If it [sexual brahmacharya, eventually] became a matter of ever-increasing joy, let no one believe that it was an easy thing for me. Even when I am past fifty-six years, I realize how hard a thing it is. Every day I realize more and more that it is like walking on the sword's edge, and I see every moment the necessity for eternal vigi-lance." [29]

We see him, throughout his life, after each new vow strenuously work-ing over himself. Each vow and labor were paralleled by a respective change in his network of social affiliations; and each change in group membership was followed by some change in his inner world and overt activities. The net result was Gandhi's continued growth in his altruistic creativity.

A still more " secular " example of the process studied is given by the life of an eminent pioneer in the planning and building of the integral co-operative community — Henri Lasserre. His growth in creative altruism consisted of the same trilateral process: in a continuous change of his social affiliations by dropping the groups inimical to his altruistic objective and by affiliating with groups or even creating new organizations (*Terre Libre* and the *Foundation for the Establishment of Integral Cooperatives* in Europe, and the *Robert Owen Foundation* and the *Canadian Fellowship for Cooperative Community*, in Canada) that helped or embodied his ideal of the integral co-operative community. This process led him eventually from Switzerland and Europe to Canada. It was followed by the reintegration of his egos, values, and activities around the supreme value of creative, free, unselfish Love — the sublime Love of the Sermon on the Mount, practiced and realized *here and now* (in contradistinction to " Moral Rearmament " and similar movements which he regarded as mainly preaching good principles but not practicing them).

Reading his autobiographical notes, one can see that several times the rearrangement of his group affiliations was followed by strenuous efforts to reintegrate respectively his inner world and overt behavior. Starting his career as a notary and lawyer, he soon came into contact with co-operative and labor organizations. This contact gradually ripened in him the conclusion that the " ownership of unearned productive property is socially undesirable."

These reflections impressed me deeply. From 1909 on I felt a vague desire to give up my inherited wealth amounting to some thousands of Swiss francs, together with the accumulated interest on it. I now took the decision to devote this money to a useful and socially just purpose. The opportunity for doing so was not long in coming.

He accordingly affiliated himself with the new (altruistic) groups and established a true co-operative community. These changes led to severing his affiliations with several persons and groups and to contacting membership in several new groups. This process was followed by a respective change in his egos, values, and overt activities; and so his whole life continued to flow in the stream of ideological and practical altruistic creativity.[30]

Like H. Lasserre, in the course of his quiet altruistic growth John Woolman found it advisable to give up his successful business and his membership in several groups as " entangling superfluities " hindering his altruistic activities. He well describes this psychological process.

The increase of business became my burden; for though my natural inclination was towards merchandise, yet I believed truth required me to live more free from outward cumbers; and there was now a strife in my mind between the two. In this exercise my prayers were put up to the Lord, who graciously heard me. Then I lessened my outward business . . . and in a while I wholly laid down merchandise, and followed my trade as a tailor by myself, having no apprentices. I also had a nursery of apple-trees. . . .[31]

He stayed out of any organization or group cultivating luxury, because "every degree of luxury hath some connection with evil."[32] Subsequently he not only severed his connections with but actively opposed all groups exploiting Indians and Negroes, defending slavery and sharp inequality, and supporting other injustices. He became identified with a few small groups resolutely but nonviolently fighting for a true moral, mental, and social ennoblement of man and human society.

Quietly, but decisively, A. Schweitzer cut off his closest ties with musical, artistic, scholastic, religious, and other cultural organizations of Europe and "buried himself" in the medical, moral, and social service to "the savages" of Equatorial Africa through his organization established there.

Similar trilateral transformations are observable in the life of Dorothy Day, Simone Weil, and other "secular" altruists.[33] The same process has been experienced by several hundreds of American Good Neighbors.[34]

These "karma yogins" or "secular altruists," born and living in the ordinary human universe, doing there their good deeds, and growing there in their love creativity, pass through the same triple operation. Some perform these operations almost simultaneously; others with some (usually slight) nonsynchronousness — one of the operations, say, group rearrangement, preceding the other two operations or one of these two preceding the other two. Some do all this with great pain, strain, and time consumption; others do it more easily and in a shorter time. But all pass through all three experiences, and all have to labor over the reintegration of their inner life and their overt activities. Especially difficult is the whole operation for the late and partly for the intermediary altruists. However, the difficulty of altruistic transformation in the conditions of the ordinary human world seems to be not essentially different from that of the hermits, pilgrims, or members of a monastery or brotherhood.

## VI

### PASSAGE TO THE CONTROL OF BIOLOGICAL — UNCONSCIOUS AND BIOCONSCIOUS — DRIVES

Having somewhat elucidated the process of the reintegration of the sociocultural egos and values, now we can pass on to a closer examination of the control of biological drives — unconscious and conscious. In this chapter the reintegration of these drives has been mentioned in passing, but it has not been described at all. The next chapter deals with one essential aspect of this control: the intensity of the mortification of the body's needs as practiced by various altruists. More specific techniques of the body's control as well as of the reintegration of egos, values, and activities are analyzed in other chapters.

## Chapter Fifteen

# Types of Control of Biological Drives

## I

### THE NEED FOR CONTROL

Love is possible only when one's unconscious drives are well controlled by the supraconscious self and by the conscious forces of the individual. The complete freedom of biological impulses and egos means a lack of integration of personality, and a perpetual anarchy within the organism. The uncontrolled impulses, emotions, and passions will drive the human animal to incessant clashes with others. Plato and Aristotle were right in calling such a human being " the worst of the beasts."

This explains why even an ordinary, normal individual must acquire, to some extent, control of his biological egos and impulses, as well as of his overt actions. Still greater must be the control in the altruistic person. Let us glance at the main types of techniques for achieving this purpose.

## II

### TECHNIQUE OF EXTREME MORTIFICATION OF THE ORGANISM

This is the rudest, most painful, and most primitive of the techniques practiced by persons and groups in various populations and at various times. The technique is based upon the belief that the flesh and its drives are the greatest enemy of God, or of the highest self. Therefore, all the needs of the organism, and especially its lusts, must be suppressed and denied as much as possible. " I kill my body, for it kills me," expressed by Dorotheus the Theban, is one of the shortest formulas of this belief.[1] Plato gives another example. " While we are in the body, and while the soul is mingled with this mass of evil," no truth is possible. " For the body is a source of endless trouble to us by reason of the mere requirement of food; and . . . by filling us as full of loves, and lusts, and fears, and fancies, and idols, and every sort of folly, it prevents our ever having so much as a thought." It is a source of wars and enmity, of turmoil and confusion, and the greatest obstacle to obtaining the truth. "All experience shows that if we would have pure knowledge of anything, we must be quit of the body, and the soul in herself must behold all things in themselves." "Thought is best when the mind . . . has as little as possible to do with the body, and has no bodily sense or feeling." Such is Plato's formula of this belief, in reference to knowledge, truth, and goodness.[2]

When literally understood, the following sayings of Christ are further formulas of this method. "If thy right eye offend thee, pluck it out"; "if thy right hand offend thee, cut it off."

Saint John of the Cross gives another variation of this prescription. The first step for the union of the soul with God, he said, is "privation and purgation of the soul of all its sensual desires." We must "mortify the concupiscence of the flesh, and the concupiscence of the eyes, and the pride of life, from which all the other desires proceed." Liberated from all the sensual pleasures and desires, "in this detachment the spiritual soul finds its quiet and repose; for, since it covets nothing, nothing wearies it when it is lifted up, and nothing oppresses it when it is cast down."[3]

This accounts, then, for the fantastically varied practices of mortification of body by many an ascetic of the East and the West, of the past and the present. Beginning with suicide as a direct solution of the problem, and ending with the cruelest forms of self-torture, the practices exhibit an unbelievable variety of self-torturing inventiveness.

Here we meet, first, hundreds of forms of fasting as a suppression of the *bodily need for food* — complete fasting for days and weeks; lifelong relative fasting in the form of eating only a little bread and drinking a little water; eating only raw herbs, or inedible garbage; or eating only by two teeth; or fasting unto death.

Second, there is the violent suppression of the *sex impulse* in all its forms, beginning with self-castration and mutilation of the sex organs, and ending with weakening of the sex impulse through fasting, strenuous physical work, destruction of all its conditioned and unconditioned stimuli; fleeing from such stimuli and environment; imposing upon the body all sorts of cooling pains like prolonged immersion in cold water or snow, dropping cold water upon the scalp or other sensitive parts of the body, opening the veins and shedding blood, etc.; not to mention hundreds of purely mental techniques for the elimination, suppression, and weakening of all kinds of erotic images, memories, associations, and desires.[4]

Third is the violent denial to the body of anything that gives *sensual pleasure* and imposition upon the body of all kinds of pains and hardships. These practices include exposure of the body to cold and hot temperatures or climatic conditions; keeping it free from the comfort of cleanliness and subject to the hardships of dust, dirt, being besmeared, and physically defiled by all kinds of pollution; wearing either nothing or dirty nd lousy rags, or horsehair undergarments, or a shirt studded by sharp nails or thorns, incessantly pricking, cutting, and scratching the body; oading the body with heavy chains or iron shirts, and ceaselessly causing o it various physical pains.

Fourth is the denial to the body of its *need of sleeping in comfortable conditions.* Most of the followers of this method of subjugation of the body regularly practiced sleeplessness for many days and nights; or reduced the period of sleep to an unbelievable minimum. In addition, they slept in conditions stripped of all comfort: on hard rocks, on the ground, without any bed or pillow, often without any blanket or cover.[5] Some of them invented and practiced sleeping on boards studded by sharp nails, or covered by sharp stones or thorns; others did not allow the body to stretch out fully or kept it in a painful posture. Again in regard to this need there have been invented hundreds of most ingenious techniques either to deny its satisfaction or to satisfy it to some extent in the most painful way possible.

Fifth is the denial to the body of its need of *physical rest and comfort.* Lying prostrate on a cold floor, without change of the body's posture for hours and days; standing upright on the feet, without any change of position for long periods; kneeling on a stone for weeks; now and then, in cases like St. Simeon Stylites, living buried up to the neck for many months and then dwelling for years on the top of a pillar, with all the hardships involved; demanding from the body an endless exertion after it had already reached the state of utter fatigue and exhaustion: these are just a few examples of the suppression of the bodily need for rest and physical relaxation.

Sixth are the practices of denying to any sense organ of the body or to all the receptors of its nervous system anything that gives or may give *sensory pleasure* and seeking for the objects, actions, thoughts, and forces that give to them pain. Beginning with viewing skulls, coffins, and other symbols of death and infirmity, and ending with avoidance of any pleasant sight, sound, fragrance, or other pleasure-giving stimuli, there are hundreds of techniques which have been practiced for this purpose.

The above listing gives an idea of the essential traits of this technique of acquiring control over the body, its needs, drives, and biological egos. The ascetics following this method sometimes competed with one another in seeing who could overtorture himself in comparison with the other self-immolators.[6]

What is to be said of this technique as a whole? In its extreme form it obviously is accessible only to very few; 99.9 per cent of human beings simply cannot stand it at all. Therefore, at best, its " therapeutic " application is very limited. Even for the insignificant fraction of the ascetics who tried to practice it, *it did not always prove to be effective.* A fraction of these ascetics failed in their task of either union with God, or becoming eminent altruists, or even acquiring a mastery over their body and its lusts. Another fraction died prematurely from their self-torture. Still another portion turned into fanatic maniacs, or into individuals reminding one of animals rather than particularly spiritualized, ennobled, and purified saints or sages. Then, asceticism and ascetics become sometimes utterly egoistic, instead of altruistic. " Man may repress his lower [biological] nature for the sake of vainglory, or pride. . . . Such a victory of spirit is not a virtue. Still worse when a self-control of spirit and concentration of will are used for harming others. Among the successful ascetics there have been not only vainglorious, hypocritical, and proud individuals, but even hateful, perfidious and cruel egotists. Morally, such an ascetic is much worse than a common drunkard, glutton or a profligate. . . . Asceticism which frees man's spirit from the shameful bodily passions only to bind it closely with the spiritual evil passions is evidently a false or unmoral asceticism. . . . The principle of asceticism become moral only conditionally, namely, when it serves the purpose of altruism rooted in compassion." [7]

Buddha, having practiced this technique amidst the self-torturing ascetics, found it quite inadequate for his purpose. According to his conclusion, this method of self-torturing does not " kill selfish personal aim, nor does it efface ego." Purely bodily exercise and self-torture " is but the cause of death, strength results alone from the mind's intention." [8]

The same is stressed in the Bhagavadgita. " He who restrains his organ of action, but continues in his mind to brood over the objects of sense whose nature is deluded, is said to be a hypocrite (a man of false conduct) But he who controls the senses (and desires) by the mind, O, Arjuna, and without attachment engages the organ of action in the path of work, he is superior." [9]

The inefficiency of this method in mastering biological impulses, such as sex or anger or vainglory, is testified to by the statements of the ascetic themselves. For instance, in the *Verba Seniorum* we read the story of a certain brother, who, in spite of all his efforts and solitary life of self-torture could not find peace of mind, and three times came to the Abbot Theodore of Pherme asking for help and advice. During the third " counselling and psychoanalytical interview" the Abbot finally asked him " Tell me now, how many years hast thou been in this [monk's] habit? " And the brother said, " Eight." And the old man said, " Believe me, I have been in this habit seventy years, and not for one day could I find peace: and thou wouldst have peace in eight? " [10] If an earnest and strenuous effort to control the bodily needs during either eight or even seventy years failed, in some degree, the method can hardly be called successful The *Verba Seniorum* and writings of several Church Fathers record similar failures in regard to sex lust, anger, hate, vainglory, gluttony, and other biological needs and passions.

On the other hand, when this method is used as a subsidiary one to a much more delicate technique of mental and psychosocial nature, it seems to have been helpful in the realization of the supreme objectives of the strong ascetics. For such strong souls it seems to have been harmless even biologically. St. Anthony, St. Paul of Thebes, St. Francis of Assisi, Henry Suso, St. Ignatius Loyola, St. John of the Cross, St. Serafim of Sarov, and many others underwent a great deal of this self-torture, and sometimes for a period of several years. The fact that they became eminent religious and moral leaders; that they acquired an extraordinary control of their bodily propensities; the fact that some of them lived an unusually long life — St. Anthony lived 105 years, St. Paul of Thebes 113 years — while the whole group of largely ascetic Christian Saints had a much longer duration of life than their nonascetic secular contemporaries: [11] these facts indicate that for some of the ascetic altruists, the technique discussed did not prove fatal or even useless. One of the reasons is possibly the additional fact that in their self-spiritualization and self-altruization the technique of torturing the body was merely subsidiary to a less physical and much more mental technique used by them. Another reason for the success possibly was their moderation in the use of this technique in the sense that they avoided inflicting upon their body tortures that irremediably damaged its vital organs, and that they imposed these hardships at the proper moment and under proper conditions.

These two last reasons are illustrated by the following cases given in the *Sayings of the Fathers*. When " a certain brother," tortured by lust, came for advice to an old ascetic and disbelieved his statement that he was free from sex temptation, the old man explained the reason, saying: " Since the time that I became a monk I have never given myself my fill of bread, nor of water, nor of sleep, and tormenting myself with appetite for these things whereby we are fed, I was not suffered to feel the stings of lust."

Another ascetic, when visited by a woman who wanted to seduce him, being "burnt with [sex] desire," lit a lamp and " put his finger into the flame," and in this way he burnt and scorched all his fingers, one by one. " When the unhappy woman saw what he was doing, she became like a stone for dread," and eventually " turned from her sins and lived in chastity for the rest of her days." [12]

There is hardly any doubt that an infliction upon the body of burning pain may counteract the tormenting sex impulse, especially when the procedure is a mere subsidiary part of a much more refined psychosocial technique.

However, even granting the efficacy of these techniques for certain persons who can take them and use them wisely, they are so painful, so wasteful, and so inaccessible to the overwhelming majority, that in their extreme forms they cannot be recommended at all. We can only be sorry for the many ascetics who practiced them, especially in view of the existence of

several other less painful and more effective techniques. After all, the self-
torturers who relied for their spiritualization and altruization mainly upon
these techniques were a peculiar sort of believers in the all-determining
power of the body: like many contemporary behavioristic educators and
materialistic physicians, they believed that spiritualization and ennoblement of an individual and acquirement of self-control can be accomplished only through a painful change in the body of the individual, and
in no other nonbodily way.[13]

## III

### TECHNIQUE OF A MODERATE AND SENSIBLE CONTROL OF THE BODY AND OF BODILY NEEDS AND EGOS

If the excessive forms of the technique discussed are wasteful, harmful,
ineffective, and inaccessible to most ordinary people, nevertheless a moderate inhibition and limitation of the bodily drives and needs, a harmonization of biological egos with one another and subordination of them to the
unified sociocultural egos, and especially to the highest self, has always
been a necessary procedure in the altruization and spiritualization of practically all the religious and moral leaders of humanity. Among such altruists we hardly meet a glutton, a profligate, a devotee of conspicuous consumption or of unlimited gratification of carnal lusts. Before their
"conversion," many altruists were such profligates and gluttons, but not
after their transfiguration. This transfiguration has been usually achieved,
among other means, through reasonable inhibition of biological propensities.

Within this general pattern of a moderate self-discipline of the body
and its urges, there are several varieties of techniques differing in degree
and secondary traits. One of these is represented by *St. Francis of Assisi's treatment of his body*. Though his *First Rule of the Friars Minor*
stated "Let us hate our body with its vices and sins, because by living
carnally it wishes to deprive us of the love of our Lord" (Art. 22),[14] nevertheless, he did not torture his body for the sake of torture; on the contrary, he tenderly called it "Brother Body" or "Donkey Body," to be
guided by its "Brother Soul." In this guidance, however, the necessary
needs of the body in food, shelter, and clothes were reduced to the very
smallest minimum, hardly endurable for most human beings; and the
amount of labor, endurance, and insensibility to all kinds of hardships demanded from the "Brother Donkey" was enormous. "Brother Donkey,
God wills it, we must hurry and do," was his usual demand put upon the
body. This tender and joyful but exacting treatment of his body gave to
Francis' soul a complete mastery over the biological man.[15] However
hard were the conditions of his body, St. Francis remained the happy and
joyful "jester of God."

Another variation of this pattern, much milder and much easier, is given by the techniques recommended by St. Francis de Sales. This eminent " director of souls " never failed to stress that the Christian God is the God of Joy and not of Fear; that man is inherently good and that " everything is to love, in love, for love and of love in the saintly Church." [16] Viewing love as the *principium et fons* of any ennoblement of our life, he recommended cultivation in this spirit of love of the whole man: his body, his heart, his sentiments, his volition, his intellect and his actions.[17] He also aimed at cultivation of the true, the beautiful, and the good: *libido sciendi, vivendi, sentiendi.*[18]

For the attainment of this perfect life, he also demands an effective control of the biological man, but by mild, mainly psychological means. The control of the body does not mean for him its torture or denial of its needs, but limitation and restraint of these needs insofar as they interfere with the realization of love to God and to man and with the ennobling spiritualization of our life. His method is one of the least ascetic among the techniques of mastery of the biological forces and egos.

Another moderate, though more ascetic, pattern is given by the techniques widely used in various monastic orders of the past and the present, Christian and non-Christian. The *Rules* of St. Pachomius, St. Basil, St. Theodore of Studium, and of St. Benedict can serve as examples for this pattern. For the sake of economy we use here only St. Benedict's *Rule*.

After practicing for three years the monastic discipline of Egypt, St. Benedict almost perished from its austerities. As a result, he introduced his comparatively mild *Rule*. " He did not endeavor to insist upon the discarded austerities and penitential exercises of the East, but sought reformation on new lines. He secured the old ideals of ascetical life by moderation and common-sense ruling over men given to prayer and labor directed and controlled by obedience to authority." [19] " The Instruments of Good Works " clearly show the altruistic objectives of St. Benedict's *Rule*.[20]

For spiritual molding of the mind and behavior of the monks many techniques are prescribed in great detail; among these are moderation in food, drink, clothing, sleep, and so on. Here, however, as in other things " let everything be done with moderation." [21] Vegetarian food is prescribed (except for the sick) twice a day, consisting " of two cooked dishes " and a pound of bread, somewhat increasing the food under conditions of great labor. This is sufficient to keep the body going and does not involve its torture. On the other hand, " nothing is more contrary to the Christian spirit than gluttony." The same rule goes for drink, allowing, however, " a pint of wine a day " when necessary. Moderate fasting is recommended, especially during Lent and similar occasions.[22] So also with clothing. It should be suitable to the climate, but ordinarily " it will be enough for each monk to have a cowl and tunic," " a scapular for working purposes, and shoes and stockings for the feet." "A mattress, blanket, coverlet and pillow are to suffice for bedding." [23]

The whole of the *Rule* is permeated by the idea of efficient control over the biological man through reasonable, moderate, all-pervading, incessant restraint of bodily needs by satisfying their minimum but denying their lusts, without any torture or indulgence. With some variations, the techniques of bodily control practiced by many other monastic orders — Christian and non-Christian — have been similar.[24]

Among the great contemporary altruists, Gandhi and Sri Aurobindo give concrete examples of this moderate asceticism. Somewhat earlier, John Woolman and George Fox, among the Friends, supply further examples. M. K. Gandhi began his ascetic self-discipline fairly early in his life: giving up meat and turning vegetarian; giving up many luxuries and physical comforts in clothing, shelter, and so on; giving up his personal fortune and property. Though married, he gave up sex life (Brahmacharya) at the age of thirty-seven; he more and more strictly inhibited anger, hatred, vainglory, vindictiveness, repulsion to lepers, fear of plague, and other passions and emotions of antisocial natures. Finally, he gave up any resistance by violence, even the killing of poisonous snakes. In brief, his moral and spiritual growth has been parallel with an increasing ascetic self-control of his body and its needs. This moderate *ascesis* was not imposed by Gandhi upon himself for its own sake or for just penalizing and torturing his body, but as a necessary means to the end of finding and serving the Truth or God.[25] On the basis of his own experience he gives us a series of prescriptions helpful in a mastery of the sex impulse, as well as of any bodily drive.

"Brahmacharya means control of the senses in thought, word and deed." For acquiring such a control in regard to the sex impulse, as well as other passions, the following factors are necessary or helpful:

1. Deep, from the bottom of the heart, quest for God or Truth or generally the highest value; 2. irrevocable determination or vow to give up the lust; 3. consecration of one's energy and activity to the realization of the high purpose; 4. incessant thought of one's duty to remain pure to one's self, to society, and the world, and to "that unseen Power which though we may never see, we all feel within us as watching and noting every impure thought and ever helping us"; 5. regulation of the persons and society we meet, our reading, recreation, food and sense organs; exposing one's self to and seeking only the good and pure society, nonreading passion-breeding novels and magazines, and reading only "the works that sustain humanity"; avoidance of theaters and cinemas; practicing only such recreations and sports that "uplift the soul"; eating not for the satisfaction of one's palate but of hunger only: "a self-indulgent man lives to eat; a self-restrained man eats to live"; frequent fastings are helpful 6. brisk walking in the open air early in the morning and at night before

going to bed; 7. early to bed and early to rise, going to bed on an empty stomach; 8. strenuous mental and physical activity of a clean and altruistic kind; 9. control of sight, hearing, and other sense organs by avoiding sights, sounds, objects, scenes, that are " tempting," " debasing and enervating " — " A Brahmachari must see only clean things and close his eyes before anything unclean; he will hear nothing obscene, smell no strong, stimulating things "; 10. as an extraneous aid, a cold bath or cold immersion which helps also to cool the passions; 11. " above all, one must not consider continence to be so difficult as to be practically impossible "; 12. " a heartfelt prayer every day for purity makes one progressively pure." [26]

The result of such a mastery over bodily drives is that to such a Brahmachari " the whole world is one vast family; he will center all his ambition in relieving the misery of mankind . . . never being stirred by passion. He will instinctively know the fountain of strength in him. . . . His humble strength will command respect of the world." [27]

Similar are the conclusions of another Hindu sage and moral educator Sri Aurobindo.[28]  On the basis of his own transfiguration from a scholar and an eminent political leader in the fight for independence of India into one of the most eminent Hindu sages and altruists, Sri Aurobindo, in his Integral Yoga, prescribes a similar control of the body as a necessary condition for obtaining the highest goal of " the truly divine love."  His system does not require any torture of the body, any asceticism for the sake of asceticism, but wise moderation in food, accompanied by frequent moderate fastings.  The same is true of other bodily needs.  In regard to sex, however, he prescribes complete chastity for those who want to achieve the highest purpose of realization of God or of " the life and love divine " during their life on this planet.  " Love humanity, serve humanity, give it a helping hand as it strives to divinize itself." [29]  " We are here to work out the Divine Will . . . for the progressive incorporation of the Supreme and the establishment of His reign upon the earth." [30]  Such is Sri Aurobindo's supreme goal.  " The whole principle of this [Integral] Yoga is to give one's self entirely to the Divine alone [and to the Divine love], and to nobody and nothing else, and to bring down into ourselves by union with the Divine Mother-Power all the transcendent light, force, wideness, peace, purity, truth-consciousness and Ananda [divine bliss] of the supramental Divine. . . . Therefore, these [any sexuality in thought, word, or deed] are absolutely forbidden in the sadhana " (spiritual discipline).  In order to master such impulses he indicates a series of prescriptions that lead not to a mere suppression of such an impulse nor to its mere sublimation (which according to his experience does not free us from it), but to a complete liberation from it.[31]

Similar self-control, as a preliminary condition, is indicated by Albert Schweitzer.  " There are no heroes of action: only heroes of renuncia-

tion and suffering," he says.  Accordingly, throughout his life, in a natural way, he disciplined his bodily needs and kept them under control,
without any spectacular asceticism.  Even such a noble value as musical
and scholarly creativity he gave up in order to go to the African jungles
and to serve there the preliterate aborigines.[32]

Another example of healthy-minded self-discipline of the body's cravings is given by John Woolman.  From early childhood he spontaneously
began to practice it, and then quietly carried it on throughout his life.
His drink was water, his food was moderate, simple, and mainly vegetarian;
he systematically refused any luxury, wealth, and material advantages in
favor of a poor, simple, but free life.  "Every degree of luxury, every demand for money inconsistent with the Divine order" leads to injustice,
"and hath some connection with evil."  "My mind, through the power of
truth, was weaned from the desire of outward greatness, and I was learning to be content with real convenience, that were not costly, so that a
way of life free from much entanglement appeared best for me, though
the income may be small. . . .  I saw that an humble man, with the blessing of the Lord, might live on a little, and that where the heart was set on
greatness, success in business did not satisfy the craving; but that commonly with an increase of wealth the desire of wealth increased."[33]  Accordingly, several times when his honest business became prosperous he
deliberately gave it up[34] "to be content with things really needful and to
avoid all superfluities."[35]  Throughout his life he carried on quietly but
incessantly self-denial of any kind of "superfluities": even some orna-
mentation and decorative carvings on a ship on which he traveled to England made his conscience uneasy.[36]  In brief, John Woolman gives us a
conspicuous example of natural, quiet, but unfailing control upon the
body and its proclivities free from self-torture as well as "superfluous indulgence."  In spite of a lack of anything spectacular in this self-mastery
it is at least as effective, unfailing, and complete as any mastery via spectacular self-immolation of the ascetics.

Finally, a purely utilitarian, sensible moderation or rational temperance
is recommended by all "reasonable and sensible" counselors of moral
health: not so much for the sake of God as much as for the purely utilitarian, "this worldly" happiness of the person.

"Be pious, diligent.  Be discreet on visits.  Beware of the harlot.  Be
prudent in speech.  Boast not of thy strength. . . .  Be not a drunkard.
Be respectful.  Learn: knowledge is useful."  These and other maxims
were given by an Egyptian scribe to his son because "emoluments, promotion and physical well-being were to be obtained thereby."[37]

Somewhat similar to these are the precepts on the *Art of Virtue* sketched
by Benjamin Franklin.  He writes to his youngest sister: " Sister, farewell
and remember that modesty, as it makes the most homely virgin amiable
and charming, so the want of it renders the most perfect beauty disagree-

able and odious." He recommends drinking of water instead of beer, because in his own experience his water drinking made him stronger and saved five shillings each week, compared with the beer-drinking workers in the London printing house.

And similarly run his maxims concerning other virtues: temperance, silence, order, resolution, frugality, industry, sincerity, justice, moderation, cleanliness, tranquility, chastity, humility. By practicing and making these virtues habitual, we can control our passions and lusts. Such a mastery is considered by him as indispensable for any good, successful, and happy life.[38]

Without further examples it can be stated that practically all eminent altruists, from the moment of their altruization, acquire almost a complete control of their bodily needs and proclivities. Some obtain it up to an ascetic degree, others up to the extent that prevents interference of such needs with the fullest discharge of the individual's altruistic duties to God and fellow men. Some acquire the mastery over their biological man with much effort, pain, and difficulty; others, like the fortunate altruists, obtain it with comparative ease by starting their self-discipline in early childhood and in a natural way continuing it throughout their life.

## IV

### Concluding Remarks

Having studied the processes and factors of altruistic growth and reintegration as they occurred in the life of altruists, and having shown the technical procedures used in these processes, now we can examine in a systematic way the main techniques of moral and spiritual training. After examining these techniques one by one, we shall pass to a study of *the three unified systems of these techniques* as they are represented by the Yoga system, the monastic system, and by the system of altruistic education in the secular brotherhood communities. The total knowledge of these techniques can possibly help in the practical task of increasing love blessings in the human universe.

# TECHNIQUES OF ALTRUISTIC TRANSFORMATION OF PERSONS AND GROUPS

PART FOUR

TECHNIQUES OF ATHLETIC TRANSFORMATION
OF PERSONS AND GROUPS

*Chapter Sixteen*

# The Ego-Centered and the Ego-Transcending Forms of Love and Techniques

The foregoing chapters clearly show that altruistic formation and transformation of human beings is an exceedingly delicate, complex, and difficult operation. There is no single magic procedure that can successfully perform it. Neither is there a standard set of operations equally applicable to all persons and groups. To be effective, the methods must vary in accordance with the many conditions and properties of the individuals and groups. In addition, even the effective methods must be supplemented and supported by a respective transmutation of the culture and social institutions of the persons and groups undergoing the altruistic change. What exactly, and in what direction, is to be changed in the existing social institutions and culture is discussed elsewhere.[1] Here the change of social and cultural environment is touched upon only slightly, insofar as it directly concerns the transformation of persons and groups.

The preceding chapters have shown that no notable altruization is possible without three mutually connected personal and sociocultural changes, namely: 1) a self-identification of the individual with some sort of altruistic values, conceived either in their sublimest or elementary form; 2) a respective rearrangement of one's egos, values, and standards; and 3) a corresponding rearrangement of one's group affiliations and environment.

Of the diverse conditions and properties of the individuals and groups, two are particularly important: 1) the characteristics of the individual or group to be altruistically formed or transformed; and 2) the level of creative altruism — its extensity, intensity, duration, purity, and adequacy — to be achieved by the formed or transformed person or group. Altruistic formation of a baby, for example, is much easier than altruistic transformation of a grown-up egotistic person. Furthermore, the effective techniques for achievement of a low-grade altruism have to be different from those of a high-grade altruism. And there are other personal and collective conditions that demand respective variations of the ways and means of successful altruization.

## II

### Ego-Transcending and Ego-Centered Systems of Altruization

For the purposes of our study the diverse techniques of altruization can be classified into two main systems of altruization: the *ego-transcending* and the *ego-centered*. Exemplified by the systems of altruization of Yoga, Zen Buddhism, the Christian monastic brotherhoods, and of a majority of the great altruists, the first method of altruization is based upon a complete transcendence of one's bioconscious and socioconscious egos and unconscious drives. Altruistic transformation in the ego-transcending system is one of the steps towards the final state of egoless pure spirituality or towards union with the suprapersonal supreme value, called " God," " Love," " Universal Self," and many other names. Psychologically, the ego-transcending system implies a more or less complete control of one's conscious and unconscious energies, thoughts, emotions, wishes, feelings, unconscious drives, and overt behavior by one's supraconscious energy. Such a control can be achieved only by a few geniuses of love. For the rank and file it is hardly accessible.

*Ego-centered altruism* does not require annihilation or complete transcendence of one's egos and unconscious drives. It views one's egos and unconscious forces as positive values and their preservation as a necessary condition for altruization. According to its postulate, a person who does not love himself or his own egos cannot love anyone else. Self-love is a necessary condition for loving others. Consequently, in order to be an altruist one does not need to transcend or annihilate his egos and unconscious drives. One needs only to be " enlightened " about his real self-interests; to keep his egos and drives in mutual harmony; to clean them from the excesses of " unenlightened selfishness "; and to train himself to co-operate with other individuals for their mutual benefit and pleasure. The ego-centered love is utilitarian, hedonistic, and " rational " in its nature. It endeavors to train the self-centered individual " to live and let live," " to respect others in order to be respected," " to be friendly to others in order that the others be friendly to you," " to help others in order to be helped by others when you need their help," " not to harm others in order that others do not harm you," " to enjoy fully your life, as long as you do not violate the enjoyments of others."

Psychologically, this form of altruization does not require a complete control of the conscious and unconscious forces by the supraconscious. Theoretically and practically it can operate through " rational " and " self-enlightened " harmonization of one's egos and unconscious drives with one another and with those of other individuals. This harmonization can be achieved through the techniques of mechanical drilling, inculcation of conditioned reflexes, of habit-forming, of " interiorization " of co-operative forms of behavior, and of scientific mentality and rational ideology. Expertly using the stimuli of pain and pleasure, of punishment and reward, of utilitarian advantage and disadvantage; of leader's example and followers' imitation; of reasonable coercion and persuasion; of scientific demonstration of utility and disutility of various forms of behavior; of inculcation of scientific verities and rational ideologies, and of building a " scientific frame of mind " in the individual: through these and similar techniques the ego-centered " socialization " of human beings can be accomplished. It can make them reasonably friendly and adjusted to one another in their social life.

The outlined difference between these two forms of altruism is responsible for several differences in the techniques of development of each form of altruism. Though each of the subsequent techniques can be used for ego-centered as well as ego-transcending altruization, the latter requires several additional techniques not necessary for ego-centered altruization. Ego-transcending altruization also demands a more rigorous use of the techniques exploited for ego-centered socialization.

A number of the ego-centered techniques are applicable even to dogs, cats, mice, and other animals. Though discovered long ago, many of these techniques have been recently rediscovered through experimentation with animals and then directly applied to human beings. The other side of the applicability of these techniques to the rank and file, and even to animals, is that they hardly ever yield the sublimest forms of creative unselfish love. They produce mainly the low-grade altruism. To raise the level of altruization to a still finer love of high intensity and wide extensity, a durable, pure, and adequate love, the techniques of the ego-centered method need to be supplemented by those of the ego-transcending method. In a sense, the ego-transcending system is a " post-graduate " system accessible only to creative Ph.D.'s of altruistic love. The ego-centered techniques are mainly fit for the " undergraduates " in this field.

Each of the surveyed techniques can be used singly; but more often than not they are used in various combinations with one another. Let us now turn to a concise analysis of these techniques.

### III

### THE MAIN TECHNIQUES OF ALTRUIZATION AND SOCIALIZATION

Like many other instrumentalities, most of the techniques of modification of human behavior can be used for good as well as bad purposes, for altruistic as well as egotistic change. An airplane can serve a charity mission and a bombing raid. A powerful drug can be used for curing as well as for poisoning purposes. The same is true about the techniques discussed. Here they are considered only as means for altruization.

Differently classified by various investigators [2] these techniques are as follows:

1. The technique of change of the individual's organism and of its processes, including the utilization of biological drives for altruistic ends, training in postures, movements, and in regulated respiration.

2. The technique of conditioned reflexes and of coercive, mechanical drilling, reinforced by punishment and reward.

3. The technique of pains and pleasures meted out to the person and his dearests.

4. The technique of altruization by public opinion pressure.

5. The technique of separation of the inimical parties.

6. The technique of utilization of a third party.

7. The technique of pacification through common enemy or common friend and cause.

8. The technique of setting a heroic moral example.

9. The technique of rational persuasion and scientific demonstration of advantages of friendship and disadvantages of enmity.

10. The technique of reinforcement of altruistic actions by emotional and unconscious forces, including the psychodramatic and sociodramatic techniques.

11. The technique of direct life experience.

12. The technique of altruization through the fine arts.

13. The technique of exposure to love of others.

14. The technique of individual creative activity.

15. The technique of collective creativity, group enhancement, and group therapy.

16. The technique of good deeds.

17. The techniques of integration and reintegration of one's egos, values, and norms of conduct.

18. The techniques of self-identification.

19. The technique of private and public prayer.

20. The technique of conscience examination.

21. The technique of private and public confession.

22. The technique of the private, public, and collective vow.

23. The techniques of psychoanalysis.

24. The technique of supraconscious meditation and creativity.

25. Auxiliary techniques of silence, repetition of short formulas, ecstasy, and " kwats."

26. The techniques of rearrangement of group affiliations.

Some of these techniques overlap and imperceptibly pass into one another. Each technique mentioned, however, has its specific point important for our purposes.

These techniques cover all the essential ways of altruistic formation and transformation. Since these techniques are well known, there is no need to describe them in detail. Concise comments are sufficient for their general characterization. It is to be added that in most of the cases of altruistic education these techniques are used in combined sets of two or more techniques.

## 1. *The Technique of Biological Change of the Individual's Organism and of Its Processes*

It is probable that there are biological states of the human organism which are conducive to kind and friendly behavior of the individual towards his fellow men, and states facilitating the individual's irritable and aggressive conduct towards others. It is uncertain, however, exactly what states of the organism are uniformly conducive to friendly conduct, and what biological conditions uniformly induce unfriendly behavior. Almost all the numerous attempts to establish uniformities in this field have not been very successful. This is true of the numerous theories of causal association of various racial types and bodily constitutions with various mental and moral characteristics, including sociality, aggressiveness, cooperativeness, egotism, and altruism.[3]

All the endeavors to establish a uniform association either of the Nordic, the Alpine, the Mediterranean, or other racial types with certain psychosocial and moral traits; or of the endomorphic, mesomorphic, and ectomorphic and other bodily constitutions with aggressiveness, sociality, complacency, ruthlessness, criminality, love of domination, solitude, sociophobia, and other characteristics have largely failed. The respective theories cannot stand a rigorous scientific test, and are contradicted by factual and logical evidence.

The same is to be said about many theories which try to prove the causal association of the biological factors of sex, age, and health with sociality or antisociality, kindness or aggressiveness, egotism or altruism. Likewise, a fairly generally accepted association of friendliness with good health, and of sickness with aggressiveness, or J. Comenius' *mens sana in corpore sano* have so many exceptions that the very existence of the claimed uniformity between these variables becomes questionable.

Even a satisfaction of all the bodily needs does not always lead to altruistic conduct; nor do hunger, thirst, and frustration of other bodily needs uniformly result in aggressive, criminal, or egotistic behavior. There is no adequate evidence for claiming even that the individuals with satiated bodily needs yield a notably higher per cent of altruists than the individuals with poorly satisfied bodily needs. As we have seen, the Freudian "frustration always generates aggression" is simply untrue,[4] as a general uniformity.

The above does not mean that there are no biological conditions conducive either to altruism or egotism. It signifies only that so far no uniform conditions of either kind, applicable to all human beings, in all cultures and situations, have been discovered. Therefore, instead of relying upon the doubtful uniformities, the wise altruistic transformer of a given individual must thoroughly study him and his conditions, and must find in each case what kind of biological change in the given individual can facilitate his altruistic development. For some individuals an improvement of their health and bodily vigor, and satisfaction of their biological needs are conducive to their becoming more friendly to others. For other individuals sickness, poor health, denial of satisfaction of many bodily needs, bodily discomfort, and even bodily torture favor their altruistic development. Almost all the catastrophic and late altruists, many saints, especially the saintly ascetics, are examples of such individuals. If we compare the extreme types of persons who pamper their bodies and satiate all their animal needs, with the ascetics and persons who meagerly satisfy only the most necessary requirements of their organism, we shall hardly find a higher per cent of altruists among the pamperers than among the ascetics or semi-ascetics.

If any generalization is possible in this matter of overindulgence and asceticism in satisfaction of one's biological needs, it may be said that *a well-tempered and law-abiding satisfaction seems to be the best for the overwhelming majority of human beings.* Overindulgence tends to make the individual a slave of his biological drives and, through that, unconsciously or consciously selfish. On the other hand, asceticism in the satisfaction of biological needs is accessible only to very few individuals: most human beings are incapable of it. A moderate and well-planned satisfaction which does not contradict the moral demands of one's sociocultural egos can be practiced by most people. It is free from the sins of overindulgence, keeps the animal in man on an even keel, and makes the individual careful and less aggressive in regard to others than does the pampering of one's biological needs. Temperance helps also to keep in harmony all biological drives and egos, giving to each its due at the proper time. The same is true of the harmony of the bio-conscious egos. Allotting to each a moderate satisfaction in turn, it does not inflate any specific need at the cost of the others, as is the case in the overindulgence.

*Postures, movements, and regulated respiration.* Of the many conditions of the body favoring friendliness, a tangible role is played by specific postures, movements, and respiration. The old and well-tested experience of the Yogi, the Buddhist, the Hinduist, the Sufist, and the Christian altruists demonstrates the facilitating influence of some of the postures and movements, and of " voluntary respiration " upon the development of friendliness towards others. The experience and techniques of the altruists and saints are increasingly supported by recent scientific studies. For instance, recent experimental studies of so-called "voluntary respiration" give a clean bill of health to the Yoga *pranayama* or complex respiratory exercises, while the experimental investigations of Dr. Thérèse Brosse and others show different "spectra" of cardiographic, electroencephalographic and other recordings of the activity of the heart, lungs, and other bodily organs under the conditions of experiencing altruistic love and hate, of mental concentration and deconcentration.[5]

Likewise, some of the ecstatic dances, practiced in many religions,[6] seem to release the aggressive tensions of the dancers and thereby help them in becoming less ego-centered and more community-minded.[7] Similarly an elimination of the inner tensions in the organism by a rational change of the poise of head, neck, and other parts of the body helps also in decreasing the individual's irritability and aggressiveness.[8]

While the ingenious techniques of postures, movements, and respiration practiced by Yogis or the saintly altruists are too difficult for the rank and file, their simplified version can be practiced by ordinary persons. If, for instance, the mastery of the Yoga respiration technique or its control of the heart activity are inaccessible for most of us, the postures of comfortable sitting or lying, and a series of deep inhalations and exhalations, in the moments of being angry or aggressive, can be practiced and can somewhat calm our emotional disturbances. A further practice in simple "voluntary respiration" along the line of the pranayama may increase our control of aggressive propensities. While without a long training the difficult art of prolonged kneeling or prostration, practiced by Christian saints, cannot be mastered by everyone, a simplified version of these can be effected with fruitful results. So, also, can the actions of either crossing or fingering a rosary with the repetition of a short praying formula or a pacifying motto. The concrete forms of these sorts of activities vary in accordance with the individual's mental and moral equipment, but in some form they can be practiced by almost everyone. Of the rich variety of the techniques of postures and actions of the eminent altruists, one can pick up those that suit him best.

Greatly neglected by science, these techniques embody a vast experience and represent an arsenal of efficacious techniques for the pacification of aggressive disturbances. Their specific religious and ritualistic forms can be modified in accordance with the mental and moral equipment of the individual, while their essential psycho-physiological properties are likely to exert an influence favorable for the development of friendly propensities. When scientifically tested and developed, these techniques of postures, movements, and respirations can serve as the instruments of altruistic education. As an important variety of the biological techniques, utilization of biological drives, even hate, for altruistic purposes can be mentioned. Further on, in Chapter Twenty-Three, this point will be developed.

So much about the factors and techniques of the bodily changes of the individual.

## 2. *The Techniques of Conditioned Reflexes and of Coercive and Mechanical Drilling, Reinforced by Pains and Pleasures, Advantages and Disadvantages for the Individual*

Unless we unduly generalize the precise meaning of conditioned reflexes and of the mechanism of their inculcation, we must be aware that not all habits are conditioned reflexes, nor are all habits established through the mechanism of conditioned reflexes. Likewise, the levers of pains and pleasures, of utility and disutility, are not operating in the inculcation of all habits and all conditioned reflexes.

On the other hand, the hedonistic and utilitarian stimuli are operative in actions that are neither conditioned reflexes nor habits. For this reason, they are distinguished in the above enumeration of techniques. Since, however, these techniques are well known, they are concisely considered here together.

The technique of conditioned reflexes, based upon more or less simultaneous stimulation by the conditioned and the unconditioned stimuli, can build a series of desirable acquired responses in the individual. Though the efficacy of the technique is limited, and it by no means succeeds in regard to all desirable responses, nevertheless, it can be used effectively for the purposes of inculcation of many altruistic responses in the individual. As a matter of fact, a portion of our friendly and aggressive actions has probably been built through the " natural " — i.e., unplanned — operation of this mechanism.

Similarly a series of apparently friendly forms of conduct can be grafted by repetitive drilling of the individual in friendly patterns of conduct. From early childhood we were drilled in saying " thank you," " how do you do," " good morning "; in waving our hand at seeing a fellow; and in many other actions of " small kindness." A large portion of our actions of politeness and courtesy has been built into us, from our earliest days, by drilling in these courteous and diplomatic responses by our parents and other members of the family, by the teachers of nursery school, kindergarten, grade, and Sunday schools. Drilling is possibly the main technique in molding soldiers' behavior in obeying not only the rules of military discipline, but in the almost automatic sacrificing of their lives on the battlefield for the welfare of their country. Many cases of drilling are done without the use either of the mechanism of the conditioned reflexes or of the painful and pleasurable stimuli. Repetition of the patterns of actions of " a good boy " or " a good girl," demanded by our parents or other educators, makes them habitual or automatically performed. " Sow an act and you will reap a habit; sow a habit and you will reap a character," correctly says the old proverb.

When to the drilling force the reinforcement of pain and pleasure, advantage and disadvantage, is added and regularly applied, these stimuli increase the effectiveness of drilling still more.

No less effectively the painful and pleasurable stimuli condition human behavior in the *nonrepetitive actions*. Beginning with a piece of candy or slight spanking, a verbal approval or disapproval, in our childhood and ending with the vast arsenal of punitive measures of criminal law and the biological, economic, political, and social rewards, painful and pleasurable stimuli incessantly condition our behavior from the moment of birth on up to the hour of death. Rejecting the claim of the extreme utilitarianists and hedonists that pain and pleasure motivation conditions *all* human actions and are the *only effective stimuli* of our behavior, we must nevertheless recognize the exceptionally important role they play in shaping our personality and our behavior. They perform this role as external and internal forces. As external stimuli they act as the totality of social sanctions rewarding the individual for his socially approved behavior and achievements, and punishing him for his " criminal " and disapproved actions by painful disadvantages. The range of the socially imposed pleasurable and painful values runs all the way from the little rewards up to the intensest pleasures, large economic fortunes, fame, and hero glorification, and from a slight disapproval and petty fine up to the capital punishment. Incessantly operating and ever-present, these social sanctions continuously influence our behavior, wishes, and aspirations. As an internal force they operate in the form of our conscious calculations of utilitarian and hedonistic advantages and disadvantages of this or that action, and of our unconscious impulses and semi-conscious propensities to obtain this or that pleasure, and to avoid this or that pain.

A large portion of our total behavior has been shaped by the incessant operation of these stimuli. Likewise, a large part of social processes are determined by these factors. And the more antisocial, selfishly aggressive, and unmanageable the individual, or the more disharmonious and innerly antagonistic the given society, the greater the role played by these forces in the life history of the individual or society. In the behavior of a truly unselfish and ethically noble person they play a comparatively insignificant role: most of his actions are motivated by his unselfish love, legal duty, moral imperative, and considerations of social well-being, regardless of the rewards and punishment, pleasure and pain which his actions may bring upon him. In the behavior of an exceptionally selfish or morally cynical person, an incomparably larger portion of his actions are determined by these utilitarian and hedonistic factors. Like a ferocious animal, only through the roughest punishment and rewards can such a person be forced to comply with the minimum of socially required moral behavior, and to abstain from the violation of the rights of others.

Likewise, when a society is torn by the intensest inner conflicts, its members begin more liberally to apply to one another the stimuli of pain and pleasure. The same is true when the tensions grow between two or more societies. Mass murder of the opponents, their wholesale imprisonment, banishment, tortures, confiscation of their property, and similar means of forcing the opponents to comply with the wishes of a given individual or clique mount to an unprecedented degree. International wars with their unrestricted destruction of an enemy and civil wars with their bloody extermination of the opposite party give examples of this conflagration of punitive measures. A systematic study of the fluctuation of the quantity and severity of punishment in the periods of an increase of tensions among several societies or within the same society well corroborates this uniformity. When the conflicts subside, the curve of punishment goes down; when they increase, the curve goes up.[9]

Side by side with the antisocial and demoralizing effects which unwise and too liberal use of the punitive and rewarding measures has produced in the life of individuals and groups, the painful stimuli have played an important role in the pacification of human societies, the unification of several inimical groups into a larger solidary society, the inhibition of criminal actions, and in the maintenance of the minimum of social and moral order in social groups. No less important has been the role of the pleasurable or rewarding levers. Along with the morally negative effects of their incompetent use, their discerning application has greatly stimulated creative efforts of individuals and groups, and has fruitfully served the purposes of moral development of persons and societies.[10]

When wisely applied, these levers of human behavior can still be fruitfully used for the purposes of socialization and altruization of human beings. Like other factors and techniques of ego-centered altruism, they can hardly produce the sublime forms of unselfish love. But they can still help in an inhibition of the rudest varieties of interindividual and intergroup aggression, and in an inculcation of the elementary forms of decent behavior in regard to others, especially in the demoralized human universe. In a society of ferocious human animals these levers often act as a strait jacket by bringing the demented members to their senses, and by building the foundation of elementary moral order. When such a foundation is laid down, the nobler, finer, and more creative stimuli of altruistic love can be applied for erection of higher levels of the personal, social and moral organization.

In order that these powerful levers of individual and group behavior can yield only the morally constructive effects and be free from disastrous consequences, the utilization of these stimuli must follow certain rules of wisdom and practical experience. Some of the main rules are as follows:

a. To persons and groups influenced by finer and nobler motivation the pain-pleasure stimuli should not be applied at all. They may cheapen the higher level of their moral organization and drag it to a much lower ego-centered level. This truth is hardly understood by many prize-giving persons and groups. Often they ceremoniously parade their rewards and prizes — for " brotherhood," " heroism," " sanctity," " service to God and humanity," and so on — and bestow them upon persons moved by much purer motives than quest for rewards. Still worse, at the present time there is a veritable mania for giving all sorts of moral, civic, religious and peace prizes to all sorts of persons by all kinds of organizations. The reward-giving ceremony is photographed for the press, televized, and broadcast by radio, often for the purposes of self-advertising the givers. Not infrequently, the moral standard of the givers as well as of the recipients of the " virtue " rewards is very questionable. As a result, the craze especially of " mutual prize-giving " by A to B, and by B to A, harms rather than helps the work of maintaining and raising the moral standards of the parties involved and of society at large. Such prize-giving tends to " pay for " the values of the kingdom of God or of supreme love by morally worthless citations, parchments, medals, publicity, and dollars. Such a " rewarding " debases the highest — moral, religious, civic — values and turns their realm into a stock exchange of commercial dealers in profaned pseudo-values.

Still more debasing are the results of punitive stimulation of the persons discharging their duties for the sake of duty, social well-being, or unselfish love. Replacement of such a high moral order by that based on coercion and punishment usually disorganizes the moral integrity of the individual and the moral order of a social group. It leads to moral regression.

b. The concrete forms of pain-pleasure stimulation must vary in accordance with the character of the individual or group and their conditions. A few disapproving or approving words quietly and kindly spoken are quite effective for one individual, while for another much stronger painful or pleasurable measures are in order. The physical sanctions are more fit for some individuals, while for others the psychological stimuli are more effective.

In general, the rewarding and punitive measures must be individualized according to the sex, age, health, mental, moral, and social characteristics of the persons or groups, and their values.

c. All punishments and rewards that may seriously harm the individual or group physically, biologically, mentally, morally, and socially must not be used at all. They defeat the purpose which they aim to serve. Capital punishment may be very effective in hindering the individual from committing a crime; but by destroying him, it defeats itself as a means of moral education. The same is true of physical and mental tortures which harm the health and mind of the punished. Besides, as a rule they evoke in the punished the emotions of hate towards the executioners, their bosses, the social order, and society at large. They demoralize also those who impose such punishments and the society at large that approves such measures.

The same is to be said of excessive rewards especially of a material kind. Woe to a person and society who discharge their duties only for the sake of ostentatious and selfish rewards. The foundation of their moral order becomes as unsafe as the proverbial sand. As has been mentioned above, excessive prizes and rewards depreciate and drag down the moral values of the individuals and groups. Another result of this commercialization of sympathy, empathy, and moral duty is a proliferation of jealousy, pride, and selfish competition in the struggle of individuals and groups for bigger and better rewards. For these and other reasons it is better to underdo than to overdo with the use of the punitive and rewarding levers of human behavior and moral order.

### 3. The Technique of Pains and Pleasures Meted Out to the Persons and Groups Dearest to the Individual

Sometimes the pitiless punishment and the richest reward are powerless to obtain from an individual or group the conduct desired by the other party. In such cases this individual or collective party often tries to force the other party to comply with its commands by extending its punishments or rewards upon all the persons and groups dear to the commanded party: upon the members of its family, the born and the unborn posterity, its tribe, and other in-groups, not to mention the posthumous threats of eternal punishments or rewards for the commanded party itself. By unlimited extending the pressure of pains and pleasures in time (for eternity) and over the number of the punished and rewarded persons, the commanding party expects to obtain from the commanded party the prescribed conduct. The history of criminal law, of the mores, and the social life of almost all societies abounds with the use of such unlimitedly extended mass punishments and rewards of the persons and groups dearest to the commanded party.

If thou shalt hearken diligently unto the voice of the Lord thy God to observe and to do all his commandments . . . the Lord will set thee on high above all nations of the earth. . . . Blessed shalt be the fruit of thy body, and the fruit of thy ground. . . . And the Lord shalt make thee plenteous in goods, in the fruit of thy body, and in the fruit of thy cattle . . . But . . . if thou wilt not hearken unto the voice of the Lord thy God . . . all these curses shall come upon thee, and overtake thee. . . . Cursed shalt be the fruit of thy body, and the fruit of thy land. . . . The Lord shall send upon thee cursing, vexation, and rebuke . . . until thou be destroyed and until thou perish quickly. [The Lord shall smite the guilty with pestilence, blindness, madness, consumption, fever, cause them to be smitten by the enemies, and so on.]

Thy carcass shall be meat unto all fowls of the air, and unto the beasts of the earth. . . . Thou shalt betroth a wife, and another man shall lie with her. . . . Thy sons and thy daughters shall be given unto another people. . . . Thou shalt beget sons and daughters, but thou shalt not enjoy them; for they shall go into captivity. . . . And thou shalt eat the fruit of thy own body, the flesh of thy sons and of thy daughters . . . in the siege, and in the straightness. . . . Then the Lord . . . will bring upon thee every sickness and every plague, untill thou be destroyed. And ye shall be left few in number.[11]

Punishment of the posterity of the guilty party up to the third or the seventh generations, punishment or rewards of the whole nation for the sin or heroic achievement of one of its members, and similar sanctions meted out to the persons and groups dear to the commanded party are other forms of this extension of the discussed stimuli in time and in number of the punished or rewarded persons.

For the sake of preserving all this creation, the most Glorious [Lord] . . . created punishment, the protector of all creatures, an incarnation of the law, framed of Brahman glory. . . . If punishment does not fall upon the criminal himself, it falls upon his sons; if not upon the sons then upon his grandsons; but transgression of law, once perpetrated, never remains without its consequences for him who performed it: he perishes with all his posterity.[12]

These law provisions of the Bible and of the Law Codes of India serve as examples of the collective punishment or rewards for the respective actions of the individual. Such an extension of the use of these levers of human behavior is fairly frequent in the collective retaliation and reward among many preliterate groups. It is found in the law codes and practices of most of the historical or " civilized " societies: in ancient Egypt, Babylonia, Iran, India, China, Japan, Greece, Rome, and the Western societies.[13]

The unlimitedly extended use of these levers continues in the law and practice of contemporary individuals and groups. Criminal gangs often threaten to kidnap or harm the members of the family of the person from whom they demand money or service. And the threatened parties often comply with their demands. The criminal codes and practice of the Soviet Union, the imposition by the Nazi and Fascist governments of collective punishments upon the whole family, village, city, or region of the guilty individual; the persecution by the American Committee on Un-American Activities of the persons " guilty by association with " or relationship to the disloyal person; the wholesale strategic or atomic bombing of the cities and the noncombatant populations of the enemy in World War II and the Korean war; or imposition of the severest punishments by the English or French authorities on whole populated regions in Malaya or Indo-China for a few rebels operating there: in these and many other forms the indiscriminate and wholesale mass application of the extended punishment for the " crime or sin " of one or a few individuals continues to be practiced on the widest scale by contemporary "civilized" persons, governments, groups, and nations.

The same can be said of the extended use of remunerative sanctions. In the past as well as in the present, in interindividual as well as in intergroup relationships, rewards of various kinds have often been extended over the persons and groups dear to the heroic individual. Beginning with the fame and glory and ending with the ennoblement, promotion, economic rewards, titles, and other blessings, the hero's family, posterity, tribe, nation, and other in-groups have often shared his rewards. Individuals have often been stimulated to follow the prescribed conduct just by the rewards for the hero himself as well as for the persons and groups dearest to him.

In so-called capitalist (contractual) societies, the mainspring for the economic activities of the members has been exactly the conscious or unconscious desire to secure the means of subsistence for the individual as well as for the members of his family. In contrast to the slave-and-self economy where the main stimulus for doing satisfactory slave work was direct coercion and harsh punishment of a lazy slave and sometimes a reward for his good work; and in contrast to the "familistic" society where the members freely work for the sake of duty and social service to the group: in contrast to these, the law order of capitalist economy does not coerce directly to work and does not punish directly for not working. It leaves the matter to the decision of its members. Leaving it to them, at the same time, it says to each member: "If you prefer not to work, that is your business. But in that case you yourself and the members of your family are likely to become paupers and will lack the necessities of life. If you work, you and your family will earn at least the minimum of the means of subsistence. It is up to you to choose which of these alternatives you prefer." Thus *the economic man* of capitalist systems is not *the egoistic man,* as many economists assume, nor the high-grade altruist working for the welfare of humanity, but the *bonus pater familias* deeply concerned with his own as well as with his family's interests and well-being. Thus, indirectly, the pressure of the well-being of his family is the mainspring of his economic activities.[14]

There is no need to prove that this motivation by the punitive and rewarding stimuli extended over the dearest persons and groups has often been effective where the pain-pleasure motivation for the individual only has failed. For these reasons in carefully considered mild forms it can be used also for the purposes of the ego-centered moral ennoblement of individuals and groups. However, the stimulation by benefits and disadvantages for the dearest to the individual needs a still greater limitation than the pain-pleasure motivation of the individual. A wise experience at once rules out all punitive measures for the dearest not responsible for the misdeeds of the individual. Only a demonstration of possible harmful consequences of too selfish conduct of the individual for his family, friends, and in-groups and an exhibition of the beneficial consequences of the individual's decent and friendly conduct for his dearests are advisable. Such demonstrations can sometimes inhibit his aggressive actions and urge him to more generous conduct.

Rewards to the dearests for the unselfish actions of the individual may possibly have a larger margin of application than do the punitive measures. But even here it is better to underdo than to overdo with the rewards. Indiscriminate and extravagant use of rewards for the dearests can lead to a decline of the responsibility of the individual and of his dearests, to a sort of moral indolence of both, to commercialization of moral values, and eventually to individual and group egotism. A person discharging a minimum of his duties just for the sake of getting reward for himself and his family is certainly better than a person failing in his duties. But the virtue of such an individual is of a low-grade utilitarian nature. As such it is fragile and unstable: having failed to get the expected reward, he may easily fail in a further discharge of his duties and service to others.

With these reservations, in a limited form the motivation by beneficial and harmful sanctions for the dearests can be used for the purposes of developing an elementary sociality in especially selfish persons and groups.

## 4. Technique of Altruization by Pressure of Public Opinion

This represents a combined variation of the preceding techniques. In a society whose members have a similar set of values, where all or an overwhelming majority of the members unanimously approve and disapprove the same forms of conduct, there is *the* public opinion of the whole society. This public opinion plays an important role in shaping the behavior of its members. It inculcates prescribed forms of conduct in each member from the moment of his birth and continues to enforce them all his life. The inestimable pressure of the uniform public opinion is not counteracted in such a case by that of any contradictory public opinion. For these reasons, the collective moral pressure effectively inhibits the members' disapproved actions and propels them to conform with the required or approved standards of conduct. It accomplishes this task often by the mildest pressure of moral opinion itself, without use of strong punitive or rewarding measures.

Quite different is the situation in a society with contradictory sets of values and norms of conduct. Strictly speaking, in such a society there is no unified public opinion. Instead, there are a multitude of different, often opposite, opinions of factions, cliques, or parties, each pushing and pulling the member of society in different directions. From the time he is born up to the time he dies, each member is exposed in such societies to mutually contradictory sets of values and rules of behavior. While one set commands " Thou shalt not kill," the other set demands " Kill your enemies "; while one set tells " Private property is sacred," the other preaches " Private property is theft." One set demands sexual chastity, the other urges " enjoy yourself, it is later than you think."

This contradiction inhibits the strong interiorization of each of the opposite rules of conduct. It makes the individual hesitant and doubtful as to which of the lines of behavior is " right " and which is " wrong." It instills a doubt in the sacredness and value of any norm of conduct. The members' moral convictions and sense of duty become somewhat vague, weak, and indetermined. Being feeble, they often fail to control the members' biological drives and selfish impulses. Not infrequently the individuals turn into " rudderless boats " of cynical relativists who feel free from moral obligations and burdens of duty.

Or, having accepted one set of values and being abliged to defend it from the criticism and attacks of the other set, the individual turns (in the process of his war against the opposite values) into a fanatic of his set and of his clique — intolerant, inimical, and " crusading " against the opposite clique by all means at his disposal. His fanaticism often gives him a beautiful ideological justification of his selfish impulses.

Moral cynicism as well as factional fanaticism, generated by the society with the conflicting public opinions, values, and commandments, lead not so much to an altruization of its members as to a proliferation of the individual and factional egotisms. In their turn these generate an intensification and barbarization of the interindividual and interfactional struggle in such a social group.

For these reasons the pressure of pseudo-public opinions hardly contributes much to the altruization of the members of a society and can hardly be used as a successful instrument of altruistic ennoblement. The contemporary Western world gives an example of this sort of human universe with excessive atomization, relativization, and contradiction of its values and moral norms. Though many a scholar still thoughtlessly talks about *the* public opinion, there are only a multitude of mutually discordant opinions of the Soviet and the Western blocs, the Communist and the anti-Communist groups, the Republican and the Democratic parties, the Catholic and the anti-Catholic factions, of the rich and the poor, of management and labor, and of hundreds of other cliques and parties. No wonder that none of these opinions has morally ennobled the Western world or has prevented the explosions of the bloodiest wars and revolutions, the cruelest mutilation of millions of noncombatant people, the most barbarous destruction of cities and villages, and of other bestialities of our age. Instead of making its members generous and friendly, these " public opinions " of our society have enormously inflated their individual and factional egotisms. As a finishing touch, for propaganda purposes the agents of these " public opinions " are using the noblest moral preachings for screening their ignoble practices. Fraud and hypocrisy are widely practiced to help their selfish rule of force.   Until this moral anarchy is ended by establishment of a unified system of values and moral norms, the bloody struggle of the factional egotisms is bound to continue.   Until such a unification, the relative ineffectiveness of the pseudo " public opinions " of our time as instruments of altruization shall continue also.

## 5. The Technique of Separation of Enemies

Any weakening of interindividual or intergroup hatred is a step towards altruization.   Mutual animosity of two or more parties can often be mitigated by separation of the inimical individuals and groups from one another.[15]   Like the separation of quarreling children into different rooms of a school, so the separation of grown-up persons into different quarters — rooms, houses, cities, or countries — mechanically stops their quarrel and any further intensification of their fight.   Given sufficient time, separation often cools their animosity, helps them to come to their senses, turns their heated emotions into mere memories, makes them carefully examine their relationships, and find fault not only with the enemy but with themselves.   " Out of sight, out of mind " works for weakening not only friendship, but also animosity.   With a lapse of time, the wounds of the past offenses tend to heal, animosity gives place to indifference or, once in a while, even to tenderness and respect for the former enemy.

Separation of inimical groups for the purposes of preventing intensification of animosities is also practiced now and then.   The secession of the plebeians to the Sacred Mount in ancient Rome (494 B.C.), separation of armies by a neutral or buffer zone in the period of truce, or emigration of a nonconformist group from the country of the dominant party are examples of this way of prevention of further conflicts.   More often than not, however, spatial separation of the inimical groups is impossible: the inimical parties simply cannot go to different quarters of the world.   In such conditions several other devices are used to serve the purpose.   Termination of diplomatic relationships between inimical states, establishment of a buffer zone between antagonistic groups, delineation of areas of activity and of spheres of influence for each group are the samples of such devices.   They serve the same purpose as the spatial separation. Not infrequently these measures help to prevent a continuation or intensification of the intergroup animosity.

The same purpose is served by establishment of a zone of indifference between the antagonistic parties, with the help of a third party.   All varieties of the separation technique in its voluntary and coercive forms (imposed by the parents or teachers on quarreling children, by police and neighbors upon quarreling grownups, by counselors, courts, and authorities upon fighting parents or gangs) are easy to apply and are often effective, at least in termination of intense conflicts and in prevention of their growth.   It is true that such techniques rarely transform enemies into friends; they serve, however, as the first steps in this direction — they help to establish "a truce" between the antagonists and to cool their hatred. This "truce" builds a ground for the operation of other techniques of pacification, for turning the enemies into either indifferent parties or even into real friends.

## 6. *The Technique of Utilization of a Third Party*

Many quarrels and fights of individuals and groups are stopped abruptly, at least for the time being, by the mere appearance of a third party at the moment of quarrel. Entrance into the room of the child of quarreling parents; an appearance of a neighbor on the scene of feuding parties, of a teacher amidst fighting pupils; of a third party before quarreling lovers; of a possible witness of feuding parties that want to keep their enmity secret — these are daily examples of the abrupt cessation of fighting of two parties by the mere appearance of a third party at the scene of a quarrel. "Be quiet, the neighbors will hear our quarrel," "Stop yelling at me, our child is listening," "Shut up, somebody's coming" are all familiar expressions of the role of a third party discussed.

The abrupt stopping of quarrels by the mere appearance of a third party is especially effective when the third party is a person of authority, love, and reverence; or when the antagonistic parties want to keep their conflict secret from all others or from a wide publicity. Still more effective is the third party when it takes upon itself the functions of a wise mediator, either chosen by the parties, or authoritatively imposed upon them by society. An understanding counselor, an expert mediator, a wise official judge, a revered moral leader, a fair-minded neighbor, and many other mediators daily succeed in the mitigation of interindividual tensions, and now and then in replacement of antagonism by either neutral attitudes or even by friendship of the parties concerned.

With a proper modification, the same can be said of the role of a third party in the mitigation of intergroup conflicts. Here, also, the mere appearance of such a third party amidst conflicting parties, and its mediating, pacifying, and reconciling roles, often exert positive effects upon the inimical, cold-warring, and hot-warring parties. The Hague Court of International Justice, and the chosen or imposed, official or unofficial mediators of labor-management conflicts give examples of the pacifying functions of the third party. In hundreds of other forms a third party plays this role in numerous intergroup antagonisms. For similar reasons an evil-minded third party can and does exert a hate-breeding influence. In the role of the *tertius gaudens*, it often keeps the flame of animosity burning. But here this sort of third party is not considered. Only third parties serving the cause of peace and friendship are meant in this section. When systematically and wisely used, the technique of the third party has served and can increasingly serve this cause.

### 7. The Technique of Pacification Through Common Enemy or Common Friend and Cause

Two important forms of the technique of mitigation of conflicts through a third party are to be specially mentioned. One is the technique of binding together inimical parties into a solidary body by setting them against a common enemy; the other is unifying them through a common friend or cause. Both techniques have been fairly successful in the weakening and termination of interindividual and intergroup antagonisms. If mutually antagonistic parties are set against their common and most dangerous enemy, this enemy often makes the parties forget their feud and unite their forces against it. The driving forces of such a unification are the self-preservation of each party, and its hate and fear of the common enemy — in other words, a set of the most powerful and most primitive emotional drives. No specific training, education, or moral nobility is required for acquiring these primitive emotions. They are inherent in the unconscious and conscious " compartments " of most human beings and groups.

This explains why this method has been widely used, since immemorial antiquity. Its recent examples are: the coalition of Russia and the Western Allies against Germany in World War I; " unification " of Stalin-Churchill-Roosevelt and their nations against Hitler in World War II; the Atlantic and the Pacific pacts against Soviet Russia and its allies at the present time; today's crusade against Communism on the part of the most heterogeneous groups — the Roman Catholics, the Protestants, the Jews, the Shintoists and Atheists, Socialists, Capitalists, Liberals, and Conservatives, and so on. In all these " coalitions," the " allies " have been united almost exclusively by the *common enemy* factor. In other conditions, these allies have often been either indifferent or antagonistic to one another.

In the selfish and hate-laden nature of the bond, which binds together the inimical parties, lies the weakness of this technique. Though once in a while in the process of common struggle against the enemy, the bond of hatred and fear of the common enemy is transformed into a tie of real comradeship and lasting friendship, more often than not, this bond breaks as easily as it is thrown around the parties. As soon as the common enemy is defeated, the coalition of the " strange bed-fellows " disintegrates. Former enmity of the temporary allies reasserts itself, and they resume their previous struggle. In it they often enter into alliance with the defeated common enemy. As soon as Germany was conquered in World War I and the coalition of Japan and Germany was defeated in World War II, the " sacred comradeship " of their opponents disintegrated: Russia and her Western allies turned into bitter enemies. For the same reason, if the Malenkov and Mao Tse-tung coalition disappears, the partners of the American coalition are likely to turn into mutual opponents.

A similar story has been repeated millions of times in interindividual and intergroup alliances of this sort. The cement of hatred and fear in regard to the common enemy as easily disintegrates as it easily binds the antagonists.

Even a temporary cessation of hostilities between inimical parties is a step towards their "truce," however, and in some cases towards lasting friendship. When wisely used, this technique can render a valuable service to the whole of humanity. For instance, at the present time, a dramatic and effective setting of the whole of mankind against its common enemies like death, disease, insanity, poverty, suffering, crime, ignorance, stupidity, from which all nations, all parties, all human beings suffer, a true crusade against these enemies could unify otherwise antagonistic persons and groups. A relentless crusade against these enemies by all humanity can mitigate fratricidal intergroup and interindividual wars. It can bind the whole of mankind into one solidary body animated by one common will to free all human beings from their greatest enemies. N. F. Fedorov, in his *Philosophy of Common Cause*,[16] developed a detailed plan of fraternization of all human beings into one real brotherhood on this basis and through this technique.

When the factor of a common enemy is reinforced by the factor of a common friend or a constructive common cause, the two factors can effectively conquer many enmities and turn them into decent relationships. Frequently a common love for their dear child helps to attenuate the antagonisms of the parents. Considerations for the health of a sick friend or reverence for a hero, or respect for the memory of the departed dear, fairly often serve as catalyzers of friendly feelings in inimical parties. An important common cause, like fighting a war or other catastrophe, or competing on a football or baseball team with other teams or in a business firm with other firms, often silences the discords of the members of the same group, and forces them to co-operate heartily for the sake of realization of their common goal. The common cause of victory in an exploded war ordinarily results in a coalition government of hitherto inimical political parties. Building of a church, or school, or hospital, or other institution equally desired by inimical parties often cancels their little animosities in their common endeavor. In hundreds of other forms the important common cause makes the feuding persons and groups bury their tensions and unite into one solidary body for the achievement of their common purpose. The combined techniques of setting against the common enemy and of uniting for achievement of common purpose have been effective in many cases and, in a carefully improved form, can serve successfully the cause of mitigation of enmities and stimulation of co-operation. When wisely planned and skillfully executed, these techniques can be more important than the techniques of indiscriminate punishments and rewards.

### 3. The Technique of Setting a Heroic Moral Example

An extraordinary creative achievement of a genius in any field — science, religion, philosophy, fine arts, ethics, politics, economics, or sport — never passes without calling forth conscious or unconscious " imitation " of the heroic example by others. Its followers may now be a few, now many; its mysterious influence sometimes infects others instantaneously and sometimes it is delayed by days, weeks, years, and decades. But the heroic example hardly ever vanishes fruitlessly, without infecting others with the desire to follow the creative genius. His magic influence is due, primarily, to the sheer power of the supraconscious creative force, regardless of the hedonistic and utilitarian advantages it entails. The creative achievements of Mozarts and Beethovens, Homers and Shakespeares, Platos and Aristotles, Galileos and Newtons, Michelangelos and Phidiases, and of other known and anonymous creators of great values always recruit followers and continuously condition the behavior of thousands and millions of people.

The same is true of the achievements of a creative genius of unselfish love. His heroic example never perishes in vain and always engenders an uncounted legion of followers. Lao-tzu and Confucius, Buddha and Mahavira, Moses and Hillel, Jesus and St. Francis of Assisi, Al Hallaj and Al Ghazzali, Gandhi and Schweitzer are striking examples of this. Still more remarkable is the fact that the heroes of unselfish love accomplish this without arms and armies, or wealth and coercive government machinery, without a control of means of communications, or other instrumentalities of influencing people and recruiting followers. Even more, they often go against the prevailing mores and powerful governments and suffer the penalty. Some 37 per cent of the Christian saintly altruists died the death of martyrs. In spite of this, these greatest apostles of love have had a much larger number of followers for a much longer time than any of the mighty monarchs, conquerors, statesmen, millionaires, dictators, and other executives of history. Chapter Four of this volume, on the Power of Love, gives other evidence of the effective influence of the actions of love upon criminals, robbers, and ordinary human beings.

In the light of this evidence it can be contended that any example of an altruistic action is bound to exert an altruistic influence upon others. The effects of heroic altruism are naturally greater than those of " small " altruistic action. But even a modest example of kindness does not remain sterile; it contributes to the moral ennoblement of others.

Elsewhere in this work and in the two Symposia of this Research Center, it is shown that a friendly approach to others is responded to by friendly reaction in some 70 to 80 per cent of the cases; [17] that small good deeds of one of the mutually inimical parties done to the other party turns their enmity into friendship; that the examples of amity of parents observed regularly by children tangibly contribute to the children's friendliness. The same can be said of other examples of ordinary unselfishness in human life.

As to the effects of a heroic example of sublime love, they are truly incalculable. They persist in time for centuries and millennia: Buddha and Jesus continue to condition tangibly countless lives though they died (as human organisms) some two thousand years ago. The total number of human beings influenced by their examples has to be reckoned by hundreds of millions and billions.

For contemporary mankind, ravaged by moral atomism and egotisms, an emergence of a great genius of love is particularly needed. One or a few such heroes of unselfish love can morally ennoble the demoralized humanity more than most of the ordinary agencies of crime prevention, of utilitarian "moral rearmaments," of police forces, and of legalistic or revolutionary movements for "justice and equity." Even if these moral agencies can help in bridling the extreme forms of selfishness, they can hardly lift the moral standards of the rank and file to the loftiest peaks of the sublimest love. Only the human incarnations of unbounded love can accomplish this task. Herein lies the limitless importance of their creative genius.

## Chapter Seventeen

# The Techniques of Altruistic Transformation (continued)

*9. The Technique of Rational Persuasion and Scientific Demonstration of Advantages of Kindness and Co-operation*

The essentials of this technique consist in a definition of the rules and patterns of altruistic behavior, in communication of these forms to the person or group involved, in the rational persuasion and scientific demonstration of various benefits of altruistic behavior for the parties and of the harmful consequences of their selfish conduct. There is an enormous fund of such theories and practices. The theories range from the elementary precepts like " crime does not pay," " hatred undermines health and shortens life," " it is profitable to be kind," " contribution to the Community Chest is your best investment," up to the intricate theological revelations, moral philosophies, ethical systems, biological, psychological, sociological, psychiatric, and other scientific theories — all demonstrating the vital, mental, spiritual, and social necessity of unselfishness, co-operation, and mutual aid, and the disastrous consequences of aggressive egotism and enmity. In recent times scientific demonstration of these verities has been particularly in vogue.

A large series of scientific studies supply experimental and other proofs that a more equitable distribution of income between labor and management brings a greater profit to the business firm; that an increase of wages stimulates a greater efficiency of labor and higher returns for the enterprise; that kindness and co-operation make us happier and build our peace of mind; that hateful emotions undermine our health; that war and bloody revolution are the worst ways of social reconstruction; that unloved and " rejected " children yield a high per cent of juvenile delinquents and psychoneurotics; and so on.

The contentions of these religious, philosophical, ethical, and scientific theories concerning the incalculable blessings of friendly co-operation and the disastrous results of an unbridled egotism are mostly valid. They are supported by a solid body of logical reasons and relevant facts. The total fund of these theories contains a multitude of the finest logical and factual reasons for persuasion in, and demonstration of, their verities. Finally, the persuasion and demonstration have been practiced since the remote past on up to the present time.

And yet, in spite of all persuasion and demonstration the technique has never been fully effective. In spite of millennia of preaching and teaching of these truths, they have been largely neglected and frequently violated in practically all societies and at all periods. Notwithstanding the continuous use of this technique in various forms, it has not turned human beings into unselfish and unaggressive creatures. It has not eradicated even the bloodiest forms of interindividual and intergroup antagonisms from human history. It has hardly even decreased egotisms and the most murderous forms of the struggle for existence. The present-day explosion of interpersonal, intergroup, and international wars, with their Apocalyptic destruction on a scale unprecedented in human history, is tragic and incontrovertible evidence of the insufficient effectiveness of this technique. Since an increase of scientific discoveries, technological inventions, schooling, and literacy for the last ten centuries has been followed by an increase of wars and aggressiveness, rather than by their decrease [1] it is evident that even the scientific variety of the use of this technique has also been somewhat unsuccessful.

The main reasons for its partial failure in altruization of human behavior are at hand. In the first place, as we already know, a human being is not a wholly rational or logical creature. *In his unconscious and bioconscious " compartments " he is neither logical nor illogical: his unconscious drives are out of the realm of logic or rationality of his intellect.* They neither have such logic nor follow it because the category of the intellect's rationality is simply inapplicable to the unconscious or semiconscious forces. The category is applicable only to the conscious state of mind and not to the unconscious. In addition, these drives operate in their own way different from a rational logic of the intellect.

A human being often becomes nonrational or irrational also when he is propelled to contradictory thoughts and actions by his contradictory conscious egos. When a man talks and acts as a member of the Christian religion with its demand " thou shalt not kill," he preaches nonkilling, and abhors and abstains from murderous actions. When he talks and acts as a patriotic member of his state at war with another state, under the pressure of his state group he preaches killing of enemies and performs the " heroic " acts of extermination of the members of the inimical state. Placed in his membership among the mutually warring groups that give to his respective egos the opposite commands, he thinks, speaks, and acts in a self-contradictory, nonlogical, and illogical manner. As we have seen before, one of his egos affirms what his other ego denies; some of his egos speak and do the things unrelated to his other egos and incoaerent from their standpoint.  As a result, his talk, writings, and actions become either self-contradictory, incoherent, or inconsistent.

Finally, in " civilized " man the nervous centers controlling our thoughts and speech-reactions have possibly become more autonomous from those that control our overt actions than in " primitive " man.  Preliterate men possibly more frequently do what they think and say, and say and think what they do.  The nervous centers controlling their thoughts, talk, and overt actions are possibly more closely interdependent than those in ' civilized " man.  If this hypothesis is valid,[2] it explains why we can quote by heart the Sermon on the Mount, can write profound commentaries on Kant's *Critique of Practical Reason*, can deliver a lofty sermon on altruistic love, and, at the same time, can remain aggressive egotists.  Being autonomous, our intellect can grasp and think the sublimest moral precepts while our actions can, at the same time, be quite opposite to our moral ideas.  Under this condition, moral persuasions and scientific demonstrations of the benefits of unselfish love can impress our intellect without affecting tangibly our overt actions.  We can well preach altruistic verities and not practice them at all.  Such are the main reasons for the behavioral ineffectiveness of the technique discussed.

In our age this ineffectiveness is particularly striking.  The existing governments and leaders, and our fellow men, show inexhaustible abundance of the fiercest contradiction between their noble preachings and ignoble practices.  We have indeed a superabundance of noble moral preachings and of scientifically demonstrated moral verities followed by an extreme scarcity of noble behavior, relationships, and policies.  Hundreds of leaders are daily quoting the Sermon on the Mount at one moment and at the next moment they are ordering massacres of thousands of " enemies," " subversives," " disloyals," and anyone who opposes them.  Almost everyone is appealing nowadays to the highest moral values, and at the same time is incessantly violating these values in his actions.  We live indeed in an age of sincere hypocrites, double-crossers, bigots, and behavioral cynics.  In its speech-reactions our age appears to be supremely altruistic; in its deeds it is strikingly " murderous." [3]

Since most of us are the members of many contradictory groups, and since our intellectual progress has made our thoughts and words fairly independent of our overt actions, the technique of rational persuasion and scientific demonstration of altruistic verities is bound to be fairly ineffective in altruization of our behavior; especially when these verities are presented to our intellect in a quiet, rational, or logical way, little disturbing our unconscious drives, emotions, and feelings.  Intellectually the technique is very successful; behavioristically it falls flat, remains on the surface of the intellect, does not penetrate into the unfathomable depths of our unconscious mind, nor releases our supraconscious potential.  In these conditions a purely intellectual communication of moral rules and ideals cannot basically change our selfish and nonmoral behavior. For its greater effectiveness the technique needs the help of other techniques of moral transformation discussed in this work. One of these helpful techniques is the technique of reinforcement of the moral preachings and teachings by the emotional and vital forces of the unconscious and by the mysterious forces of the supraconscious.

## 10. The Technique of Reinforcement of Altruistic Patterns of Conduct by Emotional, Affective, and Unconscious Forces

If a communication to, and perception of altruistic precepts by, our intellect arouses in us a strong emotional perturbation sympathetic to these precepts; if through this it touches the hidden springs of the unconscious drives and drafts them for the service of these "intellectual precepts," then the communicated ideas do not remain merely on the surface of our intellect, but penetrate into our "body and heart," our speech-reactions and overt behavior. Emotional and affective excitation breaks the barriers of the unconscious otherwise hardly penetrable for the purely intellectual ideas. It has been mentioned in the preceding section that the realm of the unconscious is largely impenetrable for the intellectual logic and scientific demonstration. The unconscious, by definition and by its nature, is incapable of thinking, either logically or illogically, scientifically or nonscientifically. Any thinking is always a conscious activity. Like white blackness, or senseless sense, an "unconscious thought" is a self-contradiction. Not being able to think, the unconscious is largely immune to the power of logical and scientific argument. Rational, inductive, deductive, mathematical, and empirical arguments glide over the surface of the unconscious, hardly penetrate its "inner sanctum," and cannot directly arouse its forces for the service of the respective ideas. To accomplish this task the intellectual ideas and proofs need the mediation and co-operation of emotional and affective factors.

Being aroused, these factors awaken the forces of the unconscious and, guided by the altruistic ideas and precepts, they help to draft the power of the unconscious instincts, reflexes, and drives for service to moral values and ideals. Under this condition, the otherwise "cold" ideas of intellect become supplied with strong driving power. They begin to influence our mind, body, and behavior. Preaching now begins to be practiced; the enormous discrepancy between the noble precepts and ignoble deeds narrows and sometimes vanishes. Persons and groups become now altruistic not only "ideologically" but also behavioristically.

Herein lies the enormous importance of affective and emotional support of our ideas, precepts, commandments, and ideals. The reinforcing emotions, feelings, and unconscious drives may be, according to the circumstances, of most different kinds ranging from empathy, sympathy, gratitude, love, reverence, admiration, benevolence, hope, respect, kindness, and various forms of joy, and pleasures, all urging a fulfillment of moral precepts, up to hate, enmity, guilt, shame, repentance, remorse, disgust, anxiety, fear, revulsion, despair, sorrow, sadness, and all sorts of pain and suffering tending to inhibit the violation of altruistic values. Likewise, through aroused emotions and feelings each of the unconscious drives of sex, hunger, thirst, breathing, moving, sleeping, and self-preserving can be drafted for the support of moral patterns of behavior. Sometimes only one or a few, and sometimes many, of these forces need to be used for the altruistic purposes.

In its essentials this verity was discovered long ago. Since the remotest past, the moral and spiritual educators of humanity well understood its importance, and through trial and error, knowledge and enormous experience, they invented a large number of ingenious techniques for emotional, affective, and unconscious support of their religious, legal, moral, and civic precepts.

Religious cults and rituals furnish us with a rich treasury of ingenious techniques serving this purpose. As a matter of fact, the main function of religious cult and ritual consists exactly in arousing and mobilizing the unconscious, emotional, and affective forces for support of the respective religious beliefs and their moral commandments. The very character of the architecture of temples and cathedrals, their sculpture, pictures, ikons, decorations and thousands of ritualistic objects — candles, lamps, ceremonial vestments, crosses, religious standards, and other cult instrumentalities — represent a multitude of the most effective stimuli for awakening the emotions, affections, and unconscious drives of the believers. Still more effectively this function is performed by sacramental rites and ritual ceremonies, by religious processions and festivities. In each society its religious services are its greatest tragedies, its intensest "psychodramas," and its most moving "sociodramas" actively played by each believer. There is hardly a greater tragedy than that of God or God's Son sacrificing Himself for redemption of man or the tragic mystery of the *Agnus Dei qui tollis peccata mundi*. There is hardly a more dramatic action than that of a sinful believer partaking the very flesh and blood of his God and Savior. There is no more moving role than that of a mortal assured in his immortality; of a greatest sinner redeemed by God's love and granted a blissful salvation.

No less important is the fact that the sacramental tragedies and mysteries are actively participated in by the believers: they do not merely look passively and listen or just "read their lines." True believers actually live their role in a most real way, and live it collectively, surrounded and co-acted by their fellow believers, by their religious and moral leaders; and they do this in the presence of, and in communion with, God Himself. Playing their role they feel themselves becoming divinized, purified, sanctified, and blessed by the grace of their Supreme Being.

This active participation and collective performance of their roles in the religious tragedies, dramas, and mysteries, in communion with the Supreme Being, enormously enhances the effectiveness of religious ceremonies.

The ritual of each important sacrament or the rites of each important service are marvelously adapted for their specific purpose. The rites of repentance, confession, and the Eucharist, the ritual of baptism or "the rites of passage," of marriage and funeral — and religion has a specific service for all the important events in human life — each of these ceremonies is different from the others, and in each the prayers spoken, the hymns sung, the music played, the postures and motions acted, the instrumentalities used, the vestments and objects employed are again ingeniously adapted for their specific purposes and for arousing corresponding kinds of affections, emotions, and primeval drives. In the Christian religion, its Requiem Mass is something very different from the rites of the Te Deum Mass; marriage consecration is different from the ritual of baptism; this from the rites of repentance, or confession, or of the Eucharist. The same can be said of the cult and ritual of all religions, beginning with the " primitive " ones and ending with the greatest religions of humanity.

Important also in religious techniques are various physical, chemical, biological, and psychosocial stimuli used: they effectively change our bodily conditions and psycho-physiological processes. Use of various intoxicants from ritual smoking and wine-drinking up to various drugs; ritual fastings and feasts; specific postures of prostration, sitting, standing, or immobility; specific motions of crossing, raising hands, head-bending, or genuflection; religious dances in their multifarious forms,[4] now pious and stately, now violent and wild; religious asceticism and so-called " religious orgies "; use of phallic and sex symbols; extensive use of the most moving music — and the great religious music is among the greatest music of humanity; similar utilization of poetical, beautiful, and dramatic language — and the great religious poetry and literature, such as the Bible, the Koran, the Vedas, the Bhagavadgita, the Mahabharata, are among the greatest literary masterpieces of mankind; a vast array of stimuli of color and forms, of touch and sight, of smell and of other sense organs: all these chemical, physical, somatic and psycho-physiological stimuli contribute their share to the mobilization of the bio-emotional forces for the service of religious and moral values.

When carefully studied and fully understood, the ritual and sacramental techniques of the great religions turn out to be among the most scientific and effective techniques for spiritual and moral transformation ever invented.

Great religions at their creative period, through their sacramental and ritualistic tragedies, dramas, and " mysteries " have been among the greatest moral educators of humanity. An overwhelming majority of the great apostles of love, like Buddha and Jesus, have come from among religious creators and leaders. Religious tragedies and dramas have possibly purified, ennobled, and achieved moral catharsis of a greater number of their believers than ennoblement and catharsis achieved by secular plays or school education.

Side by side with their universal and perennial essentials, ritualistic techniques have temporary and local elements efficacious only for a given specific group at a given period. These temporary and local elements incessantly change according to the mental, moral, and vital properties of persons and groups in the process of moral education. So modified, the essentials of these techniques can be used for moral transformation of almost all human beings and groups of our time.

Besides their religious forms, the techniques of emotional " indoctrination " are widely used by the states, political parties, civic organizations; in military training, in occupational and ethnic groups, in boy scout and similar organizations; and finally, in the school and the family moral education. Parades, demonstrations, ceremonies, festivals, pageants, badges and medals, emotionally saturated propaganda, glorification of heroes and vilification of " enemies," corresponding music, intoxicants, and other emotional stimuli are used, in various forms, degrees, and artfulness in most different organizations for reinforcement of their indoctrination.

Unfortunately, these techniques are used also for antisocial, egoistic, aggressive, even murderous " indoctrination." For the purposes of altruistic transformation, however, they represent an important instrumentality for making human beings practice the moral values they preach. Without their help, the purely intellectual precepts and ideals would be much more feeble than they are when supported by the emotional and biological forces of human nature.

As a special case of the technique discussed, Moreno's *psychodramatic and socio-dramatic techniques* need to be mentioned.[5] In their essentials these techniques represent a special variation of the technique of emotional reinforcement particularly adapted for the treatment of mental and moral disorders. By making the patient play assigned roles on the stage of the psychodramatic theater and, in sociodrama, by making the role-playing truly collective and by careful arrangement of the details of these procedures, Moreno's methods cause the players to pass through intense emotional, affective, and vital experiences working towards catharsis or mental, moral, and behavioral recovery of the patients-actors. In their carefully thought out details, these methods have many admirable sub-techniques of tangible effectiveness especially in treatment of psychoneuroses, as well as other mental and moral disorders.

11. *The Technique of Direct Life Experience*

As a specially important variation of the techniques of emotional reinforcement of ideological values and imperatives, the technique of direct life experience is to be noted. It is widely operating in real life, but is used little in moral education of persons and groups. Its essence consists in putting the individual into some real life condition in which he passes through a real and direct life experience of a specified kind. In such a direct experience the individual not only learns intellectually about the subject matter of his experience but lives it through, with all his emotions, affections, and unconscious propensities. In contrast to the "make-believe" experience of the psychodrama and sociodrama, here his experience is thoroughly genuine. His total personality participates in it as it does in his real life actions and reactions.

For these reasons the technique of direct experience is bound to be particularly effective. The lesson learned in such an experience is unforgettable and tangibly shapes one's personality and behavior. Direct experience of being hungry, thirsty, cold, dirty, of being beaten, unjustly treated, insulted, exploited, arrested, or persecuted teaches us more effectively about these experiences than the best sermons and lectures. The same is true of the direct experience of being helped in misfortune, shown sympathy in trying conditions, offered unexpected friendship, encouraged when one is downhearted, and so on. All direct life experiences develop our empathy and emotionally charged understanding of the similar experiences of others.

From this standpoint, for altruistic purposes, it is instructive for the rich to pass through the direct experience of being poor and needy; for the poor to have a direct experience of the worries, anxiety, responsibility, incessant competition, and other disturbing elements in the life of the rich. No less instructive would it be for the healthy and well-to-do to pass through the experience of sickness without medical help; for crooked and pitiless judges to pass through the life conditions of being unjustly and severely punished; for the dictatorial rulers to have a real taste of how their subjects feel under their tyranny; for a propagandist of war to live on the battlefront in the horrible conditions of the fighting soldiers; for a master to live in the conditions of a slave; for a bully to be bullied; for the rulers, commanders, and the crew of bombing squads to live in the conditions of the bombed populations; for a disloyal husband or wife to be confronted with the disloyalty of his partner; and so on. One can be sure that real life experience can teach individuals more effectively than the most eloquent sermons or artificial psychodramas and sociodramas.

In spite of its efficacy, the technique of direct life experience has several serious limitations. First, subjection of even willing persons to many direct experiences is prohibited by law. Second, still more numerous direct experiences are factually impossible. Who can force a king or dictator to become, say, for a month or a year, just a humble subject; or place the rulers and the rich in the conditions of the ruled and the poor; or put the chief and the crew of the bombing squad with their families among the bombed population; and so on? Third, many experimentations of this sort are dangerous — physically, mentally, and morally — for the individuals undergoing the direct experience. To subject for moral purposes an unfaithful husband to the life experience of unfaithfulness of his wife may cure the husband, but it is likely to morally ruin his wife, if she commits the act of unfaithfulness just for moral improvement of her husband. To leave a sick rich man without medical care or the minimum of hygienic conditions may give him a deep empathy and understanding of the sick and poor who live in unhealthy conditions and have no medical care, but this life experience can seriously damage his health.

These examples illustrate many dangers inherent in the technique of direct experience. Fourthly, in a number of cases the actual effects of the prescribed direct experience are uncertain and unknown. They may be altruistic and positive; but they may be negative and may evoke an explosion of hate, envy, and selfishness in various forms. For instance, the rich man's real life experience of being poor and needy may make him all the more anxious to stay rich, without any desire to help the poor. An aggressive bully, having been beaten and bullied, can become still more aggressive instead of turning more friendly and less cruel. As it is shown elsewhere,[6] the same kind of frustrating life experience makes some people more selfish and aggressive, and some more altruistic and helpful to others. This uncertainty of the effects of a given direct experience rules out its prescription for all cases where the effects are unknown.

These shortcomings of the technique seriously limit its use; even with these limitations, however, it still has a wide field of application. This field is much wider than that of its contemporary utilization. The efficacy of the technique warrants an extension of its employment for the purposes of creative altruization. To be sure, a wise discernment and scientific competence are needed to determine what sort of direct experience is to be prescribed to what kind of persons in order that the life experience bring the expected altruistic results. But, after all, such a discernment and competence are necessary for " prescription " of almost all techniques of medical treatment and altruization.

## 12. The Technique of Altruization through the Fine Arts

Somewhat related to the technique of emotional reinforcement of ideas, images, symbols, and patterns of conduct is the technique of use of the fine arts for the purposes of altruization. Elsewhere in this work it has been pointed out that beauty, truth, and goodness are three mutually connected supreme values and that each of these values and energies can be transformed into one another, and can contribute to a creative growth and support of the other two. This explains why the genuine fine arts can and do serve the task of altruistic ennoblement as well as that of cognition of truth. In the remote past this role of the arts was understood and widely used for moral and cognitive purposes. As we have seen above, religious and secular agencies extensively employ the fine arts for spiritualization and socialization of their members.

Among many preliterate peoples, in ancient Egypt and Babylon, India and China, Iran, Greece and Rome, the noble (sacramental and magic) fine arts "were given a divine origin," and were ascribed "a hidden meaning, hidden efficacy, and hidden charm." [7] Special religious and governmental boards were established for the development and maintenance of the noble fine arts. "To set forth correctly the successes and failures of governments, to affect Heaven and Earth, and to move spiritual beings, there is no readier instrument than poetry (and music)," states Confucius.

For the purposes of inculcation of reverence, benevolence, and of the Golden Rule in human behavior and interrelationships, Confucius composed a whole book of poetry, songs, and ceremonies. [8] Pythagoras, Plato, and Aristotle reiterated these ideas and stressed especially the mental and moral catharsis produced by the genuine fine arts. From these times on, this role of the true fine arts, in contrast to the vulgar pseudo-arts, has been restated and practiced again and again. [9]

By its nature the fine art masterpiece represents a marvelous unity which arouses simultaneously our intellectual, emotional, affective, volitional, and vital energies. Hegel well described its character, stating that:

What is demanded for artistic interest as well as for artistic creation is, speaking in general terms, a vital energy in which the universal is not present as law and maxim, but is operative in union with the soul and emotions, just as also, in the imagination, what is universal and rational is enclosed only as brought into unity with a concrete sensuous phenomenon. [10]

This "sensuous concreteness" of art phenomena, permeated by emotions and vital urges, makes the fine arts particularly fit for a powerful conveyance of concrete notions, experiences, and values charged by dynamic vital forces which influence the total man, his mind and heart, his body and soul. Art can teach many verities which cannot be taught by abstract intellectual reasoning. Nietzsche was right in defining art as "the cheerful science" accessible to many for whom conceptual thinking is often unavailable. Art's "sensuous" elements directly awaken our emotional and unconscious forces for support of its message. In addition, great art conveys to us those *universalia ante rem*, as R. Wagner puts it, or those suprarational truths which cannot be communicated by words and concepts.

For these reasons a great tragedy often moves its audience much more deeply than an eloquent sermon; a great novel or a great symphony frequently inspires us with stronger moral aspirations than an excellent scientific lecture on ethics; a masterpiece of painting or sculpture, the Parthenon or a great cathedral, uplifts us in the realm of creative spirit more efficiently than a statistical diagram, mathematical formula, or a chain of impeccable syllogisms can do.

Recent studies of the effect of music and of other fine arts [11] confirm this role of the art phenomena, and give a more detailed knowledge about their effects upon our physiological, cognitive, emotional, volitional, affective and vital processes, as well as about the uses of art stimuli for therapeutic and industrial purposes. For the sake of brevity only some of the observed effects of music will be mentioned here; but with a corresponding variation, similar effects can be claimed for other fine arts.

A series of experiments by Tarchanoff, Dutto and others shows that music increases bodily metabolism; increases or decreases (according to the character of music) muscular energy (Féré, Tarchanoff, Scripture); accelerates respiration and decreases its regularity (Binet, Guibaud, Weld); affects volume, pulse and blood pressure; lowers the threshold of sensory stimuli of different modes; stimulates emotions and moods according to the character of music (Washburn, Dickinson, Shoen, Gatewood, Hampton); influences the internal secretions (W. Cannon and others); reduces or delays fatigue; serves several therapeutic purposes, reduces patients' apprehension and fear, and often is the only medium through which the patient can be reached (Larson, Gardner, Altschuler, McGlin, Marriner). Other studies show that certain kinds of music increase industrial efficiency and output (K. Bücher, Wallaschek, Billroth, Reynolds, Ramsay), and decrease industrial accidents (Hugh), stimulate the spirit of cheerfulness, and friendliness; decrease the feeling of tiredness, unpleasantness, and irritability in the working hours (Middleton, Kerr, Benson, Spears, Cardinelli, Burris-Meyer, and others); sharpen the processes of attention and perception, decrease tensions, animosity, and antagonism (Antrim, De Bernardis, Ernst, Denny); and so on.[12]

With a proper variation, the same can be said of plays, literature, painting, sculpture, and architecture. All the genuine fine arts have been serving and can increasingly serve the tasks of the spiritual and moral ennoblement of man.

To accomplish this purpose the chosen art phenomena must be genuine art, and in each case they must be carefully adapted to the character of the persons and groups involved. Not every great masterpiece can be effective for all human beings and all social groups. Depending upon their physical, mental, moral and sociocultural equipment, only certain kinds of the fine arts are effective in the moral ennoblement of each person and collectivity. Other kinds of art phenomena, being foreign to the given individual or group, may remain ineffective or may even exert a demoralizing influence. In each case the utilized art medium must deeply move the individual or group — and for every person and collectivity a moving art medium can be found; it must move them to the higher moral, mental, and aesthetic levels.

An effective art medium usually shows the immortal values in mortals, the shining beauty in ugly phenomena, the noblest elements in ignoble appearances. It radiates the light of the highest values over the darkness of vulgarity, depravity, stupidity, and ugliness. It awakens in us empathy, sympathy, and understanding in regard to all living beings. Among the immortal art masterpieces only certain art media can accomplish this task for each given individual and society.

Viewed from this standpoint the bulk of the modern fine arts, literature, plays, movies, television, music, painting, sculpture, dancing — in their high-brow and low-brow forms — is rather unfit to be the medium of moral ennoblement for a great many persons and groups. The high-brow modern arts are mediocre in their artfulness, while the modern " popular " arts are conspicuously vulgar. For these reasons they can hardly exert the positive influence discussed. Then, the bulk of the modern arts is overwhelmingly negativistic, muckraking and " dirt-painting." They move mainly in the regions of the moral, mental, and social sewers. They depict mainly the subnormal and abnormal human beings and pathological deeds and events. Criminals and semi-criminal detectives, hypocrites, and liars; stupid, aggressive, insane, cynical, disloyal, greedy, sensual, selfish, and sexually crazy human beings are the most frequent types of personages of our literature, shows, movies, program music, painting, and sculpture. A positive type of human being is exceedingly rare in this crowd, and when it appears, it is rarely depicted as artfully as the negative types: somehow most of the positive heroes of the modern arts look like " virtuous scarecrows " and piously talking phonographs rather than full-blooded living individuals. Most of the topics of the modern fine arts are centered around the sex organs, police morgue, criminal hide-out, mental asylum, ferocious struggles, murder, vice, and money. In its bulk this art is debunking and muckraking agency: it mortalizes the immortals, uglifies the beautiful, ignobles the noble and drags all values into turbid waters.[13] Thus it can hardly perform successfully the function of man's moral and creative ennoblement in regard to most of the persons who are exposed to it and actively participate in it. Several studies show that it exerts demoralizing, disintegrating, and enervating effects rather than any constructive influence. For these reasons, its bulk can hardly be used for the purposes of altruistic transformation.

In mankind's great and rich treasury of art masterpieces, however, including the beauty of the sunset, of starry skies, and of millions of natural phenomena, there always can be found the special art medium fit for altruistic transfiguration of a given person or group. Sometimes it lies in "the small voice" of the sun reflected in a pool of water, or in a little tune of a beautiful folksong or in the joyful play of children, not to mention the chefs-d'oeuvre of the great artists and masters. With discernment the fine arts can and should be used much more than they are used now, for mental, moral, and the "total" education of mankind. Additional merit of this technique is that it works in a most enjoyable way, free from the pains and fatigue of many other techniques.

## 13. The Technique of Exposure to Friendship and Love of Others

So far, almost all the techniques discussed represent operations which are initiated and performed by agencies different from the individuals and groups passing through the process of altruization. The individuals and groups whose transformation is sought for remain comparatively passive. They do not initiate their own change, but respond rather to the stimuli set forth by others until their altruistic change progresses far enough so that they begin actively working for their own moral improvement. In this category belongs also the technique of exposure of the individuals and groups to the *genuine* friendship, love, and good will of others. This technique is possibly as effective as any of the above "passive" techniques. By *genuine* friendship is meant friendly feelings, thoughts, words, and deeds. The same is meant by genuine love or good will. Any good will is genuine only when it is manifested in inner experience, words, and overt actions. In order to be still more effective the factors of friendship or love must also be *adequate* in the sense defined elsewhere in this work (cf. Chapter Two). The technique of exposure to genuine and adequate altruistic feelings, words, and deeds of others is likely to be one of the most effective methods for altruistic purposes. In Chapter Four on the power of love and in other parts of this work a vast body of experimental, observational, clinical, statistical, historical and logical evidence is given to support this statement.

This evidence shows that unfriendly relations between inimical persons are changed into friendly relationship in a sufficiently high per cent of the cases by friendly deeds initiated by one of the antagonistic parties. And the more genuine and adequate these deeds are and the more consistently they are rendered, the higher the per cent of change tends to be. "Acceptance" of the mentally sick patient by his therapist proves to be the necessary and most important factor in curing the mental disorders. Exposure to an unexpected genuine and adequate love of many a criminal starts their transformation into honest citizens. Exposure to such a love starts the altruistic conversion of many an eminent apostle of love from his preconversion selfishness. And so on and so forth. A vast body of this sort of evidence testifies to the efficiency of this technique. Its importance is enhanced by its accessibility to almost every individual and group. No special talent or training is necessary to use it fruitfully except the decision to use it. When a necessary wisdom to make the friendship genuine and adequate is added to this good will, the efficacy of this technique notably increases. As several experiments show, however, it proves itself tangibly effective even when at its initial use friendly good deeds are done and kind words are spoken without an inner fire and enthusiasm. With a repetition of such deeds and words, according to the theory of James-Lange, the cold friendship gradually warms up until it becomes truly genuine.

The main shortcomings of this technique are two. In some circumstances its use involves the altruistic party in the danger of being attacked, harmed, insulted, or generally jeopardized by the aggressive party exposed to his love and friendship. Furthermore, in certain circumstances such an exposure to love and friendship can encourage the aggressiveness of the other party: not meeting any physical resistance to his criminal or selfish actions, and not being threatened by retaliation, the aggressor may become still more violent and criminal. Such cases happened and continue to happen.

These dangers seriously inhibit the unexceptional use of the technique. Even in the cases of the unashamed aggressors, however, it can and should be used in a combination with other techniques at the " hot " moments of aggression. At such moments, the techniques of physical resistance, of coercion by force, of punishment, and the like can be applied in order to stop the aggression, care being taken all the time, however, not to harm the aggressor seriously. The " friendly " character of these measures must be made clear to him. A loving spanking of a mischievous child at the moment of his mischief, stopping an attack of a robber without seeking the full measure of punishment possible, defending one's life without murdering the guilty party, and so on, are the examples of these measures. The attack stopped and the danger averted, the technique of the exposure to friendly actions can then be put into operation. The technique of stopping aggression with people has much in common with methods used to train dangerous animals. At the first contacts with such animals, precautionary measures of stopping their attacks by force or similar measures are sometimes necessary. But these techniques rarely, if ever, tame such animals and turn them into the trainer's friends. This result is usually achieved by friendly treatment of these animals, by feeding and giving them something they like, by caressing them, and by other kind actions. These deeds and words disarm them, remove their fear, and assure them of the good will of the tamers. The same is true of the technique of turning a ferocious dog or wild horse into one's best friend. In practically all cases of taming the dangerous animals the most effective technique is that of exposing them to the good feelings, deeds, and words of the trainers. The techniques of coercion, punishment, and other unfriendly methods have hardly ever turned any dangerous animal into a friendly creature.

In combination with the precautionary measures suggested, the technique of exposure to friendship can be used in most of the dangerous situations discussed. The animal trainers well know this and regularly use this combined method. It is a pity that in application to themselves human beings use it much less and prefer to employ intimidating, coercive, and punitive measures, often to the complete exclusion of the technique of exposure discussed. Shall we wonder that in such cases human beings regularly fail to turn enemies into friends and succeed mainly in a mutual intensification of their hatred and struggle? It is high time to apply to ourselves the privilege of the noble method of exposure granted by us to animals. To sum up: the technique discussed can and should be used much more than it is used at the present time.

## 14. The Technique of Individual Creative Activity

The creative urge is possibly one of the basic aspirations of human beings. In simple or complex form it animates practically all individuals, young and old, preliterate and civilized, dull and bright, normal or abnormal. The paleolithic man " painting " the walls of his cave or decorating his weapon; children absorbed in their manipulations of blocks or in construction of various sand buildings; a city-dweller enjoying his gardening; a housewife trying to bake a better pie or busying herself with a new arrangement of her furniture; a mother inventing a new way of handling her baby; a boy dreaming his daydreams; a factoryhand or peasant endeavoring to improve here and there his occupational work; a mediocre professor inventing a little variation on the theme of his predecessors; finally, a genius so deeply absorbed in his creative work that he neglects his health and earning his means of subsistence: these and millions of other apparently " routine " activities manifest the creative urge in both its simplest and its highest forms.

Being one of the basic and at the same time highest aspirations, the creative urge represents the focal point of human personality. It is a manifestation of the conscious mind at its best and especially of the supraconscious grace in man. As we have seen in Chapter Six, all great creative achievements are inspired by the supraconscious and are executed by the conscious mind working under the guidance of the supraconscious genius which resides in the creative person. In a small degree the voice of the supraconscious speaks also in modest creative efforts. The creative urge is thus in a sense the holy of holies of every person. It is also the most distinctive mark of his individuality, of his conscious egos, and especially of his egoless self. Creativity and individuality both mean something new, something different from what already exists and from other persons.

The creative urge is therefore one of the main forces that molds and preserves the ego-centered and especially the egoless individuality of each person: his ego-transcending self. So far as the preservation of a person's individuality is no less a basic need [14] than the preservation of his life, a free display of the creative urge is one of the main forms of man's freedom.[15] Free manifestation of the creative urge is therefore one of the main "ingredients" of man's happiness, self-respect, and peace of mind. Frustration of the creative urge means an undermining of his individuality, his freedom, and his happpiness. Most of the persons threatened by a loss of these values cannot help starting a fight for them, counterattacking the inimical forces, becoming irritable, aggressive, and unfriendly towards the antagonists. Most of the persons who can freely display their creative urge find some satisfaction in their life, are not forced to fight for their individuality, freedom, and a measure of happiness. Therefore, they are more friendly towards their fellow men and the world at large.

For these reasons, the therapy of creative activity is one of the important techniques for making human beings less selfish and less aggressive. By arranging the conditions in which a given person or group can freely engage in a desirable creative activity, the individual or group is deflected from many mischiefs, squabbles, and enmities by the much more absorbing creative thoughts and deeds. The very nature of their constructively creative work tends to ennoble them mentally and morally. They increasingly become the instrument of the best conscious activities and of the supraconscious forces, and decreasingly the animal organisms controlled by discordant biological drives and by disharmonious, narrow egos.

The importance of this technique was understood long ago, and most eminent educators have systematically used it. Among more recent educational systems, Montessori's method particularly strongly emphasizes it.

The pedagogical method . . . has for its base the [creative] liberty of the child; and liberty is activity. . . . Discipline must come through liberty. . . . The first dawning of real discipline comes through [creative] work. At a given moment it happens that a child becomes keenly interested in a piece of work, showing by the expression of his face, by his intense attention, by his perseverance in the same exercise. That child has set foot upon the road leading to discipline.

Creative work develops the child spirituality; but the child with a fuller spiritual development works better, and his improved work delights him. . . . Discipline is, therefore, not a fact but a path, a path in following which the child grasps the abstract conception of goodness with an exactitude which is fairly scientific.[16]

One of the morning exercises gives a more concrete idea of how children behave when they are freely engaging themselves in a creative work.

The child keeps still for a while, and then chooses some task he finds easy, such as arranging the colors in gradation; he continues working at this for a time, but not for very long; he passes on to some more complicated task, such as that of composing words with the movable letters, and perseveres with this for a long time (about half an hour). At this stage he ceases working, walks about the room, and appears less calm; to a superficial observer he would seem to show signs of fatigue. But after a few minutes he undertakes some much more difficult work, and becomes so deeply absorbed in this, that he shows to us he has reached the acme of his activity (additions and writing down the results). When this work is finished, his activity comes to an end in all serenity; he contemplates his handiwork for a long time, then approaches the teacher, and begins to confide in her. The appearance of the child is that of a person who is rested, satisfied, and uplifted. . . . He experiences the higher social impulses, desiring to make confidences and to hold intimate communion with other souls.[17]

Comenius, Pestalozzi, Froebel,[18] and other eminent educators voice similar opinions, based upon their extensive educational practice.

Besides educators, many thoughtful therapists advocate and use this technique as " active play therapy," " creative work therapy," or " occupational therapy " in the treatment of psychoneuroses, aggressiveness, and inner conflicts of children as well as of grownups.[19]

Furthermore, several experimental studies of the productivity, turnover, and conflicts of factory workers show that the rate of productivity is directly proportional, and the rate of turnover and aggression is inversely proportional, to the amount of a free participation of operators in the choice and change of their special jobs in the factory. An experimental group of operators autocratically assigned to their jobs showed the lowest productivity in their work and the highest rate of turnover and conflicts with the management, while an experimental group of similar workers who actively participated in the choice and change of their jobs displayed the highest productivity in their work and the lowest rate of turnover and conflicts with the management. " Through participation people find self-expression. And they feel deep satisfaction over the personal recognition and opportunity for creativity which participation provides. Participation in group decisions in matters affecting them gives them a feeling of importance, of freedom to act, of fellowship with other free persons in reaching decisions." [20]

To sum up: there is hardly any doubt that this technique is one of the most important for our purposes. What kind of creative work is to be prescribed for each person or group depends upon their interests and mental, moral, and cultural equipment. For anyone, however, some kind of creative work capable to absorb him fully can be found. The absorption in such an activity can make many people happier and less inimical than can an improvement of their standard of living or other material advantages. This is especially true of the creative geniuses. A Beethoven or a Mozart, a Newton or a Michelangelo would certainly prefer full freedom for doing his creative work in relative poverty to the position of a multi-millionaire deprived of this freedom. With their creative *élan* suppressed, such artists probably would have felt themselves unhappy, irritable, and aggressive towards all who hindered a free display of their creative genius. In a smaller degree this is also true of millions of " small creators."

It is regrettable, again, that in our age this technique is not used as much as it should be. Big and small political, economic, and other " bosses," a legion of agencies for prevention of crime, revolution, and war; administrators of reformatories and schools: most still rely on dictatorial commands, rewards, and punishments more than on the technique of creative activity. Unfortunately, also, our mechanized and " specialized " technological culture enormously limits a free display of the creative urge for millions of people. Mechanical, robot-like operations in factories, " required " texts and lecture courses in our schools, vulgarized entertainment by professionals in high-brow and low-brow music, movies, television, theater, papers, magazines, and best sellers — all these cultural activities condemn millions to the passive role of consumers of the professional " intellectual chewing gum," rather than to the role of creators. For large masses the fields of manifestation of their creative urge are limited to various " hobbies," rubber-stamp recreational activities, and the like.

This limitation is possibly one of the important factors in the nervousness, irritability, dissatisfaction, unrest, and interindividual, intergroup, and international tensions — war included — of our age. In spite of a notable improvement in material conditions of life in countries like the United States, these " syndromes " of dissatisfaction and aggressiveness are at least as great now as at any time before. One of the remedies for this seems to consist in widening the opportunities for satisfaction of the creative urge of the rank and file. The widening is urgently needed not only for altruistic purposes and for mitigation of our " wars of everyone against everyone," but also for physical and mental welfare and the cultural progress of humanity. After all, " the Supreme Creator " is possibly the most important characteristic of God. Creativity is also the most important life mission of man. It is man's royal road to the supraconscious, as well as of the supraconscious to man. It is the main way for the union of the mortal human being with the Immortal Cosmic Creator. Why then not open this royal road for all human beings?

## 15. *The Technique of Collective Creativity, Group Enhancement and Therapy*

Some creative works can successfully be done alone, without a direct participation of others. This is true especially of the great creative efforts by the men of genius. Mozart or Brahms, Shakespeare or Dante, L. Tolstoi or Isaac Newton, indeed most eminent composers, writers, scientists, philosophers, inventors, thinkers, and spiritual and moral leaders work alone in the crucial part of their creative activity. They need the fullest concentration of their supraconscious and conscious mind on the creative task without being distracted by others. The same can be said of ordinary persons engrossed in their creative work, beginning with the grade-school pupil working on his arithmetic problems and ending with the grownup trying to solve his creative task.

Side by side with the creative activities better done in solitude, there are many creative works that can be done better in a free co-operation with others interested in the same creative problem. In such collective creative enterprises the ego-taming and the ego-transcending effects of creative work are enhanced by the factor of collectivity or group influences. In free collective creativity each member is continuously stimulated, helped, heartened, and taught by other members; in this creative process the individual's little egos are largely dissolved and merged into one creative " we," with common joys and sorrows, successes and failures. In the successes each member feels himself a real creator of the accomplishments that far exceed those of one individual; in the setbacks each member is consoled by the fact of collective failure: " it is not my failure only but it is the failure of all of us." This sort of consolation enormously softens the bitterness, depression, and disillusionment attendant to individual failures. " With the world looking at you, even your death is easy," says a Russian proverb. Collective effort somehow inspires an enthusiasm impossible in many individual efforts; it enormously invigorates one's labor; often makes a drudgery enjoyable; helps a member to be absorbed by his creative task; and develops a real comradeship among the members and friendliness toward the world at large.

In brief, the effects of collective creativity are inestimable. In order that the technique of collective effort yields these results, however, it must meet several requirements. First, the ends and means of collective creative effort must be morally, mentally, and socially positive. The point is that there is not only the good but also the evil low-grade creativity of the conscious (and hardly ever of the supraconscious) mind. The creative activity of a criminal gang or of a death-spreading army can bind together its members by the bond of blood of their victims; but outside of the in-group it sows hate, destruction, and death. It makes the gang and the army into group egotists in regard to the outside world. The same can be said about any creative group collectively engaged in achievement of an antialtruistic end through morally reprehensible means. Even the collective achievement of a good end through the wrong means usually yields antialtruistic results: in such a group or person their wrong means usually become their end and the good goal becomes forgotten. This explains why innumerable group efforts of this sort regularly fail in producing moral ennoblement of either their members or the outsiders, and why the motto "A good end justifies the bad means" has hardly ever realized its end. Viewed in this light the past and the present "crusades" for spiritual, religious, or moral purposes, carried on by means of wars, "cloak and dagger diplomacy," deceit and lies, bribe and murder, have invariably failed, and will fail in realization of their good goals.[21]

Second, participation of each member in the collective enterprise must be freely chosen and freely carried on. A genuine creative act is always a free act. "Coercive creativity" is a self-contradiction. A slave forced to participate in building an Egyptian pyramid, or a prisoner of a concentration camp coerced to work in building Soviet factories and canals, can hardly be expected to be morally ennobled or to become altruistic towards his masters and the world at large. The same goes for practically all coercive participation in creative group work. This does not deny an exceptional and temporary use of the techniques of drilling, mild punishment, reward and of other low-grade techniques discussed above. But their exceptional use consists, at best, in a mere preparation of the unsocial persons to be freely captivated by creative urge. By themselves, these rough measures neither transform a coerced activity into a creative work, nor do they produce the altruistic consequences of a genuine constructive creativity.

Third, to be effective the collective enterprise must be of intense interest for all the participants. A mere gathering together of a number of persons interested in different creative tasks rarely evokes the beneficial effects mentioned above. If some members succeed in putting through their creative project in which other members are not interested, these other members will be bored and their co-operation is bound to be apparent rather than real.

If these three conditions are met, any collective creative work can serve the purposes of altruization and stimulation of the creative potential of each member. Concrete forms of such creative group endeavors are very diverse and numerous, depending on the creative interests of the individuals. Collective sewing, gardening, Red Cross work, recreational projects; the collective effort of habitual alcoholics to free themselves from alcoholism (like "Alcoholic Anonymous"), a group of former patients of psychopathic hospitals fighting together for preservation of their sanity (like the society "We Are Not Alone"); a society of previous criminals working together for prevention of their relapse into criminal activity; the collective building of a community hospital, school, church, library, recreational center; consumers' or producers' co-operative organizations; collective scientific, philosophical, religious, artistic, political, ethical, and economic creative associations — these are a few examples of the innumerable collective creative endeavors. The very fact that individuals interested in the same creative task tend to and do establish a society for realization of their common purpose well demonstrates the fruitfulness of free co-operation in creative work.

The participation of many Greeks in building the Parthenon or of thousands of medieval individuals in building a great cathedral; the spontaneous common effort of citizens of an invaded country to defend themselves; the collective endeavor of the members of a community to establish a good school; of factory workers to have a factory orchestra; of a group of compassionate persons to organize a relief work: these and other forms of creative group work have socialized their participants possibly more than a mere listening to an eloquent sermon on how to be creative, generous, and virtuous.

The preceding section has mentioned that participation of factory workers in a collective decision about some aspects of their work tends to increase their efficiency and to decrease their tensions with the management, and among themselves.[22] The same can be said of the creative participation of members of the family in family affairs, of citizens in the affairs of the state; of researchers in their common scientific project; of actors in their play; of children in their spontaneous game. And so on.

No wonder that the technique of collective creativity has also been beneficial for therapeutic purposes in regard to the patients of mental hospitals, to juvenile and grown-up delinquents, and for an alleviation of interindividual and sometimes of intergroup tensions.[23]

In the chapters of this work dealing with the techniques of the monastic brotherhoods and of the living communities of the Brothers in Paraguay, of the Mennonites, the Hutterites, and of the " boys' towns " and various " junior republics," [24] it is shown that one of the main techniques of their moral education is exactly that of creative group work. A careful study of the altruistic effects of this technique in these types of communities shows its considerable efficacy. The members of these communities are indeed notably altruistic to one another and to the outside world.

With a proper modification the same can be said of the altruistic effects of creative group work for the alleviation of material and spiritual difficulties of others. Whether such effort consists in Red Cross work, or in an active participation in collection of clothing, money, food, or books for the needy or for amelioration of school, recreation, and cultural conditions of this or that population: whatever the work, an active participation in it tangibly improves the moral behavior of the participants.

To sum up: any creative group work satisfying the above three conditions is an effective method for mitigation of selfishness and for altruistic growth of the persons involved. As this technique has few dangerous drawbacks, it should be used more than it is used at the present time.

## 16. The Technique of Good Deeds

Of all the single techniques of altruization, the technique of good deeds is possibly the most effective and the most accessible for everyone. At the same time it is the necessary companion of all the other techniques, because if their use does not result in good deeds of the respective person or group, these cannot be considered to have been changed altruistically. *Fides sine operibus mortua est*, " faith without works is dead." [25] Furthermore, the technique of good deeds has possibly the least number of dangerous drawbacks. For all these reasons it is as important a technique as any, and probably more important than most of the other techniques.

In order to fulfill successfully its altruistic function, the good deeds, performed by the subjects of transformation, must be adequate or wisely chosen, fitting well the subjects themselves as well as the addressees of the good actions.

With this reservation, performance of friendly, helpful, and loving actions can be prescribed for any person and group at any stage of their altruistic education. It can be recommended even when such a person or group profoundly dislikes the addressees, and does not have any enthusiasm for doing good deeds for them. An age-old experience, well confirmed by our experimental studies,[26] shows that after a sufficient number of repetitions, the good actions, performed at first in a cold, unenthusiastic way, begin to exert (according to James-Lange theory [27]) their influence upon the performer. "Cold" or mainly external good deeds awaken friendly emotions and affections, become hearty and spontaneously desired to be rendered. The inimical attitude towards an enemy begins to melt; cold service and cold co-operation turn into warm sympathy and good will. Eventually hate gives place to a sort of indifference, then to a real and warm friendship. Repetition of good deeds instills eventually love even towards one's enemy, as Jesus correctly stated.

The outlined change of heart is depicted only in the main line of the transformation. In actual reality, depending on many individual conditions, this main line has variations. Some of the individuals undergo the described change quickly, others slowly, with many setbacks; some reach the stage of warm friendship, others only pass from hate to indifference; finally, there are some who either remain unchanged or even regress from indifference to hate. Under the condition of a sufficient number of repetitions of adequate good deeds towards an enemy, however, the regressive change happens very rarely, if at all.

Besides changing the doer of good deeds, the technique also changes the addressees of the good actions. Even an enemy-addressee, "bombarded by good deeds" of his previous antagonist, rarely remains unresponsive. The good deeds speak louder than good words. Exposed to the friendly action of his enemy, the addressee can hardly help being forced sooner or later to re-examine his attitude to the doer and to admit eventually that his enemy behaves as a friend rather than as an enemy. Persistence in doing good deeds increases this impression, and in most of the cases progressively weakens the enmity and reinforces a responsive friendship. Such is the general course of the change in the addressee of good deeds.

In the mentioned experimental studies of this Research Center, in Chapter Four of this work on the power of love, in the preceding sections of this chapter on the technique of exposure to love, and in other chapters of this work; in several studies published in the first Symposium of this Research Center,[28] and in many other works the substantial body of evidence given demonstrates the notable effectiveness of the technique of good deeds. For the purposes of moral ennoblement, there hardly is any single technique that can compete with it. It is more effective and works faster than most of the preceding procedures, not to mention psychoanalytical and similar techniques.

Its efficacy is well confirmed also by the method of establishment of friendship between ourselves and dogs, horses, and other domestic as well as wild animals. Beginning with our " domestication " of squirrels, chipmunks, birds, and ending with acquiring the unlimited loyalty of dogs who are faithful unto death to their masters, millions of such friendships have been established mainly through the technique of good deeds on our part towards the animals. Rarely, if ever, has any friendship with them been achieved through aggressive actions or without use of the technique of good deeds.

As mentioned, its additional merits are that it can be practiced by everyone, at almost any time, and has hardly any demerits. It is regrettable that it is used much less than it should be used, especially in intergroup and international tensions. Here, the " big stick " policy, intimidation, coercion, stimulation of animosity, infliction of mutual destructions, up to the deadly technique of unlimited mass murder and total war still are overwhelmingly dominant. The use of the technique of good deeds is still contemptuously called " appeasement," " surrender," " impotence," " cowardice," and the like. In the field of politics the carnivorous policies of unteachable politicians and diplomats with the attendant human stupidity still blossom. No wonder that instead of peace and friendship such policies generate but bigger and bloodier wars. Is it not time to stop this murderous insanity?

## Chapter Eighteen

# The Techniques of Altruistic
# Transformation (concluded)

### 17. *The Techniques of the Inner Integration and Reintegration of One's Egos, Values, and Norms of Conduct*

Ego-centered and, especially, ego-transcending altruistic transformation is impossible without a corresponding change in the structure of one's egos, values, and norms of conduct, as we have seen. The altruistic integration or reintegration of egos, values, and norms of conduct has to be done by the individual himself, by his own effortful thinking, meditation, volition, and self-analysis. Other persons can help in this difficult task, but they cannot replace the active efforts of the individual himself.

The main techniques for a successful performance of this operation are: a) self-identification of the individual with unselfish love; b) private and collective prayer; c) examination of conscience; d) private and public confession; e) private and public vow; f) meditation and contemplation; g) psychoanalysis. Let us now concisely outline each of these techniques.

### 18. *The Technique of Self-Identification*

We have seen that one of the very first steps in the altruistic integration or reintegration of one's egos, values, and norms of conduct consists in a self-identification of the individual with the value of unselfish love in either its low-grade or sublimest form. The individual begins to view his " true self " as generous, kind, and friendly. He rejects the idea that his " highest self " is rampantly egoistic. If he continues to think, speak, and act selfishly, he considers such thoughts and actions as alien to his real self, as a weakness, sin, vice, and moral failure imposed upon him by his " lower nature," or by the force foreign to his true self.

At its preliminary phases the self-identification is now semi-conscious and vague; now clear but purely intellectual, without deep roots in the emotional, volitional, unconscious, and behavioral realms of the individual; and at still other times it is mainly emotional and affective without a distinct ideological definition of its nature. With its maturation, the self-identification increasingly becomes total: ideological, emotional, volitional, and behavioral.

If the self-identification stops at its initial phase, its influence does not penetrate tangibly the realm of the unconscious drives and overt actions of the individual. He remains a merely ideological or " wishful " altruist practicing little, if at all, the virtue of unselfish love he preaches. If through his efforts and interplay of various altruistic factors his self-identification progresses, it increasingly penetrates his emotional, volitional, and unconscious forces, and begins to control his overt actions. When the self-identification is mature, he becomes not only an ideological and wishful altruist, but also a behavioral altruist who actually practices what he preaches.

If the individual becomes just a good neighbor or ego-centered altruist, his self-identification with utilitarian, hedonistic, and eudaemonistic love or friendship can suffice. If, however, the individual grows into an apostle of sublimest love, he usually identifies himself (see Chapters Eight, Nine, and Ten) with the value of love at its purest and best, with Love as God or Love as the highest value.

This shows the extreme importance of the kind of value or self with which individuals and groups identify themselves. Their total personality and their behavior is tangibly conditioned by what they think and feel about their true nature. If they sincerely identify themselves with " matter," a " reflex mechanism," or with a " human animal," controlled mainly by the drives of sex, destruction, death, hunger, and by the stern laws of self-preservation and struggle for existence, such a self-identification, when sufficiently progressed, tends to turn such individuals, with their egos, values, drives, and actions, into this sort of human animal.

Herein lies the poisonous influence of Freudian and similar " therapies " that insist on this sort of self-identification of their fellow men and patients, that depict man mainly as a libidinal and aggressive creature, that interpret the greatest cultural values and creative geniuses, including Jesus, St. Paul, Buddha, St. Francis and others, in these libidinal and animalistic terms. These " therapies " utterly degrade also fatherhood, motherhood, childhood, and other values in their muckraking ideologies. In our overripe Sensate age, there is a plethora of such opinions and therapies parading under the name of modern scientific theories. Their theoretical and practical identifications of man with a perverted animal, with genital, anal, and oral libido, " id," and the instincts of death and sadistic aggressiveness have contributed a notable share to the modern demoralization of humanity and to the explosion of interindividual, intergroup, and international mass murders on a scale hitherto unknown to mankind. If we want a mitigation of this human bestiality, these phantasmagoric identifications must be replaced by those that view man not only as a perverted organism, but also as a rational mind and, especially, as a free agent of the highest and most creative supraconscious forces in the world.  Such conceptions of man's nature are not only morally ennobling, aesthetically beautifying, mentally and creatively inspiring; they are also more scientific from the standpoint of truth and real knowledge.

19. *The Technique of Private and Public Prayer*

Prayer is a most sincere communion of the individual with his highest self, or soul, or God, or with the Supreme Cosmic Power.  However conceived — and they are conceived differently by different persons, groups, and cultures — this self, or soul, or God, or the Supreme Cosmic Being is always intuited as something far transcending the individual in power, wisdom, glory, creativity, goodness, and other highest virtues.  This communion usually contains either an appeal for help in the critical situations of anguish, sickness, stress, danger, approaching death; or a spontaneous thankful and joyous gratitude in the moments of joy, victory, and success; or a desire to be in a close communion with the supreme power; or else an honest confession of one's vices and errors with an intention of freeing oneself from them in the future.

*Prayer may be vocal and silent.  It is done privately and publicly.*  Its concrete forms widely vary from person to person, society to society, culture to culture, period to period.  Varying in its historical forms, prayer in its general nature is a universal " constant " of human activity, given in all societies, at all times, and in some form indulged in by almost all individuals.  According to P. Marinier,[1] it is a reflex about as constant and universal as are the " reflexes " of sex, sleeping, or eating.  Its historical forms are the " conditioned reflexes "; its essential core represents something that can be called the " unconditioned or natural reflex."  It is practiced not only by the believers, but also by the disbelievers and atheists because these, too, indulge in a praying communion with their own " self," " soul," " ego," " conscience," " mind," " cosmic force," " destiny," " the power of the emergent evolution," " the creative power of nature," and the like.  Now and then they also appeal to something far greater than their ordinary egos or personality — especially in the moments of anguish, distress, sickness, danger, approaching death, or in the moments of great joy, victory, and success.

Prayer may be *egoistic and altruistic.*  Though gradations of these forms imperceptibly pass into each other there is, nevertheless, a profound difference between their extreme patterns.  The egoistic prayer is always an appeal for help or thanks for success in the selfish aspirations of the praying individual or group.  It has in view exclusively the interests of the praying subject.  Its rudest form is represented by the prayers for something that can be accomplished only at the cost of somebody else.  A businessman praying for successful competition with his rivals; a mother praying for victory of her own son over the competitors; a nation praying for the utter ruin of an inimical nation; a religious congregation praying for the complete destruction of an enemy by its army; a lover praying for success over his competitors; a man asking God to impose death upon his enemies; a prostitute praying for success in her trade: these prayers exemplify the most vulgar forms of egoistic prayer. They want to make God a mere helper and participant in the selfish and often bloody preoccupations of the praying persons or groups.

Somewhat less egoistic are the prayers in which the subjects ask for something personal but not necessarily injurious to others. A sick man praying for his recovery, a poor man praying for his daily bread, a mother praying for her own well-being and that of her family are examples of less egoistic prayers.

By their *content* the vulgar egoistic prayers hardly contribute anything to the spiritual and altruistic growth of the persons and groups. If anything, their content makes them selfish rather than altruistic. Even this form of prayer, however, may exert some altruistic effects — not through its content, but through the belief in, and feeling of, a power higher and nobler than the praying individual or group, through the clumsy efforts to get in touch with such a superior power, and through the desire to be a participant in it.

The subject of altruistic prayer never asks for any boon for himself at the cost of others. If he requests a grace or help or value, he always asks it for *all* or *for others*. " Give *us* this day our daily bread. And forgive *us* our debts as we forgive our debtors." It is " us " and not " me " or " my in-group " for whom the Lord's Prayer prays. In altruistic prayer one's egos are entirely transcended by a complete surrender of the praying subject to the superior power. "Thy kingdom come. Thy will be done on earth as it is in heaven. . . . For thine is the kingdom, and the power, and the glory, forever." The main objective of such a prayer is a dissolution of one's lilliputian egos, interests, and aspirations in the " Thy will be done," in the infinitely greater Supreme Being, however it is called and conceived. Altruistic prayer strives to free the supraconscious in man from the shackles of his little egos for the union with the Supreme Supraconscious. Such prayer tends to turn our organism and our unconscious and conscious mind into an instrument of the supraconscious in us and, through that, of the Cosmic Supraconscious. By transcending our unconscious and conscious forces, altruistic prayer tends to bring out our true self and to merge it with the Cosmic Self. Dissolution of our egos in it does not mean a loss of our identity; on the contrary, it signifies only the loss of the chains of the unconscious and conscious forces that shackle our true self. Our real identity is located in this self and not in the chains. Its liberation and its union with the Cosmic Self represents not denial but affirmation of our identity.

In these and many other ways altruistic prayer serves as a marvelous road for a pilgrimage to the magnificent peaks of spirituality and altruism. P. Marinier admirably describes this role of altruistic prayer.[2]

The use of prayer to obtain a satisfaction of desire [egotistic prayer] remains a primitive manifestation of spirituality. From this standpoint there is no essential difference between prostitutes going on pilgrimage to obtain success in their trade and the prisoner praying for release. Psychologically, one case is no more a departure from the tendency of the ego to satisfy and fortify itself than the other. The personal complex is only seeking to use forces beyond itself for its conservation. Still, this is a necessary stage in spirituality as in life. After all, it constitutes a first go at getting beyond the individual, for in itself it is a recognition of that which exceeds the ego, an attempt at relation and at growth. The individual can only arrive at intimate conviction of the existence of psychic forces and of their power by the way of this [egotistic] prayer. It is realization of desire that opens the gates to a higher knowledge, makes one suspect that this realization hardly brings liberty and that liberty is what genuine spirituality should necessarily lead to. When the gates of this knowledge have been passed, prayer for self becomes increasingly rare and is progressively replaced by prayer for others and for the world, and, finally, by the great oblatory and glorifying prayer in which the ego complex loses itself to exalt only the undifferentiated and Cosmic Self which contain it. Prayer, at first narcissistic and captive, becomes an expression of the tendency to self-forgetfulness, to sacrifice, to oblation.

When the ancient Vedic hymns chant the identity of all that is, when the Catholic church intones *Te Deum laudamus*, when the psalmist, in the *Canticle of the Three Hebrew Youths*, attributes to the sun and stars, to mountains and rivers, to beasts and herds a consciousness which causes them to glorify God . . . when, again, Francis of Assisi sings his *Canticle to the Sun*, prayer attains a psychological and ontological reality quite different from the asking prayer. Here we get a losing of ordinary consciousness in a larger consciousness, the cosmic consciousness. . . . This cosmic consciousness is generally attained in exceptional states and the great majority of human beings are barely capable of suspecting its existence. Of it, however, the works of great mystics, great poets and great musicians give testimony. The mighty and serene art of J. S. Bach seems here to have drawn its essential inspiration. It is also of this world of liberty the *Ninth Symphony* of Beethoven sings. . . .

Being thus, first, response to anguish, next expression, then voluntary recapture and actualization of infantile and archaic impulses favorable to transcending the ego, prayer ends by ceasing to be a request for something from someone and becomes infinite gratitude for all that exists and for all that one is. It becomes hymn, canticle, chant. . . . The praying activity first produces a departure from the surface being in which we habitually live, from the preoccupations, thoughts and sentiments which characterize it; it next permits a controlled immersion in deeper layers of the psyche where infantile and ancestral impulses have their seat; it finally opens the way to the undifferentiated and universal being which is that of cosmic consciousness and of liberty. At this point, human determinants and conditioning are seen in advance as a sport of nature which in no wise affects the deeper being or the ultimate Observer with whom it identifies itself henceforth.

Reaching this identification with the Cosmic Supraconscious, a praying person or group attains at the same time the peaks of sublime love. Everything and everybody becomes the end value in this state of consciousness. God opens in man and man becomes a son of God. At these peaks, prayer becomes a blissful meditation in which the boundary line between the meditating person and the object of his meditation vanishes — and vanish also man's egos with all their selfish drives, wishes, and ambitions.

As we shall see further, however, this sort of meditation-prayer as a lasting state is accessible only to very few heroes of spirituality and love. For the rank and file, only somewhat lower forms of meditation and altruistic prayer are accessible. Marinier correctly remarks that

prayer remains more adapted to the human state, to its contradictions, to its advances and regressions, to its weaknesses and debasements. It is not the exclusive prerogative of saint or seer. The criminal, the invalid, the outlaw, the mediocre may resort to it with equal efficacy. It is the instrument whereby each may hold even his most sordid desires up to the light which will purify them. It is a method for facilitating the individual's correct responses to situations in which ancestral experience knows the dangers and peculiarities. It is a discipline for unification of self with self and self with the world. Modern man often claims to reject it because it appears in conjunction with creeds or dogmatic conceptions to which he cannot adhere. But psychological value of prayer is independent of these creeds in their dogmatic form. . . . Modern man by refusing to pray deprives himself of the most fecund forces from his past and from his secret being. These forces remain unused, even repressed, while the individual, whose consciousness is no longer linked to the universal, flounders at the superficies of himself in an illusion of liberty which conceals profound dissociation and despicable ignorance. For the vast majority of us, prayer meanwhile remains the only [I would say one of the few] practical road to physical and moral recovery, to reconciliation with our ancestors, to comprehension and acceptance of the real, to liberty itself, for all these things have existence only in the One which it discloses to us and of which it is the first awakening within us.

As mentioned, prayer may be *vocal and silent*. Even among the saints, many (like St. Theresa, St. Francis de Sales and others) prefer silent prayer. It depends upon the individual which form of prayer is better for him. Vocal prayer may be spoken or sung either in the words of the existing, traditional, ritualistic prayers, or it may be said in the praying person's own words, spontaneously coming from his heart. Again, which of these forms is more fruitful depends upon the individual. Some pray now in the words of the traditional prayers, and now in their own words. For the majority the traditional prayers are probably easier and more fruitful: most of the approved prayers are marvelous in their meaningfulness, pointedness, and poetical beauty. The Lord's Prayer is an excellent example of these traditional prayers which permit of expression everything the individual wants to pray for. Then too, the traditional prayers make unnecessary any special effort of inventing one's own prayer. Many of us can hardly make such inventions easily, and can rarely utter words as pointed and beautiful as those of traditional prayers.

There are, however, persons and groups who can pray more earnestly in their own words coming from their deeper self. Even among the eminent altruists and saints many prayed in this way. In each case the matter has to be decided by the praying person himself.

The same is to be said of *private and public praying*. Some pray more fruitfully in private, as it is advised by Jesus. The majority probably prays more earnestly in public. Many use both forms of praying: public and private. Again among the saints and the eminent altruists a considerable number prayed alone: most of the hermits, and many living in the busy world. They follow the words of Jesus: " When thou prayest enter into thy closet, and when thou hast shut thy door, pray to thy Father which is in secret; and thy Father which seeth in secret shall reward thee openly." [3]

Collective praying has its advantages and disadvantages. Its main merit is its interstimulation, which Marinier pointedly describes. In collective praying, he says,

the Cosmic Being sings through the lips of suppliants and prays through their gestures. The god chained in each individual in collective praying breaks its chain: it speaks and acts through hundreds of thousands of tongues and arms. It rises from the multitude of consciousnesses where it was buried to transcend them in its true identity and stature. Barriers, distinctions, and separations being then effaced or blurred, its limitless power spreads through the distress zones or to the resistance foci of the great body assembled there. It is then that the hardest hearts melt, that paralytics walk, that the deaf hear, and the blind see. The physical and spiritual cures [in such collective prayers] are the fruits of the emergence of the deeper Being in the community of suppliants, of the flow of its purifying waters in the souls and bodies which are its manifestations in the universe of multiplicity.

In spite of this marvelous interstimulation, there are individuals for whom individual praying is better and moments of life when the individual prayer-meditation is more fruitful — especially when the prayer is silent or reaches its peaks of spirituality and love, or when it passes into the deepest meditation described. For such individuals and moments private prayer is better. In these conditions, the presence, words, and actions of a collectivity are but distracting obstacles. Private prayer is more suitable also for many a modern man who is skeptical in regard to creeds, dogmas, and rituals. With their rejection of dogmas and creeds they cannot earnestly pray amidst a collectivity. They can pray and do pray in their own way in private: sometimes in a room listening to Bach, Mozart, or Beethoven, sometimes in their self-analysis and " examination of conscience," and sometimes in the conditions of stress and anguish. Once in a while in these prayers they also reach the " feeling of the presence " of the cosmic power called by them " genius," " nature," " creative matter," " emergent evolution," and so on. For many a believer such names sound profane and atheistic; in fact, however, they often designate a spiritual and altruistic experience as high and pure as that of the religious saints and apostles of love. One must be able to see a genuine prayer behind the misleading names.

To sum up: altruistic prayer is one of the most accessible and fruitful ways for spiritualization and altruization of human beings and groups. The more of this sort of prayer, the better for all of us.

Supplication, worship, prayer are no superstition; they are acts more real than the acts of eating, drinking, sitting or walking. It is no exaggeration to say that they alone are real. Such worship or prayer is no flight of eloquence; it is no lip-homage. It springs from the heart. If, therefore, we achieve that purity of the heart when it is " emptied of all but love," if we keep all the chords in proper tune, they " trembling pass in music out of sight." Prayer needs no speech. I have not the slightest doubt that prayer is an unfailing means of cleansing the heart of passions. But it must be combined with the utmost humility.[4]

So Gandhi sums up his own history. Similar are the statements of practically all eminent apostles of love, based upon their own vast experience.

## 10. *The Technique of Conscience Examination*

This technique consists in one's sincere and critical appraisal of his own secret and open thoughts, wishes, words, and deeds experienced during a certain past period of his life: during the preceding twenty-four hours, or three days, or week, or month, or just from time to time. The examination of conscience tries to bring to light especially one's hidden impulses in all their ugliness and one's reprehensible thoughts, wishes, words, and deeds in all their selfish and " sinful " reality. Here the higher self of the individual carefully examines and calmly registers what the individual's conscious egos and unconscious drives have done for the preceding period. Having done so, the self brings to the attention of the individual an objective balance of his good and bad doings for the period examined. Since the operation consists in face to face communion of a person with himself, since there are no witnesses and no public, since the examination is undertaken by free violition of the individual with a view to becoming better informed about his defects, and since the individual himself is here the examiner and the examined, the judge and the judged, there is no reason for the individual to be insincere, hypocritical, or secretive. He has no motive to hide from himself his defects, vices, and selfishness, or to deceive himself by painting his shortcomings in an embellished manner. When earnestly performed, the examination of conscience " excavates " as much of one's ugliest impulses, thoughts, and deeds as the Freudian " free association " technique can do. Even more: the technique of conscience examination performs this task without the possibility of sexual misinterpretations by a psychoanalyst and without other dangers involved

in the Freudian technique. ( See on these dangers further in this chapter
in the section dealing with psychoanalysis.)

The technique of conscience examination was discovered long ago and
has been widely practiced since the remotest past. In this or that variation
it has been used as a " standard technique " for spiritual and moral transformation in the oriental and occidental monastic brotherhoods; among
the Yogis, hermits, and a multitude of secular persons and organizations
anxious to maintain their moral standards. Among others, B. Franklin
was its devotee. In his *Autobiography* and other writings [5] he tells us
that at the age of twenty-two he " conceived the bold and arduous project
of arriving at moral perfection " and for that purpose he made a catalogue
of all the main virtues: Temperance, Silence, Order, Resolution, Frugality,
Industry, Sincerity, Justice, Moderation, Cleanliness, Tranquility, Chastity, and Humility. Desirous to " acquire the habitude of all these virtues
. . . . and conceiving then, that agreeably to the advice of Pythagoras in
his Golden Verses daily examination would be necessary, I contrived the
following method for conducting that examination."

I made a little book, in which I allotted a page for each of the virtues. I ruled
each page with red ink, so as to have seven columns, one for each day of the
week, marking each column with a letter for the day. I crossed these columns
with thirteen red lines [one for each of his thirteen virtues].[6]

Each day then he marked on these pages his progress or failure in mastering one of his thirteen virtues during the particular week. Viewing
the seven columns, one for each day of a week, he could see at a glance
his accomplishments for the whole week.

Franklin's scheme represents a variation nearest to Loyola's " visual
diagram " for daily and weekly examinations of conscience. Elsewhere
in this work a more detailed analysis of the monastic and Jesuit technique
of conscience examination will be given (see Chapters Twenty and
Twenty-One).

As mentioned, the examination of conscience has many variations. The
most common variety probably consists in daily examination, either in the
morning, or before going to bed. Examination usually ends with
prayer, or a decision to continue the efforts of one's moral and spiritual
improvement. A table of one's daily accomplishments and failures
whether of the kind of St. Ignatius Loyola,[7] or of St. Francis de Sales,[8] or
of B. Franklin, helps in a quick appraisal of one's performances. A one-
sided variation of this technique consists in a concentration on one's failures. While the examination of conscience registers moral minuses as
well as pluses, the remorseful self-condemnation sees only the minuses in
one's mental, moral, and physical doings. It focuses its beam of light on
only the negative phenomena. This one-sided self-analysis has been practiced by many a saint and a good man.

There is hardly any doubt in the effectiveness of this general technique when it is performed earnestly, in a humble spirit of one's many failures and one's sincere hopes for moral and spiritual improvement. By bringing to light his selfish deeds and impulses the individual becomes aware of them, and re-lives these experiences. By this operation he passes through a process of purification similar to the catharsis following an altruistic prayer, confession, or psychodramatic role-playing or the catharsis ascribed to psychoanalytical free associations. By becoming aware of his failures the individual begins to see his problems more clearly and can fight them more fruitfully. Dissatisfaction with himself for his failures, together with an accounting of his positive accomplishments, doubly stimulates him to further efforts in his altruistic growth. Contrary to a widely spread opinion, the sense of self-dissatisfaction, guilt, and remorse does not necessarily inhibit one's altruistic endeavors, especially when this sense is accompanied by the achieved successes. If anything, a dissatisfaction with oneself is a necessary condition for redoubling one's efforts for improvement in any field. It is not a sense of guilt or angriness at oneself, but narcissistic self-satisfaction that leads to a lazy " resting on laurels." Strong self-complacency in turn weakens the individual's strivings for further creative accomplishments in moral or other endeavors. When self-dissatisfaction is coupled with positive achievements, both factors neutralize possible negative effects of each other: dissatisfaction neutralizes the dangers of self-complacency, and the successes achieved disarm the sense of hopelessness which might ensue from too great a dissatisfaction or too deep a sense of guilt. Neutralizing the negative influences of each other, both senses doubly encourage the self-examining person in continuing his struggle for moral ennoblement.

These observations are well corroborated by the facts of altruistic growth of saintly and notable altruists. An overwhelming majority of these almost continuously experienced the deepest sense of guilt, of remorse, and of intense dissatisfaction with their sins, vices, and failures. They never tried to pass them by lightly or to brush them aside as something unimportant. They rather deliberately " inflated " them. On the other hand, they never despaired in the infinite mercy of God or the Supreme Being, and hardly ever doubted the fruitfulness of their efforts. As a result they never relaxed their altruistic and spiritual efforts, and succeeded in reaching the peaks of spirituality and love.

The same is true of the great creators in other fields of culture. None of them has rested on his laurels. All have often felt a deep dissatisfaction with their works, especially in the initial phases of their creations. On the other hand, all of them have been hopeful in the final accomplishment of their masterpieces. Only the philistine scholars and artists, pharisaic moral leaders and midget creators sometimes show narcissistic self-satisfaction. The great creators hardly ever have it.

The same has to be said of a multitude of good men and women. They also work under the double stimulation of self-dissatisfaction and hopeful accomplishment. The current fad of viewing a sense of guilt, remorse or self-condemnation as an obstacle either for recovery from mental illness or for mental and moral improvement is just a dangerous Freudian phantasma without any logical or factual basis. To sum up: an earnest and sincere examination of conscience is an effective and fruitful activity in some way to be repeatedly done by almost any person who tries to maintain and improve his altruistic progress.

### 21. *The Technique of Private and Public Confession*

When conscience examination is followed by confession of one's moral and spiritual failures to somebody else or to a community, the technique of conscience examination passes into that of private and public confession. To be effective confession must be earnest and searching; it must be made to a person or group with moral prestige and integrity, or one that serves as an agent of the highest moral power; it must be preceded by an awareness of, repentance for, and an urge to be free from, the selfish impulses, thoughts, words and deeds. The public or private confessor must not condone or minimize the failures of the confessed, if they are serious; at the same time he must accept the confession in the spirit of understanding, all-forgiving love, and hopeful encouragement of the future improvement of the confessing person. In some cases the confessor may suggest or impose upon the confessed some penance as a condition of absolution from the "sins" or moral failures. When such a penance is desired by the confessing person, when it is not too severe, and in the given circumstances can serve as a lasting stimulus for altruistic activities, it can play a positive role. The life history of many saintly altruists shows that they practiced such penances and tangibly profited by their disciplinary influence. Otherwise, penance should not be imposed or suggested.

The same is true of many psychodramatic details of public confession. In Christian and other monastic brotherhoods public confessions were performed sometimes amidst an impressive setting and in the most dramatic manner. The sinner was dressed in penitential rags, his head covered with ashes; stripped of his dignified paraphernalia he had to approach the community crawling or kneeling, or in a crouched position, weeping and crying for mercy. He had to confess before the altar of God, in the presence of the monastic community with its abbot or superior; until the absolution he was often severely reprimanded and censored, and sometimes even physical chastisements were inflicted. Variations of this sort of psychodramatic confession have been practiced since ancient times, in many preliterate groups, in practically all historical societies, among religious and secular communities, in formal and informal manner. For the details of these practices see Chapters Twenty and Twenty-One.

It is easy to see the unforgettable impressiveness of this sort of confession for the "sinner" as well as for the community itself. In a real way it combines all the cathartic influence of "make-believe" psychodramatic role-playing; of "digging the dirt" by the free association technique of psychoanalysis; of the technique of the client-centered therapy; of shock therapy; and of practically all the techniques of contemporary psychodrama, sociodrama, psychoanalysis, and other "psychological" and partly psychosomatic branches of psychiatry.

On the other hand, the technique can be so strong that in many cases it defeats itself. When carelessly applied, it easily degenerates into a mere procedure of punishment of the penitent. Instead of real repentance it can evoke in him an all-depressive hopelessness, a sense of shame, insult, unjust humiliation, and hateful rage against the community and its moral values, especially when this sort of public confession is coercively imposed upon the penitent. A study of the actual cases of such confessions well corroborates this expectation: if in a number of cases its effects were salutary, in other cases they were poisonous. For this reason, even the much milder forms of psychodramatic public confession can be applied only in exceptional cases and *never* without the explicit desire of the confessing person.

The net result of a fruitful confession must be the absolution of the confessed from his sense of guilt, remorse, hopeless failure, and all the inner tensions involved. Either after the confession or fulfillment of the penance, or after the final act of purification and reunion with the supreme power through sacraments similar to the Eucharist in Christian religion, the confessed person must feel himself purified from his failures, restored in his moral integrity, and set at deep peace with himself, his fellow men, and his God, however he conceives Him.

Since the technique of confession is found functioning in some form in practically all societies at all historical periods, there is hardly any doubt as to its restorative effectiveness: otherwise, it would not be a universal "constant" of all cultures. If useless or harmful, it would have vanished long ago from the moral history of humanity. Actual study of the practices of eminent apostles of love and of good men and women corroborates this conclusion: almost all of them practiced in some form this method of moral improvement and invariably found it fruitful. An analysis of it from the standpoint of contemporary knowledge entirely justifies its wise use. As mentioned, it contains in itself practically all the sound parts of the modern psychiatric, psychological, sociological, and educational therapies. In an effective form it exerts a cathartic influence upon the confessing person; it restores his peace of mind and moral integrity; it doubly stimulates him to further efforts in his altruistic growth. When done in a public form it is reinforced by the collective force of the community, by social disapproval of his failures, and by the most power-

ful collective empathy, sympathy, and encouragement. Even more: since
the confessional " excavation " of moral defects of the confessing person i
done after an establishment in him of the positive standards of altruistic
morality, his confessional immersion into his moral and spiritual muck doe
not drown him and does not demoralize him, as it unfortunately does now
and then in the therapies which bring about such an immersion without a
preliminary establishment of his moral standards. In such circumstances
the respective individual sometimes is hopelessly sucked in by his failures
without any firm support of the previously established moral and social
values.

In a concrete form properly adapted to each modern individual o
group, the technique of public and private confession can and should be
fruitfully used more frequently than it is practiced at the present time
For a believer in one of the institutionalized religions, it can be used in it
religious forms; for a freethinker, agnostic, disbeliever, or atheist, it can
be used in one of its secular forms. A beloved member of the family, a
real friend, a respected leader, a good teacher, or moral guide can serv
the role of confessor in the secular confession. After all, we must remem
ber that all the varieties of this technique used by contemporary educators
psychiatrists, or moral counselors were not invented by them in recen
times, but are borrowed from the age-old technique of confession prac
ticed fruitfully for millennia by the rank and file, and especially by the
wisest and greatest educators of humanity.

## 22. The Technique of the Private, Public, and Collective Vow

In close connection with prayer, conscience examination, and confes
sion is the act of taking a binding vow either of abstaining from certain
selfish deeds or of doing certain altruistic actions. When, after a seriou
preparation, it is freely taken with an utmost determination to fulfill i
unfailingly, such a vow serves as an additional stimulus to altruistic
growth. In these conditions the vow marks the final step in achieving a
given altruistic activity.

On the basis of his own experience, M. Gandhi well describes its im
portant function, difficulties and joys. Without taking any vow, fo
several years before 1906, Gandhi tried to achieve Brahmacharya or com
plete sexual continence in the relations with his wife. Finally,

after full discussion and mature deliberation I took the vow in 1906. . . . I ha
great difficulty in making the final resolve. I had not the necessary strength
How was I to control my passions? . . . . But I launched forth with faith i
the sustaining power of God. . . .

As I look back upon the twenty years of the vow, I am filled with pleasure
and wonderment. The more or less succesful practice of self-control had been
going on since 1901. But the freedom and joy that came to me after taking
the vow had never been experienced before 1906. Before the vow I had been
open to being overcome by temptation at any moment. Now the vow was

ure shield against temptation. The great potentiality of *Brahmacharya* daily became more and more patent to me. For *Bramacharya* was now no process of hard penance. It was a matter of consolation and joy. Every day revealed a fresh beauty in it. But if it was a matter of ever-increasing joy, let no one believe that it was an easy thing for me.[9]

This description well points out the reinforcing role of the vow in bridling the biological and selfish impulses and in facilitating the vowed altruistic efforts; it also suggests the joy and the difficulties involved in keeping the vow unbroken. In passing, it can be noted that this description is quite typical of hundreds of similar statements by St. Augustine, St. Jerome, and other saints as well as by eminent altruists about their experience in taking and keeping their vows of chastity, humility, unselfishness, love, and other altruistic and spiritual tasks. Unanimously they stress the same points as Gandhi's description does. (See some details in Chapters Nineteen to Twenty-One of this work, dealing with the monastic and other techniques of self-control.) A vow decidedly and freely taken, after the necessary preparation, exerts this reinforcing influence indeed, and gives a sense of finality to a lasting altruistic effort, whether it is the vow of nonsmoking and nondrinking, or of not causing any harm by thought, word, and deed to any man or living creature.

This, however, cannot be said of "vows" similar to the New Year's resolutions taken every year by thousands and just as soon broken. Their authors have neither necessary preparation, nor training, nor serious determination; nor do they view their resolutions as categoric imperatives. Such vows do not do any good; rather, they leave a sense of frustration, weakness, and purposeless dissatisfaction. As such, they should not be taken or advised.

For some individuals in certain conditions the private vow is more fruitful; for others in specific conditions the public or collective vow is more effective. When the individual makes his solemn vow in the presence of a group — the family, the monastic or occupational or other community — he reinforces his determination by the forces of the community, especially if it is sympathetic with his vow. When personal forces of the individual are going to fail him in keeping his vow, his responsibility to the community, with the possibility of publicly acknowledged shame and downfall of his prestige and self-respect, often comes to his rescue. In such conditions, now and then the additional force of his public vow saves the person from breaking it. In the cases where a private vow is likely to be insufficient, the public vow can be prescribed.

In certain situations the vow taken by a collectivity as a body and by each of its members proves especially effective. In the collective vow each member is stimulated to keep it by other members and by the collectivity as a whole. Direct and indirect influence of mutual interstimulation, as well as that of the whole group, is inestimable, especially in the long-lasting and difficult spiritual and altruistic activities where the temptations to break the vow are continuous and an incessant vigilance is required for a long time, sometimes for the rest of the life of the members. A breach of the collective vow involves not only the honor and integrity of its member, but no less the honor, the prestige, the dignity and integrity of other members and of the collectivity as a moral body. If a member is unable to resist the temptation for his own sake, he often is restrained from his breach of vow by considerations of the enormous harm done to his fellow members and to the collectivity itself. When a member is in danger of breaking his vow, he is reinforced in his struggle by the experience, empathy, sympathy, and direct help of other members and of the collectivity as a whole. In free collectivities where members mutually value and respect one another, and where they all highly appreciate the collectivity itself — be it the family, religious, political, racial, national, ethnic, occupational, or other group — this restraining and helping role of the collective vow plays an important part. Collectivities like the Alcoholics Anonymous, the Boy and Girl Scouts, monastic communities, religious groups, various brotherhoods, Masonic organizations, families, and various groups with honorable *esprit de corps* can serve as examples of groups bound by an explicit or implicit collective vow. Their successes in keeping their members from a breach of their code of honor are well demonstrated and known. The spirit of mutual responsibility and sympathy, reinforced by the implicit or explicit collective vow, are the springs of these successes. For this reason, in the situations described the collective vow can be strongly recommended.

### 23. The Technique of Psychoanalysis

Since we are dealing here with techniques for moral and spiritual improvement above the average level, we are not concerned with the psychoanalytical theory and therapy of the subnormal and abnormal mental disorders. For this reason our discussion of the techniques of psychoanalysis can be brief. It can be summed up in a simple statement: *psychoanalysis has discovered hardly any new sound technique for altruistic and spiritual transformation.* Practically all the psychoanalytic techniques which are sound represent a reproduction or variation of the above-discussed techniques discovered long ago and practiced for centuries and millennia. The specifically Freudian contributions have consisted mainly in the psychoanalytical theory and therapy of mental disorders. As to the main theories of Freud and the nondiluted Freudians, their scientific invalidity has been concisely shown above, in Chapter Five. These theories are rapidly losing their scientific prestige, and are increasingly being diluted and modified by the psychoanalysts themselves.[10] The moral and social effects of these theories have been destructive rather than constructive.

As to the Freudian therapies for mental disorders, in their unmodified forms they have hardly been practiced by competent psychoanalytical therapists. As a matter of fact, their therapies have not basically differed from those of the non-psychoanalytical psychiatrists.[11]   In addition, these therapies, as mentioned, deal mainly with "adjustment" of the mentally and socially sick, and not with the moral ennoblement above the moral standard of normal persons. For all these reasons there is hardly any necessity to go into the psychoanalytical techniques for a more detailed analysis.

### 24. *The Technique of Supraconscious Meditation and Creativity*

Supraconscious meditation is something very different from the usual intellectual activity of our conscious mind. The latter is daily performed by all of us in the form of ordinary thinking. It operates in our conscious activities. It functions also in our conscious altruistic doings. The individual performing an altruistic deed is usually aware of what he is doing, why, and wherefore, and what are the results of his actions. Thinking or "meditation" here is done mainly or exclusively by our conscious mind, with little or no participation of the supraconscious mind.

In supraconscious meditation and creative activity, the conscious mind with all its egos is absorbed or dominated by the supraconscious mind. The very consciousness or awareness of the egos tends to disappear entirely. The logic and psychology of the conscious mind undergo a substantial change. The logical laws of identity and contradiction are transcended by the supralogic of the *coincidentia oppositorum* — of the identity of the opposites. The supraconscious mind resolves the contradictions and antinomies of rational logic. It does this by the total, direct, unmediated self-identification with the meditated phenomena. In this meditation, the boundary line between the meditating person and meditated object tends to disappear: the person and the object, the knower and the known, tend to become one. Such an identification is inaccessible to the conscious mind. It always remains an outsider in regard to the cognized object, and in its mediated thinking there always exists the chasm between the knower and the known. Even when we have St. Thomas' *adequatio rei et intellectus*, this chasm remains. In this sense supraconscious meditation is something far more complex than a purely intellectual activity.

When intellectual thinking enters the first stages of supraconscious meditation, the conscious mind or the "mind-stuff," as Yoga calls it, becomes a mere "handmaid" of the supraconscious mind, wholly guided and controlled by it. On these lower levels of meditation, the supraconscious concentration "is accompanied by deliberation upon coarse objects, by reflection upon subtle objects, by joy, by the feeling of personality" (*asmita*). On the highest levels of supraconscious meditation and concentration the activity of the conscious mind-stuff (*citta*) is stopped altogether. The very purpose of Patanjali's Yoga is defined as the "restriction of all the fluctuations of the mind-stuff" which by its nature is "the restless, the infatuated, the distracted" and incessantly changing.[12] As such it only hinders the supraconscious concentration and for this reason needs to be stopped in its distractive and restless dynamism. With the cessation of its activity "the feeling of personality" ceases also. "When there is restriction of all the fluctuations of the mind-stuff, there is the concentration in which there is no consciousness of an object"[13] or of personality or ego.

Similar changes are undergone by all sensations, sense-perceptions, affections, emotions, and other psychological processes (*rajas, tamas, sattva*). On the lower level of meditation and concentration they may function under the guidance and control of the supraconscious. On the highest levels of meditation, their activity is stopped also. The supraconscious meditation becomes entirely free from their interference. The meditation becomes "single-pointed," identifies itself with the object of concentration, becomes one with it. In the terms of cognition this means the direct, full, and total cognition of the object of the concentration as the supraconscious mind's own part. In the subsequent chapter on Patanjali's Yoga system something more will be said of meditation and concentration. Here it is enough to say that real meditation is one of the highest ways for moral and spiritual ennoblement.

### 25. Auxiliary Techniques of Silence, Repetition of Short Formulas, of Ecstasy and "Kwats"

Of the auxiliary techniques for reaching supraconscious meditation, the techniques of silence, of repetition of short prayer, of ecstasy and Zen "kwats and kwans" are to be mentioned.

The deeply meditating persons do their meditation in silence and often without use of any words. Many of the Persians, Hindu, the Buddhist, and the Christian saintly altruists meditated in silence. Some of them kept silence for months and years. Recently so also did Sri Aurobindo in the last few years of his life. Silence is accompanied sometimes by an immobile posture of the body lasting for hours. Silence and immobile position facilitate the single-pointedness of their meditation and restrain the interference of the dynamic mind-stuff and of the unconscious drives. In meditation about the ultimate reality which is unutterable, inexpressible, and indefinable, words, verbal terms, and concepts cannot help much; if anything, they can rather mislead by replacing the total living grasp of the inexpressible whole by one of its differentiations embodied in verbal definition. For these reasons supraconscious meditation is often going on in silence, without any words or verbal concepts.

Other meditators find a monotonous repetition of short prayers, or "mantra" or formulas helpful. It helps to "put asleep" the dynamic mind-stuff and the no less dynamic drives of the organism. The monotonous repetition of the formula is often accompanied by repetition of simple movements like fingering the beads of a rosary, or making a genuflection. These serve the same purpose of quieting the fluctuations of the conscious mind and of unconscious forces. Putting these asleep does not mean, however, a somnolence of the supraconscious. On the contrary, freed from these disturbances, it becomes open only to its "subliminal impressions" and more fully turns the meditator into its instrumentality.

As a preparation to supraconscious meditation some, like the Sufist mystics, employ violent movements and similar techniques to induce a state of ecstatic absorption by the supraconscious. As the cases of Rūmī, Al Hallaj, Al Ghazzali, Dhu'l-Nūn, Abū Yazīd, Abū Sáid and of other great Muslim mystics and saints show, this technique also helps some meditators in reaching their task.[14]

Finally, in the Zen Buddhism the technique of "kwats" and "kwans," enigmatic answers by the master to the questions of the disciples, is used for the stimulation of the supraconscious meditation. Here are two examples of the kwat and the kwan.

A monk asked Joshu, "I read in the Sutra that all things return to One, but where does this One return to?" Answered the master, "When I was in the province of Tsing I had a robe made which weighed seven chin."

When Kwazan was asked what the Buddha was, he said, "I know how to play the drum, rub-a-dub, rub-a-dub."[15]

The purpose of these seemingly incoherent answers consists in the awakening of supraconscious meditation in the disciples by a peculiar stimulation of their inner thought process. This technique follows from the basic premises of Zen cognition.

To conceive the truth as something external which is to be perceived by a perceiving subject is dualistic and appeals to the intellect for its understanding, but according to Zen we are living right in the truth, by the truth, from which we cannot be separated. . . . Zen never appeals to our reasoning faculty, but points directly at the object one wants to have. [When one of the masters was asked] "What does it mean when they say that in spite of our having it every day we do not know it?" [the master offered to the questioning person a piece of cake. When, after eating the cake, the questioning person asked again the same question, the master answered]: "Only we do not know it even when we are using it every day." [The function of these answers is] to make the seeker of the truth directly realize within himself what it is, and not to make him merely the possessor of a second-hand knowledge. "Ein begriffener Gott ist kein Gott," declares Terstegen.[16]

The real Yogis who have reached these peaks of the meditation and concentration; the real mystics who achieved the final stage of the union with the Infinite, the Unnamed, the Unutterable, the Indefinable, and the

Inexpressible, symbolically called now God, now Tao, now Nirvana or Yen, Brahman or Atman, now " the Divine Nothing " or " the All in All," now " the Cosmic Mind," " the Supraessence," " the Ground " or " the Oversoul "; the saints for hours immovably immersed in their meditation-prayer and totally absorbed in their direct vision of, and communion with, the Supreme Being: these give examples and a notion of the meditation discussed. Only those who have experienced it know its nature adequately; those of us who are not blessed by this grace can know of it only indirectly and very inadequately.

In a modified form the greatest creative geniuses reach this peak also at the moments of their highest supraconscious creativity: in arts and sciences, in religion and altruistic love, in philosophy and technology. At such moments the supraconscious turns their organism, their unconscious forces and conscious mind-stuff into its monopolistic instrumentality. At such moments of creative grace Buddha and Jesus, Plato and Kant, Mozart and Bach, Phidias and Michelangelo, Isaac Newton and their like lose the feeling of their personality, transcend their own egos, acquire an insensitiveness to the disturbing interferences of their unconscious drives, conscious mind, and their empirical milieu: they turn to be " single-pointedly " absorbed in their creative *élan* and become one with their creation. And the higher the pitch of their creative inspiration, the greater their immersion into the supraconscious. When the moments of this grace are over, they relapse back into the state of common mortals subject to the many infirmities of the human organism, of the unconscious drives, and of the conscious mind-stuff.

The same is true of supraconscious meditation and creativity in the field of moral reality. When, after many efforts of " ascendance of the ladder of moral perfection," the seekers of the all-giving and all-forgiving love reach the peaks of supraconscious meditation and creativity, they also become the mouthpieces of the supraconscious. It is at such moments of grace that they become the moral lawgivers, the moral seers, the unfailing prophets, and the immortal moral teachers of humanity. Immersed in supraconscious meditation under the bo tree for many hours, Buddha achieved his Enlightenment and discovered the eternal moral verities. Similarly, in the third month of the exodus of the Jews from Egypt, the Ten Commandments were " revealed " to Moses after his lonely meditation on the mountain.[17] During forty days of fasting and deepest meditation in the wilderness Jesus [18] discovered his Gospel of Truth and Sublimest Love. In similar meditations amidst the mountains he discovered the verities of the Beatitudes,[19] preached the immortal Sermon on the Mount, and experienced the transfiguration.[20] Likewise, after many meditations in the lonely cave Giovanni Bernardone was transformed into St. Francis of Assisi. He began then to preach and practice his Gospel of the Lady Poverty and Unbounded Love towards the whole cosmos and started his marvelous deeds of the all-giving service and all-forgiving love towards lepers, all human beings, every living creature, " the Brother Sun," " the Brother Moon," and towards the whole world. (See Chapter Twelve on the details of St. Francis' transformation.) The same can be said of practically all the apostles of love and the heroes of spirituality. They themselves unanimously acknowledge that all their moral verities were discovered and their sublimest deeds of love were done not by them as mortals, but by the supraconscious (God) that acted through them (cf. Chapters Six and Eight).

It is exactly at such moments of immersion into supraconscious meditation and creativity that the seekers of the sublimest love and spirituality discovered the eternal verities of moral and spiritual order, whether in their Taoist or Confucianist, Hinduist or Buddhist, Judaist or Jainist, Christian or Mohammedan variations. In small details these variations are somewhat different from one another. In their main themes they are, however, identical in all these religions. It is at the moments when the " chosen and anointed " are possessed by the supraconscious that the great religions are born, the eternal moral verities are uttered, the superhuman moral deeds are done, the true prophecies are spoken, the incurables are cured, the hopeless sinners are redeemed, the moral and spiritual mission of humanity is set forth, and its foundations are laid down.

What is still more significant here is the fact that many of these " anointed " discover, teach, and practice their verities without a serious labor of their conscious mind-stuff and contrary to their unconscious urges. The hour of the supraconscious grace over, they themselves as the mortals are often surprised at the thoughts, words, and deeds done by them in the state of supraconscious meditation and creativity.

It goes without saying that these peaks of supraconscious meditation and spirituality are reached only by the very few " anointed " and " chosen." For the overwhelming majority they are inaccessible.[21] For the rank and file only much lower forms of moral meditation and creativity are available — the forms dictated mainly by their conscious mind and urged by their vital needs. In spite of the lower level, however, these forms should neither be depreciated nor discounted in their influence. Such a rational meditation assumes the forms of the examination of conscience, of thinking of one's moral mistakes and improvements, of cultivation of the spirit of friendship and mutual aid, of scientific plans for improvement of one's own and of others' moral standards, for decreasing criminality, poverty, and disease, for increasing social service agencies, co-operative organizations, schools, recreation centers, youth organizations, religious institutions, community charities, and the like. Earnest thinking and doing along these planes lead the thinking individuals and the community to a notable ennoblement of their civic virtues and moral standards. In their totality these good thoughts and deeds, performed by millions, exert an enormous influence upon everyone and all. For these reasons the ordinary meditation and moral creativity of the rank and file have inestimable importance for the altruistic progress of mankind.

### Conclusions on the Integration and Reintegration of Egos, Values, Drives, and Actions

The above techniques, beginning with self-identification and ending with supraconscious meditation and creativity, are the main ways through which altruistic geniuses and craftsmen travel and reach their point of destination: a replacement of their unintegrated, disintegrated, or selfishly integrated personality by the integrated or reintegrated servant of love. The travelers ordinarily use not one but several of these techniques, in conjunction with the other techniques of altruistic growth outlined before those of the integration and reintegration. When wisely and repeatedly used, the techniques give not only ideological and vocal but also tangible behavioral transformation of the altruistic and spiritual pilgrims.

In order, however, that these techniques can be effective, they have to be paralleled by a corresponding — voluntary or involuntary — rearrangement of the pilgrims' group affiliations. Without such a rearrangement, many of these techniques can hardly be used, and, when applied, may remain largely fruitless.

### 26. The Techniques of Rearrangement of Group Affiliations

Above, in Chapters Five and Thirteen, it has been shown that each social group with which the individual is affiliated has its own ego and values in the totality of the egos and values of the individual, and its own demands upon his time, thoughts, aspirations, and deeds. In the same chapters it has been shown also that often the demands of different groups of our affiliations are mutually conflicting. Under such conditions, our egos, values, and actions representing the opposite groups also become mutually antagonistic. A person self-identifying himself with the supreme values of love and its respective groups must cut off all his affiliations with those groups whose demands contradict the love egos, love values, and love actions. Otherwise he would be, at best, only a wishful or ideological altruist, inconsistent even in his ideologies and speeches, not to mention his behavior. In such conditions he could not become a real altruist consistently doing what he preaches.

The rearrangement of one's group affiliations is not only necessary, but it is one of the most powerful factors of his progress of altruization. This factor works in two ways: negative and positive. When a would-be altruist cuts his affiliations with all the " anti-love " groups, he frees himself from all their egos, values, and pressures that inhibit his altruistic growth, make him waste an enormous energy in his inner conflicts, and impose upon him inconsistency and self-contradiction in his thoughts, aspirations, words, and deeds. Such a freedom from the inner inhibitive forces eliminates the most important obstacles for altruization, and thereby enormously helps our altruistic progress. On the other hand, affiliations with only altruistic groups positively promote our altruistic growth. Under these conditions, all altruistic groups urge and push us to altruistic conduct only. They become a unified system of forces that monopolistically push us in the same direction, inspire the same ideal, dictate the same duties, give the same kind of values, and require the same kind of deeds. The individual is pushed towards the same goal by a multitude of altruistic groups, without any competitive pressure of the anti-altruistic collectivities. The total influence of affiliations with only altruistic groups is inestimable: it is as great, and often greater, than the influence of any other single factor. This has to be stressed because the factor of group affiliations is all too often completely neglected or paid little attention by many contemporary educators, psychologists, psychiatrists, criminologists, religious and moral counselors.

To review what we have already said: this operation sometimes slightly precedes, sometimes follows the inner process of altruistic reintegration. More often the rearrangement of group affiliations goes on hand in hand with the inner reintegration. Without any exception, however, the late and the intermediary altruists had to solve and did solve this problem before they achieved the inner reintegration around Supreme Love. Some, like the hermits, solved it by cutting off all their group affiliations and isolating themselves in a wilderness. Others solved it by an explicit renunciation of all their group affiliations and by merging all their loyalties into one group, be it a monastic brotherhood, a religious group, a secular community, a specially created group, or mankind as a whole. Some solved it in other ways discussed before.

When their family opposed their altruistic or religious aspirations — and 29 per cent of the parental families of 3090 Christian saints opposed it,[22] they had to renounce their family. Doing so they followed Jesus' saying: " He that loveth father or mother more than me is not worthy of me; and he that loveth son or daughter more than me is not worthy of me." [23] When their friends, occupational, economic, or ethnic groups opposed their altruistic or religious self-dedication, they cut off their affiliations with these groups. Jesus again states correctly this renunciation by saying: " It is easier for a camel to go through the eye of a needle, than for a rich man to enter into the kingdom of God." [24] When their political party, or their caste, or religious group, or the state hindered their self-identification with love, they renounced their membership with these groups, as we have seen before.

Sometimes the individual solves the problem of reintegration without painful difficulties; sometimes the solution is exceedingly difficult, painful, and leads to martyrdom. Almost all the martyrs of the religion and ethics of love — and among 3090 Christian saints, 37 per cent died the death of martyrs, as we have seen — died because of their renunciation of the groups, especially of the state that demanded their loyalty to these "anti-love" groups and opposed their self-dedication to God as Love and Love as God. In these cases the painful rearrangement of group affiliations (and of the corresponding inner reintegration) becomes indeed the act of "taking the cross" and following the supreme value of love. Cutting off their affiliations with the anti-love groups and paying for it by their life, the martyrs of love followed the course beautifully summed up by Jesus: " He that loseth his life for my sake shall find it." [25]

The above reminds us of the importance of this operation of the rearrangement of group affiliations, already discussed in detail in Chapters Eleven, Twelve and Thirteen of this work.

### Concluding Remarks to This Section

The techniques outlined in this section represent all the main single techniques of the altruistic and spiritual transformation of man. Only the medico-pharmaceutic therapies for physical and mental diseases, and the methods of changing social institutions and cultures are omitted from this survey. The reasons for the omission of the medical techniques are obvious: these techniques, like lobotomy operations, electric shocks, injection of drugs, or hypnotherapy, belong to the field of biological, medical, and psychiatric disciplines. Since these disciplines deal with these techniques, there is no need to give any homemade duplication. They are to be determined and administered by the specialists of these branches of science. Furthermore, these therapies are applicable mainly to the subnormal, mentally and physically sick persons. In regard to the normal, and especially the supernormal altruistic individuals, they can hardly be used and be helpful. By a lobotomy operation, electric shocks, injection of a drug, prescription of a barbiturate, or hypnosis, one can hardly transform an egotist into an altruist, a sinner into a saint. For these reasons the techniques discussed are omitted.

Different are the reasons for the omission of the techniques of sociocultural change. There is not the slightest doubt that the character of the basic social institutions and culture exert an enormous influence on the psychosocial character of the individuals and groups living amidst and incessantly interacting with their institutions and culture. Elsewhere, it has been shown that personality, social institutions, and culture are three inseparable aspects of one indivisible sociocultural reality. If we want to change one of these aspects of the Sociocultural Trinity, we have to change respectively the other two aspects. Otherwise, the change in one aspect only is likely to be abortive. One cannot have an eminently altruistic population amidst egoistic social institutions and culture; and one cannot have an altruistic culture or institutions amidst an egoistic population.[26]

If we want to raise the moral standards of large populations, we must change correspondingly the mind and behavior of the individuals making these populations, and their social institutions and their cultures. This basic principle has been demonstrated in my *Reconstruction of Humanity*. It answers the questions of what exactly must be changed and how in the existing types of the family, the state, the school, and other social institutions as well as in the existing types of science, philosophy, fine arts, and other cultural systems, in order that they would mold less selfish and more creative human beings.

All this means that the paramount importance of the ways and techniques of the altruistic modification of social institutions and culture is neither overlooked, nor underestimated. If, however, the nature and the methods of their changes are not discussed fully in this work, the reason is that the scope of this work contains only the techniques of altruistic transformation of man. Altruistic change of institutions and culture does not eliminate a respective change of their members, but the techniques of the members' transformation are not identical with those of the change of social institutions and cultural systems. Even in an altruistic sociocultural milieu the individuals do not become creative and altruistic automatically. Very strenuous efforts and the use of specific techniques by the individuals themselves are necessary in order that their altruization be successful. For this reason, these techniques can be studied separately from those of sociocultural transformation.

Having outlined the above techniques and their underlying factors in their essentials, now we can continue our study of these techniques and factors in the form of the effective unified systems of moral and spiritual education of man. Of these systems we shall study the system of Yoga, the monastic systems, and the system of altruistic education in the brotherhood communities marked by notable altruism of their members and of the community as a whole. In this way we can obtain a better comprehension of these techniques and of their unified systems of moral education, as well as a deeper understanding of the dynamics and factors of the processes of altruistic growth.

We begin with an analysis of the Yoga system of altruistic and spiritual transformation.

*Chapter Nineteen*

# The Unified Techniques of Patanjali's and Other Yogas

## I

### THE BASIC IMPORTANCE OF PATANJALI'S RAJA YOGA

Whether through independent invention or, as in many cases, through diffusion from India, techniques of spiritual and moral transfiguration similar to the experimental techniques of Patanjali's Raja Yoga are found not only in all religious and philosophical schools of India [1] but in several other religions and cultures. Variations of these techniques or their truncated forms are found in Siberian shamanism, several ancient " mystery religions," in Taoism, Buddhism, Jainism, in Sufist Islam, in mystic currents of Judaism, among the Zoroastrians and other Iranian sects. They have been practiced in the Orphic, Pythagorean, and mystic currents of the Greco-Roman world: beginning with the Greco-Roman " mystery religions," Plato and the Platonists, and ending with Plotinus, the Neoplatonists, the Neo-Pythagoreans, the Cynics, the Stoics, the Gnostics, the followers of the cult of Mithra, Osiris, Isis, and other mystic and moral movements. Through Plotinus, the Neoplatonists, and other Greco-Roman influences, these techniques apparently passed into Christianity and became incorporated in its " spiritual exercises," religious and ethical training. The creed, philosophy, and ideology of these religions and ethics are different; their techniques of spiritualization are, however, similar to the Yoga techniques in many respects. [2] For this reason the techniques of Patanjali's classical Yoga deserve to be outlined somewhat more fully than many others.

Its ingenuity, experimental realism, and spiritual breadth and depth are unique in many respects. " The word Yoga occurs in the Rigveda in various senses, such as yoking or harnessing, achieving the unachieved, connection, and the like. . . . It, however, became gradually rarer and rarer in its original meaning, and it began more often to be used in the sense of yoking the senses." Instead of the original meaning of the control of the steeds, " the firm holding back of the senses, is what is called Yoga."

Eventually it "has come to be regarded as a method of attaining salvation." [3]   In terms of Patanjali's treatise, Yoga method means "the suppression of the functions of thinking principle" in the specific sense of the author; [4] or in another translation: "Yoga is concentration, which restricts fluctuations of mind-stuff. Then the Seer (that is the Self) abides in himself. At other times it (the Self) takes the same form as the fluctuations of mind-stuff." [5]

The Yoga system as a whole is a definite system of philosophy, close to the Sankhya philosophy; it is, at the same time, a system of religion, cosmology, physics, biology, ethics, psychology. And, finally, it is an elaborate method of complete liberation of the self or the immortal soul (purusha) as a pure intelligence from its connection with the prakriti, or mother nature, which is made up of three gunas (tamas, sattva, rajas) of a somewhat "material" character. [6] According to the Yoga philosophy, man is made up of the prakriti or "matter" through different combination of its "heavier and lighter" gunas (tamas, rajas, and sattva), and of self or "soul" (purusha) as a pure intelligence (though usually hidden in the folds of the prakriti). These two principles — pure intelligence and somewhat material prakriti — both are real and co-eternal. Material prakriti is ever-changing, ever in transformation and becoming. The purusha is unchangeable, everlasting being, the pure intelligence always identical to itself. [7]

In man, not only his body and biological properties of his organism are made up of the "material" prakriti, but also his mind with its sensation, memory, consciousness, emotions, ego, concepts, rational logic, and dialectic. This mind is not the purusha or self or soul. Made up mainly of the subtle forms of "matter" (sattva), the human unconscious and conscious mind with its urges, sensations, feelings, emotions, notions, and concepts is also an ever-changing, unstable, always on the move and restless form of the prakriti. As such it cannot be free from pain or pleasure, from desires and feelings, from emotions, ego, and from the will-to-be. Even as a cognitive organ the "bodily mind" or "mind-stuff" cannot attain the whole truth and nothing but the truth because its ego's perceptions, concepts, logic, and dialectic never annihilate the difference between the cognizing subject (ego) and the cognized object. As long as such a duality between the subject and object persists, and as long as the subject and object are not entirely merged into oneness, the bodily mind remains an outsider to the object, and as an outsider it never can grasp adequately any reality. Its descriptions, definitions, analyses, and measurements of the moon, or of any other object, are not the moon but merely words or mere "fingers pointing at the moon" (in terms of Zen Buddhism). [8] The concept is always concerned with something; it is never that something; it is never existential. A definition of a triangle is not a triangle: at the best we know only the relationship of the words pointing at the triangle but not the triangle itself.[9]  Still less is it possible for the bodily mind to know adequately the purusha, or the self or the soul.

In contrast to our prevalent conception of man as a dyadic " body and mind," Yoga as well as most of the Hindu and other oriental psychologies view man as a triadic being consisting of self (purusha), mind-stuff (the subtle forms of prakriti), and body (the coarse elements of prakriti). Here the self (purusha) is somewhat similar to the *nous* of the ancient Greeks and to the supraconscious as it is defined in this work.  Yoga's " mind-stuff " roughly corresponds to our " conscious mind," and Yoga's " body " corresponds to our conception of the biological organism with its unconscious, physiological processes.  From this triadic viewpoint, our dyadic ontology and psychology are grossly inadequate: they entirely miss the highest level of man's nature.[10]

Leaving out of this discussion many points of Yoga as a philosophical system, it can be indicated that the highest purpose a Yogin sets for himself is the liberation of his purusha or self from its ties with the material prakriti.  He wants to achieve *mukti* or transcendental freedom by rising above the limitations of body, life, and mind that are made of some alien or illusory stuff.  Only through such a liberation can he forever end the otherwise endless cycle of rebirths and redeaths with their inevitable egos, ignorance, pain and pleasure, tribulations and all other evils, generated by egoism acting through ignorance (avidya).  Only through the transcendental liberation can he attain full and complete truth and become a pure unsullied intelligence, eternal, indestructible, ever-identical to itself.

In difference from Kapila's Sankhya philosophy, the Yogasutra of Patanjali introduced — besides the purusha and the prakriti — an auxiliary agency, a sort of a deity (Iśvara).[11]

Isvara is the purusha that is free from any connection with the prakriti. The Yogin who reaches the transcendental liberation becomes himself identical with God (Iśvara).  " The ideal of conduct for a Yogin is the removal of ignorance and the realization of the true nature of the self," and thus ultimately a dissociation of " the soul from the bondage of matter," [12] and the attainment of " the absolute freedom of the spirit," (the *mukti*) or Buddhist Nirvana.[13]

This state of the pure intelligence is marked by an inexpressible bliss (though the bliss is a by-product), by omniscience, and by the Yogin's generally becoming divine in the best and highest sense of the term.

## II

### The Techniques of Raja Yoga

Such being the supreme objective of a true Yogin, Raja Yoga gives us a systematic method for its attainment.  This method shows the necessity of being supremely altruistic as one of the unavoidable first steps for the liberation of the self. For this reason Raja Yoga is also a system of techniques for altruistic transformation of the human individual. *Herein lies its importance for our study.*

The technique of Raja Yoga does not prescribe any particular asceticism or mortification of the flesh, as many other techniques do.[14] Instead it prescribes a system of physical and mental exercises which aim toward a full self-mastery over the body and the bodily mind. It does this through a series of procedures, each of which tries to use scientifically the properties of the body and of the bodily mind itself in order to bring them under a complete control of the self.

For a realization of this purpose, the Yogin must overcome, first, "*the five hindrances*": an undifferentiated consciousness or ignorance (avidya), feeling-of-personality or "ego," passion, hatred, and the will-to-live. Second, he must master "*the seven forms of discriminative insight.*" Third, he must practice "*the five abstentions*" from injury, lying, stealing, incontinence, from property. Fourth, he shall carry on "*the five observances*": cleanliness, contentment, self-castigation, study, and devotion to Iśvara. Fifth, he shall be trained in *the performance of postures;* sixth, in *regulation of breath* (these two steps giving an extraordinary control over the body and its processes). Seventh, he must master "*the withdrawal of the senses,*" and "*fixed attention;*" and, eighth, the "*contemplation and concentration.*"[15]

The whole course of Yoga techniques for the liberation of the self consists of "eight aids" or steps, physical and mental exercises. The first four of these are a preparation to the subsequent four. Practice in each step is not meant to be strictly chronological but somewhat simultaneous, especially the practice of the first four steps. Generally the practice of overt actions or physical exercises in postures and breathing are performed together with the prescribed mental exercises, without which purely physical exercises are ineffective for the purpose.[16] In a brief outline, these eight steps are as follows:

1. *Yama.* Unflinching practice of overt behavior of: nonkilling and noninjury (Ahimsa) by thought, word, or deed to any living being under any conditions whatsoever; complete veracity or truthfulness; speech to be employed only for the good of others and never for their injury (abstention even from speech if it is injurious to living beings); abstinence from theft, even from the very desire of unlawful or egotistic possession of things; continence (Brahmacharya) or restraint of the generative organ and control of sexual life; abstention from avariciousness in the form of the nonappropriation of things not one's own, of attachment to, and accumulation of, material things, up to nonreceiving any gifts. Through these overt practices (always discharged with a view to the liberation) the bodily mind is cleansed from impurities and brought by one step nearer

to the final goal. The same objective is pursued by the overt actions of the second step.

2. *Niyama.* Mental and behavioral practice of: external and internal cleanliness, contentment, purificatory actions, study and (for the believers in God) a complete self-surrender to God (or to the highest self), by making the God the motive of all actions. The niyamas aim to cultivate the strength of remaining steadfast during the changes of hunger and thirst, heat and cold, standing and sitting, luck and adversity, and change in social position. Generally, they aim to help in mastery of passions, emotions, and feelings that disturb the bodily mind. Self-surrender to God or to the highest value means an effacement of our ego and of all its tribulations, through the bestowal of all our actions to the Greatest Teacher or Value. By making ourselves a mere instrument in the hands of God (or His equivalent), by identifying our real self with the highest value, we are greatly helped in our endeavor of reaching our final goal. A complete transcendence of " ego-feeling " is the main objective of the niyamas, for this " ego-feeling " is one of the main hindrances to the objective of. a Yogin. The transcendence of ego-feeling means also an unselfish love: a complete self-abnegation, love for the sake of love, without any bargaining or expecting any reward for it. " By the cultivation of friendliness towards happiness, and compassion towards pain, and joy towards merit, and indifference towards demerit [the Yogin should attain] the undisturbed calm of the mind-stuff." [17]  For the believer in Iśvara or God, this transcendence of ego means love of God. " With the love of God comes, as a sure effect, the love of everyone in the universe," and self-surrender and joyful readiness to welcome pain, misery, death, even " going to hell " for the sake of love. Blessed is everything that comes from the Lover. " Ask not anything in return for your love; let your position be always that of the giver; give your love unto God, but do not ask anything in return even from Him." Such a self-surrender knows no fear, no rival, no apprehensions.[18]

Through these two steps, the Yama and the Niyama, man's body and mind are freed from egoism and ego, and are taken under a control of the higher self; man is enormously advanced toward his purpose. Practice in the yama and the niyama is done almost simultaneously with the physical practices of the next two steps which make up a part peculiar to the Yoga method and greatly facilitate the preceding, as well as subsequent, steps towards the liberation.[19]

3. *Asanas.* This step consists in a series of physical exercises in various specific postures. They aim to ease and to steady the mind and to obtain perfect control of various parts of the body: its organs, muscles, and glands. At the same time, they tend to make habitual a posture most favor-

able for the unobstructed circulation of the spiritual vital energy (Kundalini, the Serpent Power, akin to the Freudian libido, but of a spiritual nature) that has six centers along the spine, from its base (between the base of the sexual organs and the anus) to the cerebrum. This spiritual energy must be able to circulate freely along the spine with the progress of the Yogin towards his purpose. The easier and the higher it can rise the easier and fuller the process of the liberation becomes.[20]

" As a result of mastering the postures, [the Yogin] is not overcome by the extremes, by cold and heat, and by other extremes." [21]

4. *Pranayama*. Inseparable from the exercises in posture are those in breathing. According to Patanjali, in our breathing we do not merely inhale and exhale air, but are also doing so in regard to the vital energy. Therefore, being ingenious to the point of marvel, the system of these exercises has a far deeper significance than the mere expression " breathing exercises " can convey. Besides the mastery of breathing, of heart activity, and generally of the functions regulated by the autonomic nervous system, the purpose of pranayama is again restraint of our senses, steadying of our bodily mind, and loosening of the bonds between our material part and the purusha or pure intelligence. In their totality, the exercises in postures and breathing are so ingenious, complex, and precise, that they can be learned only under the guidance of a competent Guru-Yogin. When they are mastered, the results are truly astounding, especially in the control of the bodily processes, including those of heart and lung activities.

At the present time, we have sufficient evidence of these results, tested by Western scientists and registered by respective mechanical instruments, not to doubt the scientific validity and efficiency of the techniques of the asanas and pranayama. These results are such that contemporary Western science hardly can produce them, and hardly even knows their " how." Here is testimony of an eminent French medical scientist, a former chief of the Cardiological Clinic of the Medical Faculty of Paris University, Dr. Thérèse Brosse. In connection with her own experimental study in France she, together with other scientists, was sent by the French government to test and verify the Yoga techniques in postures and breathing. The result of many tests is summed up in the following lines taken from her report.

After years of training, phases of apnoea (suspension of breath) can last several hours: The longer the suspension of breathing, the greater the mastery of yoga. One of our yogis, as an experiment, had himself buried for ten hours under the observation of the medical corps of Baroda, who noted a tachycardia (rapid pulse) of 160, which quickly returned to normal. In the course of our examinations, the pneumograph registered repeatedly for ten to fifteen minutes these phases of apnoea so superficial that it was accompanied by no expansion of the thorax. By withdrawing what he calls vital energy, the yogin thus puts his body in a state of slowed-up life, comparable to that of hibernating animals. . . . The mastery of the yogin over his voluntary muscular system is such as to permit already such difficult postures, for example, as a lateral displacement of the long straight muscles of the abdomen, contracted; the result is abdominal massage. But this elective mastery is also extended to the smooth fibers, regulating at will the peristaltic and antiperistaltic motions, permitting in both directions the play of the anal or vesical sphincters and insuring by simple suction and without the help of any other instrument the penetration of liquids into the bladder or the rectum.

A still more prodigious feat was the willful control of pulse and heartbeat by the Yogis, as tested and registered by electrocardiograph, pneumograph, and other instruments.

Thus we find these yogis are masters over diverse activities. Knowing nothing about the structure of their organs, they are, however, the incontestable masters of appropriate functions. Moreover, they enjoy a magnificent state of health.[22]

5. *Pratyahara.* This step consists of withdrawal of the senses from contact with external objects or making our bodily mind introspective. Through a certain sort of mental exercises our mind is made to concentrate more and more upon itself. Becoming quite introspective its senses cease from coming into contact with external objects. The mind with all its organs becomes contemplative and self-centered. This stage imperceptibly passes into the exercises of the subsequent stages.

6. *Dharana.* These are exercises in the concentration of the bodily mind at one particular point, like the point in the heart, in the navel, the light point in the brain, the tip of the nose or of the tongue or any point in the body. By concentrating the mind on this point, by holding it to it for as long a time as possible, by not allowing it to wander to any other topic or place, the Yogin is making it steadfast, less and less wandering, less and less disturbed by any stimuli, and more and more single-pointed and self-penetrating. If one tries to perform such a concentration, he will see that without practice he cannot hold his mind at one point even for a minute. With increasing practice the duration of the concentration increases until one can hold his mind steadfast at such a point for an indefinitely long time. It goes without saying that during such a concentration our emotions, feelings, and senses all become inactive, dormant, or " frozen."

7. *Dhyana* or *meditation.* It is a continuation of the dharana, in which the object of concentration is considered from different standpoints or in its different aspects by a spontaneous flow of consciousness now free from feeling of effort. The stream of consciousness flows now by itself, unmediated and unstimulated by any extraneous force or by any break of the

conscious state. It develops by itself from the advanced concentration and goes on not so much in terms of discursive analysis or rational concepts, as much as in a superrational and superdiscursive manner.

8. *Samadhi.* This is the last step assuming the form of a superconscious transcontemplation. In this stage the duality of the subject and object disappears and both become one: "mind becomes transformed to the form of the object of contemplation." Samadhi has different degrees. He who reaches it, and especially its highest degree, reaches the goal of the liberation: becomes, at least for the period of it, a purusha or pure superconscious intelligence freed from the bondage to the "material" prakriti. "The Self's Energy of Thought becomes isolated, since it is grounded in itself, and is not again related to the *sattva* of the thinking-substance. Its continuance thus forevermore is Isolation." [23] Dr. Thérèse Brosse in her quoted work very clearly outlines the passage from the dharana to the samadhi stage.

The specific exercise of Yoga, the one which permits it to be reduced to a unique technique, is "mental concentration" or samyama. It is a concentration pushed beyond anything we can imagine, and divided into three periods. In the first, the attention is fixed upon a chosen object (a body organ, a feeling, a philosophical concept, etc.). It is a struggle against automatic mechanisms which have a tendency to distract the attention from it. The attention has to maintain itself upon the chosen object for a period of time determined by the will. It is the concentration of diffused attention and a focusing upon a single point (the single-pointedness of mind). The elements making up this first period are, therefore, triple: subject, object, and act of concentration. In the second period, consciousness loses awareness of effort and the inhibition of the unconscious processes is complete. The self has before it only the chosen object upon which the concentration, now happy and easy, can last indefinitely. There is now only a duality of subject and object; the feeling of effort has disappeared.

In the third period (samadhi), this feeling of duality of subject and object in turn disappears. The conscious being is indissolubly united to the object of its contemplation, melts into it and becomes identical with it. [24]

Being identical with the object, the Samadhi-Yogin knows it fully, without any mediation of any discursive logic or sensory observation and other "fingers pointing at the moon." Instead, he becomes identical with the moon itself.

The thing in this state does not appear as an object of consciousness, but the consciousness being divested of all "I," or "mine," becomes one with the object itself, so that there is no such notion here as "I know this," but the mind becomes one with the thing, the notions of subject and object drop off, and the result is one steady transformation of the mind as the object of its contemplation. This state brings to us the real knowledge of the thing divested of other false and illusory associations, which instead of explaining the real nature of the object, serve only to hide it all the more. The objects of this state are the grosser material objects and the senses.

In this stage mind is filled with supreme bliss or happiness.

When this stage of samadhi is reached, the Yogin directs his attention to finer and subtler objects, those from which the atoms are derived, then to still subtler ones, including the mind itself, until he reaches the last stage of samadhi or *nirodha*. " The mind in this state is in pure vacuity, so to say. . . . All the potencies [of mind and " I "] are destroyed, and at last the citta [the bodily mind] is annihilated in the sense that it returns back to prakriti, never again to bind the purusha." " Having passed beyond the bondage to prakriti, the purusha now shines forth in its own pure and ultimate freedom "; Man becomes equal to God or Iśvara.[25]

Thus, among other things, Yoga gives a solution to the eternal problem of direct and adequate cognition or the " Enlightenment " (prajna and jnana), in contradistinction to the purely discursive, indirect, logical, and observational knowledge of the intellect. This intellectual knowledge does not annihilate the unbridgeable chasm between the cognizing subject and the cognized object or reality. " When in opposing the subject and the object, philosophical theory abstracts them both from Being (reality), it makes the apprehension of Being impossible. To oppose knowledge and Being is to exclude knowledge from Being." The cognizing subject is put, under these conditions, outside of Being and the communion with Being becomes impossible for the subject of cognition. Therefore, the real cognition cannot be realized.[26]

This was understood long ago by the several Hindu and Buddhist philosophies, and was brilliantly demonstrated by their great thinkers and logicians. On the other hand, they gave us also the positive solution to the problem, namely, that the true Enlightenment and understanding, or the adequate knowledge (prajna, jnana), requires the most concentrated meditation, supersensory and superrational contemplation or mystic intuition that binds the subject and the object into one unity.

The Hindu and the Mahayana Buddhist logicians, such especially as the great Nagarjuna, Asanga, Vasubandhu, and to some extent Gotama, Dignaga and Dharmakirti (all lived between the first and the seventh century A.D.) demonstrated, with brilliant dialectical logic, that the nature of the true and whole reality " forbids every formulation by concept or speech, since they can only bifurcate reality and never directly seize it," and that " the real Buddha (or reality) can be perceived only directly by intuition "; that any attempt to cognize the true reality only through sense perception and discursive logic leads but to ignorance (avidya), and to inevitable self-contradiction of logical thought. This explains their throwing overboard sensory, logical, and dialectical cognition, so far as the true reality and its adequate comprehension are concerned. This true reality is simply " inexpressible," " unutterable," " indefinable," " indescribable " in words, notions, and concepts, by any logic or dialectic.[27] The true reality (Nirvana) is a *coincidentia oppositorium.* Thus, according to Nagarjuna:

> What neither is released, nor is it ever reached,
> What neither is annihilation, nor is it eternality,
> What never disappears, nor has it been created,
> This is Nirvana. It escapes precision (or definition). . . .

> Neither as Ens nor as a non-Ens
> Nirvana therefore can be conceived. . . .

> Insoluble are antinomic views
> Regarding what exists beyond Nirvana,
> Regarding what the end of the world is,
> Regarding its beginning.[28]

The Lankavatara Sutra puts it thus:

When thou reviewest the world with thy wisdom and compassion, it is to thee like the ethereal flower, and of which we cannot say whether it is created or vanishing, as the categories of being and non-being are inapplicable to it. . . . It is beyond the reach of mind and consciousness. . . . Of which we cannot say whether it is permanent or it is subject to destruction. . . . Real existence is where rises no thought of nature and no-nature.[29]

These thinkers well developed the dialectical method with its identity of the opposites and the dialectical thesis, antithesis, and synthesis. Many centuries later Hegel rediscovered it in the West. In difference from Hegel, however, they rejected the possibility of an adequate cognition through merely intellectual dialectic and sensory observation without the help of the superlogical or supraconscious intuition.

In their opinion the adequate cognition — the Enlightment or Illumination (prajna, jnana) — was possible only through mystic, direct intuition in the state of samadhi or its Buddhist equivalent, in which the subject of cognition and the cognized object merge into oneness. This intuition

is a faculty both intellectual and spiritual [affective and volitional], through the operation of which the soul is able to break the fetters of intellection. The latter is always dualistic inasmuch as it is cognizant of subject and object, but in the prajna . . . there is no separation between knower and known, these are all viewed in one thought, and the Enlightenment is the outcome of this. . . . Enlightenment is an absolute state of mind in which no " discrimination " takes place, and it requires a great mental effort to realize this state of viewing all things " in one thought."

Our logical and practical consciousness is too much given up to analysis and ideation. . . . We cut up realities into elements in order to understand them; but when they are put together to make the original whole, its elements stand out too conspicuously defined, and we do not view the whole " in one thought." [30]

This, as any other description of the intuitional grasp, is of course only a finger pointing at it without conveying its essence, which as such is unconveyable in any words and notions. The great Islamic thinker and mystic, ibn-Mansour Al Hallaj, hinted at it in saying " to know something adequately is to see not only the illuminated point [object we study], but also the darkness it is surrounded by." [31]

This Hindu and Buddhist solution to the problem of adequate cognition through samadhi-prajna-jnana or direct intuition goes beyond St. Thomas Aquinas's *adequatio rei et intellectus*.[32] The solution, together with the contention of an utter inadequacy of any intellectual cognition of true reality, has been flowing, with some variation, incessantly through philosophical thought and especially through the so-called mystic streams.[33]

Plato's " divine madness " as the supreme way of cognition of the true reality; Plotinus' theory of mystic cognition, influenced by the Hindu Yoga and Persian mystics: [34] and (through the influence of Plotinus and of other Neoplatonists) the mystic theories of some of the Church Fathers, like Clement of Alexandria, Origen, Pseudo-Dionysius,[35] Erigena, Maximus the Confessor, St. John of Damascus, Hugh of St. Victor, and so on, represent further variations of the mystic, intuitional theory of cognition. Meister Eckhart states the theory of the mystic union of subject and object, himself and God, explicitly. " Das Auge darin ich Gott sehe, ist dasselbe Auge, darin Gott mich sieht. Mein Auge und Gottes Auge ist ein Auge und ein Gesicht und ein Erkennen und ein Liebe."

The same is true of such mystics as Ruysbroeck,[36] St. John of the Cross,[37] the *docta ignorantia* of Nicolas of Cusa, and of J. Boehme, Pascal, and even Descartes [38] and Sir Isaac Newton (in their metaphysics). Finally, Hegel's dialectical logic is but a Western version of especially the Mahayana Buddhist dialectical logic of Nagarjuna and of others.

In various forms they all claim that the true reality cannot be adequately grasped through the rational mind of man, with its words, notions, concepts, and other abstractions which the subject of cognition makes about the cognized object. Putting himself outside of the object, a cognizing subject can never " identify himself with " or " participate " directly in the object; at best, he can only " point his finger at the moon " (through his discursive, inductive, deductive, and mathematical reasoning), never grasping the moon. Then, since the ultimate reality is infinite quantitatively and qualitatively, whatever notion, concept, definition of it is made, it is a finite notion of a finite human mind that does not exhaust the infinity at all. At best, it points only at one of the infinitely numerous " differentiations " of the Undifferentiated. Erigena's " God himself does not know what He is, because God is not what " expresses it. " What," and our categories of space, time, subject, object, causation, essence, matter, spirit, etc., are the " crutches " used by the human mind in the finite world of the prakriti. When applied to the quantitative and qualitative infinity or to the purusha, the categories and the laws of logic become inadequate. With these crutches one cannot walk far enough into the realm of the infinite true reality or the realm of the purusha. God or the ultimate reality is, among other definitions, the *coincidentia oppositorum* that transcends the law of logical contradiction. In its un-differentiated continuum it becomes indefinable, ungraspable, and inex-pressible in the terms of verbalized thought and the notions of the logical mind. Whatever we say of it, it points at only one of the ripples of the infinite ocean, but does not define the ocean itself. Only the supersensory, superlogical, unmediated merging of the object and subject into seamless oneness allows an adequate knowledge of the object or the true reality.

Finally, the problem of an unmediated cognition of the object by the subject is one of the central problems of contemporary philosophy and epistemology. The attempts of Hume and Kant (of the *Critique of Pure Reason*), of Hegel and others to solve it without obliterating the " separateness " of subject and object have failed and, therefore, made it increasingly urgent to find some variety of this unmediated knowledge. Hence, there have been various recent attempts to solve it, beginning with the revival of Soren Kierkegaard's philosophy, W. James' " will to be-lieve," H. Bergson's intuitionalism, N. Lossky's intuitivism, E. Husserl's " phenomenological " unmediated " intuition of essences," and ending with the existentialism of Heidegger-Jaspers-Sartre, not to mention the largely mystical philosophies of N. Hartmann, N. Berdyaev, L. Shestov, S. Frank, and many others. In different degrees and manners, these and many other thinkers seem to state that without an obliteration of the separateness of subject and object, no adequate cognition of the true reality is possible. And the obliteration seemingly cannot be accom-plished through purely sensory perception and logic of intellect: some sort of direct intuition is necessary for that.[39] In this way the solution to the problem which Yoga gives has uninterruptedly flowed throughout all these centuries, and is running strong in our time.

Such, in brief, is the system of techniques of Patanjali's Yoga. Begin-ning with the first and ending with the last stage, these techniques make a systematic whole designed to reach the transfiguration of man into a pure, perfect, absolutely free intelligence or God. Moral altruization in this system is only one of the means to the supreme end. In spite of that, it is love in its highest and sublimest form.[40] The system represents fur-ther a scientific combination of the physical and mental techniques per-fectly harmonized with each other. Its techniques are rightly called " experimental, concrete, actional, therapeutic and esoteric." " Thera-peutic because it suppresses ' the dolour of existence '; esoteric because it prepares the yogin for Nirvana (or for absolute final freedom), for final experience." " It does all this through concrete and immediate action, realization and experimentation" and not by abstract dogmatizing or purely ritual practices.[41]

Viewed from a broader standpoint, the Yoga technique is the boldest "technique of spiritual autonomy" of Eros, versus Agape, in the terms of Nygren.[42] It endeavors to achieve the liberation of man by man's own will, true knowledge, and desire for salvation, rather than through grace of God. In "atheistic" (Sankhya) Yoga there is no God; in Patanjali's Yoga the Iśvara is only an agency that may facilitate the progress along the path of Yoga, but in no way is a decisive factor. In the early Buddhism with its denial of God, soul, personality, substance, matter and anything static, "Man reaches salvation [quiescence, Nirvana, from endless disquieting struggle] by his own effort, through moral and intellectual perfection." [43]

In later Buddhism, especially in Zen Buddhism, man endeavors to obtain the highest "Enlightenment" (satori) also by his own effort. His liberation " is not depending on Creator's support. Zen wants absolute freedom, even from God." [44]

And what a goal does Hindu and Buddhist Yoga try to achieve! No more and no less than transcendence of Time and Space, and suspension of the basic causal law of the universe—the law of *karma*. Yoga seeks liberation from it and from the prakriti itself. Indeed,

According to Patanjali, the yogins can dominate any object and any "state" they meditate over. For the meditation of a yogin has a magical value: through meditation the yogins dominate and possess the object of the meditation; suspend the objective laws of the physical universe, modify the reality. . . . This meditation assumes a continuous universe, as a vast field of forces . . . penetrated by karma energy. . . . Any existence in this framework of the immense receptacle of living forms is in direct contact with the whole universe. The "servitude" of the soul, the eternal "cycle of existences," of re-births and re-deaths, is . . . man's participation in the fate of millions of forms that come out from [and return to] the same universal matrix. This eternal return in the universe, this endless cycle of reincarnations is in fact but an endless prolongation of larval existence. It signifies death rather than life, since according to the post-Vedic Hindu mentality, the condition of man is tragic: he cannot be either happy or free. Life on this planet is larval because it lacks spiritual freedom and beatitude — the necessary conditions of real existence. We can say that karma plays in this mentality the role of an "Inferno" to which any living form is condemned forever. . . . The aspirations of the Hindu soul for liberation from this imprisonment, for beatitude and spiritual autonomy are equivalent to a desire to avoid the Inferno, to reach the *saccitānanda, nirvana, mukti*. In spite of a pessimistic appearance of these esoteric solutions, they tend towards eternal, real and free life of the soul.[45]

The pure imprisoned purusha cannot intervene into this huge universe (prakriti). Only the forces of the bodily mind — intellect and will, through meditation — can perform this work of the liberation. Yoga points out the detailed, precise, concrete, experimental way towards the freedom. Only through the suppression of the very roots of the endless chain of reincarnations can be realized the true life of absolute freedom, truth, and beatitude: the state of *mukti*, or *Nirvana*.

Viewed in this light, then, Yoga is indeed the boldest invention of man for his own transfiguration into the pure, free, and beatific intelligence, worked by his own efforts.

So understood, the Yoga, the Sankhya, and the Buddhist *Weltanschauung* cannot be regarded as something purely passive, entirely empty, and fatalistic, something annihilating our "self," as it is commonly regarded by many Western thinkers — theologians, philosophers, moralists, and scholars.[46]

As to passivity, beginning with the *Bhagavadgita* and ending with at least four of the six Indian philosophies-religions and Buddhism, they, like Taoism, state that "Doing nothing is better than being busy doing nothing" and warn against spending one's life pursuing a legion of pseudo-values. On the other hand, they all subscribe to the *Bhagavadgita's* precepts:

"Not by abstention from work does a man attain freedom from action; nor by mere renunciation does he attain to his perfection. . . . For no one can remain even for a moment without doing work; everyone is made to act helplessly by the impulses born of nature. . . . Do thou thy allotted work, for action is better than inaction; even the maintenance of thy physical life cannot be effected without action. Perform always the work that has to be done. Thou shouldst do works also with a view to the maintenance of the world. Whatever a great man does, the same is done by others as well." And so on. The very essence of the Karma Yoga — as the path of action and work for salvation, which is as efficient as the path of knowledge of Jnana Yoga — is already a perfectly clear evidence of the nonpassivity of the *Bhagavadgita* and the Hindu and Buddhist thought. The *Bhagavadgita* advises even an active participation in war.[47]

As to the alleged extinction of the soul or even "ego" in the samadhi or Nirvana or mukti, a subjugation of the biological man and the lower ego to the control of the highest in man — his immortal and divine self, and the liberation of this self from any bondage to the material forces — is evidently not an extinction but, on the contrary, a true liberation of self, an expansion of our little biological and biopsychological egos to an unlimited divine self. Just as a liberation of the divine soul from the bondage of the flesh and the union of this soul with Godhead is not regarded by Christianity as an annihilation and extinction of the soul, so for the same reason the liberation of the self in Taoist-Hindu-Buddhist thought and in mysticism generally cannot be regarded as an extinction and annihilation of "self." Finally, the "emptiness" of Buddhism is not a real emptiness, but the divine bliss and inexpressible fullness of the Infinite

Manifold (Nirvana). Just as we do not have any reason to call a mere emptiness " the Divine Nothing " of most of the Christian mystics, we do not have any basis to call Buddhism a religion of pure negative emptiness. Such an interpretation, unfortunately still prevalent among Westerners, is really a misinterpretation of Buddhism, Taoism, Hinduism, and practically all the genuine forms of mystical religion, philosophy, and experience.

### III

### THE TECHNIQUES OF OTHER YOGAS

Besides Raja Yoga and Hatha Yoga, there are other variations of Yoga. The main of these are Bhakti Yoga, Jnana Yoga, Karma Yoga, Mantra Yoga, Laya Yoga, Tantra Yoga, and various " Integral Yogas " like that of Sri Aurobindo.[48] Their general techniques retain the essentials of Raja Yoga. The main differences from it are threefold. First, the philosophies of each of these Yogas, especially in non-Hindu and Buddhist countries, are not identical with one another and with the Sankhya-Yoga philosophy; however, they retain the general principles of the *generic* Hindu-Buddhist philosophy.[49] Second, in the above terms of Eros and Agape, the Mantra and Bhakti Yogas rely on the divine grace — Agape — more than on human efforts or Eros: the grace of God for salvation is implied by these Yogas much more than by Raja Yoga. The third difference concerns the techniques of the liberation. The main dissimilarity here consists in a reduction of the physical exercises — asanas and pranayama (postures and breathing) — of Raja Yoga and of the most intensive forms of the withdrawal of the senses, of the single-pointed concentration and meditation, and in a partial replacement of these by other techniques — by unbounded love and a complete dedication of all thoughts, feelings, deeds, and words to God (in Bhakti Yoga); by good altruistic deeds (in Karma Yoga); by true knowledge or wisdom (in Jnana Yoga);[50] and by indefatigable repetition of the *mantras* (sacred formulas), prayers, and ritual (in Mantra Yoga). Thus, according to this division, Jesus is a Bhakti-Yogin; Buddha is a Jnana-Yogin; St. Francis of Assisi is a Karma-Yogin. This difference is tied up with several secondary differences in the techniques. Thus, prayer to God in its various forms plays a much greater part in the techniques of Bhakti, Mantra, or even Jnana Yoga than in Raja Yoga. Prayer and rituals are more instrumental in the non-Indian " spiritual exercises " similar to Yoga. However, these differences are relative. All Yogas perform, to some extent, all the eight forms of Yoga exercises, giving a relative emphasis to this or that " step."

# IV

## THE INTEGRAL YOGA OF SRI AUROBINDO (1872–1951)

Sri Aurobindo's Integral Yoga is an attempt to give a synthesis of all the main Yogas and of their philosophies. It endeavors to integrate into one system their valuable parts, as well as what is valuable in the Western science and religions. The main distinctive points of the Integral Yoga are as follows:

1. Most of the surveyed Yogas and their philosophies have a somewhat negative attitude towards the world of the senses and our empirical life. The manifold sufferings of our life are viewed by the Yogas as " conditioned by our entanglement either in the meshes of prakriti (*Sankhya*), or in 'the cobwebs of maya' (*Shankara Vedanta*), or in the fetters of karma (*Buddhism*). The supreme goal of life must, therefore, consist in total liberation from Nature, in complete emancipation from the bonds of prakriti, maya, or karma." " The main endeavour of Yoga has been to realize *mukti* or transcendental freedom by rising above the limitations of body, life, and mind which are supposed to be made of some alien or illusory stuff, and to rest permanently in that state of freedom on some lofty summit of spiritual attainment " [51] (absorption in Brahman, in Nirvana, or in " Kaivalya," the state of freedom from nature or prakriti forever and ever).

In difference from this, the Integral or Purna Yoga views even the material Nature as a lower form of the true reality — the supermind — imperceptibly passing into a finer and finer form of the Divine. In the course of the evolution the matter tends to be increasingly divinized. The trend towards divinization of the whole material world is the main trend of world evolution. The prakriti is not separated from the purusha by an unbridgeable chasm, but is a " low-grade " manifestation of the Divine of which the purusha or Self is the higher form. Respectively, the highest goal of a Yogin is not simply an attainment of the transcendental *mukti* or freedom, but an active participation in the creative joy of the Divine and co-operation with it in the divinization of the empirical world and of the whole " embodied life," here and now. As Chaudhuri aptly says, the goal is " to live a life of divine activity after the attainment of individual liberation, so that Nature herself may be assisted in her liberation, that is, in the complete fruition of the creative urge concealed in her bosom. . . . Having reached the pinnacle of the supramental realization, the integral yogi is again to descend; he is to come to the point of his departure, to the physical consciousness, and he is to bring down there the light and power of the supramental Truth-Consciousness." [52]

" Our Yoga," says Sri Aurobindo, " is a double movement of ascent and descent; one rises to higher and higher levels of consciousness, but at the same time one brings down [the divine] power not only into mind and life, but in the end even into the body. And the highest of these levels is . . . the Supermind. Only when that can be brought down is a divine transformation possible in the earth-consciousness." [53]

Integral Yoga contends that the union with the Divine Supermind is possible not only in a spiritual trance or ecstatic samadhi in which the waking consciousness fades out, but also in the state of a full waking consciousness as well. Its objective is not only and not so much a transcendental liberation of the individual, as it is the divinization of the whole embodied life and the collective liberation of mankind. The Purna Yoga strives to join hands with the evolutionary, creative effort of Nature, through infusion of the Eternal in the temporal, the Supermind in matter. It endeavors to transform the empirical humanity into the divinized Supermanhood; to build progressively the " kingdom of God " in this life, on this planet, here and now.

In conformity with this goal, the techniques of the Integral Yoga are integral also. They consist mainly in dynamic self-identification of every Integral Yogin with the Supreme Creative Power — the Supermind or the Divine Mother, as it is called metaphorically by Sri Aurobindo. This Supreme Creative Power constantly guides (behind the scene) the course of the evolution of Nature and Man, and assists man's efforts to divinize himself. The Integral Yoga strives to help man's active union and cooperation with the creative Divine in the building of the divinized Supermanhood on this planet. For that purpose the co-operation of man's aspiration from below and the Supermind's grace from above is necessary.

The techniques of the Purna Yoga largely dispense with the posture and breathing exercises of Hatha Yoga and the Raja Yoga, and to some extent with Patanjali's superhuman exercises in mental concentration and withdrawing of the senses.

Likewise, Integral Yoga does not believe that its objective can be reached exclusively through religious sentiment, rituals, and endless repetition of the prayers and mantras; or exclusively through the moral force of nonviolence and good deeds; or by devotion and love; or wisdom and knowledge. Instead, its techniques require a sort of a synthesis of all these procedures: first, an unconditional opening and complete self-surrender to the Supermind or " the Divine Mother " and incessant co-operation with this Cosmic Creative Power; second, " psychisation " and then " spiritualization " of one's whole life — thoughts, words, and deeds. Third, for stilling the storms and tumult in our mental life the Integral Yoga prescribes effortful exercises to obtain successively four mental states: 1. quiet; 2. calm; 3, peace, and 4. silence. (This is not fundamentally different from the mental exercises of Raja Yoga.) Fourth, its " triple path " tries to integrate the separate ways of Raja Yoga, Karma Yoga, Jnana Yoga, and Bhakti Yoga; the path of wisdom and knowledge, of love and devotion, and of good deeds and work. It tries to enlist and to use the forces of thinking, feeling, willing emotions, and actions. In brief, the Integral Yoga endeavors to unite into one philosophical, moral, and technical system most of the positive ideas and techniques of all the other Yogas, as well as Eastern and Western philosophies, science, and techniques.

In this " integration " lies its strong and weak points. Its strong points have been emphasized above; the main weakness is a sort of eclecticism that pervades especially the techniques of Integral Yoga. Rejecting as one-sided the techniques of other Yogas, and trying to give its own system of techniques, the Purna Yoga hardly gives any of its own. It simply puts together, side by side, several techniques taken from other Yogas. Neither its prescriptions of self-opening and self-surrender; nor of co-operation with the Cosmic Power; nor psychisation and spiritualization; nor calming and stilling the bodily mind; nor the triple path, are new. They all are given and developed in other Yogas, and in the techniques of various " mystic ways " outside of India. For these reasons the Integral Yoga hardly contributes much that is original to this field.

On the other hand, by its ideological integration of several religious, philosophical, and scientific currents of the East and the West, Sri Aurobindo's " philosophy " is a notable achievement in this age of considerable aridity in these areas. His attempts to put together various techniques of spiritualization and divinization of man and humanity also make an important contribution to the field of the techniques. After all, in some way the numerous diverse procedures have to be taken stock of, and somehow have to be unified into a system. If Sri Aurobindo only partly succeeded in this task, this partial success is already of some importance. The whole task is so gigantic that no single man can achieve it in its full totality. It is up to subsequent intellectual and moral seers to bring it nearer to its full fruition. So much about the Integral Yoga.

## V

### PERVERTED TECHNIQUES OF THE PSEUDO-YOGA LIBERTINES

Finally, in passing, the perverted techniques of the Pseudo-Yoga libertines may be mentioned. Once in a while, in a religious or ethical movement persons and groups appear that pervert the creed, the moral commandments, and the techniques of spiritualization or altruization for their own egotistic purposes. The objective result of such a perversion is not an altruization but a demoralization of respective persons and groups. Among the Indian " denominations," the Tantra or the Cult of the Great Mother has been accused of such perversions. A· more careful study has shown, however, that the accusations have been largely baseless, so far as the Tantrika religion and practices are concerned.[54] If, however, now and then a few instances of perversion occur, such rare cases happen in many religious, political, and ethical movements. With this reservation, the following examples illustrate the Pseudo-Yoga techniques.

Among the Tantrikas and in the sect of the Sahajiya in Bengal, a mystical eroticism in the form of the *maithuna* is supposed to be practiced. Connected with their religious cult, a long ritual preparation takes place before the sexual act is permitted. The purpose of this preparation is to make the initiated a master of his senses and desires by the combined method of " teasing and stimulating " his sex passion and teaching him at the same time to control it, especially at the highest moment of the passion. This is achieved by the training of the initiated in a gradual approach to " the selected woman " (*nayika*): during four months he should serve her as servant, sleeping in the same room, at her feet, and not touching her; then during the next four months he sleeps on her " left side," then on her " right side," then in embracing position. Finally, he is allowed to have sexual pleasure — in order to express Nirvanic beatitude — but he must control and stop the seminal emission, even to make (by his effort) the semen go back into his body. Otherwise, he is supposed to be damned to law of karma. All this is followed by some ideologies aiming to prove that by this technique his process of liberation is accelerated, that he receives some experience of remote resemblance to egoless bliss, and so on.[55] In connection with this *maithuna*, these groups have been accused of sex and other orgies. As mentioned, a great deal in these accusations is either baseless or represents a wicked misinterpretation of the socially sanctioned, religious, and moral rituals of marriage and sex relationships. A careful study of the sexual life of the Tantrikas shows, if anything, a much purer and less loose sexual life among them than that among the populations of Western accusers.

Similar accusations have been made against many sects and movements in practically all countries, including the West: against the early Christians accused of " nocturnal orgies " by the non-Christians; against the Manichaeans, the Montanists, the Priscillianists, the Cathari, the Waldenses, the Antinomians, the Brethren of the Free Spirit, and so on, up to the contemporary sects of the Khlysty, Scopzi and others. Most of these accusations have been again baseless. Once in a while, however, among these and many other groups there happen to be a few who have been guilty of libertinian perversion of their credos and rituals for satisfaction of their lusts and sexual abnormalities.[56]

Whatever " ideological justifications " these libertines have offered, the objective result has been negative for our purposes: hardly any eminent altruist, or even spiritual leader, has ever emerged from these libertines. As a rule they seem to have remained either outstanding egotists, or at best just ordinary persons neither too altruistic nor too egotistic, neither too religious and spiritual nor too atheistic and coarsely materialistic. All such techniques are unfit for altruization; more often than not they are definitely harmful from this standpoint. In spite of their ingenious ideologies, these perverted techniques demoralize and enervate, rather than integrate their practitioners. With this we may dismiss them.

## VI

### GENERAL CONCLUSIONS ON THE YOGA TECHNIQUES

For the rank and file of human beings the techniques of Patanjali's Raja Yoga are hardly accessible. Taken as a whole they far exceed the physical and mental capabilities of the overwhelming majority of human individuals. In a diluted form, however, a part of these techniques can be practiced by the rank and file. Which techniques, and how, has been outlined in preceding chapters devoted to a study of single techniques.

By a very few " religious and moral athletes," the Raja Yoga techniques can be fruitfully used for moral and spiritual transfiguration; however, even for these few not all of these techniques are equally good and efficacious. A combination of some of these techniques with those of the other Yogas and the non-Yoga procedures seems to be more practical for a greater part of even the religious and moral leaders.

For the ordinary human beings the techniques of the Karma Yoga and the Bhakti Yoga seem to be more suitable than those of the Raja Yoga. The Karma Yoga techniques consist mainly in performance of good deeds and altruistic conduct. The Bhakti Yoga techniques are based mainly on deep devotion, self-surrender, and love of God. The Jnana Yoga techniques are mainly intellectual; the Karma Yoga techniques are predominantly " operational," based upon the retroactive effects of good actions upon the mind and conduct of the Karma Yogin; while the Bhakti Yoga techniques are preponderantly " emotional and affective," powered by the fuel of devotional emotions and feelings. The techniques of good deeds and of intense devotion to God have been used by millions, while the exacting techniques of the Raja Yoga have been practiced only by very few individuals.

The system of the techniques of each Yoga contains in itself some of the techniques of other Yogas. The Integral Yoga of Sri Aurobindo (and also the various techniques practiced by Ramakrishna) deliberately attempts to unite the main techniques of all the Yogas. In this point the Integral Yoga is on the right track. The techniques should vary in accordance with the character of the persons and groups undergoing altruistic transformation, as we have seen. In spite of this variation, all the efficacious techniques, and especially those applied to millions of the rank and file, are to be a unified mixture of the techniques of all Yogas and of many non-Yoga techniques. They have to contain some physical training, some intellectual concentration, meditation, and creativity, some emotional and affective self-discipline, and, finally, the operational performance of good deeds. Besides the supraconscious, they have to use the physical, biological, intellectual, emotional, volitional, and actional forces of an individual to empower the drive of the transformation. In brief, the most efficacious system of techniques of altruistic transformation is always integral in this or that form. What sort of integration is best for what sorts of persons and groups has to be decided by the experience of the individual and by the wisdom of his moral counselors.

*Chapter Twenty*

# The Monastic System of Techniques

## I

### COMPARATIVE SUCCESS OF MONASTIC TECHNIQUES

The monastic techniques of spiritual and altruistic transfiguration make a remarkable unified educational system. In details monastic systems of education vary from one monastic order, religion, culture, or people to another. In their basic characteristics, however, the educational techniques of the Taoist, the Hinduist, the Buddhist, the Jainist, the Christian, the Mohammedan and other monastic institutions are essentially similar. We concentrate here on a study of the educational system of the Christian monasteries. What is said of it can be said, with necessary changes, about the techniques of the non-Christian (oriental and occidental) monasteries.

In its heroic age the early Christian system of moral and religious education was remarkably efficacious. Up to about 150 A.D. the early Christians represented a society of the saints and even called themselves "saints." (See II Corinthians 1:1; Ephesians 1:1; Philippians 1:1, 4:22.) The spiritual and moral level of the early Christian communities was exceptionally high. And yet, even among these saints, there were moral and spiritual failures and some of the saintly Christians now and then committed various sinful actions.[1] Similarly, even in the heroic age of Christian monasticism, among the monks there were failures — selfish and sinful monks. The founders of the great monastic orders, like St. Basil, St. Benedict, St. Jerome, and the early historians of the Christian Church like Socrates and Isidore testify to this.[2]

In spite of these failures the moral level of the rank and file of the monks of the early centuries of our era, and throughout the early Middle Ages, was exceptionally high; in some periods and regions it was notably higher than that of the clergy.[3]

It has been said in Chapter Thirteen that monasteries gave an unusually high per cent of the saints and altruists among all Christian saints — many times higher than the per cent of the total monastic population in the total adult population of the respective countries and periods and notably higher than the per cent of the saints from the secular clergy. Likewise, many a moral crusade against the demoralization of the Christian clergy and population came from monasteries and often resulted in a healthy reformation of the members of the Christian community. All this means that in spite of their partial failure the monastic techniques for spiritual and moral training have been comparatively effective. Their effectiveness means their scientific character: otherwise, they could not be fruitful.

Let us glance at the system as a whole. A monastery is, according to St. Benedict, " a school of the Lord's service " where the brotherhood of monks under the leadership of an abbot carries on an incessant fight against human weaknesses and vices and strives to achieve the possible perfection on earth in order to prepare itself for the eternal life in the kingdom of God.[4]

According to John Cassian, " the goal of our [monks'] profession is the kingdom of God . . . while the road to it is the purity of heart without which it is impossible to arrive at this goal." [5] Love of God and love of neighbor are two main forms of the purity of heart, two main duties and activities of a monk.[6] Both loves are to be cultivated by monks. Some monks cultivated primarily the love of God, the contemplative type of monks; while others cultivated primarily the love of neighbors, the practical or altruistic type of monks.[7] Hence, these two types of monkhood: *contemplative and practical.*

The difference is, however, relative: for charity and love of neighbor was a duty of the contemplative monks no less than the duty of the practical monks. St. Anthony the Great, the father of Christian hermitage, carried on altruistic activities side by side with his contemplative eremitic life. He ennobled many a cruel person, pacified fighting persons and groups, defended the weak and unjustly oppressed, consoled the sorrow-stricken: " In brief, as a great doctor he was given by God to Egypt," says his eminent biographer, St. Athanasius.[8] St. Isaac the Syrian states that all contemplative hermits must be charitable to all living creatures and must love all human beings, because " without loving neighbors our mind cannot be enlightened by the Divine wisdom and love." [9]

Contemplative and practical monks saw in every human being a child of God superior to themselves and entitled to their service. They believed that by helping the sick, the pilgrim, the beggar, the poor, the orphan, the helpless, the oppressed, the prostitute, the criminal, the serf, and the slave, they were serving Christ himself, who also was poor, humble, and oppressed. This explains why the readiness to help the needy seems to have been unlimited among even the contemplative hermits of the Desert; why service to the needy was required by the monastic rules of St. Basil, St. Benedict, and others; and why monks were the initiators and pioneers of what we now call social service, social work, charity, and philanthropy in the declining Greco-Roman and the emerging Western worlds. They established the first orphanages, asylums, hospitals, various relief agencies for feeding the poor, for helping the needy, diverse schools, retreats for the penitents, and medical, psychiatric, and counseling services to the nonmonastic secular population. Monks' services to the human world went far beyond this relief, philanthropic, and welfare activities. At the period of the crumbling of the Greco-Roman culture, and the beginning of the " barbarian " medieval period, the monasteries, following the example of Cassiodorus, became sanctuaries where the remnants of the old cultural heritage — its literature, art, etc., — were lovingly collected and preserved " so that the world might not be submerged completely in barbarism." Monasteries established the first libraries and museums with their *scriptoriums* for copying and preserving the ancient codices. Monasteries started and developed schools and educational institutions for children, as well as for adults. Monasteries became the main art centers, and the centers for economic, political, and cultural organization of the whole medieval world.

The best in the medieval culture of the West was largely the creation of Christian monasticism. This means that the monastic system of moral, mental, and religious education of the monks as well as of the outsiders was effective indeed in its combined — contemplative and practical — forms.[10]

Now, what are the essential techniques of this monastic system of moral and religious education? How did the monasteries succeed so well in this difficult task, especially in regard to the decadent and demoralized Greco-Romans and the Western barbarians emerging on the historical scene?

## II

### MONASTIC TECHNIQUES

Here are the essentials of this system of techniques.

1. *The Supreme Goal.* It is the kingdom of God: union with God and cultivation of love of God and of neighbor. The objective is thus the supraconscious at its highest and best or the highest possible value.

2. *The Monastic Society.* In St. Basil's terms it is " a free brotherhood of the like-minded persons, of one heart and of one soul " collectively striving to realize their supreme objective through complete dedication of their lives and activities, of their body, mind, and soul to it. The whole social structure of the brotherhood is built, and the whole stream of their activities is carried on, with a view to this objective.

3. *Preliminary Testing and Selectivity.* The first concrete technique for building the monastic community was preliminary testing and selec-

tion of its prospective members. In Chapter Thirteen it has been outlined that only those aspirants who passed the test were admitted, not to
the membership, but to the body of novices as the potential candidates
for membership. In various forms this preliminary testing and selection
has been established in practically all monastic orders. John Cassian (*ca.*
360–*ca.* 435 A.D.) gives a typical picture of these operations.

In the Tabenna and Egyptian monasteries the testing ordeal was as
follows:

One who seeks to be admitted to the discipline of the monastery is never received before he gives, by lying outside the doors [of the monastery] for ten
days or even longer, an evidence of his perseverance and desire, as well as of
humility and patience. And when, prostrate at the feet of all the brethren that
pass by, and of set purpose repelled and scorned by all of them . . . ; and
when, too, covered by many insults and affronts, he has given a practical proof
of his steadfastness . . . ; and when, with the ardor of his soul thus ascertained, he is admitted [for next ordeal] . . . then the brethren inquire with
the utmost care whether he is contaminated by a single coin from his former
possessions clinging to him. . . . For they know that he cannot stay for long
under the discipline of the monastery, nor ever learn the virtue of humility
and obedience, nor be content with the poverty and difficult life of the monastery, if he knows that ever so small a sum of money has been kept hid.

The aspirants are not permitted " to bring anything in with them " to
prevent their arrogance and pride. They

must lay aside their own clothes and be clothed in others by the Abbot.
Wherefore each one on his admission is stripped of all his former possessions. . . . In the council of the brethren he is . . . stripped of his own clothes,
and clad in the dress of the monastery, so that by this he may know not only
that he has been despoiled of all his old things, but also that he has laid aside
all worldly pride, and come down to the want and poverty of Christ. . . .

[If the seeker] remains in that fervor with which he began, they give them
[clothes and possessions] to the poor. But if they find that he has been guilty
of any fault of murmuring, or of even the smallest piece of disobedience, then
they strip off from him the dress of the monastery . . . and reclothe him in his
old garments . . . and send him away.[11]

When, then, anyone has been received . . . he is not allowed to mix at once
with the congregation of the brethren, but is given into the charge of an Elder,
who lodges apart not far from the entrance of the monastery, and is entrusted
with the care of strangers and guests, and bestows all his diligence in receiving
them kindly. [During this year he is severely tested — and trained — in humility, obedience, social service, piety, and in other monastic duties.] And
when he has served there for a whole year without any complaint . . . [with
humility and patience], when he is to be admitted from this into the congregation of the brethren he is handed over to another Elder, who is placed over
ten of the juniors . . . whom he both teaches and governs.[12]

These lines give an idea of the character of the preliminary testing and
selection of the novices. The test continues for one year or more before
the seekers are admitted into the " rank of the juniors " to be trained and

taught for a full membership. The tests are not merely the paper-pencil tests or speech-reactional tests, or the interviewing, questionnaire, or other *spurious* tests commonly used by contemporary psychologists, educators, and psychiatrists, but *real* tests where the candidate is tested by real life conditions continued for a comparatively long time: one year or more. Even if he passes this preliminary test, he is still only in the position of a junior to be tested for several more years by real life conditions. Such tests are identical with the actual life tests. In comparison with the plethora of tests (mainly paper-pen-vocal-inkblot-tests)[13] flooding our social and psychological disciplines, the monastic tests are much more scientific and adequate for the purpose.

In different monastic orders of the Christian and non-Christian religions, the preliminary tests and selections somewhat vary in details, but in essentials they are similar to the above tests.[14]

4. *Complete Renunciation of All Worldly Affiliations, Values, and Possessions.* As a significant detail of the preliminary test of the novices, a renunciation of all their worldly affiliations (up to the family ties), of all their possessions, and of all the worldly values is to be specifically stressed. Following Christ's precepts that " no man can serve two masters," and that " if any man will come after me, let him deny himself, and take up his cross, and follow me," all monastic Rules impose upon the aspirants as well as upon its members the continuous duty of self-denial, and require complete renunciation of their egos with all the egos' properties and worldly possessions. As Morison correctly says, in monastic Rules " renunciation is a means, and not the end. The end is union with God. . . . Renunciation is . . . necessary condition for the attainment of Christian perfection." [15]

Let us quote a few lines from St. Basil's reasons for and interpretation of renunciation.

Renunciation is a loosening of the chains which bind us to the present material and transitory life, a freeing from human obligations, making us more ready to start on the Godward way. [Renunciation demands spatial withdrawal from the worldly society and forgetfulness of the habits of worldly sinful life.]. . . This entails no small struggle. . . . Whoever in a crowd could fulfil the precept: " If any man would come after me, let him deny himself " (Luke 9:23) — But to deny oneself means complete forgetfulness of the past and retirement from one's own will, in which it is very hard, almost impossible, for a man to succeed when he lives in promiscuous intercourse. Indeed, mixing in such a life impedes even the taking one's cross and following Christ. . . . The soul, looking at the crowd of offenders . . . has no opportunity to perceive its own sins and to become contrite by penitence for its misdeeds.[16]

Especially must he [the aspirant and novice] consider this point that the man who has chosen the life of angels has passed the confines of human nature and crossed over to the bodyless state. For this is the mark of the angelic nature, to be free from matrimonial intercourse and to think of no other beauty, but to gaze continually on the face of God.[17]

Come, then, soldier of Christ . . . set before thyself a life without house, city, or possessions. . . . Be free, released from all worldly cares. Let not love of woman enchain thee, nor solicitude for child. . . . Seek not to leave children on earth, but to lead them up to heaven; not to be joined in bodily wedlock, but to desire spiritual marriage, to rule over souls and beget spiritual children. . . . Come to a life of poverty and freedom from distraction.[18]

Such a soldier of God " contends against heat, against cold. He fights the foe and faces extreme dangers and often, it may be, death."

Besides renunciation of the family and other social ties, renunciation of property and all possessions is also necessary.

The Divine voice calls us and persuades us first to cast off the burden of great possessions by disposing of them to the needy. [Following the example of Christ and the Apostles monks should live without any private property.] He who aspires to the higher life must carry out the renunciation of possessions, because thoughts of and care for material things bring great distraction to the soul.[19]

If a monk or novice retains something as his private property,

this is contrary to the testimony in the Acts concerning them that believed, where it is written: " And not one of them said that aught of the things which he possessed was his own " (Acts 4:32). So he that says anything is his private property has made himself an alien to the Church of God and to the love of the Lord.[20]  One should be poor, not rich, according to the word of the Lord. . . . One should not be solicitous to abound in the necessaries of life, nor zealous for abundance or luxury; but should be free from every form of covetousness and adornment.[21]

These excerpts give an idea of the total and categoric renunciation of one's egos and of all the egos' ties and values demanded from the aspirants, the novices, and the full-fledged monks. As mentioned, this rule and technique is common to all Christian and non-Christian monastic communities. They all require " the complete death of the old man " in the aspirant and its replacement by a new, egoless, unselfish man, completely self-identified with God or the highest value.

St. Benedict's *Rule* sums up the renunciation saying that " from that day [of admission into the community] forward he will have no power even over his own body," [22] and that his " profession is a definitive and irrevocable act." [23]

The *Constitution of the Society of Jesus* states in regard to the novices that in order

the better to break with the world, they [the novices] must, in the beginning, avoid all communications with their friends and families. They must be satisfied to have all their letters, coming and going, read by the superior, who is to judge whether the letters are to be sent or received. All merely natural affection . . . should be ruled and governed . . . by the love of Jesus Christ who takes the place of all for those who have abandoned all to follow him.[24]

Again, this test of total renunciation is identical with life itself. Not all aspirants can stand it, especially when one considers that it is to be a life-long renunciation. Its pregnant significance has been partly discussed before. It means an abandonment of all group affiliations of the aspirant, and a reintegration of all his social bonds in and around one group, the monastery. It means an abandonment of all the old values and reintegration of the new values in and around the value of God. It means the mortal blow to one's "old man" and one's previous egos and their replacement by an unconditional egoless humility and complete obedience to the seniors.

In all these respects the nature and the technique of renunciation are ingenious. They start the transformation of the aspirant at the very first steps of his contact with the monastic community.

5. *Vow of Obedience.* When a novice passes his tests and is ready to be received into the monastic community, he must make a solemn vow of unconditional obedience to all monastic rules and to all his superiors. The technique of the solemn vow, as well as the difficult duties it imposed upon the initiated, is important in the total system of monastic techniques of moral and religious transfiguration. St. Benedict's *Rule* gives a typical description of this vow. When a novice successfully passes two months, then six months, then four months of his novitiate, carefully reading the *Rule* of St. Benedict after each of these periods,

and if, having deliberated with himself, he promises to keep all things, and to observe everything that is commanded him, then let him be received into the community, knowing that it is decreed by the law of the Rule that from that day forward he may not depart from the monastery nor shake from his neck the yoke of the Rule, which after such prolonged deliberation he was free either to refuse or to accept. ["Profession is a definitive and irrevocable act."] Let him who is to be received make before all, in the oratory, a promise of stability, conversion of manners and obedience, in the presence of God and His saints, so that, if he should ever act otherwise, he may know that he will be condemned by Him whom he mocks. Of this promise of his let him make a petition in the name of the saints whose relics are there, and of the Abbot there present. Let him write this petition with his own hand . . . and place it with his own hands upon the altar. When he has placed it there, let the novice himself presently begin this verse: "Suscipe me, Domine " . . . . And this verse let the whole community thrice answer, adding thereto "Gloria Patri." Then let the brother novice cast himself at the feet of all, that they may pray for him; and from that day let him be counted as one of the community.[25]

If one was a sincere Christian believer, as most of these novices were, the character of the vow ritual alone would not fail to leave an unforgettable impression upon the novice and would become a powerful factor in his subsequent conduct. Its potency is reinforced by the unconditional character of the obedience to the superiors irrevocably pledged by the novice. "The limit of obedience is death," say the *Rules* of St. Basil.[26] Only when the order of the superior contradicts the Holy Scripture of God's commandments can it be disobeyed. "The Holy obedience" (*sancta oboedientia*) is the basic duty of a monk. St. Ignatius Loyola in his *Constitution* eloquently stresses this.[27]

The *Constitution* of the Society of Jesus (Part VI, Chap. I) requires that

holy obedience be perfect in us in every respect, in execution, in will, and in understanding; obedience in execution consists in doing what is ordered; obedience in will, in having no other will than his from whom we receive the order; obedience in understanding, in thinking as the superior thinks, and in believing what he ordains is rightly ordained. . . . Let every one convince himself that those who live under obedience, should be led and governed by Divine Providence through their superior, *perinde ac si cadaver essent*, as a corpse would be, that allows itself to be carried here and there, and handled after any fashion; or like an old man's staff, which suffers itself to be used everywhere, and in any way, that he who holds it wishes.[28]

It is hardly necessary to add that the vow of this "corpse-like" obedience freely taken and willingly practiced tends to demolish all the egos and every vestige of egoism of the initiated monk. With a slight variation, the vow of unlimited (except by sin) obedience is the technique common to all monastic orders — Christian and non-Christian.

6. *Complete Renunciation of Private Property*. The renunciation of private possessions is required not only from the novices but no less from all the full-fledged members and the hierarchy of the monastic brotherhood.

Above all let the vice of private ownership be cut from the monastery by the roots. Let none presume to give or receive anything . . . or to keep anything as their own, either book or writing tablet or pen, or anything whatsoever; since they are permitted to have neither body nor will in their own power.

Distribution of the necessities among the brethren from the common possession of the monastery must be "made to every one, according as he had need . . . not respecting of person but considering the infirmities."[29]

No less emphatic on this point are other monastic Rules. According to John Cassian, in Egyptian monasteries even the very word "mine" was prohibited. "No one ventures to say even in word that anything is his own: and it is a great offence if there drops from the mouth of a monk such an expression as 'my book,' 'my tablets,' 'my pen,' 'my coat,' or 'my shoes.' On the other hand, the brethren must be most careful in preserving everything of the common property of the monastery; so much so that there is a slight punishment for dropping on the floor of . . . three beans."[30]

Use all care that all things in the brotherhood be common and not distributed [instructs St. Theodore of Studium]; and let nothing, not even a needle, belong to any one particular. . . . Let your body and your spirit, to say nothing of your goods, be ever divided in equality of love among all your spiritual children and brethren.[31]

The cult of the Lady Poverty of St. Francis involves also a complete renunciation of private property for any of the Friars and prohibition to even touch money.

Let none of the brothers . . . carry or receive money or coin in any manner, or cause it to be received, either for clothing, or for books, or as the price of any labor. . . . For we ought not to have more use and esteem of money and coin than of stones. And the devil seeks to blind those who desire or value it more than stones. [A brother who breaks this rule is regarded as] a false brother, a thief, a robber.[32]

This technical rule destroys radically the economic or material foundation of egoism and, together with other techniques, contributes to the destruction of the egos of the members of the community.

7. *Technique of Competition in Humility and of Ennoblement of Motivation.* This technique is directed towards the same purpose: destruction of egoism and ego-consciousness in all its forms. St. Pachomius' *Rules,* for example, prescribe *mutual competition of the brethren in humility,* in their peaceful and harmonious relationships with one another.[33]

Humility is to consider all men superior to oneself. . . . Humility is the parent of virtues. . . . [We must] strive to be last of all and servant of all. [Humility must permeate the soul of a monk and manifest itself in his behavior and manners]: He must keep his eyes down, and his soul up.[34]

St. Benedict's *Rule* treats humility at considerable length and distinguishes its twelve degrees. The *Rule* regards it as a basic virtue necessary for every Christian, and especially for a monk. Its twelve degrees are regarded by the *Rule* as " the ladder to heaven."

The first degree of humility . . . is that man always keep the fear of God before his eyes. Let him hasten to cut off the desires of the flesh.
The second degree of humility is that a man love not his own will, nor delight in gratifying his own desires. . . .
The third degree of humility is that a man for the love of God submit himself to his superior in all obedience.
The fourth degree of humility is that if in this very obedience hard and contrary things, nay even injuries, are done to him, he should embrace them patiently with silent consciousness, and not grow weary or give in.
The fifth degree . . . is to hide from one's Abbot none of the evil thoughts that beset one's heart, nor the sins committed in secret, but humbly to confess them. . . .
The sixth degree . . . is for a monk to be contented with the meanest and worst of everything, and to esteem himself a bad and worthless laborer. . . .
The seventh degree of humility is that he should not only call himself with

his tongue lower and viler than all, but also believe himself with inmost affection of heart to be so, humbling himself. . . .

The eighth degree . . . is for a monk to do nothing except what is authorized by the common Rule of the monastery or the example of his seniors.

The ninth degree is that a monk refrain his tongue from speaking, keeping silence until a question be asked him.

The tenth degree . . . is that he be not easily moved and prompt to laughter.

The eleventh degree . . . is that when a monk speaks he do so gently and without laughter, humbly, gravely, with few and reasonable words. . . .

The twelfth degree of humility is that the monk, not only in his heart, but also in his very exterior, always show his humility to all who see him: that is, in work, in the oratory, in the monastery, in the garden, on the road . . . or wherever he may be . . . with head always bent down and eyes fixed on the earth. . . .

Having therefore ascended all these degrees of humility, the monk will presently arrive at that love of God which, being perfect, casts out fear: whereby he shall begin to keep, without labor and as it were naturally, all those precepts which he had hitherto observed not without fear, no longer through dread of hell, but for the love of Christ, and of a good habit and a delight in virtue.[35]

This differentiation of the degrees of humility is self-explanatory. Its objective is the same: transcendence of egoism, development of love of God and of man, and self-identification with the highest supraconscious.

Of the details two things are to be noted. First, St. Benedict, St. Basil, and other great educators of humanity were well aware of the paramount importance of the *behavioral manifestation* of either humility or love or any virtue; even about the causal role of the external actions and postures determining the internal emotions and the state of mind. For these reasons they persistently stress the necessity of behavioral practice of the inculcated ideological virtues, because a faith without corresponding deeds is dead and impotent. And they carefully prescribe what sort of bodily posture and overt actions are most fit for a deeper " internalization " of either humility or other desirable characteristics. Hence, their advice about the posture " with head always bent down and eyes fixed on the earth," and so on.

Another important detail is the monastic founders' *theory of motivations* put at the basis of their educational system. For many individuals (but not for all because the founders require a wide individualization of the techniques in accordance with the character of each person) they find it advisable to start their education in virtue with fear of God, of hell, and with other rude and low motives, and step by step to pass to nobler and nobler motives of their spiritualization until they reach the highest motive: to do good for the sake of good itself, to love God or neighbor for the sake of love itself. This is clearly shown in the last paragraph quoted above from the *Rule* of St. Benedict. And this also permeates the theory and practice of St. Basil and of other monastic fathers.

St. Basil indicates that there are

three dispositions which by inevitable necessity lead us to obey. Either through *fear of punishment* [" slavish disposition "] or, seeking to *profit by the reward,* we fulfil the commandments for the sake of *our own benefit,* and are accordingly like *hirelings;* or else we do good *for the sake of the good itself,* and from love of Him Who gave us the law, rejoicing that we are thus thought worthy to serve the glorious God, and so we have the *disposition of sons.*

Indicating these three dispositions or motivations (which are reminiscent of Aristotle's classification of friendship into utilitarian and hedonistic pseudo-friendships and the true friendship for the sake of friendship itself), St. Basil states that the spiritual and moral education of many individuals has to begin with the rudest " slavish disposition " of fear of punishment, and eventually shall end with " the disposition of sons," doing good for the sake of the good itself.[36]

Similarly John Cassian stresses that

the beginning of our salvation is " the fear of Lord." And when this has gained an entrance into man's heart, it produces contempt of all things, and begets a forgetfulness of kinsfolk and an horror of the world itself. But by the contempt for the loss of all possessions humility is gained. . . . [Further on Cassian analyzes ten concrete manifestations of humility somewhat similar to the twelve degrees of humility of St. Benedict] And when this humility is secured, then at once it leads you on by a still higher step to love which knows no fear. . . . [Then we fulfil the commandments] no longer from regard of punishment or fear of it, but from love of goodness itself and delight in virtue. . . . Hear, then, in a few words how you can mount up to the heights of perfection without any difficulty. " The beginning of our salvation and of wisdom is . . . the fear of the Lord " (Ps. 3:10). From the fear of the Lord arises salutary compunction. From compunction of heart springs renunciation, i.e., nakedness and contempt of all possessions. From nakedness is begotten humility; from humility the mortification of desires. Through mortification of desires all faults are extirpated and decay. By driving out faults virtues shoot up and increase. By the budding of virtues purity of heart is gained. By purity of heart the perfection of . . . love is acquired.[37]

Further on, we shall return to this topic for a further study. For the present the above gives an idea of the painstaking analysis of humility and of the how and why of its cultivation in the monastic community.[38]

8. *The Supreme Love and Its Concrete Actions.* We already know that the supreme goal of a monk is the union with God, through love of God and of neighbor. The founders of monasticism and their Rules unanimously view Love as the highest value. They regard altruistic transfiguration of man as the highest perfection, the last step on " the Ladder of Paradise " where man becomes co-participant of Godhead. They all quote St. Paul's famous dictum: " But now abideth faith, hope, love, these three, and the greatest of these is love," and St. John's " God is Love." [39] *Charitas ex natura qualitatis suae est similitudo Dei, quantum*

*mortales assequi possunt . . . Charitas est status angelicus.*[40]  For John
Climacus (*ca.* 525–600), love is the last step of the thirty-step ladder of
perfection ascending to Heaven.  For St. Bernard (1090–1153), love is the
highest and the last step of perfection leading immediately to the direct
vision of God or union with God.  " Of humility, love, and contemplation
[of God], love is the central course." [41]  And similar is the evalution of
love by other monastic fathers.

Defining the general nature of love of neighbors, they broke down these
general definitions into a series of concrete actions that clearly indicate
what sort of conduct is altruistic and what is not.  Let us take a few
illustrations of each of these points.

" What is the mark of a Christian? " asks St. Basil, and answers: " To love
one another, even as Christ also loved us." [42]  " How do we discern him that
loves his brother . . .? "  " There are two prime characteristics of love: to feel
grief and anxiety when the loved one is injured; and to rejoice and strive for
his advantage."  " What manner of love ought we to have among ourselves?
Such as the Lord showed when He said: ' Love one another, even as I have
loved you.  Greater love has no man than this, that a man lay down his life for
his friends.' "

A Christian should love for the sake of love.  " He ought to be pure from all
hatred towards all men and to love his enemies."  " We are taught to show
love even unto death, on behalf both of righteous and sinners, making no dis-
stinction." [43]

These statements define the essentials of love experience and love conduct
to one's neighbors.  The general definitions of other fathers of monasticism
are similar.

They realized, however, that often general definitions are not enough;
for many, a more concrete indication of what actions are love actions,
and what are not, is needed — hence, their specification of love conduct
toward God and neighbor.  The *Rule* of St. Benedict gives a typical example.  Here is a list of actions of love of God and of neighbor, or, in the
terms of St. Benedict, a list of " the Instruments of Good Works." [44]

*Love of God.*  In the first place to love the Lord God with all one's heart,
all one's soul, and all one's strength.
To prefer nothing to the love of Christ.
To put one's hope in God.
To attribute any good that one sees in oneself to God and not to oneself.
But to recognize and always impute to oneself the evil that one does.
To desire with all spiritual longing everlasting life.
To know for certain that God sees one everywhere.
To dash down at the feet of Christ one's evil thoughts, the instant that they
come into the heart.
To listen willingly to holy reading.
To apply oneself frequently to prayer.
Daily to confess in prayer one's past sins with tears and sighs to God, and
to amend them for the time to come.

Daily to fulfil by one's deeds the commandments of God.
And never to despair of God's mercy. . . .

*Love of neighbor.* To love one's neighbor as oneself.
Not to kill.
Not to commit adultery.
Not to steal.
Not to covet.
Not to bear false witness.
To honour all men.
Not to do to another what one would not have done to oneself.
To relieve the poor.
To clothe the naked.
To visit the sick.
To bury the dead.
To help in affliction.
To console the sorrowing.
Not to gratify anger.
Not to harbour a desire of revenge.
Not to foster guile in one's heart.
Not to make a feigned [false] peace.
Not to forsake charity.
Not to render evil for evil.
To do no wrong to anyone, yea, to bear patiently wrong done to oneself.
To love one's enemies.
Not to render cursing for cursing, but rather blessing.
Not [to be] a detractor.
To hate no man.
Not to be jealous, nor to give way to envy.
Not to love strife.
To reverence seniors.
To love juniors.
To pray for one's enemies in the love of Christ.
To make peace with an adversary before setting of the sun.

*Special monk's duties.* To deny oneself, in order to follow Christ.
To chastise the body.
Not to seek after delicate living.
To love fasting.
To keep aloof from worldly actions.
Not to swear, lest perchance one forswear oneself.
To utter [speak] truth from heart and mouth.
To bear persecution for justice's sake.
Not to be proud.
Not given to wine.
Not a glutton.
Not drowsy. [Not to be given to sleep.]
Not slothful.
Not a murmurer.
To keep death daily before one's eyes.
To keep guard at all times over the actions of one's life. [To watch over the actions of one's life every hour of the day.]
To lay one's evil thoughts open to one's spiritual father.

To keep one's mouth from evil and wicked words.
Not to love much speaking.
Not to speak vain words or such as move to laughter.
Not to love much or excessive laughter.
Not to fulfil the desires of the flesh: to hate one's own will.
To obey in all things the commands of the Abbot.
Not to wish to be called holy before one is so.
To love chastity.
To fly from vainglory.

*Concluding Remarks.* Behold, these are the tools of the spiritual craft, which, if they be constantly employed day and night will gain for us from the Lord that reward which He Himself has promised. . . . And the workshop where we are to labour diligently at all these things is the cloister of the monastery, and stability in the community.[45]

The general definitions of love and the sample of concrete actions of love (detailed still more in altruistic practice) is a clear answer to the skeptical remarks of many that love is indefinable, that nobody can clearly show what actions are love actions and what are not, and that love and love actions are very relative and vague, and so on. These skeptics seem to be unaware that the main moral commandments of all great religions, of all great moral systems, and even of all criminal codes are basically identical and much more unanimous than, for instance, any scientific generalization in the social and humanistic sciences. These objections of the ethical skeptics are essentially baseless, and the monastic fathers show this baselessness especially well.

9. *The Ladder Leading to the Supreme Love.* Having concretely defined the actions of love, the monastic fathers outlined a series of concrete actions to be undertaken in a certain order to reach this goal, step by step. They call these steps "the Ladder of Paradise," or "the Degrees of Humility and Pride," or the "Scale of Ascendance to the Way, the Truth, and the Life." An example of this ladder has already been given above in St. Benedict's twelve degrees of humility. Here we add two other examples of the ladders. Like St. Benedict, St. Bernard and St. John Climacus view their ladders as "the instrument of good works," or as a practical course of actions leading the individual to the full realization of love, to the summit of Christian perfection, and to the union with God.

The diagram of the ladder constructed by St. Bernard gives a concise visual idea of the ladder or the sequence of actions of humility to be performed, and of actions of pride to be avoided, which by the twelve steps lead to the first degree of Truth, seen in ourselves by Humility, then to the second degree of Truth seen in our neighbors by Love, then to the third degree of Truth seen by direct vision of, or union with, God as the Way, the Truth, and the Life.

Here are a few comments of St. Bernard regarding this ladder. He

## Diagram Illustrating the "Scala" of St. Bernard [46]

I
am
the
Way the Truth
and
the
L
i
f
e
Third degree of Truth
seen in itself by
Direct Vision
Second degree of Truth
seen in our neighbours by
Love
First degree of Truth seen in ourselves
by
Humility

| | | | |
|---|---|---|---|
| 12 | an attitude of pious prostration | an attitude of vain curiosity | 1 |
| 11 | short, sensible and subdued speech | an unbalanced state of mind | 2 |
| 10 | abstinence from frequent laughter | silly, unreasonable merriment | 3 |
| 9 | reticence until questioned | conceit shown in excessive talking | 4 |
| 8 | observance of ordinary monastic rule | eccentricity and sense of self-importance | 5 |
| 7 | belief in and statement of inferiority to others | self-importance claiming special piety | 6 |
| 6 | admission and acknowledgment of unworthiness | presumptuous readiness to undertake anything | 7 |
| 5 | confession of sins | excuse for wrong-doing | 8 |
| 4 | endurance of hardship in spirit of obedience | unreal confession — resentment of discipline | 9 |
| 3 | obedient submission to a superior | rebellion against the ruler and the brethren | 10 |
| 2 | forbearance to press personal desire | liberty to sin | 11 |
| 1 | constant abstinence from sin from fear of God | habitual transgression in contempt of God | 12 |

The first two stages of the ascent must be made before admission to the monastery. The two last of the descent can be made only after departure or expulsion therefrom.

regards " humility as the way " towards Christ; and pride as the way from Christ. " Humility is the virtue which enables a man to see himself in his true colors and thereby to discover his worthlessness."

The whole course of ascendance to Truth consists of three main " courses ":

The first course is humility, purifying by its bitterness; the second is love, comforting by its sweetness; the third is full vision, secure in its strength. . . . The recognition of truth is gradual. . . . We seek for truth in ourselves; in our neighbors, and in its essential nature. We find it first in ourselves by severe self-scrutiny (humility), then in our neighbors by compassionate in-dulgence (love), and, finally, in its essential nature by that direct vision which belongs to the pure in heart ["the truth which is withheld from the proud, is disclosed to the humble "]. . . . For the merciful quickly discover truth in their neighbors when they extend their sympathy to them, and so kindly identify themselves with them that they feel their good and evil characteristics as if they were their own. They are weak with those that are weak, with those who are offended they burn. A sick man feels for the sick and a hun-gry man for the hungry, with familiarity the greater as his own condition approaches theirs. For as pure truth can be discovered only by one whose heart is pure, so can the sorrow of a brother be most truly felt by one whose heart is sad.[47]

Self-scrutiny reveals to us our own evil case. "Thou hypocrite, cast out first the beam out thine own eye and thus shalt thou see to cast out the mote out of thy brother's eye." . . . Pride in the mind . . . so darkens the mental vision as to hide the truth. . . . So the man who is really anxious to discover the truth must remove the beam of pride which prevents him from seeing the light. . . . Consciousness of our own shortcoming makes us merciful to those of other people. This gives us the second degree of truth. If truth thus com-pels men to look into themselves and so to learn their own worthlessness, it follows as inevitable consequence that all those things which have hitherto given them pleasure — yea, even their own selves — should become distasteful to them. . . .
The third degree of truth is the clearing of spiritual sight, so that it may gaze on holy and heavenly things. . . . If men practice perseverance in the three matters — the sorrow of repentance, the longing for righteousness, and works of mercy — they clear their spiritual sight . . . and may pass on to the direct vision [of God]. There are then three kinds of degrees of truth: we rise to the first by humble effort, to the second by loving sympathy, to the third by enraptured vision. In the first, truth is revealed in severity; in the second in pity; in the third in purity.[48]

The specific actions of humility and pride indicated in each step of the twelve-step ladder are to be performed and mastered in order that the individual can ascend to the next step. From this standpoint the ladder is a systematic " curriculum " of spiritual and moral transformation, be-ginning with the " first grade " and ending with graduation in the highest possible grade, the union with the highest value, God.[49]
St. John Climacus' *Ladder of Paradise* comprises thirty steps of the soul's ascendance to God.[50] Each step treats of a virtue to be acquired and a vice to be overcome in the soul's ascending to God from the lowest or easiest step to the highest. Only on reaching the thirtieth step does one reach Christian perfection or sanctity. The steps from the first to the seventh aim to achieve detachment of the soul from all earthly things; the steps from the eighth to the twenty-seventh consist in effortful liberation from the vices and in acquiring of virtues. The last few steps endeavor to acquire the Christian *apatheia* and the union with God by charity or love.
In making the first step the soul must renounce all earthly possessions,

abandon the vanity of profane things, strip itself of affection for riches, honors, and well-being, and detach itself from family life and all social bonds that distract it from God.

In the second step the soul must free itself from passions and all worldly "desires that produce nothing but sadness and disgust." This is achieved through meditation on the Last Judgment, and on shortness of this life, and through living constantly in the fear of God and expectation of death. Thus "denuded of all [desires] and free from all care, he can ardently follow Christ."

The third step consists in becoming a complete stranger to, and pilgrim in, this world, totally detached from it. On the wings of the acquired complete detachment from the earthly life, in the fourth stage the soul "mounts up to heaven" by cultivating obedience as "a complete surrender of one's own will" that frees us from the responsibility of our decisions and makes us "travel here below without peril and die without fear." [51] "The obedient man is like a traveller, who, being led, sleeps as he proceeds." Completely surrendering to God and not to a doubtful guide, the traveller is led by obedience to heaven and not to perdition.

The fifth and sixth steps consist in cultivation of repentance, humility, and private and public confessions of one's vices and sins. Like other fathers, John Climacus extensively analyzes the efficacy and advantages of confession, its techniques, its individualization according to the persons and conditions. As it will be shown further, he and other fathers knew about the therapy of confession and practiced its techniques with a skill probably far exceeding the knowledge and skill of most contemporary psychoanalysts and psychiatrists. Sincerity, humility, and gentleness must accompany an avowal of faults and the penitent should not hide anything however shameful it may be.

Uncover and show thy wounds to the physician and, putting shame under foot, say, "There is my wound, father, there is my sore, there is the fruit of my softness. None but I is responsible; it is indeed I who am to blame." . . . When thou comest to confess, be in attitude and expression like one condemned, with head bent down . . . and bathe with thy tears the feet of thy physician as though they were the feet of Christ. . . . Confession is without benefit unless accompanied by repentance and reparation of the fault.

Such a confession brings forgiveness for our sins and serves as a brake which stops our sliding down the slope of evil. Penitence leads to hatred of sin and to voluntary reparation by painful works. Here, as in other "steps," Climacus describes many actual cases of practicing each of these rules. In his analysis of the fifth step he gives the celebrated account of the austerities practiced by certain penitent monks whom he visited.

The sixth step recommends meditation on death as a powerful stimulus to repentance and moral ennoblement.

The seventh step deals with afflictions of the soul, compunction, and sadness that come at this stage, and that with the help of God result eventually in spiritual joy. Silence, fasting, disregard of insults, deepest humility, and "the blessed gift of tears" are the proper techniques to overcome this affliction and to turn it into happy joy. With this step the first stage of the "ladder" is climbed and the general preparation for the next stage is accomplished.

The steps from the eighth to the twenty-seventh make the second stage. Climbing these steps consists largely in a struggle against, and in liberation from, the specific vices, and in acquiring specific virtues. Thus at the eighth *gradus* one must free himself from anger and acquire gentleness. Then, at the subsequent steps one masters forgetfulness of wrongs (9th step), slander (10), talkativeness followed by cultivation of silence (11), lying (12), discouragement, tedium, wearisome lifelessness (*acedia*) that now and then attack the monks, the mystics, the hermits in their climbing the "ladder of paradise" (13), greediness and gluttony (14), acquiring temperance and chastity (15), mastering avarice (16), poverty (17), hardness of heart (18), excessive sleep (19), cultivating vigils (20), freeing oneself from cowardice (21), from all sorts of vainglory (22), from foolish pride, blasphemous and pernicious thoughts (23), developing gentle meekness and innocent simplicity (24), humility, "the virtue which destroys all vice" (25), discernment of thoughts, vices, and virtues (26). With the mastery of the above vices and acquirement of the mentioned virtues the soul is now free from all evil inclinations, and is prepared to enter "the tranquil gate of solitude" especially in the form of the eremitical life. Cultivation of this supreme peace of mind and inner calmness is the task of the twenty-seventh step. Its mastery raises the soul to the state of extraordinary prayer which is found at the twenty-eighth step. This prayer is "a familiar converse and union of man with God." It is made in few words and consists in perpetual union of the soul with God: the soul is enkindled with the divine fire, is enlightened and purified. Here St. John indicates in detail numerous functions of genuine prayer.

Oratio . . . est familiaris conversatio et conjunctio hominis cum Deo; si autem vim seu efficaciam, mundi conservatio, Dei reconciliatio, mater lacrimarum et iterum filia, propitiatio peccatorum, pons tendationum, propugnaculum adversus impetum afflictionum, bellorum oppressio et exstinctio, officium angelorum, omnium spirituum alimentum, futura laetitia, actio sempiterna, virtutum scaturgio, gratiarum divinarum conciliatrix, profectus spiritualis, nutrimentum animae, mentis illustratio, securis desperationis, spei demonstratio, tristitiae solutio, divitiae monachorum, thesaurus solitariorum, irae diminitio, speculum religiosi profectus, dimensionum index, status declaratio, futurorum significatio, gloriae futurae indicium. Oratio est vere peccantis curia, locus judicii et Domini ante generale judicium tribunal.[52]

In these few lines John Climacus indicates more fully and more accurately numerous functions and effects of genuine prayer than many a recent volume about prayer does.

At the twenty-ninth step the soul enters into Christian *apatheia*. It is the state of a Christian whose flesh is purified from all stain and is rendered, in a sense, incorruptible, as it will be after the resurrection. He is free from all vices, he controls every sense and bodily force, he practices every virtue, and is in constant union with God. His soul is now in a state superior to mortal life. *Apatheia* is a state bordering on immortal life. God dwells within such a person and rules his thoughts, words, and actions. (The *apatheia* is similar to the samadhi of Yoga, satori of the Zen Buddhism, the Enlightenment of Buddhism, and the " god-intoxication " of mystics of all religions.)

Finally, in the thirtieth step and last, are found " faith, hope, and love, these three: but the greatest of these is love " (I Cor. 13:13). Love or charity is the crowning gem of the soul's ascent towards God. Love makes man like unto God, as far as it is possible for the mortal being to be so. When the soul is immersed in, and fully permeated by, love, a kind of divine splendor radiates from it.

St. John ends his book with the prayer to Love.

Enlighten us, quench our thirst, lead us by the hand. For the one thing we seek after is to mount up to thee, who rulest all things. . . . And Love appeared to me like a queen coming forth from heaven . . . and said: " So long as thou remainest bound to thy material body thou canst never contemplate my beauty as it is. . . . But that thou mayst learn from this ladder in what order the virtues are developed, know that it is I who occupy the highest place." [53]

The above gives only a mere sketch of St. John Climacus' thirty-step system of spiritual and moral transfiguration. Throughout his work he carefully distinguishes, in respect to vices and virtues, which operations are fit for the beginners, which are for those who have reached the middle of the ladder, and which for the perfect who are near the ladder's top. At each step he indicates, in considerable detail, the best technical actions for internalization of its virtues and for liberation from the step's vices. His technical procedures are well illustrated by actual cases, observed by John Climacus, of various monks and religious pilgrims who experimented with, and successfully practiced them.

The wisdom of the book, its wealth of material, and its fine analysis explain its lasting influence upon Eastern Christian theology, ethics, and monastic organization. Stripped of its theological phraseology, it contains a large body of technical procedures to be performed for the moral and spiritual ennoblement of man.

These works give an idea of the systematic order of " moral and spiritual exercises " to be performed for altruistic and religious ennoblement of human beings. They were experimented with, and practiced for several centuries in monastic communities; and, as we have noted, with a notable success. From a purely scientific standpoint, they are to be regarded at least as effective and scientific as any therapeutic and educational system of our time.

10. *Unlimited Extensity and Equality of Love Distribution.* We already quoted St. Theodore of Studium's advice: "Let your body and your spirit . . . *be ever divided in equality of love* among all your spiritual children and brethren." Stressing that love to be granted not only to friends but also to enemies, the monastic fathers naturally demanded love to be applied equally to all members of the monastic community, without preferential cliques, in-groups, or persons. Here are a few telling lines from St. Basil's writings on this matter.

The law of love does not allow particular friendships and companionships in this common dwelling. For it is inevitable that particular affections should injure greatly the common harmony. . . . All should look at one another with an equal degree of feeling and have one standard of love for all the company. . . . All should bear a common and equal love to one another. . . . It is wrong for any private groups or parties to be found in the convent. . . . Similarly both unseemly strife and partiality are to be excluded from the convent. For from strife enmity arises, and from partiality in love and friendship suspicions and jealousies. For deprival of equal treatment is everywhere the origin and cause of envy and hostility on the part of those who are slighted. [We must] imitate the goodness of Him Who maketh the sun to arise on just and unjust alike. . . . As then God grants to all alike participation in the light, so let those who imitate God direct upon all a common and equally honorable ray of love. For where love fails, there of a surety hatred enters in its place. . . . It is fitting that love should be equal and similar on the part of all towards all.

As a finishing touch of the principle of equal and similar love of all towards all, St. Basil adds:

So let a man's parents or brothers according to the flesh, if they live in godly fashion, be cared for by all the brethren, as fathers or friends of all. . . . Bodily kinship will not affect love any more. Not even if one be the brother of another [in flesh], or the son, or daughter, will the community of blood cause greater affection to the relation as compared with the others. [Instead] whosoever shall do the will of my Father in heaven, he is my brother, and sister, and mother.[54]

The monasteries were then the most radical social groups in renunciation of private possessions and in equality of love distribution among its members and among all members of the human race. There is no other group, including communist and equalitarian groups, which have been more radical in these respects than the monastic communities. Likewise, their love distribution is of a clear-cut Agape type granted to all, including enemy, criminal, and every human being.

11. *Behavioral Practice of Love.* The monastic fathers were well aware of the danger of hypocritical preaching of love without its practice in

one's overt behavior and relationships. Therefore, they insisted strongly "that each man must confirm his profession by his own works," "that we must make ourselves examples of good works to others, each according to his ability," that love "should not be superficial but innate and fervent," "that man should be . . . steadfast in the faith and immovable from the good things that are in the Lord." "Let there be no sign of anger, unforgiveness, jealousy or contention among the monks; no gesture, movement, word, look, expression, or anything of the kind, calculated to stir a companion to wrath." "One should be solicitous and anxious for the needs of the brethren" and "strive to be last of all and servant of all." [55]

This behavioral confirmation of love is insisted upon by all monastic orders and permeates the whole life and organization of monastic community, as well as all the ladders of perfection practiced there. In the heroic age of monasticism the bulk of the monks truly practiced the noble virtues they preached. From this standpoint the techniques of the monastic fathers are strictly behavioristic. Further on we shall see that practically all the overt behavior of the monks during each twenty-four hours was organized with a view of continuous behavioral practice of love and other virtues of "the Ladder of Paradise." There hardly ever has been any organization that excelled the monastic brotherhoods in their heroic age in the rational and consistent organization of their life, behavior, and mentality for a maximal possible realization of love.

12. *Utilization of the Superindividual Forces of the Monastic Community.* Organizations like "Alcoholics Anonymous" explicitly acknowledge the insufficiency of the individual powers of an alcoholic in the fight with his alcoholism and the need of reinforcement of his efforts by the helping power of the whole group. Though often intangible, the sympathy and loving help of the group are nevertheless vitally important, and often decisive for the victory of an alcoholic over his disease. This "secret" was well known to the great educators of humanity. The loving power of the monastic brotherhood was skillfully utilized for altruization and spiritualization of its members. The whole life of a monastery was organized in such a way that each monk in his striving for Christian perfection was incessantly supported by the whole community. The whole brotherhood was an all-pervading and ever-present "Sinners Anonymous" that helped each of its brethren in his difficult climb up the ladder of Christian perfection.

This power of the whole community comes out in the very definition of the monastic group as the union of "the like-minded persons," "of one heart, one soul, and one will," "having all things in common," in a collective way striving to realize the purity and perfection of the early Christian communities. It comes out in a general principle that "all should be

harmonious with one another in the love of Christ as member in a body,"
that all should help and bear the burden of one another; that none is self-
sufficient and, therefore, every member needs to be enriched by "the
fruits of other men's gifts." The same principle lies at the basis of the
provision that the brethren all work together, pray together, suffer together, and by collective effort help one another, especially those who are
in affliction. Everyone "must rejoice with those who practice virtue
successfully and not envy them; suffer with those who suffer. . . ."

"Concerning matters of dispute among the brethren," St. Basil's Forty-
Ninth Rule orders "to bring them with any before the brotherhood for
common consideration, or else to refer them to the Superior."

Each member chooses his personal spiritual counselor from whom he
hides nothing, and to whom he opens all his secrets, vices, and troubles.
In addition to the *spiritualis pater*, he has the privilege of confessing his
sins either secretly or publicly to the Superior, or the seniors, or to the
whole community.

When the day is over and all work, both bodily and spiritual, has come to
an end, before going to rest it is fitting that each man's conscience be examined by his own heart. . . . And if anything wrong has happened, forbidden*thoughts, or unfitting conversation, or slackness in prayer . . . or desire
of the world, let the sin not be hidden, but told to the brethren, that the fault
of him who has done such wrong be healed by the prayers of all.[56]

The utilization of the loving help of the community for the therapeutic
and ameliorative improvement of each member permeates indeed the
whole monastic life and organization.

13. *Prayer and Work as the Main Activities for Moral and Spiritual
Education.* The life of a monk is an incessant alternation of prayer and
work, day and night, say St. Basil, St. Benedict, St. John Cassian, and
others; so, also, is the life of the monastic community.[57] Except for a
few hours for sleep, interrupted by night vigils, the rest of each twenty-
four-hour period is occupied by these two activities. They are regarded
as the best therapies for developing the life of Christian perfection. The
meaning of prayer and of its physical, vital, mental, moral, and other
functions was well formulated by St. John Climacus, as we have just seen.
"There is nothing which so purges our understanding of its ignorance
and our will of its depraved inclinations, as prayer; it cleanses our souls
of their imperfections, and quenches the thirst caused by the passions of
our heart," says St. Francis de Sales. Its importance explains why a considerable part of each twenty-four hours was devoted to prayer performed six, seven, eight, or twelve times each day and once or twice each
night. Prayer opened the day's activities, "so that the first movement
of the soul and mind may be dedicated to God and nothing taken into
consideration before we are gladdened by thoughts of God." "Again at
the third hour we must rise to prayer and collect the brotherhood [scat-

tered to their various occupations] and worship all together that we may become worthy to receive sanctification. . . . And then we resume our work again." [58] And so alternation of collective prayer and work goes on throughout day and night. In the Egyptian monasteries of St. Pachomius there were from six to twelve collective prayers during twenty-four hours. The Superior presided at the services, which consisted of psalms, prayers, and lessons. The Eucharist was celebrated on Saturdays and Sundays. In addition, monks were expected to meditate on their way from and to the cells and at their work.[59]

In St. Basil's monasteries there were eight prayers in twenty-four hours.

When the day is finished [vespers] let us give thanks for what has been given us during the day and for what we have done rightly, and let us confess what we have left undone, every sin whether voluntary or involuntary. . . . For to review the past day is a great safeguard against falling into the like [sin] again.[60]

John Cassian informs us that the method of praying of the Egyptian monks was in standing position, interrupted from time to time by prostration to the ground for a few moments. There were seven prayers a day.[61]

The *Rule* of St. Benedict establishes night vigils and seven day prayers: Matins or Lauds, Prime, Terce, Sext, None, Vespers, and Compline. It reminds one that during the service " mind and voice should be in harmony," " in the presence of God and of His angels." [62]

Still more time was given to prayers in the Cistercian order.[63] Monks were expected to come to the prayers promptly, at the appointed moments. In the night time, " the stragglers " were awakened by special monks. Monks arriving late were reprimanded. In the monasteries of St. Theodore of Studium, " in Lent there was a special brother appointed to go around to all kitchens and workshops at nine in the morning, and say: 'Fathers and Brothers: we die, we die, we die. Let us remember the Kingdom of Heaven.' " [64]

The details of the prayers — their ritual, the postures of the monks, standing or sitting, the gestures like crossing, genuflection, raising hands, prostration; the kind of songs sung, the prayers said, the music, intonation, and the kind of reading; the environment of the church or chapel; and hundreds of other details are highly significant. When studied carefully, they are found to be ingenious inventions greatly facilitating the expected effects of prayers. Almost all of these details have a real therapeutic and educational efficacy.

Here are a few technical instructions concerning the method of prayers. Most of the fathers follow Jesus' dictum: " But when ye pray, use not vain repetitions, as the heathen do: for they think that they shall be heard for their much speaking." (Matthew 6:7).

With all lowliness and purity of devotion we ought to offer our supplications to the Lord. . . . And let us remember that not for our much speaking, but for our purity of heart and tears of compunction, shall we be heard. Therefore prayer ought to be short and pure, except it be perchance prolonged by the inspiration of divine grace. [*The Rule of St. Benedict,* Chap. 20, pp. 183–93.]

"We must not use vain repetition in our prayers," says St. Basil.[65] St. Ignatius' three methods of praying remind one somewhat of Yoga techniques.

In the first manner of praying . . . before entering into the prayer, let me repose the spirit a little, sitting or walking as may seem better, considering whither I am going and for what. . . .

The second method of praying is to contemplate the meaning of each word of the prayer. . . . The second method of praying is that the person, kneeling or seated according as he finds himself more disposed and greater devotion leads him, keeping the eyes closed or fixed on one place without moving them about, should say *Pater,* and remain in the consideration of this word as long a time as he finds meanings, comparisons, relish and consolation in considerations appertaining to the said word; and in the same manner let him act with each word of the *Pater noster,* or with any other prayer. . . .

The third method of praying is, that with each respiration or breath, one is to pray mentally, saying a word of the *Pater noster* or of another prayer . . . in such manner that only one word is said between one respiration and another, and while the time lasts between one respiration and another, one should observe principally the meaning of such a word, or the person to whom one is reciting it, or one's own baseness.[66]

Some saints, like St. Theresa and St. Francis de Sales, preferred the silent or mental prayer to the vocal one. "The mental prayer is more pleasing to God and more profitable for the soul than the vocal prayer," states Francis de Sales.[67]

The monastic Rules prescribe in detail, then, how many and what sort of religious services have to be performed, up to the last details of the hieratic ritual of each service and each prayer.

Now let us turn to *work, as the other main method of therapy, education, and salvation.* Preoccupation with work was regarded by the fathers as important as the prayer activity.

Idleness is an enemy of the soul. . . . [Monks only] then are truly monks when they live by the labor of their hands.[68]

[Monks must] win [their] food with sweat and toil. . . . Working with their hands they eat their bread honestly.

He who is unwilling to work . . . is unworthy even to eat.[69]

Monks must produce the means of subsistence, not only for themselves but also for the poor and the needy. "Each, therefore, should put before himself as the aim in his work the service of those in want, not his own needs." [70]

John Cassian gives a comprehensive reason for the combination of work and prayer in monastic brotherhoods.

And, therefore, they supplement their prayer by the addition of labor. . . . For practicing equally the virtues of the body and of the soul, they balance what is due to the outer by what is profitable to the inner man; steadying the slippery motions of the heart and the shifting fluctuations of the thought by the weight of labor, like some strong and immovable anchor, by which the changeableness and wanderings of the heart . . . may be shut up in some perfectly secure harbor, and so . . . may not only forbid the watchful mind to give a hasty consent to any evil suggestions, but may also keep it safe from any unnecessary and idle thoughts; so that it is not easy to say which depends on the other — I mean, whether they practice their incessant manual labor for the sake of spiritual meditation, or whether it is for the sake of their continuous labors that they acquire such remarkable spiritual proficiency and light of knowledge. . . . By repeating by heart some Psalm or passage of Scripture one gives no opportunity or time for dangerous schemes or evil designs, or even for idle talk, as both mouth and heart are incessantly taken up with spiritual meditations.[71]

The above considerations explain why prayer and work were combined together, and why they were considered as the best activities for moral and religious growth.

Though work occupied most of the time of the monks, it was not to be too heavy and hard. St. Benedict and St. Basil instruct: " Let all things be done in moderation for the sake of the faint-hearted "; the workers should not be " oppressed by weight of labor "; " the weakness of the brethren must be considered by the Abbot," and so on.[72] The work and its division were rationally organized according to the ability of each member, as it was seen by the Superior and the senior members of the monastery. The work was mainly physical, only in a smaller part mental, like writing and copying manuscripts, teaching and learning. The masters and the skilled craftsmen were advised not to be proud of their skill and masterfulness. Among other things, in monastic communities use of slave labor was prohibited. " Do not obtain any slave, nor use in your private service, or in that part of the monastery over which you preside, or in the fields, man who was made in the image of God," rules St. Theodore of Studium.[73]

Difficult or unpleasant work activities were performed in rotation by everyone when his turn arrived. The main reason for that is " that both the reward of humility may be shared by all and that no one be allowed to overreach the rest of the monks even in doing good work, and that all may have rest equally." [74]

We have already seen that the " *incentive* " *for the work was neither personal profit of a monk, nor his pride, nor any selfish motive of the community. The work was a prayer and prayer was work*, both performed to the Glory of God and for the good of neighbors. " We should be anxious and work eagerly, on account of our neighbors' needs." In order " that we may have to give to him who is in need . . . one should work diligently " . . . (St. Basil prohibits neglect of work, even for)

" the sake of prayer, because . . . of love to our neighbor, in order that God by our means may bring sufficiency to the weak." [75]

Thus the early monasteries were not only the earliest organizers of collective work on a rational plan, but the communities using the noblest and most unselfish incentives for the most earnest and diligent labor. In this respect they were far ahead of their time, and are still unexcelled by any other organization. They practiced to " everyone according to his need, and from everyone according to his capacity " earlier, and possibly more successfully than socialist and communist experiments have hitherto done.

Being an unselfish work for production of the bare necessities of life, the work activities were carefully chosen: the work for production of luxuries was excluded, and only the work conducive to " the peaceable nature " of monastic life was admitted.

Generally speaking, one may recommend the choice of such arts as preserve the peaceable and untroubled nature of our life, needing neither much trouble to get the requisite material, nor much anxiety to sell what has been made, and which do not involve us in undesirable or harmful meetings with men or women. But in everything we must consider that simplicity and cheapness are set before us as our proper aim, and we must avoid serving the foolish and harmful lusts of men by working to satisfy their requirements. [76]

The production of the bare necessities helped them also to be free from excessive " worries about tomorrow," and to keep peace of mind and devotion to the main objective — realization of love of God and of neighbor.

He who has received the teaching of the Lord . . . does not occupy the soul uselessly in the cares of this life which choke the word and render it unfruitful. . . . He believes in the Lord who said: " The workman is worthy of his food," and he is in no way worried about this. But he works and is anxious not for his own sake, but for the commandment of Christ: . . . " ye ought to support the weak." . . . For to be anxious for one's own sake accuses a man of self-love; but to work for the sake of the commandment shows a disposition that loves Christ and the brethren. [77]

Such are the essentials of the labor organization pioneered by the monastic fathers. They seem to have realized, on a considerable scale and with a notable success, an unselfish, free, and most ennobling system of labor organization serving God and community. Many centuries have elapsed since this system was introduced; many efforts have been made to establish a free, noble, and unselfish labor organization. So far none of these efforts has excelled the work organization of the monastic fathers, especially in its unselfish service to God and the community.

Such are the two main normal activities — prayer and work — which were considered as the best and most efficacious techniques for climbing the ladder of perfection, as well as the best therapies for curing human frailties and mental aberrations.

*14. Continence and the Continent Standard of Living.* Moral and religious perfection demand a complete subordination of the " bodily man " to the " spiritual man " in the individual. Side by side with prayer and work, continence was considered the best means for that purpose.

The buffeting of the body and bringing of it into bondage is accomplished by nothing so much as by continence . . . by abstinence from pleasures practiced with a view to destroying the mind of the flesh and achieving the end of godliness. . . . The practice of godliness does not refer only to the pleasures of the table, but extends also to abstinence from everything that hinders religion. So that the strictly continent man will not master his stomach and be worsted by human ambition; he will not overcome base lust only, but will no longer be subject to wealth, nor any other unworthy passion, whether anger or dejection or any of the things by which untrained souls are naturally enslaved. . . . Clearly the rule of continence is necessary. . . . Continence is the beginning of spiritual life. . . . For pleasure is the great bait used by evil; owing to it we men most readily fall into sin; by it every soul is dragged to death as if by a hook. . . . We know continence to be mother of temperance; the winner of health, the potent remover of hindrances to the bearing of good fruit in Christ.[78]

The " athletes of God " cultivated continence in two ways: in acquiring mastery over their bodily lusts, drives, and pleasures; and in intentional establishment and maintenance of continent material conditions. About the techniques of mastering one's " bodily man " something has been said in Chapter Fifteen, and more will be said further on. For the present we must stress the straightforward consistency of the rule of continence with the rules of love, renunciation, prayer, work, and with the supreme objective of monastic life. All these principles, operations, and techniques make one unified system in which all the parts are in logical and empirical consistency with one another.

The principle of continence explains *the moderately ascetic material standard of living of the monks.* Neither indulgence nor mortification were favored. " No excess was desired," whether in regard to food, or drink, or sleep, or clothes, or living quarters, or any other material condition. " The gluttonous and those who make their belly their god " were condemned. The same is true of any other indulgence in pleasures. On the other hand, the *Rule* explicitly prohibit the extreme asceticism and mortification of flesh.

Let this be the best rule and method of continence, to aim neither at luxury nor ill-usage of the flesh, but in both directions to avoid excess. . . . For by both extremes equal harm is done to the soul, both when the flesh becomes unruly and through fulness of habit runs off into wrong courses, and when it is oppressed by sufferings and becomes relaxed, and feeble, and sluggish. For in such a state of body, the soul has no leisure to gaze with freedom upon the higher things, but it is perforce preoccupied with the sensation of pain and dwells upon it, depressed in sympathy with the ill-usage of the body.[79]

This statement is typical for practically all monastic orders. A widely accepted opinion that monasteries favored extreme asceticism is really baseless. Almost all monastic Constitutions contain several rules explicitly prohibiting (without special permission of the Superior) excessive fasting or other forms of extreme asceticism. One of the reasons for such prohibition is that extreme asceticism may hatch the spirit of competition, vainglory and self-pleasing which are alien to continence.[80]

From these principles the concrete rules about food, drink, sleep, and other material conditions follow. The prescribed food was mainly vegetarian, some monastic orders admitting fish (and meat for the sick) as an exception. The main drink was water, plus a very moderate amount of wine in the wine-producing countries. A similar moderate asceticism determined clothing, and all other material conditions of monastic living. They were truly "spartan" and continent; but they were sufficient to keep body and soul together.

Continence concerns not only the bodily needs of the individual, but no less his total behavior, manners, deeds, talks, and thoughts. In John Cassian's terms it demands complete self-control of "the spirits of fornication, covetousness, anger, dejection, vainglory, pride," and of other selfish aspirations.[81]

15. *Education, Charity, Punishment and Other External Measures.* The exceptionally high level of the monastic demands for moral perfection required a mobilization of all the creative powers of a monk, reinforced by the wholehearted support of his monastic community, in order that the monk and the community could reach their goal. In order to reinforce the monks in this difficult fight, the monastic fathers introduced, besides the surveyed measures, additional procedures for either prevention or repression of moral backsliding. These procedures are: examination of conscience, monastic "psychoanalysis," repentance, confession, spiritual and moral counseling, and, finally, charity, education, punishment, and other measures. Of these devices education, charity, and punishment shall be briefly mentioned at this point. The other procedures are so complex and significant that they shall be an object of a more extensive analysis in the next chapter.

Since the whole monastic regime is a unified system of moral and spiritual education, by education here is meant either education of children in monasteries or education in reading, writing, and Scripture, or "the intellectual formation" of the novices and scholastics.

In the monasteries of St. Pachomius and others there were daily sermons, lessons, and learning by heart of some parts of the Scripture, as well as teaching of reading, writing, and arithmetic.[82] Morally selective intellectual instruction of this sort was carried on in practically all monastic orders. Monasteries were the schools for the members, as well as for outsiders. In the Society of Jesus and some other orders, there was much more advanced " intellectual formation " of the novices and scholastics: instruction in grammar, logic, the humanities, rhetoric, philosophy, theology, Sacred Scripture, in Greek, Latin, and oriental languages.[83]

In St. Francis' order a purely intellectual education was appreciated much less than in the Society of Jesus. " Let not those who are ignorant of letters care to learn letters." Much more than this " book knowledge," he considered it important " to possess the spirit of the Lord," and to cultivate pure-hearted prayer, humility, and patience.[84]

Practically all monastic orders carried on mental and moral education of children, partly with a view to educating some of them for their future monastic vocation. Religious and moral values conditioned their intellectual training. Only morally sound theories were selected and taught. " Their literary studies must be appropriate to their moral ideal," says St. Basil. " The education must be carried on in the spirit of Christian love and goodness, and must educate not only the intellect but the character and conduct of the pupils." [85] " The soul must be led to practice good immediately and from the outset, while it is still plastic and soft, pliable as wax and easily molded by the shapes pressed upon it." But training must be individualized according to the ability and inclination of a child.[86]

Essentially similar was the education of children in other monastic orders. They all advised " a kind consideration, and paternally-loving attitude " towards children, and indefatigable care about their physical, mental, and moral well-being.[87] By this education the monastic communities prepared from early childhood successive generations of monastic leaders of a predominantly " fortunate type." At the same time, the educational activities of the monks helped their own moral well-being.

The same ends were served by the *charitable* activities of monks. By helping the sick and the needy, they practiced daily the commandments of unselfish love. In this way the noble preachings were regularly realized in their overt behavior and often became their " second nature." The charitable activities of monks consisted mainly in the *care of the sick* in monastic hospitals, in *distribution of alms to the needy*, and in *hospitality* rendered to all visitors of the monastery, especially to pilgrims and the poor.

We who serve the sick in the hospital are taught to serve them with such a disposition as if they were brothers of the Lord.[88]

Similar was the spirit of the service in other monastic orders.[89]

Helping the needy by giving food, clothing, shelter and other necessities was another charity regularly discharged by the monasteries. The Rules instructed monks to regard the poor and the needy as brothers, and to help them as though they were helping Christ himself. Since monks did not have their own property, the rendering of help was entrusted to a special steward who knew better who really needed help and who was asking for it from avarice. Help had to be rendered primarily to the needy, but in exceptional cases "from our superfluity the sun may arise on the evil and the good" (the familiar form of Agape love practiced in monastic institutions).[90]

The next form of charity was the *hospitality* of monasteries rendered to all visitors, but especially to the poor and the pilgrims. "Let all guests that come be received like Christ Himself. . . . Let special care and solicitude be shown in the reception of the poor and the pilgrims. . . . Let the guest be met by the superior or brethren. . . . Let them first pray together, and thus associate with one another in peace. . . . Let the superior break his fast for the sake of the guest." [91]

The specially entrusted steward (*hospitum exceptor*) and his helpers took utmost care of the visitors — washed their feet and hands, prepared clean and convenient beds, fed them well from a special kitchen, and so on.[92] However, in this care no luxury was to be practiced, "for if luxury is evil, it is to be avoided. . . . We never pass the bounds of what is necessary. Let this be the limit of our hospitality." The reception of guests and conversation with them should consist of instruction in piety and good deeds and not in idle prattle and amusement.[93]

In addition to these positive measures, the monastic Rules tried to help the monks by *mechanical devices*, like nonadmission of women into the monastery, prohibition of the monks from visiting the outside world, strict control of all their interactions with outsiders, elimination of various environmental temptations perceived by eyes, ears, and other senses; and, finally, by a series of corrective disciplinary measures.

"The gates of the monastery must be closed to women," prescribes St. Basil.[94] "Let all brothers . . . carefully avoid unbecoming looks and company of women, and let no one converse with them alone," rules St. Francis of Assisi.[95]

There is no leaving the monastery, except on fixed and necessary occasions. . . . Let leave to travel be given only to the man who is able to complete his journey with benefit to his fellow-travellers, and without damage to himself.

After each journey the monk had to give a strict account to his Superior of his actions, words, even of the "thoughts of his heart" he experienced during his travel.[96] Monks were permitted to travel usually only in groups.

For the same reason of keeping the brethren from temptations, their letters and other communications with the outside world were supervised and censored. Also books, pictures, and other visible stimuli; songs, words, and other audible stimuli; environmental objects and events, looked at, heard, and perceived by sense organs were carefully screened and selected. Anything that could have aroused sinful thoughts, desires, or actions was carefully eliminated from the monk's milieu.

Finally, if and when other measures proved insufficient, *corrective techniques of comparatively mild punishment* were sparingly practiced. The standpoint of the fathers in this matter was perfectly modern: *the vices and backslidings of a monk were considered as disease,* and the corrective means were explicitly viewed as the therapeutic measures of a doctor applied to his sick patients.

[The Superior] must be compassionate, showing long-suffering to those who through inexperience fall short in their duty, not passing sins over in silence, but meekly bearing with the restive, applying remedies to them with all kindness and delicate adjustment. He must be able to find out the proper method of cure for each fault. . . . Let the Superior employ the corrective methods on the afflicted after the example of doctors, not being angry with the sick, but fighting the disease. Let him face the illness and by more laborious regime, if necessary, cure the soul's sickness. For example, he will cure vainglory by ordering practices of humility; idle speech, by silence; excessive sleep, by watchings with prayer; bodily idleness, by labors; unseemly eating, by deprivation of food; murmuring, by separation. . . . The Superior must apply this with the disposition of a father and doctor treating his own son with sympathy and compassion according to knowledge.

[The disciplinary measures are to be chosen] with regard to the age of the culprits, their condition of soul, and the difference of their sin.[97]

In the first instance all should sympathize with him [the culprit] as a sick member of the body, and the Superior should try to cure his infirmity by his private admonitions; but, if he perseveres in disobedience and will not amend, then the Superior must correct him sharply before all the brethren and apply methods of healing by every method of exhortation. But, if after much admonition he is still unabashed, and shows no improvement in his conduct, with many tears and lamentation . . . he must cut him away from the body after the practice of doctors.[98]

These principles give a general idea of the corrective measures for violation of the Rules. The greatest punishment is expulsion from the monastic brotherhood. The slightest is a private admonition by the Superior or spiritual counselor. In between there was a series of disciplinary treatments of the moral and mental diseases of the members, such as: reproof, exclusion from the common table and oratory, excommunication for a limited time, fasting, genuflections, up to " stripes " in some (not in all) monasteries. In most of these for a serious sin, the culprit " must lie on the ground and ask for absolution " from all brethren " assembled for service until the service of prayers is finished." [99]

In the monasteries of Theodore of Studium excommunication from communion for forty days was prescribed for lying and offense; silence for forty days, and fifty daily genuflections were imposed for slander and insult; deprivation for one day of wine and forty genuflections for prattling; two hundred genuflections for laughter after *completorium* (evening service).

The punishment for fornication was expulsion of the guilty from the Franciscan order.[100] In the monasteries of St. Theodore of Studium, the following were the punishments for impulses, thoughts, and actions related to the sex drive: [101]

300 genuflections for anointing one's body during bath.

40 days fasting (on a small ration of bread and water) for having sex temptation, and 300 genuflections each day and night; if the temptation does not disappear, one must fast and make prescribed daily genuflections until the temptation disappears.

Prohibition of Communion, 40 genuflections, reading Psalm 50th, and 100 times repetition of "Lord have mercy on me" for sexual dream.

40 days' prohibition of the Communion for kissing a woman.

Excommunication from church for three years for monk and nun guilty of fornication.

Besides these measures, the *Rule* and *practice* contain other, more delicate provisions aimed at the same purpose: maintenance of chastity and prevention of the sin of fornication, sexual dreams, thoughts, and temptations.

The above shows that these corrective measures aimed not so much at punishment of a culprit as at recuperation of a sick brother from his moral infirmity.

All in all, as a system of therapeutic measures the correctives were in several respects ingenious and effective. However, they seem to have played a much less important role than other therapeutic devices such as: monastic "psychoanalysis," examination of conscience, repentance, confession, spiritual and moral counseling. Let us turn to an analysis of these techniques.

## Chapter Twenty-One

# Monastic "Psychoanalysis," Counseling, and Therapy

## I

### INTROSPECTIVE-BEHAVIORISTIC "PSYCHOANALYSIS"

St. Basil correctly remarks that the concept of sin in the New Testament is wider than in the Old Testament. While the Old Testament forbids only bad deeds and actions, the New Testament forbids also bad thoughts and passions hidden deep in the heart. "As the law [the Old Testament] forbids bad deeds, so the Gospel forbids the very hidden passions of the soul." [1] In ascribing the greatest signifiance to the hidden desires, thoughts, and passions, St. Basil, and other monastic and Christian fathers follow the view of the Gospel.

The New Testament's statement on adultery is typical for its standpoint.

Ye have heard that it was said by them of old time, Thou shalt not commit adultery: But I say unto you, That whosoever looketh on a woman to lust after her hath committed adultery with her already in his heart.[2]

The monastic fathers saw the origin and the source of man's sinful or virtuous actions "deep in the heart" or in "the mind" of human beings. Respectively their curative and perfecting therapy consisted, first, in eradication of a vice from the hidden depth of the soul and inculcation of a virtue therein; and, second, in elimination of sinful actions, and in performance of virtuous deeds, in the overt behavior of the monk. Both the inner and external aspects of human conduct were well taken care of in their analysis of human behavior and in their educational practice.

The "integral psychology" of the fathers includes these elements among its therapeutic and educational techniques: indefatigable self-analysis and examination of conscience; a spiritual counselor (*spiritualis pater*) chosen by each monk from among the wise and experienced monks to guide him in his difficult task; repentance; confessions; absolution from sin; the sacrament of Communion; demonstration and imitation of good examples; and other measures. In their totality these techniques made a remarkable system of therapeutic and educational operations hardly excelled, or even rivaled, by any system of our time. Let us look closer at the principles and ministrations of this system.

## II

### CLEANSING OF THE SOUL OR HEART OR MIND AS THE FIRST OPERATION

According to the "integral psychology" of the monastic Rules, the source of our vices or virtues is in our soul or heart or mind. If these are impure, if some vice is hidden there, our overt actions will also be impure or sinful. If the vice is eliminated from our soul, the roots of corresponding sinful actions are thereby cut off; the individual can successfully free himself from his overt vice if he translates the purity of his heart into his overt behavior. This principle is commonly accepted by Christian and non-Christian monastic Rules and by practically all the Christian fathers.

St. John Cassian develops this prescription in his *Remedies for the Eight Principal Faults:* Gluttony, Fornication, Covetousness, Anger, Dejection, Accidie, Vainglory, and Pride. The first step in one's liberation from each of these vices consists in exploration, discovery, and expulsion of the vice from the conscious and unconscious recesses of his soul. The inner cleansing done, the elimination of the vice from his overt behavior can be accomplished with a comparative economy of effort.

For instance, discussing the method of liberation from "the spirit of fornication," St. John indicates that "the seat of this malady" is not so much in the flesh as much as in the spirit or "heart," in the deepest recesses of our soul, among our most secret, least controllable, unconscious propensities which are often hidden from ourselves.

The correction of this vice flows mainly from the perfection of our heart because it is from the heart . . . that comes the virus of this malady: "For out of the heart proceed evil thoughts, murders, adulteries, fornications, thefts, false witness, blasphemies: these are the things which defile a man." (Matthew 15:19–20). Therefore, first of all, it is necessary to purify [*expiandum*] that source out of which come life and death: "Keep thy heart with all diligence; for out of it are the issues of life." (Proverbs 4:23) The flesh only obeys the directions and orders of the heart. For this reason it is necessary, with a great care, to impose a moderate fasting on the flesh lest, being fed too well, it would insolently oppose the precepts and reject its king who is the Spirit. But, if we place our trust only in mortification of the body [*in castigatione corporis*] and if the soul is not purified of its vices by divine meditation and spiritual exercises, with which it shall be occupied, we cannot climb to the sublime top of the true integrity because the malady of our soul shall infest the purity of our body. It is necessary, therefore, first of all, to purify the main thing in ourselves, "that what is inside of the cup, according to the words of the Lord, in order that what is outside of it will also become pure." [3]

He recommends, then, exploring the most secret recesses of the "heart" and chasing from there all evil thoughts and sinful desires. The perfect evidence of a successful purification of the soul consists in an absence of any seductive image or desire which may trouble the individual's rest or sleep. Though such involuntary disorders are not exactly sins, they are, however, the symptoms of the spirit's still being far from perfect and still being infected by the vice. Here Cassian formulates his theory of impure sexual dreams that sounds so modern:

> The quality of thoughts by negligence entertained in relaxations of the daytime manifests itself in the sleep of the nighttime. If then an illusion of this kind [erotic dream] occurs, it is not the sleep to be blamed but the careless passing of time that preceded it. It needs to be viewed as a manifestation of a latent inner malady.[4]

It is not the hour of night that generates in us these troubles, but that which is hidden in the intimate recesses of the soul: it breaks out as a rash on the skin, thanks to the rest of sleep, and reveals thus the secret fevers of the passions contracted by us through entertaining bad thoughts during the daytime.[5]

The urgent advice of John Cassian is that first of all one must keep indefatigable vigil over all his sense perceptions and sense organs, over his thoughts, and his desires especially. He must guard the integrity of his soul. Without inner purity no real chastity is possible.

The same operation of "excavating" all evident and hidden vices in the soul, bringing them to the daylight, opening and confessing them to the spiritual counselor or even to the whole brotherhood, is advised by the saintly author as a first step in fighting the other seven vices.

The individual should incessantly be on guard against the entrance of sin — via sense organs and others — into his heart, and especially against the sin remaining unnoticed, many times reiterates St. Basil. "When the day is over, before going to rest it is fitting that each man's conscience be examined by his own heart. Let the sin not be hidden, but told to the brethren, that the fault of him who has done such wrong be healed by the prayer of all."

For the same purpose of opening the hidden fault, one should carefully listen to the voice of his conscience or compunction. "Such compunction is God's gift" and helps in the discovery of the hidden faults.

Frequently man does not notice his sin and remains unaware of it, when it lurks in the deep unconscious recesses of his soul. In such cases the monk must listen to the voice of the more experienced and attentive brethren. "If a man not perceiving his own sin fails to condemn himself, yet he ought to trust those who can see his state more clearly than he himself." [6]

The monastic fathers view a hidden, undiscovered vice "like a festering sore in the soul," and urge again and again to discover and bring it to the light of one's own and of others' conscious attention. Any "uncleared" fault generates another. And if after clearing one vice the individual continues to sin, this means that he still has a hidden, undiscovered sin that hinders his moral recovery.

He who is drawn away by sin against his will ought to understand that he is being mastered by some other previous sin, which he serves willingly, and is henceforward led under its power even to things which he does not wish.[7]

This means that the psycho-moral diagnosis of the responsible vice was incorrect. The very fact

That he who has once repented commits again the same sin is proof that he has not purged away the prime cause of that sin, so that from it as from a root the same growth comes again necessarily. . . . Since certain sins have not their beginning in themselves but grow out of others, it is altogether necessary that he who wishes to be clean from them should remove the first causes of those sins. For example, strife and envy are not self-originated but grow from the root of love of glory. For aiming at glory in the eyes of men, one quarrels with him who has a high reputation and envies him who has a reputation superior to his own. If, then, a man who has once owned his fault of envy or strife falls into the same again, let him recognize the prime cause of his envy or strife, namely, the love of glory which is the underlying disease he is suffering from. And he ought to heal this disease of love of glory by the opposite treatment of exercises of humility — in order that, having acquired thus the disposition of humility, he may no longer fall away into the growth of love of glory. . . . And the same applies to each of such sins.[8]

These excerpts show that the monastic fathers knew well about the hidden or unconscious maladies of the human soul. The contemporary theories of the unconscious, of bringing repressed wishes into the open, and so on, were well known to the monastic educators many centuries before Freud and recent psychiatrists.

### III

### TAXONOMY AND THERAPY OF THE PRINCIPAL VICES

The monastic fathers did not stop at the general idea of the open and hidden maladies of the soul. They went much further and attempted to give " a taxonomy " of the main " faults," or " maladies," or " vices," or " sins " of the human soul, as well as their characteristics and therapies. In contrast to Freudian and related theories of one or two libidinal and destructive sources of functional mental disorders, the fathers professed a pluralistic theory of vices different from one another. Thus Cassian distinguished eight main faults or vices; St. Bernard twelve main vices; and St. John Climacus indicates a still greater number of basic sins. These eight or twelve species of vices produce a much greater number of concrete faults and wrong actions. St. Benedict's list of concrete wrong actions, given in Chapter Twenty, is an illustration of these " derivative " vices. They represent variations of the main forms of " maladies of impure soul." As a typical example of the classification, analysis, and therapy of the main vices, John Cassian's treatise on *The Remedies for the Eight Principal Faults* can serve.[9]   As mentioned, Cassian distinguishes eight principal faults or vices: the spirits of Gluttony, Fornication, Covetousness, Anger, Dejection, Accidie, Vainglory, and Pride.  The main tasks of his work are: 1. "to investigate the nature of these in all points however trifling or hidden or obsecure "; 2. "to explain with sufficient clearness the causes for them "; 3. "to bring forward fitly the cures and remedies for them."

According to Cassian "these faults, being found in everybody, are ignored by everybody [in spite of the fact that] these evil passions . . . claim for themselves dominion and a most horrible tyranny in our mortal body." [10]

As a general introduction to his analysis of each "fault," he outlines an already familiar theory that the way of Christian perfection begins with fear of the Lord and ends with the sublime and fearless love of God.[11]

Cassian's analysis of the vice of *gluttony* begins with an indication that "temperate partaking of food " that meets the necessary requirements of our body is not gluttony.

Bodily weakness [requiring food] is no hindrance to purity of heart, if only so much food is taken as the bodily weakness requires, and not what pleasure asks for.  [Even] the more delicate foods, so they conduce to bodily health, . . . need not destroy the purity of chastity, if they are taken in moderation.

The necessary amount and quality of food widely fluctuates from person to person, according to the age, sex, health, and other conditions of the body.  Gluttony begins when one becomes "overburdened beyond the measure of his appetite."  Gluttony

dulls the keenness of the mind, and when the soul as well as the flesh is surfeited, kindles the baneful and fiery incentive to vice. . . .  The belly when filled with all kinds of food gives birth to seeds of wantonness, nor can the mind, when choked with the weight of food, keep the guidance and government of the thoughts.  For not only is drunkenness with wine wont to intoxicate the mind, but excess of all kinds of food makes it weak and uncertain, and robs it of all its power of pure and clear contemplation.

The remedies against gluttony are twofold: physical and mental.  The physical remedy consists of tempered fasting, of abstinence from excessive food.  "We should exercise self-restraint in the matter of food."  Cassian disapproves of excessive fasting as much as gluttonous indulgence.

Each one should impose such a sparing diet on himself as the battle of his bodily struggle may require. . . .  A reasonable supply of food partaken of daily with moderation, is better than severe and long fasts at intervals.  Excessive fasting has been known not only to undermine the constancy of the mind, but also to weaken the power of prayers through sheer weariness of body.  The abstinence of prolonged fasts — where repletion of body follows — produces weariness for a time rather than purity and chastity.[12]

However, the physical fasting is insufficient for conquering " the spirit of gluttony," because " bodily lusts are not extinguished except by the entire rooting out of vice." " We must trample under foot gluttonous desires, and to this end the mind must be reduced not only by fasting, but also by vigils, by reading, and by frequent compunction of heart." " For it is not an external enemy whom we have to dread.  Our foe is shut up within ourselves: an internal warfare is daily waged by us; and if we are victorious in this, all external things will be made weak, and everything will be made peaceful and subdued for the soldier of Christ. . . .  We should for this reason practice bodily abstinence, that we may by it attain to a spiritual fast . . . the purity of heart.  Otherwise, our labors will be spent in vain." [13]

The second battle to be waged by the athletes of God is against " the spirit of fornication."  It is

a combat much longer and more tenacious than the combats against the other vices.  Only a few obtain complete victory in this enormous warfare which in human species begins with the appearance of puberty and does not end until all the other vices are conquered.[14]

Cassian sharply distinguishes between continence and chastity.  Continence means a perpetual struggle with the spirit of fornication, without succumbing to it but without complete victory over it.  A large number of persons achieve continence.  Chastity is a complete freedom of the flesh from any sexual propensity, image, dream, or thought.  It is an angelic state granted only to a few saints.  It is unobtainable without God's grace, *peculiare beneficium Dei*.  For victory over the spirit of fornication several external treatments supplement and help inner purification of the heart or soul.  *External* means are: no idle conversations, no angriness, no seductive sense perceptions (unconditioned and conditioned erotic stimuli), no worldly attachments and cares, few hours of sleeping, moderate fasting, solitude and withdrawl from the world " in order that the sick mind, less provoked by external forms of the vice, can arrive at a higher degree of pure contemplation and can extirpate up to the last root the pestilential source of concupiscence."

These and other external medicines are, however, utterly insufficient for achievement of victory over the sex impulse.  A complete purification of the soul from all sex elements is required.  This inner purge is much more important than the external measures.  Cassian's statements about this have already been quoted in the preceding chapter.  The inner purification is carried on through incessant *vigilance, prayer, humility, continuous feeling of God's presence, patience of heart, the fear of the Lord and desire of the celestial kingdom,* and by other monastic techniques surveyed and indicated further.[15]

Cassian explicitly stresses that all this means an endless and continuous battle of the athletes of God with sinful temptations of the flesh. One, however, should not be afraid of this perpetual battle, just as a physical athlete is not afraid of strenuous training and of his battles. Temptations are sent by God and perform an important function: the flesh must be absolutely conquered if we want to free our soul. This is clearly shown by those who are exempt from temptations because of the defective nature of their body. It is lack of danger to the chastity of their body and lack of battles against temptations that make them so lazy and so indifferent in their pursuit of virtue. Without conquest of temptations there is no chastity; without chastity there is no freedom of the soul. Herein lies the important role of temptations of the flesh and of the battle against them.

It can be noted that while the fathers regard sexual continence as a necessary condition of moral and spiritual growth, the Freudians view inhibition and then repression of unsatisfied sexual impulses as the main source of functional mental disorders, as well as of many moral, legal, and social " maladjustments." While the Freudians would deplore sex repressions and inhibitions, the monastic fathers would prescribe it. While psychoanalytical therapy consists of liberation of the sex propensity, and sometimes even in stimulation of the sex impulse, the monastic therapy vetoes all idle talks, perception of any — conditioned and unconditioned — sex stimuli, " concupiscence of eyes," ears, and other sense organs, withdrawal from all external forms of vice, and solitude. In brief, the two standpoints are almost opposite in these matters.

According to Cassian the fault of *covetousness* " is not a natural one in man, as the other faults are. . . . The love of money is outside of our nature." It is an acquired vice, not inherent in the human body, and acquired at a later period of human life.

This disease coming upon us at the later period [of our life] . . . can be the more easily guarded against and resisted. . . . If it is disregarded and once allowed to gain entrance into the heart . . . it becomes a root of all evils and gives rise to a multiplicity of incitements to sin.

Then it is extremely difficult to free ourselves from this vice, for " the love of gain becomes to a covetous person, as the belly does to others." Once entered covetousness cannot be extinguished by further gains, because the more the covetous individual has, the more he wants to have. There is no point of saturation in this vice.

Respectively the remedies against covetousness are twofold: the *external remedy* consists of " stripping one's self of everything," of any possession, of even a single last penny. " We must put an end to this madness [or " spiritual leprosy "] not by riches, but by stripping ourselves of them. For the madness of this avarice is not satisfied with any amount of riches." The *internal* remedy against avarice is complete eradication of the very desire of possession of riches. " We must not only guard against the *possession of* money, but also must expel from our souls *the desire* for it. For it will do no good not to possess money, if there exists in us the desire for getting it." [16]

Similar is Cassian's analysis of " the deadly poison of *anger* " or *hatred or irritability*.

We ought never to be angry at all, whether for good or bad reasons: we shall at once lose the light of discernment, and the security of good counsel, and our very uprightness, and the temperate character of righteousness, if the main light of our heart has been darkened by its shadow.

The only exception to this rule is anger directed at one's own anger and other defects. Otherwise, a good Christian should remain calm and maintain his peace of mind, independent of anything and anybody except his own will and his own control. " And so the fact that we are not angry ought not to result from another's perfection, but from our own virtue, which is acquired, not by somebody else's patience, but by our own long-suffering."

In order to obtain a full mastery over this vice,

we ought not only to banish it from our actions, but entirely to root it out from our inmost soul. For it will not be any good to have checked anger in words, and not to have shown it in deeds, if God sees that it remains in the secret recesses of our bosom. For the word of the Gospel bids us to destroy the roots of our faults rather than the fruits.

Among several techniques of eradication of anger, Cassian prescribes never to pray to God while we are angry, to remember daily that " we are soon to depart from the body, and that our continence and chastity, our renunciation of all possessions, our contempt of wealth, our efforts in fastings and vigils will not help us at all, if solely on account of anger and hatred eternal punishments are awarded to us."

As long as wrath and hatred of anybody remain in our soul, all other virtues are neutralized and made ineffective.[17]

Along similar lines Cassian treats the " Spirit of Dejection " and the " Spirit of Accidie." With the exception of dejection " in penitence for sin " all other forms of dejection

ruin and repress mind . . . make it impatient and rough in all the duties of work and devotion . . . make the feelings almost mad and drunk.

The athletes of God should be joyful and hopeful, and not depressed and sad.

*Accidie is " weariness or distress of heart."* Especially frequently it attacks the solitary hermits and monks. " It produces dislike of the place, disgust with the cell, disdain of brethren. . . . It also makes the man lazy and sluggish " in his prayer and work. Both " disturbances are caused in us not by the fault of other people, but by our own." Their common source is mental and physical idleness.

The remedies for dejection and accidie are, again, external and internal. The main *external remedy* is "occupational therapy," especially manual labor. "Manual labor prevents many faults. . . . A monk who works is attacked by but one devil; but an idler is tormented by countless spirits."

The *mental remedy* consists of meditation and prayer, in "keeping our mind constantly occupied with hope of the future and contemplation of the promised blessedness."

The contemplation and vision of the infinite bliss make us joyful and undismayed by the instability of this life. Knowing its transitory character, we neither become arrogant in success, nor dejected in misfortune, nor wearied in adversity. These remedies help us to remain steadfast and joyful, kind and loving, under all conditions of this life.[18]

In difference from other vices, each of which has but one main form, *vainglory and pride* have many forms and attack us from all quarters. They try to

injure the soldier of Christ in his dress, in his manner, his walk, his voice, his work, his vigils, his fasts, when he withdraws, when he reads, in his knowledge, his silence, his obedience, his humility, his patience. . . . Our elders admirably describe the nature of these maladies as like an onion and as those bulbs which when stripped of one covering are found to be sheathed in another; and as often as you strip them, you find them still protected.

This manifoldness, changeability, and variety of these vices make the fight against them extremely difficult. One form defeated, another form takes its place. Even more,

all vices when overcome grow feeble . . . but vainglory [and pride] when beaten rise again keener for the struggle.

They are especially dangerous through being mixed with virtues. They "try chiefly those who are perfect and devour with their dreadful bite those who have almost attained the consummation of virtue." There are carnal and spiritual pride and vainglory. Many a hermit and virtuous monk fall victims of the spiritual vainglory and pride. Both of these vices are the prime source of many other vices.

The remedies against them are: "the fear of God and humility, proceeding from kindness and simplicity or heart"; the yoke of obedience; unconditional surrender of one's own will; viewing oneself sincerely as unwise and foolish, refusing to do anything suggested either by vanity or pride; no boasting; no self-admiration; no belief in one's doing something remarkable; in brief, radical eradication of the roots of pride and vainglory from the individual's soul as well as from his overt actions.

Further on, a constant bearing in mind of the passion of our Lord and of humility of His saints; of the shortness of this life; of the insignificance of one's efforts in the life of the whole humanity; these and similar thoughts and images help (for the deeply religious monks and hermits) in development of humility, obedience, and other instruments for victorious fighting of vainglory and pride.[19]

Such in brief is the typical classification of main faults or vices; their characteristics; their causes and remedies. The essentials of John Cassian's psychology of the unconscious, and the hidden vices and their remedies, are shared by practically all Christian and non-Christian builders of monasticism.

# IV

## THE SECOND OPERATION: IMMEDIATE TRANSLATION OF THE INNER PURIFICATION INTO OVERT GOOD DEEDS

Any cleansing of the soul must be followed by an immediate translation of the inner change into the overt behavior of the individual; he must infallibly practice what he preaches — such was the second principle of the monastic educators of humanity. By this demand they avoided a most common mistake of many moral and religious crusaders, who seem to have been satisfied by mere "ideological" witnessing of their converts. Thousands of the converts of popular religious preachers, and others, manifest mainly this "easy" ideological conversion that hardly changes anything important in their overt behavior, and does not find any manifestation in their "good deeds."[20]

In their indefatigable demand for immediate corroboration of the inner improvement of the individual by "good works," the monastic fathers strictly followed the precept of Jesus that not everyone who incessantly calls for the name of the Lord enters the Kingdom of Heaven, but only he who does the will of the Father. There is no doubt that the demand is perfectly sound and scientific.

In fighting each of the eight vices, Cassian prescribes an actional or behavioral remedy. The remedy consists of behavioral realization of the inner improvements of the soul. "One should show forth all that is good and holy by his deeds, rather than his words."[21] Similarly, St. Basil reiterates that love of the brethren "should not be superficial, but innate and fervent," and that "each man must confirm his profession by his own works." He must not "render evil for evil. He must rather be reviled than revile, be struck than strike, be wronged than wrong, be defrauded than defraud."[22] "The mere giving up of sins is not sufficient for penitents to win salvation, but they need also the works of righteousness opposed to sin." "Love ought to express itself more in works than in words," reiterates St. Ignatius Loyola.[23]

Behavioristic also is the evidence of liberation from a sin: when the penitent ceases to repeat it, when he begins to hate the sin and to act contrary to it, such conduct is the evidence that he is cured of his vice and that God has forgiven him. The joyful bliss is another symptom of the sinner's absolution. St. Basil, St. Isaac the Syrian, St. Nilus of Sinai, St. John Cassian, and other fathers unanimously stress this behavioral symptom and evidence of the *indicium satisfactionis et indulgentiae*.

In this, as well as in many other points, the monastic fathers were radical and consistent maximalists. They did not hesitate to draw and to practice all the consequences of their premises, however radical they might appear. If possessions and private property appeared to be dangerous, they eliminated every vestige of private possessions, up to the private possessions of one's egos and personality.

If the vocation of the athletes of God required a strenuous training and complete mastery of bodily needs, they did not hesitate to impose the hardest training and to acquire the control however difficult. Viewed in this light, the whole system of monastic transfiguration of sinful men into the athletes of God was the most radical, most consistent, and most fearless educational experiment in the whole history of man's moral education.

## V

### EXAMINATION OF CONSCIENCE

Having outlined the general character of the monastic system of moral education, we can now take up one by one some of the techniques of this system. The first of such techniques is the *examination of conscience*.

It consisted of a systematic daily examination of one's deeds, thoughts, words, and most hidden movements in the soul in order to find out soberly what, if any, progress was made during the day in comparison with the previous days; what old vices remained unconquered; what new vices had crept into the soul and overt actions; what hitherto hidden vices were brought out into the open; and what old and new virtues were practiced. Examination of conscience was the most merciless exploration and excavation of one's sins or defects; a daily inventory of all the daily changes in the "statics and dynamics" of one's mental and behavioral vices and virtues.

Among other things the examination of conscience successfully performed the function of bringing out of the hidden recesses of the unconscious into the searching light of the conscious self the "repressed" or hidden impulses, desires, and ideas. This was done through constant, deliberate search of the hidden vices, as well as through a play of "free associations" of the self-examiner helped by his spiritual counselor.

The examination of conscience differed from the Freudian opening of the repressed impulses in several ways. The monastic opening of the maladies of the soul was done not before, but after an establishment of a positive moral standard in the self-analyzing person, as we have said before. The psychoanalytical operation of bringing to light of the ugly muck of the unconscious is often done without a preliminary building of a positive standard in the patient. Such a procedure frequently threatens to drown the patient without giving him a chance to come out into the sunny air of moral sanity.

Examination of conscience is performed daily, throughout many years, often throughout the whole life of the person. Its effects are continuous and lifelong. Psychoanalysis is a temporary and sporadic treatment ordinarily done in emergency conditions. For this reason its effects are also temporary. In a merciless, daily examination of his urges, thoughts, and deeds, experienced during the past twenty-four hours, furthermore, the conscience examiner deals with fresh and well-ascertained facts of his own life. He knows these facts directly and fully and, therefore, can easily put his finger upon his real troubles and their motives. In contrast to this, the psychoanalyst deals with a stranger-patient whom he knows little, and from whom he learns only a few fragments of his life experiences. In addition, most of these fragments belong to the early childhood of the patient and as such are vague, uncertain, and frequently fictitious. What a psychoanalyst excavates through his "projective tests" is also unreliable, because nobody exactly knows what the projective tests uncover and what exactly they test. No less doubtful is what the results of these tests mean and how they should be interpreted or diagnosed.[24]

In all these respects the technique of conscience examination is much more scientific and therapeutic than the technique of psychoanalytical projection, interpretation, diagnosis, and therapy.

Concrete forms of the examination of conscience somewhat vary from monastic order to order and from person to person. The following excerpts display its significance and characteristics.

When the day is finished let us give thanks for what has been given us during the day and for what we have done rightly, and let us confess what we have left undone, every sin whether voluntary or involuntary, or perhaps, unknown to us, either in word or deed or in the heart itself . . . beseeching God's mercy for all in our prayers. For to review the past day is a great safeguard against falling into the like again.[25]

St. Dorotheus recommends not only daily but weekly, monthly, and annual examinations of conscience.

There are three attitudes of man in regard to passions: either he gives himself to passions or opposes them or extirpates them. . . . Try to cut off passions before they have become habitual. . . . Everyone of us should investigate in what situation he is: does he willingly abandon himself to a passion and nourish it? or does he follow it unwillingly, not being able to resist its power? or, being carried on by habit, does he regret and repent for his sin? Does he fight it wisely or just battle one passion for the sake of another? . . . Everyone should know where is he and how far has he gone on the road of virtue. We must examine ourselves not only every day, but every week, every month, and every year. . . . After each week one must tell himself: "last week I was overburdened with such and such passion; what is the situation now?" Similarly we should examine ourselves at the end of each year. . . . Daily we should find out whether we have improved somewhat or have worsened.[26]

The most detailed development of the technique of conscience examination is given by St. Ignatius Loyola.

He prescribes three "particular" daily examinations of conscience, two of which are followed by self-examinations.

The first time is immediately upon rising in the morning, when the man ought to resolve to guard himself with diligence from that particular sin or defect which he wishes to correct and amend. The second time is after dinner, when he should ask God . . . for what he wants, for grace to remember how many times he has fallen into that particular sin or defect, and to correct himself in future. Thereupon let him make the first examination. . . . Let him run through the time hour by hour, or period by period, beginning from the hour at which he rose until the hour and moment of present examination: and let him mark on the first line of the figure [27] a point for every time that he has fallen into that particular sin or defect, and afterwards resolve anew to correct himself up till the second examination which he is to make. The third time is after supper, when the second examination will be made in the same way from hour to hour, beginning from the first examination.

Four additions follow for removing a particular sin or defect more quickly:

[1] Every time that the man falls into that sin or defect, he places his hand on his breast, grieving for having fallen.
[2] As the first line of the figure signifies the first examination and the second line the second examination, let him see at night whether there be an improvement from the first line to the second.
[3] To compare the second day with the first, and to see whether from one day to another he has amended himself.
[4] To compare one week with another and to see whether he has amended himself.

A method of making the general examination contains five points: 1. "to give thanks to God for benefits received"; 2. "to ask grace to know the sins and to cast them out"; 3. "to demand an account from the soul from the hour one rose up till the present examination, hour by hour . . . and first of thought, and then of word, and then of deed"; 4. "to ask pardon of God for the faults"; 5. "to purpose amendment with His grace." [28]

St. Ignatius gives still more specific instructions for making the examination of conscience more effective in "overcoming oneself and regulating one's life." His prescriptions and "chart" are as precise and systematic as a good physician's chart marking precisely the course of the sickness from hour to hour, from day to day.

There is hardly any doubt that when adjusted in details to the kind of individual involved, the examination of conscience proves itself as one of the instrumental therapeutic and educational techniques. For "agnostics" it may function as a purely ethical examination of conscience, devoid of religious ideology.

## VI

### TECHNIQUES OF REPENTANCE, CONFESSION, AND PURIFICATION

Examination of conscience is most closely connected with repentance, confession, and other procedures of cleansing of one's soul and behavior from sins or vices, as we saw in Chapter Eighteen. In details the techniques of these operations differ from religion to religion, culture to culture, monastery to monastery; in essentials, however, they are similar and discharge similar functions. The general purpose of these procedures is to unburden the individual from the crushing load of his sins or vices, to purify him from all impurities, to free his mind or his heart from anxiety, worry, and guilt; and to reinforce him in his strivings for moral and spiritual ennoblement.

Examination of conscience brings into the open one's faults and vices. For the self-examining person it makes the reality of these maladies unquestionable. The result of this finding is compunction, or repentance, or feeling of guilt for having these vices and, then, a wish to be free from them.

Monastic and religious institutions elaborated several ways of purification from the moral illnesses. Sometimes several of these procedures are merged together; sometimes they function separately from one another. The most common operations are *repentance, confession* and *prayer,* plus other techniques serving the same purpose. For instance, St. John Chrysostom (347–407) indicates five methods of purification from sins: 1. public confession ("if you are a sinner, enter the church and tell your sins"); 2. weeping and lamentation about one's sins; 3. humility; 4. good deeds of charity; 5. prayer.[29] Anasthasius of Sinai mentions nonjudging and noncondemning anyone, forgiving everyone all his sins, humility and repentance, weeping and tears about one's own sins, prayer, intercession of fathers and brethren, almsgiving and good deeds, soul-trying sickness and suffering, fearlessness in regard to God expressed in an insistent, pure, and trustful prayer, and so on.[30] From a broader standpoint all these ways, except prayer and work, already discussed, can be viewed as parts of the repentance and confession procedures.

The church and monastic fathers were well aware of the therapeutic, purifying, and ennobling effects of both operations. Origen (*ca.* 185–254) compares hidden, unconfessed, and unrepented sin with undigested or poisonous food in the stomach. When such a food is vomited out, there is relief. Similarly, if the sin is kept unconfessed, it poisons and sickens the sinner. When it is repented and confessed, the sin is cast out and the cause of mental and moral malady is removed. One should be careful, however, in choosing his confessor. He should be an experienced spiritual doctor (*eruditus medicus*).[31]

"Recovery, healing, improvement, purification, innocence, peace of mind" — such are the effects of confession, according to the fathers. It heals the sick conscience; reconciles the sinner with God; brings to him God's grace; saves his soul; reconciles the sinner with himself; gives him peace of mind; purifies and ennobles him morally. "Confession is the best medicine for the sick human conscience." "The sores shown to others do not become worse but are healed." "He who opens his sinful impulses to the fathers, drives them away." "An evil intention weakens at once as soon as it is confessed." "The ugly serpent of sin crawls away discredited, when it is brought by the force of confession [*virtute confessionis*] from its sinister subterranean cave into the open." "Inner impulse is the beginning and the root of sins. When it is opened, the sins are driven away by the grace of God; if it is hidden, it passes into the sin of darkness." Such are some of the effects of confession in the statements of the fathers.[32]

The concrete forms of repentance and confession vary. There have been *dramatic and undramatic, private and public, sacramental and non-sacramental, silent and spoken* varieties of repentance and confession, as we have already seen.

In the Egyptian monasteries of Pachomius there was repentance without confession in the form of individual or collective weeping about sins. Asked by one of the monks what to do with his sins, Pimen the Great (*ca.* 355–450) answered: "He who wants to redeem himself from his sins can do that by weeping; he who wants to accumulate virtue, can do that by crying; for tearful lamentation is the way transmitted to us by the Scripture and by our Fathers who said: 'Cry and lament; this is the only way.'"[33]

In most of the monasteries repentance and confession went together. In some forms they were practiced by many monastic and Christian communities because, according to St. Ephraem the Syrian, "the whole Christian Church is the Church of the repentants and the Church of the perishing."[34]

Historically, up to about 150 A.D. the early Christians regarded themselves as "the Society of the Saints," as we pointed out earlier, and were supposed to be free from sin. Even then some of them morally failed, however; the failures raised the problem of repentance.

In about the third century A.D. sins were divided into three classes: 1. light sins which were absolved without formal repentance and confession; 2. venial sins whose culprits were reunited with the Church only after public confession and expiation (in form of repentance, fasting, prayer, lamentation, for two to seven weeks) imposed by the Church; 3. mortal sins — apostasy, fornication, adultery, and murder — which led to an irrevocable exclusion of the sinner from the Society of the Saints. The mortal sinners also publicly confessed, and carried on the expiatory repentance. The Church interceded for them and prayed for them to be forgiven by God, but they were not taken back into the "Society of the Saints." About that time the task of the repentance of the mortal sinners and of their reunion with the Church was placed into the hands of a bishop to whom was given now the power of binding and absolving the sins. The bishop decided what sort of penance for how long had to be imposed upon the guilty, in order that his sins be forgiven and he be readmitted to the Church. Pope Callistus (218–23) decreed that after the fulfillment of the imposed penance, fornicators and adulterers could be readmitted into the Church. Somewhat later the readmission was extended to apostates and, finally, to murderers. In this way, with many complications and schismatic struggles, especially between the Novatians and the followers of Saint Cyprian of Carthage (ca. 200–258), the Church elaborated its system, forms, and techniques of repentance and confession. The decisions of the Carthage Council of the Church in 251 A.D. played an important role in systematization and crystallization of these forms and techniques.

They were invigorated, modified, and developed by the monastic fathers. Side by side with the sacramental forms of repentance and confession (performed according to the canonical rules with priest or bishop officiating), the monasteries introduced and enormously developed private forms of these with the freely chosen *spiritualis pater* replacing the official priest or abbot or bishop. The main forms of confession and repentance can be briefly outlined as follows.

*Public repentance and confession.* Both had the dramatic and the non-dramatic forms. As an example of a routine, daily, nondramatic repentance-confession the mentioned *Rule* of St. Basil can serve.[35] This daily therapy of the small faults was helped by the "client-centered" participation of the whole brotherhood: every one was helped by all. In more serious sins the public repentance and confession assumed in many monasteries dramatic forms. Even in the monasteries of St. Pachomius, which as a rule did not admit public confessions, admonitions were made before altar, or in the refectory publicly, in the presence of the brethren.[36]

In Benedictine and other monasteries,

. . . he who for graver offences is excommunicated from the oratory and the table must, at the hour when the work of God is being performed in the oratory, lie prostrate before the doors of the oratory, saying naught; only let him with his face on the ground and body prone, cast himself at the feet of all as they go forth from the oratory. And let him continue to do this until the

Abbot judge that satisfaction has been made. Then, when the Abbot bids him, let him come and cast himself at the feet of the Abbot, and next at those of all the brethren, that they may pray for him. And then . . . let him be received back into the choir, in such a place as the Abbot shall appoint.

This dramatic performance had to be repeated every day until the Abbot decided: " it is enough." [37]

Variations of this dramatic form of repentance and confession were widely practiced in most of the monastic orders. The public confession known as " culpa " of the Cistercian order is one of the variations.

This was one of the most curious and characteristic monastic institutions. The Cistercian rule . . . prescribes that, after the other business [of the daily Chapter], " anyone who knew himself to be in any respect an offender should ask pardon." After that " if any accusations are to be made, they should then be brought forward." This was a direct invitation to anyone who knew of any offence by another monk to disclose it. An opportunity was then given to the accused to admit or deny the accusation. If he denied it, evidence was called for, and the presiding officer gave his decision. If the offence was a serious one, the guilty monk was to be publicly whipped by some monk other than his accuser. . . . Any reference to these proceedings outside the Chapter was strictly forbidden.[38]

In other variations of public repentance and confession there were still more dramatic details like special penitential garb, special postures and actions of the culprit, dramatic intonations and prayers, questioning and answering, impressive form for imposition of penance, and so on.

For the penitent and his co-actors who deeply believed in the dogmas, cult, rituals, and moral commandments of the monastic community, this sort of public confession and repentance was indeed the intensest tragedy and an unforgettable psychodrama of which the penitent was the main tragic actor.

Staged in a sacred church or on its grounds, amidst the holy relics of the saints and the symbols of God, in His direct presence, the whole drama of the repentance and confession was likely to produce in the believers as great a catharsis as any tragedy or drama could do. From this standpoint, the whole procedure was indeed one of the most ingenious techniques of moral education ever invented. This conclusion is greatly reinforced by a study of the details of the procedures: almost each detail was marvelous from the standpoint of its fitness to the task it served.[39]

In spite of these merits, in a number of cases public repentance and confession aimed at trial and punishment for sin rather than at the improvement of the sinner. For this reason the best representatives of the cenobitic monkhood did not approve it as a regular method of confession. For the sake of moral ennoblement of the monastic society itself, and because of their compassion towards the sinners, they protested against public religious judgments meted out to the weak and the fallible.[40]     In addition they had serious apprehension as to the moral effects of the public confessions upon the listeners and public at large. One of the hermits fell into sex sin and imposed upon himself a year-long fast and repentance. In his prayer to God he says: " I shall again confess my rottenness to Thy kindness, to Thine angels and saints. If there were no temptation to others, I would have confessed my sins to the people."

The monastic moral doctors had an enormous experience in these matters, and now and then they observed demoralizing effects of the emotional public confessions of sex and other vices upon some of the listeners. These reasons explain why public confessions were practiced little in many monasteries, and why private and secret confessions to the spiritual counselor, the Superior, or the priest increasingly replaced them in many monastic orders. Here are the reasons for that.

The *Rules* of St. Basil ask: " Ought he who wishes to confess his sins to confess to all and sundry? if not, then to whom? " and answer that the confession of sins must be made

in the presence of those who are able to treat them: the same fashion should be observed in the confession of sins as in the showing of bodily diseases. As then men reveal the diseases of the body not to all or to chance comers but to those who are experienced in their treatment; so also the confession of sins ought to take place in the presence of those who are able to treat them.[41]

[The freely chosen spiritual counselor, *spiritualis pater*, is especially fit to listen to confession. St. Basil instructs every monk] to find a trustworthy guide to thy life, one who understands well how to guide those that go to God . . . for if the blind leads the blind, both shall fall into the pit.[42]

Then the Superior, the Abbot, the priest, the bishop are the persons to whom one can confess.

All things, even the secrets of the heart are to be revealed to the Superior. [Brethren] must lay bare the secrets of the heart to those brethren who are entrusted with the task of caring for weak souls tenderly and sympathetically.[43]

A poet of repentance, the Blessed Ephraem the Syrian, pointedly observes:

Repentance does not need noise, show, and pomp. It needs the confession. I instruct, pray, and beseech you to confess more often to God. Not for the sake of disgracing you before slaves similar to yourself, neither do I coerce you to open your sins to the mortal men. Open your conscience to God, to Him do you show your wounds, Him do you ask for the healing medicines. Show yourself to Him who does not reproach but cures.

Like many other monastic fathers, he sharply condemns public repentance and confession as purely external and hypocritical, ridiculous to the onlookers and offensive to God.[44] " A friend who corrects in secret is a wise doctor; he who censors publicly, only shames," says St. Isaac the Syrian.[45]

When the Blessed Moses was ordered to come to the public confession of a brother fallen into sin, he came with a basket punctured by holes and filled with sand.  While sand was pouring out of the basket, Father Moses explained to the congregation that it was not sand, but his sins falling from the basket.  In spite of his sinfulness, he added, he was expected to "judge the sins of another brother."  Hearing this "sermon in action," the brethren forgave the sinner without public confession. Many of the athletes of God viewed public confession as a sin against the Gospel's "judge not, that ye be not judged."  They saw in the sinner not a criminal to be punished, but a sick brother in need of recovery, compassion, help, and love of God.  "Christians," says Makarius the Great, "should not judge anyone: neither harlot, nor any sinner, but should look on all with simple kindness and innocent eyes.  They should neither humiliate, nor condemn, nor show repulsion to anyone; should not make any discrimination among human beings, and must embrace in their heart every human being, without any distinction between the evil and the good."  Many of the fathers preached the duty of "covering the sins of the neighbor." [46] With these moral attitudes prevailing among the founders of the monastic orders, the public forms of repentance and confession could not well flourish there and were eventually replaced by private, secret, sacramental, and especially informal repentance, confession, and moral instruction.

In discharge of these functions, a specially important role was played by the spiritual counselor, *spiritualis pater*, freely chosen by each monk for his moral and spiritual guidance.  Let us stop at a concise analysis of the role of *spiritualis pater* (equivalent to the Hindu guru, Moslem sheik), and the respective forms of mental, moral, and religious therapy as well as ennoblement, carried on through the *spiritualis pater*.

## VII

### Spiritualis Pater as Charismatic Alter Ego, Therapist, Spiritual Counselor, and Responsible Confessor

The term *spiritualis pater* (or Πνευματικὸς Πατηρ) seems to have emerged in the ascetic literature of the fourth century A.D.  It designated neither a priest, nor sacramental confessor, nor executor of a bishop's decisions, but an elderly monk, often devoid of priestly rank, marked by charismatic grace, pure life, wisdom, and experience in moral and spiritual matters. For spiritual guidance he was freely chosen and freely accepted by his monastic or secular disciple.[47]

*Spiritualis pater* was for his disciple simultaneously: closest intimate friend, loving spiritual father, most authoritative moral guide, soul-searching "psychoanalyst," alter ego of the "client-centered" therapy, confessor of the disciple, taking upon himself his sins and responsible to God for him, and a great deal more.  Of course, the above definition gives an idealized type of the spiritual father. Only a small minority of them realized this type. The majority of the spiritual fathers, especially in a later period of monasticism, fell short of this ideal.

Since this chapter deals not with the history of monasticism but with the techniques and methods of monastic education, only the best methods used by the greatest monastic educators concern us here. The best techniques and methods of spiritual counseling were practiced by the greatest and best of the spiritual fathers. This explains why further on we would be dealing only with the highest type among them. Poor moral counselors do not concern us here.

The role of the spiritual counselor was regularly performed by the abbot or the Superior of the monastery. Ex officio he was the shepherd of his flock to whom the soul of each monk was to be open, and who was responsible for each to God. But side by side with the official authorities, monasteries had certain elders freely chosen by the novice-disciple and freely accepting him for moral and spiritual guidance. The right to choose his spiritual father was the inalienable right of each novice. And the spiritual father chosen was free to accept or not to accept the monk or a secular person for spiritual guidance. Once reached, the agreement between the counselor and his disciple was regarded as unbreakable for the rest of their lives. Only in such exceptional conditions as the spiritual counselor's becoming dangerous for the moral and religious well-being of his disciple or the disciple's becoming unworthy of his spiritual guide, could the covenant between them be broken. Each novice or disciple could have only one spiritual father, though the latter could have several disciples. Ordinarily they lived together in the same cell until spiritual maturity was reached by the disciple.

The relationship between the elder and the disciple was marked by the following traits. On the part of the disciple it consisted of love, faith, and reverential awe towards the elder (similar to the feeling of the " Holy " in religion, according to R. Otto); [48] of complete surrender of his soul, mind and will to the elder, of total obedience and unreserved confessing to him of all his sins and the secret movements in his soul; of asking him for instruction in all problematic situations.

On the part of the elder the relationship consisted of the elder's unlimited love, charismatic help, and complete moral responsibility to God for the soul and body of the disciple, for all his thoughts, wishes, impulses, and actions. Complete surrender of the soul, mind, and the will of the disciple to the elder made the disciple " morally irresponsible " for his thoughts and actions, and transferred the responsibility to his spiritual father. A profound peace of mind in the disciple was one of the results of this " transference of responsibility." Such in brief was this relationship between the spiritual father and the disciple. [49]

The spiritual and moral prestige of the great spiritual fathers was exceptionally high. They were called equal to angels. Not only their souls but even their bodies were considered to be permeated by the divine grace of the Holy Ghost. They were believed to have about reached the summits of Christian perfection and became essentially God-like.[50] Their charismatic grace and their moral perfection were the foundation for their authority and the unquestionable evidence of their competence in spiritual guiding of others. Their charismatic gifts manifested themselves in telepathy or " extrasensory perception," in prophetic foresight and forecasting, in discernment and expulsion of evil spirits, in healing power, in ability to read the deepest secrets of the human soul, and other exceptional talents. As in Yoga training, however, the great spiritual fathers like St. Pachomius, St. Basil, John Cassian, Makarius the Great, and others forewarned against *cultivation* of these gifts. At best they regarded them as the low form of charisma which might even lead to temptation and moral regress. The highest evidence of charismatic grace was considered to be " the purest and perfect love " as the evidence of achieved transfiguration of human nature, as the summit of sanctity manifest in the elder's sinless thoughts, words, and actions.[51]

The complete surrender of the disciple's will to the will of the elder is called by John Climacus by the term " freewilled slavery." The disciple freely chose to become " a blessed living corpse " or " a mere instrumentality " in the hands of the spiritual guide. Except for the duty of a complete obedience to the elder, the disciple, after self-surrender, became irresponsible for his thoughts and actions. The whole responsibility fell upon the spiritual father.

The elders solemnly promised this to their disciples and added: " from now on do not worry yourself about things which do not concern you: God freed you from all cares and responsibility." The awareness of the moral irresponsibility, the feeling of freedom from " the burden of self-judgment " was in a sense pleasant. . . . He who had *spiritualis pater* left to him all the cares about himself, remained perfectly unworried about anything, and was not subject to God's condemnation.[52]

Obedience, that complete surrender of one's own will makes us " travel here below without peril and die without fear," and we are freed thereby from the responsibility of our decisions. The obedient man is like a traveller who, being led, sleeps as he proceeds [stresses St. John Climacus].[53]

On his part the spiritual father became an intercessor pleading with God for his disciple, even becoming the disciple's substitute in moral responsibility, as we have mentioned. Expressions of this tranference are:

My son! If thou fulfill my command, given for the sake of thy salvation, by the grace of God I shall not leave thou either in this or the next world. Before thy eyes I am taking now upon myself thy burden, sins, and duty, and thou has now become a new, pure, and sinless man: from now on thou shall remain pure.

Gladly I give my soul to death for thou, my brother.

Lord! either usher my [spiritual] children with me into Thy Kingdom or erase me from Thy book.[54]

By his prayers to God, by instruction, and by example the elder counselor helped the disciple in his spiritual and moral transfiguration. Now and then the elder transmitted to the pupil his charismatic gifts.[55]

Taking the moral responsibility for his pupil, the spiritual counselor naturally had to know all his sins and vices. The disciple's conscience and mind had to be completely open to him. The means for that purpose was the unreserved and most sincere confession of the pupil to his spiritual guide, confession of all the movements in his soul, of all the impulses, of all the thoughts, words, and deeds. Nothing secret could be kept from the father.

The eminent spiritual fathers were well aware of the exceptionally difficult role they had to play in this relationship. Only the elders who reached moral perfection and the grace of charisma could perform it satisfactorily. One of the conditions for a successful discharge of the guidance was an *unlimited love and a perfect empathy of the father to the disciple.* The spiritual counselor had to be simultaneously the alter ego of the disciple and a charismatic guide far transcending him in every grace. In this respect the spiritual fathers admirably performed the role of the "client-centered" therapist. "To be of assistance to you I will put aside myself. . . . I will become . . . another self for you — an alter ego of your own attitudes and feelings — a safe opportunity for you to discern yourself more clearly . . . more truely and deeply," [56] is the main attitude of the "client-centered" therapist. Here are a few statements of the spiritual fathers about this problem. Origen cautions the disciple in the choice of his spiritual father.

Be most careful in choice of your confessor. Before confessing find out whether the doctor can be infirm with the infirm, can weep with the weeping, can be compassionate and empathic.[57]

St. Basil states that the spiritual father must "care for the weak souls tenderly and sympathetically." [58]

He must be compassionate, showing long-suffering to those who through inexperience fall short in their duty . . . not passing sins over in silence but meekly bearing with the restive, applying remedies to them with all kindness and delicate adjustment.[59]

This "delicate adjustment" means: "Know that humility, authority, rebuke, exhortation, compassion, freedom of speech, kindness, severity, in a word everything has its own time." [60] Like a real virtuoso, the experienced counselor varies the techniques according to the person and conditions.

St. Bernard still more strongly stresses the role of love and empathy in the relationship between the followers of Christ.

For the merciful quickly discover truth in their neighbors when they extend their sympathy to them, and so kindly identify themselves with them that they feel their good and evil characteristics as if they were their own. They are weak with those that are weak, with those who are offended they burn. . . . A sick man feels for the sick and a hungry man for the hungry, with familiarity the greater as his own condition approaches theirs.[61]

The confessor [according to St. John Climacus], is a father, a judge, a physician, and a "spiritual man." [62]

Profound wisdom and enormous experience were necessary for the spiritual father to accomplish his task successfully. By listening to the confessions of others in the most secret sins, he exposed himself to many temptations. His imagination, emotions, and passions could not help becoming aroused and "dirtied" by the confessed intentions and actions. If he were weak, this could easily stain his own soul and lead to his own fall. This is the reason why the experienced fathers compared the persons hearing confessions with a washbasin. As St. Nilus of Sinai said:

Purifying the actions of the confessed, we cannot help becoming ourselves somewhat tarnished. A washbasin by cleansing the hands washed in it absorbs into itself the dirt of the hands. In a similar manner the person who cleanses evil passions in others cannot help becoming himself dirtied. A mere memory of the sins confessed already contaminates the mind of the confessor.[63]

Ephraem the Syrian explicitly points out that the confessor's soul tends to be demoralized by the memories of the sins listened to; that listening to confessions tends to rob the spiritual counselor of his peace of mind, and that now and then confession demoralizes the relationship between the spiritual father and the confessed. "When the spiritual son again commits the confessed passions, he begins to look at his spiritual father as at his worst enemy." Hence the unanimous advice of the monastic fathers: "If you are not inspired by the Holy Ghost, you should not wish to listen to the sins of others." [64]

In addition to this danger, the confessor's purity was threatened by the lust for power, by misuse of his authority, by pride, vanity, competition for the disciples, and other corruptive forces of the situation. This explains why practically all eminent monastic fathers indefatigably warned the prospective disciples to choose their counselors with the utmost care, to choose only those whose charismatic grace and wise experience were clearly demonstrated, and whose life and conduct were crystal-pure.

Among other things the above shows that they were well aware of what Freud calls "transference," and clearly saw that the danger of contamination threatened the confessor, therapist, or psychoanalyst. This danger is rarely stressed by the contemporary psychiatrists. Even more, the monastic fathers tried to counteract the danger by disadvising a dis-

charge of the functions of the spiritual father to all who did not demonstrate their charismatic grace, unselfish love, wise experience, purity of
mind, and sanctity of life. They looked at the functions of the moral
guide, spiritual counselor, and therapist more responsibly and scientifically
than many a modern educator, counselor, and therapist does.

Another thing to be noted is that the monastic educators were well
acquainted with the " client-centered " therapy, with real " psychoanalysis " free from the phantastic elements of the Freudian psychoanalysis,
with " conditioned response therapy," with catharsis of confession, with
dramatic and psychodramatic effects of public confessions, and with most
of the notions and procedures of contemporary psychiatry and education.

This survey does not exhaust at all the minor techniques of the public
and secret confessions, of the functions of the spiritual father, and of the
relationship between him and his disciple. It gives, however, an idea of
the enormous experience accumulated by the fathers in the field of the
moral healing and ennobling of human beings.

## VIII

### ABSOLUTION OF SINS AND THE COMMUNION

Having repented in one's vices, and having fulfilled any imposed penances, the sinner was absolved from his sin by the confessor and then, as
a final evidence of his regeneration, he was sanctioned in his purity by the
sacrament of Communion. All these procedures put an end to the agonies
and depressive moods of the sinner, and to the high tension of his mental
state. The Communion was the final evidence of the death of the sinner
and of the rebirth of a new person in the same individual.

The psycho-moral effects of these rituals upon the believer were much
greater than those of the verdict of " not guilty " upon the accused in a
court. The believing person was now absolved — empirically and spiritually — from his moral malady; he was made a new man, reunited with
God and the monastic community. His integrity, purity, self-respect,
and his divine nature were now reaffirmed and restored in a categoric
and unquestionable manner. He underwent the experience of a real
resurrection.

Let us briefly glance at the statements of the fathers about these procedures. Practically all monastic fathers state that confession has to be
followed by repentance. Otherwise, the confession is fruitless.

A soul which has lived in sins ought to depart from its sins with fear and
tears, it ought to hate its reprobate former life, and to approach God with
hope. . . . "For godly sorrow worketh repentance unto salvation." (II
Cor. 7:10)

Only the repentance, sincere in thought, desires, and actions, is fruitful.
About a penitent sinner the Gospel says: " Rejoice with me for I have

found my sheep that was lost." The fruits of repentance are " the works of righteousness opposed to sin." [65]    After purification by confession and repentance, absolution and then the Communion follow. " Participation in the body and blood of Christ is necessary for eternal life." [66]

Confession is without benefit unless accompanied by repentance and reparation of the fault.

Repentance is inseparable from compunction, or " the affliction of the soul " and " the sadness which comes from God." Eventually it produces spiritual joy.

With beginners this state of the soul produces silence, fasting, and disregard of insults. In the more perfect it inspires sentiments of deepest humility. The tears which it brings wash out the stains that have been contracted and render prayer acceptable to God.

St. John Climacus gives a remarkable analysis of the " blessed gift of tears " — and of the happy mental and moral results it produces.[67]

In early periods of monasticism the Communion did not always follow the confession. The close connection between these rituals was established in the fourth century or later. For this reason, in the earlier period, the absolution of the sins of the confessed disciple by his spiritual father sometimes followed immediately after the confession. It usually took the form of transference of responsibility upon the confessor. In some cases the spiritual father took upon himself all sins of his disciple; in other cases only one-half of the sin burden. A monk confessed the sin of fornication to his spiritual father, Lot.

Do not despair, Lot said to the sinner. There is repentance. Go, stay in the cave and fast for two days. I am taking one-half of your sin upon myself. After three weeks God revealed to the father that He accepted the repentance of the monk.[68]

The symbolic action of this transference of the sins of the confessed disciple upon the spiritual father consisted usually in putting the disciple's hand on the neck or shoulder of the father.

A monk for twenty years troubled by the demon of calumny could not free himself from his sin. He described it in detail on a parchment. Then, having come for confession to his spiritual father, he gave the parchment to him and prostrated himself at his feet.

As soon as the elder read it, he smiled and, having raised the disciple from the ground, said: " My son, put your hand upon my neck." And when the sinner did so the great elder declared: " Regardless of how many years this sin has been and will be committed by you, it is on my neck from now on; it does not concern you any more." The monk later on testified that even before he had left the cell of the elder his vice ceased to trouble him.[69]

When Leonty told his moral malady to his elder, the elder said: " Since you are helpless in this struggle, stand up and put your hand upon my shoulder." "When I stood up, weak and pale," tells Leonty, "and put my hand upon his sacred neck he told me: 'In the terrible day of the last judgment I shall answer to God for this sin which you think you have committed.' Having said this three times he ordered me to sit down and said. 'My son, since your soul resists and revolts against this temptation, you do not sin.'" [70]

In this sort of confession, the moment of transference of the sin was the most important moment: the transference absolved the sinner from his responsibility and regenerated him.

Before the absolution from sins the elder or sacramental confessor often imposed penances upon the confessed. In that case only when the penances were fulfilled the remission of sins took place. When a close connection between the confession, repentance, and Communion was established, the Communion was the crowning act of the sinner's regeneration. After establishment of this connection, only those purified by confession and penances were admitted to the sacrament of the Communion. [71]

These sacraments not only purified but conferred bliss, joy, peace, and even sanctity upon the former sinners. Hence all monastic orders prescribed them in some form. In some monasteries the monks confessed and had Communion once a week; in the monasteries of St. Pachomius each Saturday and Sunday; in other monasteries more often, even daily; in some others only a few times a year.

Taken as a whole, the set of operations of examination of conscience, of confession, repentance, absolution, and Communion, together with the specific functions performed by the *spiritualis pater* or confessor are marvelous techniques of moral regeneration and ennoblement. They proved to be delicate and effective, especially for religious persons and groups. They still remain ingenious if and when the religious vocabulary and color are replaced by purely ethical values. In their essential core, these operations represent universal and perennial methods of healing moral maladies and of ennobling human beings.

## IX

### Techniques of Prayer, Meditation, and Concentration

It has been mentioned above that the monastic life was an alternation of prayer and work. We mentioned also that public prayer occupied a large portion of every twenty-four hours and was regulated in details as to the time, duration, character, words, songs, postures, gestures, actions of every member in each of the services. No less regulated were the scenery and the religious objects used in the ritual. Each public service-prayer as sacred ritual was hieratically prescribed up to the last detail. Any deviation from the established forms was prohibited as sacrilege or religious offense.

The Rules exactly define the character of each of the daily monastic services. There is no need to reproduce the detailed regulations here. Each service was something much more impressive than, say, a classroom lecture or movie or radio speech. For the believers religious service was simultaneously intellectual instruction, moral education, and aesthetic experience. It made the believer a co-participant in God's truth, God's goodness, and God's beauty.

Even for a nonbeliever it has often been an unforgettable experience. The countless efforts of the known and unknown persons, who elaborated the ritual, the cult, and the dogmas, made them something truly great, regenerating, and beautiful. In turn the services stimulated the creative efforts of the great geniuses — be it Dante, Palestrina, Bach, Mozart, Haydn, Handel, Beethoven, up to the contemporary composers of masses, oratorios, and religious symphonies.

Side by side with public prayer, the fathers established private prayer, vocal and silent. Its forms were much less regulated than the public prayer. A great deal in private prayer was left to the initiative of the individual.

Here most of the fathers limit their intructions by recalling the precepts of the Gospel, that the prayer should be performed in secret, that before offering it to God one should free himself from enmity to neighbors, that prayer should not be too long and should not consist of many repetitious sayings, that the concentrated earnestness and intensity are more important than a mere length of praying, and so on.

In Christian and non-Christian religions the practice elaborated subsidiary techniques alleviating private praying.

If an individual wants a detailed instruction in how to pray privately, each great religion has several guidebooks in praying or spiritual exercises. *The Spiritual Exercises* of St. Ignatius Loyola and *Introduction to the Devout Life* of St. Francis de Sales are famous examples of such guidebooks. For each day of spiritual exercises these instruction books give detailed instructions on how to pray the first day, then, the second day, and so on, for each week of praying.

These instruction books are no less detailed and specific than instruction books in engineering or gardening or in any practical activity. Taken as a whole the religious guidebooks incorporate an enormous experience of generations in ethico-religious exercises. As such they have been helpful for millions of believers who preferred to use a perfect ready-made pattern to a homemade pattern of their own. A multitude of people in many fields have such a preference. The use of ready-made prayers seems to be easier than extemporaneous creation of their own forms of moral and spiritual exercises.

Finally, prayer and religious exercise for a number of ethico-religious persons assume the form of *meditation and concentration* similar to those in Yoga. Contemplative monks and mystics meditate rather than pray in the strict sense of the term. Their meditation and concentration is their prayer; and their prayer is meditation and concentration. To some extent meditation enters almost any prayer. But it becomes the main form especially for those who are advanced on the ladder of ethical and spiritual perfection: they communicate with God or the supreme reality directly, often without verbal instruments.

In the works of the monastic fathers there are many instructions on how to meditate and concentrate in prayer. In essential these instructions are fairly similar to the Yoga precepts on this matter. In some of the instructions like those of St. Ignatius even breathing exercises are mentioned.[72]

The prayer technique of the Hesychast religious school of Mt. Athos, and of some other monastic schools of the Eastern Church consisted mainly in meditation followed by somato-psychic techniques similar to those of Raja Yoga.[73]

Another device — *silence* — during work or meals or vigils was prescribed in monastic communities. One of the reasons for it was facilitation of meditation. Silence was believed to be better than an idle talk.[74]

A study of the technical rules on how to meditate and concentrate given by various religions and spiritual instructions shows a notable similarity of these techniques. The similarity suggests their solid experiential basis. They seem to stand even when they are stripped of a given religious ideology and are connected with another religious or purely moral ideology. The procedures work with Christian, Yoga, Buddhist, Mohammedan, and other ideologies. They seemingly work also with any ideology of the supraconscious or value system of truth, or goodness, or beauty.

## X

### Additional Techniques of Moral Regeneration

A few other procedures serving the same purpose of moral ennoblement can be mentioned briefly here.

*Annual or semi-annual absolution of all the offenses of each member of the monastic community by all the other members.* It usually assumed a public form. In the monasteries of St. Pachomius at the annual meeting of the monastic community (in August), "the striking scene took place when each forgave the wrongs done to him by others." [75] Similar procedures existed in other monasteries. The operation aimed to erase all tensions in the interrelationships of the monks and all the animosities accumulated in every one of them. It tried to re-establish inner peace in each member and interpersonal harmony in the whole community.

If and when the act of forgiving is performed freely and sincerely; when it is mutual and is backed by the whole community; finally, when it is followed by the overt actions of mutual reparation of the wrongs done — in these conditions the procedure is bound to be tangibly effective for the purpose.  In a variation, adjusted to the given individual and collective conditions, the procedure can be used for maintenance of harmonious — interpersonal and intergroup — relationships, and for prevention of growth of antagonisms.  If, for instance, the representatives of mutually antagonistic states, of labor and management, or of other mutually inimical groups would come to their meetings with the spirit of mutual forgiveness instead of that of mutual accusation, they would be able to come to a just and amicable solution of their problems much more successfully than they do when they are animated with the spirit of crushing the opponent, right or wrong.

*Setting Forth and Imitation of Good Example.*  Another procedure strongly stressed by the monastic fathers is setting forth and following a good example.  Especially important is the good example set forth by the Superiors.  Such a pattern is spontaneously followed by the rank and file, and becomes an important factor of moral and spiritual education.  Whether the Abbot, the Superior, and the seniors of a monastic community were democratically elected by the community, or were appointed by the higher authorities, or were selected by the stratum of equal authorities — all these forms of designating governing persons and strata existed in various monastic orders — all monastic constitutions indefatigably stress the duty of the superiors to be the virtuous models for the rank and file.  And the fathers required that the example had to be not merely verbal preaching, but actual overt conduct.  Here again the fathers show themselves " hard-headed behaviorists " not deceived by verbal hypocrisy.  The leaders had to be good indeed to be the good leaders.  Hardly any social group has stressed more than the monastic groups the principle of " *noblesse oblige* " and of the importance of the spontaneous imitation of the good example of the superiors by the rank and file.  Requiring an unconditional obedience of the novices and brethren to the superior authorities, the Rules demanded almost superhuman virtues from the leaders and governing group.

It is unlawful to put constraint upon others to do what man [bishop or abbot or superior] has not done himself. . . .  He who is set over the word should make himself an *example* to others of every good thing, practicing first what he teaches. . . .  He . . . should be merciful and compassionate, especially towards those whose souls are afflicted. . . .  He . . . must not abuse his power to insult those who are under him, nor even exalt himself over them, but must rather use his rank as an opportunity for practicing humility towards them. . . .  One must not preach the Gospel by way of contention or envy or irritation against any.  The teacher should set before himself this aim, to bring all to a perfect man, to the measure of the stature of the fullness of Christ, yet each in his own order. . . . One must instruct adversaries with forbearance and meekness. . . . One should depart from the unbelieving after exhausting every form of care towards him.[76]

St. Basil recommends a democratic method of election by the brethren of a most virtuous brother for the position of the Superior. Such a brother "should be promoted to be Superior over the rest, that his virtues may become the common property of all who imitate him." (In another place St. Basil approves also having the Superior chosen by the Superiors of other monastic communities.) [77]

Again

The Superior must make his life a clear example of every commandment of the Lord. . . . First of all humility must be practiced by him in the love of Christ that even when he is silent the example of his deeds may stand out more strongly than any word as a means of teaching. . . . Let meekness of character and lowliness of heart characterize the Superior. . . . Further, he must be compassionate, showing long-suffering to those who through inexperience fall short in their duty . . . meekly bearing with the restive, applying remedies to them with all kindness and delicate adjustment. He must be able to find out the proper method of cure for each fault, not rebuking harshly, but admonishing with meekness, watchful in present affairs, able to foresee the future, capable of contending with the strong and bearing with the infirmities of the weak, able to do and say everything that will bring his fellows to perfection. . . . Let not the Superior be elated by his high office. But let him be persuaded of this, that the care of many entails the service of many.[78]

These demands upon the true Superior are reiterated by practically all monastic fathers. They are unanimous in what really good government — the wise, loving, competent, and exemplary service of the entrusted brethren — should be; what kind of behavioral and vocal examples it must set forth; and how and why such an example is necessary and efficacious in arousing a free imitation by the others, especially by the rank and file of the brethren. The monastic fathers' views in the matter of what sort of government and leaders are good government and leaders deserve possibly as much attention as the views of Plato or Aristotle, or of any eminent thinker on this matter. In the opinion of this writer the good monastic "Superiors" are likely to be better than the good "Guardians" of Plato, and especially than the glorified evil rulers of Machiavelli, Hobbes, Marx, or Lenin.

Among other things the above shows that the role of suggestion and imitation, of "an exemplary leader and freely imitating followers" was discovered neither by G. Tarde nor by any recent educator, sociologist, or psychologist, but was well known to the monastic fathers of the past. The greatest among them not only knew of this role, but they set forth the good examples by practicing the noble verities they preached. The same cannot be said of many modern rulers and leaders, who rarely practice their noble preachings.

*Making Good Conduct Habitual.* Like other forms of energy, love energy can also be accumulated or stored, as we saw much earlier. The storing of love energy in individuals means making their love actions and reactions spontaneously habitual, interiorized, and rooted to such an extent that they become second nature. The monastic fathers knew this well and systematically cultivated habit-building of good thoughts, words, and deeds. In order to acquire humility, St. Dorotheus advises us to learn how to cut off the " desires of our will."

Through habit one becomes passionless and eventually imperturbable. . . . Try and you will build a habit of virtue. . . . When I began to learn, sciences appeared to me burdensome; I used to take a book with a fear similar to that of touching a wild beast; but after I persisted for some time, with God's help, I became so strongly habituated to books that my thirst for knowledge often made me forgetful of food, drink, and sleep.

In a similar way, one can make habitual any other virtue. Habituated virtue turns into one's second nature.[79]

St. Dorotheus and other monastic fathers warn against relapse into a vice before a strong habit of virtue is built, especially at the initial phase of habit-building. At that initial phase a single relapse into a vice which we are trying to get rid of can annul all our previous efforts. When, however, the virtuous habit becomes strong, the danger of relapse and its disastrous consequences progressively diminish. Habituated virtue gives a complete mastery over the opposite vice or sin. With this idea in mind the great organizers of the monastic brotherhoods introduced several techniques of habituation of virtues and inhibition of vices. This inhibition aimed either to break the power of a bad habit or to prevent turning a vice into a habit.

## XI

### GENERAL CONCLUSIONS ABOUT THE MONASTIC SYSTEM OF MAN'S ETHICO-RELIGIOUS PERFECTION

The analysis of the monastic system of spiritualization and altruization of human beings given in the last two chapters does not exhaust at all the quantitative and qualitative richness of the monastic techniques used for that purpose. It is hoped, however, that the outline gives the essentials of the system. Among other things the analysis shows, first, that monastic techniques were not a mere eclectic collection of various procedures, but made one unified system of moral and religious transfiguration of human beings. Second, it shows that all in all the system was ingenious in many ways and comparatively effective for especially religious persons and groups; third, that it contained practically all the main techniques of contemporary art of education, psychology, and psychiatric therapy. Fourth, in addition it contained several techniques of "climbing the ladder of Christian perfection" which are little known and practiced by the therapeutic and educational agencies of our times. Fifth, the bulk of monastic techniques were based on a deep insight into the human "heart, mind, and soul," and especially upon the profound belief in the supraconscious potential given in human beings. Sixth, the system attempted the heroic task of not merely bringing the subnormal and abnormal to the level of normal human beings; or of curing "the sick soul" from its spiritual malady; but it tried to transfigure human beings into apostles of creative love and heroes of spiritual perfection. Seventh, as the number and per cent of the monastic saints among all the saints of Christianity and other evidence show, the system at its heroic age succeeded, to a tangible degree, in this truly bold and revolutionary task of man's moral and mental ennoblement: with a reasonable degree of certainty one can say that it succeeded in its extremely difficult objective possibly more than contemporary psychiatry succeeds in a mere "adjustment" of its mentally "maladjusted" patients, or than contemporary systems achieve in re-education of juvenile and grown-up delinquents. Eighth, though the system is much more efficacious for persons who sincerely believe in the religion of a given monastic order (in its dogmas, philosophy, cult, and ritual) than for the disbelievers and agnostics, the bulk of the techniques of the system seem to remain efficacious when their religion is replaced by another altruistic, religious, moral, or philosophical system of ideas, beliefs, and imperatives of conduct — especially when these ideas articulate *Supraconscious Love*. In other words, with proper modification in accordance with the character of the individuals and groups, the monastic techniques of moral ennoblement can be fruitfully used in a nonmonastic milieu, among different religious, ethical, philosophical, and social groups. The efficacy of the techniques lies in the nature of the techniques themselves, rather than in the specific religious or other ideology connected with them. The techniques seem to be operative with all the ideologies and beliefs in the supraconscious and in the value systems of truth, goodness, love, and beauty.

For all these reasons the monastic system should be carefully studied. It can enrich us with several techniques of mental and moral therapy. Let us now pass to an examination of the system of techniques practiced in contemporary brotherhood communities.

## Chapter Twenty-Two

# Techniques of Contemporary Free Brotherhoods

## I

### THE SOCIETY OF BROTHERS

A third system of techniques of altruistic socialization is given by the educational systems of contemporary communal brotherhoods. Of these, the Society of Brothers in Paraguay, the Mennonite and the Hutterite brotherhoods are chosen here. In contrast to the multitude of short-lived, abortive, or miscarried experiments in total communal living,[1] the Mennonite and the Hutterite brotherhoods have existed for a few centuries. Because of varying social, cultural, geographic, and historic environments they have modified many secondary points of their organization during their historical existence. The essential characteristics of their way of life and organizations, however, have remained little changed. The comparatively long life of these brotherhoods testifies to the efficiency of the techniques they use for maintenance of the spirit of brotherhood in their communities. This vitality is the reason for selecting these brotherhoods for analysis of their methods of social, moral, and spiritual education. Of these, the Society of Brothers in Paraguay is singled out for the additional reasons of its heterogeneous composition and its recent establishment. If it succeeds in preserving brotherly relations among members of different races, nationalities, sexes, ages, religions, vocations, education, etc., this would show a real efficiency of its methods. The essentials of these methods are well outlined in the following statements of the Society of Brothers in Paraguay, Uruguay, and England.[2]

*Community in Two Hemispheres.* The Society of Brothers is a community group on an intentional and voluntary basis. Members hold all goods in common and work is done for the benefit of the whole group and for those who avail themselves of the help the community wishes to extend to all who are in physical or spiritual need.

The movement arose thirty-two years ago in Germany and now [1952] consists of some 850 members, men, women and children, of which number

650 live in Paraguay and 200 in England. A small group has recently been established in Montevideo, Uruguay.

*Who are They?* The Brothers are a new branch of the Hutterian movement, a community group which arose in the Sixteenth Century in Europe and has spiritual and historical connections with early Mennonites and the beginnings of Quakerism. In their golden age in Moravia, at the beginning of the Seventeenth Century, some 40,000 Hutterians lived in full community of work and goods. There are about 9,000 Hutterian descendants practicing community in some eighty " Bruderhoefe " (fraternal farms) in Canada, South Dakota, Montana and Mexico, now.

The settlements in England and South America, however, originated spontaneously from the modern world in an attempt to demonstrate that peaceful and creative community is possible today on the basis of the Early Christian way of life. The members of the Society of Brothers, on joining the group, surrender all their property and use their energies in the service of God and men for the rest of their lives without seeking a reward. Their guidance in practical conduct is the Sermon on the Mount, and they have found that the pattern of a new order of justice and love among men arises out of the free dedication of each individual, and of the group as a whole, to the need of their fellowmen, following the maxim: " Love thy neighbor as thyself."

They realize that voluntary poverty and simplicity, a harmonious and pure common life, with an open door for all, irrespective of nation, creed, race, age, sex or wealth, is the answer to the confused and frustrated condition of contemporary man, who faces the problem of spiritual and physical survival in a state of utter bewilderment. They know from experience that the need of modern man is as much spiritual as economic, as much emotional as physical, as much personal as social. Life is a whole, and its disintegration in apparently isolated spheres is one of the aspects of the present-day crisis. In the Early Church, where life was truly one, as all its multiple aspects were governed by one creative power, all the members were of one heart, one mind and one soul, and as a natural outcome of this spiritual, emotional and rational oneness, they held all their material possessions in common. In this way the germ cell of the new body socio-politic of mankind was created, which is still growing today and will eventually supersede the present order of decay and death.

The Society of Brothers does not attempt to copy the Early Christian example in an outward and mechanical way. It knows, however, that the same spirit, if allowed to govern men's life today, brings forth a community organism identical in its essential characteristics, if not in outward detail, with the Early Church at Jerusalem. These characteristics are fundamental principles without which no true community can survive or grow. They are unity of faith and action; love, embracing all and breaking down all barriers of property, class, race or creed; peace, as harmony and cooperation to the exclusion of injustice, violence and war; purity in human relationships, as faithfulness and creativeness in contrast to selfish indulgence, fear and mutual infliction of pain.

*Origin and History.* Arising out of the Continental social and religious movements of the early twenties of the present century, the community flourished in Germany . . . until the advent of National Socialism. Unwilling to compromise its deep convictions, the group emigrated to Liechtenstein . . . and England, during the years 1933-37. . . . A second move became necessary in 1940-41 owing to the war, as the community, then numbering some

350 members, was in danger of being broken up into its national components by the internment of its German members. The majority of the group moved to South America, where they were able to settle in Northern Paraguay. There, at Primavera, three communal villages were built up in the course of eleven years. . . .

A small group of three members left behind in England to wind up the affairs of the group, soon grew in numbers, and started afresh in 1942, when the Wheathill Bruderhof was founded, which now numbers some 200 people. The English and South American Bruderhoefe, although widely separated geographically, are settlements of people inspired by the same objectives: they work fully together, through a close contact for the common task and through the frequent exchange of members.

*Opportunities in Paraguay.* Primavera is situated south of the Equator. The total population of that area, in the neighborhood of 40,000, is mainly engaged in agriculture, cattle raising and lumbering. The rural population is very poor as a whole, and their health, education and general welfare have been badly neglected.

The work of the Society of Brothers arises from the character and needs of the geographical area in which they are placed. The basis of subsistence is cattle ranching, lumbering, wood industries and agriculture. A small hospital came into being as a result of the Brotherhood's counting three doctors, a bacteriologist, two pharmacists and several nurses among its members. Recognizing the great need and suffering prevalent in the neighborhood, they put their services at the disposal of the sick and ailing of the district, immediately upon arrival of the group from England in 1941. Several thousands of patients from outside the community are being treated every year. Paraguayans also avail themselves of the educational facilities which the community has to offer, and learn from the new agricultural methods introduced by the Brothers. Several families and individuals have joined the community from Paraguay, and a growing number of parents ask the Society to take their children into its schools. At a Nativity play written and produced by younger members of the community at Christmas, 1951, more than 250 neighbors came to experience the message of Christmas.

*The People in the Communities.* The members of the Society of Brothers are for the most part young, the average age of the adult members being between 35 and 45. More than 350 of the total membership of 650 are children under fifteen years of age. Most adults are married and they lead a harmonious family life. They come from many different nations and walks of life. The majority are English, German, Swiss and Dutch, with representatives from Sweden, Austria, Czechoslovakia, France, Italy, Latvia, India, Spain, North America, Argentina and Paraguay. Formerly most of them were members of many Christian denominations and movements; some were atheists and agnostics, others Jews or members of other non-Christian groups. Today they are all united in one common, living faith. Most members came from big cities, a few from rural areas, having worked in industries and offices as workers or clerks. Among the group are former merchants, teachers, doctors, mechanics, builders, engineers, clergymen, lawyers and artists. Very few were farmers. Several are university graduates. Most had a good all-round education, some hardly any learning at all. Some were well-to-do or rich, others poor, the majority middle class. Now they all work together for one common aim; all differences of race, wealth or creed are completely abolished. The old and the young, man and woman, intellectual and worker, Jew and Gentile, South American and European, have here found that they are fundamentally the same, that they all have to fight the same battle against selfishness and destructiveness within themselves. Helping one another in the fight for brotherhood, they find that they can be united spiritually and practically, acting as one body. This is their deepest joy and their greatest opportunity, and this they wish for all men alike.

*Education.* Most of the 350 children under fifteen and the 40 young people under twenty-one are children of the 90 families living in the communities in Paraguay. Some were orphans and children or young people entrusted to the care of the Brotherhood by outsiders. The education of the younger generation is one of the most important tasks of the Society of Brothers, and is regarded as the joint responsibility of all its members. Education is for and in community, the family unit being regarded as an organic and highly important part of the whole. The children live with their parents but join their respective age groups during the greater part of the day. The baby house, toddler house, kindergarten and school are important parts of every Bruderhof community. Breakfast and afternoon tea are taken in the families, whereas the bigger meals, dinner and supper, are taken in the communal dining room (each village has only one kitchen, as it has only one common purse, one communal storehouse, one laundry for all, etc.). Young people after leaving school are given an opportunity for training outside, which enables them, apart from the knowledge and skill acquired, to get to know other people and different ideas. They are thus encouraged to make an independent decision whether they want to join the community at the age of discretion, or live as other people do. Practically all of the young people choose the brotherly way of life. It is felt to be of great importance that the decision of the young people grown up in the community should be spontaneous and free.

*Contact with the Outside World.* In two South American cities, in Asunción (Paraguay) and Montevideo (Uruguay) the Brotherhood maintains houses where members live in community in an attempt to carry the message of brotherly life to people outside. These houses serve as centers for meetings and as a home for some of the young people from the communities as they train outside. They are also important economically, as most of the buying and selling activities of the Society are carried on through them, especially the one in Asunción. At regular intervals the community sends out members to other countries, mainly to Europe and North and South America, in order to make contact with other movements and seeking people, and to make the way of brotherly living more generally known through the medium of lectures and meetings. Circular letters, books, pamphlets and leaflets are published from time to time. The communities welcome guests and visitors for longer and shorter periods in Paraguay, Uruguay and England.

·        ·        ·

*And You?* The members of the Society of Brothers in South America and England feel that the message they wish to convey, by their lives rather than by fine-sounding words, has a bearing on the present world situation, and is directed to every individual striving to find a solution to the problems that beset men and women today. Community life in its fullest, creative sense, is possible. It is not restricted to any particular group of people, or to any special type. Any ordinary person can live it. You can do it yourself. The only condition is an unrestricted will and a complete dedication to this one object —

the full surrender of self. Community means freedom, freedom from fear, freedom from frustration, conflict, destructiveness, freedom from self. It alone is the true calling of man, the fulfillment of his deepest longing.

Additional details are given by Grace Rhoads, Jr., and by Eberhard C. H. Arnold.[3]

*The Community*.[4] It is understood that a guest takes an equal share in the work, of which there is plenty in a community of 600 persons established only ten years ago in the primitive conditions of sub-tropical ranch life in South America. It is remarkable what has been accomplished on a shoestring of capital in developing three villages, each with dairy, orchard and garden, one with the sawmill and wood-turnery, one with the hospital, and the third with the bakery and library. . . . One develops both some unused muscles and an admiration for the men and women who are able to do such hard work without most of the modern machinery which would be so helpful. The tiny hospital has profited greatly by a gift of a second-hand X-ray machine and is crowded with Paraguayans who come miles on horseback for treatment of hookworm, malaria, the South American equivalent of the dread Indian kala-azar, and other diseases, and who are beginning to bring their wives in numbers for pre-natal care and childbirth. . . . Shortage of labor and machines is one of the chief problems, but the hard work it involves produces a rare fellowship.

There are good times, too. Outings by the little river two miles away which reminds one of New Jersey's Rancocas Creek, celebrations of special events like engagements and the return of travellers, folk-dancing, singing, an orchestra, arts and crafts, and the walks which bring children into close contact with Nature, lighten the daily grind.

Youth takes a chief place in the community interest, as is natural when young people form half the population and a normal family has six to eight children. Lively, jolly children they are, too, cared for in baby house, toddler house, kindergarten and school through the day, joining their families at tea-time as well as breakfast, and having what one found to be an especially strong family feeling. At the two main meals the younger children eat separately in their age groups while the older ones join the adults in their common dinner and supper. Families live in apartments of one to four or possibly five rooms in long low buildings. Older children are apt to be learning a trade in another village or may be off to Asunción for their technical education in the year which it is expected young people will take in order to make up their minds whether to join the community.

*Its Principles.* The life of the group is governed by one guiding principle, that the individual must give up his will to God and be willing to follow His leadership for the community. Religion permeates all of life. No separate house is required for worship, for the " church " is the group of believers. Mealtimes are times when one attempts to realize the presence of God, as are the special meetings on Sunday and one week-day evening. At meals, after a song and a longish period of silence, some one generally reads from a book or the many letters which come from abroad. Meetings for business, held in the " Bruderschaft " or group of actual members, are somewhat like Friends' monthly meetings, with full consideration by the whole group and an opportunity for each to express his feeling of what is right. . . . One feels in this community of sixteen nationalities the same desire to reach a "sense of the meeting " that Friends strive to put into practice.

The government of the community is definitely democratic. Certain individuals are chosen as "Servants of the Word," "Witness Brothers," "Stewards " and "Housemothers " to perform certain functions, but their recommendations are always subject to group decision, "in the Light," as Friends would call it. The functions of these representatives correspond roughly to those of elders, overseers and certain committees, except that there is much more to be decided and carried out jointly in a group which shares so completely.

One finds men and women who have come from very different backgrounds, social, racial, economic, educational and religious, living here as Brothers. Paraguayans have begun to join. All are on the same plane of importance. . . .

Certain rules have been formulated in the thirty years since the group was founded in Germany by Eberhard Arnold, young Student Christian Movement secretary, following the First World War. They form a minimum of basic common belief and practice felt to be essential for the right living of the community. One rule which is considered extremely important is that no one should speak evil about another; he promises to go direct to the person involved if he finds anything wrong, and he promises to accept reproof by another. There are certain vows to be taken on becoming a novice and on joining. One promises devotion to God and one promises to remain in the community even if husband or wife should leave, the vow to God being considered higher than the one to husband or wife. There are sacraments, purely symbolic, such as baptism on being received into membership, and the Lord's supper at Easter, after one has examined his conscience for possible wrong relationships, and tried to make all right. There are lovely simple ceremonies such as when a baby is presented to the community and at the time of the harvest Thanksgiving festival, in which candles on the tables and flowers around the room make an atmosphere of quiet joy.

Joy is evident in many occasions throughout the year, especially of course at Christmas when the Christmas story is acted out even in heat which bends candles. The faces of the adults generally show a serenity and happiness rare in ordinary life. They feel they have not withdrawn from the world but are called to a life of brotherhood, based on the Sermon on the Mount and the second chapter of Acts, which makes all members one of another. If they have had to go as far as Paraguay for sanctuary, God must have a reason for it. There is a constant sense of being sustained by the group. The belief is similar to early Quakerism in its emphasis on Jesus and the Eternal Light which guides men if they but give up their will to the leading of God.

The experience certainly leads one away from egotism and gives a new sense of belonging together in the company of believers. It has transformed people who came to the group in great need, mental, physical or spiritual, or who were proud or dictatorial. Of course it does not make men perfect. All are welcomed freely to share in the life.

One of the great things for me was to know that one was not looking out for oneself at the expense of others, as one feels to be the case in saving for old age when people are starving in the world. One knows also that there is a place and service for every one, no matter how old or feeble. It is remarkable, incidentally, how the older people have stood the hot climate and the hardships. For hardships there are, in crowded living, in lack of many physical comforts to which one is accustomed, in rather monotonous diet, in climate, not to speak of the greater sacrifices of leaving family, friends and native country. The sacrifice of giving up property is usually felt to be minor. But all sacrifice seems to be forgotten in the joy of living a life of brotherhood, losing one's life rather than seeking to save it.

*Family Organization.*[5] Are integral community and family life compatible? Do they not mutually exclude one another, and, is it not a vain attempt to try to reconcile these two divergent patterns of life? In short, can only monks live in community?

Various ways have been tried to solve this dilemma. In Israel the Kibbutzim have put the education of the children almost completely into the hands of the group, although there exists a considerable variety of methods and degree in carrying out this principle. In many groups the children live away from their parents with the other children, the mother being completely free to work in one of the departments of the Kibbutz. The parents see their children daily, however, and maintain a warm parental relationship with them. This is one solution, unacceptable as it is to many. By this method the married woman of the Kibbutz is in a position to share fully in all the various activities of the group. She may, however, feel deprived of both the responsibility and the emotional satisfaction of motherhood, at least to some extent. It is important to note in this context that the Hutterian Bruderhofs, during their prime in Moravia and Slovakia in the 16th and early 17th centuries, had solved the problem of education in very much the same way.

The group farms of the Society of Brothers in England and Paraguay have worked out another solution: The family is regarded as an important unit of the larger Bruderhof organism. Whereas utimately the whole group is responsible for the education of the children and young people, this is carried out jointly by the parents and teachers (including sisters working in the baby house, toddler house and kindergarten). Frequently these who are in daily personal contact meet as a group, and find a common way of action in all educational matters. The smaller mealtimes, that is breakfast and an afternoon refreshment, are taken in the family circle, and the children share the same home with their parents. Yet during the daytime the children are cared for in their corresponding age groups. Since cooking, washing, sewing, as well as the education of the children is done communally rather than on a family household basis, the mother is able to be actively engaged in communal work, and is free to be a responsible member of the group. In the English and Paraguayan communities a careful system has been worked out in order to extend to each member an equal opportunity to attend meetings and mealtimes, which are considered important. In this way the mother of a family of six or eight children can be as active as the unmarried woman or bachelor in all the affairs of the group. This is important also for this reason, because the maturer judgment of older and more experienced members is thus available for the benefit of the whole group. The way in which this is done is quite simple: All members, men and women alike, have an average number of two evening chores per week, and therefore are able to attend meetings during the other evenings. The evening watches [" baby sitting "] during meetings are done in turns by all, and family dwellings are so grouped that only a very small number of women are required to look after the children during the evening. For Sundays when there is a morning meeting, and for special occasions like festivals, weddings, etc., a careful list is kept for both men and women by their respective coordinators so that burdens, responsibilities and joys are shared equally by all. In this way the significance of family life is fully maintained, but it is subordinated to the higher and greater unit of the whole community. The women, also those with large families, are able to take an active part in the work as much as in the spiritual and cultural activities of the group. . . .

This solution, as described above, is of necessity only possible on the basis of a deep spiritual integration of all the members into one living organism. Only where there is full mutual trust and complete confidence can the individual, the family and the community serve one purpose in full harmonious coordination, without one part hampering or destroying the other. True community, therefore, means true individuality and true family life. As it is in this case, teacher and parents carry the responsibility for each child together, both being members of the same brotherhood in which they seek clarity and unity about all questions of life. Then there is no reason why it should not be a happy, active and creative young generation which is growing up, as children, not only of their own parents, but of the whole community.

The question of family life in community is a vital one. Unless it can be solved, unless the men, the women and the children as individuals, and the family as a whole find their rightful places as living cells in the whole body, each contributing fully to the benefit of the whole in full harmony and fulfillment of their true function — unless this true organic equilibrium has been found, no true community can survive as a creative challenge of a new order of life in the face of the disintegration of present-day society.

## II

### THE HUTTERITES IN THE UNITED STATES

Joseph W. Eaton, R. J. Weil, and B. Kaplan give additional knowledge about the moral and mental sanity of the Hutterite communities in the United States and about the instrumental factors of it.[6] Some excerpts from their work follow.

" More than one out of twenty in a mental hospital. . . . One out of every ten Americans is likely to suffer a serious mental difficulty which will incapacitate them during some part of their lives." These are the best available estimates of the toll now taken by that conglomerate of ills, lumped together in the catch-all phrase of " mental disease."

There is a general impression that the Hutterites have a considerable immunity from symptoms of personal and social disorganization. Severe mental illness, requiring hospitalization, suicide, crime, juvenile delinquency and divorce — these and other indicators of personal tension so common in the American society at large — seem exceedingly rare among the more than 8,500 adherents of this religious kinship group.

What is the basis for the Hutterite reputation for good mental health? Bertha W. Clark, who travelled among them in the 1920's claims that they are entirely free of crime and notes their general contentment with life.[7] Dr. Lee Emerson Deets, whose doctor's thesis at Columbia University dealt with the Hutterites, observed an almost utopian happiness and concluded that " Compared with our society, the Hutterite community is an island of certainty and security in a river of change." A report to the Manitoba legislature by the Manitoba Civil Liberties Association claims that the Hutterites do not " contribute to the over-crowding of our mental hospitals, since the mental security derived from their system results in a complete absence of mental illness." Personal inquiry and correspondence with a large number of public officials as well as university professors who have made a systematic study of some aspect of Hutterite culture, strongly confirm the impression so well expressed by Miss Mary Waldner of the Freeman College (a Mennonite school in South Dakota close to one of the centers of Hutterite settlement): "Most observers credit them with remarkable mental health and usually credit it to the freedom from tension and conflict which they enjoy in their way of life."

Their reputation for possessing an unusual degree of peace of mind can also be traced back historically through many stages of the more than four-century-old religious sect. As early as 1669, we have a report by a Catholic novelist, Hans Jacob Christoph Grimmelshausen, about their community life. Their contentment attracted him greatly despite the "heretical opinions contrary to the general principles of the Christian Church," which he, as a devout Catholic, believed them to entertain. There was no anger, no jealousy, no vengeful spirit, no envy, no enmity, no concern about temporal things, no pride, no vanity, no gambling, no remorse; in a word, there was throughout and altogether a lovely harmony.

Nowhere in the literature can one find any significant dissent from this general picture. . . .

"No Hutterites in our hospitals," report Insane Asylum administrators in South Dakota, Montana, Manitoba, and Alberta. Outside of two patients, whom Hutterites brought in for short-term treatment in one of the Canadian provinces and five Hutterites who had some contact with a mental hygiene clinic, no record of institutional contact could be found since the immigration of the sect to North America.

A similar response was obtained from law-enforcement officers concerning crime and juvenile delinquency. . . .

Our investigation found that in the history of the sect since their coming into the United States, only one suicide, one divorce and two separations have occurred. There is no known case of parental abandonment of children and no incidence of arson, personal violence or attempted homicide. No sex crimes are known to have occurred although the Hutterites disclose knowledge of a few instances where their own strict sex mores have been violated during the present generation. These instances, to any reader of the Kinsey report, would hardly warrant the lifting of an eyebrow!

. . . Our study generally substantiates the Hutterite reputation for good personal and social adjustment, although it notes more exceptions to the trend than any superficial acquaintance with the sect would reveal.

*Co-operation.* Hutterite communities practice an unusual degree of co-operation sustained by strong common beliefs, values and a historical consciousness of identity. They hold all property in common. No wages are paid. Each person works to the best of his ability. He eats his meals in the community dining room, prepared by different women in rotation. If sick, the colony will look after him, sending him to specialists, such as the Mayo Clinic in Rochester, if local medical facilities do not seem adequate. In case of death, widows and dependents have no financial worries. The loss of a breadwinner never means the loss of bread. The Hutterite way of life provides social security from the womb to the tomb. The religious beliefs of the group assure their members a further guarantee for security beyond the tomb. It promises certain salvation to all who follow the precepts of their faith.

The co-operation also extends to the education of children. After the age of two and a half, boys and girls attend a communal kindergarten, where they spend most of the day. Later, when they go to school, they also spend many of their waking hours in the company of one another, under supervision of a Hutterite religious teacher, who is responsible for much of their discipline outside of hours when the children attend public school. Since both mother and father work for the colony, at least part of each day, older siblings assume much of the care of their younger brothers and sisters. In general, Hutterites grow up within a stable and closely-knit group of age-mates. Their imagination and expectations are influenced considerably by other children, close to them in physical and mental development. . . .

The Hutterite family performs fewer functions than in the American society. Nevertheless, there is strong attachment to and identification with their families. Children are generally wanted. Birth-control practices are considered sinful; violations of this taboo are extremely rare. The community makes many provisions to share parental burdens when families grow large. Most children are born with the help of a Hutterite midwife. The husband and the mother, or another close female relative of the woman, are present during delivery. Most Hutterites prefer the security which these familiar people and surroundings give them to what they regard as the " coldly antiseptic " atmosphere of hospitals. However, in case of complications, a doctor will be called, and the mother may be delivered in a hospital with proper instruments. After birth, the community will provide enough help to a mother for eight weeks to relieve her of all responsibility except the care of her baby. If she already has a large family, a single female relative or some other woman will volunteer to help her with sewing, washing and the many other chores connected with running a home. The Hutterite culture considers childbearing and rearing among its most important functions. Children are genuinely wanted and grow up in a community which is carefully organized to help them and their parents in this process.

The colonies are governed in secular matters by an assembly of all men who have been baptized. Women have no formal vote. In religious matters, preachers usually are allowed to make the decisions. There also is a tendency to give greater responsibility to people as they grow old. While formally their system of government might be described as a democracy with patriarchal and theocratic trends, most actual group decisions are based on common consensus. Hutterites take care to keep their villages small enough so that people really know one another well. Controversial issues are rare because leaders know how their followers think. Decisions are not commonly made against the strong opposition of even a minority.

Hutterites have a great deal of freedom within their narrow path. There is no time clock to govern their work. Their pay is never docked if they want to take a day off to visit friends or see a doctor. But this freedom is purchased at, what must seem to many outsiders, considerable restrictions. These limits are self-imposed, by custom and religion. Most Hutterites are quite conscious of their limits and are brought up to believe that " too much individualism would destroy the solidarity and peace we need to live together like a flock of sheep," to quote one of their leaders. Individuals must consult the group before they do anything not sanctioned by time-honored custom. They all wear the same clothes, homemade by the women for their families from cloth bought for the whole village. They eat together in the communal dining room, with no special diets, except for those who are ill. All homes are furnished with standardized and simple equipment. Hutterites believe it to be sinful to enjoy what they define as "worldly luxuries," such as radios, pleasure cars, fashionable clothing, jewelry and other material goods.

This puritan self-denial, however, is not coupled with a rejection of the technological developments of our age. For themselves, most Hutterites will forego running water in their homes; the old-fashioned wash basin will do. But for their chickens, they will construct the most modern coops, well designed for efficient egg-laying with running water close by. They will stock them with good breeds of hens as recommended by the Agricultural Experiment Station. Their machinery often is the most modern found in the neighborhood.

To the visitor they may appear to be a freak survival of sixteenth century peasant culture because of the way they dress, the ancient sermons they preach, the songs they sing and customs they adhere to. But in the economic realm they certainly keep up with what they call the "world." Their leaders also have considerable insight into current affairs, be they local, national or international. The Hutterites have become integrated in much of the American culture, but are trying hard to assimilate selectively. They use their religious beliefs as guides for deciding on modifications of their way of life in response to outside influences. The process can perhaps be described best as *controlled acculturation*. Only a stable community which has considerable control over its members through their allegiance and loyalty to its way of life, can make such a planned adjustment to conflicting ideas with which the community comes into contact. Although there are rumblings of deeper change, they have so far been successful in transmitting the essence of their way of life to the next generation.

*Genetic Homogeneity*. Hutterites are a predominantly youthful population. In 1949 over half (50.3%) were less than 15 years of age, against less than a third (32%) among the rural farm people of Alberta, South Dakota and Manitoba. The Hutterite birth rate is exceedingly high, 38.6 children per 1,000 people having been born to Hutterites in 1949, against 30.0 among all people in Montana or 22.1 among white rural people in the United States in general. Correspondingly, Hutterites have a low death rate; 5.3 people died for every 1,000 in 1949, against nearly 8 (7.96 among U.S. white rural people), or over 10 (10.1) among the U.S. general population. These unusual population statistics will require further checking, over a longer period of time, to make more certain of their validity. However, the phenomenal natural increase of the sect, almost entirely through natural increase, suggests that the high rate of births and low rate of deaths has been a continuous phenomenon ever since the people came to the U.S.A. There were about 300 of them in 1875 living in three colonies. Today in 1950 there are over 8,500 Hutterites living in 91 colonies, descendants from these original immigrants. (Converts, of which there are not many, are not included in these calculations.)

The Hutterites show considerable internal stability. It has been a common experience for minority groups in the U.S.A. to find themselves assimilating rapidly as they come into contact with the American way of life. Present-day Hutterites are the third to fifth generation of their people on this continent. They and their way of life have undergone many changes, but their group identity remains essentially intact. Few of their young people leave their colonies permanently. Some of the younger boys go away to "try the world." Most of them return. . . .

What makes the sect's experience even more significant is that their social system has perpetuated itself for over 400 years, often in the face of terrible persecution (or perhaps because of it, too). They are no odd mutation of history. They originated around the year 1528 when a group of Tyrolese peasants, influenced by an Anabaptist preacher named Jacob Hutter, fled to Moravia to escape persecution. Hutter exhorted his followers to restore the simple truths of the Bible, as he saw them. Among the most outstanding differences with the established churches was his belief in the sinfulness of private property, the wickedness of the use of force under any circumstances, adult baptism, refusal to take oaths and the insistence on simplicity in living conditions. In 1536 Hutter was burned at the stake after terrible tortures. For over three centuries a band of faithful, sometimes diminishing in numbers close to extinction, were forced to flee many times — from Switzerland and Austria, to Moravia, Hungary, Rumania and finally to Russia. In Russia they lived for nearly a century under the liberal conditions offered such refugees by the czarina, Catherine the Great, who was anxious to build up the economic power of her country through the attraction of skilled laborers and farmers. In the 1870's the Hutterites moved to the United States when Czar Alexander II threatened to abrogate their privileges of maintaining their own schools and of exemption from military service.

In the annals of American experiments with co-operative living, the Hutterites stand out because of their capacity to maintain permanent co-operative farm communities. The Owenites, Brook Farm, Oneida and the Amana people, to mention only a few of the roughly 300 efforts to live communally, are today only of interest to historians. The Hutterites have grown and expanded in the face of competition for their young generation with the more powerful American culture.

The Hutterites do many things differently from the way most Americans would do them. However, they are closely and deeply influenced by the larger culture. Their children attend a public school in the colony usually taught by a non-Hutterite, as the sect does not encourage its own young people to get the necessary advanced education to qualify for school teaching. They have daily business and social contact with the "world." They are more literate and capable of speaking English than many of the minority groups in the United States and Canada. However, they keep going without the incentives we need to motivate our people. Wealth, personal power and artistic adornment are considered sinful objectives. They also get along without many of the negative social controls, like imprisonment, fines, threats of loss of livelihood or loss of life itself.

The order of their society is maintained through an internalized discipline of the conscience, re-enforced through a fear of external punishment and social disapproval. The Hutterites have certain freedoms we don't have; but also many restrictions which they themselves recognize as "very hard" to adhere to. But for the most part, they do.

Our search for clues to the cultural and environmental factors in mental health is complicated by Hutterite homogeneity through heredity and a long history of biological selection. The Hutterites may have acquired some genetic or somatic immunity against certain mental diseases, in which such factors play an important role. They are one of America's most inbred groups, because of their anxiety for centuries to marry only with their religious sect. There have been few converts within the last 75 years, during which there was a natural increase of over 2,800%, almost exclusively through in-group marriages. There are now only sixteen family names among the kinship Hutterites, with eight names predominating and accounting for a considerable proportion of the entire population. There also are folk beliefs among the Hutterites about the influence of heredity on personality. Some family strains are considered constitutionally healthy or weak by them. Some American doctors, who practice among them, express similar hunches. Our research team is therefore not overlooking the possible role of genetic and somatic factors in the mental health of these people, although short of a complete genetic survey, which technically and financially cannot be made within the framework of our present study, their influence can only be assessed qualitatively.

The American bookstores are full of well advertised guides to " perfect happiness." The covers and titles of the volumes are well designed to suggest: " Read me, I cost only $3.50, won't take more than a few hours of your time and won't involve you in any real change of your life pattern! " The study of the Hutterite culture strongly suggests that mental health and ill-healths are rooted much deeper in the very essence of our personal lives and civilization.[8]

# III

## Conclusions

The preceding descriptions of the Hutterite brotherhoods — in Paraguay as well as in the United States — bring out clearly the main factors of altruism emphasized in this study. First, each member of these brotherhoods is fully identified with Supreme Love and the precepts of the Sermon on the Mount. The overwhelming majority call this supreme value " God," others — the freethinkers in the Paraguay community — call it Supreme Love or something similar. Second, the adults who join the brotherhood do so quite freely, by their own choice. Third, every member willingly surrenders his egos to the supreme value and the brotherhood. Fourth, all members have thus the common fund of the basic values of the brotherhood. Fifth, each member identifies himself or herself with the brotherhood community: through that he or she becomes free from all conflicting loyalties and group affiliations. Sixth, through the triple identifications — with the supreme love, with the basic common values, and with the brotherhood community — each member acquires: a) harmony of his egos, their sublimation to, and control of their conscious and unconscious drives by, the supreme value — God, Love, Self — with which the member identifies himself; b) harmony of the members with one another; and c) investment of their total personality in one community. Seventh, as a result of this triple " harmonization," the members are at peace with themselves, with one another, and with the world at large. Eighth, as a consequence of this, they free themselves to a considerable degree from endless worries about tomorrow, from the sense of insecurity, from gnawing ambitions, competitive antagonisms, loneliness, and ego-centered unhappiness. Ninth, reared in this atmosphere of love, the children freely grow into " fortunate altruists " and spontaneously perpetuate the brotherly way of life of their parents.

Tenth, the freedom to leave the community by those who for some reasons prefer the individualistic way of life serves as the safety valve for the community: through a free exodus or unhindered disaffiliation of the individualistic elements the brotherhood incessantly frees itself from the discordant members and maintains its brotherly unity.

In all these respects the basic principles of the brotherhood are similar to those of the monastic orders. Both of these types of organization incorporate in their structure and activity three basic principles of altruistic groups: ideological and behaverial identification of the group and of its members with the supreme value of love (called by different names); common fund of the basic values for all members; and the total affiliation of each member with the (monastic or brotherhood) community, with resulting surrender of his egos and affiliations to the supreme value of the community and the community itself.

This explains why the monastic and the "secular" communties of the Hutterite type have been comparatively long-living among many short-lived "communal groups" and why, on the other hand, an enormous majority of numerous "communal experiments" have quickly failed and disintegrated. If one carefully investigates the short-lived "brotherhoods" or "communistic experiments," one finds that these have lacked one or more of the basic conditions of altruistic group or membership. Either their members did not identify themselves with a supreme value of love and did not "sublimate" to it their egos and drives; or they have not surrendered their little egos and selfish interests to the supreme value and to the community, remaining "egotistic" and "individualistic"; or did not invest their whole personality into the community; or did not create a common fund of the basic values for all the members of the brotherhood. Being deficient in one or several of these properties, such communities could not acquire the intrapersonal integration of their members, the interpersonal harmony among their participants, and the strong unity of the community itself. These disharmonies and defects in their turn hindered the realization of most of the benefits of the true brotherhood: peace of mind, sense of security, joy of participation in a creative effort of the group; freedom from worries, ambitions and from inner anarchy of conflicting egos and drives. The communal enterprise of that sort has all the shortcomings of competitive individualistic groups, and of superficial collectivism, without the virtues of either. No wonder that such enterpises have been short-lived.

If a few of these lived longer, they did so only by becoming "coercive societies," bound together by the rude force exerted by their rulers. Such societies, exemplified by the U.S.S.R., have, of course, many altruistic threads in the interrelationships of their population; nevertheless in their main structure they are largely compulsory societies run by their rulers' coercion, pitiless punishment, coarse rewards, hate, and other semi-animal forces. Such coercive groups are the very opposite of the free altruistic community. Without the cement of compulsion, all communal bodies devoid of the above conditions of altruistic communities are liable to disintegration. They either degenerate into a competitive association of individuals and cliques, each motivated by selfish utilitarian drives, or else into a " Communistic society " of prisoners, enclosed by coercive walls, fear of punishment, greed of reward, and by the egoistic lust for power of their rulers.

# PART FIVE

# TRAGEDY AND TRANSCENDENCE OF TRIBAL ALTRUISM

PART FOUR

TRAGEDY AND TRANSCENDENCE OF TRIBAL ATTITUDE

Chapter Twenty-Three

# From Tribal Egoism to Universal Altruism

### TRAGEDY AND VICTIMS OF TRIBAL ALTRUISM-EGOISM

*If unselfish love does not extend over the whole of mankind, if it is con-*
*fined within one group — a given family, tribe, nation, race, religious de-*
*nomination, political party, trade union, caste, social class or any part of*
*humanity — such an in-group altruism tends to generate an out-group*
*antagonism. And the more intense and exclusive the in-group solidarity*
*of its members, the more unavoidable are the clashes between the group*
*and the rest of humanity.* Herein lies the tragedy of tribal altruism not
extended over the whole of mankind or over everyone and all. An exclusive love of one's own group makes its members indifferent or even
aggressive towards other groups and outsiders. The members of " my
group, right or wrong " cannot help treating the rest of humanity as a
mere means for their group. If its well-being can be obtained only at the
cost of the outsiders, the group does not hesitate to attack, to exploit, and
to misuse the rest of mankind in any way in which it can accomplish this
task. Its narrow in-group altruism turns — for the outsiders — into an
aggressive group egoism.

Mo-tzu (*ca.* 475–393 B.C.) well described this egoism of a tribal altruist.

A thief loves [*ai*] his own family and does not love other families, hence he
steals from other families in order to benefit his own family. Each grandee
loves his own clan and does not love other clans, hence he causes disturbances
to other clans to benefit his own clan. Each feudal lord loves his own state
and does not love other states, so he attacks other states in order to benefit his
own state. The causes of all disturbances . . . lie herein. . . . It is always
from want of equal love to all.[1]

This idea of Mo-tzu was reiterated in Chinese Confucianism by Han Yü
(A.D. 768–824), Jou Dun-yi (1017–1073), Jang Dzai (1020–1077), and
Wang Shou-ren (1472–1529).

" Imperialistic " encroachments of any selfish group are opposed, first
of all, by *all persons whose love behavior extends over other groups and*

*especially over the whole of humanity.* They cannot approve aggressive misdeeds of an exclusive tribal loyalty. Their universal or more extensive [2] love cannot help clashing with the narrow, tribal love of the group. Hence the conflict between such persons and the group. Hence the persecution of such individuals by the group. Hence the tragic martyrdom of the apostles of universal love, who have been condemned to death, imprisoned, banished, tortured, and variously persecuted by the partisans of tribal loyalty. Socrates, Jesus, St. Peter, St. Paul, Al Hallaj, Gandhi and some 37 per cent of the saintly Christian altruists are eminent examples of its victims. The total number of the martyrs of tribal patriotism of various political, ethnic, racial, religious, economic, occupational, and other collectivities with exclusive in-group solidarity has been enormous in human history.

Jesus well understood this clash between the two types, and the persecution of the universal altruists by the tribal ones, when he said to his disciples: "And ye shall be hated of all men for my name's sake. . . ." "Think not that I am come to send peace on earth: I came not to send peace, but a sword. For I am come to set a man at variance against his father, and the daughter against her mother." [3] Almost any universal altruist is bound to become a " subversive enemy " to be persecuted by the " patriotic " tribal altruists. In this sense the eternal tragedy of the *agnus Dei qui tollis peccata mundi* continues in human history unabated. The tribal patriots of " the Athenian Committee on un-Athenian Activities " condemned to death Socrates; " the Jewish Committee on un-Jewish Activities " crucified Jesus; " the Muslim Committee on un-Muslim Activities " quartered and burned Al Hallaj; the self-appointed guardians of Hindu Orthodoxy shot Gandhi for his " un-Orthodox " activities. The annals of history are sprinkled with the blood of altruistic " heretics and schismatics " put to death by the tribal " orthodox " religions; indeed, each page of these annals is soaked in the blood of altruistic " subversives " executed by the tribal state governments. Most of the political parties, racial, occupational, national, and other groups have been guilty in persecution of their " disloyal " members whose " disloyalty " consisted exactly in extension of their love far beyond the boundaries of the respective organization. And so this drama is continued up to this day when a multitude of " patriotic governments " and " crusading committees " relentlessly persecute many a " disloyal " altruist in the name of Communist, Socialist, Liberal, Conservative, Fascist, Democratic, Capitalist, Labor, Atheist, Religious, and other tribal solidarities and lilliputian in-group patriotisms. And so far, no end of this tragedy is visible.

*Another, much larger class of victims of tribal altruism is made up of these groups themselves.* By their narrow in-group solidarity these groups bring upon themselves disastrous consequences of their own egoism and often dig their own graves. As the overwhelming majority of organized groups are guilty — in various degrees — of tribal egoism, and as the total membership of all such organizations embraces almost the whole mankind, mankind itself becomes a victim of its own tribal selfishness. Since an exclusive in-group altruism turns into an out-group egoism, an intergroup conflict becomes unavoidable in such a situation. An aggressive struggle of a group for its own aggrandizement calls forth a counter-attack of the encroached groups against the aggressor. The result is a relentless intergroup struggle for existence and domination. Whether in the form of a cold or a hot war, this intergroup warfare has gone on incessantly in human history, and has filled its annals with the most deadly, most bloody, and most shameful deeds of Homo sapiens. An exclusive tribal solidarity — known also as tribal patriotism, tribal loyalty, and tribal altruism — has mercilessly set man against man, and group against group. It has killed more human beings and destroyed more cities and villages than all the epidemics, hurricanes, storms, floods, earthquakes, and volcanic eruptions taken together. It has brought upon mankind more suffering than any other catastrophe. Tribal solidarity has been the greatest curse and the most merciless Nemesis of humanity's tribal egoism and moral stupidity. It has been responsible for all the interstate and inter-religious wars, and for all the interracial, interethnic, intertribal, inter-caste, and interclass wars, as well as for all the cold wars between masters and slaves, patricians and plebeians, nobility and serfs, the rich and the poor, the privileged and the underdogs, the rulers and the ruled, capitalists and proletarians, labor and management, " the chosen " and " the inferior people," and for hundreds of other intergroup conflicts. Mountains of corpses and seas of human blood have been sacrificed to the Moloch of warfare of exclusive tribal solidarities. In an endless rhythm of today's victors and tomorrow's victims, the groups have been succeeding one another in this process of mutual extermination. And as long as tribal altruism-egoism continues, the intergroup warfare is bound to continue also.

## II

### First Steps for Elimination of Intergroup Warfare

If the curse of intergroup warfare is to be ended or, at least, notably diminished, the necessary step towards this task consists evidently in *extension of everybody's altruistic conduct far beyond the membership of his own groups, eventually over the whole of mankind, or over everybody and all!* When every human being is actually treated by every other human being as an end value; when no truly harmful action is committed by anybody against anybody; when one's joy and sorrow become everybody's joy and sorrow; when everyone is responsible for everyone; when everybody is spontaneously prompted to help, within his capacity, everyone who needs help; in brief, when everyone behaves as dear brother or sister to everybody: then, and only then, altruistic love is extended over the whole of humanity. With such an extension of creative love, all exclusive tribal solidarities are cleansed of their egoistic poison. With such a purification the very roots of intergroup warfare are cut off; with the roots destroyed, the warfare itself is bound to die out. Such is the prescription for elimination of the curse of intergroup conflicts from the human universe.

In order that this prescription can have practical value it needs further clarifications, and especially practical specifications as to where the prescribed " medical ingredients " can be obtained, how " the medicine " is to be used, and how the sick humanity can be induced to " swallow it."

The prescription, let us note, does not mean an annulment of differentiation of mankind into multifarious groups and cultural organizations. In a good family the parents and children are different from one another; however, this difference does not hinder their intense love for one another. Sex, age, and somatic differences of individuals are not an obstacle for mutual love of man and woman, of the old and the young, of the strong and the weak. Neither racial, national, ethnic, occupational, cultural, educational, political, nor religious dissimilarity is an impediment for mutual friendship when these differences are rightly perceived as mutually enriching each of the parties concerned, or when they are regarded as multicolored manifestations of the creative genius of humanity. The eminent altruists have loved most different persons and groups, and have had no difficulty in loving especially those who were different from themselves.

The musical treasury of mankind would have been enormously impoverished if all the musical masterpieces had consisted of only Beethoven-like or Bach-like music. The great literature of humanity would have been poor indeed if it had contained only Homer-like or Shakespeare-like literature. The religious creativity of many would have been quite limited if it had created only one great religion, be it Taoism or Hinduism or Christianity. The same is true of philosophy and architecture, painting and drama, folkways and mores, ethics and law, economics and politics, persons and social groups. A monotonous similarity of all human beings, of all social groups, and of all cultures would have turned the human universe into a realm of a uniformly grayish boredom. Even more: it would have demonstrated a notable lack of creative genius in human history because the very essence of creativity is an untiring invention of ever-new values, different from the existing ones. Monotonous similarity marks not an ever-varying creative activity, but an ever repeated automatism of reflexes and instincts. Only under exclusive domination of reflexological automatisms is endless mechanical repetition of similar actions by the members of a few, biologically fixed, types of human organism possible. In that case, however, the species of Homo sapiens would have been but one of the animal species little different from the rest of the animal kingdom. It was a great fortune for man to be blessed by the grace of creativity at the very beginning of his history. Due to this grace he has been able to create ever-new differentiations of individuals, groups, and cultural values. These differentiations testify to the boon of creative genius in man, in the multiplicity of human social groups, and in man's multicolored and inexhaustible cultural achievements.

It is not the grace of creativity and its differentiations that are responsible for incessant interpersonal and intergroup warfare. History exhibits to us thousands of dissimilar families and millions of heterogeneous persons who have at various periods peacefully lived side by side in mutual harmony. If dissimilarity were the cause of interpersonal and intergroup conflicts, such a peaceful coexistence of heterogeneous individuals and collectivities would have been impossible. If it has occurred many times, as it undoubtedly has, then the real cause of the warfare lies not in these differentiations, but in something else — namely, in *the poison of tribal selfishness* that infiltrated in the differentiated societies and their members. *This poison consists exactly of the restricted extensity and exclusiveness of their tribal love or solidarity.* If this hypothesis is correct, then the disease can be cured only by extension of solidarity or love to include everyone and all. This extension does not require elimination of all interpersonal and intergroup dissimilarities. It requires only a thorough cleaning of individuals and groups from the poison of exclusive selfishness.

If this diagnosis is correct, can the prescription of the universal love be carried through? Can one indeed love equally every human being, the strangers and the enemies as much as the members of his family and friends? Is not such love a biological and psychological impossibility?

Taken literally, the prescription is impossible for the overwhelming majority of human beings; however, the extension of love over the whole of mankind neither means nor requires an equal distribution of love among all human beings. At its initial stage it means three things: first, that *everyone* loves the members of his family and the limited circle of his friends and acquaintances as his special part of humanity chosen by and entrusted to him for this purpose. If everyone does so, every member of the human race will find himself loving and loved by the members of his special groups. Under such conditions not a single person in the whole human population remains unloved and not loving. Second, universal love means that *everyone* must abstain from all actions harmful to any human being. Through this *neminem laedere* in the whole human race nobody remains hated, harmed, and seriously mistreated by other human beings. Third, it means that *everyone*, within his capacity, extends his loving hand beyond his special group to *everybody* who is in need of help and warm sympathy — first of all, in one's immediate community and second, in the whole human universe. If *everybody* does so in regard to the persons in his own community, then every human being will find the needed loving help from his community. If each community does the same in regard to other communities in need of help, then the whole human population will be blessed by, at least, the minimum of love and vital help. Under these conditions in the whole mankind there will be found not a single person lonely, forsaken, unloved, or unhelped. This extension of love can be done privately and publicly, in individual and social forms. If now and then it requires sacrifice on the part of the individual and his group, such sacrifice is to be gladly given. If every person and group do so, these sacrifices will be repaid by other individuals and groups when the sacrificing persons and groups are in need of help. Viewed so, the sacrifices are but a form of a mutual insurance of all human beings against possible insecurity and misfortune.

Such is the meaning of the universal love at its initial stage. It is easily seen that it does not contain anything utopian or impossible. At this stage it represents but a development of the existing " network of love," and an increased inhibition of the interhuman aggression. Once established in this initial form, it will in the course of time and practice spontaneously develop into ever richer, nobler, and more perfect universal love.

If wisely guided and earnestly executed, the initial phase of universal love can be achieved without serious difficulty and at a much cheaper cost in the terms of death, suffering, and destruction, than the price to be paid in this sort of " money " for continuation of tribal loyalties and tribal warfare. Within the life cycle of one or two generations this phase will bring mankind much closer to the ideal of security, brotherhood, and peace on the earth, than the leaders and followers of tribal patriotisms have been able to do for millennia or can do in the future. Here are some of the *practical* prescriptions as to what the first steps of realization of the universal solidarity should consist in, and how they should be carried through, to bring mankind nearer to this objective.

These prescriptions utilize not only man's supraconscious and the noblest conscious potentialities, but also man's unconscious and even egoistic drives.

## III

### UNIVERSALIZATION OF LOVE THROUGH HATRED AND THE HOLY WAR AGAINST THE COMMON ENEMIES OF THE WHOLE OF MANKIND

Hatred is still one of the most powerful emotions of man and one of the most efficient " motors " of human behavior. In an overwhelming majority of human beings it cannot be quickly eliminated or even greatly weakened. It can, however, be rechanneled for serving different "works" and "operations." Hitherto it has "powered" mainly interindividual and intergroup conflicts. Instead of this function, its power can be used for extension of love and for binding mankind into one solidary body. How? *By redirecting the power of hatred from its present channels of interindividual and intertribal conflicts into a new "pipe line" serving the sacred war of humanity against the most terrible, most implacable, eternal, and common enemies of every human being, every group, and of the whole of mankind: against death, physical and mental disease, gravest criminality, stupidity, ignorance, interhuman strife, ugliness, poverty, fruitless suffering, nature's calamities, interhuman hatred itself, and a host of other forces inimical to every man's creative growth and everybody's vital, mental, and moral well-being.*

Instead of setting man against man, and group against group, the power of hatred can be directed against these eternal and universal enemies of humanity. They are so formidable that the whole reservoir of mankind's hatred can easily be spent in this fight. Their merciless pressure is so enormous that everybody's fighting impulses can find the fullest satisfaction in this sacred war. Their tyranny is so painfully felt by every individual and group that everyone can be aroused against these enemies of all human beings. With a minimum of teaching, preaching, and propaganda, everybody's patriotic ethos and pathos in this sacred war can be easily incited, maintained and exalted to the highest pitch of intensity ever reached in any tribal war. Likewise, the loftiest ideologies of sanctification of the holy war can be created easily because only this war of the united humanity against its nonhuman enemies is free from religious objections, moral injustice, and from the vital, mental, economic, and social destructions inherent in all interpersonal and intergroup wars. It is the only war truly sacred for the whole of mankind in contrast to tribal wars glorified by the victor and cursed by the victim. If Hitler as the common enemy could temporarily bind together Stalin, Roosevelt, and Churchill; if the Kremlin Communist government, as the common enemy, could unify into one military alliance the most heterogeneous governments of the Western bloc; still more easily can mankind be unified into one permanent solidary body by its perennial common enemies.

To sum up: if a fraction of the resources spent for inciting tribal wars is used for arousing the holy war of humanity against its nonhuman adversaries, the most powerful — intellectual, emotional, and volitional — unification of the whole of mankind for such a war can be accomplished. In the fervent ethos and pathos of such a crusade some of the tribal conflicts will vanish, others will decrease, still others will be pushed to the backstage of history. In the radiance of the brightest and purest halo of this crusade, the smoky little fires of tribal wars will become unnoticeable and will cease to attract tired human pilgrims. In this way the elemental power of hatred will be destroying interhuman hatred, the aggressive

propensities of man will be fighting interhuman aggressions, and the
"fighting instincts" of man will be serving the task of the unification of
humanity freed from interhuman wars.[4]

That this plan is *perfectly realistic* is demonstrated by the body of evidence given in Chapter Four of this book. Its striking corroboration is
recently supplied by the United Nations, as well as by the "Point Four"
program of the United States. While the selfish policies of practically all
the member states of the United Nations, carried on through its outra-
geously tribal Security Council, Political Section and General Assembly,
have ruined Korea, killed millions of human beings, and inflicted an untold amount of suffering upon vast multitudes, in contrast to these deadly
results its supratribal war against the common enemies of mankind —
against death, disease, poverty, ignorance, etc. — carried on through its
UNESCO and relief agencies, have produced notably fruitful results far
exceeding the meagerness of the funds appropriated for this purpose.
Only this holy, supratribal fight of the United Nations against the common enemies of humanity has been constructively successful.

The same is true of the foreign policy of the United States or of the
Soviet Union. Being in its bulk selfishly tribal, the American foreign
policy has produced mainly disastrous results — destructive not only for
the Soviet-Chinese bloc, but also for the Western bloc and the United
States itself. This tribal policy, carried on by the American military
forces, ruined Korea, killed millions of human beings, resuscitated the
hatred of Americans for the nations of the Soviet bloc and the hatred of
these nations for the United States. It has wasted the enormous moral
prestige of the American nation, killed and wounded one hundred and
thirty thousand of its beloved sons, fruitlessly squandered billions of dollars, turned the great democratic nation into an increasingly totalitarian
police-state, and caused many other great damages. In contrast to it, the
American "Point Four" policy, being free from the tribal egoism of the
main American foreign policy, has tangibly helped the vital, mental, moral,
economic, and cultural well-being of millions of human beings, in spite
of the miserly funds appropriated for this task. The same is still more
true of the policies of the Soviet Union and its satellites. Their Communist tribal policies have spread mainly death and destruction over their
own nation, as well as over others. On the other hand, their little "supratribal" crusade against the nonhuman enemies of humanity has been
amply rewarded by the fruitful results accomplished.

Without any hesitation it can be predicted that this uniformity of destructive results of tribal crusades and of constructive consequences of
the supratribal "holy war" will repeat itself in the future policies of all
states, and of the United Nations. It is high time we learn this simple
verity and reap the benefits of its consistent practice.

# IV

## PACIFICATION OF HUMANITY THROUGH COMPETITION IN NATURE'S HARNESSING, IN LOVE, AND HUMILITY

Like hatred, the unconscious and conscious competition for superiority and domination is deeply ingrained in man, and especially in modern man. Beginning with the competition for the largest possible share of material wealth and sensual pleasures of "gracious" eating, drinking, clothing, and love-making, and ending with the rivalry for superiority in physical might, in sport, in scientific, philosophical, artistic, religious and moral achievements, this competitive drive animates most of the activities of most of human beings. Even the missionary zeal of propagation of one's own religion, scientific theory, or moral standards is largely "fueled" by the competitive drive. Explicitly or implicitly, any missionary activity presupposes one's deep conviction in the superiority of his own brand of religion, scientific theory, philosophical doctrine, aesthetic patterns, or way of life. In this sense these activities are also competitive, "imperialistic," and imbued with selfish pride in one's own superiority over all the others. Especially when they claim a monopoly of being the only "way, the truth, and the life."

Being so deeply ingrained in "human nature," competition can hardly be quickly extirpated from man's organism and behavior. But like hatred, it can be redirected from serving the tasks of interhuman conflicts to the service of pacification, stimulation of creative efforts, and eventually of enfeeblement of the competitive drive itself.

Instead of tribal competition as to who can kill the greatest number of human "enemies," or destroy the largest number of factories, railroad stations, or city blocks, this prepotent drive can find still fuller satisfaction in competition for saving human lives, or in building new houses, mills, villages, and cities. In place of rivalry as to who can invent the most efficacious instruments of death and destruction, it can be used for invention of the best means for improvement of economic conditions, physical and mental health, moral integrity, creative ability, and social well-being of all human beings. In lieu of competitive money-making or improving one's own group's well-being at the cost of other groups — through military spoliation, exploitation, or by taking advantage of other groups' ignorance, simple-mindedness, or inability to compete — the competitive "instinct" can be fully gratified by rivalry in finding new natural resources, in harnessing new forces of nature, and in putting them at the service of all persons and groups. In this sort of constructive competition the competitive drive of an overwhelming majority can find purer, fuller, and better satisfaction than in predatory rivalries at the cost of other members of the human family.

Generally, competition in discovering, creating, and harnessing forces of nature and putting them at the service of mankind can give the fullest outlet to all competitive drives of all human beings. Through this outlet it can dry up the total reservoir of competitive forces of humanity, and leave nothing for the destructive and predatory competition.

Perhaps a still more effective way of elimination of the destructive, parasitic, and predatory forms of competition is the replacement of the competition in aggressiveness by that in unselfish love, of rivalry for superiority by that for humility. In the preceding chapters we have seen that all the genuine altruists regard ego-centered pride and the sense of one's own superiority as the greatest obstacles for moral perfection. Likewise, these altruists and their systems of moral training unanimously recommend cultivation of humility as the highest virtue, and as the necessary condition for realization of other virtues. The only competition they allow is the competition in humility and unselfish service. Based upon their vast experience, this prescription appears to be scientifically sound especially for those who aspire to reach the sublime levels of unselfishness and spirituality.

For its awakening and satisfaction, the competitive urge is not limited to one specific objective, say, winning a baseball championship or a Nobel prize. It can be aroused and satisfied by competition for different values. Unselfish love or humility can successfully be one of the most important competitive values. To a tangible extent it has played this role in practically all societies and at all periods. In the societies with dominant Ideational culture like medieval Europe, the Hindu society at several periods, the Early Buddhist, the Stoic, the Cynic societies, or the oriental and occidental monastic communities — in such Ideational cultures unselfish love and humility have been the greatest, and often the only permitted, competitive value. A competitive attainment of the highest levels of love and humility has been considered there as the attainment of the highest possible goal, far transcending all other distinctions. "Sainthood," "holiness," "the highest rung on the Ladder of Paradise," "the state of Godliness," "angelic state," "the state of Man-God" — such have been the names given to this goal. In such societies competition for humility and unselfish love has been considered as the greatest and the most desirable of all competitions. This means that the values of purest love and humility can easily arouse the competitive urge and intensify it to the highest limit.

In Sensate societies, with their ego-centered competition for material values, unselfish love and humility do not have as great a competitive force as they have in Ideational cultures. But even in Sensate societies their competitive value is by no means insignificant. In our Sensate age the prestige, influence, and glory of M. Gandhi, A. Schweitzer, Sister E. Kenny, and of other humble servants of humanity are hardly lower than those of the top-dictators, top-generals, top-captains of industry and finance, top-scientists, top-artists, and of other top-climbers of the ladder of Sensate superiorities. Even in a selfishly tribal cultural atmosphere competition for these values can be as contagious as the aggressive competition for power, wealth, "pride of the ego" and "concupiscence of flesh," and for other evanescent distinctions and hollow superiorities.

At the future stock market of values, the price of the "bonds" of unselfish love and of the "shares" of humility is likely to go up. Contemporary mankind is in an increasingly urgent need of these scarce values. Painfully suffering from an overabundance of all sorts of aggressiveness, being threatened in its very survival by competitive counterfeit-values, mankind can save itself only through a notable decrease in these aggressive competitions and by a notable increase in unselfish love and humility. For this reason the competition for these values is likely to increase in the future.

If, to this naturally arising trend, the intentional efforts for reinforcement of competition in love and humility are added, there is hardly any doubt in a successful growth of this sort of competition. A fraction of the resources spent for predatory competition is sufficient to open the gates for the flood of powerful competition in these moral values. A notable increase of this kind of rivalry, together with that of creative, supratribal, competition in harnessing the forces of nature for the service of humanity, are capable of tangibly decreasing the predatory competitions in the human universe. Such a change means an enormous progress in the extension of love over the whole of humanity and the unification of mankind into one solidary family, largely freed from tribal wars and interhuman quarrels.

Viewed in this perspective, the existing foreign policy of the Eastern and the Western blocs of nations is the most obsolescent, uncreative, and war-breeding policy of a carnivorous human animal. It is the age-old competitive policy of *si vis pacem para bellum*, of the "peace through power," deterrence, coercion, exploitation, and destruction of the "enemy" by all means available. It does not try to overcome the tribal conflicts by creation of new natural resources, by invention of new vital economic and social values, by competition in mutual service, reconciliation, and humility. Instead of enriching all tribal parties through the creative effort and ennobling them through mutual love and restraint of their selfishness, it destroys the existing resources and impoverishes all parties. Instead of lifting them to higher moral levels, it turns the parties into the worst mass murderers and destructive human beasts. Shall we wonder at the utter failure of this policy in giving peace to humanity? Practiced and preached for millennia, this carnivorous tribal competition has made the twentieth century the bloodiest and most barbarous period out of all preceding centuries of human history, so far as international and civil wars are concerned.[5] Likewise, it has not decreased interpersonal wars and crimes. In anno Domini 1954 the grave criminality especially of juvenile delinquents stands as high as at any previous period, and certainly much higher than in most of the preceding decades and centuries. There is no hope for this sort of murderous competition's bringing the bliss of peace to humanity. Instead, it is likely to inflict irreparable harm upon the human race. In this situation, the replacement of carnivorous competition by constructive rivalry in creativity, love, and humility becomes not a matter of utopian luxury, but that of the sternest necessity. The above shows that such a replacement is quite possible, and that the power of the competitive urge can indeed be put at the service of unification and pacification of mankind.

## V

### Solidarization of Humanity Through Other Biological Drives

What has been said about utilization of hatred, the "fighting instinct," and the competitive urge for extension of love over the whole of mankind can be said about practically all unconscious urges of the human organism, its reflexes and instincts, its biological needs, with all its mechanisms involved. Beginning with its instinct for self-preservation, sex impulse, avoidance of pain and quest for pleasure, and ending with its need for food and other life necessities, all these biological forces can be fruitfully used for the purposes of pacification of humanity. The conversion of these forces from breeders of interhuman conflicts into agencies of interhuman solidarity can be accomplished in the same ways as the conversion of hate, fighting and competitive urges — namely, by elimination of the bloodiest manifestations of these drives, by creation of new abundant resources for their satisfaction, and by utilization of the mechanisms of these drives for constructive purposes.

To begin with, none of the murderous interhuman conflicts increases the existing global amount of life necessities. As a rule, in all interpersonal and intergroup wars a portion of these necessities is always destroyed. Mankind as a whole is always a loser in all such conflicts. They invariably increase the number of people lacking the minimum of means of subsistence and make satisfaction of their biological needs more difficult and less possible. If now and then they temporarily enrich the victors, they do it at the cost of victims and the rest of humanity. Furthermore, this enrichment is usually short-lived: today's victor invariably becomes tomorrow's victim, impoverished and robbed in its turn. The coercive "redistributions" of life necessities in the endless struggle of tribal victors and victims never increases but invariably decreases the existing global amount of means of subsistence through destruction of its part in the conflicts.

In addition to depriving many of the possibility of satisfaction of their biological needs, the predatory conflicts directly clash with man's instinct for self-preservation by killing, mutilating, and endangering the life of the fighting multitudes. By inflicting an untold amount of pain, fear, and anxiety upon the fighting parties, the tribal struggles go also against man's propensity for avoiding pain and striving for pleasure.

In all these ways the interhuman clashes operate against man's biological drives, against their full satisfaction, and against the vital interests of human organisms. With the exception of purely temporary and local situations, where biological needs of an individual or a small group can be satisfied at the cost of others, the durable and universal satisfactions of man's biological drives are inhibited by interhuman conflicts. The drives fully and easily can be satisfied more in the conditions of a peaceful and unified humanity than in those of wars of everybody against everybody. For these reasons the drives can easily be converted into the allies of universal peace and their power can be enlisted for the service of interhuman solidarity.

Still more powerfully is this conversion reinforced by the fact that only through discovery of new natural resources, and through invention of better ways of utilization of immense sources of cosmic energy for the needs of humanity, can mankind's means of subsistence be increased and can its material and cultural standards be improved, without impoverishing any part of humanity. By its nature this creative activity has nothing to do with interhuman conflicts. It is performed more successfully in peaceful conditions than in those of interhuman warfare. It enriches everyone and all at the cost of the harnessed forces of the cosmos, and not at the cost of another part of mankind. Only this creative work gives an ever-fuller satisfaction of man's biological needs. It fulfills the highest mission of man on this planet and fully justifies his very existence in this empirical world. For this decisive reason, the biological drives are and can increasingly be the natural servants and allies of this creative activity. Together with it they can increasingly serve the task of extension of solidarity over the whole human race.

The above outlines the how and why of utilization of biological forces for the establishment of peaceful harmony in the whole human universe. Still more easily can the mechanisms of reflexes, instincts, and drives be used for this task. In the preceding chapters on various techniques of altruistic transformation, the survey begins with the techniques of a well-tempered satisfaction of biological needs, of practicing certain postures, movements, and voluntary respiration, of the conditioned reflexes and mechanical drilling, reinforced by the technique of consequent mild pains and pleasures. All these techniques are based upon a use of the biological mechanisms of the human organism. Their concise analysis has shown how these mechanisms can be utilized for the altruistic education of human beings. Out of the factors of interhuman enmity, they can easily be turned into mechanisms of interhuman friendship. For an additional illustration we shall take here only the mechanisms of conditioned reflexes and of habit-building. What is said about these mechanisms can be said about the others.

If from the moment of birth every child is treated lovingly by his parents, siblings, and others who are in face to face interaction with him, and if he is consistently " conditioned " to treat all human beings in a friendly way as sacred end values, regardless of their sex, age, color, creed, nationality, social position, and so on; when such a treatment and conditioning is done consistently, with all the necessary operations involved, this sort of utilization of the mechanisms of conditioned reflexes and of habit-formation will produce a rich harvest of human beings friendly to all human beings, compassionate, co-operative, and helpful members of mankind. And let it be stressed that such a conditioning can be achieved as easily as training in aggressiveness, animosity, prideful selfishness, and in misuse of others for one's self-aggrandizement. There is nothing utopian in this statement. It is corroborated by numerous experimental studies of conditioned reflexes and of the mechanisms of their inculcation, reinforcement, radiation, transference, and extinction.

It is true that for a success of altruistic conditioning, the most consistent inhibition of each of the child's unfriendly actions-reactions and encouragement of each of his friendly reflexes is necessary. A few other conditions for an effective inculcation of conditioned responses have to be met also. But the totality of these requirements are neither too burdensome nor too intricate to be managed by intelligent parents, siblings, playmates, educators, and interactors with the child.

It is true also that this consistency has to be extended over several spheres of the child's activity which at the present time are the breeding fields of children's aggressiveness and demoralization. All murderous toys, like guns, tanks, bombers, soldiers, etc., have to be tabooed as toys of education for murder. Many games like " Cops and Robbers " or " Cowboys and Indians " killing one another; many children's movies which teach the lessons of ferocious murder, sex lust, mishandling of man by man — such things have to be abolished. The same goes for the bulk of comic books, " children's magazines," and other " children's stories " which are too poisonous even for grownups.

A great deal in the total education and environment of children has to be changed, also. Beginning with the inculcation of all sorts of aggressive tribal patriotisms, and ending with all forms of glorification of the struggle for existence, predatory competitions, selfish self-aggrandizement at the cost of others — all this must go, too. Glorifying mythologies of an office boy becoming president of the biggest bank, of a military hero who killed hundreds of enemies, of a general who destroyed cities and industrial centers of the enemy, of a political boss who hoodwinked all his opponents, of a scientist who invented the deadliest means of destruction — these and other glorifications of interhuman strife, with its cult of success and defeat, victor and victim, have to be either abolished or given as examples of the tragical misfortune of the parties concerned.

All this has to be done because inconsistent conditioning now in friendship and now in enmity cannot mold consistently friendly human beings. This inconsistency is exactly the reason why the existing education of children often fails to produce kind and friendly youths, and why it yields so many juvenile delinquents and " civilized barbarians." In their schools, Sunday schools, or in their church they are conditioned in the precepts of the Sermon on the Mount and in love to all humanity. In their games, reading, amusements, their social milieu, sometimes even in their family, they are conditioned in enmity, crime, deceit, egoism, and aggressiveness. A mere war in Korea or elsewhere is sufficient to wipe out their total conditioning in love. A mere game of Cowboys and Indians is enough to erase all the precepts of " love your neighbors," and " love your enemy." An exposure to a few sex-murder-war-movies, or listening to a few aggressive political or " patriotic " speeches, washes out most of the conditioned " reflexes " of love to humanity.

To sum up: self-contradictory use of the mechanisms of conditioned reflexes and of habit formation cannot mold unaggressive and friendly human beings. On the other hand, when these mechanisms are consistently employed for inculcation of friendly actions-reactions only, they serve the task of altruization of man with a notable degree of success. When *every* person is used as a conditional stimulus for building altruistic responses, these mechanisms help in extension of friendly conduct beyond one's own tribes, over the whole of humanity.

With a corresponding variation the same can be said of other biological mechanisms and propensities. Out of the factors of interhuman enmity they also can be turned into the agencies of harmonization of the whole human universe.

## VI

### TRANSCENDENCE OF INDIVIDUAL AND TRIBAL EGOISMS THROUGH CONSCIOUS SCIENTIFIC EFFORTS

The dynamic capacity and creative ability of the conscious, rational mind can serve the task of solidarization of humanity in several important ways. First, in co-operation with, and controlled by, the supraconscious, creative scientific efforts can serve immeasurably the whole of mankind by discovering and creating new resources for satisfaction of its vital, mental, moral, and sociocultural needs. Potentially the cosmic world surrounding mankind as well as mankind itself contain an unlimited amount of such resources. If discovered and harnessed, they can abundantly supply all the means for the fullest satisfaction of all human needs. When successfully discharged, the inventive and creative activity makes unnecessary interhuman struggle for the means of subsistence that has hitherto cursed human history. Through this service, the rational mind eliminates one of the most important factors of interhuman conflicts and thus contributes greatly to the cause of harmonization of the whole human universe. For this reason, the constructive scientific activity should be developed to its possible maximum. Instead of wasting billions for interhuman struggle and for the sterile, often poisonous, machinations of politicians, these billions used for expanding scientific efforts will enrich humanity beyond the most optimistic expectations.

In the second place, this rational activity must be concentrated entirely upon constructive discoveries and inventions, and no part of it is to be wasted for invention of destructive means of interhuman warfare. This requirement is again perfectly practical because truly creative scientists and inventors would rather joyfully serve the God of Creation and Love than the Satan of Destruction and Hate.

In the third place, the rational scientific thought can increasingly convince even the most cynical partisans of interindividual and tribal warfare that in the long run crime as well as all interhuman warfares do not pay, and they do not bring to the parties involved either lasting economic well-being, or genuine peace of mind and happiness, or improved health and increased chances of biological survival. From a purely utilitarian and hedonistic standpoint, interhuman conflicts are disutilitarian and predominantly painful, rather than pleasurable for all the parties concerned.

Like the drunken orgy of a criminal, the orgy and fortunes of each victorious party are invariably short-lived and sooner or later have to be paid for by its being defeated, killed, exploited, enslaved, imprisoned, and treated in the same painful way in which it had treated its victims. The personal fortunes or tribal organizations for whose sake the parties carry on their warfare are mortal and have a limited life span. The average life span of contemporary small competitive business organizations like grocery-drug-shoe-hardware stores is about 3 years; that of big business organizations, listed on the stock exchange, is about 24 or 28 years. An overwhelming majority of the noble, aristocratic, or richest families die out within 100 years; a small portion survive for a longer time, but hardly any top-family survives for more than 300 years. Their prosperous and elevated position is still more short-lived than their social and biological life span. The proverbial three generations from shirt sleeves to shirt sleeves are rarely exceeded. The same is true of the royal families. Most of the ancient Egyptian dynasties lasted on the average of about 150 years; the Chinese dynasties about 300 years; the European dynasties from a few days up to 269 and 304 years, and none for a longer period. With the exception of a few states like ancient Egypt or China, thirty-six of the existing sovereign states have existed less than 100 years. A large majority of the living sovereign states have existed less than 200 years.[6]

This means that the life span of particularly aggressive and competitive organizations, like states, political parties, economic enterprises, royal, aristocratic, and richest families — all regarded as particularly durable — is in fact very limited. Among other things it is much shorter than the life span of less aggressive and more altruistic organizations like the great religions propagating love to much larger parts of humanity or even to all mankind. The religious organizations of Hinduism, Buddhism, Taoism, Confucianism, Judaism, Jainism, Christianity, and Mohammedanism have already existed from some 3,500 years to 1,300 years; and they do not show, as yet, definite signs of disappearance. Moreover, during their limited life span states, political parties, economic organizations, and top-families experience many ups and downs, the rhythm of victories followed by defeats, of pleasures and advantages followed by sufferings and disfranchisements. All this shows that the tribal organizations for whose sake individuals and groups killed and got killed, robbed, raped, and exploited and were robbed, raped, and misused in their turn, happened to be evanescent structures built on sand and crumbling to pieces in a short period of time. From a truly rational standpoint, the vast multitude of victims of intertribal struggles of such organizations have been perishing in vain and their sufferings have been tragically wasted.

As to the comparative life spans of the aggressively egoistic and unaggressive altruistic human beings, the aggressive egoists and the leaders of aggressive social organizations have, as a general rule, a shorter life span than the saintly altruists and friendly good neighbors of the same countries and periods. The aggressive enmity, predatory ambition, strenuous competition, and insatiable pride of the egoistic individuals seems to adversely affect their physical, moral, and mental well-being in spite of a " conspicuous consumption," luxurious living, and full satisfaction of their biological needs. On the other hand deep peace of mind, friendliness towards others, and devotion to God, Love, and Moral Duty seems to invigorate the health and prolong the life span of eminent and saintly altruists, in spite of their ascetic practices, lack of necessities, and other supposedly unhealthy conditions of their life and activity.

This generalization is well supported by many sets of evidences: a) By the comparatively short life span of criminals, wretched kind of life they live, and by the highest rate of death by violence they die. b) By the data of psychosomatic medicine showing the negative influence of hateful, aggressive, and inimical emotions upon physical, moral, and mental health of individuals. c) By a shorter life duration of monarchs and rulers in comparison with that of other prominent men in less aggressive or non-aggressive occupations: 53.6 years is the average life span for 272 monarchs studied; 67.5 is the average for 1,013 historical persons studied — theologians, clericals, scientists, scholars, architects, authors, artists, musicians, jurists, judges, statesmen, etc. — of about the same centuries and countries as the monarchs.[7] d) By the exceptionally high per cent of mental disease of monarchs and rulers.[8] e) By the decreasing life duration of the later generations of monarchs of the same dynasty. f) By the life-shortening effects of strenuous political activity on American presidents, vice-presidents, senators, and congressmen: their actual duration of life is by 7 to 30 per cent shorter in comparison with the expected longevity.[9] g) By the exceptionally high rate of criminality, and especially gravest criminality, of absolute monarchs, dictators, and unlimited rulers of even powerful religious organizations, like the Roman Catholic popes or cardinals in the periods of the supremacy of their absolute power over the secular power of kings.[10] h) By the exceptionally high rate of death by violence among the monarchs, presidents, dictators, and rulers of the state: of 423 monarchs studied 135 or 31.9 per cent died by violence. The rate fluctuates from zero for the Danish and Spanish monarchs for the last two centuries up to 66.3 per cent of the monarchs of the Roman Empire. While in the United States in 1921 among all the causes of death 7.2 per cent were caused by violence, 12.1 per cent of the presidents of the United States and France died by violence. The rate of violent death among other historical persons in less aggressive pursuits has been much lower: from 0.3 and 0.8 to 10 per cent.[11]

On the other hand, the life span of the saintly and eminent altruists has been far above that of their contemporaries. In spite of their asceticism, fastings, long vigils, and lack of many necessities they lived longer than their contemporaries, or even the monarchs and rulers of their time.[12]

It is true that among the Christian Catholic saints the rate of death by violence was also exceptionally high during especially the first centuries of Christianity; all in all 37 per cent of them died by violent death.[13] But in contrast to the violent death of the aggressive rulers killing and killed in their mutual struggle, the saints died as the martyrs of love and spirituality at the hands of the intolerant rulers and state governments. The universal altruists are always victims and never killers. The vigorous vitality and comparatively long life of altruists are due to the beneficial effects of friendly emotions and altruistic disposition upon the health, longevity, and well-being of the individuals. An increasing knowledge of biological, medical, psychological, and social sciences confirms this conclusion. Other conditions being equal, friendly and altruistic persons tend to have healthier, longer, and happier lives than aggressive and hate-ridden individuals.

In many other ways, the rational, scientific mind can convincingly demonstrate the truth of the proposition that crime and interhuman conflicts do not pay, and are nonutilitarian and nonhedonistic in their nature and long-time results. Through this enlightening service, rational thought can contribute a great deal to unification and pacification of mankind and to redirection of its aggressive propensities against its nonhuman enemies.

In the fourth place, rational thought can help this task by scientific study of the conflicting values, life philosophies, and ethical principles of the antagonistic groups and persons, and by elaboration of the system of values, philosophy, and ethics that transcends all tribal systems in the validity of its truth and in the adequacy of its ethics for the purposes of harmonization and unification of the whole of mankind. Elsewhere I have shown that " the main cause of internal or international peace is the presence in each of the interacting societies of a well-integrated system of basic values and their norms of conduct, all of which are compatible with one another, practiced by the societies involved, and based upon the Golden Rule. In a given universe of societies or within a particular society the probability of peace varies directly with the integration of the systems of basic values and their mutual compatability. When their integration and compatability decline, especially suddenly and sharply, the chances for international, or civil, or interindividual war increase." [14]

Starting with different premises, and in his own way, Professor F. S. C. Northrop has well demonstrated the decisive importance of such a universal and perennial system of values — transcending all the tribal value systems — for the internal and international peace of humanity.[15]

If the ultimate foundation and goal of such a system are rooted in the supraconscious, the logical and empirical demonstration of its superiority over the tribal value systems is the task of rational, scientific thought. Only scientific proofs of this superiority can be convincing for the overwhelming majority of human beings, and especially for its utilitarian and " practical " leaders.

In the fifth place, science can render an inestimable service to this task by inventory of the known and invention of the new effective techniques of altruistic ennoblement of individuals, social institutions, and culture. Our enormous ignorance of love's properties, of the efficient ways of its production, accumulation, and distribution, of the efficacious techniques of moral transformation has been stressed many times in this work. This ignorance is responsible for the comparative impotency of the multitude of existing organizations for moral education, moral rearmament, and pacification of mankind. In spite of the enormous number of such agencies consisting potentially of all the families, all the schools, all the religious organizations, of all the governmental, civic and social work agencies, of all the pacifistic and special organizations for moral rearmament, for elimination of conflicts between labor and management, between Christians and Jews, between different races, nationalities, and so on; in spite of the commendable efforts of these organizations — the actual results of their indefatigable labor have been pitifully modest. They have failed not only in elimination of interhuman strifes; but even in a mere decrease of interpersonal, intergroup, and international bloody conflicts. Criminality as the sharpest form of interpersonal strife; bloody civil wars as the barbarous forms of intergroup clashes; and gigantic international wars are ravaging mankind at the present time as much as at any previous period of human history. Even more: all these strifes are now more rampant, more frequent, and more deadly than they have been during the preceding twenty-five centuries of Greco-Roman and Western history. This ugly fact is the decisive evidence of a meager success and of a big failure of all the organizations discussed.

One of the main reasons for this failure is the prevailing ignorance of love phenomena and of the techniques of altruistic education. The main — and sometimes the only — technique the discussed organizations use is the speech-reactional technique in its variations of sermons, lectures, discussions, conferences, oral and printed propaganda, listening and reading, movies and television. The technique aims mainly to change opinions and ideologies of the adversaries and of the public involved.

Now and then it succeeds in such a change. But it rarely changes the overt behavior and deeply rooted selfish tendencies of the parties involved. In contemporary man with his deep chasm between his noble ideologies and ignoble practices, the speech-reactional and visual techniques leave the sources of personal and tribal conflicts essentially untouched. They fail either to eliminate or even to diminish interhuman warfare. Even speech-reactional changes effected by the technique are not always truly altruistic. Often the new opinions and ideologies are used by the parties for beautification, rationalization, and reinforcement of their old ugly interests. Remaining as strong as before, these interests now cover themselves by new verbal garments, put on new ideologies and under new slogans continue their aggressive crusades without diminishing by one iota their venomous virulence.

The members of these organizations tend to overestimate the effectiveness of their work. They feverishly expand their speech-reactional and movie activities and by this superficial expansion they measure their success and proudly bestow upon one another various prizes for brotherhood and for service to peace and humanity. Such indulgences are comprehensible and excusable. Unfortunately, the ugly reality of the unrivaled human warfare going on now does not support these illusions, and enormously deflates the inflated belief in a successful discharge of their mission.

Only in a small degree is their comparative failure due to their own fault: only insofar as they do not use other available techniques surveyed in the preceding chapters. The main reason for their failure lies in the continued ignorance of truly effective methods of moral transformation, of the true nature of man, and of the sociocultural universe generally.

Only with a considerable increase of our knowledge of these mysterious phenomena can much more fruitful techniques be discovered, and much greater progress in fraternization of human beings be made. This increased knowledge can be obtained mainly through scientific study of these problems. Concentrating its efforts on such a study scientific thought can again immensely help mankind in its moral progress.

In the sixth place, rational thought can facilitate this task by deepening and increasing our knowledge of man, man's institutions, culture, and of the total human universe. The existing knowledge of especially the intangible and perhaps most important aspects of these phenomena is still very limited. Knowing them better we can devise better means for successful solution of man's important practical needs.

In the seventh place, scientific study is indispensable for solution of two additional problems of pacification of humanity namely: a) which of numerous techniques are most fit for whom and under what conditions; and b) the problem of adequacy of love. In medical science each kind of illness requires its own specific medicine, and even the specific medicine has to be varied in accordance with the variety of human organisms treated. Similarly, in the task of altrustic education the techniques must vary in accordance with the specific properties and conditions of the individuals or groups. This individualization and differentiation of the techniques for each specific case can be accomplished only by scientific research.

In the introductory chapters of this work the meaning of the adequacy of love was defined and its importance was indicated. In order that one's unselfish love can produce the desired beneficial consequences, one has to know what sort of actions create these results in the easiest and fullest form. The choice of such adequate actions requires a sufficient knowledge of the causal consequences of various actions-reactions in diverse conditions and for different persons. This knowledge does not come by itself, and can be furnished only by scientific study of these phenomena. Otherwise, without this knowledge, the best-intentioned love may choose the wrong kind of activity and may lead to disastrous results for the loving and the loved parties instead of beneficial ones. A loving mother pampering her child may spoil him. A statesman with the most charitable intentions starting a wrong kind of policy may unchain the forces of hate and bring about destructive warfare in place of peaceful improvement of his own and other nations.

The existing knowledge of the causal consequences of various human actions is very meager. For the purposes of making numerous actions of love adequate, it needs to be greatly increased. This enrichment of knowledge can be accomplished only through the cognizing activity of our rational mind.

In these and similar ways, an effortful concentration of conscious, scientific thought on these problems can surely decrease interhuman antagonisms and enormously promote creative and moral ennoblement of the human species. Through mobilization of the best scientific brains available, these results can be obtained within a comparatively short period of a few decades. The governments, the foundations, the private philanthropists can hardly make better use of their resources than by the investment of their funds for this sort of scientific research.

## VII

### THE SUPREME ROLE OF THE SUPRACONSCIOUS IN MORAL ENNOBLEMENT OF MANKIND

In spite of the immensely important role which the unconscious and conscious forces of man can play in elimination of interhuman strife and in extension of solidarity over the whole of humanity, these forces alone cannot successfully accomplish this task without the guidance, control, and creative support of the supraconscious. From the preceding chapters we already know that this supraconscious is undescribable by any words and indefinable by any concepts.

It infinitely transcends any human ego, I or me, and is egoless in this sense. It is different from, and superior to, man's unconscious and conscious mind. It is the fountainhead of man's greatest creative achievements in all fields of constructive creativity.

Axioms of the supraconscious are the ultimate basis of the validity of mathematical, logical, and empirical truths and of the methods of validation or proving these truths.[16] We know also that only through the supraconscious union of the knower with the known is direct, unmediated cognition possible (see Chapters Six and Nineteen). Likewise, the truth that the "unselfish and creative love is the supreme moral value" is an axiom of the supraconscious. It was "revealed" long ago through its human instrumentalities: the great apostles of love, moral sages, and religious seers. Belonging to most different cultures and periods they voice this axiom and its moral imperatives as unanimously as any scientific truth has ever been voiced by scientists of different societies and periods. It is needless to add that *a posteriori* this axiom is confirmed by the total experience of mankind throughout its history. All constructive systems of ethics, with their mathematical, logical, and empirical proofs, are based upon this axiom. Without its certitude, the logical and empirical arguments of all the humanist, utilitarian, and hedonistic ethics of mutual aid, solidarity, co-operation, and friendship, become perfectly relativistic, unconvincing, and as questionable as the arguments of the ethics of hate, enmity, and interhuman warfare. We know also that "no sublime love is possible without the supraconscious" (see Chapters Eight, Nine, and Ten).

This outline of some of the supreme functions of the supraconscious reminds us of the exceptionally important role which the supraconscious forces play and can play in the moral progress of humanity.

The supraconscious can help in this task in many ways. First, a mere awareness of the fact that the total man is neither a mere organism, nor a mere unconscious and conscious being, but also an embodiment of the supraconscious, can greatly contribute to the moral ennoblement of mankind. Self-identification with the supraconscious as one's highest and truest self is the first decisive step in man's altruistic progress. If the self-identification remains on its purely ideological or speech-reactional level, it does not produce a radical change of one's total personality and behavior. We have seen that in all societies there always have been many self-identified and self-appointed "sons of God" who behaved themselves like human beasts. Fortunately, however, in many other persons, the self-identification, once started, develops far beyond the speech-reactional or ideological level and progressively encompasses their emotional, volitional, and behavioral spheres of being. As soon as self-identification with the supraconscious reaches these depths, it begins to transform the total personality and behavior of the respective individuals. The supraconscious begins to mold them in its own image, acquires an increasing control over their conscious and unconscious behavior, activates their creative potential generally and their altruistic creativity especially. It tends increasingly to transform the total man into a superman who feels, thinks, speaks, and behaves like a true " son of God."

If a mere ideological self-identification with the Highest Form of Being is not enough to change a human organism into a true son of God, it, nevertheless, is *the first necessary step for such a transformation.* Herein lies its importance. Otherwise; " If I am just an animal, I can behave only as animal and nothing else can be expected from me. Animal state is my natural state. If the supreme law of the animal world is the merciless struggle for existence, as an animal, I am subjected to this law and can and should but mercilessly fight for my own existence by all means at my disposal." This animalistic self-identification, greatly fostered under the name of science for the last century, is tangibly responsible for the scientifically calculated beastly wars, bloody revolutions, and cold-blooded mistreatment of man by man in this " supercivilized," " scientific and technological " twentieth century. If this tragic self-degradation of man and its terrible consequences are to be ended, all animalistic self-identifications of man must be replaced by the conception of the total man as the unconscious, conscious, and especially the supraconscious being. And the deeper and more universally this revolution in man's conception of man's true nature is accomplished, the greater becomes the creative unification and " divinization " of mankind.

In spite of its importance as one of the first steps towards divinization of man the purely ideological self-identification with the supraconscious is insufficient for creative and altruistic transmutation of one's personality and behavior. For that purpose, the self-identification must permeate also the unconscious, emotional, volitional and, finally, behavioral spheres of the individual. This task is accomplished easily if the individual starts a respective training in his childhood. The analyzed cases of our fortunate altruists give the details of this way of total self-identification and of gracious growth in sublime love. If the individual does not have this fortune in his childhood and youth, he has to undergo a conversion similar to that of the late and catastrophic altruists. Only by strenuous labor and pertinacity can he transform his purely ideological self-identification into the total self-identification with the supraconscious. It hardly ever comes by itself. Like a beautiful flower, it requires careful and effortful cultivation.

Many of the surveyed techniques of altruization can immeasurably help in this task. The techniques of good deeds, prayer, meditation, of reintegration of one's values, egos, and norms of conduct around the supraconscious generally and sublime love particularly; the techniques of conscience examination, confession, silence, and creativity; sometimes the techniques of ecstasy and for those who can use it the techniques of Yoga or of the monastic brotherhoods assisted by the techniques of voluntary respiration, postures, control of bodily processes, of conditioned responses, and so on, can be very helpful.

Sometimes, a use of corresponding "precipitants of conversion" may be advisable.

Finally, the technique of rearrangement of one's social affiliations is a necessary concomitant of the above techniques. For extension of love over all mankind, the rearrangement of one's social affiliations means the following operations: a) cutting off one's affiliations with all activities — individual and collective — that contradict the imperatives of the universal and supratribal love, no matter by what persons or groups such activities are carried on; b) affiliation with all activities that realize this imperative of universal love, regardless by what persons or groups they are practiced; c) replacement of loyalty to all tribal altruisms-egoisms by that to the whole humanity or to everyone and all; d) unreserved abstention from participation in all aggressive, violent, and especially murderous inter-human strifes and in mistreatments of man by man; e) fervent and fearless practice of the imperative of love towards all human beings; f) courageous opposition to all anti-love activities and tribal egoisms, but only by activities of love and nonviolent resistance, and never by the violent means of irreparable harming and extermination of the opponents. This does not mean an absolute exclusion of use of force, say, in the cases where human beast tortures an innocent child and in similar situations. Force can be used for prevention and termination of such actions, but only insofar as it is necessary for stopping such brutalities and, as far as possible, without irreparable harming of the aggressive brutes.

In terms of persons and groups, this rearrangement of social affiliations means two kinds of group membership: a) permanent affiliation with persons and groups that practice consistently the imperative of universal love towards all human beings; b) fluid, temporary, and only partial affiliations with persons and groups of tribal character: insofar as they practice the activities of universal love, one must wholeheartedly support these and be a member of such groups; insofar as they carry on tribal or personal aggressive policies, one must oppose them and decisively dis-affiliate oneself from such persons and groups in the periods of their selfish activities.

The outlined plan of rearrangement of one's social affiliations is the ideal or maximal plan — the plan as it should be at its purest and best. It goes without saying that this ideal plan can be reached only by a small fraction of human beings. The majority can climb only to the lower ridges of this towering peak. In spite of this, each step towards it repre-sents moral progress of humanity, and the outlined visibility of the peak guides the multitude of pilgrims in their pilgrimage towards the moral " holy of holies."

All these techniques for the total self-identification with the supra-conscious can be used, to a considerable extent, by every individual, in any sociocultural environment, even in the environment inimical to the supraconscious imperatives of the universal love. The unfavorable socio-cultural milieu would, however, greatly increase the difficulties of the persons striving to attain this goal. Besides the enormous obstacles in-herent in the process of the total self-identification, such persons must overcome the gigantic resistance and continuous animosity of their tribal fellow men, institutions, and culture. Often they may be subjected to cruel persecution and even to death by martyrdom. All this makes the achievement of the task discussed possible only for a few heroes of love in such an environment. In these conditions others can climb only a few steps on this " ladder of moral perfection."

Quite different is the situation in a society whose institutions and culture favor their members' total self-identification with the supracon-scious. When the family, the state, and other basic institutions strive to educate their members as the real children of a unified humanity; when the culture of a given group, beginning with its science and philosophy, and ending with its religion, fine arts, law, ethics, economics, and politics, articulates and consistently carries out the ideal of universal and supra-tribal solidarity; these social and cultural forces immeasurably help their members in their total self-identification and in their progress towards the ideal of universal love.

Factually these processes of the moral ennoblement of the individuals and of the socio-cultural milieu are interdependent: moral progress of the individuals generates the moral ennoblement of their social institutions and culture; the moral improvement of culture and social institutions promotes altruistic transformation of their members.[17]   While only a few individuals of heroic stature and in an exceptionally fortunate situation can climb the peak of moral perfection in a tribal society with its low-grade moral culture, much larger numbers can do it in a society and culture favorable to such an endeavor.

The supraconscious helps in this task also through creation of *the greatest heroes of the sublimest love*.   We already know that the great apostles of love become such heroes through their attainment of total self-identification with the supraconscious.   As true heroes in any other field, they inspire vast multitudes to imitate their magnificent examples.   Through this imitation a few heroes of love raise the moral standards of the masses far more effectively than thousands of ethical *raisonneurs* and " rational preachers " can do.   For moral ennoblement of humanity the emergence of one hero of love, like St. Francis or Gandhi, is more important than the publication of thousands of utilitarian, hedonistic, and " rational " books on ethics.   Through this form of manifestation the supraconscious grace has rendered and can increasingly render an inestimable service to the cause of universal love.

The supraconscious serves this cause also *through giving to humanity the highest moral value around which all other positive values can be harmoniously integrated, while all the pseudo-values can be clearly discerned and discarded, as void or negative values*.   The preceding chapters have shown that integration or reintegration of moral values around one supreme value is a necessary condition for moral sanity, and especially for altruistic integrity of persons and groups.

By their nature all tribal, Sensate, utilitarian, and hedonistic moral values are relative, conditional, atomistic, ever-changing, and self-contradictory.   What is good for Stalin and the Communists is bad for Churchill and the anti-Communists; what is " right " for the colonial masters is " wrong " for the subjugated colonial peoples.   What is pleasurable for a ravisher is painful for the ravished; what is useful for the rich is often harmful for the poor.   What is " patriotic " for one tribe, state, race, ethnic group, occupational union, class, or political party is " criminal " for the inimical tribe, state, or party.   All such values are similar to the proverbial precept: " If I steal my neighbor's wife it is good; if he steals my wife it is bad."   Being relativistic all such values and precepts tend, in the immanent process of their development, to become increasingly relativistic and contradictory until they become devoid of any binding power, any prestige and value for all except the tribe or the individual who profess it.   Such exactly is the situation with all tribal and Sensate moral values of the present time.   They are all turned now into mere " smoke screens," " rationalizations," " derivations," " façade-ideologies," or " beautiful fronts " hiding ugly tribal interests.[18]

Obviously all values of this sort cannot serve the function of the supreme value around which all moral values of all persons, tribes, and groups of humanity can be integrated into one universal system. Only the moral value which is axiomatic, universal, perennial, and which transcends all tribal, conditional, ever-changing, Sensate values can be the rallying point for the universal integration of all positive moral values. We already know that only the *sublime love, unbounded in its extensity, maximal in its intensity, purity, duration and adequacy, inseparable from the perfect truth and blameless beauty* meets all the requirements of the supreme moral value. The supraconscious intuition reveals it as the ultimate moral axiom and imperative; the rational thought demonstrates its logical adequacy; and sensory experience furnishes the *a posteriori* evidence of its empirical validity. It transcends all personal and tribal loves and all utilitarian and hedonistic values. At the same time, it encompasses all these values by assigning to them their proper place in its all-transcending unity. It clearly differentiates itself from all pseudo-moral values that are either void of love or negate and contradict it: from hatred, enmity, moral indifference, cynicism, nihilism, hypocrisy, from individual and collective selfishness.

Being universal, perennial, and infinitely creative the sublime love is acceptable for all human beings. Only it can integrate into one unified system the multitude of diverse moral values of different individuals and groups and can place each value at its proper place and rank in its vast system.

As mentioned, this supreme value was supraconsciously intuited long ago by the inspired apostles of love, by the great moral teachers of humanity, by founders of all genuine religions, by the true sages, seers, and prophets of practically all countries, cultures, and periods. In slightly different terms like love, compassion, sympathy, mercy, benevolence, reverence, friendship, Eros, Agape, the Golden Rule, mutual aid, co-operation, and so on, they unanimously affirm the supreme love as the highest moral value and its imperatives as the universal and perennial moral commandments. In spite of their very different cultural, social, and historical background, they make their affirmation with a certitude and unanimity at least as great as that of scientists asserting the validity of the best-verified scientific proposition.

This supreme moral value has also been confirmed by the moral values and imperatives of practically all social groups so far as they prescribe the in-group conduct of their members. Folkways, mores, taboos, legal and moral rules of practically all social groups have invariably prescribed, required, and recommended mutually helpful, friendly, or loving conduct of the members of the same group to one another. The main limitations of their moral values have been their narrow tribalism, and, often, a low grade of solidarity. Notwithstanding these shortcomings, their moral commandments have invariably been the commandments of love, but not of hate; of mutual aid and solidarity, but not of mutual strife and animosity; of in-group altruism, but not of in-group egoism. In other words, the intratribal moral values of practically all groups which have existed in human history have unanimously voiced the same principle of love that more perfectly has been voiced by the great moral leaders of humanity.[19]

To sum up: emanating from the supraconscious, validated by logical reasons and confirmed *a posteriori* by sensory experience, the universal sublime love is the supreme value around which all moral values can be integrated into one ethical system valid for the whole of humanity.

By repeatedly revealing the supreme love as the holy of holies of all moral values, the supraconscious has rendered and can increasingly render the greatest service to humanity in its realization of the supreme moral ideal in the human universe.

Another basic service to this task is accomplished by the supraconscious through its being the fountainhead of creativity in all fields of culture. Chapter Six has shown that almost all great creative achievements have been started by the supraconscious inspiration or genius. Without its wonderful springs, the full-flowing creative stream in human history would long ago have dried up to a mere trickle of mediocre discoveries, inventions, and creations of the conscious mind. Without the supraconscious source of creativity neither scientific discoveries nor technological inventions would have been as numerous and great as they are; nor can they triumphantly grow in the future without the supraconscious. In order that they can render the inestimable help, described above, in the moral ennoblement of humanity, the scientific research and inventive activity of the conscious mind need an incessant inspiring support of the supraconscious genius. For this reason, all the creative achievements of science, technology, the fine arts, religion, philosophy, ethics, economics or politics that enormously help mankind in its unification and pacification are to be credited not only to the conscious mind, but in no less a degree to the supraconscious genius also. Anything that can increase its circulation in the present and future human universe, anything that augments the human share of its inexhaustible creative grace can inestimably promote the task of vital, mental, moral, and social progress of the human race. Cultivation and multiplication of the supraconscious genius in the human cosmos is possibly the most hopeful way for a creative solution of humanity's difficult problems. For this reason, the prevalent neglect of the supraconscious by scientists, scholars, governments, foundations, universities, and other agencies is not only shortsighted but truly ruinous. It undermines the most important roots of the most important tree in the human garden — its tree of creativity without which Homo sapiens would have been but one of innumerable animal species.

Replacement of this policy by that of maximal fostering of research in the mysterious properties of the supraconscious, and of invention of the ways of a more abundant circulation of its grace in the human world is the most urgent need of the present time. Without the supraconscious genius the main mission of humanity on this planet — its creative mission — cannot be successfully continued. Without its continuation, the human race is bound to degenerate and die out. Becoming increasingly uncreative, Homo sapiens cannot fall back for its survival upon a well-functioning mechanism of reflexes and instincts. As mentioned above, this mechanism has been irretrievably damaged in the course of human evolution and cannot be fully repaired.

Any species devoid of the supraconscious and conscious creativity and of the sound mechanism of reflexes and instincts does not have any chance for survival. It is doomed to perish on account of the absence of a wise controlling force in the organism of its members. It is high time that this elementary truth be fully understood by everyone, and especially by the existing rulers and leaders of humanity. As the fountainhead of human creativity the supraconscious has been helping mankind not only in its historical mission, but even in its survival. By this role it has rendered another service to man and his moral ennoblement. If carefully cultivated, it can increasingly assist the human race in this task.

The above outlines the main functions of the supraconscious in the survival, creative growth, and moral ennoblement of the human race. In all these respects its role has been truly decisive. It remains paramount also for the future of humanity. We must do our best to cultivate the supraconscious potential in everyone of us. Our research bodies must concentrate their activity on a most intensive study of this ground of all real values. The chosen few that are graced by the creative genius must help us in bringing its grace to distressed humanity. Using the known methods of release of the supraconscious in every person: the techniques of good deeds, meditation, contemplation, prayer, moral purification, conscious examination, self-identification with and self-surrender to it, the technique of mimesis of the creative heroes of love, the techniques of Yoga, and others, we have a good chance to increase its fructifying circulation in the human universe. By indefatigable efforts in discovering new techniques for this purpose we may find more effective means of its multiplication in the human family.

Finally, by becoming conscious of the paramount importance of the supraconscious and by earnest striving for its grace, we can activate its creative potential and its control over our conscious and unconscious forces. By all these means we can break the thick prison walls erected by prevalent pseudo-science around the supraconscious. By denying its reality, by asserting the animalistic nature of man, by suppressing the creative manifestation of the supraconscious through the prevalent educational methods and many other ways this pseudo-science has greatly inhibited the manifestation of the supraconscious forces in man. The time has come when these prison walls must be broken and full freedom for the activities of the supraconscious be secured. Blessed by its grace mankind can resume its creative march towards the fulfillment of its greatest hopes and highest ideals.

# VIII

## CONCLUSION

The preceding paragraphs show the egoistic nature of all tribal altruisms, their inevitable conflicts, and their innumerable victims. The conclusions make clear the necessity of transcendence of all tribal solidarities by the universal solidarity of mankind, if interhuman warfare is to be eliminated from the human universe. Further on, this chapter seriously contends that an approximate realization of the ideal of pacified humanity is neither impossible nor is it a mere utopian dream. However difficult is its attainment, it must be achieved for the simple reason of survival of creative mankind itself. This attainment is not a matter of fanciful choice, but that of stern necessity. The destiny's categoric ultimatum of " to be or not to be " can be answered positively only through extension of solidarity over the whole human race and through creative ennoblement of its nature.

This hopeful answer is backed up by the practical plan of how this objective can be reached. The plan demands, first, mobilization of the unconscious, conscious, and supraconscious forces of man for this " holy war " of the united mankind against its eternal and implacable enemies: death, disease, stupidity, ignorance, criminality, sterile suffering, poverty, and the like. Second, the plan shows how the power of the unconscious antisocial drives, like hatred, self-preservation, egoism, competition, and so on, can be redirected into the channels serving this purpose. Third, it shows how the mechanisms of the unconditioned and conditioned reflexes can be used for unification and pacification of humanity. Fourth, how the powers of the rational thought and conscious scientific activity can help in this task, and fifth, how the supraconscious genius of humanity can render supreme guidance and creative assistance in this undertaking.

So organized and unified into one magnificent force, the existing unconscious, conscious, and supraconscious powers of man are sufficient for elimination of most of the interhuman wars, as well for a splendid renaissance of man himself, of his culture and social universe. As soon as these powers are organized according to the plan, they will begin their work and in a comparatively short time will achieve the results far exceeding the best expectations. By the mysterious forces of destiny mankind is confronted with a stern dilemma: either to continue its predatory policies of individual and tribal selfishness that lead it to its inevitable doom, or to embark upon the policies of universal solidarity that brings humanity to the aspired for heaven on the earth. It is up to everyone of us which of the two roads we prefer to choose.

# Notes

1. See my *Leaves from a Russian Dairy* (Boston, 1950), p. 310.
2. A. H. Maslow, "Love in Healthy People," in Ashley Montagu, ed., *The Meaning of Love* (New York, 1953), pp. 57-58.

## CHAPTER ONE
### THE MANIFOLDNESS OF LOVE AND ITS MAIN ASPECTS

1. I John 4:7, 8, 16. See: St. Francis de Sales, *Treatise on the Love of God* (Westminster, 1942); E. Swedenborg, *De Divino Amore et de Divino Sapientia* (New York, 1890).
2. P. Tillich, *The Protestant Era* (Chicago, 1948), p. 160.
3. A. Nygren, *Agape and Eros* (London: Society for Promoting Christian Knowledge, 1937), Vol. I, pp. 165, 171, *et passim*.
4. See among recent writers D. de Rougemont, *L'Amour et l'Occident* (Paris, 1939), translated into English by Montgomery Belgion under the title *Passion and Society; Love in the Western World*, American ed.; P. Rousselot, *Pour l'Histoire du Problème de l'Amour au Moyen Âge* (Münster, 1908); M. C. D'Arcy, *The Mind and Heart of Love* (London, 1947); S. Radhakrishnan, *The Bhagavadgita* (New York, 1948), pp. 62 ff.; Sri Aurobindo, *The Life Divine* (New York, 1949), pp. 187-189.
5. In the Upanishads and the Bhagavadgita, "in Bhakti the grace of God is earned to an extent; in prapatti it is freely bestowed"; S. Radhakrishnan, *op. cit.*, p. 62.
6. G. P. Fedotov, *A Treasury of Russian Spirituality* (New York, 1948), p. 229.
7. See for instance Sri Aurobindo, *Bases of Yoga* (Calcutta, 1936) pp. 12 ff., *et passim; The Life Divine*, pp. 874, 892 f., 925 f. See further Chap. 19 of this work.
8. See W. W. Jaeger, *Paideia: The Ideals of Greek Culture* (Oxford, 1939), Vol. I, pp. 34-77, 122, 134-147, 160 ff., 204 ff., 235 ff., 265-282, *et passim;* also Vols. II and III, *passim;* S. Ranulf, *The Jealousy of the Gods and Criminal Law at Athens* (London-Copenhagen, 1933-34), Vol. I, pp. 32-42, 112, 148, *et passim;* P. Sorokin, *Dynamics* (New York, 1937-1941), Vol. II, pp. 490 ff.
9. M. C. D'Arcy, *The Mind and Heart of Love* (London, 1947), pp. 255, 312, 320, *et passim*. Unfortunately all these authors, including even D'Arcy, make several mistakes in their interpretations of these forms of love and of various (especially oriental) religions and philosophies from this standpoint. One of these mistakes is the tendency to view oriental philosophies and religions as the epitome of a dark, romantic, passionate Eros in which the ego or self or personality loses itself entirely in the mystic union with Brahma or nirvana and ends in a self-immolation. Such a conception is incorrect. As mentioned, oriental religions and philosophies contain in themselves both forms of love, Eros and Agape, some stressing the Eros type, others the Agape type, but almost always containing both. The same is true of Pythagoreanism, Gnosticism, Neoplatonism, Manichaeanism, and medieval movements like Priscillianism and Catharism, described by de Rougemont as advocating only love as a dark passion — irrational, ecstatic, self-effacing, leading to self-destruction and self-immolation.

10. H. Diels, *Fragmente der Vorsokratiker* (Berlin, 1912), Vol. I, Empedocles, Fragment 17; Vol. II, pp. 1–2, 6–13. "In one movement all things coalesce into a unity in Love; in another they all separate in the enmity of Strife."

11. See also Swami Vivekananda, *Karma-Yoga* (New York, 1945), pp. 10–12; Sri Aurobindo, *The Life Divine, passim.*

12. I Corinthians 13:4–8, 13.

13. M. K. Gandhi, *Self-Restraint versus Self-Indulgence* (Ahmedabad, 1928), p. 102.

14. P. Tillich, *op. cit.*, xxv.

15. See the cited works of St. Francis de Sales and E. Swedenborg. See also N. F. Fedorov, *Filosofia obschevo dela* (*The Philosophy of Common Cause*) new edition (Kharbin, 1928–30); V. Solovyev, *The Meaning of Love* (English tr., London, 1945); especially Solovyev's *Opravdanyie Dobra* (*Justification of Good*) and *Nravstvennya Osnovy Zhizni* (*The Spiritual Bases of Life*) in his *Works* (*Sobranyie Sotchinenyi*) (St. Petersburg, 2nd ed., 1913), Vols. VIII and III. Fedorov evolved a comprehensive plan for a reconstruction of humanity in this direction, with the goal of conquering death as the greatest universal evil of humanity. See his work mentioned.

16. V. Solovyev, *The Spiritual Bases of Life*, Vol. III, pp. 35–52.

17. *Ibid.*, Vol. III, pp. 35–52. Somewhat similar ideas were expressed some thirty years later by Sri Aurobindo in his *The Life Divine.*

18. *Ibid.*, Vol. III, p. 351, *et passim.* See also Solovyev's other works mentioned and Fedorov, *op. cit.*

19. See N. Wiener, *Cybernetics* (New York, 1948), where the universal form of "communication" is well analyzed.

20. See Ashley Montagu, *On Being Human* (New York, 1950), for an excellent summary of various forms of co-operation and mutual aid as the basic biological processes. See also Ch. Nicolle, *Biologie de l'invention* (Paris, 1932), pp. 78 ff.; H. S. Jennings, *The Beginning of Social Behavior in Unicellular Organism* (University of Pennsylvania, 1941).

21. See Peter Kropotkin, *Mutual Aid* (London, 1902); W. C. Allee, *Animal Aggregations* (Chicago, 1931); *The Social Life of Animals* (New York, 1938); E. F. Darling, *Bird Flocks and the Breeding Cycle* (Cambridge, 1938); A. E. Emerson, "The Biological Basis of Social Cooperation," *Illinois Academy of Science Transactions*, Vol. XXXIX, 1946; R. Gerard, "Higher Level of Integration," in *Biological Symposia*, Vol. VIII, 1942; R. S. Little, *General Biology and Philosophy of Organism* (Chicago, 1945); S. J. Holmes, *Life and Morals* (New York, 1948); Charles Sherrington, *Man on His Nature* (New York, 1941); Sri Aurobindo, *The Life Divine.*

22. W. C. Allee, "Where Angels Fear to Tread," *Science*, Vol. XCVII, 1943, pp. 518–25. See other considerations and facts in Ashley Montagu's and other cited works.

23. See M. Scheler, *Das Wesen und die Formen der Sympathie* (1929); N. Berdyaev, *Solitude and Society* (London, 1938), pp. 194 ff.; P. E. Johnson, *Christian Love* (New York, 1951). For other forms, see my *Society, Culture, Personality,* Chap. 5.

24. Aristotle, *The Nicomachean Ethics*, Bk. IX, 1166a; Bk. VIII, 1156a; Cicero, "On Friendship," Everyman's Library Edition, p. 179, *et passim.*

25. V. Solovyev, *The Meaning of Love* (London, 1945), pp. 21, 44, *et passim.*

26. V. Solovyev, *Justification of Good*, Vol. VIII, p. 99; Berdyaev, *op. cit.*, Chap. 4.

27. V. Solovyev, *The Meaning of Love*, pp. 22, 44, 53, 59, *et passim.* "Without love there is no self-fulfilment of personality," N. Berdyaev, *op. cit.*, p. 195. See a development of these ideas in Sri Aurobindo's *The Life Divine*, pp. 187 ff., 874, *et passim.*

28. See the data and literature in P. Sorokin, *Society, Culture, and Personality* (New York, 1947), p. 8 ff.; also P. Sorokin, *Altruistic Love: A Study of American "Good Neighbors" and Christian Saints* (Boston, 1950).

29. See E. Swedenborg, *op. cit.*, pp. 96 ff.; Swami Vivekananda, *Karma-Yoga*, pp. 10–13.

30. Swami Vivekananda, *Bhakti-Yoga*, pp. 88–89.
31. See, on the life span and longevity of various social organizations (states, business empires, political parties, educational institutions, religious organizations, and so on), my *Society, Culture, and Personality*, Chaps. 34 and 47. Whereas the average duration of business empires is about 28 years, and of empires built hastily through conquest is from a few years to a few centuries, the great religious organizations are the most long-lived of practically all social groups and cultural systems. They have already been living for one or several millennia.
32. Philippians 4:7. "Peace I leave with you, my peace I give unto you: not as the world giveth, give I unto you. Let not your heart be troubled, neither let it be afraid" – John 14:27.
33. Swami Vivekananda, *Bhakti-Yoga*, p. 104. The ordinary joy of love is illustrated by what St. Tychon's companion (Chebotarev) says of him: "On the days when St. Tychon had received the greatest number of poor and distributed the greatest amount of money and other alms, he appeared especially cheerful and joyous. But on the days when he had been solicited only by a few or none at all, he would be sad and depressed. . . . He was like Job – the eye of the blind and the feet of the lame. His doors were always open to beggars and wanderers (and even criminals), who found food, drink, and rest under his roof." G. P. Fedotov, *op. cit.*, p. 199.

## CHAPTER TWO

## THE FIVE-DIMENSIONAL UNIVERSE OF PSYCHOSOCIAL LOVE

1. Swami Vivekananda, *Lectures from Colombo to Almora* (Mayavati, 1944), p. 175. "Not only do I seek nothing that is earthly, but I seek nothing even in heaven except you, my God and Creator" (St. Tychon) is another formulation of it.
2. Swami Vivekananda, *Karma-Yoga and Bhakti-Yoga* (New York, 1945) pp. 86–89.
3. Among other things, such a blind "romantic" love – a sort of fever – is the main reason for the instability and short life of contemporary marriage. See de Rougemont, "The Crisis of the Modern Couple," R. N. Anshen, ed., *The Family: Its Function and Destiny* (New York, 1949), Chap. 16.
4. See *The Bhagavadgita*, tr. S. Radhakrishnan (New York, 1948).
5. Even Jesus used such a rough grading. "*Greater* love hath no man than this, that a man lay down his life for his friends" (John 15:13). J. Bentham and other utilitarians do the same in their "moral arithmetics," though unfortunately they tend to look at their rough appraisal of various "utilities" as a real measurement; this is an error.
6. See P. Sorokin, *Altruistic Love*.
7. See P. Sorokin, "Experimente zur Soziologie," *Zeitschrift für Völkerpsychologie und Soziologie* (March, 1928), pp. 1–10; P. Sorokin and others, "An Experimental Study of Efficiency of Work," *Amer. Journal of Sociology*, Vol. XXXV: 765–782 (1930).
8. See P. Sorokin, *Altruistic Love*, Chap. 20.
9. See P. Sorokin, "Affiliative and Hostile Tendencies of College Students," in P. Sorokin, ed., *Explorations in Altruistic Love and Behavior*, pp. 277 ff.
10. See J. B. Maller, *Cooperation and Competition: An Experimental Study in Motivation* (New York, 1929), Chap. 12. The somewhat different results obtained by B. A. Wright may be due to the fact that the choice of toys for friends and strangers was not actual but only imaginary and speech-reactional; and to several other conditions of the experiment. See B. A. Wright, *Selfishness, Guilt-Feeling and Social Distance;* and *Fairness and Generosity*. Both studies are unpublished theses (University of Iowa, 1940 and 1942).
11. This is somewhat similar to a "feed-back" process. See N. Wiener, *Cybernetics* (New York, 1948), pp. 151 ff., *et passim*.
12. Almost all the papers in the mentioned Symposium: *Explorations in Altruistic Love and Behavior*, especially N. Rashevsky's, R. Hyde's, M. Greenblatt's, G. Allport's, Sorokin's, testify to this.

13. We shall see that all great and small apostles of love have always had enemies who hated, vilified, persecuted, and even murdered them. Some 37 per cent of the Christian saints died as martyrs; see my *Altruistic Love*.
14. L. Massignon, *La Passion d'Al Hallaj* (Paris, 1914-21), pp. 6–7; see there the testimony of his son, his servant, and the minutes of court procedure and statements of the witnesses.
15. M. Gandhi, *An Autobiography, or The Story of My Experiments with Truth* (Ahmedabad, 1929), Vol. II, pp. 21–22, 151, *et passim*, 590–593.
16. *Albert Schweitzer: An Anthology*, Charles R. Joy, ed. (Boston, 1947), pp. 109, 129, 155.
17. V. N. Il'in, *Prepodobny Serafim Sarovsky* (St. Serafim of Sarov) (Paris, 1925), pp. 29–31, 124, *et passim*. Here, by the way, we see Gandhi's ahimsa (nonviolence) practiced in full and under the most trying conditions. Also, despite the severe asceticism of Serafim, his God was a joyful God of love and of indescribable bliss, and not a stern and mournful God of revenge.
18. On familistic and contractual relationships, see my *Society, Culture, and Personality* (New York, 1947), Chap. 5.
19. See V. Solovyev, *The Meaning of Love;* D. de Rougemont, *Love in the Western World;* also his "The Crisis of the Modern Couple," *loc. cit.*
20. See on this further Chaps. 5 and 6 of this work; also my *Reconstruction of Humanity*, Chap. 13; and *Social and Cultural Dynamics*, Vol. IV, Chap. 16.
21. See the literature and quotations on this in my *Dynamics*, Vol. I, Chap. 12, *et passim;* H. Read, *Education Throught Art* (London, 1943).
22. See on the "aesthetic component" and on art as a "pure intuition," F. S. C. Northrop, *The Meeting of East and West* (New York, 1946); Martin Johnson, *Art and Scientific Thought* (London, 1944); B. Croce, *Aesthetics* (London, 1909), pp. 385 ff. Nietzsche's fine arts as "a merry science," R. Wagner's theory of the fine arts as giving us the cognition of the ultimate reality, "*universalia ante rem,*" are but a few variations of this well-established fact of cognitive functions of the fine arts.
23. R. H. Schauffler, *Beethoven* (New York, 1934), pp. 278–279, 349, 383.
24. See C. I. Lewis, *An Analysis of Knowledge and Valuation* (La Salle, 1947); see there also a history of this basic problem. Further see P. H. Furfey, *The Scope and Method of Sociology* (New York, 1953), Chap. 4; H. Hart, "Value-Judgments in Sociology," *Amer. Sociol. Rev.*, 3:862–867 (1938); H. Becker, "Supreme Values and the Sociologist," *Amer. Sociol. Rev.* 6:155–172 (1941); W. M. Urban, "Axiology," in D. D. Runes, ed., *Twentieth Century Philosophy* (New York, 1943); St. Thomas, *Summa Theologica*, I, q.5, a.6, and II–II, q.145, a.3.
25. See on this my "Theses on the Effects of Science, Particularly Social and Humanistic Sciences, upon International Tensions and Solidarity," in *Learning and World Affairs*, ed. L. Bryson, L. Finkelstein, R. MacIver (New York, 1948).
26. See the data on this in my *Reconstruction of Humanity* (Boston, 1948), Part I, *et passim*. See also there the relevant literature.

## CHAPTER THREE

### TENTATIVE CONSIDERATIONS ON PRODUCTION, ACCUMULATION, AND DISTRIBUTION OF LOVE ENERGY

1. The term energy is used here in its general sense of "capacity of acting or producing an effect" or "capacity for performing work" (*Webster's Dictionary*).
2. To many the expression "production, accumulation, and transmission of love energy" may sound somewhat strange and paradoxical. Yet many of the eminent altruists and saints well understood the problem and even used similar expressions. The statements of Serafim of Sarov about the true goal of Christian life may serve as an example: "The true aim of our Christian life is to acquire (and accumulate) the Holy Spirit of God. . . . To acquire is the same as to gain. . . . You understand what acquiring money means. Acquiring God's Spirit, it's all the same. . . . The aim in life of ordinary people is to acquire or make money, and

for the nobility it is, in addition, to receive honors, distinctions, and other rewards for their services to the government. The acquisition of God's Spirit [or love] is also capital, but grace-giving and eternal, and it is gained in very similar ways, almost the same ways as monetary, social and temporal capital. . . . Earthly goods are virtuous acts performed for Christ's sake and conferring on us the grace of the Holy Spirit." G. P. Fedotov, *A Treasury of Russian Spirituality* (New York, 1948), pp. 267 ff.; V. N. Il'in, *Prepodobny Serafim Sarovsky* (*Blessed Serafim of Sarov*) (Paris, 1925), pp. 105 ff. Thus there may be and should be a special "economics and sociology of generation, accumulation, and distribution of love energy." Of course the principles and laws of such a discipline are bound to be very different from, often contradictory to, those of the economics and sociology of the generation, accumulation, distribution, and consumption of material commodities.

3. On the various forms of a hero's influence, see besides T. Carlyle's famous *Heroes, Hero Worship and the Heroic in History* (London 1841); Gerald Johnson, *American Heroes and Hero Worship* (New York, 1943); D. Wecter, *The Hero in America* (New York, 1941); O. E. Klapp, "Hero Worship in America," *Amer. Soc. Review*, Vol. XIV, pp. 53-62 (1949); S. Czarnowski, *Le culte des héros et les conditiones sociales* (Paris, 1919); H. Delehay, *Sanctus, essai sur le culte des saints dans l'antiquité* (Bruxelles, 1927); L. R. Farnell, *Greek Hero Cults* (Oxford, 1921); F. R. S. Raglan, *The Hero, a study in Tradition, Myth, and Drama* (London, 1936); D. W. Riddle, *The Martyrs, a Study in Social Control* (Chicago, 1932); G. M. Mecklin, *Passing of the Saints: a Study of a Cultural Type* (Chicago, 1941); P. Sorokin, *Altruistic Love*.

4. See further Parts III and IV of this work.

5. Some of the critiques of my *Reconstruction of Humanity* baselessly ascribed to me the idea that I aspired to make everybody a Yogin or an ascetic or a St. Francis. Such an idea never entered my mind.

6. See on this, and on what exactly must be changed in the existing family, political, economic, and other institutions to make them more love-productive and less hate-radiating, my *Reconstruction of Humanity*, Chaps. 9, 10, 11.

7. For what is meant by "culture," "cultural system," and "cultural congeries," what is the total structure of culture, and how cultural systems differ from organized social groups or institutions or social systems, see my *Society, Culture, and Personality*, Chaps. 4, 8, 17, 18, *et passim*.

8. See, on the negative effects and on what exactly must be changed in the main cultural systems in order to make them more altruistic and creative, my *Reconstruction of Humanity*, Chaps. 6-8; also my *Social and Cultural Dynamics* (all four volumes), and *Crisis of Our Age*.

9. See the actual figures on the movement of wars and other evidence in my *Reconstruction* and *Dynamics*.

## CHAPTER FOUR
### POWER OF CREATIVE LOVE

1. See on Sensate culture and mentality P. Sorokin, *Social and Cultural Dynamics* (New York, 1937-41), 4 vols.; P. Sorokin, *Crisis of Our Age* (New York, 1941); F. R. Cowell, *History, Civilization and Culture: An Introduction to the Historical and Social Philosophy of Pitirim A. Sorokin* (London, 1952); J. Maquet, *The Sociology of Knowledge* (Boston, 1951).

2. See on these theories P. Sorokin, *Contemporary Sociological Theories* (New York, 1928). A further criticism of all these theories, their tests and techniques will be given in my forthcoming *Fads, Delusions, and Myths in Modern Sociology, Psychology and Anthropology*.

3. A. Ruth Fry, *Victories Without Violence* (published by the author, Suffolk, 1951), p. 19.

4. Allan A. Hunter, *Courage in Both Hands* (New York, 1951), p. 9; taken from

William Hughes's journal, 1945 (also reported by BBC, August 15, 1948, by W. Maude Brayshaw).

5. See H. B. White and W. Price, "Brazil Opens the West," *Saturday Evening Post*, March 15, 1947, pp. 24–25.

6. See W. J. Bender, *Nonresistance in Colonial Pennsylvania* (Scottdale, Pa., 1932).

7. Edward Thomas, ed., *Quaker Adventures: Experiences of Twenty-Three Adventurers in International Understanding* (New York, London, 1921), p. 14.

8. *Ibid.*, p. 15.

9. *Ibid.*, pp. 15–16.

10. *Ibid.*, pp. 17–18.

11. *Ibid.*, pp. 12–13.

12. For many facts of this sort see *Quaker Adventures, passim.*

13. A. Ruth Fry, *op. cit.*, pp. 48–49.

14. *Ibid.*, pp. 37–41.

15. *Ibid.*, pp. 23–26.

16. From *Fellowship*, Jan., 1945, Vol. II, No. 1; A. A. Hunter, *op. cit.*, pp. 5–7.

17. Hunter, *op. cit.*, p. 7.

18. *Ibid.*, p. 11.

19. *Ibid.*, pp. 13–17.

20. *Ibid.*, pp. 21–23.

21. *Ibid.*, pp. 28–29.

22. *Ibid.*, pp. 29–30.

23. *Ibid.*, pp. 33–37.

24. *Ibid.*, pp. 40–43.

25. See similar facts in Allan A. Hunter, *Three Trumpets Sound;* C. F. Andrews, "Mahatma Gandhi," *The Canadian Student*, Vol. 12, No. 1; Richard Gregg; *The Power of Non-violence* (Lippincott, 1934); J. C. Winslow and Verrier Elwyn, *Gandhi's The Dawn of Indian Freedom* (Revell, 1931).

26. *Fellowship*, Nov., 1945.

27. Hunter, *op. cit.*, pp. 48–50.

28. *Ibid.*, pp. 56–58.

29. Allan A. Hunter, *Out of the Far East* (Friendship Press, 1934).

30. Observation made in Hecht House Nursery School, February, 1952.

31. Hu Shih, *The Development of Logical Method in China* (Shanghai, 1922).

32. Sir Ernest Bennett, *Christian Pacifist*, April, 1942, pp. 68–9.

33. M. A. Best, *Rebel Saints* (New York, 1925).

34. A. Hunter, *op. cit.*, pp. 69–70.

35. Margaret T. Applegarth, *Right Here, Right Now* (New York, 1950), pp. 11–12.

36. C. F. Andrews, *Sadhu Sundar Singh* (New York, 1934).

37. *The Messenger of Peace*, supplement to the *American Friend*, April 16, 1931.

38. Michi Kawai, *My Lantern* (Tokyo, 1930), pp. 6–11.

39. William James, *The Varieties of Religious Experience* (New York, 1903), pp. 281–83.

40. Allan A. Hunter, *Youth's Adventure* (New York, 1925).

41. A. Hunter, *op. cit.*, p. 77.

42. J. H. Franklin, *Ministers of Mercy*, Chap. I, Missionary Education Movement (New York, 1919); A. M. Pennell, *Pennell of the Afghan Frontier* (New York, 1920), p. 6.

43. C. F. Andrews, *What I Owe to Christ* (New York, 1932), pp. 245–6.

44. William James, *op. cit.*, p. 359.

45. A. Hunter, *op. cit.*, pp. 82–83.

46. See J. Mark Thompson, "Experimentation with the Technique of Good Deeds in Transformation of Inimical into Amicable Relationships," in P. Sorokin, ed., Symposium on *Forms and Techniques of Altruistic and Spiritual Growth* (Beacon Press, Boston, 1954).

47. See R. W. Hyde and H. Kandler, "Altruism and Psychiatric Nursing," in the same Symposium.

48. See H. Eichorn and R. W. Hyde, "Friendly and Unfriendly Interactions in the Mental Hospital," in P. Sorokin, ed., *Explorations in Altruistic Love and Behavior* (Boston, 1950), pp. 258–260.

49. P. Sorokin, "Affiliative and Hostile Tendencies of College Students," *Explorations,* pp. 289–90.

50. P. Sorokin, "Dynamics of Interpersonal Friendship and Enmity," in P. Sorokin, ed., Symposium on *Forms and Techniques of Altruistic and Spiritual Growth.*

51. See K. Lewin, R. Lippitt, R. K. White, "Patterns of Aggressive Behavior," *Journal of Social Psychology,* 10:271–299, 1939.

52. M. E. Bonney, "A Sociometric Study," *Sociometry,* 9:21–47, 1946.

53. M. D. Fite, "Aggressive Behavior in Young Children," *Genetic Psychology Monographs,* 22:151–319, 1940.

54. See L. Bender, S. Keiser, and P. Schilder, "Studies in Aggressiveness," II, *Genetic Psychology Monographs,* 18:546–564, 1938; G. H. Reeve, "General Principles," *American Journal of Orthopsychiatry,* 13:411–414, 1943.

55. See on the meaning of the "adequate" love above, Chap. 2.

56. P. Sorokin, *Altruistic Love,* pp. 100–101.

57. See on the factors of suicide P. Sorokin, *Society, Culture, and Personality* (New York, 1947), pp. 8 ff. See there also the literature on this problem.

58. See on psychosomatic disturbances L. J. Saul, "Physiological Effects of Emotional Tensions," in J. McV. Hunt, ed., *Personality and the Behavior Disorders* (New York, 1944), pp. 269–305; see the other literature given there.

59. *N. Y. Times,* April 27, 1952. See similar cases in Montagu's *On Being Human.*

60. See the facts and evidence in J. W. Eaton, R. J. Weil, and Bert Kaplan, "The Hutterite Mental Health Study," *Mennonite Quarterly Review,* January, 1951; B. W. Clark, "The Hutterian Communities," *Journal of Political Economy,* 32:357–374, 468–486, 1924; L. E. Deets, *The Hutterites: A Study of Social Cohesion* (Gettysburg, 1939).

61. See the results in R. P. Knight, "Evaluation of the Results of Psychoanalytic Therapy," *American Journal of Psychiatry,* 98:434–446, 1941; K. E. Appel, "Psychiatric Therapy," in J. McV. Hunt, *op. cit.,* pp. 1107–1163; L. Kessel and Harold T. Hyman, "The Value of Psychoanalysis as a Therapeutic Procedure," *Journal of American Medical Assn.,* 101:1612–1615 (1933); A. Salter, *The Case Against Psychoanalysis* (New York, 1952); C. R. Rogers, N. J. Raskin, and others, "A Coordinated Research in Psychotherapy," *Journal of Consulting Psychology,* 13:149–220, 1949.

62. K. E. Appel, *op. cit.,* p. 1155.

63. F. E. Fiedler, "The Concept of an Ideal Therapeutic Relationship," *Journal of Consulting Psychology,* 14:239–245, 1950.

64. F. E. Fiedler, "A Comparison of Therapeutic Relationships in Psychoanalytic, Nondirective, and Adlerian Therapy," *Journal of Consulting Psychology,* 14:436–445, 1950.

65. S. G. Estes, "The Therapeutic Relationships in the Dynamics of Cure," *Journal of Consulting Psychology,* 12:76–81, 1948.

66. R. W. White, *The Abnormal Personality* (New York, 1948), p. 334.

67. C. R. Rogers, *Client-Centered Therapy* (Boston, 1951), pp. 37–38.

68. *Ibid.,* p. 159. See also pp. 51–52, 69, 74, 158–161, *et passim.* Like many other therapists, Rogers correctly indicates the ineffectiveness of a faked, insincere, sham-love or friendship. Such a simulacrum of love does not work.

69. See K. Menninger, *Love Against Hate* (New York, 1942), pp. 6, 128–29, 136, 262, *et passim.* Where Menninger repeats the Freudian concept of love he unduly reduces it to the sexual variety. Fortunately, in many places of his book Menninger forgets Freudian concepts and gives an analysis of love and of its functions far more adequate than Freudian misconceptions.
    Cf. the studies of J. Seeman, E. T. Sheerer, D. Stock, G. Haigh, A. E. Hoffman, A. C. Carr, in "A Coordinated Research in Psychotherapy," *loc. cit.;* P. E. Kauffman and V. C. Raimy, "Two Methods of Assessing Therapeutic Process,"

*Journal of Abnormal and Social Psychology*, 44:379–385, 1949; E. G. Boring, "Was This Anaylsis a Success," *Journal of Abnormal and Social Psychology*, 35:4–10, 11–16, 1940; W. U. Snyder, "An Investigation of the Nature of Non-Directive Therapy," *Journal of General Psychology*, 33:193–223, 1945.

70. See P. Sorokin, "Love: Its Aspects," in *Explorations*, pp. 27 ff.

71. See on this I. N. Korner, "Ego Involvement and the Process of Disengagement," *Journal of Consulting Psychology*, 14:206–209, 1950; J. Seeman, "Clinical Opinion on the Role of Therapist Adjustment in Psychotherapy," *Journal of Consulting Psychology*, 14:49–52, 1950.

72. See Ashley Montagu, *On Being Human* (New York, 1950). See there the details, the evidence, and the main literature.

73. See Peter Kropotkin, *Mutual Aid* (London, 1902); W. C. Allee, *Animal Aggregations* (Chicago, 1931); *The Social Life of Animals* (New York, 1938); E. F. Darling, *Bird Flocks and the Breeding Cycle* (Cambridge, 1938); A. E. Emerson, "The Biological Basis of Social Cooperation," *Illinois Academy of Science Transactions*, Vol. XXXIX, 1946; R. Gerard, "Higher Level of Integration," in *Biological Symposia*, Vol. VIII, 1942; R. S. Little, *General Biology and Philosophy of Organism* (Chicago, 1945); S. J. Holmes, *Life and Morals* (New York, 1948); Charles Sherrington, *Man on His Nature* (New York, 1941).

74. W. C. Allee, "Where Angels Fear to Tread," *Science*, Vol. XCVII, 1943, pp. 518–25.

75. See above, Chapter One.

76. See the main works and data in A. Montagu's *On Being Human*.

77. P. Sorokin, *Reconstruction of Humanity* (Boston, 1948), pp. 67–68.

78. See A. Montagu, *On Being Human;* M. Merrill, *Problems of Child Delinquency* (New York, 1947); H. Witmer, "The Outcome of Treatment in a Child Guidance Clinic," *Smith College in Social Work*, Vol. 3, 1933; W. Warren, "Conduct Disorders in Children," *British Journal of Delinquency*, 1:164–186, 1951; C. Burt, *The Young Delinquent* (London, 1925); E. Shilder, "Family Disintegration and the Boy Delinquent," *Journal of Criminal Law and Criminology*, 8:709–732, 1918; W. A. Lunden, *Juvenile Delinquency* (Pittsburgh, 1936); S. and E. Glueck, *Unraveling Juvenile Delinquency* (New York, 1950). See also Chapter Eleven of the present work.

79. See P. Sorokin, *Altruistic Love*, pp. 136–37, 245.

80. See the details of the life and activities of Asoka in D. R. Bhandarkar, *Asoka* (Calcutta, 1932); V. A. Smith, *Asoka, the Buddhist Emperor of India* (Oxford, 1909).

81. P. Sorokin, *Social and Cultural Dynamics* (New York, 1937), Vol. 3, p. 352. See there a systematic study of all the wars and of the peace periods in the history of the countries mentioned from 600 B.C. up to A.D. 1925.

82. For the actual data on the movement of wars in the last twenty-five centuries and for the evidence of the twentieth century's being the bloodiest of all these centuries, see *ibid.*, pp. 259–382.

83. See for all such periods Sorokin, *Dynamics*, Vol. 3, pp. 259–380.

84. For the full evidence of the statements on the constructive sterility and destructive success of war-built empires and hate-inspired revolutions, see P. Sorokin, *Sociology of Revolution* (Philadelphia, 1924); *Leaves from a Russian Diary*, 2nd ed. (Boston, 1950), the essay: "Thirty Years After"; *Social and Cultural Dynamics*, Vol. 3, pp. 383–508 (which gives so far the only existing study of all the revolutions and important internal disturbances from 600 B.C. up to A.D. 1925, in the history of Greece, Rome, Byzantium, France, Germany, Austria, England, Italy, Spain, the Netherlands, Russia, Poland, Lithuania); *S.O.S.: The Meaning of Our Crisis* (Boston, 1951); *Man and Society in Calamity* (New York, 1942). In these works a vast body of factual evidence is given in favor of the summary statements of this chapter.

85. See R. Trumbul, "Holy Man Who Walks in Gandhi's Step," *New York Times*, Magazine Section, February 10, 1952, pp. 13–30.

86. See on this P. Sorokin, *Society, Culture, and Personality*, Chaps. 5, 6, 7.

## CHAPTER FIVE
### MENTAL STRUCTURE AND ENERGIES OF MAN

1. For details see P. Sorokin, *Reconstruction of Humanity* (Boston, 1948), Chap. 5; A. Montagu, *On Being Human* (New York, 1950), *passim;* P. Sorokin, *Society, Culture, and Personality* (New York, 1947), Chaps. 19, 48; P. Sorokin, ed., *Explorations in Altruistic Love and Behavior* (Boston, 1951).
2. Subsequent summaries of Freud's theories are based upon several of his works published in Freud's *Collected Papers*, Vols. I–IV (London, 1924, 1925), *General Introduction to Psychoanalysis* (New York, 1943), *A New Series of Introductory Lectures in Psychoanalysis* (New York, 1933); *Three Contributions to the Theory of Sex* (Washington, 1930). A concise analysis of Freud's theories of the unconscious and of the mental apparatus generally is given in E. Glover's *Freud or Jung* (New York, 1950), Chaps. 1 and 2, and in C. Thompson's *Psychoanalysis: Evolution and Development* (New York, 1951), *passim.*
3. The conspicuous illogic and bizarreness of Freudian thought about ego and superego can be seen even from E. Glover's *Freud or Jung*, in spite of all the efforts of Glover to glorify and justify his teacher; see especially pp. 22–24, 54 ff. The same is true of C. Thompson's *Psychoanalysis*. A more serious criticism of Freud can be found in Jan D. Suttie, *The Origin of Love and Hatred* (London, 1935); A. Salter, *The Case Against Psychoanalysis* (New York, 1952); and in many other works.

## CHAPTER SIX
### THE SUPRACONSCIOUS IN MAN'S MENTAL STRUCTURE, CREATIVITY, AND COGNITION

1. See the data and evidence in P. Sorokin, *Society, Culture, and Personality*, Chaps. 35–44; *Dynamics*, Vols. I–IV, *passim*. For the saints as geniuses in goodness see *Altruistic Love*, Chaps. 37, 38.
2. See *The Yoga System of Patanjali*, tr. by J. H. Woods (Cambridge, 1927), Book I *et passim;* D. T. Suzuki, *Essays in Zen-Buddhism* (New York, 1949), pp. 30–35, 227 ff., 261 ff.
3. Lao-tzu, "Canon of Reason and Virtue," i, ii, iii, *et passim*, in W. S. A. Pott, *Chinese Political Philosophy* (New York, 1925), pp. 103 ff.; Lin Tung-Chi, "The Chinese Mind; Its Taoist Substratum," *Journal of the History of Ideas*, June, 1947.
4. See K. W. Wild, *Intuition* (Cambridge University Press, 1938); N. Lossky, *Sensory, Intellectual, and Mystical Intuition* (Paris, 1938). After surveying and analyzing the meaning of *intuition* in the works of many philosophers and thinkers (Spinoza, Bergson, J. S. Mill, Jung, Croce and others), Wild finds the following common elements in the intuition concept of all these thinkers: " An intuition is an immediate awareness by a subject of some particular entity, without such aid from the senses or from reason as would account for that awareness." "Reason and all other forms of knowing are dependent" upon this intuitive awareness. "Intuition is not alternative to reason (or to senses); its minimum function is to form a basis for reason, and its wider function is to deal with what is unaccessible to reason. . . . It gives a peculiar feeling of unity between subject and object. . . . Intuition gives us insight into reality as opposed to, or supplementing, appearance." The supraconscious "intuition is an endowment of specially gifted people." Wild, *op. cit.*, pp. 226 ff.

For a survey and analysis of the *supraconscious* or "genius" in recent biological, psychological, and philosophical theories, see N. D. M. Hirsh, *Genius and Creative Intelligence* (Cambridge, 1931), pp. 232 ff., *et passim;* Charles Nicolle, *Biologie de l'Invention* (Paris, 1932), Chap. 1; P. Sorokin, *Social and Cultural Dynamics* (New York, 1941), Vol. IV, pp. 746 ff.; J. Hadamard, *The Psychology of Invention in the Mathematical Field* (Princeton, 1945); S. Voronoff, *Du Cretin au Génie* (New York, 1941), pp. 35 ff. See other literature in Sorokin, *Dynamics*.

5. Frederic W. H. Myers, *Human Personality and Its Survival of Bodily Death* (New York, 1903), Vol. I, pp. 78 ff. Myers summed up the data given by Prof. Scrupture (in *American Journal of Psychology*, April 1891), by Binet (in *Revue Philosophique*, 1895), and by others.

6. *Ibid.*, Vol. I, pp. 80 ff.

7. See details in Myers' work.

8. Most recent case of a calculating wizard is reported by *N. Y. Times* (October 26, 1952): "Johannesburg. David de Klerk Smith, mathematical wizard of the Johannesburg stock-exchange, can outfigure calculating machines. David, 27-year-old bookkeeper, can subtract and multiply faster than figures can be written down. In fifteen seconds he calculated how many times a wheel with a fifteen foot diameter would revolve in fifteen miles. In ten seconds he reckoned that 4,789 multiplied by 8,362 equalled 40,045,618. To multiply forty-seven to the fifth power took him ten seconds. He took thirty-nine seconds to solve another highly involved problem against 142 seconds of calculating machinery."

9. H. Poincaré, *Science et Méthode* (Paris, 1908), pp. 52–55.

10. H. Poincaré, *Inventions Mathématiques* (Paris, 1908).

11. G. Birkhoff, "Intuition, Reason and Faith in Science," *Science*, December 30, 1938, p. 603.

12. See E. Meyerson, *Du Chéminement de la Pensée* (Paris, 1931), Vol. I, Chap. 1; Vol. III, pp. 719–754; F. Gonseth, *Fondements de Mathématiques* (Paris, 1926); G. Hardy, "Mathematical Proof," *Mind*, Vol. 38, New Series, No. 149.

13. J. Hadamard, *The Psychology of Invention in the Mathematical Field* (Princeton, 1945), pp. 41 ff., 60 ff., 97, 112, *et passim*. See also S. Voronoff, *op. cit.*, pp. 53 ff.

14. See L. T. More, *Isaac Newton* (New York, 1934), pp. 41 ff., 56, 288, *et passim.* "As a mathematician he seemed to grasp the solution of a problem immediately."

15. E. Kretschmer, *The Psychology of Men of Genius* (London, 1931), p. 141.

16. C. Bernard, *Leçon d'Ouverture* (Paris, 1857), pp. 7, 36, 82.

17. See E. D. Hutchinson, *How to Think Creatively* (New York, 1944), pp. 18–19; see many other facts in J. Liebig, *Reden and Abhandlungen* (Leipzig, 1897), pp. 249 ff.; E. Meyerson, *De l'Explication dans les Sciences* (Paris, 2nd ed.), pp. 597 ff.; E. von Hartmann, *Philosophy of the Unconscious* (London, 1931), Vol. I, pp. 243–372, Vol. II, pp. 1–44; A. L. Porterfield, *Creative Factors in Scientific Research* (Durham, 1941), Chap. 5; W. Platt and Ross A. Baker, "The Relation of Scientific Hunch to Research," *Jour. of Chemical Education*, 8:1969–2002 (1931); H. E. Durkin, "Trial-and-Error," *Arch. Psychol.*, No. 210 (1937); J. G. Miller, "Discrimination Without Awareness," *Amer. J. of Psych.*, 52:562–578 (1939); L. E. Baker, "The Influence of Subliminal Stimuli upon Verbal Behavior," *J. of Exper. Psychology*, 20:84–100 (1937); P. H. Furfey, *The Scope and Method of Sociology* (New York, 1953), Chap. 7; G. Polya, *How to Solve It* (Princeton, 1945), pp. 158 ff.

18. See for details J. Venn, *The Principles of Empirical or Inductive Logic* (London, 1907), pp. 129–133. Also see A. Comte, *Positive Philosophy*, tr. by Martineau (New York, 1885), Vol. I, pp. 40–41; *Positive Polity* (London, 1875), Vol. I, pp. 97, 257, 321, Vol. II, pp 7 ff.

19. See, for instance, A. Eddington, *Philosophy of Physical Science* (New York, 1939); I. Langmuir, "Science, Common Sense and Decency," *New York Times*, Dec. 27, 1942; I. Lapshin, *Philosophy of Invention and Invention in Philosophy* (in Russian, Prague, 1924); F. S. C. Northrop, *The Meeting of East and West* (New York, 1946), Chaps. XII, XIII, *et passim;* L. Dechèsne, "La Pensée Inconsciente dans la Recherche Scientifique," *Bulletin de la Classe des Lettres, Academie Royale de Belgique*, Tome xxxiii, 1947, pp. 169–174; R. Ulich, *Man and Reality* (New Haven, 1948), The Hazen Pamphlets, No. 21; E. W. Sinnott, "Science and the Whole Man," *American Scientist*, Vol. 36, 1948, pp. 127–138,

and *Two Roads to Truth* (New York, 1953); H. O. Taylor, *Fact: The Romance of Mind* (New York, 1932); H. Dingle, *Through Science to Philosophy* (Oxford, 1937); J. H. Leuba, "Intuition," *Forum*, May, 1928; H. Margenau, *The Nature of Physical Reality* (New York, 1950).

20. See the literature and details in my *Social and Cultural Dynamics*, Vol. IV, pp. 746 ff. and E. von Hartmann, *Philosophy of the Unconscious.*

21. See I. I. Sikorsky, *The Story of the Winged-S* (New York, 1942), p. 227; see the whole Chap. 22, where intuition as "a sixth sense" is well analyzed.

22. J. Rossman, *The Psychology of Inventors* (Washington, 1931), pp. 101–106. See also E. D. Hutchinson, *How to Think Creatively*, where a large number of similar facts are given, pp. 18–30, *et passim;* and S. Voronoff, *op. cit.*, pp. 64 ff.

23. J. de Maistre, *Examen de la Philosophie de Bacon* (Paris, 1836), Vol. I, pp. 67 ff. Not without reason de Maistre claims that inventions and discoveries are hardly ever made according to the rational rules of Bacon.

24. A. P. Usher, *A History of Mechanical Inventions* (New York, 1929), pp. 28 ff; H. S. Hatfield, *The Inventor and His World* (London, New York, 1931); J. M. Montmasson, *Invention and the Unconscious* (London, 1932); J. Venn, *op. cit.*, pp. 352 ff.; L. Dechèsne, *op. cit.* See also other literature in my *Dynamics*, Vol. IV, pp. 754 ff.; Voronoff, *op. cit.*, pp. 35 ff., 64 ff., 129 ff.

25. See E. von Hartmann, *op. cit.*, Vol. I, pp. 293 ff.; R. A. Wilson, *The Miraculous Birth of Language* (New York, 1949).

26. F. Nietzsche, *Werke* (Taschenausgabe), Vol. VII, pp. xxiv ff.

27. O. Jahn, *W. A. Mozart* (Leipzig, 1856–59), Vol. III, pp. 423–25. It is to be noted in passing that the creativity of a genius graced by the supraconscious proceeds fast and results in a large quantitative output compared with that of the mediocrities working within much longer time. While the average output of a mediocre professor is about two or three volumes for life, most of the eminent scholars and thinkers whose works make history in social or humanistic or philosophical science have been much more prolific and most of their works were written in a comparatively short time. Ibn-Khaldun wrote his *Prolegomena* (three large volumes in quarto) within one year; G. Vico wrote his *New Science* within some four months. Mozart, Pergolesi, Purcell, Mendelssohn, Schubert, and several other great composers died in their thirtieth year or soon after. And yet the total output of their works is something exceeding many times the total output of mediocre composers who died in their seventies. The real masters wrote a suite or concerto or symphony sometimes within a short period of a few hours, a few days, or a few weeks. Handel's twelve *Concerti Grossi* were composed within one month; his *Messiah* in twenty-four days. Telemann, Mozart, Bach, and Haydn could compose a suite within the time necessary to write a long letter to a friend. This explains why the total output of eminent composers was enormous: hundreds of operas, suites, concerti, symphonies, masses, etc. The same applies to the creative geniuses in other fields.

The supraconscious is possibly responsible also for the frequent precocity of genius. Conscious ability requires long training while the supraconscious seems to be able to manifest itself in a comparatively short period. Here are typical examples of the precocity of genius:

*Mozart:* played piano at age 3; wrote a concerto for the clavichord at age 4; at that age, also, was able to play a piece on the violin without ever having been taught how. He completed his first opera at age 12. . . . He would suddenly stop walking, take out his notebook, and start writing notes feverishly, saying to his comrades: "Don't speak to me or interrupt me; they are singing in my ears, I must note it down."

*Franz Lizst:* Began playing piano at age 6; gave concerts from age 8 on, composed his first opera "Don Sancho" at age 14.

*Schubert:* Wrote sonatas, symphonies, and operas at age 11 and 12; at age 15 his musical production was already prodigious.

*K. M. Weber:* Wrote six symphonies, three sonatas, and an opera at age 12;

at 13, wrote a two-act opera, "Das Stumme Waldmädchen"; and at age 14, wrote the opera "Peter Schmol and His Neighbor."

*F. Mendelssohn:* Wrote a psalm at age 12, the overture "Sommernachtstraum" at age 17, and had written four operas by the age 15.

*Friedrich Gauss:* Worked arithmetical problems and traced geometrical figures in the dust at age 3.

*Blaise Pascal:* His father, a mathematician, encouraged the son to study Latin and Greek; he was told only that geometry consisted in the proper drawing of figures and the arranging and determination of their parts in their relations to one another. On the basis of this information, and with no other guidance whatsoever, Pascal proceeded to cover the walls and floor of his recreation room with geometrical figures, axioms, and theorems, all the way to Euclid's 32nd proposition in his first book on geometry; he had invented a mathematical system at age 12, thereby, entirely independent of outside guidance. At 16, he had composed a treatise on conic sections; at 18, he had invented a mathematical machine for making complicated calculations.

*Ampère:* Performed mathematical calculations with pebbles before he could read or write, and by the age 4 performed mental calculations as well.

*Alexis Claude Clairaut:* In 1726, at age 13, read a paper on four curves of his own invention before the Academy of Sciences. At 18, he was admitted to that academy after publication of his researches on curvilinear relationships.

*Jose Comas Sola:* A Spanish astronomer who, in 1877, at age 10, wrote his first work on astronomy. He produced a second work at age 12, and at age 13 observed sun spots through a small telescope.

*Brunswick:* In 1780, at age 3, solved mathematical problems and also (like Pascal and Gauss) traced geometrical figures in the dust.

Leaving mathematics and music and entering the art of painting, precocity is just as evident, although the ability to manipulate the tools of artistic production does not appear at quite as early an age:

*Raphael:* Began drawing at age 8, had some drawings accepted at the Academy in Venice at age 12, and was already famous at 19.

*Claude Joseph Vernet:* At age 4, used crayons well; was famous at age 20.

*Greuze* made his first work (public appearance) at age 8; *Giotto* started at 10; *Dürer* at 15; *Titian, Rubens, Jordaens,* were also very precocious.

*Bernini:* Completed his first sculpture at age 10; *Grasser* was sculpturing statues at age 13.

*Dante:* Composed a sonnet to Beatrice at age 9; *Tasso* and *Byron* began writing at age 10 to 12.

*Victor Hugo:* Had written over 3,000 verses by age 14; also, had begun two tragedies by that time.

*Goethe:* Wrote dialogues and other pieces between age 6 and 8; wrote his first theatrical play at age 10; wrote "Thoughts on the Descent of Jesus Christ into Hell" at age 15.

*Pushkin:* Wrote his first poem and his comedy "L'Escamoteur" at age 10.

*Pico della Mirandola:* Was familiar with Latin, Greek, Hebrew, Arabic, and Chaldean while still a child.

*Ralph W. Emerson:* Wrote the poem "Fortus" at age 12.

*Goldoni:* Produced a comedy at age 8.

*Ovid:* Spoke in verse from the time of childhood.

*Shakespeare:* Wrote all his historic plays before age 34.

*Ellius Quirine Visconti:* Gave sermons at age 6.

*Bossuet:* Gave sermons at age 12.

*Fénelon:* Gave sermons at age 15.

A large number of other examples of precocity could be added to this list.

28. R. H. Schauffler, *Beethoven* (New York, 1934), pp. 553, 279, 63–64.
29. W. Niemann, *Brahms* (New York, 1929), p. 11; see also E. D. Hutchinson, *How to Think Creatively,* p. 30.

30. C. D. Bowen and Barbara von Meck, *"Beloved Friend"* — *The Story of Tchaikovsky and N. von Meck* (New York, 1937), pp. 206, 216–18.

31. M. Proust, *La Prisonnière*, Vol. II, p. 73.

32. P. Chabaneix, *Le Subconscient chez les Artists, les Savants et les Ecrivains* (Paris, 1897); T. Ribot, *Creative Imagination* (New York, 1906); E. von Hartmann, *op. cit.;* also F. W. H. Myers, *op. cit.*, Vol. I, pp. 89 ff.

33. H. Delacroix, *Psychologie de l'Art* (Paris, 1927), pp. 189–98. See also K. W. Wild, *op. cit.*, Chap. VIII; S. Voronoff, *op. cit.*, pp. 64 ff.; C. Patrick, "Creative Thought in Poets," *Arch. Psychol.*, No. 178 (1935), "Creative Thought in Artists," *J. of Psychol.*, 4:35–73 (1935); G. Wallas, *The Art of Thought* (New York, 1926).

34. *The Bhagavadgita*, tr. by S. Radhakrishnan (New York, 1948), p. 62.

35. See H. Brinton, *Children of Light* (New York, 1938), p. 406.

36. B. Croce, *The Essence of Aesthetics* (London, 1921), pp. 33, *et passim*.

37. G. Birkhoff, *Aesthetic Measure* (Harvard University Press, 1933), pp. 6, 216, *et passim*. See further K. W. Wild, *op. cit.*, Chap. 8; E. von Hartmann, *op. cit.*, Vol. I, pp. 269–293.

38. For a detailed study of all the prohibited and punishable actions in various law codes — of preliterate groups, the Greco-Roman and early Barbarian codes of the West, and the most recent criminal codes of Soviet Russia, Hitlerite Germany, Fascist Italy — see my *Social and Cultural Dynamics*, Vol. II, Chaps. 13, 14, 15. The study shows that the main crimes in all these codes remain essentially the same. Changes concern either secondary misdemeanors or details, or less essential elements of the criminal actions.

39. E. von Hartmann, *op. cit.*, Vol. II, p. 39.

40. A. N. Whitehead, *Adventures of Ideas* (New York, 1933), p. 138.

41. A. Eddington, *op. cit.*, pp. 221–23.

42. See J. B. Rhine, *The Reach of the Mind* (New York, 1947) and *New Frontiers of the Mind* (New York, 1937); J. B. Rhine, J. G. Pratt, B. M. Smith, C. E. Stuart, and J. A. Greenwood, *Extra-Sensory Perception After Sixty Years* (New York, 1940); W. W. Carrington, *Thought Transference* (New York, 1946); then the volumes of the *Journal of Parapsychology* and *Proceedings of Society for Psychical Research*; A. Smith, *The Psychic Source Book* (New York, 1951); S. David Kahn, "Studies in Extrasensory Perception," *Proceedings of Amer. Soc. Psychical Research*, SSV: 1–45, 1952.

## CHAPTER SEVEN
### FORMS AND WAYS OF PERSONALITY INTEGRATION AND CREATIVITY

1. See H. Bergson, *Creative Evolution* (London, 1913), also his *Les Deux Sources de la Morale et de la Réligion* (Paris, 1932); F. Matthias Alexander, *Man's Supreme Inheritance* (New York, 1918), *The Use of the Self* (New York, 1932), *The Universal Constant in Living* (New York, 1941); T. Burrow, *The Neurosis of Man* (New York, 1949).

2. See on this P. Sorokin, *Society, Culture, and Personality*, pp. 63 ff., *et passim*; P. Sorokin, *Reconstruction of Humanity*, Chap. 6.

3. See the classification of the most important social groups in P. Sorokin, *Society, Culture, and Personality*, Chaps. 10–15.

## CHAPTER EIGHT
### SUPREME LOVE AND THE SUPRACONSCIOUS

1. R. A. Nicholson, "Mysticism," in Sir Thomas Arnold and A. Guillaume, *The Legacy of Islam* (Oxford, 1931), p. 218.

2. Al Ghazzali, *The Confessions*, tr. C. Field (London, 1909), pp. 47–48.

3. St. Theresa of Jesus: *The Life, Relations, Maxims and Foundations Written by the Saint* (New York, 1911), pp. 62 ff., 74–76, *et passim*. St. Pachomius the

Great says that only when one "becomes the temple of the Holy Ghost" can one do the deeds of sublime love. St. John Climacus states that saints do not say anything of their own; they say and do what God pleases to say and do through His saints. See *Annales du musée Guimet*, Vol. XVII, pp. 523–33; Migne, *Patrologia*, P. G. Vol. LXXXVIII, 1057. Similar statements are made by St. John the Prophet and others. They all reiterate Jesus' statements to His apostles: "When they deliver you up [to governors], take no thought how and what ye shall speak: for it shall be given you in that same hour what ye shall speak. For it is not ye that speak, but the Spirit of your Father which speaketh in you" (Matthew 10:19, 20).

4. See A. Schweitzer, *The Philosophy of Civilization* (New York, 1949), pp. 76–81, 92–93, *et passim*. See also his *Mysticism of Paul, the Apostle* (New York, 1931), and *My Life and Thought* (London, 1933), pp. 172–3, 254, 259–60.

5. *An Autobiography: The Story of My Experiments with Truth* by M. K. Gandhi, tr. by Mahadev Desai (Public Affairs Press, Washington, D.C., 1948), p. 175.

6. *Ibid.*, pp. 95–96.

7. *Ibid.*, pp. 4–8, 614–16. "A knowledge of religion, as distinguished from experience, seems but chaff in the moments of trials" (p. 94).

8. M. M. Davy, *The Mysticism of Simone Weil* (Boston, 1951), pp. 33, 53–54, *et passim*. Also Simone Weil, *Waiting for God*, tr. by E. Craufurd (New York, 1951).

9. Dorothy Day, *On Pilgrimage* (New York, 1948), pp. 8–10, *et passim; The Long Loneliness* (New York, 1952), *passim*.

10. V. N. Il'in, *Prepodobny Serafim Sarovsky* (Paris, 1925), pp. 38, 60, 161–62, 46, *et passim*.

11. P. Sabatier, *Life of St. Francis of Assisi* (New York, 1927), pp. 84, 338.

12. *The Journal of John Woolman* (Boston, 1909), pp. 61–63, 94, 34–36, *et passim*.

13. Saint Bernard, *The Twelve Degrees of Humility and of Pride*, tr. Barton R. V. Mills (New York, 1939), p. 40.

14. An analysis of their system of moral education is given in Chaps. 20 and 21 of this work.

15. Swami Nikhilananda, *Ramakrishna* (New York, 1948), pp. 96–97, 194–95. See also *Life of Ramakrishna*, compiled from various authentic sources (Advaita Ashrama), 4th ed., pp. 73 ff., 173 ff., *et passim; The Life of Swami Vivekananda*, by his Eastern and Western disciples, 2 vols. (Advaita Ashrama), Vol. I, Chaps. 8, 9, *et passim*. An analysis of their techniques is given further.

16. *The Book of Discipline of the Religious Society of Friends* (Philadelphia, 1943), p. 7.

17. P. N. Malov, *Dukhoborzy* (Thrums, Canada, 1948), pp. 268–69, 164 ff.

18. See the *Mennonite Life* and *Mennonite Quarterly Review:* these magazines give a good account of the life, mentality, aspirations, and behavior of the Mennonites and the Hutterites. See further Chap. 22 of this work.

19. Quoted from the manuscript of G. Briton on these prophets and their techniques of altruization, prepared for the Harvard Research Center in Creative Altruism.

20. See P. Sorokin, *Altruistic Love* (Boston, 1950), p. 57.

21. "The Texts of Taoism," in the *Sacred Books of the East* (Oxford, 1891), Vol. XL, pp. 3–4, 251–52, and throughout "The Classic of Purity" and "The Writings of Kwang-Tze."

22. Lao-tzu, "Canon of Reason and Virtue," in W. S. A. Pott, *Chinese Political Philosophy* (New York, 1925), pp. 103–107.

23. H. H. Dubs, "Development of Altruism in Confucianism," in W. R. Inge and L. P. Jacks, eds., *Radhakrishnan* (New York, 1951), pp. 267–275.

24. *Matsya Purana*, CLXVII, 13–25. See also H. Zimmer, *Myths and Symbols in Indian Art and Civilization* (Washington, 1946), pp. 49–50.

25. *The Yoga System of Patanjali*, tr. J. H. Woods (Harvard University Press, 1927), p. 71, 3–6.

26. See Th. Stcherbatsky, *Buddhist Logic*, 2 vols. (Leningrad, 1932), Vol. I, pp. 1–27.

Also his *The Central Conception of Buddhism* (London, 1923); *The Conception of Buddhist Nirvana* (Leningrad, 1927).

27. *The Bhagavadgita*, tr. by S. Radhakrishnan (New York, 1948), pp. 190–198. See also D. T. Suzuki, *Essays in Zen Buddhism* (New York, 1949), Essays I, V, *et passim;* S. Radhakrishnan, *Indian Philosophy*, 2 vols. (London, 1929).

28. On these systems of ethics and on their fluctuation in Greece, Rome, and the Western world, see P. Sorokin, *Social and Cultural Dynamics* (New York, 1937), Vol. II, Chap. 13.

29. Plato, *Phaedo*, in *The Works of Plato*, tr. B. Jowett (The Dial Press, New York), pp. 195–201, 217–18, 224, 267, *et passim*. Similar ideas are developed in his other dialogues, especially in the *Republic* and *The Laws*. In the *Phaedo*, however, Plato's formulations are especially similar to those of the Sankhya, Yoga, Vedenta, and Buddhist philosophies. This similarity is the reason for the conjecture that Plato visited India during his travel and came into contact with India thought systems. See on this Swami Vividishananda, "Mysticism and Reincarnation in Greece," in C. Isherwood, ed., *Vedanta for Modern Man* (New York, 1951), pp. 205–13.

30. Similar principles were stated by practically all the numerous representatives of "the ethics of principles," "the ethics of love," and even by a few eudaemonistic leaders, listed under these categories in my *Dynamics*, Vol. II, pp. 706–712.

31. John 14:6–26; also 15.

32. I Cor. 2:16.

33. Gal. 2:20.

34. *Confessions of St. Augustine*, tr. E. B. Pusey (Everyman's Library), Bk. X, 40–42.

35. See their names in my *Dynamics*, Vol. II, pp. 706–08.

36. E. Underhill, *Mysticism: A Study in the Nature and Development of Man's Spiritual Consciousness* (London, 1930), pp. 85, 169–208.

37. See a fuller list of the notable leaders of the ethics of love in my *Dynamics*, Vol. II, pp. 706–08.

38. J. A. Comenius, *The Way of Light* (Liverpool, London, 1938), pp. 18, 30, *et passim*.

39. F. Froebel, *The Education of Man* (New York, 1912), pp. 1–3, *et passim*. See also his *Autobiography* (London, 1886).

40. A. Comte, *System of Positive Polity* (London, 1875), Vol. I, pp. 257, 10–11, 69–71, 341.

41. L. Tolstoi, *The Law of Love and the Law of Violence*, tr. by M. K. Tolstoi (New York, 1948), pp. 17, 27, 35, 74, 82, 93, 104.

42. See the details in C. F. Chassell, *The Relationship Between Morality and Intellect* (New York, 1935), pp. 25–133, 377–470, *et passim*.

43. The data on the number of universities and institutions of higher learning are taken from the official *Minerva Jahrbuch der Gelehrten Welt* (Berlin, 1930). Other data are from P. Sorokin, *Dynamics*, Vol. II, Chap. 3, Vol. III, Chaps. 9–14, which should be consulted for the details and for the method of computation of the indexes of wars and revolutions.

44. See *Explorations in Altruistic Love and Behavior*, ed. P. Sorokin; Ashley Montagu, *On Being Human*, P. Sorokin, *Reconstruction of Humanity*, pp. 67 ff.

## CHAPTER NINE

### THREE TYPES OF ALTRUISTS AND THREE COURSES OF ALTRUISTIC GROWTH

1. On the why and how of creativity of nations and cultural groups in history see P. Sorokin, *Social Philosophies of an Age of Crisis* (Boston, 1951), Chaps. 12, 13, 14.

2. See P. Sorokin, *Society, Culture, Personality* (New York, 1947), pp. 540 ff.

3. See P. Sorokin, *Social Philosophies, passim*.

4. See many examples for Christianity in F. R. Webber, *Church Symbolism* (Cleveland, 1927); for Hinduism and Buddhism see H. Zimmer, *Myths and Symbols in Indian Art and Civilization*.

5. See A. Schweitzer, *My Life and Thought* (London, 1933), also *Memoirs of Childhood and Youth* (New York, 1931); John Farrow, *Damien the Leper* (New York, 1937); *The Journal of John Woolman* (Boston, 1909); A. F. Koni, *Feodor Petrovitch Haas* (Moscow, 1914); V. N. Il'in, *Prepodobny Serafim Sarovsky* (Paris, 1925); B. Franklin, *The Autobiography;* E. K. Sanders, *St. François de Sales* (New York, 1928); G. P. Fedotov, *A Treasury of Russian Spirituality* (New York, 1948); W. Thomson, *Pioneer in Community — H. Lasserre's Contribution to the Fully Cooperative Society* (Toronto, 1949).

6. *The Journal,* pp. 52–55.

7. *Ibid.,* p. 51.

8. William Caton and other Quakers apparently belong among the fortunate altruists also. See H. H. Brinton, *Children of Light* (New York, 1938).

9. See H. H. Brinton, *Guide to Quaker Practice* (Pendle Hill, Pa., 1943), *Quaker Education in Theory and Practice* (Pendle Hill, Pa., 1940).

10. A. F. Koni, *op, cit.,* p. 37.

11. John Farrow, *Damien the Leper* (New York, 1937), pp. 79–81.

12. A. Schweitzer, *My Life and Thought,* pp. 102 ff. By the way, note how much nobler and simpler is this psychology than the current psychoanalytical and other "physiodirty" interpretations. We do not see here anything of "frustration," libido complexes, escapism from unhappiness, or other Freudian phantasmagoric factors.

13. See V. Il'in, *op. cit.,* Chaps. 1–3; I. Andreev, *Prepodobny Serafim Sarovsky* (München, 1946), pp. 4–10; G. P. Fedotov, *A Treasury,* pp. 246 ff.

14. See A. F. Koni, *op. cit., passim.*

15. *The Journal of John Woolman,* p. 58; cf. pp. 80–81, 92, 94, 103–109, *et passim.*

16. E. K. Sanders, *op. cit.,* pp. 1–11; F. Vincent, *Saint François de Sales, Directeur d'ames* (Paris, 1923), pp. 10 ff., 56, 235, *et passim.*

17. See Fedotov, *op. cit.,* pp. 186 ff.; Z. Gippius, *St. Tychon of Zadonsk* (in Russian, Paris, 1923).

18. Benjamin Franklin, *The Autobiography* (Pocket Book Edition), pp. 5–6 *et passim.*

19. W. Thomson, *Pioneer in Community,* pp. 5 ff., 74 ff., 95 ff.

20. See P. Sorokin, *Altruistic Love* (Boston, 1950), pp. 59 ff., 149 ff., 245.

21. *Vita B. Antonii,* xv.

22. Asvaghosha Bodhisattva, *Life of Buddha,* tr. by S. Beal (The Colonial Press, N. Y., n.d.), pp. 305 ff., 319 ff.

23. *Ibid.,* pp. 375–397. Early Buddhism denied the reality of any substance or things: "no Matter, no Substance, no Continuous Space, no Time, no Ego, no Soul, no Personality, no God." The world consists of some seventy-five elements ("dharmas") which as "instant points" are in incessant process of momentary flashing and disappearing. A person is also but an incessant stream of such "instant points." The whole reality is but "momentary flashes of efficient energy of these separate elements without any substance in them, perpetual becoming, a flow of existential moments." The only force that holds these momentary separate elements are "the laws of physical and moral causation" (including Karma). These laws steer the course of these elements. "The port of destination is Salvation in the sense of eternal Quiescence of every vestige of life (Nirvana)." Man through the course of Yoga meditation, "through moral and intellectual perfection," can reach this Nirvana and can stop forever the endless cycle of rebirths and redeaths. Th. Stcherbatsky, *Buddhist Logic* (Leningrad, 1932), pp. 3 ff., *et passim.* See also his other works cited.

24. *Life of Buddha,* pp. 380, 397.

25. "The early Buddhist community consisted of recluses possessing neither family nor property, assembling twice a month for open confession of their sins and engaged in the practice of austerity, meditation, and philosophic discussion." Stcherbatsky, *Buddhist Logic,* p. 71.

26. R. Fülöp-Miller, *The Saints that Moved the World* (New York, 1945), pp. 163–65.

27. P. Sabatier, *Life of St. Francis* (New York, 1922), pp. 12, 14, 16.

28. Fülöp-Miller, *op. cit.*, p. 167.
29. *Ibid.*, p. 170.
30. P. Sabatier, *op. cit.*, pp. 23 ff.
31. P. Sabatier, *op. cit.*, pp. 61 ff. Fülöp-Miller, *op. cit.*, pp. 173 ff.
32. See the details in P. Sabatier, *op. cit.*, pp. 26–27; Fülöp-Miller, *op. cit.*, pp. 170–174.
33. Sabatier, *op. cit.*, p. 337.
34. Charles J. Dutton, *The Samaritans of Molokai* (New York, 1932), p. 174.
35. *Ibid.*, pp. 174–76.
36. *Ibid.*, pp. 177 ff., 199 ff.
37. *Ibid.*, p. 179.
38. *Ibid*, pp. 191–92.
39. *Autobiographie de St. Ignace de Loyola*, tr. E. Thibaut (Paris, Bruxelles, 1924), pp. 31 ff.; H. D. Sedgwick, *Ignatius Loyola* (New York, 1923), pp. 10 ff.
40. *Autobiographie*, pp. 34–35; Sedgwick, *op. cit.*, pp. 14–15.
41. As a matter of fact, Ludolf's book contained several basic principles of St. Ignatius' *Spiritual Exercises*. See Sedgwick, *op. cit.*, pp. 16–18.
42. *Autobiographie*, pp. 36–38; Sedgwick, *op. cit.*, pp. 18–22.
43. *Autobiographie*, pp. 41–42; Sedgwick, pp. 22–23.
44. *The Confessions of St. Augustine*, tr. E. B. Pusey (Everyman's Library Ed.), p. 158.
45. *Ibid.*, p. 163.
46. *Ibid.*, p. 148.
47. *Ibid.*, p. 169.
48. *Ibid.*, pp. 170–71.
49. See *ibid.*, Bk. ix.
50. M. M. Davy, *The Mysticism of Simone Weil*, pp. 6–7.
51. See Simone Weil's *Le pesanteur et la Grace*, *L'enraciment*, *Attente de Dieu*, and *La connaissance surnaturelle* for her religion, ethics, and philosophy. See also M. M. Davy, *op. cit.*, pp. 19–21, 45, *et passim*.
52. *Life of Sri Ramakrishna*, compiled from various authentic sources (Advaita Ashrama, n.d.), 4th ed., pp. 69–71, *et passim*.
53. See also Swami Nikhilananda, *Ramakrishna* (New York, 1948).
54. *Acts*, Chaps. 7, 8, 9, 22.
55. See P. Sorokin, *Altruistic Love*, pp. 59 ff., 149 ff., 245.
56. The numerous momentary "conversions" occurring supposedly after one or two hours of talks and songs in "holy-rolling" and "emotionally charged" revivals are either perfectly superficial, changing little or nothing in the conduct and mind of the "momentary converts," or else the overt phase was preceded by a much longer latent phase of "prerevival" reintegration of egos, values, group affiliations and new self-identification of such momentary converts.
57. See Fedotov, *op. cit.*, pp. 16 ff.
58. P. Sorokin, *Altruistic Love*, pp. 136–37.
59. See W. K. Clarke, *St. Basil the Great* (Cambridge University Press, 1913); E. F. Morison, *St. Basil and His Rule* (Oxford University Press, 1912); G. V. Florovsky, *Vostochnyie Otzy Chetvertago Veka* (Paris, 1931).
60. *Gandhi's Autobiography* (*The Story of My Experiments with Truth*, by M. K. Gandhi) (Washington, 1948), pp. 16–17.
61. *Ibid.*, pp. 47–50.
62. *Ibid.*, pp. 50–51.
63. *Ibid.*, pp. 40–41.
64. By the way, the greatest poet of Russia, Pushkin, and several other eminent creators are also greatly indebted in their creativity to their illiterate old nurses who loved them and were loved by them.
65. St. Theresa of Jesus: *The Life, Relations, Maxims and Foundations, Written by the Saint* (New York, 1911), pp. 2–3, 12–13.
66. *Ibid.*, p. 5.
67. *Ibid.*, p. 8.
68. *Ibid.*, pp. 10–14.

## CHAPTER TEN
### IDEOLOGICAL AND BEHAVIORAL ALTRUISTIC SELF-IDENTIFICATION

1. P. Sorokin, *Altruistic Love*, pp. 42 ff.
2. P. Sorokin, *Man and Society in Calamity* (New York, 1942), p. 165.
3. *Ibid.*, pp. 164–65, 192–93. See there many other examples of this type given in various societies and periods. See also J. Burckhardt, *The Civilization of the Renaissance in Italy* (London, 1898), pp. 272 ff.
4. For a detailed analysis of the extent to which the ideological and behavioral culture of the individuals and group is integrated, and what are different forms of personality's unintegration or disintegration, see P. Sorokin, *Society, Culture, and Personality*, Chaps. 17, 18, 19.
5. P. Sorokin, *Reconstruction of Humanity*, pp. 42–43.
6. See P. Sorokin. *S.O.S.: The Meaning of Our Crisis* (Boston, 1951), Chaps. 1–4.
7. The evidence for this statement will be published in a study on *The Criminality of Ruling Groups* by P. Sorokin and W. Lunden.
8. An unpublished study by myself, and N. Wright, Jr.
9. See A. C. Underwood, *Conversion: Christian and Non-Christian* (London, 1927), Chap. 7; E. D. Starbuck, *Psychology of Religion* (London, 1899), pp. 360, 357; W. James, *The Varieties of Religious Experience* (Modern Library Ed.), pp. 251–253.
10. See on this ideology of early Buddhism Th. Stcherbatsky, *Buddhist Logic* (Leningrad, 1932), "Buddhism denied a God, it denied the Soul, it denied Eternity. . . . By the champions of all other established religions in India, the Buddhists were generally regarded as arrogant nihilists." "No Matter, no Substance, no Ego, no Personality, only separate elements, momentary flashes of energy without any substance in them, perpetual becoming" is the second characteristic of early Buddhism. "The leading idea of Buddhist analysis of personality was a moral one." (Vol. I, pp. 2–5.)
11. G. W. Allport, J. M. Gillespie, I. Young, "The Religion of the Post-War College Student," *Journal of Psychology*, 1948, pp. 3–33; G. W. Allport, *The Individual and His Religion* (New York, 1950), Chap. 2.
12. P. Sorokin, *Altruistic Love*, pp. 42–46. See there the details about these irreligious altruists.
13. Matthew 6:1–8.

## CHAPTER ELEVEN
### FACTORS IN THE EARLY INTEGRATION OF THE FORTUNATE ALTRUISTS

1. A recent example of this karmic theory, based upon a study of the records of an American psychic, Edgar Cayce, is given in Gina Cerminara's *Many Mansions* (New York, 1950).
2. Practically all of the karmic diagnoses of Edgar Cayce, and Cerminara's assertions remain completely dogmatic, without a shred of real evidence. See Cerminara's *Many Mansions*.
3. For corroboration of this criticism see P. Sorokin, *Social and Cultural Dynamics*, Vol. 4, Chaps. 9, 10, 11, 13.
4. See on this P. Sorokin, *Social Philosophies of An Age of Crisis*, pp. 230 ff.
5. See L. Ron Hubbard, *Dianetics* (New York, 1950), pp. 60 ff.
6. Even Dr. J. A. Winter (who wrote an enthusiastic "Introduction" to Hubbard's *Dianetics*) in his later book, *A Doctor's Report on Dianetics*, had to secede from Hubbard and had to expose many charlatanish claims of dianetics: that often its techniques do not cure, that sometimes they harm, that he never has seen any single "clear" (completely cured person), and so on. Similarly negative conclusions have to be applied to several other therapeutic theories, like A. L. Kitselman's E-Therapy (Institute of Integration, San Francisco, 1951) and

others luxuriously proliferating in the credulous age of ours and finding a large number of naive clients.

7. For other variations of these theories see Sorokin's *Social and Cultural Dynamics*, Vol. 4, Chap. 10.

8. See a detailed analysis and criticism of these theories in P. Sorokin, *Contemporary Sociological Theories*, Chaps. 2, 3; *Dynamics*, Vol. 4, Chaps. 9, 10, 11.

9. See on this P. Sorokin, *Altruistic Love*, pp. 108–121.

10. See. E. Kretschmer, *Physique and Character* (New York, 1925); E. A. Hooton, *Crime and the Man* (Cambridge, 1939); *Young Man, You Are Normal* (New York, 1945); W. H. Sheldon, *The Varieties of Human Physique* (New York, 1940); W. H. Sheldon and S. S. Stevens, *The Varieties of Temperament* (New York, 1942); W. H. Sheldon with E. M. Hartl and E. McDermott, *Varieties of Delinquent Youth: An Introduction to Constitutional Psychiatry* (New York, 1949); C. W. Heath, *What People Are* (Cambridge, 1945); C. C. Seltzer, "Body Disproportions and Dominant Personality Traits," *Psychosomatic Medicine* (1946) and "The Relationship Between the Masculine Component and Personality," *Amer. Journal of Physical Anthropology* (1945); T. Ferguson and James Cunnison, *The Young Wage Earner* (Glasgow, 1951).

11. Cf. a detailed critical analysis of these in P. A. Sorokin's *Contemporary Sociological Theories*, Chap. 5.

12. For a more detailed criticism, see E. Sutherland, "Critique of Sheldon's Varieties of Delinquent Youths," *Am. Soc. Review*, 16:10–13 (1951).

13. K. F. Schluessler and D. R. Cressey, "Personality Characteristics of Criminals," *Am. Journal of Sociology*, 55:476–484 (1950); see also P. Sorokin, *Reconstruction of Humanity*, pp. 68–74.

14. G. Gorer and J. Rickman, *The People of Great Russia* (London, 1949) pp. 122–153, 221–223, *et passim.* See also G. Gorer, *The American People* (New York, 1948); M. Mead, *Soviet Attitudes Toward Authority* (New York, 1951). Many other characteristics, ascribed by these psychoanalytical anthropologists to the American people (like "rejection of father," predominantly "feminine" character of American conscience, etc.) or to the Russian people ("diffused guilt," "avalanche fantasies," etc.), are attributed in a purely impressionistic and dogmatic way without almost any evidence.

15. "The Hsiao King or Classic of Filial Piety," *Sacred Books of the East* (Oxford, 1879), Vol. III, pp. 466–488.

16. See P. Sorokin, *Social Mobility* (New York, 1927), Chaps. 17–18; H. Hartshorne and M. May, "Testing the Knowledge of Right and Wrong," *Religious Education*, XXI (1926), p. 545. See further P. Sorokin, C. Zimmerman, and J. Galpin, *Source Book in Rural Sociology* (Minneapolis, 1929), Vol. 2, Chap. 10; C. C. Zimmerman, *The Family and Civilization* (New York, 1947).

17. For the details, see my *Contemporary Sociological Theories*, Chap. 2.

18. S. and E. Glueck, *Unraveling Juvenile Delinquency* (New York, 1950), p. 115.

19. *Ibid.*, Chaps. 4, 8, 9, 10, 11. See also S. S. Glueck, *1,000 Juvenile Delinquents* (New York, 1934); S. and E. Glueck, *500 Delinquent Women* (New York, 1934); S. and E. Glueck, *Juvenile Delinquents Grown Up* (Boston, 1940).

20. E. Shilder, "Family Disintegration and the Boy Delinquent," *Journal of Criminal Law and Criminology*, 8:709–732 (1918).

21. C. Burt, *The Young Delinquent* (London, 1925).

22. W. Warren, "Conduct Disorders in Children Aged Five to Fifteen Years," *The British Journal of Delinquency*, 1:164–186 (1951).

23. M. Merrill, *Problems of Child Delinquency* (New York, 1947).

24. H. Witmer and Students, "The Outcome of Treatment in a Child Guidance Clinic," *Smith College Studies in Social Work*, Vol. 3 (1933), p. 370.

25. P. Wiers, *Economic Factors in Michigan Delinquency* (New York, 1944), pp. 31–36, 52 ff.

26. See W. Healy and A. Bronner, *New Light on Delinquency* (New Haven, 1936); H. Shulman, "The Family and Juvenile Delinquency," *The Annals of the American Academy of Political and Social Science*, 261:21–31 (1949); H. Hart-

shorne and M. A. May, *Studies in Deceit* (New York, 1928), *Studies in Service and Self-Control* (New York, 1929); S. Breckinridge and G. Abbott, *The Delinquent Child and the Home* (New York, 1912).

27. P. Sorokin, "Affiliative and Hostile Tendencies of College Students," in *Explorations in Altruistic Love and Behavior* (Boston, 1950), pp. 264–66, 272. Cf. W. D. Wall, "Happiness and Unhappiness in the Childhood and Adolescence," *British Journal of Psychology*, 38:191–208 (1948)

28. P. Sorokin, *Altruistic Love* (Boston, 1950), pp. 25–28; 30–32.

29. P. Sorokin, *ibid.*, pp. 136–37, 245. *Explorations*, pp. 277–78. As most of the students are unmarried, they naturally do not mention spouse or child. Those who are married often put their spouse or child at the first and the second place among the dearest.

30. P. Sorokin, *Altruistic Love*, pp. 70 ff.

31. W. Boeck, *Das Mitleid bei Kindern* (Giessen, 1909).

32. H. Hartshorne, M. A. May, and F. K. Shuttleworth, *Studies in the Nature of Character* (New York, 1930), pp. 98–99.

33. W. Lunden, "Socio-Legal Norms of Delinquents and Non-Delinquents," in P. Sorokin, ed., *Forms and Techniques of Altruistic and Spiritual Growth, A Symposium* (Boston, 1954); G. Allport, *The Individual and His Religion* (New York, 1950), p. 39.

34. R. J. Havighurst and H. Taba, *Adolescent Character and Personality* (New York, 1949), pp. 190, 233.

35. See R. M. Bakwin and H. Bakwin, *Psychologic Care During Infancy and Childhood* (New York, 1942), pp. 295 ff.; M. Ribble, *The Rights of Infants* (New York, 1943), pp. 4–7.

36. L. G. Lowrey, "Personality Disorder and Early Institutional Care" in *American Journal of Orthopsychiatry*, 10:576–585 (1935). See also A. Montagu, *On Being Human* (New York, 1950), pp. 55 ff.; W. Goldfarb, "The Effects of Early Institutional Care on Adolescent Personality," *Journal of Experimental Education*, 1943, p. 128. See further literature in Montagu's book.

37. F. Bodman, "Child Psychiatry in War-Time Britain," *Journal of Educ. Psychology* 29:293–301 (1938).

38. See H. Miller and D. W. Baruch, "A Study of Hostility in Allergic Children," *Am. Journal of Orthopsychiatry*, 20:506–519 (1950); H. Lippman, "Psychoanalitic," *Am. Journal of Orthopsychiatry*, 13:415–418 (1943); L. Bender, S. Keiser, and P. Schilder, "Studies in Aggressiveness," *Genetic Psychology Monographs*, 22:151–319 (1940); M. E. Bonney, "A Sociometric Study," *Sociometry*, 9:21–47 (1946); H. Orlansky, "Infant Care and Personality," *Psychological Bulletin*, 46:6–45 (1949); J. Bowlby, "The Study and Reduction of Group Tensions in the Family," *Human Relations*, 2:123–29.

39. P. Sorokin, *Altruistic Love*, pp. 136–37.

40. For a fully developed classification of the most powerful or influential social groups consult P. Sorokin, *Society, Culture and Personality*, Chaps. 8 to 14.

41. *Altruistic Love*, pp. 140–41.

42. *Ibid.*, pp. 57–58.

43. P. Sorokin, *Explorations*, pp. 265–66.

44. P. Sorokin and C. Q. Berger, *Time-Budgets of Human Behavior* (Cambridge, 1939), p. 153.


## CHAPTER TWELVE

### INNER CONFLICTS AND PRECIPITATING FACTORS OF THE LATE ALTRUISTS

1. See the facts and details in A. C. Underwood, *Conversions: Christian and Non-Christian* (New York, 1925), Chaps. 11, 12; E. D. Starbuck, *Psychology of Religion* (London, 1899), pp. 278 ff.; W. James, *The Varieties of Religious Experience* (Modern Library Edition), Chaps. 7 and 8.

2. I am quoting from W. James's translation in his *Varieties of Religious Experience*, pp. 151–52.

3. W. James, *ibid.*, pp. 154–55.

4. *Ibid.*, p. 156. See there several other descriptions of the preconversion state of the late religious and altruistic converts.

5. See E. Underhill, *Mysticism: A Study in the Nature and Development of Man's Spiritual Consciousness* (London, 1930), pp. 169 ff.

6. E. D. Hutchinson, *How to Think Creatively* (New York, 1944), pp. 3–17.

7. Ibid., pp. 19 ff.

8. A detailed analysis and a body of empirical evidence about these " noncreative " ways of the resolution of inner conflicts is given in my *S.O.S.: The Meaning of Our Crisis* (Boston, 1951), Chap. 4.

9. Norman Cameron, " The Functional Psychoses," in J. McV. Hunt, ed., *Personality and the Behavior Disorders* (New York, 1944), p. 882.

10. See on the causes of suicide E. Durkheim, *Le Suicide* (Paris, 1912); M. Halbwachs, *Les causes du suicide* (Paris, 1930); P. Sorokin, *Society, Culture, and Personality*, pp. 8 ff.

11. I. P. Pavlov's experiments with dogs and J. H. Masserman's experiments with cats show that conflicting motivations or stimuli (roughly corresponding to the conflicts of egos, values, groups) regularly produce neuroses, especially when the conflicting motivations or stimuli are about equal in their power. See I. P. Pavlov, *Conditioned Reflexes* (New York, 1927), pp. 133, 290–292; J. H. Masserman, " Experimental Neuroses," *American Journal of Orthopsychiatry*, 14:636–643, 1944.

12. M. D. Fite's study shows that at the root of aggressiveness of children are the multilinear conflicts of rules, standards, and patterns of behavior they were exposed to in their homes, in the school, and in their environment generally. See M. D. Fite, " Aggressive Behavior in Young Children," *Genetic Psychology Monographs*, 22:151–319, 1940.

13. P. Sorokin, *S. O. S.*, p. 100.

14. See Asvaghosha's *Life of Buddha*, Chap. 1; Rhys Davids, *Buddhism* (London, 1903).

15. Swami Nikhilananda, *Ramakrishna* (New York, 1948), pp. 283–85; P. K. Acharya, " The Renunciation and Last Days of Sri Chaitanya," *Eur-Asia*, Vol. II, August 1948, pp. 589–93.

16. H. Waddell, *The Desert Fathers*, pp. 114 ff., 272 ff., 297 ff.

17. Z. Gippius, *Sviatoy Tychon Sadonsky* (Paris, 1928), pp. 9, 10; G. P. Fedotov, *A Treasury of Russian Spirituality*, pp. 190–91.

18. John of Ruysbroeck, *Adornment of the Spiritual Marriage* (London, 1916), pp. 7–10.

19. H. Waddell, *op. cit.*, p. 112.

20. A. F. Koni, *op. cit.*, pp. 189–90.

21. G. P. Fedotov, *A Treasury of Russian Spirituality*, pp. 211–12.

22. For the details see *The Life of Swami Vivekananda*, Vol. I, pp. 58–63.

23. P. Sorokin, *Altruistic Love*, pp. 59–61, 148.

24. P. Sorokin, *Explorations*, p. 274.

25. An unpublished study by G. Allport, *The Individual and His Religion*, p. 39.

26. H. Eichorn and R. W. Hyde, " Friendly and Unfriendly Interactions in the Mental Hospital," *Explorations*, p. 258.

27. P. Sorokin, " Affiliative and Hostile Tendencies of College Students," *ibid.*, pp. 389–90.

28. P. Sorokin, " Dynamics of Interpersonal Friendship and Enmity," in P. Sorokin, ed., *Forms and Techniques of Altruistic and Spiritual Growth: A Symposium* (Boston, 1954).

29. K. Lewin, R. Lippitt, R. K. White, " Patterns of Aggressive Behavior," *Journal of Social Psychology*, 10:271–299; 1939. A number of other studies corroborate the old uniformity that aggressiveness begets aggressiveness and love begets love. Cf. L. Bender, S. Keiser, and P. Schilder, " Studies in Aggressiveness," II, *Genetic Psychology Monographs*, 18:546–564, 1938; G. H. Reeve, " General Principles," *Amer. Journal of Orthopsychiatry*, 13:411–414, 1943; S. Keiser and P. Schilder, " A Study of Criminal Aggressiveness," *Genetic Psychology Monographs*, 18:361–409, 1936.

30. J. M. Thompson, "Experimentation with the Technique of Good Deeds," in *Forms and Techniques of Altruistic and Spiritual Growth*.

31. R. M. Brickner, "The Paranoid," *American Journal of Orthopsychiatry*, 13:400–410, 1943. M. E. Bonney, "A Sociometric Study," *Sociometry*, 9:21–47, 1946.

32. M. D. Fite, "Aggressive Behavior in Young Children," *Genetic Psychology Monographs*, 22:151–319, 1940.

33. Cf. M. Greenblatt, "Altruism in the Psychotherapeutic Relationship," in *Explorations*, pp. 188–194; F. Alexander and T. M. French, *Psychoanalytic Therapy* (New York, 1946), Chap. 4; K. Menninger, *Love Against Hate* (New York, 1942). See also the studies of F. Fiedler, E. Sheerer, C. R. Rogers, and others.

34. *The Journal*, pp. 96–97, 153.

35. A. Yelchaninov, "Fragments of a Diary," in G. P. Fedotov, *op. cit.*, pp. 422–426.

36. A. J. Toynbee, *Civilization on Trial* (New York, 1948), pp. 234, 248, 260, *et passim*.

37. S. Freud, "Mourning and Melancholia" in *Collected Papers* (London, 1934), Vol. 4; *A General Introduction to Psychoanalysis* (New York, 1920). In his *Beyond the Pleasure Principle* (London, 1922), Freud, however, notably changed his explanation of aggression. In this work he viewed it, especially its masochistic and sadistic forms, as a manifestation of a *death instinct* — the second primary instinct, side by side with his libido. The very change of Freud's view in this matter is symptomatic of the deep fallacy of his notions. He could not fail to observe that "frustration," viewed as a block to pleasure-seeking or pain-avoiding, often produces suicide, increase of internal control, unselfish sacrifice and altruization of individuals. He tried, however, to explain all such phenomena as "aggression directed against the individual himself or self-aggression." Such a generalization of frustration-aggression got him into new and worse difficulties; it explicitly contradicted his "basic pleasure-seeking and pain-avoiding principle." Suicide, self-torture, self-immolation, self-control where the frustrated individual intentionally avoids many pleasures and seeks many pains are evident contradictions to his basic "pleasure principle." Furthermore, by extending the concept of aggression, which always means aggression against somebody or something else than the self of the aggressive person, he made his concept of aggression void of any definite meaning. The result was the complete failure of his theory of the pleasure principle and of frustration-aggression. This failure made him look for a different theory that could explain all these phenomena in a more satisfactory way. Such a theory was provided by Freud in his "death instinct." This theory, in turn, is yet more fallacious than his preceding theory. It is contradicted by a legion of uncontroversial facts and irrefutable logical evidence. For this reason Freud later on practically abandoned it and left the whole matter in a messy state as concerns his theories. This footnote equally applies to a host of psychological, psychiatric, and sociological theories that blindly follow Freud and are "more Freudian than Freud himself." He, at least, saw the irremediable shortcomings of his theories, whereas these lilliputian "Freudians" do not exhibit any of the insight of their master.

38. J. Dollard and others, *Frustration and Aggression* (New Haven, 1939), pp. 1, 2, 27, *et passim*.

39. *Ibid.*, pp. 46 ff. See note 37 above, which applies to this blind repetition of Freudian mistakes. As a humorous detail, however, these authors find that "other conditions being constant, self-aggression should be a relatively non-preferred type of [aggressive] expression which will not occur unless other forms of expression are even more strongly inhibited." Quite a revelation! Or, here is another example of their generalization: "the occurrence of any act of aggression is assumed to reduce the instigation to aggression" (pp. 48, 50). Thus, if a bully freely bullies, his subsequent "instigation to bully" is reduced; if a rapist freely rapes a victim, his unhindered raping reduces the instigation to subsequent raping. It is high time that the production of this sort of nonsense, which pretentiously claims to fall in the realm of scientific generalizations, be stopped.

40. Sometimes they react intentionally in this way, for the sake of *captatio benevolentiae*. M. de Montaigne noted "that men by various ways arrive at the same

end. The most usual way of appeasing the indignations of such as we have offended, when we find that we absolutely lie at their mercy, is by submission to move them to pity; and yet, bravery, constancy, and resolution [*aggression*, P.A.S.], though quite contrary means, have sometimes produced the same effect." Edward, Prince of Wales, Scanderbeg, and Conrad III did not spare the submissives but spared the courageous and proud among the conquered, while Dionysius the Elder, or Alexander the Great, did the opposite. See *The Essays of Michel de Montaigne* (London, 1913), Vol. I, Chap. 1. Two similar types are observed among dogs. Some try to be subservient and approach a frustrating agent on all fours; others are aggressive. Among the dogs of I. Pavlov's laboratory there were conspicuous examples of both types (respectively named by Pavlov). In the cited study of K. Lewin, R. Lippitt, and R. K. White, in four autocratic groups the boys showed an extremely nonaggressive, apathetic pattern of behavior.

41. See H. von Hentig, "Physical Disability, Mental Conflict, and Social Crises," *Journal of Social Issues*, Fall, 1948, pp. 21–27.
42. G. S. Jallentyre, *The Life of Mirabeau* (New York, 1912), pp. 4–5.
43. From this standpoint Toynbee's analysis of "challenge and response," of a too favorable and too unfavorable environment in the generation of "civilizations," is additional repudiation of the criticized theory of frustration-aggression. See his *A Study of History* (Oxford, 1933), Vol. I.
44. Cf. R. Fülöp-Miller, *The Saints that Moved the World*, pp. 165 ff.; P. Sabatier, *Life of St. Francis of Assisi* (New York, 1927), pp. 15 ff.
45. D. D. Knowles, *The Monastic Order in England* (Cambridge, 1940), p. 38.
46. St. Augustine, *The Confessions* (Everyman's Library, New York, 1932), Bks. IV and IX.
47. C. Creighton, *History of Epidemics in England* (Cambridge, 1891), Vol. I, p. 6.
48. St. Theresa of Jesus, *op. cit.*, Chaps. 4–6.
49. Cf. I. Giordani, *St. Paul* (New York, 1946), pp. 8 ff.
50. Acts 9:4–9.
51. Al Ghazzali, *op. cit.*, pp. 44 ff. Also A. C. Underwood, *Conversions*, pp. 68 ff.; W. James, *The Varieties of Religious Experience*, p. 403.
52. Underwood, *op. cit.*, pp. 55–56.
53. *Ibid.*, Chap. 11.
54. A. Wautier D'Aygalliers, *Ruysbroeck*, pp. 68–70.
55. P. K. Acharya, *op. cit.*, pp. 589–93.
56. Z. Gippius, *Sviatoy Tychon Sadonsky* (Paris, 1928), pp. 9–10.
57. Cf. K. R. S. Iyengar, *Sri Aurobindo* (Calcutta, 1945), pp. 176 ff.
58. Il'in, *op. cit.*, pp. 20–21.
59. See on these Sante de Sanctis, *Religious Conversion. A Bio-Psychological Study*, pp. 44 ff.
60. Cf. P. Sorokin, *Man and Society in Calamity*, p. 167.
61. R. H. J. Steuart, *Diversity in Holiness* (New York, 1937), pp. 41 ff.
62. *Ibid.*, pp. 101 ff.
63. Cf. P. Sorokin, *Man and Society in Calamity*, pp. 165–166; J. Burckhardt, *The Civilization of the Renaissance in Italy* (London, 1898), pp. 501, 541–44.
64. Cf. P. Sorokin, *Altruistic Love*, pp. 60, 149; P. Sorokin, ed., *Explorations*, pp. 274 ff.; G. Allport, *The Individual and His Religion*, pp. 7, 39.
65. See the facts in *Man and Society in Calamity*, pp. 164–65.
66. See many significant details of this, *ibid.*, pp. 169 ff.
67. Cf. *Man and Society in Calamity*, *passim*, and Chaps. 10–12.
68. See the facts, *ibid.*, Chaps. 10–12, *et passim*.
69. The emergence and development of these reactions for the period before 1940 in the twentieth century, and for the periods of great wars, revolutions, and other calamities during preceding centuries, is given in my *Social and Cultural Dynamics* (1937–41), *Crisis of Our Age* (1941), *Man and Society in Calamity* (1943).
70. See the evidence in *Dynamics*, Vol. 3; *Society, Culture and Personality* (1947), Chaps. 31–33; *S. O. S.: The Meaning of Our Crisis*, Chaps. 1–3.
71. See on this my *Dynamics*, and *Crisis of Our Age*.

72. See P. Sorokin, *Man and Society in Calamity*, Chaps. 9–12; *S. O. S.: The Meaning of Our Crisis*, Chap. 4.
73. P. Sorokin, *Man and Society in Calamity*, pp. 159–61, *et passim*.
74. For a detailed analysis of these forms of polarization in the decade 1940–50, see P. Sorokin, *S. O. S.: The Meaning of Our Crisis*, Chap. 4.
75. *Altruistic Love*, p. 60; *Explorations*, p. 274.

CHAPTER THIRTEEN

TYPES OF ALTRUISTIC REARRANGEMENT OF GROUP AFFILIATIONS AND ENVIRONMENT

1. See T. W. Rhys Davids, *Buddhist India* (London, 1903); B. C. Law, "A Short Account of the Wandering Teachers," and "Gautama Buddha and the Paribrajakas," in *Journal of Asiatic Society of Bengal* (1918, 1919, 1925).
2. "Then was Jesus led up of the Spirit into the wilderness to be tempted of the devil." Matthew 4:1.
3. *The Spiritual Exercises of St. Ignatius Loyola*, ed. O. Shipley (London, 1840), p. 13.
4. *The Ascetic Works of Saint Basil*, tr. W. K. L. Clarke (London, 1925), pp. 81, 159.
5. On these types see P. Sorokin, *Dynamics*, Vol. 1, pp. 66–101.
6. A. J. Toynbee, *A Study of History* (Oxford, 1939), Vol. III, pp. 248 ff., Vol. IV, pp. 33–34, 233; Vol. VI, pp. 150–151, 170–171, 238–240, *et passim* in all volumes.
7. *Ibid.*, Vol. III, p. 248. See there concrete illustrations.
8. "The Sayings of the Fathers" ("Verba Seniorum"), translated from the Greek by Pelagius the Deacon and John the Subdeacon, in English translation by H. Waddell, *The Desert Fathers* (London, 1934), pp. 91–95, *et passim*. See also H. Bremond, "Les Pères du Désert" in his *Divertissements devant l'Arche* (Paris, 1930).
9. G. P. Fedotov, *op. cit.*, pp. 238–39.
10. See *Apastamba*, in *The Sacred Books of the East*, Vol. II (Oxford, 1879), pp. 151 ff; *Gautama, ibid.*, Chap. 3.
11. Asvaghosha Bodhisattva, *Life of Buddha*, tr. by S. Beal (New York, Colonial Press, n.d.), pp. 319 ff.
12. See E. J. Rapson, ed., *The Cambridge History of India*, Vol. I (New York, 1922), Chap. 4, p. 151.
13. See The Texts of Taoism, "The Classic of Purity," and "The Writings of Kwang-ze," *Sacred Books of the East*, Vol. XL, pp. 251 ff., 3 ff., *et passim*.
14. L. Massignon, *La Passion d'Al Hallaj* (Paris, 1914–21), pp. 10, 25 ff., 115 ff. Al Hallaj, as one of the greatest Mohammedan mystics, philosophers, and altruists, several times in his life retired into solitude for one or more years. So did also other Mohammedan thinkers, saints, and mystics. See R. A. Nicholson, *The Mystics of Islam* (London, 1914); R. A. Nicholson, "Mysticism," in T. Arnold and A. Guillaume, *The Legacy of Islam* (Oxford, 1931), pp. 210–238.
15. Swami Prabhavananda, *The Eternal Companion. Brahamananda* (Hollywood, 1944), p. 109. See also Sri Aurobindo, *The Bases of Yoga* (Calcutta, 1936), pp. 3, 16, 132–33.
16. St. Isaac the Syrian, "Renunciation of the World," in *Khristianskoje Chtenije*, 1822, No. 3, p. 5.
17. G. Florovsky, *The Eastern Fathers of the Fourth Century*, in Russian (Paris, 1931), p. 61.
18. St. Basil, "The Longer Rules," 2, 7, 24; "The Shorter Rules," 212; "de Fide," in *The Ascetic Works of Saint Basil*, tr. W. K. L. Clarke, pp. 97, 153–54, 166, 303, *et passim*.
19. E. F. Morison, *St. Basil and His Rule* (London, 1912), p. 23.
20. "The Longer Rules," 7, *The Ascetic Works of Saint Basil*, pp. 162–166, *et passim*. Similar views are expressed by St. Jerome; see *Select Letters of St. Jerome*, tr. F. A. Wright (London, 1933), pp. 423 ff.
21. *The Rule of St. Benedict*, A Commentary by the Right Rev. Dom Paul Delatte, tr. Dom Justin McCann (London, 1921), Chap. 1, pp. 25–33. Cf. St. Jerome, *op. cit.*, pp. 137 ff.

22. See *The Lausiac History of Palladius*, tr. W. K. L. Clarke (New York, 1918), pp. 112–115. In this history the angel tells Pachomius in his eremitic cave: "You have successfully ordered your own life. So it is superfluous to remain sitting in your cave. Up! Go out and collect all the young monks and dwell with them and according to the model which I now give you, so legislate for them." See also A. Gardner, *Theodore of Studium* (London, 1905), pp. 71–74; G. V. Florovsky, *The Byzantine Fathers of the Centuries Vth to VIIIth* (Paris, 1933), in Russian, pp. 176–77; Dorotheus, "Doctrinae," in Migne's *Patrologiae Cursus*, Series Graeca, tomus LXXXVIII (1860), columns 1617–1838.

23. *The Lausiac History of Palladius*, p. 115.

24. Matthew 22:37–39.

25. H. Waddell, *The Desert Fathers*, p. 61 ff.

26. H. Bergson, *Les Deux Sources de la Morale et de la Religion* (Paris, 1932), pp. 245–51.

27. *The Journal of John Woolman*, p. 260.

28. Al Ghazzali, *The Confessions*, pp. 8–9; Nawal Ali, *Religious and Moral Teachings of Al Ghazzali* (Baroda, 1921), pp. 15–20.

29. Swami Vivekananda, *Jnana Yoga* (New York, 1939), pp. iii, iv. See the full text in D. T. Suzuki, *The Training of the Zen Buddhist Monk* (Kyoto, 1934), pp. 5–6.

30. Kahlil Gibran, *The Prophet* (New York, 1942), p. 24. For India and the East see the quoted works of Rhys Davids and B. C. Law. Also C. Eliot, *Hinduism and Buddhism* (London, 1921), 3 vols.

31. See on this P. Sorokin, *Social Mobility* (New York, 1927), pp. 516–29.

32. See on this P. Sorokin, *The Reconstruction of Humanity*, Chap. 10, *et passim*; *Social Mobility*, Chaps. 8, 9.

33. D. T. Suzuki, *The Training of the Zen Buddhist Monk*, pp. 3–4, 37; *Essays in Zen Buddhism*, pp. 317 ff.

34. *The Ascetic Works of Saint Basil*, pp. 145, 163, 166, *et passim*.

35. *The Rules of St. Benedict*, pp. 18, 63–68; Regulae Pachomii, 179, in *Patrologiae Cursus Completus*, Series Prima, tomus XXIII (1845), 83.

36. J. C. Hannah, *Christian Monasticism* (New York, 1925), p. 156.

37. H. B. Workman, *The Evolution of the Monastic Ideal* (London, 1927), p. 272.

38. "First Rule of the Friars Minor," 17, in *The Writings of St. Francis of Assisi*, tr. P. Robinson (Philadelphia, 1906), p. 55.

39. D. D. Knowles, *The Monastic Order in England* (Cambridge, 1940), p. 20.

40. *Ibid.*, p. 451 ff.

41. *Altruistic Love*, pp. 155, 243.

42. Among other things their decline is shown by the rapid decrease of the number of Christian Saints during the last two centuries. See P. Sorokin, *Altruistic Love*, Chap. 37.

43. Cf. the evidence in P. Sorokin, *Reconstruction of Humanity*, Chap. 3, pp. 73–76. See also Chap. 8 of present volume.

44. See *Altruistic Love*.

45. The hermit-altruists well understood this. Paphnutius was shown by God that a former robber, a sinful man of degraded life, living in a village and earning his bread by song, "the headman of the village nearby," and a certain merchant were as saintly and virtuous in the eyes of God as the saintly monks and Paphnutius himself. Having met them and learned of their good deeds, performed amidst their sinful life and environment, the great hermit said to the robber: "I have done naught like that: yet I think it may have come to thine ears that the name of Paphnutius is famous among the monks. God hath shown me that thou hast no less merit before him than I" (H. Waddell, *The Desert Fathers*, pp. 67–70). "The true saint," says the great Persian mystic and altruist Abū Saïd (A.D. 967–1049), "goes in and out amongst the people and eats and sleeps with them and buys and sells in the market, and marries, and takes part in social intercourse, and never forgets God for a single moment." Viewing loving kindness and charity as the highest value, he knew no better way of attaining to God but by bringing joy to everybody's heart. Viewing the union with God not as an intermittent and occasional experience, but as a permanent extinction of the individual's ego,

and assumption of the divine nature (through sublimest love), he forbade his disciples religious pilgrimage to the Ka'ba, called it contemptuously a "mere stone house," viewed religious rituals as unnecessary and regarded the altruistic life in the ordinary world the highest and best way to God. On Abū Sáïd, see R. A. Nicholson, "Mysticism," in T. Arnold and A. Guillaume, *The Legacy of Islam*, pp. 219–20.

46. See in P. Sorokin's *Altruistic Love* the trend of decreasing number of saintly altruists for the last two centuries, and especially for the last century, Chaps. 37, 38.

## CHAPTER FOURTEEN
### TRIALS AND PAINS OF REINTEGRATION OF BEHAVIOR

1. *Select Letters of St. Jerome*, tr. F. A. Wright (London, 1933), pp. 67–69.
2. *Ibid.*, pp. 125–129.
3. *Life of Sri Ramakrishna*, compiled from various authentic sources (Advaita Ashrama), 4th ed., p. 62.
4. *Ibid.*, pp. 67–68.
5. *Ibid.*, pp. 68–69.
6. *Ibid.*, pp. 70–71.
7. *Ibid.*, p. 404.
8. Swami Nikhilananda, *Ramakrishna* (New York, 1948), p. 272.
9. Al Ghazzali, *The Confessions* (London, 1909), p. 20.
10. *Ibid.*, pp. 41–43.
11. *Ibid.*, pp. 42–49, 60.
12. *Apastamba*, Prashna I, Patala I, Khanda I, 11–19; Khanda II, 19–41; Patala II, 5.2–3, *et seq. The Laws of Manu*, III; *Gautama*, Chaps. 1, 2, 3. In the *Sacred Books of the East*, edited by M. Müller, Vol. II (Oxford, 1879), Vol. XXXIII (Oxford, 1889). See also P. Sorokin, *Social Mobility*, Chap. 9.
13. Suzuki, *The Training*, pp. 3–4.
14. *Ibid.*, pp. 5–6.
15. *Ibid.*, Chap. 1, *et passim*. For a system of moral and spiritual education in the contemporary ashram of Sri Aurobindo, see G. E. Monod-Herzen, "The Yoga of Sri Aurobindo," in P. Sorokin, ed., *Forms and Techniques of Altruistic and Spiritual Growth*.
16. Regulae Pachomii, 49, 3, 11, 23, 157, in Migne's *Patrologiae Cursus Completus*, Series Prima, t. XXIII, 61–86.
17. St. Basil, "The Longer Rules," 10; "The Shorter Rules," 112, 132; "Another Ascetic Discourse," 2. In *The Ascetic Works of Saint Basil*, pp. 142, 170–172, 271, 279.
18. St. Basil, *ibid.*, pp. 167–169.
19. *Rules of St. Benedict*, tr. D. J. McCann (London, 1921), Chap. 58, pp. 367–405.
20. *Ibid.*, pp. 1–5.
21. See A. Gardner, *Theodore of Studium*, Art. 24, p. 82.
22. "The Constitutions," in Père P. Dudon, *St. Ignatius Loyola*, tr. W. J. Young (Milwaukee, 1949), pp. 285–307; H. D. Sedgwick, *op. cit.*, Chap. 21.
23. *The Writings of St. Francis of Assisi*, pp. 33–34, 55. Similar are the requirements of Cistercian Order; see *Translations of Christian Literature*, Series II, Latin Texts. See also St. Bernard, "The Twelve Degrees of Humility and Pride," tr. Barton R. V. Mills (London, 1929), pp. 22 ff.
24. *The Ascetic Works of Saint Basil*, p. 123.
25. St. Jerome, *Select Letters*, pp. 423–29.
26. Psychiatrists and psychologists are still talking in terms of one ego or self per individual. This one ego or self is usually poorly defined and, when spoken as being "confused, split, self-contradictory and self-conflicting," it becomes perfectly meaningless. Such an "ego" or "self" is hardly possible: for any self-conflicting or self-contradictory ego ceases to be ego. "Ego" means always one indivisible unity; one "sticking out" *I* which being *I* and *ego* does not admit any self-contradiction, any self-conflicting tension. A self-fighting ego is no ego any

more; it is either "has been ego," now all smashed and broken into pieces, or, more frequently, it is at least two antagonistic egos fighting each other.

It is regrettable also that psychiatric theories and therapies still largely ignore the process of rearrangement of group affiliations of their patients. They still undervalue its importance in the trilateral operation of transformation of the individual. When psychoanalysts consider it, they use it in its worst form of "transference" or making the patient's association with the analyst the dominant, often exclusive and monopolistic, form of the client's social affiliation. Without disrespect to psychiatrists, one can firmly state that no psychiatrist can be so all-sufficient, all-filling, and all-fulfilling as to be able to replace all social groups of his patient. However helpful, the company of the psychiatrist cannot be a substitute for all social affiliations of the client. Shall we wonder, therefore, that the results of transference are often disastrous: the client becomes entirely dependent upon his psychiatrist and incapable to carry on independent life activities. Instead of being "adjusted," he becomes hopelessly "maladjusted."

When the reorganization of the client's social ties is entirely ignored, and the client is left in the same constellation of group membership in which he was before the treatment — the constellation which was largely responsible for his mental conflicts — the treatment often remains fruitless, no matter whether it is psychoanalytic or psychodramatic or client-centered or any other.

27. Carl R. Rogers, *Client-Centered Therapy* (Boston, 1951), pp. 77 ff., 83, 95, 136, 150.
28. Charles J. Dutton, *The Samaritans of Molokai*, pp. 178–79, 183–195.
29. M. Gandhi, *Autobiography* (Washington, 1948), pp. 256–60.
30. W. Thomson, *Pioneer in Community*, pp. 8 ff.
31. *The Journal of John Woolman*, pp. 91–92.
32. *Ibid.*, p. 93.
33. See Dorothy Day, *The Long Loneliness* (New York, 1952), pp. 148 ff., *et passim;* Marie-Magdeleine Davy, *The Mysticism of Simone Weil.*
34. See Sorokin, *Altruistic Love.*

CHAPTER FIFTEEN

TYPES OF CONTROL OF BIOLOGICAL DRIVES

1. *Paradisus Heraclidus*, 1, in *Vitae Patrum*, Appendix, 2nd ed. (Antwerp, 1628).
2. Plato, "Phaedo," *The Works of Plato* (The Dial Press, New York, n.d.), pp. 196–98, *et passim.*
3. *The Works of Saint John of the Cross* (London, 1934), Vol. I, pp. 18–63, *et passim.* Similar are the prescriptions for the "liberation of the divine part of the soul" in Hinduism, Buddhism, Sufism, Taoism, mystic Christianity, though as we shall see, the *techniques* of this liberation differ somewhat one from another. About a deeper meaning and the constructive purposes of mortification ascesis see A. Bloom, "Yoga and Christian Spiritual Techniques," in P. Sorokin, ed., *Forms and Techniques of Altruistic and Spiritual Growth;* also *Collection Irénikon*, XX, No. 3, 1947, "La Prière de Jesus par un Moine de l'Eglise d'Orient."
4. A rich variety of all these techniques of self-torturing in its many forms can be found (for the oriental self-torturers) in *Life of Buddha* by Asvaghosha Bodhisattva, pp. 331 ff.; in cited works of B. C. Law, T. W. Rhys Davids; also M. Eliade, *Yoga*, (Paris, 1936), pp. 179, 182, 204, *et passim.* For Christian self-torturers see Rosweyde's *Vitae Patrum* and Migne's *Patres Latini* and *Patres Graeci*, as well as any full series of the *Lives of the Saints; The Works of John Cassian*, tr. Rev. E. C. S. Gibson in *A Select Library of Nicene and Post-Nicene Fathers*, Second Series, Vol. XI (New York, 1894); O. Hardman, *The Ideals of Asceticism* (London, 1924).
5. See *Select Letters of St. Jerome*, tr. F. A. Wright, pp. 67 ff., 125 ff.
6. See *Select Letters of St. Jerome*, p. 137; *Life of Buddha*, pp. 331 ff., *et passim.*
7. V. Solovyev, *Opravdanyie Dobra* (Justification of Good), *Works*, 2nd ed. (St. Petersburg, 1913, in Russian), Vol. VIII, p. 84. St. Basil, St. Jerome, St. Benedict, and other Fathers also criticize this false asceticism. See St. Jerome, *op. cit.*, pp. 137, 407 ff., 427 ff.

8. *Life of Buddha*, p. 332.
9. Bhagavadgita, III, 6, 7. "To be free from desire, from the illusion of personal interest, is the true non-action and not the physical abstention from the activity. When one's egoism is removed . . . one works as God works." Free from desire and attachment, one acts out of profoundest depth of his inner being, governed by his supraconscious self. Comments of S. Radhakrishnan, *ibid.*, pp. 133–34.
10. H. Waddell, *op. cit.*, pp. 123–24. See also *Select Letters of St. Jerome*, pp. 421, 425–27.
11. See P. Sorokin, *Altruistic Love*, pp. 100–105.
12. H. Waddell, *op. cit.*, pp. 115–16.
13. Confronted with this excessive asceticism, one has to agree, to some extent, with V. Solovyev's *Diplomat* who prefers a mere courtesy or politeness to asceticism (Solovyev, "Three Conversations," *Works*, Vol. 10, pp. 120 ff., 155 ff.).
14. *The Writings of St. Francis of Assisi*, tr. P. Robinson (Philadelphia, 1906), p. 55.
15. See R. Fülöp-Miller, *The Saints that Moved the World*, pp. 180 ff.; P. Sabatier, *Life of St. Francis of Assisi*, pp. 17 ff., 57 ff.
16. See St. Francis de Sales, *Treatise on the Love of God*, tr. H. B. Mackey (Westminster, Maryland, 1942), Book IV and *passim*.
17. Saint François de Sales, "Introduction á la vie dévote," in *Oevres complétes* (Edition d'Annecy, 1892–1918), Vol. III, pp. 14–15.
18. Cf. F. Vincent, *Saint François de Sales, Directeur d'Âmes* (Paris, 1923), pp. 218 ff. This is an excellent analysis of the *techniques* of St. Francis in moral counseling and guidance of human beings: their body, mind, and volition.
19. *The Rule of Saint Benedict*, tr. Cardinal Gasquet (London, 1925), pp. xviii-xix.
20. *Ibid.*, Chap. 4. See on the details of monastic techniques further, Chapters Twenty and Twenty-One of the present work.
21. See Chaps. Twenty and Twenty-One of this work.
22. *Ibid.*, Chaps. 39, 40, 48.
23. *Ibid.*, Chap. 4.
24. For Buddhist and Zen Buddhist orders, see D. T. Suzuki, *The Training of the Zen-Buddhist Monk*. See also the cited *Rules* of St. Pachomius, St. Basil, St. Theodore of Studium, St. Francis, of the Cistercian Order, of Ignatius Loyola and the Society of Jesus, and other monastic orders.
25. See M. K. Gandhi, *The Story of My Experiment with Truth* (Ahmedabad, 1927), Vol. I, pp. 57, 70 ff., 143 ff., 484, *et passim;* Vol. II, pp. 58, 92 ff., 150 ff., 292 ff., *et passim*. Also M. K. Gandhi, *Self-Restraint vs. Self-Indulgence* (Ahmedabad, 1928), *passim*.
26. M. K. Gandhi, *The Story*, Vol. I, pp. 474–92; *Self-Restraint*, pp. ix-xi, 101–111.
27. *Self-Restraint*, pp. 101–2. Gandhi, on the basis of his own experience and other empirical evidence, firmly states that the results of such a self-control are unbelievably beneficial from the physical, mental, moral and any standpoint. This explains also his completely negative attitude towards contraceptive means, etc., as extremely demoralizing, debilitating, and disintegrating – physically, morally, and mentally, not to mention their deadly consequences (in the long run) for the future of a nation. Reiterating the conclusions of Paul Bureau's sociological study of the disastrous consequences of artificial birth control and sexual laxity for the French nation (*Towards Moral Bankruptcy*, tr. Mary Scharlieb from the French original *D'Indiscipline des moeurs*), he says that "The future is for the nations who are chaste." See *Self-Restraint, passim*.
28. On his life see K. R. Srinivasa Iyengar, *Sri Aurobindo* (Calcutta, 1945); H. Chaudhuri, *Sri Aurobindo* (Calcutta, 1951).
29. Sri Aurobindo, *The Yoga and Its Objects* (Calcutta, 1931), p. 5.
30. Sri Aurobindo, *Words of the Mother*, pp. 39–40.
31. Sri Aurobindo, *Bases of Yoga* (Calcutta, 1936), pp. 164–67. Like Gandhi, and practically all the Hindu Yogis, Buddhist, Taoist, Christian and other eminent altruists and moral educators, Sri Aurobindo finds Freudian and similar techniques of "opening up the lower subconscious and raising up all that is foul and obscure in it" highly dangerous, harmful, and utterly unscientific. "One should begin by a positive not a negative experience, by bringing down something of the divine

nature, calm, light, equanimity, purity, divine strength into the parts of the conscious being that have to be changed; only when that has been sufficiently done and there is a firm positive basis, is it safe to raise up the concealed subconscious adverse elements, in order to destroy and eliminate them by the strength of the divine calm, light, force and knowledge." *Ibid.*, pp. 221 ff.

32. A. Schweitzer, *My Life and Thought* (London, 1933), pp. 102 ff., 110 ff.; *Memoirs of Childhood and Youth* (New York, 1931), *passim*.
33. *The Journal of John Woolman* (Boston, 1909), pp. 17, 68, 93, *et passim*.
34. *Ibid.*, p. 91.
35. *Ibid.*, p. 239.
36. *Ibid.*, p. 239.
37. A. Erman, *The Literature of the Ancient Egyptians*, tr. A. M. Blackman (London, 1927), pp. 132–34.
38. *Benjamin Franklin on the Art of Virtue* (Franklin Institute, Philadelphia, 1938). In his *Autobiography* he gives a number of practical prescriptions for acquiring in an easy way this mastery.

## Chapter Sixteen
### The Ego-Centered and the Ego-Transcending Forms of Love

1. On the change of social institutions and culture see P. Sorokin, *Reconstruction of Humanity*, Chaps. 6–11.
2. For various classifications see F. E. Lumly, *Means of Social Control* (New York, 1925); E. A. Ross, *Social Control* (New York, 1922); H. Hartshorne, *Character in Human Relations* (New York, 1932); G. W. Allport, "Techniques for Reducing Group Prejudice" in P. Sorokin, ed., *Forms and Techniques of Altruistic and Spiritual Growth*.
3. On various racial theories and their fallacies see P. Sorokin, *Contemporary Sociological Theories*, Chap. 5; on diverse bodily constitutions as factors of mental, social, and moral characteristics see P. Sorokin, *Reconstruction of Humanity*, chap. 5; M. F. Ashley Montagu, *Man's Most Dangerous Myth* (New York, 1952); E. Sutherland, "Critique of Sheldon's Varieties of Delinquent Youth," *Am. Soc. Review*, XVI: 10–14, 1951. Cf. also Chap. Eleven of this work.
4. See Chap. Twelve above for the evidence against this pseudo-uniformity; also P. Sorokin, *S. O. S.: The Meaning of Our Crisis* (Boston, 1951), Chap. 4.
5. See Th. Brosse, "Contribution to the Psycho-Physiological Study of Altruism," in P. Sorokin, ed., *Forms and Techniques of Altruistic and Spiritual Growth*. See there also R. Godel, "The Contemporary Sciences and the Liberative Experience of Yoga," E. Dermenghem, "Yoga and Sufism: Ecstasy Techniques in Islam," W. Bischler, "Yoga and the Physiological and Therapeutic Effects of Voluntary Respiration." Cf. W. Michel, *La Respiration Volontaire* (Paris, 1951); K. T. Behanan, *Yoga: A Scientific Evaluation* (New York, 1937). Also M. Greenblatt and B. Sittinger, "Electroencephalographic Aspects of Normal, Psychopathic, and Homicidal Personality," in P. Sorokin, ed., *Explorations in Altruistic Love and Behavior*.
6. See E. Dermenghem's paper in *Forms and Techniques etc.*
7. The same can be said about this role in many primitive and great religions. Side by side with the pacifying ecstatic dances there are, of course, the ecstatic dances serving the opposite purpose: war dances are an example of these. The wide use of the techniques of ecstatic dances and of other violent motions for war and peace purposes suggests their effectiveness in conditioning aggressive or friendly behavior. This role of the dances and other ritualistic motions is still little known.
8. See F. P. Jones, "A Mechanism for Change," in P. Sorokin, ed., *Forms and Techniques of Altruistic and Spiritual Growth*.
9. For the details and evidence of this uniformity see P. Sorokin, *Social and Cultural Dynamics*, Vol. 2, Chaps. 14, 15; P. Sorokin, *Sociology of Revolution* (Philadelphia, 1925), *passim;* P. Sorokin, *Society, Culture, and Personality*, Chaps. 30–33.
10. See on this role P. Sorokin, *Crime and Punishment, Achievement and Reward*, in Russian (St. Petersburg, 1913); P. Sorokin, "The Laws of Evolution of Punish-

ment," in Russian, in *Novyia Idei v Pravovedenii*, No. 3 (St. Petersburg, 1915); N. Makarewicz, *Einführung in die Philosophie des Strafrechts* (Vienna, 1896). See the literature given in these works.

11. Deuteronomy, Chap. 28.
12. *The Laws of Manu*, I, 31; IV, 173–174; VII, 14; cf. also *Apastamba*, I, 2–3.
13. For the facts see P. Sorokin, "The Laws of Evolution of Punishment," *Social and Cultural Dynamics*, Vol. 2, Chap. 15; W. Robson, *Civilization and the Growth of Law* (New York, 1936); A. S. Diamond, *Primitive Law* (London, 1935); G. Glotz, *La solidarité de la famille dans le droit criminel en Grèce* (Paris, 1904). Also see other literature in these works.
14. See on this M. I. Tugan-Baranovsky, *Foundations of Political Economy*, in Russian (Riga, 1924).
15. L. F. Richardson has shown that most wars have been between adjacent states and "that the number of a state's external wars has a positive correlation of .77 with the number of its frontiers." L. F. Richardson, "Contiguity and Deadly Quarrels," *Journ. of Royal Statist. Society*, CXV: 219–231, 1952.
16. N. F. Federov, *Filosofia obschevo dela* (Kharbin, 1928–30).
17. See the papers of H. Eichorn and R. W. Hyde, G. Allport, P. Sorokin, Swami Akhilananda in P. Sorokin, ed., *Explorations in Altruistic Love and Behavior;* and several papers in P. Sorokin, ed., *Forms and Techniques of Altruistic and Spiritual Growth*.

## Chapter Seventeen
### The Techniques of Altruistic Transformation

1. Cf. the statistical data about the movements of wars, revolutions, scientific discoveries, technological inventions, schools and literacy in P. Sorokin, *Reconstruction of Humanity*, Chap. 3; *Social and Cultural Dynamics*, Vols. II and III.
2. See on this hypothesis Trigant Burrow, *The Neurosis of Man* (New York, 1949); W. E. Galt, "Our Mother Tongue — Etymological Implications of the Social Neurosis," *The Psychoanalytic Review*, XXX: 241–262, 1943.
3. See on this P. Sorokin, *Crisis of Our Age*, Chap. 4; *S. O. S.: The Meaning of Our Crisis*, Chap. 1–4.
4. Cf. W. O. E. Oesterley, *The Sacred Dance: a Study in Comparative Folklore* (Cambridge, 1923); T. and M. Kinney, *The Dance, Its Place in Art and Life* (New York, 1936); H. Bergson, *The Two Sources of Morality and Religion* (London, 1935); C. Sachs, *World History of Dance* (London, 1938).
5. See J. L. Moreno, "Psychodramatic Production Techniques," in P. Sorokin, ed., *Forms and Techniques of Altruistic and Spiritual Growth;* "Psychodramatic Treatment of Psychoses," in *Sociometry*, Vol. III, No. 2, 1940; "Psychodrama and the Psychopathology of Inter-Personal Relations," *Sociometry*, Vol. I, No. 1, 1937; several other papers of Moreno on psychodrama and sociodrama in the journal *Group Psychotherapy*, in Vols. I–VI; and a series of *Psychodrama Monographs* edited by Moreno: *Sociodrama, Psychodramatic Treatment of Performance Neurosis, Mental Catharsis and the Psychodrama*, and other monographs by other authors in this series.
6. P. Sorokin, *S. O. S.*, Chap. 5; see also Chap. Twelve in this work.
7. J. Combarieu, *Histoire de la musique* (Paris, 1913), Vol. I, pp. 221 ff. See the literature and an outline of history of the views on the nature and functions of the fine arts in P. Sorokin, *Dynamics*, Vol. I, Chaps. 5–15.
8. "The Shih King," in the *Sacred Books of the East*, Vol. III. For details, see P. Sorokin, *Dynamics*, Vol. I, pp. 534 ff.
9. See *Dynamics*, Vol. I, Chaps. 5–15.
10. Hegel, *The Philosophy of Fine Arts*, tr. F. P. B. Osmaston (London, 1920), Vol. I, pp. 12–13.
11. See a survey and analysis of these studies in D. Soibelman, *Therapeutic and Industrial Uses of Music* (New York, 1948); Ch. M. Diserens, *The Influence of Music on Behavior* (New York, 1926); H. Read, *Education Through Art* (London,

1943); H. Read, "The Grass Roots of Art," *Problems of Contemporary Art*, No. 2 (New York, 1947); Hans Syz, "Education Through Art," *Psychiatry*, Vol. X, 1947; P. Sorokin, *Dynamics*, Vol. I; K. Antrim, "Music Molds Our Emotions," *Etude*, 65:429, August, 1947; De Bernardis and K. Ernst, "Picture and Music," *National Education Association Journal*, November, 1948; A. Denny, "Bank Notes and Musical Notes," *Manhattan Savings Banks Organ Musicales*, 66:409, 1948. See a vast literature in these works. Also L. P. Jacks, *Education Through Recreation* (London, 1932); S. R. Slavson, *Recreation and the Total Personality* (New York, 1946).

12. See Soibelman's, Diserens' and other works mentioned in the preceding footnote.

13. See a most detailed analysis of the modern fine arts from this standpoint in P. Sorokin, *Dynamics*, Vol. I, *Crisis of Our Age*, Chap. 2; F. R. Cowell, *History, Civilization and Culture: An Introduction to Historical and Social Philosophy of P. Sorokin* (Boston, 1952), Chaps. 3, 4.

14. On the importance of the struggle for individuality as different from the struggle for existence, see N. K. Mikhailovsky, *Struggle for Individuality* (*Borba za Individualnost*) in his *Works* (in Russian).

15. On the importance and forms of freedom see P. Sorokin, *Society, Culture and Personality*, Chap. 30; I. P. Pavlov, *Conditioned Reflexes* (Oxford, 1927), pp. 12 ff.; L. Le Fevre, *Liberty and Restraint* (New York, 1931).

16. M. Montessori, *The Montessori Method* (New York, 1912), pp. 86, 93, 350–353.

17. M. Montessori, *The Advanced Montessori Method* (New York, 1917), pp. 97 ff. See in these works many important details of the technique as well as of the behavior of children engaged in a free creative activity.

18. See F. Froebel, *The Education of Man* (New York, 1912), pp. 54 ff. Also his *Pedagogics of the Kindergarten* (New York, 1895); *Education by Development* (New York, 1899); *Autobiography* (London, 1886); J. A. Comenius, *The Way of Light* (London, 1938), pp. 18 ff.

19. See J. C. Solomon, "Active Play Therapy," *Amer. Journal of Orthopsychiatry*, VIII: 479–497, 1938; S. R. Slavson, "The Treatment of Aggression: Through Group Therapy," *ibid.*, XIII: 419–427, 1943; G. H. Reeve, "The Treatment of Aggression: General Principles," *ibid.*, XIII: 411–414, 1943. See in the same journal the papers on aggression therapy by H. Lippman, R. Brickner, S. Kaufman, in Vols. XIII and XIV. See further the studies of S. Keiser, P. Shilder, L. Bender, referred to in Chaps. Four and Eleven of this work.

20. *Commission on the Social Sciences*, Report No. 5, November, 1952. See the details of this experimental study in *Human Relations* by L. Coch and J. R. P. French, available at the Research Center for Group Dynamics, University of Michigan.

21. Cf. A. Huxley, *Ends and Means* (London, 1937).

22. Cf. F. J. Roethlisberger and W. J. Dickson, *Management and the Worker* (Cambridge, 1942); F. J. Roethlisberger, *Management and Morale* (Cambridge, 1941); E. Mayo, *The Human Problems of an Industrial Civilization* (New York, 1941), *Social Problems of an Industrial Civilization* (Cambridge, 1945).

23. See on group therapy J. Bierer, *Therapeutic Social Clubs* (London, 1948); M. B. Clinard, "The Group Approach to Social Reintegration," *Amer. Sociol. Review*, April, 1949; B. Gabriel, "Group Treatment of Adolescent Girls," *Journal of Orthopsychiatry*, Vol. XIV, No. 2; P. Halmos, *Solitude and Privacy* (London, 1952); L. Wulfe, *The Reilly Plan* (London, 1945); J. Worthy, *Soviet Psychiatry* (Baltimore, 1950); J. Halliday, *Psychosocial Medicine* (London, 1948); J. W. Klapman, *Group Psychotherapy* (London, 1946); J. Lowrey, "Group Treatment for Mothers," *Amer. Journal of Orthopsychiatry*, October, 1944; J. L. Moreno, *Group Psychotherapy, A Symposium* (New York, 1945); B. S. Morgan, *Individuality in a Collective World* (London, 1936); S. R. Slavson, *Introduction to Group Therapy* (New York, 1943); *The Practice of Group Therapy* (London, 1947); W. Lunden, "Antagonism and Altruism Among Prisoners," in P. Sorokin, ed., *Forms and Techniques of Altruistic and Spiritual Growth*.

24. See also C. Krahn, J. W. Fretz, R. Kreider, "Altruism in Mennonite Life," E. Arnold, "Education for Altruism," R. Kita, K. Nagaya, "How Altruism is

Cultivated in Zen," all in *Forms and Techniques of Altruistic and Spiritual Growth.*

25. James 2:20.

26. J. M. Thompson, "Experimentation with the Technique of Good Deeds," P. Sorokin, "Dynamics of Interpersonal Friendship and Enmity," R. W. Hyde and H. Kandler, "Altruism in Psychiatric Nursing," all in P. Sorokin, ed., *Forms and Techniques of Altruistic and Spiritual Growth.*

27. The described retroactive influence of our good deeds upon our emotions, feelings, wishes, ideas, and inner experience is only a concrete case of a much more general uniformity. "The mechanical reproduction of a gesture frequently has a retroactive influence on the mind of the performer. It is possible to laugh oneself into a gay mood; a dejected attitude deliberately assumed may evoke a sad mood; the mere use of the gestures and overt expressions of rage is often sufficient to produce this emotion. Postures and actions have a real and profound, if indirect, influence on our manners of thinking, feeling, and willing. . . . The actions through which sentiments are expressed reinforce the sentiments and may even evoke them in their absence. . . . The most profound practical psychologists, such as Loyola and Pascal, recommended overt religious acts as the best means for creating a religious mood. . . . Dogs who fight playfully with one another often end in a serious fight. The elaborate Chinese ceremonial was deliberately invented by Confucius, who, like Loyola, was convinced that gestures reinforce feelings. The solemn ritual of the Catholic Church exerts a powerful influence upon the souls of people — even of those having little faith." See P. Sorokin, *Society, Culture and Personality,* pp. 58–59. Also C. G. Lange, *The Emotions* (Baltimore, 1922); W. James, "What Is an Emotion," in *Mind,* Vol. IX, 1884; C. Morgan, *Habit and Instinct* (London, 1896); J. Payot, *Education de la volonté* (Paris, 1907); P. Levy, *L'education de la volonté* (Paris, 1920); P. Guyot, *Education et Hérédité* (Paris, 1910).

28. See in P. Sorokin, ed., *Explorations in Altruistic Love and Behavior,* studies of R. W. Hyde and H. Eichorn, G. W. Allport, M. Ashley Montagu, Th. Brosse, P. Sorokin. See also P. Sorokin, *Altruistic Love;* Ashley Montagu, *On Being Human;* P. Kropotkin, *Mutual Aid* (New York, 1925). In these works a vast literature is given on the power of love and the effects of good deeds.

## Chapter Eighteen
### The Techniques of Altruistic Transformation (concluded)

1. "Reflections on Prayer," in P. Sorokin, ed., *Forms and Techniques of Altruistic and Spiritual Growth.*

2. P. Mariner, *Réflexions sur la Prière* (Genève, 1952).

3. Matthew 6:6.

4. Gandhi's *Autobiography* (Washington, 1948), p. 96.

5. *The Art of Virtue* (Philadelphia, 1938), pp. 12 ff.

6. For Franklin's comments on the "felicity" of his life, see Chapter Nine above.

7. *Spiritual Exercises of St. Ignatius* (New York, 1914).

8. Cf. St. François de Sales, *Introduction to the Devout Life* (Westminster, 1948).

9. Gandhi's *Autobiography,* pp. 256–57. See there a more detailed description of his mastery of one of the most powerful drives of man's unconscious and conscious energies.

10. It should be noted that at the present time there are very few Freudians who accept most of Freud's theories in their undiluted form. Most psychoanalysts, after paying their compliments to these theories, either explicitly reject them or modify them to such an extent that in their diluted Freudianism there remains very little from Freud's theories. Clara Thompson's *Psychoanalysis, Evolution and Development* (New York, 1951), is typical in this respect. Each chapter in this book begins with a eulogy of Freud's discoveries and ends with a criticism and rejection of these, coined in mild words but fairly hard in their meanings.

Similar dilution and criticism is shown by the works of other psychoanalysts like E. Fromm, K. Menninger, K. Horney, A. Kardiner, F. Alexander, and others, not to mention the much earlier deviations of Freudian collaborators like C. C. Jung, A. Adler, and others. Other former Freudians like T. Burrow and J. D. Suttie (in his *The Origin of Love and Hatred*, London, 1935) flatly reject Freudian theories, and Suttie even entitles Chapter Thirteen of his book the "Freudian Theory Is Itself a Disease." Finally, the non-Freudian psychiatrists and psychologists, including one of the teachers of Freud, P. Janet (in his *L'Evolution Psychologique de la Personalité*, Paris, 1929, pp. 145 ff. *et passim*) reject Freud's theories as entirely untenable. A pointed criticism of these theories was recently given in A. Salter's *The Case Against Psycho-Analysis* (New York, 1952). See there some of the critical literature. This increasing crumbling of Freudianism does not hinder some psychoanalysts from making valuable contributions to the psychiatric and psychological theories, but almost all such contributions greatly deviate from Freud's theories.

11. Cf. on this J. D. Suttie's *The Origin of Love and Hatred*, Chap. 13, *et passim;* also the referred studies of R. P. Knight, K. E. Appel, L. Kessel, H. Hyman, C. R. Rogers, N. J. Raskin, E. F. Fiedler, and others.
12. The *Yoga System of Patanjali or The Ancient Hindu Doctrine of Concentration of Mind*, tr. J. H. Woods (Cambridge, 1927), pp. 3–12.
13. *Ibid.*, pp. 4–5.
14. See on this technique of ecstasy E. Dermenghem, "Yoga and Sufism: Ecstasy Techniques in Islam," in P. Sorokin, ed., *Forms and Techniques of Altruistic and Spiritual Growth*. Sir Thomas Arnold and Alfred Guillaume, *The Legacy of Islam* (Oxford, 1931), chap. "Mysticism" by R. A. Nicholson; Al Ghazzali, *The Confessions* (London, 1900); L. Massignon, *La Passion d'Al Hallaj* (Paris, 1914–21).
15. D. T. Suzuki, *Essays in Zen Buddhism* (New York, 1949), pp. 281 ff.
16. *Ibid.*, pp. 290–92. See there and in other works of Suzuki (quoted elsewhere in this work) the details of the technique of kwat and kwan. See also R. Kita and K. Nagaya, "How Altruism Is Cultivated in Zen," and H. Benoit, "Progressive Doctrines," in *Forms and Techniques etc.*
17. Exodus 19:3
18. Matthew 4:1–2. It is significant also that Matthew says: "Then was Jesus *led up of the spirit* into the wilderness."
19. Matthew 5:1–2
20. Matthew 17:1–3. On the high mountain he "was transfigured; and his face did shine as the sun, and his raiment was white as the light." This radiation of love and light by the face of a true genius of altruism is noticeable in a milder form even on the face of many a kind and unselfish person.
21. This does not hinder some pathetic and psychoneurotic persons from believing and asserting that they have become the chosen mouthpieces of God or Jesus. Such self-annointed believers occur also among the sensational "evangelists," among the drawing room and political precinct's "crusaders of God," and among the "religious converts" who "come to Jesus" by the easy way of listening for an hour or so to the theatrical exhibitionism of a haranguing "evangelist."

Similar claims for being the anointed instruments of God are made also by the cunning racketeers in sham-religiosity, sham-spirituality, and sham-morality; by various soothsayers of radio-television and the best-selling press. We investigated 73 of the easily made converts, and found that one of these did not change at all his overt behavior in altruistic direction; 37 changed mainly their speech-reactions, and the rest remained about what they were before "the conversion."

There is no need to say that none of these "self-anointed" and "self-sanctified" individuals have any relationship to the supraconscious meditation and creativity. As a number of letters to me show, some of them are pathetic persons with a heavy load of suffering which is largely responsible for this sort of self-consolation. Others are cunning businessmen reaping large profits through exploitation of "the business of religion and moral rearmament." The majority are pedestrian "spiritualizers and moralizers" who honestly try to improve their fellow men through the means suggested by their intellect and rarely, if ever, by the supraconscious creative spirit. All of them do not belong to the truly anointed geniuses of moral and spiritual creativeness.

22. P. Sorokin, *Altruistic Love*, pp. 136-37.
23. Matthew 10:37.
24. Matthew 19:24.
25. Matthew 10:39.
26. See P. Sorokin, *Society, Culture, and Personality*, pp. 63 ff. and *passim:* the whole volume is a demonstration of these elementary truths, unfortunately all too often forgotten.

## Chapter Nineteen
### The Unified Techniques of Patanjali's and Other Yogas

1. "In all Indian systems the ultimate instrument of salvation is Yoga." Th. Stcherbatsky, *The Central Conception of Buddhism* (London, 1923), p. 51. About the origin and development of Yoga, as well as about its different forms and aspects see P. Sorokin, ed., *Forms and Techniques of Altruistic and Spiritual Growth: A Symposium.* The greater part of this symposium consists of the studies of eminent specialists dealing with various problems of Yoga.
2. See on this universality of Yoga techniques M. Eliade, *Yoga* (Paris, 1936), pp. 199, 213, 222, 247, *et passim;* M. Mauss, "Rapports historique entre la mystique hindoue et la mystique occidental," *Congrès d'histoire du Christianisme* (Paris, 1928). Some of the techniques of the great Sufist mystics, like Al Hallaj, were borrowed from India during Al Hallaj's stay there. Some other Sufist techniques were taken from Christianity and Judaism. Cf. L. Massignon, *La Passion d'Al Hallaj* (Paris, 1914-21), pp. 80, 87, 113.
3. S. N. Dasgupta, *Yoga Philosophy*, (University of Calcutta, 1930), pp. 39-46. Cf. especially many comments of the Hindu sages on Yoga in *The Yoga System of Patanjali*, tr. J. H. Woods (Cambridge, 1927). See also a brief analysis of various Yogas in H. Chaudhuri, *Sri Aurobindo* (Calcutta, 1951), Chaps. 4-7, and in the Symposium *Forms and Techniques etc.* mentioned.
4. *The Yoga Aphorisms of Patanjali*, tr. R. Mitra (Calcutta, 1883), p. xxvi.
5. *The Yoga System of Patanjali*, pp. 3-19.
6. In its early form Yoga is very old; Patanjali apparently was a systematizer of it. His biography and even the period when he lived are unknown, and are guessed by different scholars all the way from the pre-Buddhist period (6th century B.C.) up to A.D. 16th century. Most probable is the period between the fourth and the second century B.C. Cf. Dasgupta, *op. cit.*, pp. 54-69; *The Yoga Aphorisms*, Preface; *The Yoga System of Patanjali*, Introduction.
7. Other Yogas, like the Hatha Yoga, the Laya Yoga, the Bhakti and Karma Yogas, the Integral Yoga of Sri Aurobindo, the Tantric, Vaishnavist, Vedantist, or various Buddhist Yogas, have philosophical backgrounds somewhat different from the Sankhya philosophy taken by Patanjali's Yoga (with some modification).
8. Cf. the profoundest and sharpest epistemological and dialectic analysis of this problem in the treatises of the great Buddhist logicians of the first few centuries of our era — Gotama, Nagarjuna, Asanga, Vasubandhu, Dignaga, Dharmakirti — in Th. Stcherbatsky, *Buddhist Logic*, 2 vols. (Leningrad, 1932).
9. Recent "semantics" pompously claims the great discovery that "the word is not the thing; the map is not the territory." See R. Meyers, "The Nervous System and General Semantics," *Etc.*, Vol. V, No, 4, 1948, p. 232. We see that not only the discovery but even the phrase "the word is not the thing" was discovered some two thousand years ago.
10. On the triadic ontology and psychology of Yoga and of other Hindu, Buddhist, Sufist, and Orthodox Christian ontologies and psychologies, see the studies of T. Brosse, J. Masui, A. Bloom, R. Kita, H. Benoit, and others in P. Sorokin, ed., *Forms and Techniques of Altruistic and Spiritual Growth: A Symposium.* Also

see Swami Akhilananda, *Hindu Psychology* (New York, 1946); Sri Aurobindo, *The Life Divine* (New York, 1949).

11. Kapila's Sankhya philosophy does not admit any God, except the two co-eternal principles of purusha and prakriti; for this reason many call it atheistic. Patanjali's Yogastura admits, in addition to these two principles, Iśvara as a regulator of the world order by his very proximity. However, except for Iśvara's helping function in the process of the liberation, it does not play a basic role in the Yoga philosophy. Its techniques can work without God, and Yoga can be atheistic as well as religious. See about this Dasgupta, *op. cit.*, pp. 98–99, 245 ff.

12. Dasgupta, *op. cit.*, pp. 301, 315.

13. See Th. Stcherbatsky, *The Central Conception of Buddhism* (London, 1923); also his *The Conception of Buddhist Nirvana* (Leningrad, 1927).

14. "A Yoga must avoid the two extremes of luxury and austerity. He must not fast, or torture his flesh": Swami Vivekananda, *Raja-Yoga*, sixth ed. (London-New York, 1901), p. 16; *The Yoga System of Patanjali*, pp. 181 ff.

15. *The Yoga System of Patanjali*, Bks. II, III.

16. They are effective for the purposes of the Hatha Yoga whose objective is to purge the body of all dross and impurity that hinder a free circulation of vital energy, and to acquire thereby supernormal powers, including health, long life, etc.

17. *The Yoga System of Patanjali*, p. 71.

18. Swami Vivekananda, *Karma-Yoga and Bhakti-Yoga* (New York, 1945), pp. 78 ff., 87 ff. About the eight steps of Raja Yoga, see Swami Vivekananda, *Raja-Yoga*, p. 17 ff.; Dasgupta, *op. cit.*, pp. 302 ff.; S. N. Dasgupta, *The Study of Patanjali* (University of Calcutta, 1920), pp. 140 ff.; *The Yoga System of Patanjali*. See also the Symposium *Forms and Techniques etc.*

19. This moral purification is equally prescribed for the liberation by the creeds and philosophies which, like the Early Buddhism, were thoroughly atheistic, with a denial of the existence of God, soul, ego, personality, any substance, any matter. Such theories admitted only the reality of 75 elements or dharmas or, in other classification, 12 "bases" of cognition, or 18 elements of gotra that make up an individual stream of life (santaña). The whole world for the Early Buddhist was but an incessant stream of momentary flashes appearing and disappearing, united only by the causal (physical and moral) laws. Among these elements 10 are morally neutral for reaching the absolute quiescence or Nirvana (conceived as a sort of universal entropy at that stage of Buddhism), 18 are unfavorable – namely, ignorance, carelessness, indolence, disturbed mind, irreverence, hypocrisy, anger, jealousy, injuring others, deceit, perfidy, self-admiration, etc.; and 10 are universally good: purity of mind, courage in good actions, equanimity, humility, aversion to objectionable things, absence of hatred, causing no injury, mental dexterity, acquiring and preserving good qualities, compassion and love. Early Buddhism appeared as a message of compassion, noninjury, and love. Practice in these virtues was regarded as absolutely necessary for moving along the path of the liberation. This shows, by the way, that a creed or ideology may be "atheistic" and yet demand and promote the sublimest altruism. Such persons and movements are a minority (in comparison with "religious and idealistic" creeds); nevertheless, they have always occurred. For more about the Early Buddhism see Th. Stcherbatsky, *The Central Conception of Buddhism*, *passim* and Appendix II; also his *Buddhist Logic*, and *The Conception of Buddhist Nirvana*. "The Buddhist way to deliverance consisted in three-fold discipline: moral rules (*śila*) tranquilization (*samādhi*) and wisdom (*prajnā*)": Suzuki, *Essays in Zen Buddhism*, p. 69.

20. On Kundalini see V. Rele, *The Mysterious Kundalini* (Bombay, 1929); A. Avalon, *The Serpent Power* (Madras, 1924); T. Brosse, "Contribution to the Experimental Study of Altruism," in P. Sorokin, ed., *Forms and Techniques etc.*

21. *The Yoga System of Patanjali*, p. 192; Dasgupta, *The Study of Patanjali*, p. 151.

22. T. Brosse, "A Psychophysiological Study," *Main Currents in Modern Thought*, July, 1946, pp. 77–84. See there the photographs, electrocardiograms. See also Brosse's later experimental studies in her "Contribution" in P. Sorokin's Sympo-

sium *Forms and Techniques etc.* Further see K. T. Behanan's *Yoga, A Scientific Evaluation* (New York, 1937), which contains photographs and a report on similar findings; G. Coster, *Yoga and Western Psychology* (Oxford University Press, 1935); Sir John Woodroffe, *The Serpent Power* (Madras, 1924).

This mastery was the reason why these steps gave birth to the *Hatha Yoga* – a purely physical system of exercises or gymnastics for maintenance of health, longevity, and development of the body. See *Hatha Yoga Pradīpīka* (Bombay, 1893); Th. Bernard, *Hatha Yoga* (New York, 1944).

23. *The Yoga-System of Patanjali*, III; IV, p. 347.

24. T. Brosse, *op. cit.*, p. 80. See also Brosse's "Contribution" in Sorokin's Symposium. In this pioneer study, Brosse gives some 60 cardiographic and other instrumental curves of the physiological changes in the organism of Yogis undergoing these states of samyama.

25. Dasgupta, *ibid.*, pp. 338–47.

26. N. Berdyaev, *Solitude and Society* (London, 1938), p. 48.

27. Th. Stcherbatsky, *The Conception of Buddhist Nirvana*, pp. 42–45, *et passim.* See there also the translation of the *Clearworded*, Nagarjuna's *Treatise on Relativity* with comment by Candrakirti. See also Th. Stcherbatsky, *The Central Conception of Buddhism* (London, 1923), *passim*, and especially Stcherbatsky's fundamental *Buddhist Logic*; G. Tucci, *Pre-Dignaga Buddhist Logic* (Baroda, 1930); J. H. Woods, "La théorie de la connaissance dans le système du Yoga," *Journal Asiatique*, 1918, pp. 385–89; D. M. Datta, *The Six Ways of Knowing* (London, 1932).

28. Stcherbatsky, *The Conception*, pp. 74–76.

29. D. T. Suzuki, *Essays in Zen Buddhism* (First Series), pp. 76–77.

30. *Ibid.*, pp. 113–114.

31. About Al Hallaj see L. Massignon, *La Passion d'Al Hallaj*; also L. Massignon, *Lexique technique de la Mystique Mussulmane* (Paris, 1922). Reality (God) "exceeds any limit of imagination and intellection of thinkers, any conceptual power of our understanding, and any capacity to define (through our intellect)." "O, my God! I say Thou transcends everything that is said about Thou by Thy friends, as well as by Thy enemies taken together. Glorious Sovereign! I say Thou transcends all the *tasbih* of those who say about Thou 'Glory to Thou!'" and all the *tahlil* of those who say: 'No Divinity'; Thou transcends all the concepts of those who have conceived Thou." Through his own mystic (Yoga) experience he claimed he succeeded in eliminating his "ego" and identifying his essence with God's essence. Hence, his habitual statements, like: "Thou assigned to this actual witness [Al Hallaj] Thy divine essence, Thy own 'itselfness!' Thou has proclaimed Thy essence through my created essence." For such teachings he was proclaimed a heretic and condemned to death through crucifixion, cutting off his legs and arms, through hanging and burning the remains. See *La Passion*, pp. 523–24, 790, 6–7, *et passim; Lexique, passim.* A complete disillusionment in the capacity of the reason and senses to obtain a full truth led another great Muslim thinker, Al Ghazzali, to the ecstatic intuition and superrational meditation as the main ways of adequate cognition. Somewhat similar standpoint is taken by two other Muslims, the Persian poet and mystic Rūmī (1207–1273) and Abū Sáíd (967–1049). See Al Ghazzali, *Confessions; Some Religious and Moral Teachings*, tr. Syed Nawas Ali (Baroda, 1921); also R. A. Nicholson, *Rūmī: Selections* (London, 1950); D. B. Macdonald, *Muslim Theology* (London, 1903).

32. We are told that after the mystic vision of God, Dec. 6, 1273, St. Thomas stopped his work on the *Summa* and wanted even to destroy it, saying that "his puny work was as so much straw." Becoming mystic, St. Thomas saw all the inadequacy of his purely intellectualistic writings. See R. M. Coffey, *The Man from Rocca Sicca* (Milwaukee, 1944), pp. 123 ff.

33. See the names of the Greco-Roman and the Western mystics in P. Sorokin, *Social and Cultural Dynamics*, Vol. II, pp. 639–642. Among the main philosophies of the Greco-Roman and the Western world, mysticism is exceeded only by empiricism and rationalism in the number of the thinkers of each current. In some

periods mysticism was the strongest current. See the details and fluctuation of mysticism during some 26 centuries, *Ibid.*, Vol. II, Chap. I.

34. In Plotinus' biography by his direct disciple, Porphyry, we read that Plotinus "became eager to investigate the Persian methods and the system adopted among the Indians," and that "four times, during the period I passed with him, he achieved this Term [unification with "all transcendent God"], by no mere latent fitness, but by the ineffable Act" [mystic trance or samadhi]. *Plotinus: The Ethical Treatises*, tr. S. MacKenna, Vol. I (London, 1917), "Porphyry: On the Life of Plotinus," pp. 3, 24.

35. Cf. *Oeuvres Complètes du Pseudo-Denis, l'Aréopagite*, ed. M. de Candillac (Paris, 1943); C. E. Roet, *Dionysius the Areopagite* (New York, 1920).

36. See John of Ruysbroeck, *The Adornment of the Spiritual Marriage, The Sparkling Stone* and *The Book of Supreme Truth* (London, 1916). See a historical survey of this mystic-intuitional current in the West in A. Wautier-D'Aygalliers, *Ruysbroeck* (London, 1925); R. Ulich, *Man and Reality: Dimensions of Human Experience*, The Hazen Pamphlets, No. 21 (New Haven, n.d.).

37. See St. John's *Works.*

38. On the mysticism of Descartes see Wautier-D'Aygalliers, *op. cit.*, pp. 310 ff.

39. See a survey of the problem in contemporary philosophy in N. Berdyaev, *Solitude and Society;* S. Frank, *Nepostijimoie* (The Unconceivable) (Paris, 1939); R. Ulich, *op. cit.*

40. Yoga asserts further that with the progress along the Yoga course various extraordinary powers automatically develop in the Yogin, such as knowledge of previous life, and of the minds of others; levitation in the air; power over animals and human beings; disappearance; healing of various physical and mental diseases; non-burning in fire; and so on. However, the Yogin is advised to disregard all these temptations and not to deviate from his true path. On these powers, up to the alchemical elixir of longevity and other magical "miracles" supposedly performed by several Yogins and witnessed by various observers, see M. Eliade, *Yoga*, quoted, Chap. 8: "Le Yoga et l'alchimie"; O. Leroy, *La levitation* (Paris, 1928); R. Schmidt, *Fakire und Fakirtum* (Berlin, 1921); J. Masui (ed.) *Approches de l'Inde* (Les cahiers du Sud, 1949). Also see M. Eliade, "Shamanism and Indian Yoga Techniques," in Sorokin's Symposium, *Forms and Techniques etc.*

41. Eliade, *Yoga*, pp. 168 ff., 196 ff.

42. Nygren and others distinguish two fundamental forms of love: Eros and Agape. Heavenly Eros "is a detachment from the things of sense and an endeavour to attain to the higher, heavenly world" by man's own actions and merits. Agape is "an uncaused, spontaneous, regardless to merits, grace of God to man." These two forms of love have been running parallel in Christianity. See A. Nygren, *Agape and Eros* (London, 1937), pp. 165 ff., *et passim.* M. C. D'Arcy, *The Mind and Heart of Love* (London, 1947); S. Radhakrishnan, *The Bhagavadgita* (New York, 1948); Sri Aurobindo, *The Life Divine* (New York, 1949). See the discussion on this in Chapter One of the present work.

43. Th. Stcherbatsky, *Buddhist Logic*, Vol. I, pp. 2–7.

44. D. T. Suzuki, *Essays in Zen Buddhism.* First Series, p. 247. See also the papers of R. Godel on "Liberative Experience of Yoga," H. Benoit, "Progressive Doctrines and Doctrine Abrupt," A. Migot, "Buddhist Yoga," R. Kita and K. Nagaya, "How Altruism Is Cultivated in Zen," in P. Sorokin's Symposium, *Forms and Techniques etc.*

45. M. Eliade, *Yoga*, pp. 307–11.

46. Cf. for instance V. Solovyev, "The Justification of Good," *Works* (in Russian, 2nd ed., St. Petersburg, 1903), Vol. 8; M. C. D'Arcy, *The Mind and Heart of Love* (London, 1945); A. Schweitzer, *Indian Thought and Its Development* (New York, 1936).

47. *The Bhagavadgita*, tr. S. Radhakrishnan (New York, 1948), II:31–38; III:3–20; *et passim.*

48. See Swami Vivekananda, *Jnana-Yoga* (New York, 1939); also his *Karma-Yoga* and *Bhakti-Yoga* (New York, 1945); Swami Pavitrananda, *Common Sense about*

*Yoga* (Mayavati, 1944); Sri Aurobindo Ghose, *The Ideal of the Karma Yogin* (Chandernagore, 1921); also his *Bases of Yoga* (Calcutta, 1936); *The Yoga and Its Objects* (Calcutta, 1931); *The Life Divine,* 2 vols. (New York, 1949); H. Chaudhuri, *Sri Aurobindo* (Calcutta, 1951). See also J. H. Masui: "The Principal Yogas," A. Migot: "Buddhist Yoga," G. Monod-Herzen: "The Yoga of Sri Aurobindo," all in P. Sorokin, ed., *Forms and Techniques etc.*

49. Cf. Dasgupta's quoted works; Sir John Woodroffe, *Shakti and Shakta* (Madras-London, 1929), Chap. 1; also most of the works quoted in this chapter.

50. However, "Jnana as mentioned is not a mere intellectual affair. It is much more than what we understand by knowledge. It is intuition or self-knowledge in the fullest sense, of actual living in the Absolute Experience. It is actual identification with the Reality." Ordinary knowledge of sensory, empirical phenomena is contemptuously called *Jnana-Candhus.* "I prefer an ignorant man to a Jnana-Candhu," says Yoga. B. L. Atreya, *The Philosophy of the Yoga-Vāsistha* (Madras, 1936), p. 435. In Buddhism it is prajñā, as "immaculate wisdom" vs. *mati* as ordinary knowledge. Th. Stcherbatsky, *The Central Conception of Buddhism,* p. 50.

51. H. Chaudhuri, *Sri Aurobindo,* pp. 44–45.

52. Chaudhuri, *op. cit.,* p. 46.

53. Sri Aurobindo, *The Riddle of This World,* pp. 2–3; *The Life Divine,* pp. 34 ff., 232 ff. Passing by, it is to be noted that the idea of the descent of the liberated Yogin back into the empirical world is not so new as Chaudhuri says. In Buddhist sutra, the *Lankavatra,* we are told that there are two classes of "the liberated" or "Enlightened" Yogis: the Archats who desire Nirvana, or quiescent bliss only for themselves and want to stay in Nirvana forever, and the Bodhisattvas who, after attaining the true Buddhahood, do not desire Nirvana's bliss just for themselves, and turn back or descend to assist humanity in its long road to the Enlightenment and Nirvana. In Christianity, Jesus, the Virgin Mary, and some of the saints and the mystics also function in this role. They descend to humanity and help it in its salvation. The Son of God became man in order to help mankind in its divinization and salvation. One of the first acts of Christ after his bodily death was his descent into and liberation of the souls from the Inferno.

Similarly, the idea of the evolutionary divinization of the whole material and bodily world is also not quite new. Among other thinkers, Clement of Alexandria, N. F. Fedorov, and then V. Solovyev, developed it in as great detail as Sri Aurobindo. See N. F. Fedorov, *Filosofia obschevo dela* (The Philosophy of Common Cause) (new edition, Kharbin, 1928–30) and V. Solovyev, "Lectures on God-Man," "The Justification of Good," and the "Spiritual Foundations of Life" in his *Works* (in Russian), (St. Petersburg, 2nd ed., 1903), Vols. III, VIII; Eugène de Faye, *Clément d'Alexandrie* (Paris, 1898), pp. 256–293.

54. Cf. on that Sir John Woodroffe, *Shakti and Shakta* (Madras-London, 1929), Chap. XXVII, *et passim.*

55. See the details, literature, and sources in M. Eliade, *Yoga,* pp. 209, 212, 231 ff., 238, 243 ff.

56. See on this Sir John Woodroffe, *op. cit.,* pp. 593 ff.

## Chapter Twenty

### The Monastic System of Techniques

1. See on this "The Shepherd of Hermas," II, 2; P. H. Batiffol, "Les Origines de la Penitence" in *Études d'histoire et de Théologie Positive,* Vol. I (Paris, 1902), pp. 45–78; A. von Harnack, *Dogmengeschichte,* 3rd ed., Vol. I, pp. 406 ff.; S. Smirnov, *Dukhovny Otetz (Spiritualis Pater)* (Sergiev Posad, 1906), pp. 222 ff., 264–265, 298.

2. See St. Jerome, *Select Letters,* pp. 137 ff., especially his exposure of the Remnuoth class of monks; St. Benedict's castigation of the Sarabaites and the Gyrovaques classes of monks, in *The Rule of St. Benedict,* pp. 29 ff. For a general criticism of the moral defects of the monks and the clergy of the first few centuries of the Christian era, see the writings of Socrates, Sozomen, and of the Blessed Isidore in Migne, *Patrologia,* P.G., Vol. LXVII, 613–616, 1457–1460; LXXVIII, 1497–1500.

3. Smirnov, *op. cit.*, pp. 168 ff., 296–310.
4. *The Rule of St. Benedict*, Prologue, pp. 1 ff.
5. "Finis quidem nostrae professionis, ut diximus, regnum Dei seu regnum coelorum est, destinatio vero, id est scorpos, puritas cordis, sine qua ad illum finem impossible est quempiam pervenire," *Conl.* I, 4; Le Chanoine Léon Christiani, *Jean Cassien* (Editions de Fontenelle, 1946), Vol. II, p. 13.
6. St. Basil, "The Longer Rules," 2; "The Shorter Rules," 212.
7. About two types of monks see S. Smirnov, *op. cit.*, pp. 178 ff.; I. V. Popov, "Mystic Justification of Asceticism in the Works of Makarius the Great," in *Bogoslovsky Vestnik*, June, 1905, pp. 246–251.
8. See St. Athanasius, *The Life of St. Anthony the Hermit* (London, 1932); Chaps. 87–88; in Migne, *op. cit.*, P.G., Vol. XXVI, 964–965.
9. Sancti Isaaci Syri, *Opera* (Lipsiae, 1770), pp. 443–444, 457–549.
10. On the altruistic, social welfare, and cultural activities of monasteries see S. Smirnov, *op. cit.*, pp. 178–216; I. C. Hannah, *Christian Monasticism* (New York, 1925), *passim*; R. Fülöp-Miller, *The Saints That Moved the World*, pp. 70–93.
11. John Cassian, *The Twelve Books on the Institutes of the Coenobia, and the Remedies for the Eight Principal Faults*, tr. C. S. Gibson (Oxford-London, 1894), pp. 219–222, in *A Select Library of Nicene and Post-Nicene Fathers of the Christian Church*, Second Series, Vol. XI.
12. *Ibid.*, pp. 220–21.
13. Almost all of the contemporary "scientific" tests are utterly unreliable and unscientific: nobody knows what they test (except paper-pen-vocal operations), what their results mean, and how reliable they are. See about this in my forthcoming work: *Fads, Fashions, and Myths in Modern Sociology, Psychology, and Anthropology*.
14. In Chapter Thirteen a brief description of variations of these tests has been given. Testing and selection continued even *after the admission of the* aspirant to the monastic body. St. Pachomius expelled 100 monks out of some 300 monks of his monastery during the first years of its existence. Less severe but still rigid selection continued to operate in all monastic orders. Cf. *Annales du Musée Guimet*, t. XVII, pp. 511, 207–209. S. Smirnov, *op. cit.*, p. 79.
15. E. F. Morison, *St. Basil and His Rule* (London-New York, 1912), pp. 31–34.
16. St. Basil, "The Longer Rules," 5–8, *loc. cit.*, pp. 159–169; "The Shorter Rules," 2, 237, pp. 231, 317.
17. St. Basil, "An Ascetic Discourse," 1, *The Ascetic Works of St. Basil*, p. 135.
18. "Preliminary Sketch of Ascetic Life," *Ibid.*, pp. 55–57.
19. "Another Ascetic Discourse," *Ibid.*, p. 141; "De Renunciatione," *Ibid.*, pp. 60–63.
20. "The Shorter Rules," 85, *Ibid.*, p. 262.
21. "The Morals," 48:2–4, *Ibid.*, p. 113.
22. *The Rule of St. Benedict*, Chaps. 58–60, pp. 418–22.
23. *Ibid.*, p. 393.
24. Père Paul Dudon, *St. Ignatius Loyola*, p. 295, *Constitution*, (I, c. IV, nn. 1–7). Similar are the requirements in Zen Buddhist monasteries; see D. T. Suzuki, *The Training of the Zen-Buddhist Monk*, Chaps. 1, 2.
25. *The Rule of St. Benedict*, Chaps. 58, 59.
26. "The Shorter Rules," 114, 119, *op. cit.*, pp. 272–274.
27. P. Dudon, *op. cit.*, p. 299.
28. H. D. Sedgwick, *Ignatius Loyola*, pp. 221–22.
29. *The Rule of St. Benedict*, Chaps. 33–37.
30. John Cassian, *The Twelve Books*, Bk. 4, Chap. 13, pp. 6–7.
31. A. Gardner, *Theodore of Studium*, pp. 71–74; Migne, *Patrologia*, S.G. t. XCIV (1860), col. 1703–1720.
32. *The Writings of Saint Francis of Assisi*, pp. 41–42.
33. "Sitque inter eos pax et concordia, et libenter majoribus subjiciuntur . . . et invicem de humilitate certantes." *Regulae*, 179. *The Lausiac History of Palladius*, p. 83.
34. St. Basil, "The Shorter Rules," 198; "De Renunciatio," *op. cit.*, pp. 63–64.
35. *The Rule of St. Benedict*, quoted, Chap. 7, pp. 100–130.

36. St. Basil, *op. cit.*, pp. 74, 307.
37. John Cassian, *The Twelve Books*, Bk. IV, Chaps. 39–43, pp. 232–33. See a detailed development of these ideas and respective techniques in St. Bernard, *The Twelve Degrees of Humility and Pride*, tr. B. R. V. Mills (London, 1929); St. John Climachus, *Ladder of Paradise* in Migne's *op. cit.*, S.G., t. LXXXVIII, S. Joannis Abbatis vulgo *Climaci Scala Paradisi*, col. 631–1164; P. Pourrat, *Christian Spirituality* (London, 1922), Vol. I, pp. 284–294.
38. See also Migne, *op. cit.*, S.G., t. LXXXVI, Sancti Isaacs Syri, *De Contemptu mundi liber*, col. 811–886.
39. St. Basil, *op. cit.*, p. 97.
40. S. Joannis Abbatus vulgo Climaci *Scala Paradisi*, in Migne, *op. cit.*, S.G., t. LXXXVIII, col. 1155 and 1159.
41. St. Bernard, *The Twelve Degrees of Humility and Pride*, pp. 8, 14–15.
42. St. Basil, *op. cit.*, p. 131.
43. *Ibid.*, pp. 131, 195, 244, 288, 295, 299.
44. *The Rule of St. Benedict*, Chap. 4.
45. *The Rule of St. Benedict*, pp. 61–82.
46. St. Bernard, *The Twelve Degrees of Humility and Pride*, tr. B. R. V. Mills (London, 1929), p. 8. "This 'scala' or 'ladder' as constructed by St. Bernard, exhibits the plan and purpose of the treatise. The diagram appended is an attempt to show how, in his opinion, the degrees of humility and of pride correspond to and counterbalance each other."
47. Here we have a clear-cut knowledge of the role of sympathy and empathy for understanding of other human beings generally and for "self-therapy" and the "client-centered therapy" especially. Further on we shall see that the monastic fathers well knew all the precepts and tricks of practically all branches of contemporary psychiatry, clinical psychology, and science of education.
48. St. Bernard, *The Twelve Degrees*, pp. 10–40.
49. The direct enraptured vision of St. Bernard is about identical with the samadhi of Yoga, satori of Zen Buddhism, and a complete union of the knower with the known as the only adequate cognition discussed in the preceding chapter.
50. See S. Joannis Abbatus vulgo Climaci Opera Omnia *Scala Paradisi*, in Migne, *op. cit.*, S. G., v. LXXXVIII, col. 631–1164.
51. Here St. John indicates "the security function of obedience" preferred to insecurity of the self-responsible decisions, the point supposedly discovered by recent psychoanalysts like E. Fromm and others. See E. Fromm, *Escape From Freedom* (New York, 1941), and *Man for Himself* (New York, 1947).
52. *Op. cit.*, v. LXXXVIII, col. 1130. See also P. Marinier, "Reflections on Prayer," in Sorokin's Symposium, *Forms and Types etc.*
53. *Ibid.*, col. 1155–1159. Cf. also P. Pourrat, *Christian Spirituality From the Time of Our Lord Till the Dawn of the Middle Ages* (London, 1922), pp. 284–294.
54. *The Ascetic Works of Saint Basil*, pp. 138–143, 197–198, 300.
55. St. Basil, *op. cit.*, pp. 65, 109–11, 114, 138, 288, 318.
56. St. Basil, *op. cit.*, pp. 139, *et passim*.
57. *Ibid.*, pp. 75–82; *The Rule of St. Benedict*, pp. 53–58; John Cassian, *op. cit.*, pp. 13–15.
58. St. Basil, *op. cit.*
59. *Regulae*, 8–28, pp. 17–18.
60. St. Basil, *op. cit.*, p. 209.
61. John Cassian, *op. cit.*, pp. 8–13.
62. Pp. 40–53.
63. St. Bernard, *op. cit.*, pp. 25–26.
64. "Const. Stud.," 23, *loc. cit.*, pp. 24–25.
65. *Op. cit.*, p. 116.
66. *The Spiritual Exercises*, pp. 108–114.
67. *Introduction to the Devout Life*, tr. A. Ross (Westminster, Maryland, 1948), p. 77.
68. *The Rule of St. Benedict*, Chap. 48, pp. 53–58.
69. St. Basil, *op. cit.*, p. 114.

70. St. Basil, *op. cit.*, pp. 75–82.
71. John Cassian, *op. cit.*, Bk. II, Chap. 15, pp. 13–15.
72. *The Rule of St. Benedict*, Chaps. 35, 48, 53, 57.
73. A. Gardner, *op. cit.*, pp. 25–27; St. Basil, *op. cit.*, pp. 172–73.
74. St. Basil, *op. cit.*, pp. 144, 136, 306.
75. *Ibid.*, pp. 206, 283.
76. St. Basil, *op. cit.*, pp. 210–211.
77. *Ibid.*, pp. 332–33.
78. St. Basil, *op. cit.*, pp. 178–182.
79. St. Basil, *op. cit.*, pp. 68, 85–87, 136–37, 252–277, 281, 302; *The Rule of St. Benedict*, Chap. 39, Pachomius' *Regulae*, 179; *loc. cit.*, pp. 32 ff.
80. St. Basil, *op. cit.*, p. 280.
81. St. Basil, *op. cit.*, pp. 109, 139, 239, 284; St. Benedict, *Rules*, Chap. 6, pp. 66–67; *The Lausiac History*, p. 25.
82. *The Lausiac History*, pp. 25–26.
83. P. Dudon, *op. cit.*, pp. 298–99.
84. St. Francis, "Second Rule," Chap. 10.
85. St. Basil, *op. cit.*, pp. 97–98.
86. *Ibid.*, p. 98.
87. Cf. *The Rule of St. Benedict*, Chaps. 30, 37, 63, 70; A. Gardner, *op. cit.*, pp. 31–32.
88. St. Basil, *op. cit.*, p. 286.
89. Cf. *The Rule of St. Benedict*, Chap. 36. *Regulae* of Pachomius, 40, 42, 46, 126–29; *Const. Monasterii Studii*, 67–70.
90. St. Basil, *op. cit.*, pp. 264, 268, 346. Essentially similar are the provisions and the spirit of charity in the Constitutions of other monastic orders.
91. *The Rule of St. Benedict*, Chap. 53.
92. *Const. Monasterii Studii*, 82–84; *Regulae Pachomii*, 50–51.
93. St. Basil, *op. cit.*, pp. 137, 184–86, 351.
94. St. Basil, *op. cit.*, p. 137.
95. St. Francis, "The First Rule," Chaps. 12, 13.
96. St. Basil, *ibid.*, p. 143.
97. St. Basil, *op. cit.*, 216, 222–23, 267–268.
98. *Ibid.*, pp. 193–94.
99. Cf. *The Rule of St. Benedict*, Chaps. 23–30; John Cassian, *op. cit.*, Bk. iv, Chap. 16; P. Dudon, *op. cit.*, 297 ff., St. Francis, "First Rule," Chap. 5.
100. St. Francis, "The First Rule," Chaps. 12, 13.
101. A. Gardner, *op. cit.*, pp. 19–20; *Descriptio Constitutionis Monasterii Studii*, II.

## Chapter Twenty-One
### Monastic "Psychoanalysis," Counseling, and Therapy

1. St. Basil, "Moralia," 43, 1; *op. cit.*, p. 112.
2. Matthew 5:27–28.
3. John Cassian, *De Institutis Coenobiorum*, VI, 2.
4. *Ibid.*, VI, 11.
5. *Ibid.*, VI, 11.
6. St. Basil, *op. cit.*, pp. 71, 139, 236, 346.
7. *Ibid.*, p. 108.
8. *Ibid.*, p. 340 ff.
9. It makes Books Four to Twelve of his treatise: *The Twelve Books on the Institutes of the Coenobia, and the Remedies for the Eight Principal Faults*, tr. Rev. E. C. S. Gibson, in *A Select Library of Nicene and Post-Nicene Fathers of the Christian Church*, Vol. XI (Oxford and London, 1894). In this edition Book VI, on the Spirit of Fornication, is entirely omitted.
10. *Ibid.*, p. 234.
11. *Ibid.*, p. 232. Somewhat harsher is St. Ignatius' standpoint. "Although to serve our Lord much for pure love is above all to be esteemed, yet we ought also to praise much the fear of His Divine Majesty; because not only filial fear . . . but

even servile fear . . . helps much towards coming forth from mortal sin." St. Ignatius Loyola, *The Spiritual Exercises*, ed. Rev. C. Lattey (London, 1928), p. 163.

12. *Ibid.*, pp. 234–236.
13. *Ibid.*, pp. 236–242.
14. *Institut.* VI, 1. Cf. also Christiani, *Jean Cassien* (Editions de Fontenelle, 1946), vol. II, Chap. VI.
15. *Ibid.*, VI, 2–20.
16. *The Twelve Books on the Institutes*, VII, pp. 248–257.
17. *Ibid.*, VIII, pp. 257–264.
18. *Ibid.*, IX, X, pp. 264–275.
19. *Ibid.*, XI, XII, pp. 275–290.
20. The studies mentioned above show this clearly in regard to the overwhelming majority of the converts of these "crusades." In most of the cases these "ideological conversions" are but the easiest and cheapest self-gratification of selfish psychoneurotics or disintegrated, confused, and lost souls. Sometimes the converts are but clever politicians who find in their "conversion" and "ethico-religious verbiage" an excellent smoke screen for a successful pursuit of their crooked schemes and ignoble objectives.
21. *The Rule of Saint Benedict*, Chap. 2.
22. St. Basil, *op. cit.*, pp. 73–74, 110, 138, 318, 339 ff.
23. *The Spiritual Exercises*, ed. Rev. C. Lattey (London, 1928), pp. 105–107.
24. See about the unreliability of the projective tests G. W. Allport, "The Trend in Motivational Theory," *Amer. J. of Orthopsychiatry*, XXIII: 107–109, 1953; S. de Grazia, *Errors of Psychotherapy* (New York, 1952), Chaps. V, VII.
25. St. Basil, *op. cit.*, p. 208.
26. S. P. n. Dorothei, *Expositiones et Doctrinae Diversae*, XI, in Migne, *op. cit.*, S.G., t. LXXXVIII (1860).
27. St. Ignatius gives a special figure on which each failure or improvement is to be marked in such a way as to show visually the positive and negative changes in the individual at the end of each day and week. Benjamin Franklin's diagram, mentioned in Chapter 9, is a variation of St. Ignatius' schedule.
28. *The Spiritual Exercises of St. Ignatius*, tr. by a Benedictine of Stanbrook, edited by C. Lattey (London, 1928), pp. 13–21.
29. See Migne, *op. cit.*, P.G., t. XLIX, col. 285 ff.
30. For a careful analysis of the procedures of purification see Smirnov, *op. cit.*, pp. 81 ff. Also N. S. Souvorov, "K istorii nravstvennago outchenyia," *Vizantyisky Vremennik*, 1903, I, 55 ff. As an interesting detail many monastic and church fathers stress *tears, weeping*, and *lamentations* as one of the ways of absolution from sins. The therapeutic importance of tears and crying seems to be notably overlooked by contemporary psychiatry and educational art.
31. "Si autem ipse sui accusator fiat, dum accusat semetipsum et confitetur simul emovit et delictus." Origen, *Hom. II in psalm*, Migne, *op. cit.*, P.G., t. XII, 1386.
32. Migne, P.G. t. XXXI, 632–33; t. LXXXVIII, 681, 705; t. XL, 1149.
33. Migne, *Apophthegmata*, P.G., t. LXV, 333, 304. See similar statement of St. Anthony, Migne, P.G., t. XL, 1037.
34. Efrem Syrin, *Tvorenyia*, IV, 181 (Russian translation).
35. St. Basil, *op. cit.*, p. 139.
36. *Regulae*, 131–135. "Omnis correptio ita fiat, ut distincti sint qui corripiuntur; stentque in majori collecta, et in vescendi loco."
37. *The Rules of St. Benedict*, pp. 294–96.
38. St. Bernard, *The Twelve Degrees of Humility*, Introduction: "Life in a Cistercian Monastery," pp. 29–30.
39. Here are two examples of public confessions. One monk was sexually tempted for fourteen years. In despair "he came into the church and confessed his sinful temptation in the presence of the congregation. The whole congregation decided to labor for him by praying to God during seven days. The temptation ceased." (Migne, P.L., t. LXXIII, col. 877.)

A brigand came to a monastery and asked to be admitted to its membership. Having learned of his grave crimes, the Superior demanded his public confession.

The brigand agreed. " The Superior gathered together his flock of 330 monks for Sunday service. During the service, after reading the Gospel, the culprit was brought to the church. He was dragged by several brethren. They were striking him lightly. His hands were bound behind his back; he was garbed in a hair-shirt; his head was sprinkled with ashes. . . . Suddenly a piercing lament was heard. . . . Nobody knew what was happening. When the penitent approached the church entrance, the Superior called: " Stop, thou are unworthy to enter here." Stricken by the voice of the shepherd (coming from the holy altar), the culprit fell upon his face in fear and trembling. So he lay down on the ground and wept. The Superior advised him to confess in detail all his sins in the presence of the congregation. Terrified, he confessed one by one all his horrible sins revolting to listen to, not only the carnal — natural and unnatural, with hu-mans and animals — but also murders, and many others unfit to listen to or to be recorded. When he finished his confession, the Superior ordered to admit him into the brotherhood." (Migne, P.G., t. LXXXVIII, 681–684.)

40. See Smirnov, *op. cit.*, p. 90.
41. St. Basil, *op. cit.*, pp. 313–14.
42. *Ibid.*, pp. 53, 64.
43. *Ibid.*, pp. 192–93.
44. St. Ephraem, *Opera*, III, p. 458.
45. *Khristianskoye Tschtenyie*, 1829, No. 2, pp. 259–60.
46. See the facts and teachings on this problem in Migne's *Apophthegmata*, P.G., t. LXV, 352, 337, 373, 325. *Annales du musée Guimet*, t. XXV, p. 220. S. Smir-nov, *op. cit.*, pp. 90 ff.
47. See an excellent analysis of the nature and functions of the *spiritualis pater* in S. Smirnov, *op. cit.*, also K. Holl, *Enthusiasmus und Bussgewalt beim griechischen Mönchtum* (Leipzig, 1898).
48. See R. Otto, *The Idea of the Holy* (Oxford, 1925). A believer not only loves God, but has also reverential awe for Him or for the Holy, as the "*mysterium tremendum et fascinosum.*"
49. See many significant details in Smirnov's and Holl's works mentioned.
50. Clement of Alexandria and other Church Fathers subscribed to the gnostic theory of man's divinization. Cf. E. de Faye, *Clément d'Alexandrie* (Paris, 1898), pp. 183–199, 256–293.
51. Migne, P.G., t. XXXIV, 1161; Migne, P.L., t. XLIX, 6:425–436; I. V. Popov, "Mystic Justification of Asceticism," *Bogoslovsky Vestnik*, November, 1904, pp. 562–65; S. Smirnov, *op. cit.*, pp. 43 ff.; *Annales du musée Guimet*, t. XVII, p. 676.
52. Smirnov, *op. cit.*, p. 63; Migne, P.G., t. LXXXVIII, 1681.
53. P. Pourrat, *op. cit.*, p. 287.
54. See the details in Smirnov, *op. cit.*, pp. 68–69.
55. Transmission of charismatic gift from the spiritual father to the disciple is noted in many cultures: Elijah transmitted it through his mantle to Elisha; St. Simeon the Stylite transmitted to Daniel the Stylite; eminent Hindu gurus or Muslim sheiks are often mentioned as handing it down to their disciples. Among early monastic fathers such a transmission is mentioned fairly frequently.
56. C. R. Rogers, *Client-Centered Therapy* (Boston, 1951), p. 35. This therapy does not stress as yet the fact that the therapist has to be also a guide quite different from the patient.
57. " Proba prius medicum, cui debeas causam langoris exponere, qui sciat infirmari cum infirmante, flere cum flente, qui condolendi et compatiendi noverit disci-plinam." (Migne, P.G., t. XII, 1386.)
58. St. Basil, *op. cit.*, pp. 192–93.
59. *Ibid.*, " The Shorter Rules," 43.
60. *Ibid.*, pp. 271–72.
61. St. Bernard, *The Twelve Degrees*, pp. 17–19.
62. P. Pourrat, *op. cit.*, p. 288.
63. Migne, P.G., t. LXXIX, p. 756.
64. *Opera*, II, 61.

65. St. Basil, *op. cit.*, pp. 233–34.
66. *Ibid.*, pp. 292–93.
67. P. Pourrat, *op. cit.*, pp. 288–290. St. John's *Scala paradisi*, "Gradus V, and Gradus VII." In this point the therapy of the monastic fathers notably differs from that of many psychiatrists and educators, who try to erase as soon as possible the feeling of guilt, sadness, "affliction of the soul" of the patients and their depressive moods. The monastic and Christian fathers generally regard repentance with its sadness, sense of guilt, fear, and tears beneficial for the patient, even necessary, before the final absolution by Communion.
68. Migne, P.G., t. LXV, 256; Migne, P.L., t. LXXIII, 975.
69. Migne, P.G., LXXXVIII, 980.
70. *Acta Sanctorum*, Julii, t. III, "Vita S. Stephani," c. 124, pp. 522–23.
71. See the historical details of the relationships between confession, repentance, and Communion in Smirnov's quoted work, pp. 135–156.
72. St. Ignatius, *The Spiritual Exercises*, pp. 111–113.
73. See A. Bloom, "Yoga and Christian Spiritual Techniques," in P. Sorokin, ed., Symposium on *Forms and Techniques etc.* See there the details and literature.
74. See John Cassian, *The Institutes of Coenobia*, Chaps. 14–18, Bk. IV, pp. 211 ff.; *Regula Pachomii*, 68, 116; *The Rules of St. Benedict*, pp. 265–69; St. Isaac, the Syrian, *Khristianskoye Tschtenyie*, 1829, pp. 267–69.
75. *Regulae*, 27; W. H. Mackean, *Christian Monasticism in Egypt* (London, New York, 1920), pp. 99–100.
76. St. Basil, *op. cit.*, pp. 121–125.
77. *Ibid.*, p. 216.
78. *Ibid.*, pp. 216, 196.
79. St. Dorotheus, "Sermons," in *Khristianskoye Tschtenyie*, 1830, pp. 259–73.

## CHAPTER TWENTY-TWO
### TECHNIQUES OF CONTEMPORARY FREE BROTHERHOODS

1. See J. H. Noyes, *American Socialisms* (Philadelphia, 1870); C. Nordhoff, *Communistic Societies of the United States* (London, 1875); E. S. Bates, *The American Faith* (New York, 1940); M. Holloway, *Heavens on Earth: Utopian Communities in America*, 1680–1880 (New York, 1951); Davis, *Contemporary Social Movements* (New York, 1930).
2. Taken from *Toward Community Living in Our Time*, by the Society of Brothers in Paraguay, Uruguay, and England.
3. G. Rhoads, Jr., "The Society of Brothers in Paraguay," *The Friend*, Ninth Month 20, 1951. She visited the Society in 1951 and lived there for some time as a working guest. E. C. H. Arnold is a leader of the society. See his paper "Education for Altruism," in P. Sorokin's Symposium, *Forms and Techniques of Altruistic and Spiritual Growth*.
4. The following sections are taken from G. Rhoads, Jr., *op. cit.*
5. The following sections are taken from E. C. H. Arnold's paper on the family.
6. Joseph W. Eaton, Robert J. Weil, and Bert Kaplan, "The Hutterite Mental Health Study," *Mennonite Quarterly Review*, January, 1951.
7. See bibliographical references in Eaton's study.
8. Closely similar to the Hutterite communities are the Mennonite communities in the United States. One of the main differences between these is the limited admission of private property by the Mennonite brotherhoods. See on the inner and educational organization of the Mennonite brotherhoods "Altruism in Mennonite Life" by C. Krahn, J. W. Fretz, and R. Kreider in P. Sorokin, ed., *Forms and Techniques of Altruistic and Spiritual Growth*. See there the details and the literature. What is said of these communities largely applies to the *Quaker* communities, to the *Dukhobors*, the *Molokans* and several other brotherly communities. About the Dukhobors see P. N. Malov, *Dukhobortzy*, in Russian (Thrums, 1948).

## CHAPTER TWENTY-THREE
### FROM TRIBAL EGOISM TO UNIVERSAL ALTRUISM

1. *Mei*, p. 79. See an excellent analysis of the problem in Chinese Confucianism in H. H. Dubs' "The Development of Altruism in Confucianism," W. R. Inge, L. P. Jacks eds., *Radhakrishnan* (New York, 1951), pp. 267–75.
2. See above on extensity of love, in Chap. Two.
3. Matthew 10:22, 34, 35.
4. Similar ideas have been expressed by many ancient and modern thinkers, beginning with the Chinese thinkers Lao-tzu, Mo-tzu, Han Yü, and ending with W. James, and especially N. F. Fedorov in recent times. See W. James, "The Moral Equivalent of War," *International Conciliation*, No. 27 (New York, February, 1910); and N. F. Fedorov, *Filosofia obschevo dela* (The Philosophy of Common Cause), new ed. (Kharbin, 1928–30).
5. See the statistics of wars and internal revolutionary disturbances from 600 B.C. to A.D. 1925 in P. Sorokin, *Social and Cultural Dynamics*, Vol. III, Chaps. 9–14.
6. See the detailed data and the sources in P. Sorokin, *Society, Culture, and Personality*, Chap. 34.
7. See the detailed data and literature in P. Sorokin, "Monarchs and Rulers," *Social Forces*, IV:22–35, 1925.
8. *Ibid.*, pp. 525 ff., 1926.
9. *Ibid.*, pp. 23 ff. See also I. Fisher, "The Mortality of Our Public Men," *Publications of Amer. Statistical Association*, XV:35–49, 1916–17.
10. In my forthcoming publication on the *Criminality of the Ruling Groups* it will be shown that, strictly separating the crimes which monarchs or rulers had to commit for the *raison d'état* from the purely personal crimes of patricide, filicide, fratricide, matricide, uxorcide, and murder generally, among the English kings there was one murderer for every three English monarchs. Among other monarchs the rate is not very different. Likewise, the rate of criminality of the ruling group of even democratic countries is much higher than that of their citizens or subjects. Lord Acton's dictum "power tends to corrupt and absolute power tends to corrupt absolutely" is correct. With an increasing limitation of the power of monarchs, rulers, presidents, popes, for the last few centuries, their criminality, especially grave criminality has been decreasing also.
11. For the details see P. Sorokin, "Monarchs and Rulers," *loc. cit.*, pp. 523 ff.
12. See P. Sorokin, *Altruistic Love*, pp. 100–105.
13. *Ibid.*, pp. 148 ff.
14. P. Sorokin, *Society, Culture, and Personality*, pp. 507–8. See there the evidence and the literature in Chaps. 31, 32, 33. See still fuller evidence in P. Sorokin, *Social and Cultural Dynamics*, Vol. III, Chaps. 9–14; and in P. Sorokin, *Russia and the United States*, 2nd ed. (London, 1950), Chaps. 10, 11, 12.
15. See F. S. C. Northrop, *The Meeting of East and West* (New York, 1946); *Taming of Nations* (New York, 1952); "Philosophical Anthropology and World Law," in P. Sorokin's *Forms and Techniques of Altruistic and Spiritual Growth*.
16. See on this P. Sorokin, *Social and Cultural Dynamics*, Vol. IV, Chap. 16.
17. See on this P. Sorokin, *Reconstruction of Humanity, passim; Society, Culture, and Personality*, Chap. 3, *et passim.*
18. See on this P. Sorokin, *Crisis of Our Age*, Chap. 4; *Social and Cultural Dynamics*, Vol. II, Chaps. 13, 14, 15.
19. This unanimity of legal and ethical commandments of all societies at all periods of human history is strikingly demonstrated by the essential similarity of the main moral commandments of all religions, of legal and moral rules of practically all human groups (so far as the in-group behavior of their members is concerned), and by criminal codes of all societies.

   Side by side with the crimes varying from society to society, and from period to period, the gravest crimes of practically all criminal codes are essentially similar and consist of the actions of the most anti-social nature, like murder or infliction of serious bodily, mental, moral and social harm upon the members of an in-group. In other words, the religious, moral, and legal values of all peoples require, recommend, and articulate the principle of love in various degrees of extensity, purity, and adequacy, and prohibit the actions that assert the opposite values of hate and enmity. The prevalent anthropological and sociological views about an unlimited relativity, diversity, and contradictoriness of moral values of different persons and groups enormously exaggerate the discordance of moral values, and entirely overlook the basic concordance, universality, and perennialness of the central moral values. Insofar these views are fallacious. See the detailed study of moral systems and criminal codes in P. Sorokin, *Social and Cultural Dynamics*, Vol. II, Chaps. 13, 14, 15. See there also the literature on this problem.

# Index of Names

# Index of Subjects